# WHO OWNS OUT

From Space debris to asteroid strikes to anti-satellite weapons, humanity's rapid expansion into Space raises major environmental, safety and security challenges. In this book, Michael Byers and Aaron Boley, an international lawyer and an astrophysicist, identify and interrogate these challenges and propose actionable solutions. They explore essential questions, from 'How do we ensure that all of humanity benefits from the development of Space, and not just the world's richest people?' to 'Is it possible to avoid war in Space?' Byers and Boley explain the essential aspects of Space science, international law, and global governance in a fully transdisciplinary and highly accessible way. Addressing the latest and emerging developments in Space, they equip readers with the knowledge and tools to engage in current and critically important legal, policy and scientific debates concerning the future development of Space. This title is also available as Open Access on Cambridge Core.

MICHAEL BYERS holds the Canada Research Chair in Global Politics and International Law at the University of British Columbia. Professor Byers co-directs the Outer Space Institute, a global network of Space experts united by their commitment to transdisciplinary research that addresses grand challenges in the exploration and use of Space.

AARON BOLEY holds the Canada Research Chair in Planetary Astronomy at the University of British Columbia. Professor Boley co-directs the Outer Space Institute and conducts research into planetary dynamics, astrophysical discs, meteoritics, artificial satellites and space sustainability.

CAMBRIDGE STUDIES IN INTERNATIONAL AND
COMPARATIVE LAW: 176

Established in 1946, this series produces high quality, reflective and innovative scholarship in the field of public international law. It publishes works on international law that are of a theoretical, historical, cross-disciplinary or doctrinal nature. The series also welcomes books providing insights from private international law, comparative law and transnational studies which inform international legal thought and practice more generally.

The series seeks to publish views from diverse legal traditions and perspectives, and of any geographical origin. In this respect it invites studies offering regional perspectives on core *problématiques* of international law, and in the same vein, it appreciates contrasts and debates between diverging approaches. Accordingly, books offering new or less orthodox perspectives are very much welcome. Works of a generalist character are greatly valued and the series is also open to studies on specific areas, institutions or problems. Translations of the most outstanding works published in other languages are also considered.

After seventy years, Cambridge Studies in International and Comparative Law sets the standard for international legal scholarship and will continue to define the discipline as it evolves in the years to come.

*Series Editors*

Larissa van den Herik

*Professor of Public International Law, Grotius Centre for International
Legal Studies, Leiden University*

Jean d'Aspremont

*Professor of International Law, University of Manchester and Sciences Po
Law School*

*A list of books in the series can be found at the end of this volume.*

# WHO OWNS OUTER SPACE?

## International Law, Astrophysics and the Sustainable Development of Space

MICHAEL BYERS

*University of British Columbia, Vancouver*

AARON BOLEY

*University of British Columbia, Vancouver*

CAMBRIDGE
UNIVERSITY PRESS

Shaftesbury Road, Cambridge CB2 8EA, United Kingdom

One Liberty Plaza, 20th Floor, New York, NY 10006, USA

477 Williamstown Road, Port Melbourne, VIC 3207, Australia

314–321, 3rd Floor, Plot 3, Splendor Forum, Jasola District Centre, New Delhi – 110025, India

103 Penang Road, #05-06/07, Visioncrest Commercial, Singapore 238467

Cambridge University Press is part of Cambridge University Press & Assessment,
a department of the University of Cambridge.

We share the University's mission to contribute to society through the pursuit of
education, learning and research at the highest international levels of excellence.

www.cambridge.org
Information on this title: www.cambridge.org/9781108497831

DOI: 10.1017/9781108597135

First published 2023

*A catalogue record for this publication is available from the British Library.*

*Library of Congress Cataloging-in-Publication Data*
Names: Byers, Michael, author. | Boley, Aaron, author.
Title: Who owns outer space? : international law, astrophysics, and the sustainable development of space / Michael
Byers, University of British Columbia, Vancouver; Aaron Boley, University of British Columbia, Vancouver.
Description: Cambridge, United Kingdom ; New York, NY : Cambridge University Press, 2022. | Series:
Cambridge studies in international and comparative law | Includes bibliographical references and index.
Identifiers: LCCN 2022041638 (print) | LCCN 2022041639 (ebook) | ISBN 9781108497831 (hardback) |
ISBN 9781108721875 (paperback) | ISBN 9781108597135 (epub)
Subjects: LCSH: Space law. | Space tourism. | Space mining–Law and legislation. | Outer space–Exploration–
International cooperation. | Astrophysics. | Artificial satellites.
Classification: LCC KZD1145 .B94 2022 (print) | LCC KZD1145 (ebook) | DDC 341.4/7–dc23/eng/20220930
LC record available at https://lccn.loc.gov/2022041638
LC ebook record available at https://lccn.loc.gov/2022041639

ISBN 978-1-108-49783-1 Hardback
ISBN 978-1-108-72187-5 Paperback

For Katharine and Karen, Cameron and Fraser, and Elise and Noelle

# CONTENTS

*List of Figures*     viii
*Acknowledgements*     x
*Note*     xii

Introduction     1

1   Space Tourism     11

2   Mega-constellations     46

3   Mega-constellations and International Law     77

4   Abandoned Rocket Bodies     114

5   Space Mining     130

6   Planetary Defence     186

7   Space Security     258

8   Anti-satellite Weapons and International Law     300

9   Conclusion: Where to from Here?     359

*Bibliography*     372
*Index*     390

# FIGURES

1.1 A comparison between suborbital and orbital flight trajectories   18

2.1 Image of a star cluster with multiple satellite streaks passing through the field of view   47

2.2 Cumulative growth curves of artificial objects in orbit   53

2.3 Top: inclinations of active and defunct satellites as a function of orbital altitude; bottom: spatial density of objects in orbit as a function of altitude   56

2.4 Spatial density of objects in orbit as a function of altitude, including possible densities of several proposed satellite constellations   59

4.1 Apogee–perigee distribution of abandoned rocket bodies in orbit   116

4.2 Image streak due to a tumbling abandoned rocket body in orbit   117

4.3 Photograph of a piece of rocket that survived re-entry and landed on Earth's surface   119

4.4 Casualty expectations based on abandoned rocket bodies in orbit, along with a breakdown of contributions by launching states or regions   123

4.5 Curves for two rocket body weighting functions, representing the fraction of time spent over each latitude   124

4.6 Population density curve and a total rocket body weighting function projected onto a world map   124

5.1 Map of the Moon's south and north poles   133

5.2 Image of asteroid Bennu taken by *OSIRIS-REx* spacecraft   134

5.3 Orbital diagram showing Mercury, Venus, Earth, Mars and Bennu   135

5.4 Photograph of NASA Administrator Jim Bridenstine, President Donald Trump, VP Mike Pence and Second Lady Karen Pence watching a rocket launch   158

6.1 Photograph of Lake Manicouagan, which was created by a five-kilometre-diameter asteroid   187

6.2 Fireball and bolide data projected onto a world map   188

6.3 Near-Earth asteroid discovery curves, cumulative with time   192

6.4 Visualisation of the minimum orbital intersection distance (MOID) between a Bennu-like asteroid orbit and Earth   194

6.5 B-plane figure showing simulation results of different deflection scenarios for the hypothetical impactor 2019 PDC   198

6.6 Comet 67P/Churyumov–Gerasimenko, in a mosaic of four photographs from
ESA's *Rosetta* spacecraft   209
6.7 The expected damage due to an airburst from a 60-metre asteroid   217
6.8 Keyhole map for the 2029 flyby of Apophis   253
7.1 Gabbard plot showing the apogee–perigee distribution of tracked fragments
resulting from India's ASAT weapon test   268
7.2 Fraction of USA 193 and Microsat-R debris de-orbited by the number of months
after the events   269
7.3 Orbital trajectories for 340 pieces of debris from the Russian ASAT
weapon test   271
7.4 The increase in tracked debris across different altitudes due to the Russian ASAT
weapon test   272
7.5 Ballistic trajectories for three different profiles, showing a depressed, an efficient
and a high-altitude trajectory   284
7.6 Simplified example of ballistic missile flight times corresponding to depressed,
efficient and high-altitude trajectories   284
7.7 Depiction of the FTG-15 ICBM interception test   286
7.8 Surviving debris resulting from the catastrophic break-up of a missile during an
FTG-15-like ICBM interception test   287
7.9 A depiction of the Lagrange points for a simple dynamical model involving two
massive bodies   291
7.10 Artist's illustration of plans for a new DARPA program   293
8.1 Density of debris in orbit as of 27 January 2022 due to ASAT weapon tests   303
8.2 Photograph of Indian ballistic missile defence interceptor being launched for ASAT
weapon test   304

# ACKNOWLEDGEMENTS

This book is the direct result of our first meeting with each other, in November 2017. That meeting only took place because Philippe Tortell – who currently heads up the Department of Earth, Ocean and Atmospheric Sciences at UBC – knew of our common interest in the policy implications of human activities in Space. His introduction led to several sessions in a campus pub – followed by the creation of the Outer Space Institute, a number of co-authored articles, and then the writing of this book. For this, we are very grateful.

Numerous colleagues took time out of their busy schedules to read and comment on draft chapters. We are grateful to Adam Bower, Philip De Man, Gerhard Drolshagen, Steven Freeland, James Green, Brian Israel, Ram Jakhu, David Koplow, Paul Meyer, James Clay Moltz, Gregor Novak, Erin Pobjie, Haley Rice and Aaron Rosengren. Any remaining mistakes are our own.

Other colleagues shared their expertise in three workshops organised by the Outer Space Institute on core topics of this book. We are grateful to Timiebi Aganaba, Tony Azzarelli, Jennifer Busler, Jeffery Chancellor, Christopher Chyba, Mac Evans, Robin J. Frank, Brett Gladman, Veronique Glaude, V. Gopalakrishnan, Alice Gorman, Laura Grego, Andrea Harrington, Tanya Harrison, Paul Hickson, Yukun Huang, Tara Ivanochko, Moriba Jah, Catherine Johnson, Christopher Johnson, Phyllis Johnson, David Kendall, Elynne Kinney, Ryder McKeown, Xavier Pasco, MV Ramana, Melissa Rice, Sara Russell, Victoria Samson, Janis Sarra, Gregor Sharp, Ken Skublics, John Spray, Cassandra Steer, Lucy Stojak, Peter Suedfeld, Mark Sundahl, Gonzalo Tancredi, Brian Weeden, Jessica West, Paul Wiegert, Jan Wörner and Tanja Masson-Zwaan. We are further grateful to several individuals who attended these workshops, but whom we cannot identify by name.

We are thankful for the literally thousands of students who have inspired our thinking with their energy, ideas and tough questions. Some of those students contributed to this book in various ways as research assistants: Shahed Aljermashi, Andi Jordan, Rebecca Rogers, Paul André Narvestad, Logan Fladeland, Edmond Ng, Charlotte Hook, Sarah Thiele (who contributed to some of the analysis and plots), Ewan Wright (who likewise contributed to analysis and plots) and Val Muzik (who organised a pivotal workshop on Salt Spring Island in January 2020).

Andrew Simon-Butler deserves special mention, for editing most of the book and ensuring accuracy and consistency in the footnotes. Andrew Falle also deserves special mention, for serving as a research assistant and then as the research co-ordinator of the Outer Space Institute – running the show while his directors were absent for long periods of writing.

While a teenager, George Sipos aspired to be an astrophysicist before life took him in other literary and artistic directions. This book has benefited greatly from his interest and editorial skills. We are also grateful for the efforts of everyone at Cambridge University Press, especially Finola O'Sullivan, who commissioned this book shortly before her early retirement. She saw the potential in a transdisciplinary approach to these cutting-edge issues and guided the project forward with wisdom and enthusiasm.

Most importantly, we are grateful for the love, patience and good humour of our partners, Katharine Byers and Karen Samuel Boley (who both provided feedback on much of the writing and pointed out several opportunities for wordplay), and our children, Cameron, Fraser, Elise, and Noelle. Cameron initiated a father–son trip to see the first SpaceX launch-and-landing at Cape Canaveral in December 2015, thus sparking Michael's interest in Space. Elise's wonderful artwork graces the cover of the book.

Michael Byers and Aaron Boley

********

# NOTE

Some portions of this book build on our earlier co-authored writings.

Chapter 5 draws on 'US policy puts the safe development of space at risk', (2020) 370:6513 *Science* 174–75.

Chapter 2 expands on 'Satellite mega-constellations create risks in Low Earth Orbit, the atmosphere and on Earth', (2021) 11:1 *Scientific Reports* 1–8.

Chapter 7 draws on 'Cis-lunar space and the security dilemma', (2022) 78:1 *Bulletin of the Atomic Scientists* 17–21.

Chapter 4 is based on 'Unnecessary risks created by uncontrolled rocket reentries', (2022) *Nature Astronomy* 1-5, at https://doi.org/10.1038/s41550-022-01718-8 (co-authored with Ewan Wright and Cameron Byers).

Portions of other chapters draw, less directly, on five essays published in the Saturday Comment section of the *Globe and Mail*, and one op-ed in the same newspaper.

~

# Introduction

The asteroid 101955 Bennu is just a pile of rubble, weakly held together by its own gravity, the remnants of a catastrophic event that occurred a billion years ago. But Bennu is also a bearer of both life and death, containing clues about the origins of life on Earth while, at the same time, having the potential to destroy humanity. For over time, the agencies of physics and chance have brought the 500-metre-wide asteroid onto an orbit very near to Earth.

A robotic spacecraft named *OSIRIS-REx* set out in September 2016 to make contact with Bennu. After many rehearsals, flying close to Bennu each time, the spacecraft made a brief landing – a 'touch-and-go' that enabled it to collect a sample from the asteroid's surface. Once *OSIRIS-REx* returns to Earth, scientists will spend decades analysing the 60 grams (or more) of material, which might turn out to include amino acids, the building blocks of life.

The *OSIRIS-REx* mission, however, is about more than science. NASA readily admits that the visit to Bennu is a prelude for possible mining operations, with governments and private companies hoping to extract water from asteroids to make rocket fuel – thus enabling further Space exploration and, perhaps, an off-Earth economy.[1] But some states oppose these plans, arguing that Space mining, were it to happen, would be illegal in the absence of a widely agreed multilateral regime. They point to the 1967 Outer Space Treaty, which prohibits 'national appropriation' and declares the exploration and use of Space to be 'the province of all [hu]mankind'. There are also reasons to worry that Space mining, if done without adequate oversight, could create risks – including the low-probability, high-consequence risk of an asteroid being inadvertently redirected onto an Earth impact trajectory.

---

[1] 'Space' is capitalized throughout this book to distinguish it from other uses of the word.

1

Many current human activities in Space, and others planned or contemplated, raise the fundamental question: who owns Outer Space?

This book provides a detailed examination of a number of these activities and the different challenges they give rise to. But before we dive into the details, here are five more vignettes that serve as an introductory sampling of major challenges arising from the human development of Space.

### Who Owns Outer Space?

A little Pomeranian called Saba missed out on the chance to join Sharon and Mark Hagle on the first of their four planned flights to Space, though Blue Origin did offer the dog a consolation prize – a specially fitted flight suit! As for the Hagles, they already have tickets for Virgin Galactic and are now in talks with SpaceX. Travelling to Space is an 'extraordinary' experience for the Florida-based couple, whose previous adventures included swimming with whales and abseiling into caves. 'My thought is you go, I go,' Sharon said of her 73-year-old property developer husband. 'Mark has always taken me out of my comfort zone.'

More and more of the world's ultra-rich are travelling to Space as tourists on short sub-orbital flights or much longer orbital flights, with increasing numbers going to the International Space Station. Trips around the Moon might also become a reality soon. Hollywood, unsatisfied with the visual effects provided by CGI or parabolic flights on aeroplanes, is right behind them, with Tom Cruise expected to fly to the International Space Station for a film shoot soon. It is all great fun, of course, unless one considers the environmental impacts.

### Who Owns Outer Space?

The Soviet spy satellite Kosmos 1408, launched in 1982, ran out of propellant decades ago and became just another piece of Space junk . . . until it found a new purpose in life. It was chosen as a target for a powerful military to demonstrate a capability that everyone already knew it possessed – to destroy a satellite at will.

A ground-launched missile struck the 1,750 kg satellite at a relative speed of at least 20,000 kilometres per hour, creating a huge explosion and, at the same time, more than a thousand pieces of high-velocity space debris large enough to be tracked by ground-based radar. Tens of thousands of smaller but still potentially lethal pieces were also undoubtably created, many of them on elliptical orbits that cross the orbits of thousands of operational satellites, as well as the International Space Station and China's new Tiangong Space station. Immediately after the explosion, astronauts, cosmonauts and taikonauts retreated into the shelter of their capsules, which are hardened for atmospheric re-entry, and closed the hatches while the highest concentrations of debris flew by. That was not the end of the story, however. Some of the debris will remain in orbit for many years, posing an ongoing threat to all satellites, including many operational satellites belonging to Russia itself, the state that took this dangerous and completely unnecessary action.

## Who Owns Outer Space?

A recently released framework for proposed mining activities on the Moon and other celestial bodies, called the Artemis Accords, includes a proposal to place 'safety zones' around these activities. The concept is borrowed from the quite different context of offshore oil drilling on Earth and from the United Nations Convention on the Law of the Sea.

'How can anyone be against safety?'

The assurances from Space agencies and foreign ministries are almost paternalistic in tone. At a minimum, the idea of safety zones seems like a solution in search of a problem, establishing a mechanism for drawing boundaries around ill-defined future activities. What is missing from such assurances is regard for the core principles set out in the 1967 Outer Space Treaty, that the exploration and use of Space is the 'province of all [hu]mankind', and that 'national appropriation' of the Moon and other celestial bodies is prohibited.

The reasoning advanced by the proponents of safety zones might almost be amusing if it did not contain within it the seeds of conflict. 'The boundaries are just advisory. They do not exclude anyone.' But will the United States say the same thing when astronauts or robots from another spacefaring state enter one of their safety zones without permission? How long do they expect these safety zones to remain in place, given that Space mining might require some of the most expensive infrastructure ever constructed? The answer: 'They're just temporary. They will only be used for co-ordination.'

Then why not just co-ordinate? Why are lines needed at all?

## Who Owns Outer Space?

SpaceX recently moved the bulk of its operations from California to Texas, attracted by the Lone Star State's low taxes and minimal regulations. The move may also have contained an implicit threat to the US government: the now-dominant Space actor could up stakes again, but next time to another country. Luxembourg, a well-established tax haven, would be an obvious place to incorporate. Although a tiny European country, it provides a friendly home for two of the world's largest operators of communications satellites in geosynchronous Earth orbit (GEO), and, in 2017, adopted legislation to facilitate commercial Space mining. SpaceX, meanwhile, has already acquired two large oil-drilling platforms that could be used to allow launches, quite literally, offshore.

Having launched more than 3,000 satellites since 2019, SpaceX now controls large swaths of Earth's most desirable orbits. Should one company, or indeed any actor, be allowed to use the most valuable parts of low Earth orbit (LEO) to such an extent that its use effectively excludes other actors from operating there safely? At what point does SpaceX exceed the carrying capacity of LEO and degrade spaceflight safety for everyone?

Tighter regulations are coming. But those regulations will be the result of negotiations, and companies, knowing this, are now working to establish the strongest possible negotiating positions. The emergence of Luxembourg and other 'flag-of-convenience' states in the Space domain will certainly help those who seek to minimise regulation.

SpaceX only exists because of NASA contracts provided to it when it was a fragile start-up. It still relies on NASA and US Space Force contracts for revenue, but the company is growing ever more powerful, launching thousands of satellites each year and planning missions to both the Moon and Mars. At some point, governments may find that they are negotiating with a leviathan that is both able and willing to transcend all boundaries.

## Who Owns Outer Space?

In April 2019, *Beresheet*, a spacecraft owned by an Israeli foundation, became the first ever privately owned spacecraft to attempt a Moon landing. It ended up crashing onto the Moon's desolate landscape, destroying not only itself and its instruments, but also, most likely, its passengers. Those passengers were tardigrades, also known as 'water bears'. They had been smuggled aboard for no discernible purpose except, perhaps, for their mere presence – so that someone back on Earth could boast about where he had sent them.

Tardigrades are the hardiest life form known to humans, and it is at least conceivable that a few of them remain in a condition of deep stasis on the surface of the Moon, waiting to be reanimated under the right conditions. Yet the decision to place tardigrades in a Moon lander has received only muted criticism, when it should have been strongly and widely condemned. The real issue is not whether any tardigrades might have survived the journey, but that someone deliberately and successfully plotted to put life forms from Earth on another celestial body. A similar action, taken on Mars or one of the moons of Saturn or Jupiter, could wipe out any extraterrestrial life that might be present there – at enormous loss to science, and therefore to humanity's under-standing of itself.

## So Who Owns Outer Space?

All six of these vignettes concern real-life developments that took place between 2019 and 2022, when we were writing this book. We include them here to highlight the many ways in which people, states and companies think about Space, as well as how they go about their activities there. They also show how actions and decisions made today will matter greatly to all of humanity in the years and decades ahead. What succeed-ing generations choose to do will also be important, of course, and we cannot envisage all future scenarios. However, we and others already see major challenges ahead. Some of these require substantial shifts in the way Space is being used, while others may just require adopting more cautious behaviours. Either way, humanity needs to work together and take appropriate steps now, including developing new rules where neces-sary, if we are to avoid several extremely bad outcomes – not only in the long term, but including within just the next few years.

Many people believe that Space belongs to all of us. In January 2022, the Outer Space Institute partnered with the Angus Reid Group to survey a random sample of American adults about their opinions on Space. Of the 1,520 respondents, 81 per cent of them 'agreed' or 'strongly agreed' with the statement 'Outer space should belong to everyone; no one country should be able to claim control over it.'

Others are of the opinion that, far from Space belonging to everyone, it belongs to no one, and, for this reason, that no parts of it can be owned.

Yet others agree that nobody owns Space, in general, but believe parts of it can indeed be owned.

Whichever position is taken, one inevitably runs into questions concerning actions – for example, what restrictions should be in place if somebody wishes to mine an asteroid or the Moon? Is it acceptable to mine asteroids, just because there are so many of them? Or if parts of Space can be owned, which parts? An entire asteroid, a small lunar crater, or perhaps only extracted resources? Finally, there is the most important question of all: who decides on the existence and content of rules, and on their application to specific situations?

Whatever Space is, states, companies and even wealthy individuals are rushing to assert dominance over it – to exploit resources, to pursue science and exploration, and, in some cases, simply to show off. Many of these actors are enormously enthusiastic about the technological and economic achievements that might be possible in Space. Far fewer of them seem to have given much thought to the considerable risks for Space missions, for those who undertake them, and for the environment in Space and on Earth.

This book examines a selection of 'grand challenges' that have emerged very recently because of the rapid expansion of human activity in Space. By 'grand challenges' we mean problems that exist on a scale that implicates all of humanity and must be solved for our civilisation to prosper, and indeed, in some cases, to survive. The most recent of these challenges is the invasion of Ukraine, which has brought the risk of an all-out nuclear war back into sharp focus. Russia's actions matter for this book because they threaten the political cornerstone of Space governance, namely the six decades of close co-operation between Moscow and Washington that led, first to the creation of the United Nations Committee on the Peaceful Uses of Outer Space in 1958, and then the International Space Station. It is there, on the ISS, that, thankfully, that Russian cosmonauts and Western astronauts still work side by side.

It should be apparent that grand challenges cannot be understood from a single disciplinary perspective, or even multiple disciplines working independently. Legal and policy solutions must be grounded in a firm understanding of the constraints imposed by physics and the uncertainty in our knowledge of events and outcomes. And although innovation and technological advances continually open new pathways for humanity to use and explore Space, it should also be apparent that no grand challenge has a purely 'technical' solution. As with climate change, pandemics and inter-state wars, grand challenges in Space require solutions that are grounded in a firm understanding of why and how countries co-operate, and how they seek to stabilise and channel that co-operation through international law. For all these reasons, this book takes a transdisciplinary approach to investigating grand challenges and identifying possible solutions. From start to finish, we have fully integrated our expertise in astrophysics, international law and international relations.

Space debris is an excellent example of a grand challenge that can only be solved through transdisciplinary research and analysis. Yet most people conceptualise the problem in ways that make the problem worse. They see Earth orbit as a near-infinite and therefore inexhaustible void, when it is in fact a finite resource. It is the same kind of misunderstanding that led to the plastics crisis in the oceans, and the climate change crisis in the atmosphere. If you throw enough stuff away, even the largest environment will become overloaded and begin to break down.

When multiple actors are contributing to the overload, we have a 'tragedy of the commons' – the quintessential 'collective-action problem', whose dominant feature is that individual actors can believe that everyone else must take steps to solve the problem, while not taking those steps themselves. These non-co-operative actors are 'free riders' who make no changes to their own behaviour while enjoying the additional benefits of everyone else's co-operation. Thus one path towards 'sustainable development' is to foster co-operation and discourage free riding.

All of the terms in quotation marks in the previous paragraph will be familiar to many readers. We use them to underline the point that Space is properly seen as an issue of global environmental politics, using many of the same conceptual and analytical tools.

But while many are familiar with the above concepts, we must recognise that the 'Space-is-big' mentality persists and has very powerful supporters, including Elon Musk. In December 2021, the founder and CEO of SpaceX assured the *Financial Times* that 'tens of billions' of satellites could safely be placed in LEO. 'Space is just extremely enormous, and satellites are very tiny,' he said. According to Musk, orbital shells as shallow as ten metres could be employed, in which case, 'A couple of thousand satellites is nothing. It's like, hey, here's a couple of thousand of cars on Earth – it's nothing.'

The comparison might seem to make sense at first glance, with some types of satellites having similar sizes to cars, at least without their solar panels. But there are serious flaws in this thinking. Cars barely move when compared with satellites, which orbit the Earth every one and a half to two hours in LEO. Satellites thus sweep out a large volume each orbit, with lots of potential for interactions. Cars, moreover, are very manoeuvrable and can slow down when traffic becomes congested. Satellites can make only minor course corrections, barely changing speed. There are also vast numbers of small, undetectable but still lethal pieces of debris and meteoroids to contend with, as well as destructive, unexpected equipment failures such as battery explosions.

Indeed, a major satellite–satellite collision has already taken place, with Iridium 33 and Kosmos 2251 striking each other in 2009 – a time when there was a relatively low density of satellites in orbit. Today, the congestion in LEO is only increasing, stressing operators seeking to maintain a safe working environment for their satellites.

Technological advances can play an important positive role, including various levels of automation that will aid human decision making and enable satellite-based collision avoidance. But caution is required. Automation can still lead to catastrophic failures, as we have seen in the aviation industry. Moreover, if a technology allows for the dense operation of satellites, then the increased efficiency and accessibility of LEO can stimulate even higher demand for its use.[2] This, in turn, can lead to even greater densities and with them renewed stress on the environment. Of particular concern are the consequences of any debris-generating event that takes place in a crowded orbital region, due to the corresponding elevated risk of knock-on collisions.

The growing awareness of humanity's reliance on LEO is bringing the Space debris challenge into the spotlight, and with it ideas to clean up the orbital mess. Even so, most of the proposed solutions that aim to 'clean up' debris do not, or cannot, account for the still-lethal pieces that are too small to be tracked. The automated collision avoidance systems noted above would enable satellites to dodge large debris and other satellites, assuming no errors, but they cannot avoid small debris and meteoroids. And while some technologies, such as those that would enable large rocket bodies to be removed from orbit, will have to be part of an overall solution, they do not address the fundamental problem of overuse, which

---

[2] This hypothetical situation highlights a class of well-known problems associated with the Jevons paradox, which observes that technological improvements, by increasing the efficiency with which a resource is used, reduce its cost and thereby increase demand, negating the efficiency gains.

is continuing at breakneck speed and seems destined to overrun any technological 'fix'.

Sustainable development of Space will only come with the adoption of new best practices. One example, for the sake of the present discussion, might be to limit the number of satellites that a single company can launch – to incentivise operators to focus on increasing the longevity, capabilities and resilience of individual satellites, rather than building huge constellations of cheap mass-produced ones. Restrictions like this, if done well, would not undermine the commercial development of Space. They would instead maximise the potential for long-term growth while minimising environmental and other negative impacts in Space and on Earth. There are many good examples of sustainable resource management on Earth, often involving two or more otherwise competing countries, such as the four-decades of ongoing co-operation between Norway and Russia to both protect – and thus, over time, maximise – the world's largest cod fishery in the Barents Sea.

Of course, if limiting access to a resource turns out to be part of the solution, one immediately runs into questions of governance and of who, ultimately, gets to decide. But even on issues that involve hundreds of states, and that concern 'areas beyond national jurisdiction', there are many good Earth-bound examples of how this can be achieved. We discuss some of these examples in this book, in part to inspire those who worry that Space might become a 'Wild West' dominated by a few powerful and antagonistic actors. There is, indeed, another way.

At the same time, the best forms of governance take a light touch, intervening in human ingenuity and enterprise only when necessary. For this reason, understanding the ways in which Space is a resource, how it is being used and whether it is being depleted is critical to establishing effective and equitable long-term management. In ecological terms, it requires knowing what any given actor's 'footprint' is in Space, and what the 'carrying capacities' are for different orbital regions. This directly ties into the concept of Space as an environment, which is finally gaining international recognition, as well as into recognising that the Space and Earth environments constitute a single interconnected environment. This book supports this understanding by showing how Space activities, whether launches, re-entries, or the placement of thousands of reflective objects in the sky, can cause environmental damage and interfere with activities on the surface of the planet.

We thus come full circle. The expertise of Space scientists is needed to identify challenges before they become unsurmountable, and to propose practicable solutions. Social scientists and lawyers are needed to ensure that solutions are politically feasible, and to carry them forward into lasting rules and institutions. Engineers are needed to develop technologies that can be used in beneficial ways, with environmental scientists guiding us forward by identifying what is beneficial, and what might not be.

# Space Tourism

## 1.1 Introduction

Dennis Tito launched into Space on a Soyuz rocket in 2001, alongside two Russian cosmonauts. The American investment manager spent eight happy days on the International Space Station (ISS) before returning to Earth. But while Tito had previously worked as an engineer at NASA's Jet Propulsion Laboratory, he had not participated in the same highly competitive selection process as the astronauts and cosmonauts on the ISS. Instead, he paid US$20 million to a private company called Space Adventures, which arranged his transport and made him the first ever Space tourist.[1]

Over the next decade, six other individuals followed Tito's path to the ISS, paying around US$20 million to 25 million each. Microsoft software architect Charles Simonyi enjoyed his first trip so much in 2007 that he went back in 2009. All these trips were taken on Russian government-owned rockets and spacecraft. But now, private companies are taking Space tourism in a new direction by developing their own capabilities to send paying customers to Space, in a variety of ways.

Two types of Space tourism are presently under way: suborbital and orbital. A third, lunar tourism, will likely follow in the next decade or two. While several ventures have failed, three companies began launching tourists in 2021: Virgin Galactic, Blue Origin and SpaceX. The emergence of Space tourism raises a host of difficult issues. One example is the environmental impact of launches on the atmosphere and the corresponding implications for climate change. Another is the contribution of Space tourism to the Space debris crisis in low Earth orbit (LEO).

Space tourism also raises difficult questions of international law. Some of these, such as legal responsibility for Space debris, are addressed in

---

[1] 'World's first space tourist 10 years on: Dennis Tito', *BBC News* (30 April 2011), online: www.bbc.com/news/science-environment-13208329.

other chapters of this book. In this chapter, we focus on issues of specific relevance to Space tourism, including whether states have a duty to rescue tourists in distress.


## 1.2   Suborbital Tourism

Sir Richard Branson  rode a white rocket plane to the edge of Space on 11 July 2021. His mission: 'Evaluating the customer spaceflight experience' on Virgin Galactic's *SpaceShipTwo*.[2]

Branson has a long history of taking already cool enterprises, adding the Virgin brand, and making them even cooler. In 2004, a small US company called Scaled Composites won the US$10 million Ansari X-Prize by twice flying an experimental rocket plane, *SpaceShipOne*, to an altitude higher than 100 kilometres. Impressed by the global attention attained by the feat, Sir Richard hired Scaled Composites to build him a spacecraft based on *SpaceShipOne*'s design.[3]

That rocket plane, *SpaceShipTwo*, launches at an altitude of between 40,000 and 50,000 feet after being released from the underside of a twin-fuselage, four-jet-engine aircraft.[4] It can carry two pilots and six paying passengers to an altitude of 80 kilometres – the  lowest and easiest-to-reach definition of Space, and thus the most profitable. Eighty kilometres is approximately the transition point between two upper levels of the atmosphere: the mesosphere and the thermosphere. It is the altitude where, in the 1960s, US Air Force pilots flying the X-15 rocket plane earned their astronaut wings.

However, the use of the 'mesopause' to define the boundary of Space is done for convenience and not because it is physically relevant. The location of the mesopause is not exactly 80 kilometres and varies depending on seasonal and other factors. The US Air Force chose 80 kilometres (actually, it chose 50 statute miles, or 80.47 kilometres) because it was a round number, and probably because the X-15 could reach there!

---

[2] Paul Brinkmann, 'British billionaire Richard Branson plans to soar into space Sunday', *UPI* (9 July 2021), online: www.upi.com/Science_News/2021/07/09/richard-branson-virgin-galactic-flight-space/1121625768487.

[3] Nicholas Schmidle, *Virgin Galactic and the Making of a Modern Astronaut* (New York: Henry Holt & Co, 2021).

[4] It is common practice to use feet for aircraft altitudes, and kilometres in Space.

Eighty kilometres has never been widely accepted as the boundary of Space. Following the lead of the non-governmental Fédération aéronautique internationale, most states use a 100-kilometre threshold – the so-called 'Kármán Line' – to define the start of Space.[5] Yet this too is an arbitrary choice, based on the ostensible upper limit of aerodynamic flight, i.e. above the highest altitude achievable using only aerodynamic lift.[6] Complicating matters further, some satellites on stable but highly elliptical orbits have perigees below 100 kilometres.

Arguments over the location of the boundary between Earth and Space will certainly continue, with Jonathan McDowell having recently mounted a science-based defence of 80 kilometres.[7] But does it really matter? No one argues whether the International Space Station is in Space. Likewise, satellites placed in orbit, even those in very low Earth orbit (VLEO), are deemed to be spacecraft without question. Rather, the location of the boundary seems to be most pertinent to counting the number of Space flights conducted by states – and to determining who gets to be called an astronaut. Missile defence and other security-related activities taking place within the transitional zone between the atmosphere and Space raise difficult questions, including those discussed in Chapter 7 of this book. Yet none of these questions would be solved by having a widely agreed boundary.

It is the advent of suborbital Space tourism that has brought this long-lasting and previously irrelevant debate among international lawyers into the public consciousness. The question of who gets to call themselves an astronaut suddenly matters, not least to Branson, who has invested about half of his fortune in the expectation that most people will consider 80 kilometres good enough.[8] After all, who would pay US$450,000 to call themselves an 'almost astronaut'? Blue Origin, which took its first

---

[5] See generally Michael Byers and Andrew Simon-Butler, 'Outer Space' in Anne Peters, ed, *Max Planck Encyclopedia of Public International Law* (Oxford: Oxford University Press, article last modified Oct 2020), online: opil.ouplaw.com/view/10.1093/law:epil/9780199231690/law-9780199231690-e1202; Bin Cheng, 'The legal regime of airspace and outer space: The boundary problem. Functionalism versus spatialism: The major premises' (1980) 5 *Annals of Air & Space Law* 323.

[6] For reference, the United States' high-altitude Lockheed U-2 spy planes can only reportedly reach about 24 kilometres.

[7] Jonathan C McDowell, 'The edge of space: Revisiting the Karman Line' (2018) 151 *Acta Astronautica* 668.

[8] Benjamin Stupples, 'Richard Branson richer than ever from Reddit traders and space plans', *Bloomberg* (2 February 2021), online: www.bloomberg.com/news/articles/2021-02-02/branson-richer-than-ever-from-reddit-traders-and-space-plans.

tourists above 100 kilometres on 20 July 2021, is already marketing flights on its *New Shepard* rocket as offering something that Virgin Galactic and *SpaceShipTwo* cannot – reaching an altitude that everyone accepts is in Space.[9]

To complicate things yet further, we need to ask ourselves whether altitude alone is even a sensible way to define an astronaut. Flying on a commercial airliner does not make you an aviator. Riding in a ferry does not make you a mariner. Perhaps we should distinguish between the flight crew and the passengers when deciding whether someone has earned the title of 'astronaut', as we might normally think of pilots earning their wings. The United States' Federal Aviation Administration (FAA) weighed in on this just as Branson and his rival Jeff Bezos were making claims to being astronauts, writing that individuals will only be considered 'commercial astronauts' if they meet the altitude requirements (50 miles in this case) and 'demonstrated activities during flight that were essential to public safety, or contributed to human space flight safety'.[10] We agree: anyone who guides a rocket plane to 80 kilometres on dozens, perhaps hundreds, of occasions will be demonstrating an awesome level of skill and courage. Those who sit at the controls of *SpaceShipTwo* deserve their astronaut wings. As for the passengers, or those who evaluate the customer spaceflight experience, stepping into a rocket is a necessary but insufficient condition for those wings.

Whether astronauts or 'astro-nots', getting launched to 80 kilometres takes courage – or perhaps a certain lack of awareness. Spaceflight is always perilous; even among national Space agencies, missions are never treated as routine. Based on its design and early performance, the Space Shuttle was estimated to have an overall failure rate of about 1 per cent.[11] In the end, two spacecraft were lost out of 135 missions. Virgin Galactic faces unique safety challenges since *SpaceShipTwo* is manoeuvered by pilots while becoming supersonic and climbing to an altitude that is eight

---

[9] See Blue Origin, 'From the beginning, New Shepard was designed to fly above the Kármán line so none of our astronauts have an asterisk next to their name. For 96% of the world's population, space begins 100 kilometres up at the internationally recognized Kármán line' (9 June 2021 at 11:33), online: *Twitter* twitter.com/blueorigin/status/1413521627116032001.

[10] FAA Commercial Space Astronaut Wings Program, FAA Order 8800.2 (20 July 2021), online: www.faa.gov/documentLibrary/media/Order/FAA_Order_8800.2.pdf.

[11] RP Feynman, 'Volume 2: Appendix F – Personal observations on reliability of shuttle', *Report of the Presidential Commission on the Space Shuttle Challenger Accident* (1986), online: history.nasa.gov/rogersrep/v2appf.htm.

times that used by commercial airliners. In 2014, a pilot error led to a fatal accident during a test flight.[12]

Another risk derives from the fact that Virgin Galactic does not provide pressurised spacesuits to its crew or passengers. This choice seems strange when considering that pressurised suits have always been viewed as a necessity by Space agencies for both launch and re-entry. In 1961, when 'Ham the Chimp' was launched on a Mercury-Redstone rocket by the United States, a pressurised suit saved his life after the capsule sprung a leak.

The lack of pressurised suits cannot be a question of style. Beginning with Yuri Gagarin and Alan Shepard, such suits are part of the idealistic image of an astronaut. The pressurised Space suits used by SpaceX on Crew Dragon are both functional and fashionable. Virgin Galactic's decision not to provide such suits might be part of an effort to make Space travel seem routine – just as Stanley Kubrick did, more than half a century ago, in the 'Blue Danube' scene in *2001: A Space Odyssey*. If so, it is dangerously misleading. The start and finish of a *SpaceShipTwo* voyage would seem familiar to anyone who has travelled on a private jet, or even a commercial airliner. However, it is the elements in between – the rocket-propelled climb to 80 kilometres, the upward rotation ('feathering') of the twin tail rudders to increase drag and stability for re-entry, the transition from free fall back to flight – that are unusual and therefore perilous.

Branson's selection of 11 July 2021 for his first flight was part of an aggressive marketing strategy since it enabled him to beat his rival to the limelight. Bezos, the founder of Amazon, the so-called online 'Everything Store', had announced the previous month that he would be launching on 20 July 2021, the anniversary of the Apollo Moon landing.

Bezos achieved that success: strapping himself in alongside three other passengers, launching to over 100 kilometres, and landing safely. But then, after alighting, one of the world's richest men proceeded to humiliate both himself and Space tourism generally by thanking Amazon's customers and low-salaried employees because they 'paid for all of this'.[13]

---

[12] Tariq Malik, 'Deadly SpaceShipTwo crash caused by co-pilot error: NTSB', *Space.com* (28 July 2015), online: www.space.com/30073-virgin-galactic-spaceshiptwo-crash-pilot-error.html.

[13] Gino Spocchia, 'Jeff Bezos criticised by Amazon workers and customers after thanking them for funding space launch', *The Independent* (28 July 2021), online: www.independent.co.uk/news/world/americas/amazon-workers-slam-jeff-bezos-b1887944.html.

This callous statement, and the unmistakably phallic shape of Bezos's spacecraft, combined to make him a ripe target for ridicule on the Internet and late-night television.

The spacecraft was developed by Bezos's privately owned company Blue Origin. Named *New Shepard* after the first American in Space, its stubby rocket propels a small but still bulbous capsule onto a ballistic trajectory before returning to the launch site and landing on legs. The capsule, designed for six passengers, delivers several minutes of weightlessness before returning to Earth using parachutes.

Unlike Virgin Galactic, both the rocket and the capsule are automated; no crew is required. As with Virgin Galactic, pressurised spacesuits are not provided. With no path for emergency decision making within the capsule, and no physical protection if the capsule leaks or is punctured by a micrometeoroid or Space debris, *New Shepard* passengers are essentially thrill-seekers on a potentially dangerous carnival ride.

Another important difference between Blue Origin's and Virgin Galactic's approach is that *New Shepard* reaches the 100-kilometre threshold. This ensures that its passengers can be widely accepted as genuine astronauts, if altitude is a sufficient criterion. Achieving this threshold was particularly important for 82-year-old Wally Funk, who flew with Bezos on 20 July 2021. Funk was one of the 'Mercury 13' – highly skilled pilots who, in the 1960s, were never selected for the astronaut program only because they were women.

### 1.3   Orbital Tourism

'Can't get it up (to orbit) lol' – That is what Elon Musk tweeted in April 2021, after Blue Origin complained to NASA about SpaceX winning a US$2.9 billion contract to construct a lunar lander. The CEO of SpaceX and Tesla could himself have travelled to Space, had he wished to do so, since SpaceX had begun transporting NASA astronauts to the ISS in November 2020.

Orbital tourism is more complicated and expensive than suborbital tourism because the spacecraft must reach orbital speeds of approximately 7.7 kilometres per second (about 28,000 kilometres per hour), depending on the altitude. Orbital tourists also spend more time in Space and travel farther from Earth – in the case of the ISS, between 370 and 460 kilometres. SpaceX's recently developed human-rated spacecraft, Crew Dragon, not only provides transport to the ISS for astronauts from NASA and other Space agencies; it also offers a passenger service to orbit for those able and willing to pay the hefty ticket price.

SpaceX is the first company to launch tourists into orbit on its own equipment. Some of the flights are arranged by Space Adventures, the same company that set up Dennis Tito's flight on Soyuz, while others are arranged by a company called Axiom. Axiom is charging US$55 million for an eight-day visit to the ISS. The first of such trips to the ISS took place in April 2022. Known as Axiom-1, it involved former NASA astronaut and Axiom vice president Michael López-Alegría, along with three wealthy investors. Three more trips are already planned.[14] Access to the ISS has been negotiated with NASA and not with all the ISS partner states, following the precedent established by Space Adventures and the Russian Space Agency (Roscosmos) beginning with Tito's 2001 flight.

Axiom is sensitive to criticisms directed at Space tourism, with López-Alegría emphasising, 'We are not space tourists. I think there is an important role for space tourism, but it is not what Axiom is about.'[15] The company and its customers all point to the eight weeks of intensive training involved. Passenger Larry Connor noted that those flying on Axiom-1 'spent anywhere from 750 to 1000 hours of training' in comparison to the '10 to 15 hours training, 5 to 10 minutes in space' done by those who take suborbital flights.[16] However, the company's president, Michael Suffredini, has admitted that 'while we do endeavor to train to the same level as our NASA colleagues, I'm not sure that we do all the way up to that'.[17]

It is nonetheless fair to distinguish between passengers on suborbital flights and those on orbital flights. Figure 1.1 depicts the difference in scale for these two forms of spaceflight. Moreover, as Suffrendini said, 'the crew has been trained on the systems they will need to interact with, including the research systems. So, they're fully trained on that. They're also trained on what not to interact with'.[18] There is thus some

[14] Mike Wall, 'SpaceX to fly 3 more private astronaut missions to space station for Axiom Space', *Space.com* (2 June 2021), online: www.space.com/spacex-axiom-deal-more-private-astronaut-missions.

[15] Jamie Groh, 'Axiom delays launch of all-private mission to the ISS until no earlier than April 8', *Florida Today* (3 April 2022), online: www.floridatoday.com/story/tech/science/space/2022/04/03/nasa-axiom-spacex-ready-first-private-mission-space-station/7192788001.

[16] Kenneth Chang, 'Private astronauts launching to space station don't want to be "tourists"', *New York Times* (8 April 2022), online: www.nytimes.com/2022/04/08/science/axiom-launch-nasa-spacex.html.

[17] Groh, op. cit.

[18] Ibid.

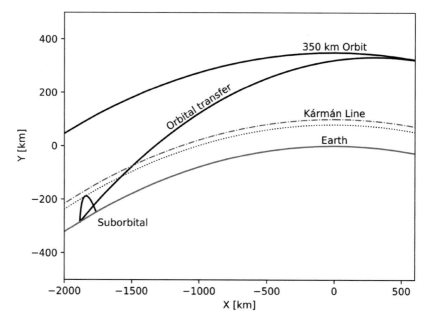

**Figure 1.1**  A comparison between suborbital and orbital flight trajectories. The blue curve represents the surface of the Earth, the grey dotted curve is the 80-kilometre altitude mark, and the red dot-dashed curve is the Kármán line. The Earth's surface passes through $X,Y = 0,0$ on this plot. (Note that the axes have different scales.) The suborbital flight (small, inverted U on the left) is an example of a trajectory that just reaches the 80-kilometre threshold. The much larger curve, including its initial 'transfer' orbit, is illustrative of an orbital launch, which imagines a 'delta-V' at an altitude of 350 kilometres that places the rocket into a circular orbit.

potential blending between the categories of passenger and crew member if passengers are indeed trained to use critical Crew Dragon systems and not just to resist urges to push buttons. Axiom further tries to use the 'experiments' and research that the passengers conduct, including naked-eye Earth observing or monitoring their personal health, to avoid the 'tourist' label. Still, with all this in mind, it is telling to consider SpaceX's own send-off to the self-styled Axiom-1 astronauts: 'Thanks for flying Falcon 9. You guys enjoy your trip to that wonderful space station in the sky.'[19]

---

[19] Chang, op. cit.

The real difference might be that Axiom is now moving forward with plans to provide its own module to house tourists on the station from 2024.[20] Thus the Axiom spaceflight passengers are contributing to experience building for Axiom, NASA and SpaceX – experience in taking the wealthy to Space.

When the ISS is decommissioned, around 2028–2030, Axiom plans to detach its module and use it as part of a commercial Space station. Presumably, this orbital hotel will be advertised to potential guests as both luxurious and entertaining, just like the spaceliners in the 1997 Bruce Willis film *The Fifth Element* and the 2007 *Doctor Who* 'Christmas Special', starring Kylie Minogue and entitled 'Voyage of the Damned'. It will, no doubt, also facilitate some 'science'.

Independently of all this, American software billionaire Jared Isaacman booked a Crew Dragon for a four-person, three-day free-flying orbital flight in September 2021.[21] The mission, named Inspiration4, did not visit the ISS and therefore did not require the involvement of NASA.[22] Nor was a SpaceX astronaut present on the fully automated spacecraft. Although the four tourists remained in contact with SpaceX mission control, they were otherwise on their own. The spacecraft travelled on an elliptical orbit with an apogee of 585 kilometres, giving the tourists an enhanced view of Earth against the backdrop of Space.

Isaacman enjoyed the experience so much that he promptly booked three more missions with SpaceX.[23] The first, named Polaris Dawn, will

---

[20] National Aeronautics and Space Administration (NASA), news release, 20-007, 'NASA selects first commercial destination module for International Space Station' (27 January 2020), online: www.nasa.gov/press-release/nasa-selects-first-commercial-destination-module-for-international-space-station. Adding a module always involves safety risks, as demonstrated in August 2021 when the thrusters on the new Russian module Nauka began firing after docking, putting the entire ISS at peril. See Joey Roulette, 'Uncontrolled firing from Russian module causes brief "tug of war" on International Space Station', *The Verge* (29 July 2021), online: www.theverge.com/2021/7/29/22600306/uncontrolled-firing-from-russian-module-causes-brief-tug-of-war-on-international-space-station. Those risks will likely be higher with a first-time commercial operator.

[21] Tom Huddleston Jr, 'Meet the billionaire commanding SpaceX's all-civilian mission – he dropped out of high school to start his business', *CNBC* (7 February 2021), online: www.cnbc.com/2021/02/07/billionaire-high-school-dropout-is-leading-spacex-mission.html.

[22] For an overview of the mission, see Vicky Stein and Scott Dutfield, 'Inspiration4: The first all-civilian spaceflight on SpaceX Dragon', *Space.com* (5 January 2022), online: www.space.com/inspiration4-spacex.html.

[23] Stephen Clark, 'Billionaire plans three more flights with SpaceX, culminating in Starship mission', *Spaceflight Now* (14 February 2022), online: spaceflightnow.com/2022/02/14/billionaire-plans-three-more-flights-with-spacex-culminating-in-starship-mission.

attempt to break the 1,372-kilometre altitude record for astronaut flight in Earth orbit, held by Pete Conrad and Dick Gordon from Gemini 11 in 1966. It will also involve 'extravehicular activity' (EVA), making Isaacman the first tourist to 'walk' in Space. Neither SpaceX nor Isaacman has revealed the cost of these missions, but individually they are likely to be much less expensive than a visit to the ISS would be.

Roscosmos is also returning to Space tourism. Thanks to NASA's Commercial Crew Program, which enables astronauts from the United States and NASA partner states to fly on SpaceX Falcon 9 rockets and Crew Dragon spacecraft from US soil, Soyuz seats formerly occupied by Western astronauts can now be used for tourists. In October 2021, actor Yulia Peresild and filmmaker Klim Shipenko visited the ISS to shoot scenes for a Russian Space-and-medical drama entitled *Challenge*.[24] The trip had its own promotional aspect, with the Russian state-owned television Channel One providing live coverage and then Roscosmos director general Dmitry Rogozin being listed as co-director of the film. There might even be an element of geopolitical competition involved, with news of the Russian plan being released after then NASA Administrator Jim Bridenstine announced on Twitter that Tom Cruise and producer Doug Liman would travel to the ISS with SpaceX to film scenes for a new movie.[25] The date of Cruise and Liman's trip, initially reported as October 2021, remains uncertain.

Then, in December 2021, Japanese fashion billionaire Yusaku Maezawa visited the ISS in a Soyuz spacecraft, accompanied by film-maker Yozo Hirano, who documented his flight. Eric Anderson, the CEO of Space Adventures, the company that arranged the excursion, explained that boredom was a motivating factor for Maezawa: 'there's only so much fine dining and other things that he could do'.[26] Separately, the Japanese tycoon has an agreement with SpaceX that should see him, along with

[24] Joey Roulette, 'Russian film crew wraps space station shoot and returns to Earth', *New York Times* (17 October 2021), online: www.nytimes.com/2021/10/17/science/russia-film-space-station.html.

[25] See Jim Bridenstine, 'NASA is excited to work with @TomCruise on a film aboard the @Space_Station! We need popular media to inspire a new generation of engineers and scientists to make @NASA's ambitious plans a reality' (5 May 2020 at 15:21), *Twitter* (on file with authors).

[26] Joey Roulette, 'Japanese billionaire arrives at space station for 12-day tourist trip', *New York Times* (8 December 2021), online: www.nytimes.com/2021/12/08/science/yusaku-maezawa-space-station.html.

eight others he selects, fly around the Moon in the company's new interplanetary spacecraft, Starship, in 2023.[27]

As this new wave of Space tourism demonstrates, off-Earth travel is often romanticised, with the dangers either minimised or, more often, completely ignored. Yet accidents and other emergencies are inevitable. Emergencies involving Space tourists will raise difficult issues, such as whether the international duty to rescue astronauts extends to them.

## 1.4   The Duty to Rescue

In the 2015 film *The Martian*, NASA's efforts to rescue astronaut Mark Watney (played by Matt Damon) suffer a seemingly catastrophic failure when a rocket loaded with emergency supplies explodes shortly after launch. The camera cuts to Beijing, where scientists at the China National Space Administration are deliberating whether to offer a newly developed, still secret rocket to NASA for use in a rescue mission. The Chinese rocket plays an essential role in enabling the American astronaut to be saved, in the best possible depiction of a key principle of international Space law in action: the duty to rescue astronauts in distress.

The duty to rescue astronauts was first set out in the 1967 Outer Space Treaty (OST).[28] The opening sentence of Article V reads, 'States Parties to the Treaty shall regard astronauts as envoys of [hu]mankind in outer space and shall render to them all possible assistance in the event of accident, distress, or emergency landing on the territory of another State Party or on the high seas.'[29] Article V goes on to specify that astronauts 'shall be safely and promptly returned to the State of registry of their space vehicle', that astronauts carrying out activities in Space and on celestial bodies 'shall render all possible assistance to the astronauts of other States Parties', and that parties have an additional duty to 'immediately inform' the other parties or the UN secretary general of 'any phenomena they discover in outer space, including the moon and other celestial bodies, which could constitute a danger to the life or health of astronauts'.[30]

[27] Yusaku Maezawa's Moon mission website advertises '8 crew members wanted! For the mission to the Moon in 2023' (2021), online: dearmoon.earth.
[28] Treaty on Principles Governing the Activities of States in the Exploration and Use of Outer Space, Including the Moon and Other Celestial Bodies, 27 January 1967, 610 UNTS 205 (entered into force 10 October 1967) (Outer Space Treaty).
[29] Ibid. Art. V.
[30] Ibid. As we explain in Chapter 2, the Chinese Mission to the United Nations office in Vienna referred to the latter duty when, in December 2021, it reported to the UN

The importance attached to the rescue of astronauts during the early years of human spaceflight was demonstrated by the fact that a second treaty, devoted to this specific topic, was concluded almost immediately. This second treaty – the 1968 Agreement on the Rescue of Astronauts, the Return of Astronauts and the Return of Objects Launched into Outer Space (Rescue Agreement)[31] – was 'negotiated backstage' in confidential talks between American and Soviet diplomats, with the other delegations to the United Nations being given less than one week to consider the final text.[32] This accelerated process unfortunately resulted in several ambiguities or errors that have bedevilled international Space lawyers ever since.

Fortunately, however, and as we explain in the next section, these ambiguities or errors can be resolved through a systematic exercise in treaty interpretation, with the result being a duty to rescue that is comprehensive in both geographic scope and the range of persons to which it applies. This outcome is consistent with the humanitarian objectives behind the rescue provision in the OST, as well as the Rescue Agreement. It is also well suited to current developments in human spaceflight.

## 1.5   The 1968 Rescue Agreement

Article 3 of the Rescue Agreement provides that, if

> the personnel of a spacecraft have alighted on the high seas or in any other place not under the jurisdiction of any State, those Contracting Parties which are in a position to do so shall, if necessary, extend assistance in search and rescue operations for such personnel to assure their speedy rescue.[33]

---

secretary general that the Chinese Space Station had manoeuvered on two occasions to avoid potential collisions with Starlink satellites.

[31] Agreement on the Rescue of Astronauts, the Return of Astronauts and the Return of Objects Launched into Outer Space, 22 April 1968, 672 UNTS 119 (entered into force 3 December 1968) (Rescue Agreement).

[32] Bin Cheng, 'The 1968 astronauts agreement or how not to make a treaty' (1969) 23 *Year Book of World Affairs* 185, reproduced in Bin Cheng, *Studies in International Space Law* (Oxford: Oxford University Press, 1999) 265 at 273. As Cheng explains, the 1963 UN Declaration of Legal Principles Governing the Activities of States in the Exploration and Uses of Outer Space and the 1967 Outer Space Treaty were also the result of backstage US–USSR negotiations followed by greatly curtailed public proceedings.

[33] Rescue Agreement, op. cit., Art. 3.

Article 5 of the Rescue Agreement introduces a new requirement, namely that a state, when requested, return 'space objects or component parts' discovered 'in territory under its jurisdiction or on the high seas or in any other place not under the jurisdiction of any State'.[34] Space objects or component parts are not granted the same priority as the personnel of spacecraft, as the state is only required to 'take such steps as it finds practicable' to recover them. Moreover, the 'launching authority' is required to reimburse any expenses incurred in fulfilling this obligation.

The Rescue Agreement also expands the geographic scope of the duty to rescue. Article V of the OST, by specifying that the duty applies on the 'territory of another State Party or on the high seas', would seem to implicitly exclude both Antarctica and Space – except in those circumstances where a state already has astronauts in Space or on a celestial body, in which case those astronauts 'shall render all possible assistance to the astronauts of other States Parties'.[35] Article 3 of the Rescue Agreement fills these possible gaps with the words 'any other place not under the jurisdiction of any State'.[36] It also specifies that, with regard to persons in distress in such a place, a state that is 'in a position to do so shall, if necessary, extend assistance in search and rescue operations for such personnel to assure their speedy rescue'.

It is important to note that the phrase 'in a position to do so' provides considerable discretion to the state, which is the only entity capable of deciding whether it truly has the equipment and personnel ready and able to provide 'necessary' assistance.[37] It is also clear that efforts to assist should not be made against the wishes of the state of registration of the spacecraft in distress. With all those qualifiers noted, such assistance might, in some circumstances, extend to launching a spacecraft on a rescue mission.

---

[34] Ibid., Art. 5.
[35] Outer Space Treaty, op. cit., Art. V.
[36] Rescue Agreement, op. cit., Art. 3.
[37] Steven Wood, 'The scope of international obligations to extend rescue assistance to "astronauts" and "personnel" under the Outer Space Treaty and the Return and Rescue Agreement', in Jan Wouters, Philip De Man and Rik Hansen, eds., *Commercial Uses of Space and Space Tourism: Legal and Policy Aspects* (Cheltenham: Edward Elgar, 2017) 44 at 62, citing Paul G Dembling and Daniel M Arons, 'The treaty on rescue and return of astronauts and space objects' (1968) 9:3 *William and Mary Law Review* 649 at 649–650; R Cargill Hall, 'Rescue and return of astronauts on Earth and in outer space' (1962) 63:2 *American Journal of International Law* 197 at 205; Francis Lyall and Paul B Larsen, *Space Law: A Treatise* (Farnham: Ashgate Publishing, 2009) at 140.

At the same time, the drafters of the Rescue Agreement created some confusion by including the word 'alighted' in Article 3, i.e. 'the personnel of a spacecraft have alighted on the high seas or in any other place not under the jurisdiction of any State'.[38] Several experts have argued that, as a consequence, the duty to rescue only applies when personnel have descended and landed on Earth or a celestial body, and not when they are in distress in orbit or deep Space.[39]

This concern over 'alighted' seems misplaced, however, once the international rules on treaty interpretation are applied in a systematic manner to the issue. These rules, set out in Articles 31 and 32 of the 1969 Vienna Convention on the Law of Treaties, are widely accepted as codifying pre-existing customary international law and can therefore be applied to an earlier treaty[40] – in this case, a treaty concluded just one year prior.[41] Article 31 of the Vienna Convention reads, 'A treaty shall be interpreted in good faith in accordance with the ordinary meaning to be given to the terms of the treaty in their context and in the light of its object and purpose.'[42] There are thus three elements to any treaty interpretation, which are normally assessed in turn: the ordinary meaning of the terms; their context within the treaty, including its preamble; and the object and purpose of the treaty. Regarding ordinary meaning, we need to look for the meaning at the time the treaty was concluded, and not the meaning today.[43]

---

[38] Mark J Sundahl, 'The duty to rescue space tourists and return private spacecraft' (2009) 35:1 *Journal of Space Law* 169.

[39] Wood, op. cit. at 57–58, citing CQ Christol, *The Modern International Law of Outer Space* (New York: Pergamon Press, 1982) at 171–72; Dembling and Arons, op. cit. at 649; Hall, op. cit. at 206; Sundahl, ibid. at 169.

[40] Customary international law is one of the three primary sources of international law. It is unwritten and results from a combination of 'state practice' and '*opinio juris*' (i.e. a sense of legal obligation or legal relevance), as explained in greater detail in Chapters 5 and 8.

[41] Vienna Convention on the Law of Treaties, 23 May 1969, 1155 UNTS 331 (entered into force 27 January 1980) (Vienna Convention). The International Court of Justice has often stated that the Vienna Convention codifies customary international law. See e.g. *Legal Consequences of the Construction of a Wall in the Occupied Palestinian Territory*, Advisory Opinion, [2004] ICJ Reports 136 at 174, para. 94; *Armed Activities on the Territory of the Congo* (*Democratic Republic of the Congo v. Rwanda*), [2006] ICJ Reports 6 at 51–52, para. 125; *Case Concerning Kasikili/Sedudu Island* (*Botswana v. Namibia*), [1999] ICJ Reports 1045 at 1059, para. 18. For the pre-existing rules of customary international law, see Lord McNair, *The Law of Treaties* (Oxford: Oxford University Press, 1961) (republished 1986).

[42] Vienna Convention, op. cit., Art. 31.

[43] Anthony D'Amato, 'International law, intertemporal problems', in R Bernhardt, ed, *Encyclopedia of Public International Law* (Oxford: Oxford University Press, 1992) 1234.

Article 32 of the Vienna Convention then allows for recourse to 'supplementary means of interpretation', including the preparatory work of the treaty (i.e. the official negotiating records, referred to as the *travaux préparatoires*) and the circumstances of its conclusion. But such recourse may only be made 'to confirm the meaning resulting from the application of article 31', or 'to determine the meaning when the interpretation according to article 31: (a) leaves the meaning ambiguous or obscure; or (b) leads to a result which is manifestly absurd or unreasonable'.[44]

And so, we begin our treaty interpretation of Article 3 of the Rescue Agreement with a consideration of the ordinary meaning of the term 'alight' in the phrase 'the personnel of a spacecraft have alighted on the high seas or in any other place not under the jurisdiction of any State'.[45]

The verb 'alight' is defined in the *Merriam-Webster Dictionary* as:

1. To come down from something (such as a vehicle): such as
   a. Dismount
   b. Deplane
2. To descend from or as if from the air and come to rest: land, settle.
3. *Archaic*: to come by chance.[46]

Although a present-day dictionary refers to this last meaning as 'archaic', we should remember that the Rescue Agreement was drafted more than half a century ago, by diplomats who themselves would have been about half a century old.

Steven Wood cites the 1913 version of *Webster's Revised Unabridged Dictionary* ('to come or chance (upon)') and the 1891 *Century Dictionary and Cyclopedia* ('to fall (upon); come (upon) accidentally, or without design; light: as, to alight on a particular passage in a book, or on a particular fact; to alight on a rare plant').[47] It seems plausible, if not likely, that there were three alternative meanings of 'alight' in ordinary usage in 1968.

---

There is an exception for 'relative terms' – expressions such as 'suitable, appropriate, convenient' that are 'not stereotyped as at the date of the treaty but must be understood in the light of the progress of events'. McNair, op. cit. at 467.

[44] Vienna Convention, op. cit., Art. 31.
[45] Rescue Agreement, op. cit., Art. 3.
[46] Merriam-Webster, 'alight' (last modified 25 March 2022), online: *Merriam-Webster.com Dictionary*, at www.merriam-webster.com/dictionary/alight.
[47] Wood, op. cit. at 61.

And again, ordinary meaning is only the first part of a Vienna Convention Article 31 interpretation. We turn now to the 'context' of Article 3, namely the rest of the treaty, including its preamble, all of which supports a broader interpretation.

The preamble of the Rescue Agreement is short and all of it is relevant to the interpretation:

> The Contracting Parties,
>
> Noting the great importance of the Treaty on Principles Governing the Activities of States in the Exploration and Use of Outer Space, including the Moon and Other Celestial Bodies, which calls for the rendering of all possible assistance to astronauts in the event of accident, distress or emergency landing, the prompt and safe return of astronauts, and the return of objects launched into outer space,
>
> Desiring to develop and give further concrete expression to these duties,
>
> Wishing to promote international co-operation in the peaceful exploration and use of outer space,
>
> Prompted by sentiments of humanity,
>
> Have agreed on the following: . . .[48]

Note the emphasis on the obligation in the OST to render 'all possible assistance to astronauts in the event of accident, distress or emergency landing', and the fact that this obligation (being referred to here with approval in the preamble to the Rescue Agreement) is not limited to emergency landings. Also note the phrase 'sentiments of humanity', which supports an expansive application that does not distinguish between the different possible locations of the personnel in distress.

Then there is the first part of Article 1 of the Rescue Agreement, which reads,

> Each Contracting Party which receives information or discovers that the personnel of a spacecraft have suffered accident or are experiencing conditions of distress or have made an emergency or unintended landing in territory under its jurisdiction or on the high seas or in any other place not under the jurisdiction of any State . . .

Note, again, that the scope of this provision extends well beyond landings to include any personnel who 'have suffered accident or are experiencing conditions of distress'.

---

[48] Rescue Agreement, op. cit., preamble.

The final stage of our Article 31 interpretation concerns the 'object and purpose' of the treaty, which in this case is clearly humanitarian. Indeed, the very short preamble to the Rescue Agreement states that it is 'Prompted by sentiments of humanity'. The rapid conclusion of the Rescue Agreement was motivated, in significant part, by two fatal spacecraft accidents (one American, one Soviet) in 1967.[49]

Moreover, as Wood explains, the Rescue Agreement 'evidences its humanitarian nature through the decision not to condition the obligations to rescue or return "personnel of a spacecraft" upon their State(s) of national origin', and thus 'the universal nature of these obligations and the intention to ensure the safety and safe return of all spacecraft personnel'.[50]

This humanitarian object and purpose call for a broad reading that does not distinguish between people in peril. Indeed, a more restrictive reading would have disturbing consequences. It is difficult to imagine that the humanitarian goals of the Rescue Agreement would exclude the personnel of a spacecraft that became distressed in orbit and was unable to descend safely to Earth. Would the drafters of the treaty have wanted the personnel of the spacecraft to attempt a dangerous crash landing before Article 3 applied?[51]

Since the systematic Article 31 interpretation conducted here does not result 'in any ambiguity or obscurity, or a result which is manifestly absurd or unreasonable', the matter is settled. Article 3 of the Rescue Agreement applies everywhere. There is no option to resort to the 'supplementary means of interpretation' referred to in Article 32 of the Vienna Convention to find support for another conclusion.

Wood is more generous to those who advocate for a more restrictive interpretation, accepting that the disagreements over Article 3 open the door to an examination of the 'supplementary means of interpretation' by generating a result that is 'ambiguous or obscure' or even 'manifestly absurd or unreasonable'. He writes,

> Recognizing these various arguments and examples supporting the opposing interpretations of 'have alighted' as alternatively referring to either the spacecraft or personnel, ambiguity and confusion exist

---

[49] Dembling and Arons, op. cit. at 638; Remy Melina, 'The fallen heroes of human spaceflight', *Space.com* (11 April 2011), online: www.space.com/11353-human-spaceflight-deaths-50-years-space-missions.html.

[50] Wood, op. cit. at 49.

[51] Ibid. at 59.

regarding the ordinary meaning of this term. Under the VCLT [Vienna Convention], confusion caused by ambiguous meaning calls for reconsideration of the intended ordinary meaning through consultation of the *travaux préparatoires* and other supplementary sources of interpretation. Further, preconditioning the duty to render assistance on spacecraft landing or personnel disembarking contravenes the humanitarian purposes of the ARRA [Rescue Agreement] and results in absurd consequences, especially where a State Party is well positioned to extend assistance to those in need.[52]

To paraphrase Wood in more succinct terms, the customary international law of treaty interpretation requires that 'an alternative meaning for "have alighted" consistent with the purposes and objectives of the ARRA must be investigated' to avoid an inconsistent and therefore absurd result,[53] i.e. a restrictive interpretation.

As Wood then explains,

> [T]he *travaux préparatoires* include a statement made to the UNGA by French delegate Mr Berard. In his statement, a recapitulation of previous statements before COPUOS and the Legal Subcommittee, Mr Berard indicated that the ARRA is meant to apply 'to search and rescue undertaken not only on the Earth and in its atmosphere, but also in outer space and on celestial bodies'.[54]

Further to this, under Article 32 of the Vienna Convention one could also consider the circumstances of the conclusion of the Rescue Agreement. These circumstances include the two fatal accidents in 1967, as mentioned above. They also include the broader history of the duty to rescue in other areas of international law, including at sea and following aviation accidents.

As we explain in Chapter 6 on planetary defence, the duty to rescue is included in numerous treaties, including the 1914 International Convention for the Safety of Life at Sea (SOLAS Convention),[55] the 1944 Convention on International Civil Aviation (Chicago Convention),[56]

---

[52]  Ibid.

[53]  Ibid.

[54]  Ibid. at 60, citing UNGAOR, 22nd Sess, 1640th Plen Mtg, UN Doc A/PV1640 (1967) [provisional] at paras. 77, 80, online: https://digitallibrary.un.org/record/742766?ln=en

[55]  International Convention for the Safety of Life at Sea, 1 November 1974, 1184 UNTS 278 ch V, reg 15 (entered into force 25 May 1980) (SOLAS Convention).

[56]  Convention on International Civil Aviation, 7 December 1944, 15 UNTS 295 Annex 12 (7th ed, 2001), Art. 2.1.2 (entered into force 4 April 1947) (Chicago Convention).

the 1979 International Convention on Maritime Search and Rescue (SAR Convention),[57] and the 1982 United Nations Convention on the Law of the Sea (UNCLOS),[58] as well as numerous regional and bilateral treaties. The drafters of the Rescue Agreement were operating within a legal and political context where the duty to rescue was well recognised as extending to all areas beyond national jurisdiction and all persons in distress.

Together, the OST and the Rescue Agreement provided rules on rescue and return that were appropriate for the early decades of human Space travel, when any accidents or emergencies would have involved astronauts from national Space agencies. Today, however, the advent of Space tourism has introduced some new legal uncertainties.

## 1.6   The Duty to Rescue and Commercial Spacecraft

Government astronauts on a commercial spacecraft – for instance, NASA astronauts on a SpaceX Crew Dragon – are clearly covered by the Rescue Agreement. But does the duty to rescue extend to rescuing someone who is not employed by a government, and who is on a commercial spacecraft that is not under contract with a government?

The OST is not limited in scope to state actors. For example, the first two sentences of Article VI read,

> States Parties to the Treaty shall bear international responsibility for national activities in outer space, including the moon and other celestial bodies, whether such activities are carried on by governmental agencies or by non-governmental entities, and for assuring that national activities are carried out in conformity with the provisions set forth in the present Treaty. The activities of non-governmental entities in outer space, including the moon and other celestial bodies, shall require authorization and continuing supervision by the appropriate State Party to the Treaty.[59]

Within the international legal system, Space law is unusual in making states responsible for all the actions of non-governmental entities. The responsibility extends to liability, as Article VII of the OST makes clear:

---

[57] International Convention on Maritime Search and Rescue, 27 April 1979, 1405 UNTS 119 Annex, ch 2, Art. 2.1.1 (entered into force 22 June 1985, including amendments adopted in 1998 and 2004) (SAR Convention).

[58] United Nations Convention on the Law of the Sea, 10 December 1982, 1833 UNTS 397 Art. 98 (1) (entered into force 16 November 1994) (UNCLOS).

[59] Outer Space Treaty, op. cit., Art. VI.

> Each State Party to the Treaty that launches or procures the launching of
> an object into outer space, including the moon and other celestial bodies,
> and each State Party from whose territory or facility an object is launched,
> is internationally liable for damage to another State Party to the Treaty or
> to its natural or juridical persons by such object or its component parts on
> the Earth, in air space or in outer space, including the moon and other
> celestial bodies.[60]

Similarly, nothing in the OST or the Rescue Agreement indicates that the
duty to rescue is limited to government spacecraft and government
employees.

The term 'spacecraft' is used throughout the Rescue Agreement. When
the approach to interpretation required by customary international law
and the 1969 Vienna Convention on the Law of Treaties is applied to
'spacecraft', it becomes clear that the term includes commercial vehicles.
First, the ordinary meaning of 'spacecraft', as defined by the *Merriam-
Webster Dictionary*, is broad in scope, namely, 'a vehicle that is used for
travel in outer space'.[61] Second, the context – i.e. the rest of the Rescue
Agreement – includes the preamble, with its reference to the OST calling
for 'the rendering of all possible assistance to astronauts in the event of
accident, distress or emergency landing' and its statement that the Rescue
Agreement was 'prompted by sentiments of humanity'.[62] Further to this,
Article 1 and other provisions of the Rescue Agreement do not refer to
the state that owns a spacecraft but rather to the 'launching authority'.
This choice of words corresponds with the assignment, to states, of
responsibility and liability for all the actions of non-governmental
entities – in Articles VI and VII of the OST, as reproduced above.

Then there is the change in terminology, as between the OST and the
Rescue Agreement, from 'astronauts' to 'personnel of a spacecraft'. As
Mark Sundahl explains, the broader language used in the Rescue
Agreement is controlling, because the Rescue Agreement was concluded
after the OST:

> [T]he Rescue Agreement supersedes the Outer Space Treaty with respect
> to the duty to rescue under the *lex posteriori* rule. The Rescue Agreement
> employs the phrase 'personnel of a spacecraft' to describe the beneficiaries
> of the duty to rescue rather than 'astronaut' – and this inconsistency is

---

[60] Ibid. Art. VII.

[61] Merriam-Webster, 'spacecraft' (last modified 20 April 2022), online: *Merriam-Webster.
com Dictionary* www.merriam-webster.com/dictionary/spacecraft.

[62] Rescue Agreement, op. cit., preamble.

resolved in favor of the later treaty. As a result, space tourism companies only need to concern themselves with the question of whether 'personnel' includes their passengers.[63]

As part of our Vienna Convention Article 31 interpretation, we must also consider the object and purpose of the Rescue Agreement, which (as we saw above) is humanitarian. This too supports an interpretation that encompasses commercial spacecraft.

Finally, under Article 32 of the Vienna Convention we can confirm this interpretive outcome by considering the circumstances of the Rescue Agreement's conclusion. As they were above, the 1914 SOLAS and 1944 Chicago Conventions are highly relevant here, since the duty to rescue in those early and widely ratified treaties extends to commercial vessels and aircraft. There is, as a result, no doubt that the obligations in the Rescue Agreement extend beyond rescuing government employees, to include at a minimum the rescue of non-governmental crew members.

### 1.7 The Duty to Rescue and Non-governmental Passengers on Commercial Spacecraft

Does the term 'personnel of a spacecraft' in the Rescue Agreement extend to non-government passengers on commercial spacecraft? The first step in answering this question concerns the 'ordinary meaning' of the term 'personnel', as part of a Vienna Convention Article 31 interpretation.

'Personnel' is defined in the *Merriam-Webster Dictionary* as:

1. a body of persons usually employed (as in a factory or organization).
2. a division of an organization concerned with personnel.[64]

It seems reasonable to conclude that the ordinary meaning of 'personnel' includes some degree of function or service.

Turning to the 'context' provided by the rest of the Rescue Agreement, we noted above that the preamble supports a broad interpretation of the duty to rescue. At the same time, however, the treaty's full title might suggest a narrower interpretation of 'personnel', one that excludes people who are not playing a functional role. Again, that title is: Agreement on the Rescue of Astronauts, the Return of Astronauts and the Return of Objects Launched into Outer Space. The term 'personnel of a spacecraft'

---

[63] Sundahl, op. cit. at 185.
[64] Merriam-Webster, 'personnel' (last modified 27 April 2022), online: *Merriam-Webster. com Dictionary* www.merriam-webster.com/dictionary/personnel.

appears later, in the text of this treaty. All that being said, from the point of view of pop culture and general public perception, the term 'astronaut' was and is widely understood to include everyone who has travelled to Space, with few in the media questioning whether Jeff Bezos and Wally Funk achieved 'astronaut' status.

As for the 'object and purpose' of the Rescue Agreement, the preamble explains that the agreement was 'prompted by sentiments of humanity', which supports the argument that it 'should be interpreted as applying to all persons involved in a space tourism flight'.[65] One can also discern object and purpose in the variety of terms used in the four Space treaties concluded between 1967 and 1974:[66] 'astronauts', 'personnel of a space object', 'personnel of a spacecraft', and 'persons on board a space object', which together indicate a principle of ensuring that 'the protection provided by the Space treaties covers all persons participating in Space flights'.[67]

As a result of this Article 31 interpretation, we conclude that 'personnel of a spacecraft' includes everyone on board. But we should confirm this interpretation, as we are permitted to do under Article 32 of the Vienna Convention, through an examination of 'supplementary means of interpretation' in the form of the *travaux préparatoires*.

The official records of the negotiations of the Rescue Agreement, which began as early as 1962, reveal an intent, on the part of the drafters, to be as inclusive as possible in terms of the beneficiaries of the duty to rescue. In 1964, for example, Working Group I of the Legal Subcommittee of the United Nations Committee on the Peaceful Uses of Outer Space (COPUOS) reviewed draft treaty proposals from both the United States and the Soviet Union, as well as a joint proposal from Canada and Australia. The records of the working group reveal that, initially, the term 'astronaut' had been suggested to take the place of 'crew' or 'personnel' as 'it means all those persons who have been in outer

---

[65] Steven Freeland, 'Up, up and . . . back: The emergence of space tourism and its impact on the international law of outer space' (2005) 6:1 *Chicago Journal of International Law* 10.

[66] Outer Space Treaty, op. cit.; Rescue Agreement, op. cit.; Convention on International Liability for Damage Caused by Space Objects, 29 March 1972, 961 UNTS 187 (entered into force 1 September 1972) (Liability Convention); Convention on Registration of Objects Launched into Outer Space, 12 November 1974, 1023 UNTS 15 (entered into force 15 September 1976) (Registration Convention).

[67] Vladlen S Vereschetin, 'Astronauts', in Anne Peters, ed, *Max Planck Encyclopedia of Public International Law* (Oxford: Oxford University Press, article last modified Jan 2006), online: opil.ouplaw.com/view/10.1093/law:epil/9780199231690/law-9780199231690-e1141.

space and have performed there certain duties'.[68] In response, the term 'crew' was suggested because it 'is relevant for the purpose of the Agreement since only in the distant future will space objects be used for pleasure trips'.[69] At one point an alternative phrase, 'persons on board a spacecraft', was advanced but then rejected out of concern that it would leave out personnel who had 'abandon[ed] the craft before landing'.[70] Most notably, however, is that the term 'personnel' was suggested because it 'is wider than the term "crew" and thus more preferable for the purpose of the Agreement'.[71]

Further to this, Wood points out that the OST

> constitutes an excellent supplemental source to inform the interpretation of 'personnel' because it forms the basis on which the ARRA [Rescue Agreement] was built and because it was adopted in the same year as the ARRA. OST Article VIII stipulates that States of registration 'shall retain jurisdiction and control over [their space] object, and over any personnel thereof'. This provides exceptional support to the position that the ordinary meaning of the term 'personnel' included private passengers at the time the ARRA was concluded.[72]

Last but perhaps not least, we can also consider the circumstances of the conclusion of the Rescue Agreement. Once again, these circumstances include the SOLAS and Chicago Conventions, where the duty to rescue includes the passengers on ships and aircraft. Indeed, the negotiation of the SOLAS Convention was prompted by the large number of passengers who died during the sinking of the RMS *Titanic* two years earlier.[73] On

---

[68] Committee on the Peaceful Uses of Outer Space, *Report of the Legal Subcommittee on the Work of the Second Part of Its Third Session (5–23 October 1964) to the Committee on the Peaceful Uses of Outer Space – Part I: Assistance to and Return of Astronauts and Space Objects. Summary of Points Raised in Discussions of Working Group I (Continued)*, UNGAOR, UN Doc A/AC.105/21/add.2 (23 October 1964) at 6, online: www.unoosa .org/pdf/reports/ac105/AC105_021E-ra.pdf.

[69] Ibid.

[70] Ibid.

[71] Ibid.

[72] Wood, op. cit. at 54; although the Rescue Agreement was opened for signature on 22 April 1968, the final stages of its negotiation were in 1967 (the year the OST was signed and entered into force), with the Rescue Agreement unanimously adopted by resolution of the General Assembly on 19 December 1967; *Agreement on the Rescue and Return of Astronauts, the Return of Astronauts and the Return of Objects Launched into Outer Space*, GA Res 2345 (XXII), UNGAOR, 22nd sess, 1640th Plen Mtg, UN Doc A/ RES/22/2345 (19 December 1967).

[73] Catherine Phillips and Jaideep Sirkar, 'The International Conference on Safety of Life at Sea, 1914', (Summer 2012) 69:2 *Coast Guard Proceedings: Journal of Safety & Security at*

this basis, as well as for the reasons above, we conclude that the term 'personnel of a spacecraft', and therefore the duty to rescue, extend to rescuing non-government passengers on commercial spacecraft.

## 1.8   The Duty to Rescue and Suborbital Flights

As we explained above, there is no agreement on where airspace ends and Space begins. This lack of agreement creates uncertainties as to the legal regime applicable to suborbital flights. Virgin Galactic flights reach altitudes just above 80 kilometres, which some consider to be Space, and others do not. Blue Origin flights reach altitudes just above 100 kilometres, which is unarguably Space, but they will not achieve orbit and are therefore akin to intercontinental ballistic missiles (ICBMs) which cross through Space but are not generally regarded as subject to international Space law.[74]

In the context of the duty to rescue, the uncertainty whether air law or Space law applies is unlikely to create practical problems. Unlike ICBMs, the vehicles used by Virgin Galactic and Blue Origin land very close to their launch sites, and therefore within the territory of the same state. Even if an accidental landing were somehow to occur on the territory of another state, or on the high seas, a duty to rescue would always exist – whether under the Rescue Agreement; the Chicago Convention on Civil Aviation; or the combined provisions of the SOLAS Convention (Regulation V-33), SAR Convention and UNCLOS (Art. 98). Finally, no crew or passengers from a suborbital flight will ever require a rescue in Space, since their vehicle would not remain there for more than a few minutes, even after an accident.

At the same time, determining which legal regime applies to a suborbital flight will have consequences for the liability regime that applies, as well as for the registration of the vehicle. The liability regime in airspace is fundamentally different from the liability regime in Space. In airspace, liability is based on fault (of the air carrier), and states are not responsible for the actions of private airlines and other non-governmental entities.

---

Sea 27, online: www.dco.uscg.mil/Portals/9/DCO%20Documents/Proceedings%20Magazine/ Archive/2012/Vol69_No2_Sum2012.pdf.

[74] Indeed, the issue of ICBMs was avoided in the drafting of the OST, which only prohibits the stationing of nuclear weapons in orbit or anywhere else in Space. See Rex J Zedalis and Catherine L Wade, 'Anti-satellite weapons and the Outer Space Treaty of 1967' (1978) 8:3 *California Western International Law Journal* 454 at 465.

Under the 1972 Convention on the International Liability for Damage
Caused by Space Objects (Liability Convention),[75] there is absolute liability of a 'launching state' for damage caused by its Space object 'on the
surface of the earth or to aircraft in flight' (Art. II) and fault-based liability
for damage caused elsewhere, i.e. in Space (Art. III). Moreover, under the
OST, states are responsible for any damage (Art. VII), including damage
caused by 'national activities' undertaken by 'non-governmental entities'
(Art. VI), such as suborbital tourism companies incorporated within, or
launching from, their territory.

Stephan Hobe argues that we can determine which legal regime applies
to suborbital flights by examining, among other things, (1) the way the
vehicle leaves the Earth's surface and (2) the vehicle's intended purpose.[76]
From this, a differentiation between aircraft and spacecraft can be made,
allowing the respective legal regimes to be applied appropriately.[77]

Some suborbital vehicles, such as Virgin Galactic's *SpaceShipTwo*, are
ferried to a high altitude by an aircraft before being released, at which
point they continue upwards under their own rocket power. As Hobe
explains, while the vehicle is attached to the aircraft, the combined units
should be dealt with under air law because they exhibit the 'technical
functions such as flight pattern and maneuverability' of an aircraft.[78]
Indeed, the definition of an aircraft under the Chicago Convention is:
'Any machine that can derive support in the atmosphere from the
reactions of the air'.[79]

Once the vehicle detaches from the aircraft and engages its rocket
engines, Hobe argues that it should be considered a 'space object'.[80] This
argument has merit, given the language of Article VII of the OST, which
reads,

> Each State Party to the Treaty that launches or procures the launching of an
> object into outer space, including the moon and other celestial bodies, and
> each State Party from whose territory or facility an object is launched, is
> internationally liable for damage to another State Party to the Treaty or to its
> natural or juridical persons by such object or its component parts on the Earth,
> in air space or in outer space, including the moon and other celestial bodies.[81]

[75] Liability Convention, op. cit.
[76] Stephan Hobe, 'Legal aspects of space tourism' (2007) 86:2 *Nebraska Law Review* 442.
[77] Ibid.
[78] Ibid at 443.
[79] Chicago Convention, op. cit., Annex 7, ch 1.
[80] Hobe, op. cit. at 443.
[81] Outer Space Treaty, op. cit., Art. VII.

The key words here are 'into outer space', which, again, begins no more than 100 kilometres above the Earth. The Liability Convention follows the approach of the OST, adding only that '[t]he term "space object" includes component parts of a space object as well as its launch vehicle and parts thereof.'[82] And it makes sense for the Liability Convention to apply to suborbital flights when they are in Space, since a suborbital vehicle could cause damage even during its brief time there. However, this conclusion might not apply to *SpaceShipTwo*, depending on whether one considers the boundary of Space to be 80 or 100 kilometres.

Determining the applicable legal regime will also be important with regard to any damage caused by the vehicle during its return to Earth. Article II of the Liability Convention reads, 'A launching State shall be absolutely liable to pay compensation for damage caused by its space object on the surface of the earth or to aircraft in flight.'[83] Again, under international air law, it is the airline that is liable and not a state. Moreover, the liability is fault-based under air law rather than absolute as in Space law.

The Liability Convention applying to suborbital flights (at least those which reach above 100 kilometres) does not mean that the Registration Convention is likewise applicable. For the first sentence of Article II of the Registration Convention reads, 'When a space object is launched *into earth orbit or beyond*, the launching State shall register the space object by means of an entry in an appropriate registry which it shall maintain'.[84]

Some experts have argued that suborbital flights could, for the purposes of the Registration Convention, be treated as failed attempts to launch into Space. The argument seeks to draw on the fact that a spacecraft which is intended to be launched into orbit, but which fails to achieve orbit, remains governed by the Space law regime. However, a suborbital vehicle does not fail to reach orbit by accident; it fails to reach orbit by design. Achieving orbit is never a possibility because the vehicle cannot achieve orbital speeds.

The limited state practice on this matter does not help to clarify things. The FAA has been licensing Blue Origin and Virgin Galactic's flights as 'commercial space transportation' under Chapter III, Title 14, of the Code of Federal Regulations. However, Title 14 includes both aeronautics and Space and the FAA is of course the Federal *Aviation* Administration.

---

[82] Liability Convention, op. cit., Art. I(d).
[83] Ibid. Art. II.
[84] Registration Convention, op. cit., Art. II, added emphasis.

Moreover, *SpaceShipTwo* has also been registered by the FAA as an aircraft and more specifically a 'glider'.[85] This makes sense because, during most of its flight, i.e. during the ferry ride to 50,000 feet, and then during its return to Earth, *SpaceShipTwo* fits the definition of an aircraft under the Chicago Convention, i.e. 'Any machine that can derive support in the atmosphere from the reactions of the air'.[86] *New Shepard*, which does not have wings, does not fit the definition and could not be so registered.

At the international level, applying the Registration Convention to suborbital vehicles would serve little purpose, since the point of registration is to publicise the presence of human-made objects in Space, and suborbital vehicles only spend a couple of minutes at the lowest fringes of Space. In other words, it makes sense for the Liability Convention to apply to suborbital flights, and for the Registration Convention not to do so. There is no reason why the geographic reaches of the treaties should be the same, since they deal with different issues.

Again, in terms of the duty to rescue, all this concerns a distinction without a difference. The duty to rescue applies everywhere on Earth, under either the Rescue Agreement, the Chicago Convention, the SOLAS Convention, the SAR Convention and/or UNCLOS. It also exists, as we explain in Chapter 6, as a universally applicable rule of customary international law.

The duty to rescue is a central principle of international Space law; so central, in fact, that the 1968 Rescue Agreement was concluded almost immediately after the 1967 OST to elaborate, via a dedicated treaty, on the duty to rescue as already set out in the OST. Although the drafters of the two treaties might not have foreseen that Space tourists would fly on commercial spacecraft in the 2020s, they worded the duty to rescue in broad terms, and with the clear intent of having it apply to all human beings engaged in Space travel.

Rescues in orbit, on the Moon and other celestial bodies and in deep Space will be difficult and expensive. But they will occur. At sea, states take the duty to rescue seriously, sometimes deploying aircraft and ships thousands of kilometres to save the crews of foreign ships and boats, whether publicly or privately owned. Although this practice is not always consistent – as sadly sometimes those same states look away when the

---

[85] To find the registration for *SpaceShipTwo*, search N202VG at 'Aircraft Inquiry' (2022), online: *FAA* registry.faa.gov/aircraftinquiry/Search/NNumberInquiry.
[86] Chicago Convention, op. cit., Annex 7, ch 1.

human beings in distress are economic migrants or even refugees – international rules can exist without uniform practice or coercive enforcement.

The duty to rescue is not coupled with a right to be reimbursed for costs. Article 5(5) of the Rescue Agreement sets out an obligation, on the part of the launching authority, to bear the '[e]xpenses incurred in fulfilling obligations to recover and return a space object or its component parts'. But the absence of a similar provision concerning the duty to rescue confirms that the rescuer bears the costs. This raises the question whether there is a need for new international rules, or perhaps a compensation fund, to reduce the costs to states or companies when they engage in rescue missions. For instance, Space companies could be required to carry insurance for the costs incurred by any rescuer. Alternatively, or additionally, Space companies could be required to maintain a rescue capability whenever they have human beings in Space. Consider the best practice demonstrated by NASA, which held a Saturn V/Apollo and then a Space Shuttle on standby whenever it had astronauts in Space. Today, SpaceX provides the same readily available backup with Falcon 9/Crew Dragon. Again, it is important to note that this issue will not arise with suborbital flights, which will always return to Earth even if something goes wrong.

## 1.9   Climate Impacts

There is nothing inherently wrong about finding new and cheaper ways to access Space. The development of commercial spacecraft could lead to innovations of general value. The problem, rather, is one of volume, with humanity already struggling to limit its collective impacts on the atmosphere. Richard Branson and Jeff Bezos are clearly planning for a very large number of tourist flights. In 2018, Branson said, 'There are, we believe, millions of people who would love to go to space, and we want to tap into those people. If you can create the best – the best hotel chain, the best clubs, the best spaceship company – it'll become very valuable.'[87] Coming from someone who once spent a lot of time and energy cultivating an image as a climate change activist, this embrace of Space tourism represents a stunning turnaround.[88]

---

[87] Nicholas Schmidle, *Virgin Galactic and the Making of a Modern Astronaut* (New York: Henry Holt & Co, 2021) 213.

[88] For a sharp assessment of Branson's record on climate change, see Naomi Klein, 'The hypocrisy behind the big business climate change battle', *The Guardian* (13 September 2014), online: www.theguardian.com/environment/2014/sep/13/greenwashing-sticky-business-naomi-klein.

In 2010, the development of *SpaceShipTwo* prompted a peer-reviewed study which predicted that 'emissions from a fleet of 1000 launches per year of suborbital rockets would create a persistent layer of black carbon particles in the northern stratosphere that could cause potentially significant changes in the global atmospheric circulation and distributions of ozone and temperature'.[89] Although the study was not specific to the form of synthetic rubber used as fuel in *SpaceShipTwo*'s 'hybrid' rocket motor, it emphasised that the black carbon produced in the upper atmosphere by such rockets could have a 'radiative forcing effect' that exceeds, by several orders of magnitude, the climate impact of their carbon dioxide emissions. Specifically, the study estimates that

> after one decade of suborbital hybrid rocket launches at the assumed rate, [radiative forcing] from the accumulated [black carbon] for these 10,000 launches will exceed [radiative forcing] from the associated $CO_2$ emissions by a factor of about $10^5$. As long as the launch rate is maintained, the $CO_2$ climate forcing for this fleet would be minuscule compared to the [black carbon] forcing. Accordingly, assessments of climate forcing for passenger and cargo rockets that consider only $CO_2$ emissions [citation removed] underestimate rockets' contribution to climate change by many orders of magnitude.[90]

This point is critical. A significant amount of the public discussion concerning climate impacts of human activities is focused on $CO_2$ emissions, and for good reason. But this cannot be at the expense of dismissing contributions from other substances that are much more relevant to rocket launches. Even water vapour placed into the upper atmosphere has the potential to form mesospheric clouds, for which the climate impacts are not fully understood.

The FAA overlooked the issue of black carbon when it conducted an environmental impact assessment of *SpaceShipTwo* in 2012.[91] The FAA did consider small particulate matter, including soot, in the exhaust of *WhiteKnightTwo* – the aircraft that ferries *SpaceShipTwo* to over 40,000 feet. However, it did not investigate the soot production by *SpaceShipTwo* in any capacity, citing the lack of data on particulate matter for the rocket

---

[89] Martin Ross, Michael Mills and Darin Toohey, 'Potential climate impact of black carbon emitted by rockets' (2010) 37:24 *Geophysical Research Letters* L24810.

[90] Ibid.

[91] FAA, 'Final environmental assessment for the launch and reentry of SpaceShipTwo reusable suborbital rockets at the Mojave air and space port', Federal Aviation Administration (May 2012), online: www.faa.gov/about/office_org/headquarters_offices/ast/media/20120502_Mojave_SS2_Final_EAandFONSI.pdf.

plane. This is a clear failure. For by limiting itself to 'data-driven' decisions (i.e. those that can be based on existing data), the FAA is treating as irrelevant scientifically well-informed models that show that soot in the upper atmosphere can have a substantial climate impact. It also implicitly supports the notion that companies can avoid rigorous environmental impact assessments by declining to make data available or simply not acquiring the necessary data in the first place.

But this does not mean that the rest of us should give Branson and Virgin Galactic a pass on their cumulative, potentially massive, climate impacts. Indeed, the 2010 peer-reviewed study concluded that the buildup of black carbon from all these joyrides to the edge of Space might, over a decade, cause as much damage to the atmosphere as all subsonic aviation – in other words, all the goods and millions of people transported by air around the world each day.[92] What if all the efforts the rest of us are making to mitigate climate change – whether paying carbon taxes, retrofitting buildings, buying electric cars, or avoiding long-haul vacations – are about to be nullified by the wealthiest 0.1 per cent engaging in Space tourism? Virgin Galactic should be required to address its potential climate impacts, including from black carbon, with publicly accessible data – or limit flights until it adopts a less-polluting fuel.

*New Shepard* is powered by liquid hydrogen and liquid oxygen, which is at face value a clean-burning fuel – as Blue Origin gleefully points out.[93] But all liquid fuels will affect mesospheric cloud formation,[94] for which the full climate effects, as well as other implications for the atmosphere, are poorly understood. Moreover, all fuels have impacts, and it is essential that the full spectrum of impacts is evaluated for understanding how rocket launches will alter Earth's environment. Focusing on just, for example, comparing today's rocket $CO_2$ emissions with those from aviation and shipping will miss numerous other factors and provide a distorted view of the consequences of human Space use.

---

[92] Ross, Mills and Toohey, op. cit.

[93] See Blue Origin (9 June 2021 at 11:33), online: *Twitter* twitter.com/blueorigin/status/ 1413521627116032001. The tweet, which includes a side-by-side comparison of *SpaceShipTwo* and *New Shepard*, actually cites Martin Ross and James Vedda, 'The policy and science of rocket emissions', Center for Space Policy and Strategy, the Aerospace Corporation (2018), online: https://aerospace.org/sites/default/files/2018-05/ RocketEmissions_0.pdf.

[94] JA Dallas, S. Raval, JP Alvarez Gaitan, S Saydam and AG Dempster, 'The environmental impact of emissions from space launches: A comprehensive review' (2020) 255 *Journal of Cleaner Production* 120209.

Orbital launches are generally worse for the atmosphere than suborbital launches since it takes more energy – more combustion – to achieve orbital speeds. SpaceX's Falcon 9 rockets are powered by kerosene and liquid oxygen, with the consumption of the kerosene injecting black carbon into the upper atmosphere. Such launches also often leave spent rocket stages and other objects behind in low Earth orbit and geosynchronous transfer orbits, increasing the operational hazards for thousands of satellites as well as the ISS and China's new Tiangong Space station.

SpaceX's new Starship will be fully reuseable and powered by methane and liquid oxygen, a somewhat more environmental combination that will, nevertheless, affect mesospheric cloud formation and still produce soot. Moreover, Elon Musk is planning to use Starship to shuttle fuel for deep Space missions departing from low Earth orbit, and for point-to-point travel on Earth itself. In numerous presentations and other public comments, Musk has made clear that he anticipates launching Starship spacecraft hundreds if not thousands of times each year. Indeed, in an e-mail to SpaceX employees in November 2021, obtained by CNBC, he warned that the company faced a 'genuine risk of bankruptcy if we cannot achieve a Starship flight rate of at least once every two weeks next year.'[95] Musk was most certainly exaggerating the threat of bankruptcy, since SpaceX is a privately held company that could raise vast amounts of money by going public on the New York Stock Exchange. But more importantly, the sustainability of all this activity must be questioned. Although some of the opportunities provided by these launches will undoubtedly benefit humanity, other aspects, such as Space tourism, will not. Again, it is all a question of volume – and with that, agreed limits on what states and private companies can do.

### 1.10    Who Will Rescue the Martians?

NASA has plans to establish a permanent human presence on the Moon, while Elon Musk claims that a self-sustaining community[96] on Mars is his principal motivation for building both SpaceX and Tesla (with

---

[95] Michael Sheetz, 'Elon Musk tells SpaceX employees that Starship engine crisis is creating a "risk of bankruptcy"', *CNBC* (30 November 2021), online: www.cnbc.com/2021/11/30/elon-musk-to-spacex-starships-raptor-engine-crisis-risks-bankruptcy.html.

[96] We prefer the term 'community' to the historically loaded terms 'settlement' and 'colony'.

revenue from car sales being necessary to fund the most expensive operation yet undertaken by humankind).

The potential for communities on the Moon and Mars raises all kinds of fascinating legal and policy issues, especially in the context of commercial missions where the spacecraft, habitations, and life-support systems belong to a private corporation. In democratic countries, there are some human and labour rights that cannot be surrendered through employment contracts, including the right to leave a job after due notice, but will these rights be available to people living in a SpaceX complex on Mars? There is also the issue of children born on Mars, and whether they might be compelled to work for SpaceX when they are adults. If not, what obligations, if any, does the company owe to them? There is also the issue of the right to self-determination, which should be available to a community in Space, not least because of its vast distance from the 'colonial power'.[97] Relatedly, there are issues involving sovereignty and territoriality. Will permanent habitations on Mars require some compromise on the prohibition on 'national appropriation of the Moon and other celestial bodies', as set out in Article II of the Outer Space Treaty? Might they require 'safety zones', as proposed by the Artemis Accords,[98] and could these be permanent – and legally opposable to other actors?

We will leave these issues for another book, except for the issue of the duty to rescue, which arises because of Article 3 of the Rescue Agreement. Again, that provision states that if

> the personnel of a spacecraft have alighted on the high seas or in any other place not under the jurisdiction of any State, those Contracting Parties which are in a position to do so shall, if necessary, extend assistance in search and rescue operations for such personnel to assure their speedy rescue.[99]

The question is, does Article 3 extend to people who have alighted on the Moon or Mars, not because of an emergency, but because they plan to stay there? In short, if people who are happily *living* on the Moon or Mars subsequently have an accident, or a medical emergency, or perhaps run out of supplies, can they benefit from this specific treaty provision? The answer, clearly, is 'no'.

---

[97] Michael Byers, 'Elon Musk, president of Mars?', *Washington Post* (22 January 2016), online:   www.washingtonpost.com/opinions/elon-musk-president-of-mars/2016/01/22/732f1520-bfc7-11e5-bcda-62a36b394160_story.html.

[98] See discussion in Chapter 5 below.

[99] Rescue Agreement, op. cit., Art. 3.

But this is not the end of the enquiry. To answer the broader question, whether there is a duty to rescue, we have to go back to the second paragraph of Article V of the OST, which reads, 'In carrying on activities in outer space and on celestial bodies, the astronauts of one State Party shall render all possible assistance to the astronauts of other States Parties.'[100] This general obligation to 'render all possible assistance' to 'astronauts carrying on activities ... on celestial bodies' is not limited to accidents occurring during the landing and 'alighting'. Nor is this general obligation superseded by the otherwise more specific provisions of the later-in-time Rescue Agreement, because they do not address this issue. So yes, the duty to rescue applies with regard to people living on the Moon or Mars, at least for now and the foreseeable future. We need not argue whether such individuals are considered to be tourists or part of the crew or something else. In fact, other terms may very well emerge to describe people who live for extended periods away from Earth or have never lived on Earth. As already discussed, 'astronaut' is intended to be broad in scope for the purposes of the Rescue Agreement.

Moreover, this duty to rescue people in distress on other celestial bodies likely also exists in customary international law, as a logical extension to our finding above that the duty to rescue applies everywhere on Earth. There is no apparent reason, either in treaty or in state practice, to think that a generally applicable rule of customary international law does not apply in Space. Indeed, Article III of the OST reads, 'States Parties to the Treaty shall carry on activities in the exploration and use of outer space, including the moon and other celestial bodies, in accordance with international law, including the Charter of the United Nations.'[101] The explicit mention of the UN Charter makes it clear that 'international law' in this context means international law in general, not just the specialised rules of international Space law.

But again, the duty to rescue is never absolute: a state has the discretion to decide that a rescue mission is impossible, unlikely to succeed, or simply too dangerous or expensive to attempt. Each situation will also depend on the facts specific to it. A refusal to mount a self-evidently feasible rescue mission to a nearby Moon base, with rovers and sufficient fuel and supplies available, might constitute a clear breach of the duty to rescue, but most other decisions will be less obvious. Even Hollywood

---

[100] Outer Space Treaty, op. cit., Art. V.
[101] Ibid. Art. III.

seems to recognise this: in *The Martian*, the Chinese provided a rocket, but did not put any of their own personnel at risk.

## 1.11   Conclusion

Richard Branson  is the king of self-promotion, with an ability to draw in A-list celebrities to boost his own stature. Lady Gaga, Justin Bieber, Leonardo DiCaprio, Brad Pitt, Angelina Jolie, Katy Perry, Russell Brand, and Rihanna are all rumoured to have reservations on *SpaceShipTwo*.[102] All this celebrity comes with a large dose of cynicism. Prospective Space tourists have expressed a desire to engage in 'exploration' and to view our fragile 'blue marble' against the backdrop of the void. This last desire is often expressed alongside the goal of raising environmental awareness, including the need for those of us who have stayed on Earth to change our personal behaviours.

In 2009, Cirque du Soleil founder Guy Laliberté became Canada's first Space tourist, travelling to the ISS for 12 days on a Soyuz rocket. He claimed the journey as a business expense – a 'social and poetic mission' to raise awareness about the need for improved access to fresh water. Let that sink in. Some of the richest people in the world are paying to launch themselves into Space and then asking for the taxpayers to subsidise their joyride. Fortunately, the Tax Court of Canada disagreed, ruling that 'the motivating, essential and overwhelmingly primary purpose of the travel was personal'.[103] Appealed by Laliberté, this judgment was unanimously upheld by Canada's Federal Court of Appeal.[104]

Most of these wannabe astronauts prefer the terms 'private astronauts' and 'spaceflight participants' to 'Space tourists.' They sometimes also profess a desire to test themselves against new challenges, likening their trip to those taken by the first astronauts, or high-risk adventure sports such as summiting Mount Everest or sailing singlehandedly round the

---

[102] Not all celebrities have jumped on this bandwagon. When Billy Eilish was asked if she wanted to go to Space, she replied, 'I would literally rather do anything else.' Sophia June, 'Billie Eilish says she'd "literally rather do anything else" than go to space', *Nylon* (October 2021), online: www.nylon.com/life/billie-eilish-hates-space.

[103] *Laliberté v. The Queen*, 2018 TCC 186 at para. 11; see Sidhartha Banerjee, 'Tax court rules Cirque's Guy Laliberte's 2009 space trip was a taxable benefit', *Globe and Mail* (14 September 2018), online: www.theglobeandmail.com/canada/article-tax-court-rules-guy-lalibertes-2009-space-trip-was-a-taxable-benefit-2. The court did allow 10 per cent of the trip to be claimed as a business expense.

[104] *Laliberté v. Canada*, 2020 FCA 97.

world. But make no mistake: they use deep pockets to bypass rigorous selection processes; undergo minimal training, particularly for suborbital flights; and have little to no real inflight responsibility. It is perhaps sobering to point out that 'Ham the Chimp' was trained to perform a mission-critical job – pushing a lever to test reaction times in Space.

Projects like Axiom, while still a form of tourism, do have some potential for advancing human spaceflight through collaboration with NASA and other Space agencies. Indeed, the United States and its allies are counting on such companies to provide next-generation Space stations. But a healthy dose of skepticism is still needed, with Axiom's current focus being on building the most expensive and elite of travel lounges.

Some of those journeying into Space will push boundaries, and these individuals could have a positive impact on crewed Space exploration, even if it is by being thrill-seeking guinea pigs who pay their own way. But many Space tourists are simply engaged in a form of extinction tourism. They are like passengers on an Arctic cruise ship,[105] spewing greenhouse gases as they travel to the melting ice – to see it before it's gone. And yet states have a duty to rescue them if something goes wrong.

---

[105] Michael Byers, 'Arctic cruises: Fun for tourists, bad for the environment', *Globe and Mail* (18 April 2016), online: www.theglobeandmail.com/opinion/arctic-cruises-great-for-tourists-bad-for-the-environment/article29648307.

# 2

---

## Mega-constellations

### 2.1  Introduction

As the COVID-19 pandemic preoccupied most of Earth's inhabitants in July 2020, the night sky provided a much-needed distraction. NEOWISE, the brightest comet seen in the northern hemisphere since the passage of Hale–Bopp in 1997, painted the heavens with its brilliant twin tails.

But NEOWISE was not the only new feature in the sky. 'Trains' of satellites crossed the sky in large numbers, with some widely shared images showing the comet being 'photobombed' by a dense overlay of white lines produced by SpaceX's Starlink satellites.[1] It might be tempting to dismiss this event as a one-off – an unlucky chance alignment between NEOWISE and a single payload of about 60 recently launched satellites undergoing orbit-raising manoeuvres. But consider Figure 2.1, a wide-field image showing a 'globular cluster' of stars and the comet C/2020 T2 (Palomar), which was produced from two hours of image stacking.[2] The image is full of both bright and faint streaks from Starlink and other satellites. Sadly, a clear picture of the sky is quickly becoming something of the past.

Until recently, those wanting to escape the effects of terrestrial light pollution could leave cities and travel to the countryside. Indeed, 'dark-sky spaces' have been recognised and protected around the world,

---

[1]  See Julien H Girard, '17 30-second images of the comet added up by @cielodecanarias, completely photobombed by @elonmusk's #Starlink satellites. It's a few hundreds of them right now, there will be a few thousands in the near future. @SpaceX is committed to coating orienting them better but still . . .' (22 July 2020 at 17:41), *Twitter*, online: twitter .com/djulik/status/1286053695956881409.

[2]  Globular clusters are old and massive star clusters, containing hundreds of thousands of stars, all held together by and orbiting each other through their mutual gravitational interactions. 'Stacking' multiple exposures to produce an image can provide many advantages over a single, long exposure. The multitude of satellite streaks is the result of each image in the 'stack' having a different set of streaks.

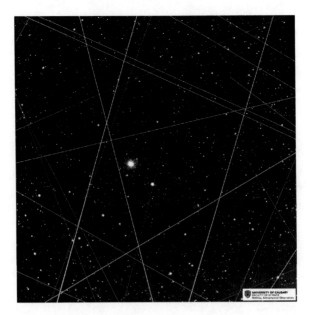

**Figure 2.1**   An image of M3 (NGC 5272), a globular star cluster, along with comet C/ 2020 T2 (Palomar), which is near the red cursor. The image was produced from a two-hour series of observations by the Rothney Astrophysical Observatory's Baker–Nunn telescope. The multitude of bright and faint streaks are individual satellites.

and stargazing has become a form of tourism.[3] But increasingly there is nowhere, and therefore no way, to escape the pollution from the thousands of satellites being launched each year.

Should Starlink and other so-called 'mega-constellations' come to fruition without brightness mitigation, the night sky as we know it could be lost. Indeed, anyone looking up at the stars as they had done in their youth could very well could see one in ten 'stars' moving – because they are not stars at all.[4] Adding to the confusion, such a dizzying dance of satellite movements could further create an optical illusion, so that suddenly all the lights in the sky appear to be in motion, making it difficult to track which are actual stars and which are something else.

[3] International Dark Sky Association Headquarters, 'International Dark Sky Place' (January 2022), International Dark-Sky Association, online: www.darksky.org/our-work/conserva tion/idsp.

[4] Samantha M Lawler, Aaron C Boley and Hanno Rein, 'Visibility predictions for near-future satellite megaconstellations: Latitudes near 50° will experience the worst light pollution' (2022) 163:1 *Astronomical Journal* 21.

Light pollution and a loss of natural and cultural heritage, however, are not the only problems that come with mega-constellations.

The era of mega-constellations began around 2019. Until then, the sight of a satellite was usually a cause of excitement – an ordinary person's glimpse at the marvel of Space exploration. Indeed, as of 2019 there were 'only' about 3,000 satellites in low Earth orbit (LEO), about half of which were functional. Moreover, before mega-constellations, there were just individual satellites and small 'constellations' – groups of satellites that work together to provide some kind of service, such as the global positioning system (GPS), with its 31 satellites. Iridium has provided satellite phone services for decades with a constellation that presently contains 76 satellites. Planet Labs provides Earth imaging for farmers, forestry companies, other businesses and governments from a constellation of 200 satellites, while SiriusXM satellite radio operates from just a handful of satellites. A mega-constellation,[5] by contrast, is designed to provide low-cost, low-latency, high-bandwidth Internet around the world from thousands or even tens of thousands of satellites in LEO.

SpaceX's Starlink constellation has been the first out of the gate. Its initial deployment phase was largely completed in 2020 with 1,440 satellites placed into a single 'orbital shell' – a collection of circular orbits having the same altitude, in this case 550 kilometres. SpaceX now operates more than 3,000 satellites or approximately 50 per cent of all active satellites in orbit (LEO to GEO, i.e. geosynchronous orbit),[6] and is well on its way to placing an already licensed 12,000 satellites into orbit.[7] Yet this is only its 'Gen1' design. The company has already filed for permission from the US Federal Communications Commission (FCC) to add a further 30,000 satellites, the

---

[5] Scientists often refer to mega-constellations as 'large constellations' or 'satcons', though both these terms downplay the order-of-magnitude change in numbers over early constellations. The nomenclature is further complicated by the fact that it would be more accurate to use the prefix 'kilo' rather than 'mega' for thousands of satellites.

[6] For updates, see Jonathan McDowell, 'Starlink statistics', *Jonathan's Space Pages*, online: https://planet4589.org/space/stats/star/starstats.html.

[7] For Gen1 of SpaceX's (Space Exploration Holdings, LLC) Starlink filings and modifications with the Federal Communications Commission (FCC), see the technical attachments of the following: Patricia Paoletta, 'Application for fixed satellite service by Space Exploration Holdings, LLC, SAT-LOA-20161115-00118' (29 March 2018), FCC, online: fcc.report/IBFS/SAT-LOA-20161115-00118; Patricia Paoletta, 'Application for fixed satellite service by Space Exploration Holdings, LLC, SAT-LOA-20170301-00027' (15 November 2018), *FCC*, online: fcc.report/IBFS/SAT-LOA-20170301-00027; William Wiltshire, 'Application for fixed satellite service by Space Exploration Holdings, LLC, SAT-MOD-20200417-00037' (27 April 2021), *FCC*, online: https://fcc.report/IBFS/SAT-MOD-20200417-00037.

so-called 'Gen2' design.[8] Other companies have similar plans for mega-constellations, including OneWeb (7,000 satellites, of which 394 have already been launched),[9] Amazon/Kuiper (3236 satellites),[10] and Guo Wang/StarNet (13,000 satellites).[11] In what could seem like a dramatic escalation, in 2021 Rwanda filed 'advanced publication information' with the International Telecommunication Union (ITU) for two constellations that would have more than 300,000 satellites between them – assuming the filing can be taken at face value. However, the Rwandan company in question, Marvel Space Communications,[12] might be planning to sell off all or some of any radio spectrum rights that it obtains, rather than placing that many satellites into orbit itself. It is also possible that at this time the company does not know exactly what its desired constellation will look like, but wants to lay claim to as much spectrum and orbital Space as it can while it sorts out the details. Since the Rwandan filing, other states have also filed advanced publication information for additional mega-constellations, including Canada for Kepler (114,852 satellites)[13] and the US for Astra Space (13,600 satellites).[14]

---

[8] For Gen2 of SpaceX's Starlink filing, see William Wiltshire, 'Application for fixed satellite service by Space Exploration Holdings, LLC, SAT-LOA-20200526-00055' (14 January 2022), *FCC*, online: fcc.report/IBFS/SAT-LOA-20200526-00055.

[9] For OneWeb's phase 1 and 2 filings, see Brian D Weimer, 'Application for fixed satellite service by WorldVu Satellites Limited, SAT-MPL-20210112-00007' (12 January 2021), *FCC*, online: fcc.report/IBFS/SAT-MPL-20210112-00007.

[10] For Amazon/Kuiper's filings, see Jennifer D Hindin, 'Application for fixed satellite service by Kuiper Systems LLC, SAT-LOA-20190704-00057' (30 July 2020), *FCC*, online: fcc .report/IBFS/SAT-LOA-20190704-00057.

[11] Larry Press, 'A new Chinese broadband Internet constellation' (2 October 2020), *CircleID*, online (blog): circleid.com/posts/20201002-a-new-chinese-broadband-satellite-constellation.

[12] The name of the company may be linked to the film *Black Panther*, which was produced by Marvel Studios about a fictional country named Wakanda, located in roughly the same area as Rwanda. Wakanda is an extremely advanced country, disguising its wealth and capabilities as a small developing country.

[13] Jeff Foust, 'Satellite operators criticize "extreme" megaconstellation filings', *SpaceNews* (14 December 2021), online: spacenews.com/satellite-operators-criticize-extreme-mega constellation-filings. Kepler is not planning to launch all these satellites itself. Rather, its business model involves installing small data terminals on 'smallsats' and 'nanosats' being launched by its customers. These terminals will connect to Kepler's own relatively small constellation of satellites, which will then pass signals onward to ground stations, creating 'always-on, real-time connectivity to space-based assets' that would otherwise lack this constant connectivity. Craig Bamford, 'Spire Global to test Kepler's Aether communication terminal and service', *SpaceQ* (20 December 2021), online: spaceq.ca/ spire-global-to-test-keplers-aether-communication-terminal-and-service.

[14] Jeff Foust, 'Astra files FCC application for 13,600-satellite constellation', *SpaceNews* (5 November 2021), online: spacenews.com/astra-files-fcc-application-for-13600-satel lite-constellation.

Although the current governance system for LEO is slowly changing, it remains ill-equipped to handle very large systems of satellites. In this chapter, we outline how the current direction of development – essentially the application of the 'consumer electronic product model' to satellites – could lead to multiple tragedies of the commons. Some of these are well known, such as a loss of access to certain orbits because of Space debris, while others have received insufficient attention thus far, including changes to the chemistry of Earth's upper atmosphere and increased dangers on Earth's surface from re-entered debris. The heavy use of certain orbital regions might also result in the de facto exclusion of other actors from them, violating the 1967 Outer Space Treaty, which among other things designates Space as 'free for exploration and use for all States without discrimination of any kind' and that this exploration and use of Space is 'the province of all [hu]mankind' (Art. I).[15] In the next chapter, we address some of the legal issues arising from collisions and Space debris, as well as from the effects of light pollution on astronomy.

We conclude that all these challenges associated with mega-constellations should be addressed in a co-ordinated manner through multilateral law-making, whether at the United Nations, at the Inter-Agency Space Debris Coordination Committee (IADC), or via an ad hoc process, rather than in an unco-ordinated manner through different national systems. Multilateral law-making has already delivered solutions to similar challenges regarding civil aviation in international air space and commercial shipping on the high seas.

Most importantly, mega-constellations require a shift in perspectives and policies. Instead of looking at single satellites, we need to evaluate systems of thousands of satellites, launched by multiple states and companies, all operating within a shared ecosystem. We use the term 'ecosystem' to underline an obvious but necessary point: the closer regions of Space are part of Earth's environment. Mega-constellations are on track to exceed the limits of that environment, with negative consequences for all of humanity.

## 2.2   Why Mega-constellations?

The thinking behind mega-constellations is simple, at least in general terms. Companies want to offer low-latency, reliable broadband Internet

---

[15] Treaty on Principles Governing the Activities of States in the Exploration and Use of Outer Space, Including the Moon and Other Celestial Bodies, 27 January 1967, 610 UNTS 205 Art. VI (entered into force 10 October 1967) (Outer Space Treaty).

connectivity regardless of user location. They are betting that, with enough users in remote and rural communities and on ships, trains, planes and automobiles, the winners in the race to industrialise LEO will create and capture a profitable long-term market. Whether these companies are right remains to be seen. It is possible that the difference between success and failure will ultimately be in the hands of military rather than civilian customers, since global low-latency connectivity delivered via thousands of satellites could offer a strategic advantage, for some applications, over higher-latency systems delivered by a much smaller number of satellites in higher orbits. For instance, it is widely assumed that the connectivity provided by a mega-constellation will be more resilient to attack, due to the large number of targets that would have to be struck to disrupt, disable or destroy the entire system.[16]

Another benefit cited by the proponents of mega-constellations is that connectivity will be brought to rural and remote communities, Indigenous peoples and those in the least-developed countries, places that often lack fibre-optic cables and other infrastructure that many of us now take for granted. Internet connectivity also creates opportunities for remote learning and 'telehealth', two services that have gained prominence during the COVID-19 pandemic. Yet some early analyses have questioned whether these promises are achievable. People who are not already well off may be prevented from accessing mega-constellations due to high subscription costs and the need for some ground-link infrastructure.[17] Iridium has built a successful business of providing satellite phones to emergency services and shipping and mining companies, but at several dollars per minute of connectivity, its customer base remains small. Larger constellations aim to find millions of customers, and it remains to be seen whether long-term profitability can be achieved – especially once multiple systems are offering the same service. Again, it may be that a single large customer, such as a military, is needed for any individual mega-constellation to succeed.

It is further possible that, as technology changes, the market for Internet connectivity from Space will flatten or contract. We see a hint of this already. The Hoh, an Indigenous people in northern Washington State, were among the first early users of the Starlink constellation.

---

[16] We question this assumption in the conclusion to this book.

[17] Meredith L Rawls, Heidi B Thiemann, Victor Chemin, Lucianne Walkowicz, Mike W Peel and Yan G Grange, 'Satellite constellation Internet affordability and need' (2020) 4:10 *Research Notes of the AAS* 189.

However, they see this as a temporary measure, with the long-term goal being fibre connectivity – for reliability reasons as well as a desire to be their own service provider.[18]

Space debris is also an issue. With several companies already launching thousands of satellites, the cumulative amount of all the material in orbit is increasing rapidly (and most importantly, in terms of collision risk, so too is the total cross-section). Elon Musk claims that billions of satellites can be operated safely in LEO,[19] but this is not generally true, particularly as more operators become involved, or if we take into account random events such as malfunctions, accidental explosions on orbit (of which there are about five each year) and meteoroid strikes. Musk also ignores the threat of lethal, non-trackable debris, which can only partly be addressed through improved detection-and-tracking technology. Over time, the cost of collisions could exceed the technological and economic advantages of LEO, pushing global satellite communications back to GEO.

## 2.3   Space Debris and Orbital Congestion

Figure 2.2 shows the  growth of on-orbit infrastructure over time, including tracked debris, payloads (active and defunct satellites) and abandoned rocket bodies. The term 'tracked debris' refers to those pieces that are large enough to be catalogued and reliably reacquired through observations, with sizes typically ten centimetres in diameter or larger. For cataloguing purposes, and as discussed here, 'tracked debris' excludes defunct satellites and rocket bodies. The latter are, of course, forms of debris but are discussed separately on account of their significant mass, and correspondingly their potential to be sources for the 'tracked debris' population, as discussed further below. Debris numbers are also incomplete, in that some objects with diameters greater than ten centimetres will not yet have been identified and tracked. Nor do they include smaller debris, which is likely much more numerous, with about one million

---

[18] Joshua Sokol, 'The fault in our stars: Satellite swarms are threatening the night sky. Is low-Earth orbit the next great crucible of environmental conflict?', *Science*, 7 October 2021, online: www.science.org/content/article/satellite-swarms-are-threatening-night-sky-creating-new-zone-environmental-conflict.

[19] Richard Waters, 'Elon Musk rejects claims he is squeezing out rivals in space', *Financial Times* (29 December 2021), online: www.ft.com/content/18dc896f-e92f-41f7-9259-69cfd8d61011.

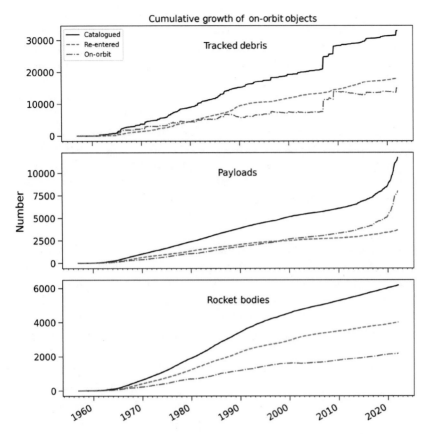

**Figure 2.2** Cumulative on-orbit distribution functions (all orbits) for tracked debris (top), payloads (middle) and rocket bodies (bottom). The 'on-orbit' curves are just the difference between the 'catalogued' and 'decayed' curves. The 2007 and 2009 debris spikes are a Chinese anti-satellite test and the Iridium 33–Kosmos 2251 collision respectively, while the 2021 spike is the Russian anti-satellite weapon test. The recent, rapid rise of the satellite (payload) curve represents NewSpace. This figure was produced using data obtained from the USSPACECOM satellite catalogue (www.space-track.org) and cross-referencing with on-orbit fragmentation records (Phillip D Anz-Meador et al., *History of On-Orbit Satellite Fragmentations*, 15th ed (Houston: NASA, 2018). All orbits are included. Sudden rises in the debris curves are typically due to fragmentation events.

pieces being inferred for sizes greater than one centimetre in diameter. All these pieces pose a threat to satellites, spacecraft, and astronauts due to their orbits criss-crossing at high relative speeds. The debris is generated by accidental explosions, collisions and degradation in the harsh Space environment. Debris can also result from the intentional destruction of objects in orbit, as discussed in Chapters 7 and 8. Whatever the cause, fragmentation of objects in orbit increases the cross-section of orbiting material, and with it the probability of collisions over time. Eventually, collisions could become the dominant factor changing the orbital environment, a situation called the Kessler–Cour–Palais syndrome, which could in some scenarios lead to a collisional chain reaction – essentially, runaway Space debris.[20]

There is a natural clearing process for debris due to atmospheric drag, caused by the presence of some gas in the lower portions of LEO. This clearing action is highlighted by the fraction of debris that has de-orbited. However, the production of debris is outpacing this self-cleaning behaviour. More worrisome are the sudden jumps in the debris population, owing to the 2007 Chinese anti-satellite weapon test, the 2009 Iridium 33–Kosmos 2251 collision, and most recently the 2021 Russian anti-satellite weapon test. Unfortunately, these jumps might provide a glimpse of what to expect as we industrialise Earth orbits.

Also shown in Figure 2.2 are the growth and decay curves of rocket bodies, i.e. rocket stages that have been abandoned in orbit after use. While fewest in number, they have the greatest mass of all the derelict objects in orbit and are a major source of debris generation. We discuss rocket bodies at length in Chapter 4.

Finally, the payload curves represent the growth of active and defunct satellites. There was a steady rise in the number of satellites in orbit until 2015, which then transitioned to a sudden rise in 2019. This change in slope serves as an environmental definition for the start of 'NewSpace' – an era dominated by commercial Space actors and mega-constellations.

Simulations of the long-term evolution of debris suggest that LEO is already in the early and still slow-moving stages of the Kessler–Cour–Palais syndrome.[21] This could potentially be managed through active debris removal – a technologically feasible process, though very expensive

---

[20] Donald J Kessler and Burton G Cour-Palais, 'Collision frequency of artificial satellites: The creation of a debris belt' (1978) 83:A6 *Journal of Geophysical Research* 2637.

[21] J-C Liou and NL Johnson, 'Risks in space from orbiting debris' (2006) 311 *Science* 340.

and perhaps legally contentious.[22] But that potentiality does not reduce the seriousness of the current situation: the addition of mega-constellations and the general proliferation of 'small' satellites in LEO is stressing the orbital environment, and it is doing so at astonishing speed.[23]

Although the volume of Space is large, each individual satellite and every satellite system has specific functions, requiring specific altitudes and inclinations (Figure 2.3).[24] This increases congestion in certain regions of LEO and requires active management for station-keeping and collision avoidance.[25] Improved Space situational awareness is required, with data from satellite operators as well as from ground- and Space-based sensors being widely and freely shared.[26] Improved communication among satellite operators is also necessary. For example, in 2019,

---

[22] Legal contention might arise if one state attempted to retrieve a space object launched by another state without the launch state's permission. States retain jurisdiction and legal responsibility over spacecraft that have stopped functioning, or even have fragmented, with the Liability Convention defining 'space object' as including 'component parts of a space object as well as its launch vehicle and parts thereof'. Convention on International Liability for Damage Caused by Space Objects, 29 March 1972, 961 UNTS 187 Art. I(d) (entered into force 1 September 1972) (Liability Convention). But the retrieval would not entail returning the defunct object to the Earth's surface; rather, it would be directed onto a re-entry trajectory where it would 'burn up'. As a result, the 'launch state' would have little to be concerned about.

[23] A Rossi, A Petit and D McKnight, 'Short-term space safety analysis of LEO constellations and clusters' (2020) 175 *Acta Astronautica* 476; Samantha Le May, Steve Gehly, BA Carter and Sven Flegel, 'Space debris collision probability analysis for proposed global broadband constellations' (2018) 151 *Acta Astronautica* 445; J-C Liou, M Matney, A Vavrin, A Manis and D Gates, 'NASA ODPO's large constellation study' (2018) 22:3 *Orbital Debris Quarterly News* 4; D Vavrin and A Manis, 'CubeSat Study Project Review' (2018) 22: 1 *Orbital Debris Quarterly News* 6.

[24] Orbital inclination, in this context, describes how 'tilted' an orbit is relative to Earth's equator. An inclination of zero degrees means the orbit is in the same plane as Earth's equator, while an inclination of 90 degrees means the orbit goes directly over Earth's poles. An inclination greater than 90 degrees means the orbit of the object has a 'retrograde' orbital sense. For example, an orbiting object with an inclination of zero degrees and another with an inclination of 180 degrees would both orbit about Earth's equator, but one would do so in a clockwise motion and the other in a counterclockwise motion, as viewed from a pole.

[25] Nathan Reiland, Aaron J Rosengren, Renu Malhotra and Claudio Bombardelli, 'Assessing and minimizing collisions in satellite mega-constellations' (2021) 67:11 *Advances in Space Research* 3755.

[26] US Senate Committee on Commerce, Science, and Transportation, 'Statement of Dr Moriba K Jah on space missions of global importance: Planetary defense, space weather protection, and space situational awareness' (12 February 2020), online: www.commerce.senate.gov/services/files/F15B56A1-9134-43D8-B072-65F6CD2ADCEA.

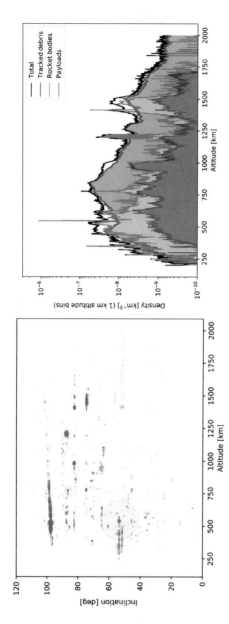

**Figure 2.3** Orbital distribution and density information for objects in low Earth orbit. Left: distribution of payloads (active and defunct satellites), binned to the nearest kilometre in altitude and one degree in orbital inclination. The centre of each circle represents the position on the diagram, and the size of the circle is proportional to the number of satellites within the given parameter space. Right: number density of different resident Space objects (RSOs) based on one-kilometre radial bins, averaged over the entire sky. Because most RSOs are on at least slightly elliptical orbits, the contribution of a given object to an orbital shell is weighted by the time that object spends in the shell. Despite significant parameter space, satellites are clustered in their orbits due to mission requirements. The emerging Starlink cluster at 550 kilometres and 53° inclination is already evident in both plots. For more on the construction of these plots, see Aaron Boley and Michael Byers, 'Satellite mega-constellations create risks in low earth orbit, the atmosphere and on Earth', (2021) 11 *Scientific Reports* 10642.

the European Space Agency (ESA) moved an Earth-observation satellite to avoid colliding with a Starlink satellite, after failing to reach SpaceX by e-mail.[27]

Then, in December 2021, China reported that its Space station had manoeuvered on two occasions, on 1 July and 21 October 2021, to avoid potential collisions with Starlink satellites.[28] One of those satellites had moved into a nearby orbit, resulting in a 'close encounter', while the other was moving unpredictably. China emphasised that the United States was legally responsible for SpaceX's activities and for ensuring that they complied with the Outer Space Treaty.[29] There is insufficient information about these incidents to determine objectively what caused them. There may have been a breach in spaceflight safety, a possibility complicated by the lack of any rules concerning what constitutes a 'safe' distance for a 'conjunction' (i.e. a close approach). It is also possible, and possibly more likely, that SpaceX and the China National Space Administration (CNSA) have different decision matrices for ensuring on-orbit safety. Equally possible, as with the ESA incident in 2019, is that SpaceX and CNSA lack an effective channel of communication, one that would have enabled them to co-ordinate their actions.

Such channels of communication are needed between all spacecraft operators. Earlier in 2021, SpaceX and the National Aeronautics and Space Administration (NASA) announced that they would be co-operating to reduce the risk of collisions arising from their on-orbit activities.

---

[27] Mike Wall, 'European satellite dodges potential collision with SpaceX Starlink craft', *Space.com* (3 Sept 2019), online: www.space.com/spacex-starlink-esa-satellite-collision-avoidance.html.

[28] Permanent mission of China to the United Nations (Vienna), 'Information furnished in conformity with the Treaty on Principles Governing the Activities of States in the Exploration and Use of Outer Space, including the Moon and Other Celestial Bodies', Note verbal, UN Doc A/AC.105/1262 (3 December 2021), online: www.unoosa.org/oosa/en/oosadoc/data/documents/2021/aac.105/aac.1051262_0.html. The report was made to the UN secretary general, pursuant to Article V of the OST, which provides that 'States Parties to the Treaty shall immediately inform the other States Parties to the Treaty or the Secretary-General of the United Nations of any phenomena they discover in outer space, including the Moon and other celestial bodies, which could constitute a danger to the life or health of astronauts.' Outer Space Treaty, Art. V.

[29] Permanent mission of China to the United Nations (Vienna), op. cit. Article VI of the OST reads, 'States Parties to the Treaty shall bear international responsibility for national activities in outer space, including the moon and other celestial bodies, whether such activities are carried on by governmental agencies or by non-governmental entities, and for assuring that national activities are carried out in conformity with the provisions set forth in the present Treaty.'

However, this agreement is between only one operator and one agency,[30] although, according to SpaceX, efforts to share data with other operators are now under way.[31] Such efforts at co-operation clearly need to include other governments, and especially China and Russia. Just as importantly, internationally adopted 'right-of-way' rules are needed to prevent games of 'chicken',[32] as companies, seeking to preserve thruster fuel and avoid service interruptions, wait for the other operator to move its satellite first.

### 2.4   Increased Collision Risk

Mega-constellations are composed of relatively low-cost, mass-produced satellites with few backup systems. This 'consumer electronic product model' allows for short upgrade cycles and rapid expansions of capabilities, but it also results in considerable amounts of discarded equipment and therefore increased collisional risks. Although SpaceX will actively de-orbit its satellites at the end of their five- to six-year operational lives, this process will take six months, so roughly 10 per cent will be de-orbiting at any time. If other companies do likewise, thousands of de-orbiting satellites will be slowly passing through the same congested region. Because satellites in higher orbital shells will by necessity pass through all lower shells, stresses on Space traffic management will be enhanced, raising the risk of collisions. Construction flaws and other malfunctions will increase these numbers, with the long-term failure rate being difficult to project. It should further be recognised that such congestion affects all orbital operations, including in GEO, due to the need to perform orbit-raising manoeuvres (i.e. 'GEO-transfer' orbits) that repeatedly pass through LEO for several weeks or months. Indeed, a collision between an LEO object and a GEO transfer object would create a debris 'family' that passes through all near-Earth orbital Space. Again, it is important to remember that SpaceX will be just one of many

---

[30] National Aeronautics and Space Administration (NASA), news release, 21-011, 'NASA, SpaceX sign joint spaceflight safety agreement' (18 March 2021), online: www.nasa.gov/press-release/nasa-spacex-sign-joint-spaceflight-safety-agreement.

[31] Jeff Foust, 'SpaceX emphasizes coordination with other satellite operators', *SpaceNews* (16 Sept 2021), online: spacenews.com/spacex-emphasizes-coordination-with-other-satellite-operators.

[32] On the oceans, such rules are known as 'rules of the road'. See Convention on the International Regulations for Preventing Collisions at Sea, 20 October 1972, 1050 UNTS 16 (entered into force 15 July 1977).

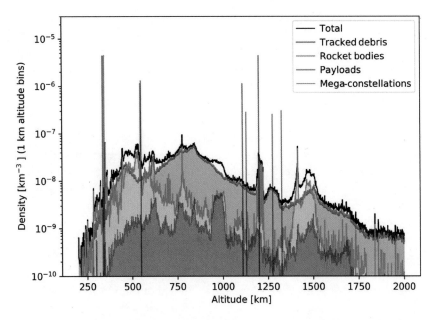

**Figure 2.4** Satellite density distribution in LEO with 65,000 satellites from four mega-constellations (Starlink, OneWeb, Kuiper and StarNet). Areas of potentially high congestion and collision risk are represented by the large spikes in orbital density. The collision risk is further heightened by debris that is too small to be tracked or when collision avoidance manoeuvres are impossible for other reasons. For more on our methods, see Boley and Byers, op. cit.

companies engaging in such practices in a congested environment, creating a serious collective action problem with no easy fix.

Figure 2.4 depicts some of the congestion that we can expect to see. It is similar to the righthand plot in Figure 2.3, but includes the Starlink, OneWeb, Amazon/Kuiper and Guo Wang/StarNet mega-constellations as filed (and amended) with the FCC and/or ITU, for a total of about 65,000 satellites. The large spikes show the considerable density of satellites in orbital shells. The total cross-section within these regions is high, and a satellite fragmentation, for any reason, at one of those altitudes could lead to multiple collisions and large-scale debris generation.

De-orbiting satellites will be tracked while operational satellites can be manoeuvred to avoid close conjunctions with them, with other satellites and with trackable debris. But effective collision avoidance often depends on ongoing communication and co-operation between operators, which, as noted above, is at present ad hoc and voluntary. The situation could become more, not less, complicated, as autonomous collision avoidance systems are developed. In April 2021, SpaceX sent a letter to the FCC about how, in the face of one upcoming conjunction, OneWeb requested that SpaceX turn off its autonomous collision avoidance system so that OneWeb could safely manoeuver its satellite out of the way.[33]

SpaceX also points to its automatic collision avoidance technology to justify the high density of its satellites in individual shells. But in August 2021, it emerged that the system is currently entirely dependent on the standard (and not always accurate) conjunction warnings provided by the United States Space Command (USSPACECOM).[34] Unresponsive satellites add a further collision risk. Worse yet, SpaceX's collision assessments, at least according to their FCC filings, do not account for untracked, lethal debris (i.e. pieces with diameters of less than about ten centimetres and larger than a few millimetres),[35] including untracked debris decaying through the shells used by Starlink. Using simple estimates,[36] the probability that a single piece of untracked debris will hit any satellite in the Starlink 550-kilometre shell is about 0.003 after one year. Thus if, at any time, there are just over 200 pieces of untracked debris decaying through the 550-kilometre orbital shell, there is roughly a 50 per cent chance that there will be one or more collisions between satellites in the shell and a piece of untracked debris.[37] While not all collisions will lead to catastrophic failures, they will still degrade the orbital environmental by producing additional debris and wearing down satellites. And it only takes one collision with a significant fragmentation outcome to produce large amounts of debris, which in turn could produce widespread satellite failures within an orbital shell.

---

[33] Letter from David Goldman, SpaceX director of satellite policy, to Marlene H Dortch, secretary, FCC, regarding application SAT-MOD-20200417-00037 (20 April 2021). See also Joey Roulette, 'OneWeb, SpaceX satellites dodged a potential collision in orbit', *The Verge* (9 April 2021), online: www.theverge.com/2021/4/9/22374262/oneweb-spacex-sat ellites-dodgedpotential-collision-orbit-space-force.

[34] Jonathan McDowell, 'SpaceX have released a bit more info on the "automatic" collision avoidance that some people have been confused about. As suspected, what they mean is that they rely on conjunction warnings generated by SpaceForce radar tracking which are uploaded to the satellites' (22 August 2021 at 15:26), online: *Twitter* twitter.com/planet4589/status/1429525312577183746.

[35] Le May et al., op. cit.

[36] Aaron Boley and Michael Byers, 'Satellite mega-constellations create risks in low Earth orbit, the atmosphere and on Earth' (2021) 11 *Scientific Reports* 10642, 1 at 5–6.

[37] Ibid.

Moreover, fragmentation events are never confined to their local orbits. As Chapters 7 and 8 explain, India's 2019 anti-satellite weapon test was conducted at an altitude below 300 kilometres in a good-faith effort to minimise long-lived debris. Nevertheless, some tracked debris (and presumably a larger amount of untracked but still lethal debris) was placed in orbits with apogees greater than 1,000 kilometres. As of January 2022, there was one piece of tracked debris from that test still in orbit. Pieces of such long-lived debris have high eccentricities and thus can cross multiple orbital shells twice per orbit. Yet all these collision risks associated with mega-constellations have not received due consideration, in part because of the FCC's practice of considering only the per-satellite collision risk when issuing licences for mega-constellations composed of thousands of satellites.[38]

The collision risks associated with meteoroids have also been largely ignored, presumably because the cross-section of on-orbit infrastructure has, until recently, been relatively low. Moreover, unlike collisions with debris, collisions with meteoroids are unavoidable, which reduces the options available to any government or company wishing to reduce the risks.

Meteoroids are composed of natural material that is between about 30 microns and one metre in diameter.[39] Their main source is ejected pieces of asteroids and comets. Much smaller objects are called 'dust', and larger objects are thought to be more asteroid-like, although this is a definition of convenience more than anything else. In any event, the cumulative meteoroid flux for masses of greater than 0.01 gram is about $1.2 \times 10^{-4}$ meteoroids per square metre per year.[40] Such masses could cause significant damage to satellites, even if they do not result in catastrophic fragmentation,[41] in part because meteoroids can attain

---

[38] Mike Lindsay (chief technology officer, Astroscale), 'Another thread about sat collision probability. This time let's talk about regulations, as the FCC has just solicited input about how to regulate collision risk. As we know, risk can be computed as = 1–(1–Pc)^N where Pc = each sat's collision probability and N = # of sats' (19 October 2020 at 8:55), online: *Twitter* twitter.com/mikeclindsay/status/1318174030583656449.

[39] International Astronomical Union, 'Meteors & meteorites: The IAU definitions of meteor terms' (2022), online: *International Astronomical Union* www.iau.org/public/themes/meteors_and_meteorites.

[40] Eberhard Grün, Herbert A Zook, Hugo Fechtig and RH Giese, 'Collisional balance of the meteoritic complex' (1985) 62:2 *Icarus* 244.

[41] Althea V Moorhead, Aaron Kingery and Steven Ehlert, 'NASA's meteoroid engineering Model 3 and its ability to replicate spacecraft impact rates' (2020) 57:1 *Journal of Spacecraft and Rockets* 160.

much higher impact speeds than orbital debris. Assuming a Starlink constellation of only 12,000 satellites (i.e. the Gen1 design), there is about a 50 per cent chance of 15 or more meteoroid impacts (or a 99.7 per cent chance of one or more meteoroid impacts) per year at a mass of more than 0.01 gram.[42] Adding more satellites will only increase the number of events per year.

Many satellites are designed with shielding, but damaging events that might be rare to a single satellite will become common when measured across all orbital infrastructure. Therefore, while orbital debris will likely remain the most significant threat to mega-constellations, we can also anticipate regular satellite failures due to meteoroid impacts. Again, this is a result of the total cross-section on orbit, and not strictly the total number of satellites. So even small satellites in sufficiently large numbers – such as the 114,852 satellites for which Kepler has filed advanced publication information – could give rise to regular debris-generating events from collisions with either debris or meteoroids.

One response to all these concerns about congestion and collisions is for operators to construct mega-constellations out of fewer satellites. But with more and more operators entering LEO, even this would only provide a partial solution. For this reason, it is critically important that spacefaring states and satellite companies, individually and collectively, take an all-of-LEO approach to evaluating the effects of the construction and maintenance of any one constellation, and then to mitigating the cumulative effects of all constellations.

## 2.5   Surface Impacts

Re-entering rocket stages pose growing safety and environmental risks on the Earth's surface, as we explain at length in Chapter 4. SpaceX is a relatively responsible actor in this regard, as the first stages of SpaceX rockets are usually landed and reused, while second stages are usually controlled through re-entry and deposited in remote areas of ocean. Unfortunately, these best practices are not being followed – or cannot yet be followed – by other launch providers. For example, the first stages of the Soyuz rockets employed by OneWeb until February 2022 (when Russia invaded Ukraine) are not reusable, nor are the second-stage re-entries controllable. OneWeb has since signed a contract to use India's

---

[42] This calculation assumes that each satellite has a cross-section of about four square metres.

Geosynchronous Satellite Launch Vehicle,[43] which is similarly limited. The Vulcan Centaur rockets that will be used by Amazon/Kuiper suffer from the same limitations, as do the Long March rockets that will likely be employed by Guo Wang/StarNet.

Satellite re-entries pose their own risks – including that of killing people – since re-entering orbiting material often does not demise ('burn up') completely in the atmosphere.[44] To get a feel for the numbers, consider the early FCC filings made by SpaceX for its Starlink satellites. The typical 'casualty risk' per satellite was listed as about 1:20,000 (the highest risk was 1:17,400),[45] meeting NASA's risk threshold of 1:10,000 per object. The satellites were (and still are) expected to last between five and six years, with a full replacement of the constellation occurring on that timescale. This meant that every replacement cycle of the 12,000 satellites in Starlink Gen1 carried a 45 per cent probability of one or more casualties from the re-entering satellites ($P = exp\,(-12000/20000) \approx 45\%$). If this were extended to Starlink's full 42,000 satellites (Gen1 and Gen2 taken together), the probability of one or more casualties per replacement cycle would be 88 per cent. Again, we are talking here about the statistical likelihood of people getting killed by a satellite impact. Fortunately, the issue was identified during the FCC's 'open consultation' process.[46] SpaceX responded by changing some components to make its satellites fully demisable and therefore of no threat to people on the Earth's surface. However, the effects of these changes will have to be verified, and it remains to be seen whether other operators will follow this new best practice.

Even controlled re-entries can be problematic if the re-entering rocket stage or satellite contains hazardous materials.[47] In 1978, a Soviet

---

[43] Jonathan Amos, 'OneWeb: UK satellite firm does deal to use Indian rockets', *BBC* (21 April 2022) online: www.bbc.com/news/science-environment-61175261.

[44] William H Ailor, 'Large constellation disposal hazards' (20 January 2020), Center for Space Policy and Strategy, *The Aerospace Corporation*, online: aerospace.org/sites/default/files/2020-01/Ailor_LgConstDisposal_20200113.pdf.

[45] Patricia Paoletta, 'Application for fixed satellite service by Space Exploration Holdings, LLC, SAT-LOA-20170301-00027' (15 November 2018), *FCC*, online: fcc.report/IBFS/SAT-LOA-20170301-00027.

[46] William Wiltshire, 'Application for fixed satellite service by Space Exploration Holdings, LLC, SAT-MOD-20200417-00037' (27 April 2021), *FCC*, online: https://fcc.report/IBFS/SAT-MOD-20200417-00037.

[47] Carmen Pardini and Luciano Anselmo, 'Uncontrolled re-entries of spacecraft and rocket bodies: A statistical overview over the last decade' (2019) 6 *Journal of Space Engineering Safety* 30; Michael Byers and Cameron Byers, 'Toxic splash: Russian rocket stages dropped in Arctic waters raise health, environmental and legal concerns' (2017) 53:6 *Polar Record* 580.

surveillance satellite malfunctioned, re-entered the atmosphere in an uncontrolled manner, and spread radioactive material over 120,000 square kilometres of northern Canada.[48] In 2008, the United States Navy used a ship-based missile to destroy a malfunctioning military satellite just before it entered the atmosphere.[49] The mission, named Operation Burnt Frost, was justified on the ground that it prevented 450 kg of unspent highly toxic hydrazine thruster fuel from reaching the surface.

Cumulative impacts must also be considered, especially in the ocean environments where most controlled re-entries end up.[50] In the 1990s, Pacific island states opposed the Sea Launch project because of environmental concerns, including from discarded rocket stages.[51] In 2016, Inuit in the Canadian Arctic protested the Russian practice of disposing hydrazine-fuelled rocket stages in Pikialasorsuaq (North Water Polynya), a biologically rich area of year-round open water.[52]

## 2.6    Atmospheric Effects

### 2.6.1    Re-entering Satellites

The demise of satellite components during re-entry introduces a further problem since none of their material actually disappears. It is, instead, converted into very large numbers of fine particulates, atoms and molecules having the same cumulative mass. To get a sense of this, again consider Starlink satellites, which have an estimated dry mass of about

---

[48] Canada presented a claim of CDN$6 million for the cleanup, citing the Outer Space Treaty and the Liability Convention. After three rounds of negotiations, the Soviet Union, while not admitting liability, agreed to pay half that amount 'in full and final settlement of all matters connected with the disintegration of the Soviet satellite Cosmos-954'. Olga A Volynskaya, 'Landmark space-related accidents and the progress of space law' (2013) 62 *Zeitschrift für Luft- und Weltraumrecht* (German Journal of Air and Space Law) 220 at 226; Protocol between the Government of Canada and the Government of the Union of Soviet Socialist Republics, E103429, Can TS 1981 No 8, online: www.treaty-accord.gc.ca/text-texte.aspx?id=103429.

[49] Nicholas L Johnson, 'Operation Burnt Frost: A view from inside' (2021) 56 *Space Policy* 101411.

[50] Vito De Lucia and Viviana Iavicoli, 'From outer space to ocean depths: The "spacecraft cemetery" and the protection of the marine environment in areas beyond national jurisdiction' (2019) 49:2 *California Western International Law Journal* 345.

[51] Colin Woodward, 'High-seas launch worries islanders', *Christian Science Monitor* (22 September 1999), online: www.csmonitor.com/1999/0922/p5s1.html.

[52] Bob Weber, 'Inuit angered by Russian rocket splashdown in the Arctic', *Globe and Mail* (3 June 2016), online: www.theglobeandmail.com/news/national/inuit-angered-by-rus sian-rocket-splashdown-in-the-arctic/article30273826.

260 kg. Although we do not know their composition, we assume that most of the mass is an aluminium alloy. If 80 per cent of the mass is aluminium, and Gen1 includes 12,000 satellites, there will be 2,500 tonnes of aluminium in total. A five-year cycle would thus see on average about 1.4 tonnes re-entering Earth's atmosphere daily. While small compared to the 54 daily tonnes of meteoroid material,[53] most meteoroids contain less than 1 per cent aluminium by mass.[54] Thus, depending on the atmospheric residence time of material from re-entered satellites, each mega-constellation could produce fine particulates that greatly exceed natural forms of high-altitude atmospheric aluminium deposition, especially if the full numbers of envisaged satellites are launched. Gen1 and Gen2 of Starlink combined, with 42,000 satellites, would lead to about five tonnes of aluminium entering the atmosphere each day, an order of magnitude above natural levels.

Anthropogenic (i.e. human-caused) deposition of aluminium in the atmosphere has long been proposed in the context of geoengineering as a way to increase Earth's albedo – essentially, reflecting solar energy back into Space to slow global warming.[55] Recent work, however, suggests that alumina, the most typical product of aluminium reacting with the molecules naturally present in the atmosphere, might have a net warming effect through the absorption of longer-wavelength radiation.[56] Said differently, it reflects visible light but absorbs infrared. In any event, these geoengineering proposals have been scientifically controversial because of the identified and as yet unidentified risks, with controlled experiments encountering substantial opposition.[57] Mega-constellations will now begin this process as an uncontrolled experiment.[58] One could

---

[53] Gerhard Drolshagen, Detlef Koschny, Sandra Drolshagen, Jana Kretschmer and Björn Poppe, 'Mass accumulation of earth from interplanetary dust, meteoroids, asteroids, and comets' (2017) 143 *Planetary and Space Science* 21.

[54] Katharina Lodders, 'Solar system abundances of the elements', in Aruna Goswami and B Eswar Reddy, eds., *Principles and Perspectives in Cosmochemistry* (Berlin: Springer, 2010) 379.

[55] David W Keith, 'Geoengineering the climate: History and prospect' (2000) 25 *Annual Review of Energy and the Environment* 245.

[56] Martin Ross and Patti Sheaffer, 'Radiative forcing caused by rocket engine emissions' (2014) 2:4 *Earth's Future* 117.

[57] Edward A Parson and David W Keith, 'End the deadlock on governance of geoengineering research' (2013) 339 *Science* 1278.

[58] Debra Werner, 'Aerospace Corp. raises questions about pollutants produced during satellite and rocket reentry', *SpaceNews* (11 December 2020), online: https://spacenews.com/aerospace-agu-reentry-pollution.

imagine Elon Musk, whose concerns about both climate change and government interference are well known, being comfortable with the geoengineering aspect of Starlink, as well as with the unadvertised and unilateral manner in which it is being done. But again, the overall effects of alumina on the climate are not settled. There is also the not insignificant issue of Musk lacking any legitimacy or authority to make decisions for the rest of humanity.

Our calculations above are rough but bolstered by the more detailed work of Leonard Schulz and Karl-Heinz Glassmeier. They calculate the current annual influx into the atmosphere as *already* involving 0.89 kilotonne per year (kt/yr) of anthropogenic material, of which 0.09 kt/yr is injected in atomic form and 0.26 kt/yr as aerosols.[59] The rest of the material (0.54 kt/yr) reaches the surface, at least for the situations they explore. Of the injected elements, they find aluminium to be the most abundant (0.21 kt/yr or about 0.6 tonne per day).

Schulz and Glassmeier then calculate the influx in a 'Scenario 1' involving 19,400 satellites. Here, the annual anthropogenic influx increases to 2.7 kt/yr, with 1.6 kt/yr being injected into the atmosphere: 1.2 kt/yr as aerosols, 0.4 kt/yr in atomic form. Again, aluminium is the largest part of the injection (0.8 kt). They further calculate the influx in a 'Scenario 2' involving 75,000 satellites. Here, the annual anthropogenic mass influx increases to 8.1 kt/yr, with 4.9 kt/yr being injected into the atmosphere: 3.7 kt/yr as aerosols, 1.2 kt/yr in atomic form. Once again, aluminium is the largest part of the injection at 2.5 kt/yr or about seven tonnes per day. Making satellites fully demisable for safety reasons will tend to increase these values, creating an apparent trade-off between protecting people from being struck by Space objects, on the one hand, and climate impacts – which have their own safety implications – on the other.

Schulz and Glassmeier also warn that:

> There are many different possible effects on the atmosphere that are caused by an increased injection. Aerosols, respectively dust particles affect the stratosphere and mesosphere by acting as condensation nuclei contributing to the formation of high-altitude clouds. Additionally, they impact the chemistry in the upper atmosphere with possible effects on the D layer ion chemistry and the ozone layer. The large amount of aerosols injected by the ablation of anthropogenic material may also have an effect

---

[59] Leonard Schulz and Karl-Heinz Glassmeier 'On the anthropogenic and natural injection of matter into Earth's atmosphere' (2021) 67:3 *Advances in Space Research* 1002.

on Earth's climate as aerosols in the high-altitude atmosphere have a negative radiative forcing effect. Injected atoms partially ionize during ablation and thus contribute to the ionospheric layers. Furthermore, injected metal atoms form metal layers where the injected particles can have various different chemical reactions with other injected material, as well as atmosphere atoms and molecules.[60]

One thing is clear: the deposition of large amounts of aluminium into the upper atmosphere from re-entering mega-constellation satellites will affect the upper atmosphere, even if we do not yet know the scale of those impacts or understand all the complex interactions involved.

### 2.6.2   Rocket Launches

The act of putting satellites into Space can itself affect the atmosphere. While cumulative carbon dioxide emissions from rocket launches are currently small compared to other sources, $CO_2$ alone is a misleading metric. Black carbon produced by kerosene-fuelled rockets such as SpaceX's Falcon 9 and alumina particles produced by solid-fuelled rockets lead to instantaneous radiative forcing. As we discuss in Chapter 1 above with regard to Virgin Galactic's *SpaceShipTwo*, modelling of the cumulative effect of emissions from 1,000 annual launches of hydrocarbon-fuelled rockets found that, after one decade, the black carbon would result in radiative forcing comparable to that from all subsonic aviation.[61] Although 1,000 launches annually is ten times the current rate, the construction and renewal of multiple mega-constellations will require dramatic increases in launches. Current launches likely cause significant radiative forcing already.[62]

Rockets fuelled with liquid hydrogen do not produce black carbon but require larger tanks and therefore larger rockets, with solid-fuelled boosters often being used to increase payload capacity. SpaceX's new Starship, which could soon be launching 400 Starlink satellites at a time,[63] will be fuelled by methane, the combustion of which still produces

---

[60]   Ibid. at 1015 (citations omitted).

[61]   Martin Ross, Michael Mills and Darin Toohey, 'Potential climate impact of black carbon emitted by rockets' (2010) 37:24 *Geophysical Research Letters* L24810.

[62]   Martin Ross and Patti Sheaffer, 'Radiative forcing caused by rocket engine emissions' (2014) 2:4 *Earth's Future* 117.

[63]   Eric Ralph, 'SpaceX CEO Elon Musk says Starship will take over Starlink launches', *Teslarati* (11 June 2021), online: www.teslarati.com/spacex-starlink-launches-starship-takeover.

black carbon that will contribute to radiative forcing, although it is expected to do so to a lesser extent than kerosene rockets. All liquid fuels will affect mesospheric cloud formation,[64] with potential impacts on the upper atmosphere.

Rockets threaten the ozone layer directly by depositing radicals into the stratosphere,[65] with solid-fuelled rockets causing the most damage per launch because of the hydrogen chloride and alumina they contain.[66] Amazon's recent purchase of Vulcan Centaur rockets to launch its Kuiper satellites poses a particular concern,[67] since each rocket will include multiple boosters,[68] each composed of 48,000 kg of solid fuel composed of hydroxyl-terminated polybutadiene mixed with aluminium.[69] As before, a single rocket has a negligible impact, but rocket launches in sufficient numbers could well be problematic. The radicals from rocket launches can also indirectly affect the ozone layer by altering the radiation balance and thus the temperature of the upper atmosphere, which in turn alters the reaction rates of ozone chemistry. A hotter stratosphere will tend to result in more ozone depletion.

Re-entering rockets, even reusable ones, require some consideration too. The intense heat of atmospheric re-entry will create radicals of $NO_x$ (the generic scientific term for nitrogen oxide and nitrogen dioxide), a process that does not require any ablation from the rocket.[70] Radicals have an unpaired electron and are therefore very chemically reactive, and

[64] JA Dallas, S. Raval, JP Alvarez Gaitan, S Saydam and AG Dempster, 'The environmental impact of emissions from space launches: A comprehensive review' (2020) 255 *Journal of Cleaner Production* 120209.

[65] Ross, Mills and Toohey, op. cit.

[66] Ibid.

[67] United Launch Alliance, 'Amazon signs contract with United Launch Alliance for 38 Project Kuiper launches on Vulcan Centaur', 5 April 2022, online: www.ulalaunch .com/about/news/2022/04/05/amazon-signs-contract-with-united-launch-alliance-for-38-project-kuiper-launches-on-vulcan-centaur.

[68] Sandra Erwin, 'Northrop Grumman expects a $2 billion order from ULA for solid rocket boosters', *SpaceNews* (28 April 2022), online: https://spacenews.com/northrop-grum man-expects-a-2-billion-order-from-ula-for-solid-rocket-boosters.

[69] Northrop Grumman, GEM MOTOR SERIES, GEM 63XL, n.d., online: www .northropgrumman.com/wp-content/uploads/GEM-Motor-Series.pdf.

[70] Erik JL Larson, Robert W Portmann, Karen H Rosenlof, David W Fahey, John S Daniel and Martin N Ross, 'Global atmospheric response to emissions from a proposed reusable space launch system' (2017) 5:1 *Earth's Future* 37; Seong-Hyeon Park, Javier Navarro Laboulais, Pénélope Leyland and Stefano Mischler, 'Re-entry survival analysis and ground risk assessment of space debris considering by-products generation' (2021) 179 *Acta Astronautica* 604-618.

when formed or mixed into the stratosphere they will deplete ozone. So far, meteoroids account for most of the $NO_x$ production from atmospheric entries, but near-future uses of Space could see this natural process, too, surpassed by anthropogenic production.

In short, when it comes to launching satellites and other spacecraft, there is no such thing as a 'green' rocket. At best, there is an environmental budget, so to speak, of launches that the Earth–Space system can handle before human activity will have a large disruptive effect. At worst, that threshold has already been reached.

## 2.7 Occupying Orbital Shells

From 1848 to 1855, the California Gold Rush brought 300,000 people to the newest part of the United States. The miners found themselves in a situation of relative lawlessness since Mexico's laws no longer applied to the territory and no new laws had yet been adopted to regulate access to gold. The result was an informal system of 'staking claims' whereby the first to begin mining a location could exclude others through his presence, though he would risk seeing his claim 'jumped' if he left, even briefly.[71] Later, when laws on gold mining were finally adopted, they perpetuated this system of 'free mining'. Not until 1866 and 1870 were shaft miners and placer miners respectively able to register and thus protect their claims.[72]

Today, the occupation and use of orbital shells appear to bear certain similarities. National regulators such as the FCC are assigning orbital shells to mega-constellations on a first-come–first-served basis, without assessing the effects on other states. These effects could include making any addition of further satellites to those shells too dangerous to contemplate. This de facto occupation of orbital shells may violate Article I of the 1967 Outer Space Treaty, which designates the exploration and use of Space as 'the province of all [hu]mankind' and 'free for exploration and use for all States without discrimination of any kind'. Article II further states, 'Outer space ... is not subject to national appropriation by claim of sovereignty, by means of use or occupation, or by any other means.' Although regulators are not claiming sovereignty over orbital shells, allowing national companies to saturate them with

---

[71] Donald J Pisani, '"I am resolved not to interfere, but permit all to work freely": The gold rush and American resource law' (Winter 1998–1999) 77:4 *California History* 123.
[72] Ibid.

satellites could easily be considered appropriation by 'other means'. Lastly, Article IX requires that Space activities be conducted 'with due regard to the corresponding interests of all other States Parties to the Treaty'.[73]

Mega-constellation operators and their regulators could respond that they are exercising the right to explore and use Space without discrimination, that the use of an orbital shell is time-limited as a result of the licence, and that the satellites will be actively de-orbited.[74] They could also argue that some states have been using slots in geostationary orbit for decades, resulting in the de facto exclusion of others from any given slot without this being considered appropriation. However, the use of slots in geostationary orbit is mediated by the ITU, which does not play the same role in LEO.

Single states and operators should not be allowed to de facto occupy orbital shells by saturating them with satellites. Of course, what constitutes saturation will depend on technologies as well as different tolerances of risk. But the challenge of defining acceptable levels of use, while preserving access for others, is a reason for international governance and not a convincing argument against it. No single state is likely to handle this matter appropriately unless it co-ordinates with other spacefaring states, in the absence of which tragedies of the commons could easily arise. Institutionally, the easiest option may be to extend the ITU's role to LEO. Other options might include assigning the regulation of different orbital shells to different states, much like air traffic control in busy regions of international airspace, where reciprocity is the primary incentive for reasonable behaviour.[75] Even then, something like the International Civil Aviation Organization (ICAO), which co-ordinates international air traffic control, might be needed. The development of internationally accepted 'right-of-way' rules could also help, similar to the priority

---

[73] Outer Space Treaty, Art. IX.

[74] Christopher D Johnson, 'The legal status of megaLEO constellations and concerns about appropriation of large swaths of Earth orbit', in Joseph N Pelton and Scott Madry, eds., *Handbook of Small Satellites* (Cham: Springer, 2020) 1337.

[75] For example, air traffic control in the North Atlantic region is shared, through geographically assigned 'control areas' (CTAs), between the United States, Canada, the United Kingdom, Portugal, Denmark, Norway and Iceland, with the 'Reykjavik CTA' extending from 61°N to the North Pole and from 76°W to the Greenwich meridian. See Government of Iceland, 'About the Reykjavik Control Area: Oceanic Control Area' (2022), online: *Isavia* www.isavia.is/en/corporate/air-navigation/reykjavik-control-centre/reykjavik-control-area.

rules that have long guided ships and boats on the world's oceans,[76] though such rules only help to prevent imminent collisions and do not address the larger issue of congestion.

## 2.8 Radio Spectrum

Another 'rush' is occurring over radio spectrum. The ITU is involved in the allocation of frequencies to communications satellites. Under its binding instruments, namely the ITU 'Constitution and Convention',[77] as well as the subsidiary 'Radio Regulations',[78] states must treat frequencies as limited resources to which others have equitable access. At the same time, however, the ITU clearly sees the Radio Regulations as facilitative rather than constraining, writing that they 'enable the introduction of new applications of radiocommunication technology while ensuring the efficient use of radio-frequency spectrum, i.e. the operation of as many systems as possible, without interference.'[79]

Satellite companies are not party to these instruments and do not deal directly with the ITU. They apply for and obtain licences from their national regulator, which early in the planning process files a general description of the satellites with the ITU, including the frequencies and orbits they will use.[80] Under the Radio Regulations, a company is required to co-ordinate with any satellite system that might be affected

---

[76] Most of these rules were codified in the Convention on the International Regulations for Preventing Collisions at Sea, 20 October 1972, 1050 UNTS 16 (entered into force 15 July 1977). For a similar suggestion, see Neel V Patel, 'To solve space traffic woes, look to the high seas', *MIT Technology Review* (23 August 2021), online: www.technologyreview.com/2021/08/23/1032386/space-traffic-maritime-law-ruth-stilwell (reporting on the views of Ruth Stilwell).

[77] The most recent 1992 version of the Constitution and Convention is available at treaties .un.org/doc/Publication/UNTS/Volume%201825/volume-1825-I-31251-English.pdf. The Constitution and Convention is a treaty that, so far, has been ratified by 193 states, i.e. virtually all, including all of the spacefaring states. Constitution and Convention of the International Telecommunication Union, 22 December 1992, 1825–26 UNTS (entered into force 1 July 1994).

[78] The most recent version of the Radio Regulations is available at International Telecommunication Union (ITU), 'Radio Regulations' (2020), *ITU*, online: www.itu.int/pub/R-REG-RR-2020.

[79] International Telecommunication Union (ITU), 'Non-geostationary satellite systems' (June 2021), *ITU*, online: www.itu.int/en/mediacentre/backgrounders/Pages/Non-geostationary-satellite-systems.aspx.

[80] Tony Azzarelli, 'Obtaining landing licenses and permission to operate LEO constellations on a global basis', in Joseph N Pelton and Scott Madry, eds., *Handbook of Small Satellites* (Cham: Springer, 2020) 1287.

by its own planned system; indeed, such filings are identified as 'co-ordination requests'. Under the Rules of Procedure,[81] the two companies are then required to work with the ITU Radiocommunication Bureau to find a way for both systems to coexist. The highly technical character of these requirements and procedures reflects the advanced nature of the ITU as an international organisation, albeit one with a limited mandate – i.e. radio spectrum – that constrains its ability to address the fast-growing problems of physical congestion and debris.

In 2019, the ITU responded to the development of mega-constellations by adopting a 'milestone-based regulatory approach', whereby listing a 'non-geosynchronous (non-GSO) satellite system' in its Master International Frequency Register requires the deployment of certain percentages of the system by certain times.[82] Simply put, operators must deploy 10 per cent of the proposed satellites within two years 'of the end of the current regulatory period for bringing into use', 50 per cent within five years, and 100 percent within seven years. The idea is to ensure that the Register 'reasonably reflects the actual deployment of such non-GSO satellite systems in specific radio-frequency bands and services', to prevent 'radio-frequency spectrum warehousing', and to facilitate the 'coordination, notification and registration of frequency assignments'.[83] The hope is that operators will now delay having their national regulator file for radio spectrum until the designs, funding, manufacturing capability and a launch provider for their satellites are all in place.

This new approach has its problems, the first of which is that the two-, five-, and seven-year milestones come after 'the end of the current regulatory period for bringing into use' – a period that is itself seven years long and begins after the first satellite in the system has been launched. This means that a company can launch a single satellite as a 'placeholder' and immediately obtain spectrum sufficient for the entire system, even if it then does nothing for seven years. That spectrum is then unavailable to others. In fact, a company can place *any* satellite as a placeholder – i.e. not necessarily one that will become part of the system.

[81] International Telecommunication Union (ITU), 'Rules of Procedure' (2021), *ITU* , online: www.itu.int/pub/R-REG-ROP/en.

[82] International Telecommunication Union, press release, 'ITU World Radiocommunication Conference adopts new regulatory procedures for non-geostationary satellites' (20 November 2019), *ITU*, online: www.itu.int/en/mediacentre/Pages/2019-PR23.aspx.

[83] International Telecommunication Union (ITU), 'Non-geostationary satellite systems' (June 2021), *ITU*, online: www.itu.int/en/mediacentre/backgrounders/Pages/Non-geostationary-satellite-systems.aspx.

Third parties are already offering the placement of a temporary satellite as a contractable service.[84]

A second problem concerns the penalty for failing to meet the milestones, which is simply a reduction in the number of satellites approved by the ITU. As a result, companies might be incentivised to apply for spectrum for a much larger number of satellites than they intend ultimately to launch.

A third problem is that a company that obtains spectrum may sell all or part of it to another company during the seven-year 'bringing-into-force' period or at any point during the subsequent seven years of milestones. In other words, a company might seek and obtain spectrum for the sole purpose of selling it to the highest bidder. Or it might seek and obtain more spectrum than it needs, with a view to selling the excess.

These problems could all converge in Rwanda's 2021 filings for 327,320 satellites on behalf of Marvel Space Communications – more than 50 times the total number of satellites currently in operation. The satellites are to be placed in elliptical orbits with perigees around 280 kilometres and apogees around 600 kilometres. They will weigh about ten kilograms each, have antennas extending 3.5 metres, be connected optically to each other, and cost less than €10,000 each to manufacture. Achieving these design and cost parameters would be quite an accomplishment, especially for a country that does not yet have its own Space industry or launch capacity. All this suggests that Marvel Space Communications does not intend to meet the ITU milestones, and that something else is going on.

According to *The Telegraph*, the filing 'has triggered concern and speculation in the space industry. If the plans are approved by the UN [i.e. the ITU[85]], even if Rwanda never launches a satellite, it could sell its rights on. One source said the project was "strategically very serious . . . 300,000 satellites with minimal regulation up for sale to the highest bidder".'[86] Another report suggests that the plan is targeted at the European Commission, which may have as much as €6 billion available

[84] See e.g. Surrey Satellite Technology Ltd (SSTL), 'Bring-into-use satellites' (2022), *SSTL*, online: www.sstl.co.uk/what-we-do/bring-into-use-spacecraft.

[85] The ITU is a 'specialized agency' of the United Nations.

[86] Matthew Field, 'OneWeb founder wants to flood space with 300,000 satellites from Rwanda', *The Telegraph* (7 November 2021), online: www.telegraph.co.uk/technology/2021/11/07/oneweb-founder-wants-flood-space-300000-satellites-rwanda.

for a Europe-based mega-constellation.[87] Such a system could, presumably, help European Union (EU) states avoid becoming overly dependent on the mega-constellations currently under development in the UK, the USA and China. The fact that Rwanda made the initial filings with the ITU would pose no impediment to this becoming a European project.

Adding to the mystery, multiple reports suggest that the Rwandan filings were instigated by Greg Wyler,[88] who founded OneWeb and served as its CEO until 2020 , when the United Kingdom rescued the company from bankruptcy – reputedly under the impression that a broadband mega-constellation in LEO could serve as a global positioning system and thus replace the EU's medium Earth orbit-based Galileo system for post-Brexit Britain.[89] In 2020, Wyler's connections with the Rwandan government were the subject of investigative journalism by European Investigative Collaborations, a group of media organisations that includes *Der Spiegel*, *El Mundo*, *Le Soir*, *Politiken* and the Croatian newsmagazine *Nacional*, where an eyebrow-raising report on Wyler's activities was published.[90]

On a more positive note, satellites having such a relatively low mass, large surface area and low perigee would easily comply with the Inter-Agency Space Debris Coordination Committee (IADC) 25-year de-orbiting guideline without needing active de-orbiting technology.[91] But such an approach would mean that this de-orbiting process is largely uncontrolled. The satellites would still pose a collision risk, in part because of their very large number and therefore high cumulative cross-section. Moreover, if we take the ITU filings at face value, the orbits are elliptical rather than concentrated into orbital shells, and so each of these 327,320 satellites would cross the orbits of the International

---

[87] Michel Cabirol, 'Greg Wyler: Le come-back fracassant de l'enfant terrible du spatial', *La Tribune* (5 November 2021), online: www.latribune.fr/entreprises-finance/industrie/aero nautique-defense/greg-wyler-le-come-back-fracassant-de-l-enfant-terrible-du-spatial-895751.html.

[88] Field, op. cit.

[89] Alex Hern, 'We've bought the wrong satellites': UK tech gamble baffles experts', *The Guardian* (26 June 2020), online: www.theguardian.com/science/2020/jun/26/satellite-experts-oneweb-investment-uk-galileo-brexit.

[90] Blaž Zgaga and Yann Philippin, 'The offshore schemes of the American satellite king', *Nacional* (13 October 2020), online: www.nacional.hr/the-offshore-schemes-of-the-ameri can-satellite-king.

[91] See Inter-Agency Space Debris Coordination Committee, 'IADC Space Debris Mitigation Guidelines' (March 2020), *NASA*, online: orbitaldebris.jsc.nasa.gov/library/iadc-space-debris-guidelines-revision-2.pdf.

Space Station, China's new Tiangong Space station, all of SpaceX's Starlink satellites and many other satellites as well. And they would each do so twice every 90 minutes or so!

It might be tempting to think of this Rwandan filing as being a special case. In some respects, it is, most obviously in the conspicuously large number of satellites involved. However, as noted above, the Kepler filings are also for more than 100,000 satellites, of which Kepler envisages only a small fraction will be its own satellites. The plan is for the rest of the constellations to be made up of third-party satellites with Kepler transmitters attached.[92] Regardless, this distinction of ownership should not distract us from the main issue, which is that these companies might actually use all or a large fraction of their filed orbits, adding literally hundreds of thousands of new satellites to LEO. And even these ambitious filings hide the full scale of what is occurring, since cumulative use must also be considered.

Between 1 January 2021 and 31 January 2022, over 1.5 million satellite slots were filed in the ITU's 'as-received' database.[93] Interpreting these numbers must be done cautiously, as many slots will be left unused and there are some duplications in the database. But even if only a small fraction of these systems succeed in moving from paper to orbit, it could fundamentally change orbital congestion. To put this in perspective, only about 0.4 per cent of the proposed satellite slots (for this one year alone) would need to be used to exceed the current number of active satellites. Moreover, some of the most highly sought-after orbital altitudes are between 500 and 600 kilometres, with potential congestion extending to 1,200 kilometres. Thus, interwoven with the larger and manoeuvrable mega-constellation satellites, including Starlink and OneWeb, will be a potentially much larger number of small, cheap, unmanoeuvrable satellites.

In summary, the ITU system for allocating spectrum to 'non-geosynchronous satellite systems' creates multiple incentives for companies to seek as much spectrum as possible as quickly as possible. The system feeds a gold-rush mentality, and, with it, the overpopulation of LEO with low-cost, mass-produced satellites, adding to the already high collision risks and thus the Space debris crisis. Moreover, some of these systems may well be abandoned after construction if one or more companies goes

---

[92] See discussion at *supra* note 13.
[93] These numbers are based directly on the ITU 'as-received' filings, compiled by Outer Space Institute junior fellows Andrew Falle and Ewan Wright.

bankrupt in what is likely to be a highly competitive market. And yet the ITU seems to be encouraging rather than seeking to slow these developments, or otherwise to steer them in a sustainable direction. Unless something changes, we may well see upwards of 100,000 satellites in LEO by 2030. This would constitute a massive change in the orbital environment, the consequences of which are not yet fully understood.

Fortunately, states will soon have an opportunity to expand the scope of the ITU's mandate so that it can address these new and growing challenges. The next World Radiocommunication Conference will begin in the United Arab Emirates in November 2023. Under Article 55 of the ITU Constitution, any member state may propose any amendment to that instrument.[94] If more than half of the delegations to the conference concur, the proposal will then be debated and put to a vote – with two-thirds support being required to make the change. The revised constitution is then opened for ratifications.

---

[94] Constitution and Convention of the International Telecommunication Union, 22 December 1992, 1825–26 UNTS (entered into force 1 July 1994), Art. 55.

# 3

# Mega-constellations and International Law

The rapid development of satellite mega-constellations raises difficult issues of international law. Some issues are of immediate relevance; others are more distant.[1] The first section of this chapter addresses the issue of liability for collisions involving satellites, as it might play out in both international law and domestic legal systems. Establishing 'causation' – demonstrating that the actions of one satellite operator caused a specific collision with another Space object and resulted in damage – could be a challenge. This challenge could be especially difficult in the context of knock-on collisions, where debris from an initial collision later collides with one or more spacecraft, including satellites. Such a collision occurred in 2013 when debris from a 2007 Chinese anti-satellite (ASAT) weapon test collided with and disabled a Russian satellite.[2] A second challenge concerns determining, in the absence of binding international rules on the design and operation of satellites, what is reasonable behaviour, and therefore what constitutes negligence. As we will see, non-binding guidelines and industry practices could be helpful in making such determinations.

The second section of this chapter addresses the interference to astronomy that is increasingly resulting from the construction of mega-constellations. A full interpretation of the Outer Space Treaty, in

---

[1] One somewhat distant issue concerns the application of competition law, whether international or domestic, in the quite plausible scenario where one company, or several companies from one state, secure an effective monopoly over the provision of broadband Internet from satellites. See Lucien Rapp and Maria Topka, 'Small satellite constellations, infrastructure shift and space market regulation', in Annette Froehlich, ed, *Legal Aspects around Satellite Constellations: Volume 2* (Cham: Springer, 2021) 1. An analogous issue concerns the application of competition law to globally dominant tech firms such as Google, as to which, see Maurice Stucke and Allen Grunes, *Big Data and Competition Policy* (Oxford: Oxford University Press, 2016).

[2] Melissa Gray, 'Chinese space debris hits Russian satellite, scientists say', *CNN* (9 March 2013), online: www.cnn.com/2013/03/09/tech/satellite-hit.

accordance with the international rules on treaty interpretation, leads us
to the conclusion that states are already required to take certain steps –
including conducting an environmental impact assessment – before
licensing mega-constellations, because of the obligation of 'due regard
to the corresponding interests of all other States Parties to the Treaty'.

### 3.1   Collisions Involving Satellites

Treaties and customary international law are sometimes referred to
collectively as 'hard law' because they contain binding obligations that,
when violated, can have direct consequences. Such consequences include
empowering other states to engage in 'countermeasures' – actions such as
economic sanctions that would be illegal under normal circumstances,
but are rendered legal as a response to the initial violation.[3]

'Soft law' is a term used for non-binding instruments such as resolutions adopted by the United Nations General Assembly or guidelines
produced by other bodies, including subsidiary organs of the United
Nations, such as the  Committee on the Peaceful Uses of Outer Space
(COPUOS).[4] These non-binding instruments cannot be enforced and
therefore, by themselves, allow for 'free riding', whereby individual actors
can save costs through non-compliance while benefiting from the compliance of others. As we explained in the Introduction to this book, in the
context of any shared resource, free riding can lead to a 'tragedy of the
commons'.[5] This is exactly what has been happening in Earth's atmosphere as a result of greenhouse gas emissions, and what now needs to be
avoided in low Earth orbit (LEO).

Soft law nevertheless remains significant, in part because non-binding
instruments can still influence state behaviour, and in part because
they sometimes serve as precursors to the negotiation of treaties or

---

[3] International Law Commission, Draft Articles on Responsibility of States for
Internationally Wrongful Acts, with commentaries, UNGAOR, 56th Sess, Supp No 10,
UN Doc A/56/10 (2001) at 128 et seq., online: legal.un.org/ilc/texts/instruments/english/
commentaries/9_6_2001.pdf. These draft articles were commended to governments by the
UN General Assembly in its resolution *Responsibility of States for Internationally
Wrongful Acts*, GA Res 56/83, UNGAOR, 56th Sess, 85th Plen Mtg, UN Doc A/RES/56/
83 (2001).

[4] Irmgard Marboe, ed, *Soft Law in Outer Space: The Function of Non-binding Norms in
International Space Law* (Vienna: Böhlau Verlag, 2012).

[5] Garrett Hardin, 'The Tragedy of the Commons' (1968) 162:3859 *Science* 1243.

the development of customary international law.[6] For instance, the 1948 Universal Declaration of Human Rights was the precursor to numerous human rights treaties, including the 1976 International Covenant on Civil and Political Rights and the 1984 Convention against Torture. It is also widely considered to have contributed to the development of customary international law, to the point where most of its provisions are now considered to have that status. Moreover, 'soft' rules of international law are often implemented in domestic legal systems through legislation and regulations – becoming 'hard law' adopted by national and subnational governments. Domestic courts also look to resolutions and guidelines produced internationally, for instance when assessing whether a particular action was negligent.

### 3.1.1    Soft Law

#### 3.1.1.1    Inter-Agency Space Debris Coordination Committee Guidelines

The Inter-Agency Space Debris Coordination Committee (IADC) is currently made up of representatives from 13 space agencies, including NASA, Roscosmos, the China National Space Administration (CNSA) and the European Space Agency (ESA). In 2007, the IADC stated that direct re-entry (i.e. atmospheric 'burn-up') at the end of a satellite's operational life is preferred, and recommended that such de-orbiting conclude within 25 years.[7] But while this 25-year guideline is widely accepted, it is poorly suited to mega-constellations made up of thousands of satellites with short operational lives. It also overlooks placement, with satellites at higher altitudes producing relatively high collision probabilities when de-orbiting timescales are long, as they pass slowly through lower orbits.[8]

The IADC also recommended that collision avoidance and end-of-life de-orbiting technologies be included in satellites. But these measures add costs, and in 2017 the IADC reported that adherence to its guidelines was

---

[6] Hema Nadarajah, 'Soft law and international relations: The Arctic, outer space, and climate change' (PhD thesis, University of British Columbia, 2020), online: dx.doi.org/10 .14288/1.0394919.

[7] Inter-Agency Space Debris Coordination Committee (IADC), 'Space Debris Mitigation Guidelines – first revision' (2007), *United Nations Office for Outer Space Affairs*, online: www.unoosa.org/documents/pdf/spacelaw/sd/IADC_space_debris_mitigation_guidelines .pdf.

[8] Hugh G Lewis, 'Understanding long-term orbital debris population dynamics' (2020) 7:3 *Journal of Space Safety Engineering* 164.

'insufficient and no apparent trend towards a better implementation is observed'.[9] More recent analyses indicate that compliance with the end-of-life guidelines is now improving, at least on some metrics, and in 2022 the Federal Communications Commission (FCC) adopted a five-year rule for US operators.[10] Yet these improvements appear to be driven mostly by SpaceX's own practices, which may or may not be followed by other mega-constellation operators. Moreover, they do not by themselves constitute an overall change in collective behaviour, since the enormous presence of SpaceX in LEO could simply be diluting averaged metrics on non-compliance even if the absolute rate of non-compliance remains the same (i.e. if some number of satellites fail to meet de-orbiting guidelines each year).

### 3.1.1.2   UN Space Debris Mitigation Guidelines

COPUOS adopted seven Space Debris Mitigation Guidelines in 2007,[11] the same year as the IADC Guidelines. The titles of the UN guidelines are indicative of their content:

1. Limit debris released during normal operations.
2. Minimize the potential for break-ups during operational phases.
3. Limit the probability of accidental collision in orbit.
4. Avoid intentional destruction and other harmful activities.
5. Minimize potential for post-mission break-ups resulting from stored energy.
6. Limit the long-term presence of spacecraft and launch vehicle orbital stages in the low-Earth orbit (LEO) region after the end of their mission.
7. Limit the long-term interference of spacecraft and launch vehicle orbital stages with the geosynchronous Earth orbit (GEO) region after the end of their mission.

---

[9] IADC, 'An overview of the IADC annual activities' (presentation delivered at the 54th Session of the Scientific and Technical Subcommittee of the Committee on the Peaceful Uses of Outer Space, Vienna, 1 February 2017), online: www.unoosa.org/documents/pdf/copuos/stsc/2017/tech-16E.pdf.

[10] ESA Space Debris Office, 'ESA's annual space environment report' (2022), European Space Agency (ESA) Ref No GEN-DB-LOG-00288-OPS-SD, online: www.sdo.esoc.esa.int/environment_report/Space_Environment_Report_latest.pdf. 'FCC Adopts New '5-Year Rule' for Deorbiting Satellites', (29 Sept 2022), online: https://www.fcc.gov/document/fcc-adopts-new-5-year-rule-deorbiting-satellites.

[11] United Nations Office for Outer Space Affairs (UNOOSA), *Space Debris Mitigations Guidelines of the Committee on the Peaceful Uses of Outer Space* (Vienna: United Nations, 2010), online: www.unoosa.org/oosa/oosadoc/data/documents/2010/stspace/stspace49_0.html.

Apart from Guideline 4, which we address in Chapter 8 in the context of anti-satellite weapons, the guidelines are couched in the general terms of 'limit' and 'minimize'. This makes measuring compliance difficult, at least in many circumstances. However, when an operator makes no effort to limit or minimise these behaviors, it will, self-evidently, not be complying and could legitimately be criticised on that basis. In this way, even these generally worded provisions can provide reasons – and justifications – for public, governmental or broader industry pressure.

The UN guidelines, moreover, were and remain very widely supported. Since COPUOS operates on a consensus basis, the guidelines were supported from the outset by all its then 67 member states, which included almost all the spacefaring states (except Israel, which joined COPUOS in 2015).[12] When the UN General Assembly endorsed the guidelines later in 2007, it stated that they 'reflect the existing practices as developed by a number of national and international organizations'.[13]

Several spacefaring states quickly implemented the 2007 guidelines within their domestic legal systems, notably China and Russia.[14] More recent follow-up developments at the domestic level include a 2019 update to NASA's Orbital Debris Mitigation Standard Practices (ODMSP),[15] and the 2018 adoption of Australia's Space (Launches and Returns) Act, which makes a Space debris mitigation strategy a launch requirement. The strategy must be based on internationally recognised guidelines or standards, such as those of the UN or the IADC.[16]

---

[12] If one considers spacefaring states as those which have launched orbital spacecraft, North Korea, which achieved orbital launch capability in 2012, is the only spacefaring state that is not currently one of the now 102 members of COPUOS.

[13] *International Cooperation in the Peaceful Uses of Outer Space*, GA Res 62/217, UNGAOR, 62nd Sess, 79th Plen Mtg, UN Doc A/RES/62/217 (2007) at para. 27.

[14] Yun Zhao, *National Space Law in China* (Leiden: Brill Nijhoff, 2015) at 218. Russian Federation, 'National Standard of the Russian Federation GOSTR52925-2008', cited in Y Makarov, G Raykunov, S Kolchin, S Loginov, M Mikhailov and M Yakovlev, 'Russian Federation activity on space debris mitigation', Federal Space Agency of Russia (2010), online: www.tsi.lv/sites/default/files/editor/science/Conferences/SPACE/makarov.pdf.

[15] National Aeronautics and Space Administration (NASA), 'US Government Orbital Debris Mitigation Standard Practices, November 2019 update' (2019), *NASA*, online: orbitaldebris.jsc.nasa.gov/library/usg_orbital_debris_mitigation_standard_practices_november_2019.pdf. The first version of the ODMSP was adopted in 2001. See NASA Orbital Debris Program Office, 'Debris mitigation' (2022), *NASA*, online: orbitaldebris.jsc.nasa.gov/mitigation.

[16] UNOOSA, 'Compendium – Space debris mitigation standards adopted by states and international organizations' (17 June 2021) at 8–9, *UNOOSA*, online: www.unoosa.org/documents/pdf/spacelaw/sd/Space_Debris_Compendium_COPUOS_17_june_2021.pdf.

The 2007 guidelines also found their way into legally binding require-ments via the International Organization for Standardization (ISO), a non-governmental organisation that in 2010 adopted a stringent set of Space Debris Mitigation Requirements for all unmanned satellites and spacecraft 'launched into, or passing through, near-Earth space'.[17] These requirements, which were updated in 2011 and again in 2019, are 'intended to reduce the growth of space debris by ensuring that spacecraft and launch vehicle orbital stages are designed, operated and disposed of in a manner that prevents them from generating debris throughout their orbital lifetime'.[18] Among other things, all new satellites must be able to de-orbit to Earth, or boost themselves into graveyard orbits at the end of their lifespan (which, while an improvement, is not a sustainable practice[19]). The ISO Space Debris Mitigation Requirements are not legally binding. However, in 2015 they were adopted by the European Cooperation for Space Standardization, an initiative, led by the 22-member-state European Space Agency, that seeks to develop a coherent, single set of user-friendly standards for use in all European Space activ-ities.[20] And the standards adopted by the European Cooperation for Space Standardization are applied – in a binding manner – to all ESA projects.[21]

---

[17] International Organization for Standardization (ISO), 'ISO 24113:2010, space systems – space debris mitigation requirements' (July 2010), *ISO*, online: www.iso.org/standard/42034.html.

[18] ISO, 'ISO 24113:2011, space systems – space debris mitigation requirements' (May 2011), *ISO*, online: www.iso.org/standard/57239.html; ISO, 'ISO 24113:2019, space systems – space debris mitigation requirements' (July 2019), *ISO*, online: www.iso.org/standard/72383.html.

[19] When GEO satellites reach the end of their life, they are manoeuvred into an orbital region at least 200 kilometres above GEO. A satellite in this fairly stable region is said to be on a 'graveyard orbit'. While this removes the spacecraft from highly desirable GEO locations, the decommissioned satellites are left uncontrolled. The collision risk between them is currently small, but material at that altitude does not clear easily and thus will continue to build, and could eventually threaten the GEO region. Moreover, break-up events and meteoroid strikes in nearby orbits could create problematic debris for GEO. See European Organisation for the Exploitation of Meteorological Satellites (EUMETSAT), 'Where old satellites go to die', *Phys.Org* (3 April 2017), online: phys.org/news/2017-04-satellites-die.html.

[20] ESA, 'European cooperation for space standardization (ECSS)' (2022), *ECSS*, online: ecss.nl.

[21] ESA, 'Mitigating space debris generation' (2022), *ESA*, online: www.esa.int/Safety_Security/Space_Debris/Mitigating_space_debris_generation.

### 3.1.1.3 UN Guidelines for the Long-Term Sustainability of Outer Space Activities

In 2019, COPUOS adopted 21 'Guidelines for the Long-Term Sustainability of Outer Space Activities'.[22] Although the text below each guideline contains permissive language (e.g. 'should'), the guidelines themselves still provide markers against which an absence of effort at debris avoidance or mitigation can be measured. For example, the following five guidelines can be used to assess whether a satellite operator took reasonable measures to prevent collisions in orbit:

B.1 Provide updated contact information and share information on space objects and orbital events.

B.2 Improve accuracy of orbital data on space objects and enhance the practice and utility of sharing orbital information on space objects.

B.3 Promote the collection, sharing and dissemination of space debris monitoring information.

B.4 Perform conjunction assessment during all orbital phases of controlled flight.

B.5 Develop practical approaches for pre-launch conjunction assessment.

In addition to providing reasons – and justifications – for applying pressure on non-compliant satellite operators, these and other international guidelines could become highly relevant after a collision or some other event causing damage, when the issue of liability arises.

### 3.1.2 Liability for Collisions

In other domains, such as the world's oceans, major disasters have led to policy changes, law-making and litigation at both the national and international levels. As we explain in Chapter 4, the 1989 *Exxon Valdez* oil spill prompted the United States and then the International Maritime Organization to require that new oil tankers be constructed with double hulls. This safety measure increased the cost of shipbuilding but reduced the prevalence of spills, which of course carry their own environmental and economic costs. In the domain of climate change, a combination of

---

[22] Committee on the Peaceful Uses of Outer Space, 'Guidelines for the Long-term Sustainability of Outer Space Activities', Annex II in *Report of the Committee on the Peaceful Uses of Outer Space, Sixty-second session (12–21 June 2019)*, UNGAOR, 74th Sess, Supp No 20, UN Doc A/74/20, online: www.unoosa.org/res/oosadoc/data/documents/2019/a/a7420_0_html/V1906077.pdf.

damaging effects and improved scientific understandings has led to litigation in domestic courts based on the fast-developing ability of climate scientists to establish causation between, for instance, the historic greenhouse gas emissions of a fossil-fuel company, and a precise portion of global sea level rise.[23] No plaintiff has won such a case in the United States, yet, due to courts deferring to executive action on these issues.[24] But as with lung cancer victims and the tobacco industry, which fought off legal actions for decades before agreeing to large settlements,[25] the ability to establish causation offers those who have suffered losses from sea level rise, such as coastal municipalities, the possibility of obtaining similar settlements or damage awards.

All this prompts us to consider the legal consequences that would flow from a collision in LEO that resulted in substantial financial losses to one or more satellite operators. And let us be clear: the losses could be very substantial indeed. In a worst-case scenario involving a collisional cascade, hundreds, perhaps even thousands, of satellites could be disabled or destroyed, although this outcome might take considerable time to develop.

### 3.1.3   Establishing Fault

One major issue concerns the establishment of fault, since under Article III of the 1972 Liability Convention, liability in orbit is fault-based:

> In the event of damage being caused elsewhere than on the surface of the earth to a space object of one launching State or to persons or property on board such a space object by a space object of another launching State, the latter shall be liable only if the damage is due to its fault or the fault of persons for whom it is responsible.[26]

This therefore leads us to ask, what constitutes fault in the design, construction and operation of satellites? For example, would failing to

---

[23] Michael Byers, Kelsey Franks and Andrew Gage, 'The internationalization of climate damages litigation' (2017) 7:2 *Washington Journal of Environmental Law and Policy* 264.

[24] See e.g. Jonathan Stempel and Sebastien Malo, 'Oil companies defeat New York City appeal over global warming', *Reuters* (1 April 2001), online: www.reuters.com/article/us-global-warming-new-york-idUSKBN2BO5O0.

[25] Michael Givel and Stanton A Glantz, 'The "global settlement" with the tobacco industry: 6 years later' (2004) 94:2 *American Journal of Public Health* 218.

[26] Convention on International Liability for Damage Caused by Space Objects, 29 March 1972, 961 UNTS 187 Art. III (entered into force 1 September 1972) (Liability Convention).

include active de-orbiting technology in a satellite, or failing to retain sufficient propellant for this purpose, constitute fault if the satellite later collided with another satellite after running out of fuel? Or would following the IADC's 25-year guideline for de-orbiting relieve the company of fault, even if the satellite was involved in a collision after spending many years in orbit with its propellant exhausted, unable to manoeuvre out of the way of incoming trackable debris?[27] International guidelines could help to determine liability, depending on what they say, which may in turn depend on when they were adopted. Again, the IADC guidelines were adopted in 2007, before mega-constellations dramatically increased the surface area of material in LEO and therefore the collision risk, particularly from small but still lethal non-trackable debris.

Can we measure a company's behaviour against that of other companies, especially if there is a widespread and consistent practice in the industry, to determine whether it was acting reasonably? Could negligence be established on the basis that a company's satellites had an anomalously high failure rate, leading to a higher-than-normal risk of collisions with other satellites and trackable debris?

What constitutes fault will be continually evolving, due in part to new technologies, and to greater risks associated with a higher density of satellites and debris, growing concerns about Space debris among governments, and changing practices – including on the part of Space agencies, national regulators and other state actors.[28]

### 3.1.4   Liability for Indirect Damage?

Another important question concerns whether liability will be limited to direct damage only, or whether indirect damage is included. Indirect damage could arise from a knock-on collision, in other words a piece of debris from the first collision striking another satellite in a secondary collision – as, again, has happened already. It might also include the costs incurred by other operators as they seek to avoid such knock-on collisions by, for instance, engaging in more frequent manoeuvres which thereby use up more thruster fuel, shortening the operational lifespan of their satellites. In the case of satellites that are not part of a large constellation, indirect damage could also include the loss of services

---

[27] IADC, 'Space Debris Mitigation Guidelines – first revision', op. cit.

[28] Note, also, that this 'state practice' can, over time, contribute to the development or change of customary international law.

provided by a satellite that has been disabled by a collision. Imagine, for instance, a small country with a single Earth-imaging satellite (perhaps used to support food production) that is forced to buy expensive imagery from foreign commercial operators after its satellite is disabled by a collision.[29]

As it happens, liability for damage from knock-on collisions is addressed in Article IV of the Liability Convention, which reads:

1. In the event of damage being caused elsewhere than on the surface of the earth to a space object of one launching State or to persons or property on board such a space object by a space object of another launching State, *and of damage thereby being caused to a third State or to its natural or juridical persons*, the first two States shall be jointly and severally liable to the third State, to the extent indicated by the following:
   (a) If the damage has been caused to the third State on the surface of the earth or to aircraft in flight, their liability to the third State shall be absolute;
   (b) If the damage has been caused to a space object of the third State or to persons or property on board that space object elsewhere than on the surface of the earth, their liability to the third State shall be based on the fault of either of the first two States or on the fault of persons for whom either is responsible.
2. In all cases of joint and several liability referred to in paragraph 1 of this article, the burden of compensation for the damage shall be apportioned between the first two States in accordance with the extent to which they were at fault; if the extent of the fault of each of these States cannot be established, the burden of compensation shall be apportioned equally between them. Such apportionment shall be without prejudice to the right of the third State to seek the entire compensation due under this Convention from any or all of the launching States which are jointly and severally liable.[30]

Article IV thus captures situations where the initial collision is the result of fault on the part of just one operator, as well as situations where both

---

[29] This example, while hypothetical, has already been prefigured. In 2013, Ecuador partially lost its first satellite (of two) to debris due to a presumed collision with Russian space junk. See 'Ecuador tries to fix satellite after space debris crash', *BBC News* (27 May 2013), online: www.bbc.com/news/world-latin-america-22678919.

[30] Liability Convention, op. cit., Art. IV, added emphasis.

operators are at fault. In the former situation, the single operator is solely liable for the damage caused by the knock-on collision, while in the latter situation, the two operators share responsibility, with the 'burden of compensation' being apportioned between them 'in accordance with the extent to which they were at fault'.

### 3.1.5   At the International Level, States Are Liable, Not Companies

The picture is further complicated by the fact that, under the Liability Convention, states are the ones liable for damage caused by a 'space object', not the satellite companies themselves. This is because, under Article III, liability attaches to the 'launching state'. This is consistent with Article VI of the Outer Space Treaty, the first sentence of which stipulates that 'States Parties to the Treaty shall bear international responsibility for national activities in outer space ... whether such activities are carried on by governmental agencies or by non-governmental entities, and for assuring that national activities are carried out in conformity with the provisions set forth in the present Treaty.'

There can be up to four launching states associated with any Space object, namely the state that launches the Space object, the state that procures the launch, the state from whose territory a Space object is launched, and the state from whose facility a Space object is launched. For instance, in 2007 Russia launched a satellite for Canada from the territory of Kazakhstan and specifically from Russia's Baikonur Cosmodrome, which is located there; in this case, there were three launch states, with Russia fulfilling two of the criteria.

It is also important to note that there is no time limit on liability.[31] Once a state has become a launching state, it remains so until the Space object is no longer capable of causing damage – including if that damage occurs after the object has become defunct, and even if it breaks into multiple fragments. Finally, the launching state(s) remain the same even if the Space object is later sold to another state, with 'on-orbit' transfers occurring with some frequency today.[32]

---

[31] The only time limits concern the making of a claim for compensation, which must take place within one year of the occurrence of the damage, or within 'one year following the date on which the State could reasonably be expected to have learned of the facts through the exercise of due diligence'. Ibid., Art. X.

[32] There is nothing in the 1972 Liability Convention on the transfer of ownership of Space objects between states or non-governmental actors from different states; as a result, the launching states remain responsible for any damage occurring after a sale. Launching

For all these reasons, most spacefaring states have domestic laws that entitle the government to recover, from the private owner or operator of the Space object, some portion of the compensation the state must provide under the Liability Convention after a fault-based accident in Space or for any damage caused by a Space object on the Earth's surface.[33] These 'indemnification regimes' also provide clarity to industry on how much insurance is required and whether the government will pursue Space companies to recover all or part of the financial loss. Most spacefaring states require Space companies to carry third-party liability insurance to a specified amount, and then cover any claims that exceed that level.

Enforcement might, however, pose a challenge. To date, there is only one known instance where a state has submitted a claim to another state under the Liability Convention. The claim was made by Canada against the Soviet Union after Kosmos 954 re-entered the atmosphere in 1978 and spread radioactive debris across the Northwest Territories. The claim, as it turns out, was settled, as envisaged under the Liability Convention, through negotiations between the two parties.[34] The Liability Convention does, however, enable a party to request the establishment of a claims commission if negotiations fail, though disputing

states can protect themselves against this risk, for example, by insisting that an indemnification agreement is part of any contract of sale. In some instances, such as when the 'launch state' status was acquired solely by procuring the launch, they might be able to transfer that status through the conclusion of a bilateral treaty. Finally, the regular rules of 'state succession', which apply when states merge, break apart or decolonise, will apply to 'launch state' status because it is treaty-based. For various scenarios and possible solutions, see Setsuko Aoki, 'Satellite ownership transfers and the liability of the launching states' (presentation delivered at the IISL/ECSL Symposium at the 51st Session of the Legal Subcommittee of the Committee on the Peaceful Uses of Outer Space, Vienna, 19 March 2012), online: www.unoosa.org/pdf/pres/lsc2012/symp-03E.pdf. On state succession and treaties in general, see Matthew Craven, *The Decolonization of International Law: State Succession and the Law of Treaties* (Oxford: Oxford University Press, 2009).

[33] See e.g. Space Activities Act 1998 (Australia); Law of 17 September 2005 on the Activities of Launching, Flight Operations, or Guidance of Space Objects (Belgium); Tort Law of the People's Republic of China, Art. 76 (China); Space Operations Act 2008 (France); Law Concerning Japan Aerospace Exploration Agency, Law No. 151 of 13 December 2002 (Japan); Law of the Russian Federation No 5663-1 of August 20, 1993 on Space Activities (Russia); Space Liability Act, Law No. 8852 of December 21, 2007 (South Korea); Act on Space Activities, 1982:963 (Sweden); Outer Space Act 1986 (United Kingdom); 51 USC Ch 509, Commercial Space Launch Activities (United States).

[34] Olga A Volynskaya, 'Landmark space-related accidents and the progress of space law' (2013) 62 *Zeitschrift für Luft -und Weltraumrecht* (German Journal of Air and Space Law) 220.

parties are not required to accept the commission's decision. As Article XIX explains, 'The decision of the Commission shall be final and binding if the parties have so agreed; otherwise the Commission shall render a final and recommendatory award, which the parties shall consider in good faith.' This was not a problem in 1978, when a mutually agreed outcome was achieved between Canada and the Soviet Union.

### 3.1.6   Liability and National Courts

The infrequent use of the Liability Convention and the potential enforcement challenges make it likely that national courts will eventually become involved when satellites are damaged due to alleged fault on the part of other operators. The involvement of national courts is made more likely by the dramatic increase in the number of private operators, who might prefer to seek their own remedies rather than trust national governments to do so on their behalf. In common law systems such as the United States, the United Kingdom, Canada, Australia and New Zealand such suits would be grounded in tort law and specifically the tort of negligence[35] – a failure to behave with the level of care that someone of ordinary prudence would have exercised under the same circumstances.[36]

As we explained above, international guidelines and industry practices can help national courts to determine whether a satellite operator was acting reasonably. For instance, an operator launching mega-constellation satellites today without end-of-life de-orbiting technology might well be acting irresponsibly and therefore negligently.

Assessing the 'reasonableness' of behaviour is one thing, but determining 'causation' for damage is another. Establishing causation can be especially difficult for the secondary and tertiary effects of a negligent action, for example damage caused to satellites by debris from a previous collision, or damage caused to governments, companies or individuals on Earth from the loss of the services provided by those satellites. But again, just as advances in medical science opened the door to litigation against

---

[35] Tort law concerns acts or omissions that give rise to injury or harm to others and amount to civil (as opposed to criminal) wrongs.

[36] For an interesting analysis of how negligence might be determined in the event of damage caused during a 'rendezvous and proximity operation', and specifically the on-orbit servicing of a satellite, see Christopher Newman, Ralph Dinsley and William Ralston, 'Introducing the law games: Predicting legal liability and fault in satellite operations' (2021) 67:11 *Advances in Space Research* 3785.

tobacco companies, and advances in climate science are now opening the door to climate change litigation against fossil-fuel companies, we can expect that advances in Space situational awareness (SSA) will dramatically reduce uncertainties concerning causation for secondary collisions involving trackable debris, and thus strengthen the role of liability as an incentive for good behaviour in Space. For example, the California-based company LeoLabs uses its own network of ground-based phased-arrayed radars to provide SSA to satellite companies, including 'conjunction' warnings that can enable satellites to be moved out of the way of an impending collision.[37] A similar, more recent entrant is Hawaii-based Privateer, backed by Apple co-founder Steve Wozniak and significantly involving Space environmentalist and aerospace engineer Moriba Jah, which is developing 'knowledge graph technology' to provide satellite operators a comprehensive real-time map of Space objects.[38] The SSA obtained and catalogued by these companies could be used to supplement data obtained and catalogued by national governments, most notably USSPACECOM, in determining causation for an actual collision. In other words, it could be employed not only prospectively to predict possible collisions and thus help prevent them, but also retrospectively to determine what happened.

Smaller non-trackable debris will, however, remain a lethal threat to satellites, notwithstanding advances in SSA, and establishing causation for a collision will be impossible in some circumstances. But in a growing number of instances improved SSA will help with event-linking, even if only on the balance of probabilities – which, as it happens, is the standard required in tort cases in the United States and other common law countries.

### 3.1.7   International Law-Making before, Not after, a Major Disaster

Collisions are still infrequent enough that satellite operators might continue to treat them, and the even smaller risk of having to pay compensation, as simply a 'cost of doing business' in an inherently risky domain.[39] And with a tragedy of the commons emerging quickly, it seems unwise to

---

[37] See 'LeoLabs – The Mapping Platform for Space' (2022), *LeoLabs Inc.*, online: www .leolabs.space.

[38] See 'Privateer' (2022), *Privateer Space Inc.*, online: www.privateer.com.

[39] See e.g. Kenneth S Abraham, 'Environmental Liability and the Limits of Insurance' (1988) 88:5 *Columbia Law Review* 942 at 957: 'Ordinary strict liability is a cost of doing business that enterprises and their insurers can anticipate and finance, even when the damages imposed are not worth avoiding.'

count on litigation in national courts to ensure the global adoption of best practices in time to ward off a major disaster. Strong regulatory action is required on the part of most, if not all, national governments. The best way to achieve this 'collective action' and to prevent 'free riding' and the emergence of 'flag-of-convenience' states is through multilateral agreements that set clear standards and provide transparency and accountability for them. Skeptics of this approach should once again consider the double-hull requirement for oil tankers, which has been adopted by all the major shipping states and is now followed, without deviation, by the shipbuilding industry worldwide.

We should not have to wait for a major disaster like the Exxon Valdez oil spill to generate the political will necessary for effective international law-making. Collisions involving mega-constellation satellites are entirely foreseeable. They have the potential to create vast amounts of long-lasting debris, including debris that is untrackable but still lethal, with severe consequences for the future use of LEO, for the global economy and even for human safety. The time to act is now.

## 3.2   Astronomy, Mega-constellations, and International Law

Astronomy is the oldest way humanity has explored the cosmos. It is a science that cultivates an understanding of Earth's place in the universe and has a long and continuing history of testing fundamental laws of physics. There is a direct connection between Tycho Brahe's early observations, analysed and understood by Johannes Kepler, and the development of Newtonian gravity. 'Newton's cannonball', a thought experiment that Newton used to demonstrate the principles of an orbit, is really just an artificial satellite. Astronomy later provided the primary tests for Einstein's 'general relativity', a more complete theory of gravity, and played a critical role in understanding processes such as nuclear fusion.

It is already well established that mega-constellations threaten astronomy.[40] Astronomers have been pushing for reductions in the

---

[40] Robert Massey, Sara Lucatello and Piero Benvenuti, 'The challenge of satellite megaconstellations' (2020) 4 *Nature Astronomy* 1022; Aparna Venkatesan, James Lowenthal, Parvathy Prem and Monica Vidaurri, 'The impact of satellite constellations on space as an ancestral global commons' (2020) 4 *Nature Astronomy* 1043; Miroslav Kocifaj, Frantisek Kundracik, John C. Barentine and Salvador Bará, 'The proliferation of space objects is a rapidly increasing source of artificial night sky brightness' (2021) 504:1 *Monthly Notices of the Royal Astronomical Society: Letters* L40; American Astronomical Society (AAS), 'Impact of satellite constellations on optical astronomy and recommendations

number and brightness of Starlink satellites since an image from a telescope in Chile was ruined in 2019.[41] SpaceX responded by adding visors to its satellites, which has reduced their brightness but still left them bright to telescopes and visible to the naked eye for a non-trivial amount of time.[42] Especially vulnerable are both next-generation sky surveys, which seek to catalogue all visible bodies, and observations close to the horizon, especially near sunrise and sunset. These surveys and observations are critical for detecting and tracking near-Earth objects for planetary defence.

Radio astronomy is also threatened since mega-constellations will require frequencies additional to those traditionally used by communications systems on the ground.[43] Portions of spectrum that are protected for radio astronomy could be encroached upon through 'out-of-band emissions'. The vast number of fast-moving transmitting stations (i.e. individual satellites within mega-constellations) will cause further interference. Although new analysis methods could mitigate some of these effects, data loss is inevitable, increasing the time needed for each radio astronomy study and limiting the overall amount of science that can be done.

The figure at the beginning of Chapter 2 shows how satellites have already created bright streaks across telescope images. There are also transient moments of interference, such as visual flares from specular (mirror-like) reflections – essentially, sunlight glinting brightly off a satellite's surface. The first commercial constellation, launched by Iridium in the 1990s to provide global satellite phone coverage, produced flares that were so bright and predictable that they became widely referred to as 'Iridium flares'. Radio astronomy has also already experienced interference from terrestrial and Space-borne sources, including communications satellites in both geosynchronous (GEO) and low Earth orbit (LEO).

---

towards mitigations' (2020), ed. Constance Walker and Jeffrey Hall ['SATCON1 Report'], online: aas.org/sites/default/files/2020-08/SATCON1-Report.pdf; AAS, 'Report of the SATCON2 workshop' (2021), ed. Constance Walker and Jeffrey Hall ['SATCON2 Report'], online: baas.aas.org/pub/2021i0205/release/1; International Astronomical Union (IAU) and UNOOSA, 'Dark and quiet skies for science and society – Report and recommendations' (2021), ed. Constance Walker and Simonetta Di Pippo ['Dark and Quiet Skies I Report'], online: www.iau.org/static/publications/dqskies-book-29-12-20 .pdf; IAU and UNOOSA, 'Dark and Quiet Skies II for Science and Society – Working Group Reports' (2022), ed. Constance Walker and Piero Benvenuti ['Dark and Quiet Skies II Report'], online: doi.org/10.5281/zenodo.5874725.

[41]  IAU, announcement, ann19035, 'IAU statement on satellite constellations' (3 June 2019), online: www.iau.org/news/announcements/detail/ann19035.

[42]  AAS, 'SATCON1 report', op. cit.

[43]  Ibid.

Mega-constellations could magnify these problems to the point where the effects on astronomy become intolerable. Several major astronomy-led initiatives have emerged in response, including SATCON 1 and 2, as well as the International Astronomical Union and UN Office for Outer Space Affairs co-sponsored Dark and Quiet Skies.[44] In what follows, we focus on the effects of mega-constellations on optical astronomy, in part because visual interference also threatens natural and cultural heritage. This includes the ability – perhaps even the right – of every human being to observe and enjoy the night sky.

### 3.2.1    Astronomical Concerns

The principal concern for astronomers is that satellites are bright and there are increasing numbers of them. Data loss from a single streak is one thing, but some satellites are so bright that imaging taken by some of the world's major astronomical facilities will develop detector-specific artefacts. One example is 'ghost' streaks, which are additional streaks in the image caused by the response of the detector electronics to localised overexposures of light.[45] Moreover, wide-field, long-exposure work will experience real multiple streaks per image.[46] Data will be lost, while the extra 'noise' from all these bright sources will make it more difficult to detect faint objects, including asteroids and comets.

Satellites also increase the potential for misidentified phenomena through transient features such as 'rare flares' – flares that occur only infrequently with a single satellite but could be quite common with a constellation comprising thousands of satellites. Even satellites and other large objects in high orbits will create noise. This is not hypothetical; some claims of new discoveries about the universe have already been based on misidentified Space debris.[47]

---

[44] Ibid.; AAS, 'SATCON2 report', op. cit; IAU and UNOOSA, 'Dark and quiet skies I report', op. cit; IAU and UNOOSA, 'Dark and quiet skies II report', op. cit. See also Giuliana Rotola and Andrew Williams, 'Regulatory Context of Conflicting Uses of Outer Space: Astronomy and Satellite Constellations' (2021) 46:4/5 Air and Space Law 545.

[45] AAS, 'SATCON1 report', op. cit.

[46] Samantha Lawler, Aaron Boley and Hanno Rein, 'Visibility predictions for near-future satellite megaconstellations: Latitudes near 50° will experience the worst light pollution' (2022) 163:1 Astronomical Journal 21.

[47] Tereza Pultarova, 'The oldest gamma-ray burst ever discovered was just a piece of space junk', Space.com (7 October 2021), online: www.space.com/oldest-gamma-ray-burst-space-junk-mistake.

The unseen might also be problematic for astronomy: satellites that are in Earth's shadow can still pass in front of stars and other astronomical objects, blocking their light in what astronomers call 'occultations'. Although most research programmes will be unaffected, at least for now, rapid time-domain astronomy[48] could eventually suffer in some cases.[49] In a related issue, satellites transiting in front of the Sun in sufficient numbers could interfere with ground-based solar observing.

Astronomers have been co-ordinating with the satellite industry to establish a set of informal guidelines to address some of the above issues. Based on modelling how satellites can affect observing facilities and amateur sky watchers, several important recommendations have been made.[50] We reproduce two of these guidelines here, followed by additional explanation:

I. Priority No. 1: Address the visible brightness of the satellites as seen from the ground.
   A. Objective: Reduce brightness to minimize impact on astronomy and night sky observers
   B. Guidelines:
      1. Endeavor to reach the fainter of these in all phases of a constellation:
         a)  Unaided eye visibility: $V > 7.0$ mag where $V$ is the photopic vision sensitivity curve.[51] Or

---

[48] Time-domain astronomy is a broad field that explores how properties of astronomical objects, such as brightness and light spectrum, vary with time.

[49] Most satellite occultations will be too rapid to cause substantial interference with observing programmes. However, as astronomers push the limits of observatories to detect ever-faster variability in the sky, satellite occultations could become a major source of noise. One near-future program might already stand to be affected as soon as it comes online – the TAOS II search for small astronomical bodies orbiting beyond Neptune. See Academia Sinica Institute of Astronomy and Astrophysics (ASIAA), 'TAOS II: The transneptunian automated occultation survey' (2021), ASIAA, online: taos2.asiaa.sinica.edu.tw.

[50] IAU and UNOOSA, 'Dark and quiet skies II report', op. cit., ch 4.

[51] An astronomical magnitude ('mag') is a measurement of the brightness of an object based on the logarithm of the flux. Specifically, the magnitude is defined as $m = -2.5 \ log_{10}(F) + C$, where $C$ is a constant and $F$ is the observed flux in a bandpass (region of the spectrum). A larger magnitude signifies a fainter source. For example an object with a magnitude of 10 is fainter than an object with a magnitude of 5, and an object with a magnitude of –5 is brighter still.

b) $V > 7 + 2.5 \ log_{10}\left(\frac{r_{orbit}}{550 \ km}\right)$, equivalent to $44\times\left(\frac{550 \ km}{r_{orbit}}\right)$ watts/steradian,[52] where $r_{orbit}$ is the mean altitude of the satellite orbit in kilometres and $V$ in this case is the Johnson $V$ bandpass at 550 nanometres.[53]

. . .

II. Priority No. 2: Address the visibility impact on astronomical sciences of large constellations of LEO satellites with altitudes above 600 kilometres
   A. Objective: Navigate the balance between constellation size and altitude to allow achievement of satellite service objectives while minimizing impact on astronomy
   B. Guidelines
      1. Endeavor to have satellite constellations operate in orbits with altitudes below about 600 kilometres, if practicable, when consistent with operational and safety objectives and constraints, in order to minimize the rate of sunlight streaks in the dark hours between evening and morning twilight for the largest-aperture telescopes.
      2. If the constellation cannot be planned for altitudes below ~600 kilometres, the impact on astronomical observations would still be reduced on balance if the constellation designers were to choose a lower rather than higher operational altitude.[54]

. . .

The motivation behind these recommended guidelines can be understood as follows. Guideline 1a under Priority No. 1 is just a statement that the satellites should be undetectable by the unaided eye. Guideline 1b, also under Priority No. 1, is a little more complicated, but can be understood conceptually. All other things being equal, a satellite's brightness will depend on the square of the inverse distance between the observer and the satellite; satellites on lower orbits are brighter than satellites on more distant orbits. However, the speed of a satellite's motion across the sky also depends on the orbit and the observer–object distance, with satellites in lower orbits 'moving' faster. If a bright object moves across a detector

---

[52] Watt is a measure of energy per time and steradian is an angular area (in this case, square radians).
[53] IAU and UNOOSA, 'Dark and quiet skies II report', op. cit. at 237.
[54] Ibid. at 238.

quickly, its impact on the detector is reduced, as compared to when that same object is moving slowly or is stationary. In other words, spreading the light out reduces the negative effects, and a bright satellite with a dim streak is preferred over a dim satellite with a bright streak. This is part of the rationale for the brightness limit and why the satellite's mean altitude is included in the equation in the way that it is. The goal of the limit is to minimise the creation of 'ghost' features at major astronomical facilities, as mentioned above. The limit is still far from optimal, as satellites that meet this requirement could still be easily observable in even small telescopes.

The reason for Priority No. 2 and associated guidelines is that keeping satellites below 600 kilometres will tend to limit the number of satellites that are sunlit – i.e. not in Earth's shadow – between twilight hours, at low latitudes nearer the equator throughout the year. Although science such as the detection of near-Earth objects (and therefore planetary defence) will continue to be affected, most observing plans will see limited adverse effects.

Not all astronomers agree with a 600-kilometre altitude limit for mega-constellations, with at least three concerns having been voiced. First, placing satellites at lower altitudes than what might be optimal from an engineering perspective could have an unintended consequence – namely that operators might need more satellites to provide the same level of service. The reason for this is that a satellite at a lower altitude will have a smaller coverage area ('beam footprint') on Earth's surface. Second, it is not clear what effect a 600-kilometre limit might have on other issues of Space sustainability. On the one hand, because it would ensure that satellites are placed in the region of LEO most strongly influenced by gas drag and therefore orbital decay,[55] over time this could help ensure a clean orbital environment after satellites become defunct or other debris is generated. On the other hand, however, a 600-kilometre limit would increase the densification of orbits, thus increasing – potentially quite dramatically – the likelihood and consequences of collisions.

A third concern is with the brightness of the satellites in an absolute sense. If brightness limits are not achieved, then the preference indicated above for placing mega-constellations at lower altitudes could lead to larger numbers of satellites visible to the naked eye. And even if the brightness limits are followed, they may be met only part of the time due to variability. Moreover, these recommended limits are heavily

---

[55] Earth's upper atmosphere extends into LEO, albeit with very low gas densities. An object moving through gas feels a resistance against its motion, called 'gas drag'.

biased towards astronomical facilities at low latitudes. At moderate and high latitudes, the 600-kilometre threshold is of little assistance, with bright satellites visible throughout the night during summer.[56] This has additional substantial implications for natural and cultural heritage.

Already, most people have lost nearly all visible contact with the night sky due to terrestrial light pollution. However, many can still escape cities and their attendant light pollution to experience skies that are almost as dark as our ancestors once knew them. To those who have not experienced it, it is difficult to describe the impact that seeing the Milky Way can have on one's sense of self. Seeing a sky replete with stars can inspire one to imagine a universe of possibilities. Yet if the proposed mega-constellations are completed as planned, without steps taken to reduce their visibility, those of us who live at moderately high latitudes will no longer be able to retreat to the countryside to see a dark, star-filled sky. Instead of the night sky as we have known it for millennia, one out of every ten stars will be a satellite streaking across the sky.[57]

As mentioned, several satellite companies, notably SpaceX and Amazon, are now taking the concerns of astronomers seriously and working with them towards brightness mitigation, with some moderate success. However, the proposed brightness limits have not yet been achieved, with measurements of on-orbit satellites demonstrating significant brightness variations.[58] Some companies are concerned that if some licensing states impose rules on brightness and others do not, this could lead to a competitive disadvantage for themselves – assuming that the measures necessary to reduce brightness require operational compromises. But seen from a broader perspective, these sorts of concern are hardly new.

---

[56] Recent work by Lawler and colleagues has demonstrated that the Starlink 550-kilometre shell will heavily impact the night sky at close to 50° latitude and that the satellites are indeed observable all night long. See Lawler, Boley and Rein, op. cit; and Aaron C Boley, Ewan Wright, Samantha Lawler, Paul Hickson and Dave Balam, 'Plaskett 1.8 metre observations of Starlink satellites' (2022) 163:5 *Astronomical Journal* 199. This issue was recognised in the Priority No. 2 guidelines of the 'Dark and quiet skies II report' through a note: 'The altitude of the LEO satellite constellation does not have a uniform impact on observations around the world. Lower orbit altitudes impact programs disproportionately at latitudes outside of +35 and –35 [deg], and increasing the number of satellites on orbit impacts programs that depend on observations in twilight, such as those for planetary defense. Further, if the satellites are not dimmer than naked-eye brightness natural and cultural heritage may be affected'. See IAU and UNOOSA, 'Dark and quiet skies II report', op. cit. at 238.

[57] Lawler, Boley and Rein, op. cit.

[58] IAU and UNOOSA, 'Dark and quiet skies II report', op. cit.; Boley et al., op. cit.

Over time, comparable concerns have been voiced in nearly every industry that operates internationally, with a common response being multilateral negotiations leading to internationally agreed rules. Done well,
these rules ensure that every actor is subject to the same standards, thus
discouraging 'free riding' and the emergence of 'flags of convenience'.
However, before recommending the establishment of such standards,
we first need to ask whether international law already requires states
to prevent, or at least reduce, the interference caused to astronomical
observatories located in – or operated by – other countries?

### 3.2.2   Astronomy and International Law

In previous chapters, we interpreted relevant provisions of the Outer
Space Treaty[59] in accordance with the customary international law rules
on treaty interpretation, as codified in the Vienna Convention on the
Law of Treaties.[60] We will do so again here. Our interpretation will lead
to several conclusions. First, mega-constellations and astronomical
observatories constitute two competing exercises of the freedom of
'exploration and use' of Space. Second, this situation engages a duty of
'due regard' on the part of states receiving licensing requests for mega-
constellations. The duty is owed to states that operate, host, supervise or
otherwise contribute to telescopes that could be impeded by light pollution from satellites. Since the Outer Space Treaty does not tell us what the
duty of 'due regard' entails, we will – in accordance with the Vienna
Convention – look to the ordinary meaning of the term, to its context –
including the preamble and other articles of the treaty – as well as to the
object and purpose of the treaty. We will also look to general rules of
international law, such as the duty not to cause harm to other states, as
well as more recent legal advances such as the precautionary principle.

---

[59] Treaty on Principles Governing the Activities of States in the Exploration and Use of
Outer Space, Including the Moon and Other Celestial Bodies, 27 January 1967, 610 UNTS
205 (entered into force 10 October 1967) (Outer Space Treaty).

[60] Vienna Convention on the Law of Treaties, 23 May 1969, 1155 UNTS 331 (entered into
force 27 January 1980) (Vienna Convention). The International Court of Justice has often
stated that the Vienna Convention codifies customary international law. See e.g. *Case
Concerning Kasikili/Sedudu Island* (*Botswana* v. *Namibia*), [1999] ICJ Rep 1045 at 1059,
para. 18; *Legal Consequences of the Construction of a Wall in the Occupied Palestinian
Territory*, Advisory Opinion, [2004] ICJ Rep 136 at 174, para. 94; *Armed Activities on the
Territory of the Congo* (*Democratic Republic of the Congo* v. *Rwanda*), [2006] ICJ Rep 6 at
51–52, para. 125. For the pre-existing rules of customary international law, see Lord
McNair, *The Law of Treaties* (Oxford: Oxford University Press, 1961) (republished 1986).

As we will explain, the precautionary principle, as accepted and applied today, includes a requirement to conduct environmental impact assessments of any planned project having potentially deleterious international effects, and then, when necessary, to take action to protect against the assessed harm. In the case of Starlink, the US government never conducted an environmental impact assessment of the potential for tens of thousands of satellites in LEO to cause harm, including to astronomy, even though, under the Outer Space Treaty, the Liability Convention and customary international law, governments are responsible for all 'national activities' in Space. The United States might not be alone in acting contrary to international law here: other states, such as the United Kingdom, with its OneWeb project, could well be engaged in similar violations.

This chapter will conclude with a consideration of how states that have licensed mega-constellations without environmental impact assessments could be brought into compliance with international law. This includes pausing the construction of mega-constellations until such assessments can take place.

### 3.2.3    Interpreting the Outer Space Treaty

#### 3.2.3.1    Is Astronomy a Form of 'Exploration and Use'?

Article I of the Outer Space Treaty reads,

> The exploration and use of outer space, including the moon and other celestial bodies, shall be carried out for the benefit and in the interests of all countries, irrespective of their degree of economic or scientific development, and shall be the province of all [hu]mankind.
>
> Outer space, including the moon and other celestial bodies, shall be free for exploration and use by all States without discrimination of any kind, on a basis of equality and in accordance with international law, and there shall be free access to all areas of celestial bodies.
>
> There shall be freedom of scientific investigation in outer space, including the moon and other celestial bodies, and States shall facilitate and encourage international co-operation in such investigation.[61]

The terms 'exploration' and 'use' are not defined in the Outer Space Treaty. Nobody disputes that operating communications satellites in LEO constitutes 'use', but what about astronomy conducted from

---

[61] Outer Space Treaty, op. cit., Art. I.

ground-based telescopes? In accordance with Article 31 of the Vienna Convention, we look first to 'the ordinary meaning to be given to the terms of the treaty'.

**3.2.3.1.1  Ordinary Meaning**  According to the *Merriam-Webster Dictionary*, the noun form of 'use' has many definitions, with the first of the normal usages being the most relevant here:

1 a: the act or practice of employing something
   b: the fact or state of being used
   c: method or manner of employing or applying something.[62]

Several entries for the transitive verb form of 'use' are also of relevance:

1: to put into action or service: avail oneself of: employ
2: to expend or consume by putting to use – often used with *up*
. . .
5: to carry out a purpose or action by means of.[63]

Astronomy has long had the practice of putting Space 'into service' for understanding natural phenomena, discovering and testing physical laws, and enjoying the cosmos. Indeed, for many states, including space-faring states, astronomy remains the primary means by which Space is explored.

This brings us to 'exploration'. The verb is more helpful here, as exploration is just the act of exploring. We turn again to the *Merriam-Webster Dictionary*:

Transitive
1 a: to investigate, study, or analyze: look into
   b: to become familiar with by testing or experimenting
2: to travel over (new territory) for adventure or discovery
3: to examine especially for diagnostic purposes
Intransitive
1: to make or conduct a systematic search.[64]

---

[62]  Merriam-Webster, 'Use' (2022), *Merriam-Webster.com Dictionary*, online: www.merriam-webster.com/dictionary/use.
[63]  Ibid.
[64]  Merriam-Webster, 'Explore' (2022), *Merriam-Webster.com Dictionary*, online: www.merriam-webster.com/dictionary/explore.

Before analysing 'to explore' further, we should also consider the definition of 'astronomy'. The same *Merriam-Webster Dictionary* defines it as 'the study of objects and matter outside the earth's atmosphere and of their physical and chemical properties'.[65] In practice, an astronomer would likely describe astronomy as an observational science that seeks to understand and study the Solar System, the galaxy and the universe, as well as to understand Earth's place in all of these. It is also used to test physical laws.

Astronomy fulfils the above first and third definitions of 'exploration' for the transitive mood, as well as the definition of the intransitive. In ordinary usage, it seems uncontroversial that astronomy is a form of exploring Space; indeed, it is the original and oldest way that this has been done.

### 3.2.3.1.2 The Context of the Terms

Article 31 of the Vienna Convention further requires that we look to the 'ordinary meaning to be given to the terms of the treaty in their context', which includes the full text of the treaty, including its preamble.

Of relevance here, two similar but different phrases are found throughout the Outer Space Treaty: 'activities in the exploration and use of outer space' and 'activities in outer space'. The former phrase appears in Articles III, IX (twice) and XIII, while the latter appears in Articles V, VI (three times), IX and XI. There is nothing to suggest that the terms were employed interchangeably or accidentally – the drafting of these provisions took place over a considerable period of time, with many international lawyers involved. We can therefore be confident that the drafters of the Outer Space Treaty intended them to mean different things, with the most logical explanation being that 'activities in the exploration and use of outer space' can include activities on Earth's surface, such as astronomy.

To highlight this point, here are a few examples of the different terms as they are used in the Outer Space Treaty. The first part of Article III reads, 'States Parties to the Treaty shall carry on activities in the exploration and use of outer space, including the moon and other celestial bodies, in accordance with international law'. In contrast, the middle paragraph of Article V reads, 'In carrying on activities in outer space and on celestial bodies, the astronauts of one State Party shall render all possible assistance to the astronauts of other States Parties.' The

---

[65] Merriam-Webster, 'Astronomy' (2022), *Merriam-Webster.com Dictionary*, online: www .merriam-webster.com/dictionary/astronomy.

astronaut activities referred to in Article V take place in Space, while the terminology in Article III is more encompassing. This, and our analysis of the context of the term more broadly, indicate that 'exploration and use' includes Earth-based activities such as astronomy.

### 3.2.3.1.3 The Object and Purpose of the Treaty

Article 31 of the Vienna Convention  further requires that we look to the ordinary meaning to be given to the terms of the treaty 'in the light of its [the treaty's] object and purpose.' The object and purpose of the Outer Space Treaty are made clear in its preamble, which includes the following lines:

> Recognizing the common interest of all [hu]mankind in the progress of the exploration and use of outer space for peaceful purposes,
>     Believing that the exploration and use of outer space should be carried on for the benefit of all peoples irrespective of the degree of their economic or scientific development,
>     Desiring to contribute to broad international co-operation in *the scientific as well as the legal aspects of the exploration and use of outer space* for peaceful purposes . . .[66]

The object and purpose of the Outer Space Treaty accordingly include the advancement of knowledge about Space, with 'exploration and use' explicitly encompassing 'scientific . . . aspects' as declared in this preamble. Given that astronomy is the original and oldest way that humanity has studied Space and continues to provide significantly more scientific knowledge to our understanding of it than spacecraft and astronauts, this treaty's object and purpose convincingly support an interpretation of 'exploration and use' that includes astronomy.

### 3.2.3.1.4 Supplementary Means of Interpretation

Under Article 32 of the Vienna Convention, recourse may be had to 'supplementary means of interpretation', including 'the preparatory work of the treaty and the circumstances of its conclusion'. But such recourse may only be had

> to confirm the meaning resulting from the application of article 31, or to determine the meaning when the interpretation according to article 31:
>
> (a) leaves the meaning ambiguous or obscure; or
> (b) leads to a result which is manifestly absurd or unreasonable.[67]

---

[66] Outer Space Treaty, op. cit., preamble, emphasis added.
[67] Vienna Convention, op. cit., Art. 32.

The Article 31 interpretation we have conducted above does not fulfill the criteria in Article 32(a) or (b), in that the resulting meaning is both clear and reasonable – i.e. astronomy is a form of 'exploration and use'. For this reason, we can only look to 'the preparatory work of the treaty and the circumstances of its conclusion' to confirm our interpretation. As it happens, the circumstances of the Outer Space Treaty's conclusion provide this confirmation. We discuss two aspects of those circumstances here: the 1959 Antarctic Treaty and the West Ford experiment of 1961–1963.

The 1959 Antarctic Treaty is relevant to the conclusion of the 1967 Outer Space Treaty for three reasons.[68] First, both treaties were unusual for their time because they concerned an 'area beyond national jurisdiction'. Second, the negotiators of the Outer Space Treaty had deep knowledge of the Antarctic Treaty. They drew directly on its language and readily admitted its influence on their thinking.[69] Third, the Antarctic Treaty places considerable importance on a 'freedom of scientific investigation' (Preamble; Art. II), including by requiring co-operation and transparency between the parties in their scientific research (Art. III). It reflects a broad conception of scientific investigation unlimited by sovereignty or boundaries.[70] The Antarctic Treaty thus supports an interpretation of 'exploration and use of outer space' that includes astronomy.

The West Ford experiment, conducted by the US military from 1961 to 1963, involved the launch and release of millions of small copper needles into LEO for the purpose of creating an artificial belt around the Earth to reflect long-range radio waves from ground stations. The Soviet Union and other states complained that no prior consultation with the global scientific community had taken place. Radio astronomers complained that the experiment had the potential to interfere with their observations, with the International Astronomical Union expressing 'great concern' about 'the grave danger that some future space projects might seriously interfere with astronomical observations in the optical as well as in the radio domain' and maintaining that 'no group has the right

---

[68] The Antarctic Treaty, 1 December 1959, 402 UNTS 71 (entered into force 23 June 1961).

[69] US, *Treaty on Outer Space: Hearings before the Committee on Foreign Relations United States Senate*, 90th Cong (1967) at 80 (Deputy Secretary of Defense Cyrus R Vance).

[70] Although slightly off point, it is interesting to note that Antarctica has served as a base for major astronomical operations. See Michael G Burton, 'Astronomy in Antarctica' (2010) 18:4 *Astronomy and Astrophysics Review* 417.

to change the Earth's environment in any significant way without full international study and agreement'.[71]

These concerns led to the Scientific and Technical Subcommittee of COPUOS recommending, in May 1963, that COPUOS turn its attention 'to the urgency and the importance of the problem of preventing potentially harmful interference with peaceful uses of outer space'.[72] The Soviet Union and the United States then negotiated a draft declaration, which was adopted without change by COPUOS in November 1963 and shortly thereafter was adopted by the United Nations General Assembly as the Declaration of Legal Principles Governing the Activities of States in the Exploration and Use of Outer Space ('Resolution 1962').

Principle 6 of Resolution 1962 reads,

> In the exploration and use of outer space, States shall be guided by the principle of co-operation and mutual assistance and shall conduct all their activities in outer space with due regard for the corresponding interests of other States. If a State has reason to believe that an outer space activity or experiment planned by it or its nationals would cause potentially harmful interference with activities of other States in the peaceful exploration and use of outer space, it shall undertake appropriate international consultations before proceeding with any such activity or experiment. A State which has reason to believe that an outer space activity or experiment planned by another State would cause potentially harmful interference with activities in the peaceful exploration and use of outer space may request consultation concerning the activity or experiment.[73]

Some three years later, Principle 6 became the basis for Article IX of the Outer Space Treaty, thus creating a direct originating connection between the threat posed to astronomy by the West Ford experiment and Space being 'free for exploration and use'. It is difficult to imagine a clearer confirmation that the term 'exploration and use of outer space' in its international law context has therefore always included astronomy and continues to do so.

---

[71] IAU, 'Resolution No. 1' (XI General Assembly of the IAU, Berkeley, 1961) at 4, online: www.iau.org/static/resolutions/IAU1961_French.pdf.

[72] US, Department of State, *US Participation in the UN: Report by the President to the Congress for the Year 1961* (Pub 7675) (International Organization and Conference Series 51, August 1964) at 30; See also Sergio Marchisio, 'Article IX', in Stephan Hobe, Bernhard Schmidt-Tedd and Kai-Uwe Schrog, eds., *Cologne Commentary on Space Law: Volume 1* (Cologne: Carl Heymanns Verlag, 2009) 169.

[73] *Declaration of Legal Principles Governing the Activities of States in the Exploration and Use of Outer Space*, GA Res 1962 (XVIII), UNGAOR, 18th Sess, 1280th Plen Mtg, UN Doc A/RES/1962(XVIII) (1963) at 15.

### 3.2.3.2    The Duty of 'Due Regard'

So far, our application of the rules on treaty interpretation has determined that mega-constellations and astronomical observatories constitute two competing exercises of the freedom of 'exploration and use' of Space. This now takes us, again, to Article IX of the Outer Space Treaty, and particularly the obligation of 'due regard'.

Article IX reads in full,

> *In the exploration and use of outer space, including the moon and other celestial bodies, States Parties* to the Treaty shall be guided by the principle of co-operation and mutual assistance and *shall conduct all their activities in outer space*, including the moon and other celestial bodies, *with due regard to the corresponding interests of all other States Parties to the Treaty.* States Parties to the Treaty shall pursue studies of outer space, including the moon and other celestial bodies, and conduct exploration of them so as to avoid their harmful contamination and also adverse changes in the environment of the Earth resulting from the introduction of extraterrestrial matter and, where necessary, shall adopt appropriate measures for this purpose. If a State Party to the Treaty has reason to believe that an activity or experiment planned by it or its nationals in outer space, including the moon and other celestial bodies, would cause potentially harmful interference with activities of other States Parties in the peaceful exploration and use of outer space, including the moon and other celestial bodies, it shall undertake appropriate international consultations before proceeding with any such activity or experiment. A State Party to the Treaty which has reason to believe that an activity or experiment planned by another State Party in outer space, including the moon and other celestial bodies, would cause potentially harmful interference with activities in the peaceful exploration and use of outer space, including the moon and other celestial bodies, may request consultation concerning the activity or experiment.[74]

**3.2.3.2.1    The Ordinary Meaning of the Terms**    The *Merriam-Webster Dictionary* identifies 'with due regard to' as an idiom meaning 'with the proper care or concern for'.[75] *Black's Law Dictionary* defines 'due regard' as 'to give a fair consideration to and give sufficient attention to all of the facts'.[76] Both these definitions indicate that the duty is one of care and that it likely extends across different and potentially changing circumstances.

---

[74] Outer Space Treaty, op. cit., Art. IX, emphasis added.
[75] Merriam-Webster, 'with due regard to' (2022), *Merriam-Webster.com Dictionary*, online: www.merriam-webster.com/dictionary/with%20due%20regard%20to.
[76] *Black's Law Dictionary*, 'What is due regard?' (2022), *The Law Dictionary.org*, online: thelawdictionary.org/due-regard.

**3.2.3.2.2   The Context of the Terms**   For the purposes of treaty interpretation, the context includes the rest of Article IX, which tells us what
'due regard' means – namely not causing 'potentially harmful interference with activities of other States Parties in the peaceful exploration and
use of outer space'. Although Article IX adds a further requirement to
'undertake appropriate international consultations' if there is reason to
believe that a planned 'activity or experiment' will cause such interference, there is nothing in the Outer Space Treaty to suggest that a state
that undertakes consultations is thereafter free to proceed with its 'potentially harmful' plans as originally designed, or is somehow excused from
legal responsibility if harm does in fact arise. As a result, the obligation of
due regard is not to cause 'potentially harmful interference with activities
of other States Parties in the peaceful exploration and use of outer space',
full stop.

**3.2.3.2.3   The Object and Purpose of the Treaty**   The preamble to the
Outer Space Treaty, including the passages quoted above, indicates that
its object and purpose are to ensure that Space remains open to all states
through the maintenance of peace and the pursuit of international co-
operation. This supports a broad and meaningful interpretation of 'due
regard'.

**3.2.3.2.4   Relevant Rules of International Law**   Article 31(3)(c) of the
Vienna Convention stipulates, 'There shall be taken into account,
together with the context ... (c) any relevant rules of international law
applicable in the relations between the parties.'

These relevant rules are not limited only to those that existed when the
Outer Space Treaty was concluded in 1967 but also include rules that
have developed since. Indeed, what is required by 'due regard' under
international law will almost always evolve over time due to new knowledge, circumstances and technologies. 'Due regard' is what Lord McNair
referred to as a 'relative term'. As the author of the definitive *The Law of
Treaties* explained, 'Expressions such as "suitable, appropriate, convenient", occurring in a treaty are not stereotyped as at the date of the treaty
but must be understood in the light of the progress of events'.[77]

The duty of due regard, interpreted in accordance with developments since 1967, engages the now well-established rule of customary

---

[77] McNair, op. cit. at 467.

international law set out in Principle 21 of the 1972 Stockholm Declaration: 'States have ... the responsibility to ensure that activities within their jurisdiction or control do not cause damage to the environment of other states or of areas beyond the limits of national jurisdiction'.[78] This was reaffirmed by Principle 2 of the 1992 Rio Declaration.[79] Many multilateral environmental treaties now include the obligation not to cause damage to the environment of other states or of areas beyond the limits of national jurisdiction,[80] and the International Court of Justice has referred to this rule on numerous occasions.[81]

The duty of due regard, interpreted in accordance with developments since 1967, also engages the precautionary principle. Principle 15 of the Rio Declaration reads, 'In order to protect the environment, the precautionary approach shall be widely applied by States according to their capabilities. Where there are threats of serious or irreversible damage, lack of full scientific certainty shall not be used as a reason for postponing cost-effective measures to prevent environmental degradation'.[82] Similarly, Article 3(3) of the 1992 UN Framework Convention on Climate Change reads, 'Parties should take precautionary measures to anticipate, prevent or minimize the causes of climate change and mitigate its adverse effects. Where there are threats of serious or irreversible damage, lack of full

---

[78] *Report of the UN Conference on the Human Environment* ('Stockholm Declaration'), Stockholm, UN Doc A/CONF48/14/Rev1 (1972) at 3.

[79] *Report of the United Nations Conference on Environment and Development* ('Rio Declaration'), Rio de Janeiro, UN Doc A/CONF.151/26/Rev.1(Vol. I) (1992) at 3.

[80] See e.g. United Nations Convention on the Law of the Sea, 10 December 1982, 1833 UNTS 397 Art. 194(2) (entered into force 16 November 1994): 'States shall take all measures necessary to ensure that activities under their jurisdiction or control are so conducted as not to cause damage by pollution to other States and their environment, and that pollution arising from incidents or activities under their jurisdiction or control does not spread beyond the areas where they exercise sovereign rights in accordance with this Convention'; Convention on Biological Diversity, 5 June 1992, 1760 UNTS 79 Art. 3 (entered into force 29 December 1993): 'States have, in accordance with the Charter of the United Nations and the principles of international law, the sovereign right to exploit their own resources pursuant to their own environmental policies, and the responsibility to ensure that activities within their jurisdiction or control do not cause damage to the environment of other States or of areas beyond the limits of national jurisdiction.'

[81] See, e.g.: *Legality of the Threat or Use of Nuclear Weapons*, Advisory Opinion, [1996] ICJ Rep 226 at 241, para. 29; *Case Concerning the Gabčíkovo-Nagymaros Project* (*Hungary v. Slovakia*), [1997] ICJ Rep 7 at 41, para. 53.

[82] Rio Declaration, op. cit. at 6.

scientific certainty should not be used as a reason for postponing such measures.'[83]

Today, the precautionary principle entails a responsibility to conduct an environmental impact assessment prior to authorising an activity that could cause damage to the environment of areas beyond the limits of national jurisdiction.[84] Space is the quintessential area beyond national jurisdiction. Yet the US government, and specifically the FCC, did not conduct an environmental impact assessment for Starlink before issuing a licence for 12,000 satellites. That omission, in our assessment, violates both the Outer Space Treaty and customary international law. Other states, such as the United Kingdom when it licensed OneWeb's mega-constellation, may have engaged in similar contraventions. To avoid ongoing and further violations of international law, the construction of these mega-constellations should be paused until environmental impact assessments can take place.

Although the existence of a legal requirement to pause the construction of mega-constellations might seem surprising to non-lawyers, 'cessation' is a well-established remedy in public international law. As Francesca Capone recently explained in the *Max Planck Encyclopedia of Public International Law*,

> The State responsible for the commission of a wrongful act is under an obligation to cease the conduct and to offer appropriate assurances, normally given verbally, and guarantees of non-repetition, such as preventive measures to be taken to avoid repetition of the breach. The function of cessation is twofold: to end the violation and protect the continuing validity and effectiveness of the primary rule. Thus, it safeguards both the rights of the State injured and the interests of the international community as a whole.[85]

All that being said, the conduct of an environmental impact assessment will not necessarily prevent a violation of international law. A government

---

[83] *United Nations Framework Convention on Climate Change*, 9 May 1992, 1771 UNTS 107 Art. 3(3) (entered into force 21 March 194).

[84] See *Case Concerning Pulp Mills on the River Uruguay (Argentina v. Uruguay)*, [2010] ICJ Rep 14 at 79, para. 197; *Certain Activities Carried Out by Nicaragua in the Border Area (Costa Rica v. Nicaragua)*, 2015 ICJ Rep 665 at 706, para. 104. See also Ulrich Beyerlin and Thilo Marauhn, *International Environmental Law* (Oxford: Hart, 2011) at 54.

[85] Francesca Capone, 'Remedies', in Anne Peters, ed, *Max Planck Encyclopedia of Public International Law* (Oxford: Oxford University Press, article last modified Oct 2020), online: opil.ouplaw.com/view/10.1093/law:epil/9780199231690/law-9780199231690-e1089.

that conducted an environmental impact assessment and then licensed a mega-constellation in defiance of its findings would be contravening the obligation of due regard, as would one that conducted an environment impact assessment in a manner that was not objective or scientifically rigorous. A state negatively impacted by a mega-constellation (for instance, a state that hosted, operated, or otherwise supported astronomical observatories) would still be entitled to protest, make a claim, seek third-party dispute settlement or engage in countermeasures, just like any state suffering damage because of a violation of any other rule of international law.

### 3.2.3.3   Conclusion to the Treaty Interpretation

In the absence of environmental impact assessments, the continued operation of mega-constellations violates international law. This is because harm is being caused to astronomy, and therefore to other states' freedom of exploration and use of Space, in a manner that contravenes the obligation of due regard.

Diplomatic negotiations will be needed to find mutually agreeable solutions for mega-constellation licensing states and those states that host, operate or otherwise support astronomical observatories. In the meantime, licensing states will need to mitigate the harm being caused, with respect to both satellites in orbit and any satellites they plan to launch. Regarding the latter, environmental impact assessments are required, followed by licensing conditions that significantly reduce light pollution from single satellites as well as their cumulative effects. This requires a pause on further mega-constellation development until assessments and mitigation plans can be put into place.

At the same time, the needs of astronomy do not pose an absolute impediment to the use of LEO. Mega-constellations also constitute an exercise of the freedom of 'use' and exploration of Space. The two activities must therefore occur in balance, and there is presently no consensus on what that balance should look like. Until a consensus is found, international law favours astronomy, and not the further development of mega-constellations – since we know that the latter causes harm to the former, but not the other way around.

### 3.2.4   Mega-constellations in US Courts

The US government's failure to conduct an environmental impact assessment before licensing Starlink has also given rise to a case currently progressing through the US federal courts, although this litigation concerns US domestic law and not the international law discussed above.

In 2018, the FCC granted SpaceX approval to place 4,408 Starlink satellites at altitudes of 1,100 to 1,300 kilometres.[86] One year later, it granted a licence modification allowing SpaceX to reduce the orbital altitude of 1,584 of those satellites by half. In April 2021, the FCC issued another licence modification allowing the remaining 2,824 satellites to be lowered to altitudes of 540 to 570 kilometres. A separate and further 7,518 Starlink satellites, also approved in 2018, did not require a licence modification because their initial FCC approval was for altitudes of 335 to 346 kilometres.

At no point did the FCC conduct an environmental impact assessment prior to any of these approvals or licence modifications. It later justified this approach on the basis that satellites fall into a category of actions 'that normally do not have a significant effect on the human environment'.[87] In other words, a categorical exclusion was claimed, deeming an environmental assessment unnecessary without further consideration. While such exclusions are permitted under the US National Environmental Policy Act, it was done under the incorrect premise that satellites would not have an impact on the environment.

Viasat is a long-established company based in Carlsbad, California that specialises in providing secure communications for Western militaries and Internet services for passengers on commercial airliners from satellites located in GEO. The company's more than US$2 billion in annual revenue reflects the almost insatiable demand of the US military and intelligence services for Space-based broadband, including for the operation of armed drones. However, as discussed in Chapter 2, communications from satellites in GEO have a certain amount of 'latency' (i.e. signal delay) compared to satellites in LEO. The difference is about 240 milliseconds versus 10 milliseconds or less, enough to be of importance for some applications. This, along with the relatively low cost of mass-produced satellites launched on reusable rockets, makes Starlink a major commercial threat to Viasat's established business model. This

---

[86] The history of the Starlink approvals is summarised in FCC, 'Federal Communications Commission's opposition to Viasat's motion for stay pending judicial review', in *Viasat Inc.* v. *Federal Communications Commission*, US Court of Appeals, DC Circuit, USCA Case #21-1123, Document #1902327 (14 June 2021), online: docs.fcc.gov/public/attach ments/DOC-373276A1.pdf.

[87] Ibid., at 5–6.

threat was confirmed in September 2021, when the US Department of Defense's Commercial Satellite Communication Office released a draft request for proposals (RFP) for 'Proliferated Low Earth Orbit Satellite-Based Commercial Services'.[88] Under this RFP, up to US$875 million worth of US government orders for satellite-based services operating from LEO will be made available.

In May 2021, Viasat sought judicial review of the FCC's licensing decisions on Starlink before the US Court of Appeals, District of Columbia Circuit, arguing that the licences were improperly granted. At the same time, the company requested a 'stay' which, if granted, would have prevented SpaceX from launching more satellites until the court could determine whether the licences had been wrongly issued. In July 2021, the court denied the stay but granted a motion to expedite the appeal, with final briefs submitted in October 2021 followed by oral arguments. A similar case, brought by satellite television provider Dish Network, was consolidated with Viasat's action by the court.

Viasat contended that the FCC had failed to comply with the US National Environmental Policy Act because it refused to conduct *any* environmental assessment before approving the Starlink mega-constellation. Viasat argued that such an assessment was necessary because of several identifiable environmental risks, including light pollution, orbital debris and climate impacts from both launches and satellite re-entries.

In their responses before the court, neither the FCC nor SpaceX addressed the substance of Viasat's complaints. They instead focused on the question whether Viasat has 'standing' to bring the case, given that it operates in GEO rather than LEO and therefore, arguably, is not affected by Starlink's plans. In response, Viasat asserted that it has plans for satellites in LEO, satellites that will be threatened by the large number of satellites that SpaceX is launching. It also claims that communications from its satellites in GEO could be substantially affected by having to broadcast through an increasingly radio-busy LEO to reach Earth. Surprisingly, Viasat has not argued that its satellites destined for GEO are threatened by Starlink satellites in the several weeks immediately following their launch when they are passing through LEO each 'GEO transfer orbit'. Nor has it argued that it is being detrimentally affected by

---

[88] Sandra Erwin, 'DoD eager to leverage LEO broadband constellations', *SpaceNews* (15 November 2021), online: spacenews.com/dod-eager-to-leverage-leo-broadband-constellations.

the launch windows to GEO becoming ever more constrained by the proliferation of satellites in LEO. As we explain in Chapter 7, a collision between a satellite on a GEO transfer orbit and another satellite in LEO would be problematic for all orbits.

The currently ongoing Viasat versus SpaceX case is important because of the issues it raises, and because of the US federal courts' ultimate decision on the matter. This importance extends to the influence of these proceedings on international law. The Statute of the International Court of Justice identifies 'judicial decisions' as 'subsidiary means for the determination of rules of law',[89] and this is generally understood to include the decisions of national courts.[90] Those same national court decisions can also contribute as state practice to the making or changing of customary international law.[91]

Just as significantly, the proceedings and decisions of national courts can expose and elaborate issues that need to be dealt with internationally, and thus serve as an impetus for intergovernmental negotiations and treaty-making. Although Viasat is arguably not the ideal litigant for what could be an important test case, due to the issue of standing, law is not always made and changed by perfect plaintiffs. More important is that this US domestic case is drawing unprecedented attention to the environmental risks associated with mega-constellations, which can only be a positive in terms of promoting international action.

### 3.2.5    Bringing Licensing States into Compliance with International Law

The effort to bring licensing states into compliance with international law will likely require several strategies, one diplomatic, the other legal. The issue of mega-constellations and astronomy would benefit greatly from having national governments raise concerns, issue diplomatic protests,

---

[89] *Statute of the International Court of Justice*, 26 June 1945, Can TS 1945 No 7 Art. 38(1)(4) (entered into force 24 October 1945).

[90] Hugh Thirlway, *Sources of International Law*, 2nd ed (Oxford: Oxford University Press, 2019) at 140. See also 'Draft conclusions on identification of customary international law', in *Report of the International Law Commission Seventieth Session*, UNGAOR, 73rd Sess, Supp No 10, UN Doc A/73/10 at 121 (conclusion 13(2)) – 'Regard may be had, as appropriate, to decisions of national courts concerning the existence and content of rules of customary international law, as a subsidiary means for the determination of such rules.'

[91] Thirlway, op. cit. at 140.

propose resolutions at international organisations and engage dispute settlement measures. International law applies principally between states, not scientists, scientific associations or satellite companies. In the absence of a state champion, astronomers are just experts identifying problems; they themselves suffer from an issue of standing in the international context as they have no 'international legal personality'.

To date, policy advocacy on this issue has focused on the satellite companies themselves, on national regulatory agencies such as the FCC, and soon – we expect – on highly specialised sub-bodies of international organisations such as the Scientific and Technical Subcommittee of COPUOS. It may be time to raise the profile of this issue further by convincing one or more states to advance a draft United Nations General Assembly resolution on mega-constellations and light pollution. Potentially, such a resolution could include a request for a non-binding but still authoritative 'advisory opinion' from the International Court of Justice (ICJ), which would constitute the first time a case concerning issues of international Space law was determined by this court. Since the ICJ deals only with public international law – i.e. the law that applies primarily between nation states – that request should focus on the harm caused to states that host, operate or support major observatories, though it could also usefully emphasise that the harm is caused to all humankind.

# 4

# Abandoned Rocket Bodies

More than six decades after the launch of Sputnik, most rocket bodies used to send payloads into Space are still abandoned in orbit. So far, only SpaceX has the capacity to bring the 'core stage' of its rockets back to Earth and land it on four legs. When Space X uses a Falcon 9 rocket to launch Starlink satellites to low Earth orbit (LEO), the core stage usually returns to a landing pad or a barge in the ocean and is often reused. However, launch sequences vary between rocket models, and even SpaceX abandons rocket bodies in orbit sometimes.

The term 'rocket body' is shorthand for more specific terminology. 'Boosters', 'core stage' or 'first stage', and 'upper stage' might seem like familiar terms, but there can still be some confusion in their use. Boosters are parts of rockets that support the launch sequence but never themselves achieve orbit. Instead, they are dropped suborbitally, albeit with some precision, into designated areas, usually in the ocean. The core stage is typically the most substantial section of a rocket. In some designs, it achieves orbit during launch and is either brought back to Earth in a controlled manner or abandoned in orbit. Many rockets also have one or more upper stages, which provide additional boosts to the 'payload', usually made up of one or more satellites. Although upper stages are sometimes brought back to Earth in a controlled manner, most are abandoned in orbit as operators choose to maximise the lifting potential of the rocket by not reserving fuel for a potentially large de-orbit burn. In what follows we use 'rocket body' as a general term that is not specific to a stage. In 2021, over 60 per cent of launches to LEO resulted in at least one rocket body being abandoned in orbit.

There are two main categories of atmospheric re-entry: 'controlled' and 'uncontrolled'. Controlled re-entries are achieved by using thrust to place the rocket body onto an orbit with a low perigee, timed in such a way that the re-entering object is directed towards a landing pad or recovery zone in the case of reusable systems, or to a remote area of ocean for expendable systems. By contrast, when a rocket body is simply abandoned on an orbit with a sufficiently low perigee, gas drag gradually reduces its altitude and eventually causes it to re-enter the atmosphere in an uncontrolled manner,[1] which can occur at any point under its flight path. This means that the location of the 'debris field' will not generally be known in advance.

While it may be self-evident, it is critical to recognise that, both collectively and individually, rocket bodies contain substantial mass and surface area. This has implications for debris generation, light pollution and re-entry casualty risks. Because we have already discussed space debris and light pollution in previous chapters, we will only touch on those first two issues briefly here, before moving on to a more substantial discussion of the third issue: casualty risks associated with uncontrolled rocket body re-entries.

## 4.1   Space Debris Generation

Abandoned rocket bodies are large tumbling objects that remain in orbit for days, months or years – and cannot be manoeuvred to avoid collisions. Their cross-sections provide ample surface area for impacts with other rocket bodies, derelict satellites, tracked and untracked space debris, and meteoroids. Worse yet, rocket bodies are not necessarily inert, with certain designs prone to explosions and fragmentation due to residual fuel, overpressure or other processes.[2]

Figure 4.1 shows the apogee–perigee distribution of those rocket bodies currently in orbit with perigees below 1,000 kilometres. Many of the orbits are eccentric, traversing large swathes of Earth's orbital regions, from LEO to GEO (geosynchronous Earth orbit). Any fragmentation event thus has the potential to spread debris throughout the entire orbital environment. Moreover, because they are among the most massive objects in orbit, a single major collision has the potential to cause large changes in the total amount of debris. Many rocket bodies also form 'orbital clusters'. To put it another way, 'families' of rocket bodies, along

---

[1]  Earth's upper atmosphere extends into LEO, albeit with very low gas densities. An object moving through gas feels a resistance against its motion, called 'gas drag'.

[2]  A detailed account of fragmentation events in orbit, including rocket bodies, is given by Phillip D Anz-Meador, John N Opiela, Debra Shoots and J-C Liou, *History of On-Orbit Satellite Fragmentations*, 15th ed (Houston: National Aeronautics and Space Administration, 2018).

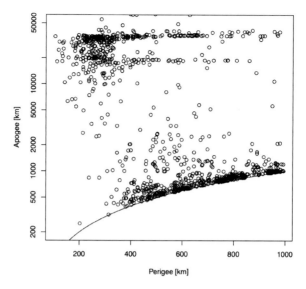

**Figure 4.1**   Apogee and perigee of abandoned rocket bodies in orbit. Recall that perigee is an object's closest approach to Earth and apogee is the most distant part of its orbit. Only rocket bodies with perigees below 1,000 kilometres are shown. The $y$ axis has logarithmic spacing on account of the apogees extending from LEO to GEO. The curve delineates the physical parameter space; an object exactly on the curve would have an apogee that is equal to its perigee, and thus have a circular orbit. Many rocket bodies, some the size of a school bus, relentlessly pass through the entire satellite field about Earth and cannot be controlled. Data are from the USSPACECOM satellite catalogue, accessed 26 April 2022.

with derelict satellites, share certain orbital characteristics and therefore have frequent close approaches with each other. This increases the risk of collisions and poses a major threat to the orbital environment.[3] The dangers of Space debris have been covered extensively in Chapter 2, and we will not repeat that discussion here. The point, simply, is to highlight that it is not just mega-constellations of satellites that put the safe and sustainable development of Space at risk.

---

[3]   Michael J Nicolls and Darren McKnight, 'Collision risk assessment for derelict objects in low-earth orbit' (paper delivered at the First International Orbital Debris Conference, Sugar Land, TX, 9–12 December 2019), online: www.hou.usra.edu/meetings/orbitaldeb ris2019/orbital2019paper/pdf/6096.pdf.

**Figure 4.2**    An image of an SL-6 R/B(2) streaking across the sky (NORAD ID: 16911), an abandoned upper stage of a Soviet Molniya rocket with a perigee of 4,753 kilometres and apogee of 34,964 kilometres. Despite being at a range of about 7,400 kilometres from the observatory at the time of observation, the rocket body is very bright. Its brightness also varies due to rapid tumbling, creating additional challenges for astronomers. The image was taken by the DAO 1.8-metre Plaskett Telescope as part of a rocket body characterisation study. The dark horizontal streaks are known defects in the detector. Credit: D. Balam and A. Boley.

## 4.2   Light Pollution

In Chapters 2 and 3, we discussed light pollution from satellites. However, light pollution from rocket bodies is also a concern, particularly given their large numbers and sizes. As illustrated in Figure 4.2, even rocket bodies at great distances from an observatory can be bright. And since many are on elliptical orbits that largely keep them out of Earth's shadow, they are illuminated for greater periods of time than satellites in LEO, making many of them visible to telescopes throughout the night. Moreover, rocket bodies that are tumbling present challenges to astronomers additional to the unwanted presence of bright streaks. Their tumbling causes variability of light that can interfere with automated image processing and cause confusion in 'processing pipelines', such as those designed to look for variability in astronomical objects. Rocket bodies may also be a source of very small, non-lethal debris brought about through meteoroid impacts, Space debris impacts, fragmentation events and surface degradation. Although such debris may not be a major concern for satellites and other spacecraft, it is a growing one for astronomers. For while such pieces have very little mass, they could have a large cumulative surface area and thus scatter a non-negligible amount of sunlight. The net effect could be that such small debris becomes a source of diffuse scattered light at night, increasing the sky brightness.[4] This type of brightening would not be noticeable to the human eye, but could still affect sensitive astronomical observations.

### 4.3    Uncontrolled Rocket Body Re-entries

Not only do abandoned rocket bodies create problems when they are in orbit, but also any uncontrolled re-entries into Earth's atmosphere create dangers for people on the surface.

As a striking example, in May 2020, the 20-tonne main body of a Long March 5B rocket re-entered the atmosphere in an uncontrolled manner after being used to launch an unmanned experimental crew capsule. Debris from the rocket body, including a 12-metre-long pipe, struck two villages in Ivory Coast, causing damage to several buildings.[5] Then, one year later, the 20-tonne main body of another Long March 5B rocket made an uncontrolled re-entry after being used to launch part of China's new Tiangong Space station into LEO.[6] This time, the debris crashed into the Indian Ocean. These two rocket stages were the heaviest objects to re-enter in an uncontrolled manner since the Soviet Union's Salyut-7 Space station in 1991.[7]

In April 2022, a metal ring with a diameter of three metres landed in a village in India, along with a cylinder-like object about 50 centimetres in diameter.[8] Fortunately, there were no injuries or property damage.

---

[4]  Miroslav Kocifaj, Frantisek Kundracik, John C Barentine and Salvador Bará, 'The proliferation of space objects is a rapidly increasing source of artificial night sky brightness' (2021) 504:1 *Monthly Notices of the Royal Astronomical Society: Letters* L40.

[5]  Jonathan O'Callaghan, 'Chinese rocket debris may have fallen on villages in the Ivory Coast after an uncontrolled re-entry', *Forbes* (12 May 2020), online: www.forbes.com/sites/jonathanocallaghan/2020/05/12/parts-of-a-chinese-rocket-may-have-fallen-on-an-african-village.

[6]  European Space Operations Centre, 'Context of the Long March 5B core stage re-entry' (6 May 2021), *European Space Agency*, online: reentry.esoc.esa.int/home/blog/long-march-5b-reentry.

[7]  Ibid.

[8]  Park Si-soo, 'India examining crashed space debris suspected to be parts of China's Long March rocket', *SpaceNews* (19 April 2022), online: spacenews.com/india-examining-crashed-space-debris-suspected-to-be-parts-of-chinas-long-march-rocket.

**Figure 4.3** Part of a re-entered rocket body. According to Jonathan McDowell of the Harvard & Smithsonian Center for Astrophysics, who posted this photograph on Twitter on 3 April 2022, 'This 3-meter-diameter ring is consistent with being part of the CZ-3B third stage tankage. It was found in Sindewahi (79.6E 20.3N) in eastern Maharashtra.' See twitter.com/planet4589/status/1510658292640534534.

According to Jonathan McDowell, who posted a picture of the metal ring on Twitter, the objects were likely from the third stage of a Chinese Chang Zheng 3B rocket that had been launched in February 2021.[9]

China has been criticised, including by US government officials, for imposing the re-entry risks of its rockets on the world.[10] However, in the absence of any international consensus on the acceptable level of risk, other spacefaring states – including the United States – make similar choices concerning uncontrolled re-entries. In 2016, the second stage of a SpaceX rocket was abandoned in orbit and re-entered one month later over Indonesia, with two intact refrigerator-sized fuel tanks reaching

[9] Jonathan McDowell, 'I believe this is the reentry of a Chinese rocket stage, the third stage of the Chang Zheng 3B serial number Y77 which was launched in Feb 2021 – it was expected to reenter in the next hour or so and the track is a good match' (2 April 2022 at 11:15), *Twitter*, online: twitter.com/planet4589/status/1510274696524279810; Jonathan McDowell, 'This 3-meter-diameter ring is consistent with being part of the CZ-3B third stage tankage. It was found in Sindewahi (79.6E 20.3N) in eastern Maharshtra. (thanks @DrSachinW for forwarding the image)' (3 April 2022 at 12:39), *Twitter*, online: twitter .com/planet4589/status/1510658292640534534.

[10] NASA, press release, 21-060, 'NASA administrator statement on Chinese rocket debris' (8 May 2021), online www.nasa.gov/press-release/nasa-administrator-statement-on-chi nese-rocket-debris.

the ground.[11] In June 2022, SpaceX abandoned another second stage after lifting an Egyptian communications satellite into a geosynchronous transfer orbit.[12]

The added technological complexity and cost involved in achieving controlled re-entries help to explain the shortage of international rules on this matter. Moreover, casualty risks are usually assessed on a launch-by-launch basis, which keeps them low and makes it easier for governments to justify uncontrolled re-entries. However, as humanity's use of Space expands, cumulative risks should also be considered. Launch providers have access to technologies and mission designs today that could eliminate the need for most uncontrolled re-entries. The challenge, in an increasingly diverse and competitive Space launch market, is not only to raise safety standards but also to ensure that everyone is subject to them, and all this needs to be done without creating unreasonable barriers to new entrants.

### 4.3.1  Assessing Casualty Risk

As indicated above, over 60 per cent of launches to LEO in 2021 resulted in a rocket body being abandoned in orbit. If these rocket bodies are not involved in either a catastrophic collision or an explosion in orbit but in due course return to Earth intact, a substantial fraction of their mass will survive the heat of atmospheric re-entry as debris.[13] Many of the surviving pieces are potentially lethal, posing serious risks on land, at sea and to people in aeroplanes.

In the United States, the Orbital Debris Mitigation Standard Practices (ODMSP) apply to all launches and include a requirement that the risk of casualty from a re-entering rocket body be below a threshold of one in 10,000.[14] However, in practice these requirements can be waived. The US Air Force waived the ODMSP requirements for 37 of the 66 launches

---

[11] Patrick Blau, 'SpaceX rocket parts rain down over Indonesia', *SpaceFlight101* (26 September 2016), online: spaceflight101.com/falcon-9-jcsat-16/spacex-rocket-parts-rain-down-over-indonesia.

[12] SpaceX, 'Nilesat 301 Mission', 8 June 2022, www.spacex.com/launches/nilesat-301.

[13] William H Ailor, 'Large constellation disposal hazards' (20 January 2020), Center for Space Policy and Strategy, *The Aerospace Corporation*, online: aerospace.org/sites/default/files/2020-01/Ailor_LgConstDisposal_20200113.pdf.

[14] US government, 'Orbital Debris Mitigation Standard Practices – November 2019 update' (November 2019), *NASA*, online: orbitaldebris.jsc.nasa.gov/library/usg_orbital_debris_mitigation_standard_practices_november_2019.pdf.

conducted for them between 2011 and 2018, on the ground that it would be too expensive to replace non-compliant rockets with compliant ones.[15] NASA also waived the requirements seven times between 2008 and 2018, including for an Atlas V launch in 2015 where the casualty risk was estimated at one in 600.[16]

The threshold of one in 10,000 for casualty risk is arbitrary,[17] and makes even less sense in an era when new technologies and mission profiles enable controlled re-entries. It also fails to address low-risk, high-consequence outcomes, such as a piece of a rocket stage crashing into a high-density city or a large passenger aircraft. In the latter case, even a small piece could cause hundreds of casualties.[18]

Internationally, there is no clear and widely agreed casualty risk threshold. The 2010 UN Space Debris Mitigation Guidelines recommend that re-entering spacecraft not pose 'an undue risk to people or property', but do not define what this means.[19] The 2018 UN Guidelines for the Long-Term Sustainability of Outer Space Activities call on national governments to address risks associated with the uncontrolled re-entry of Space objects, but do not specify how.[20] There is no binding treaty that addresses rocket body re-entries, apart from the 1972 Liability Convention which stipulates that a 'launching State shall be absolutely liable to pay compensation for damage caused by its Space object on the surface of the earth or to aircraft in flight'.[21]

---

[15] Quentin Verspieren, 'The US Air Force compliance with the Orbital Debris Mitigation Standard Practices' (paper delivered at the Advanced Maui Optical and Space Surveillance Technologies Conference, virtual, 16–18 September 2020), online: amostech.com/TechnicalPapers/2020/Orbital-Debris/Verspieren.pdf.

[16] JC Liou, 'Orbital debris briefing' (8 December 2017), NASA, online: ntrs.nasa.gov/citations/20170011662.

[17] NASA, 'Process for limiting orbital debris', NASA technical standard NASA-STD-8719.14B (25 April 2019), online: essp.larc.nasa.gov/EVI-6/pdf_files/nasa-std-8719.14b.pdf.

[18] Ailor, op. cit.

[19] United Nations Office for Outer Space Affairs (UNOOSA), Space Debris Mitigation Guidelines of the Committee on the Peaceful Uses of Outer Space (Vienna: United Nations, 2010), online: www.unoosa.org/pdf/publications/st_space_49E.pdf.

[20] Committee on the Peaceful Uses of Outer Space, Guidelines for the Long-Term Sustainability of Outer Space Activities, 61st Sess, UN Doc A/AC.105/2018/CRP.20 (27 June 2018), online: www.unoosa.org/res/oosadoc/data/documents/2018/aac_1052018crp/aac_1052018crp_20_0_html/AC105_2018_CRP20E.pdf.

[21] Convention on International Liability for Damage Caused by Space Objects, 29 March 1972, 961 UNTS 187 (entered into force 1 September 1972) (Liability Convention).

In Chapter 3, we discussed the issue of liability in the context of mega-constellations, collisions and Space debris. In that context, and others, the possibility of liability might help to induce good behaviour. However, on the issue of re-entering rocket bodies, governments have apparently chosen to bear the slight risk of having to compensate for one or more casualties, rather than require launch providers to make expensive technological or mission design changes. As in some other areas of government and commercial activity, 'liability risk' is treated as just another cost of doing business.[22] This approach may be made easier by the fact that the casualty risk is disproportionately borne by the populations of some of the poorest states in the world.

As Figure 4.4 demonstrates, most of the rocket bodies in orbit, and therefore most of the contributions to casualty risk, come from the powerful spacefaring states. And yet most of these rocket bodies are concentrated in orbital inclinations that correspond, more or less, with heavily populated regions of the Global South.[23]

During the past 30 years, over 1,500 rocket bodies have de-orbited.[24] We estimate that approximately 70 per cent de-orbited in an uncontrolled manner, corresponding to a casualty expectation of 0.015 events per square metre. This means that, on the face of it, if the average rocket body were to cause a casualty area of ten square metres, there was roughly a 14 per cent chance of one or more casualties over this time. Fortunately, there has been no such event reported, but the estimate emphasises that the incurred risk has been far from negligible.

The future risk can be modelled in several ways; we explore two and illustrate them in Figure 4.5. Both these models (and Figure 4.6) use the 'weighting function', which is the distribution of 'weights' for each latitude, with each weight set by the fraction of time that an object with

[22] Kenneth S Abraham, 'Environmental liability and the limits of insurance' (1988) 88:5 *Columbia Law Review* 942–57.

[23] In Figure 4.4, casualty risk, analysed as 'casualty expectation', has been calculated on a per-square-metre basis. For more on the methods used in this chapter, see Michael Byers, Ewan Wright, Aaron Boley and Cameron Byers, 'Unnecessary risks created by uncontrolled rocket reentries' (2022) 6 *Nature Astronomy* 1-5, online: https://doi.org/10.1038/s41550-022-01718-8.

[24] From 4 May 1992 to 5 May 2022. See Combined Force Space Component Command, 'Satellite catalog' (2022), *United States Space Force*, online: www.space-track.org.

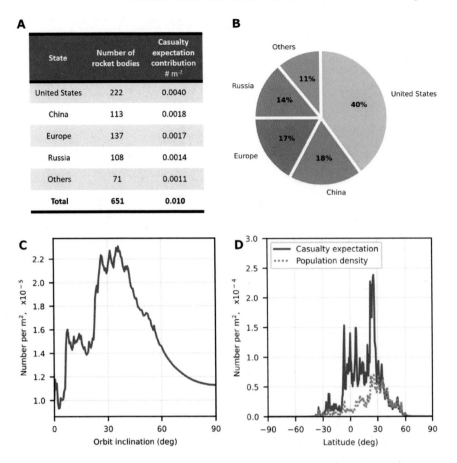

**Figure 4.4**   Casualty expectations. A Number of rocket bodies with perigee <
600 kilometres and associated global casualty expectation (CE) for spacefaring states
with large contributions (Europe treated as a single unit). B Pie chart of the proportion
of the total global CE contributed by each state. C Standard CE as a function of orbital
inclination for a re-entry and the 2020 global population (as distributed under those
inclinations). D CE of rocket bodies currently in orbit by latitude and population
density. CE is the number of casualties per square metre of casualty area as described by
R. Patera (2008) 45:15 *Journal of Spacecraft and Rockets* 1031–41. Casualty area, which
is the total area over which debris could cause a casualty for a given re-entry, is not
modelled. In all panels, only rocket bodies with perigees at or below 600 kilometres are
included, based on the US Space Force Satellite Catalogue as of 5 May 2022. This
approximates the population of long-lived abandoned rocket bodies that might
reasonably be expected to de-orbit. Credit: Ewan Wright.

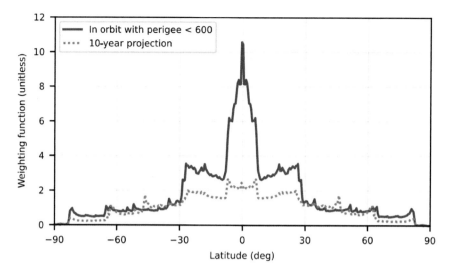

**Figure 4.5**  Rocket body weighting functions. Each curve is the sum of the rocket bodies' normalised time spent over each latitude. Two models are shown: the sum of all rocket bodies currently in orbit with perigee under 600 kilometres and a ten-year projection based on the rocket bodies that re-entered uncontrolled from 4 May 1992 to 5 May 2022. Credit: Ewan Wright.

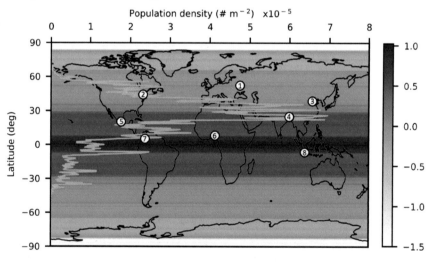

**Figure 4.6**  Population density by latitude (orange plot) and rocket body weighting function (blue logarithmic heatmap) overlaid on a world map. Some major and high-risk cities are labelled: 1 Moscow, 2 Washington, DC, 3 Beijing, 4 Dhaka, 5 Mexico City, 6 Lagos, 7 Bogota, 8 Jakarta. Credit: Ewan Wright.

a given inclination spends over that latitude.[25] Assuming again that each re-entry spreads lethal debris over an area of ten square metres, we conclude that current practices have on the order of a 10 per cent chance of one or more casualties over a decade.

First, the long-term risk resulting from the build-up of rocket bodies in orbit can be estimated by looking at rocket body orbits that have a perigee lower than 600 kilometres, with this perigee representing an imperfect but plausible division between rocket bodies that will de-orbit in the coming decades and those that require much longer timescales. For this cut-off, there are 651 rocket bodies, with a corresponding casualty expectation of 0.001 per square metre. As a second alternative, we can take the trend of rocket body re-entries from the past 30 years and apply it to the next ten years, in which case there is a corresponding casualty risk of 0.006 per square metre. Both these estimates are conservative as the number of rocket launches is increasing quickly.[26]

Each rocket body is abandoned at a specific orbital inclination, and these are not evenly distributed. On-orbit rocket bodies are concentrated at inclinations where they spend most of their time above the lower latitudes. This is because many of the rocket bodies that lead to uncontrolled re-entries are associated with launches to geosynchronous orbits, located near the equator.[27] As we illustrate in Figure 4.6, the cumulative risk from rocket body re-entries is significantly higher in the states of the Global South, as compared to the major spacefaring states. The latitudes of Jakarta, Dhaka, Mexico City, Bogotá and Lagos are at least three times as likely as those of Washington, DC, New York, Beijing and Moscow to

---

[25] An object on a zero-degree inclination orbit would have a 'weighting function' that is unity at the equator and zero everywhere else, while an object on a polar orbit would have a weighting function that is a constant for all latitudes. For other inclinations, an individual orbit will have a weighting function with peaks at the latitudes close to the value of the orbital inclination, a U-shaped distribution between the peaks, and weights of zero at latitudes higher than the inclination. An individual weighting function is normalised such that its integration over all latitudes is unity. The casualty expectation is thus set by (1) calculating the weighting function for each rocket body in a given distribution, (2) summing in each latitude bin all of the resulting weighting functions, (3) multiplying the world population densities at each latitude by the corresponding summed weight and (4) summing the results over all latitudes. For more on the methods used in this chapter, see Byers et al., op. cit.

[26] Eric Berger, 'The world just set a record for sending the most rockets into orbit', ArsTechnica (3 January 2022), online: arstechnica.com/science/2022/01/thanks-to-china-and-spacex-the-world-set-an-orbital-launch-record-in-2021.

[27] Combined Force Space Component Command, op. cit.

have a rocket body re-enter over them, under one estimate, based on the current rocket body population in orbit.

This situation, of risks from activities in the developed world being borne disproportionately by populations in the developing world, is hardly unprecedented. Powerful states often externalise costs and impose them on others, with greenhouse gas emissions being just one example.[28] The disproportionate risk from rocket bodies is further exacerbated by poverty, with buildings in the Global South typically providing a lower degree of protection; according to NASA, approximately 80 per cent of the world's population lives 'unprotected or in lightly sheltered structures providing limited protection against falling debris'.[29]

### 4.3.2   Switching to Controlled Re-entries

Due to technological advances, allowing rocket bodies to re-enter in an uncontrolled manner is increasingly becoming a choice rather than a necessity. Controlled re-entries require engines that can reignite, enabling the launch provider to direct the rocket body away from populated areas, usually into a remote area of ocean.[30] Some older rocket models that lack reignitable engines are still used by some launch providers; these will need to be upgraded or replaced to achieve a safe, controlled re-entry regime.

Performing a controlled re-entry also requires having extra fuel on board, above and beyond that required for launching the payload. Some launch providers operating modern rockets with reignitable engines deplete the fuel on board to boost the payload as high as possible, thus saving customers time – since otherwise the payload will have to use its own thrusters to slowly raise its orbit. But in doing so, the providers deny themselves the opportunity for a controlled re-entry. Such an approach to mission design will have to be changed to achieve a safe, controlled re-entry regime.

Most of these measures cost money. In the case of the Delta IV rocket, the US government reportedly granted waivers because of the costs of upgrades,[31] even though, as the entity procuring these launches,

---

[28] Daniel Faber, *Capitalizing on Environmental Injustice: The Polluter–Industrial Complex in the Age of Globalization* (Lanham, MD: Rowman and Littlefield, 2008).

[29] NASA, 'Process for limiting orbital debris', op. cit.

[30] Vito De Lucia and Viviana Iavicoli, 'From outer space to ocean depths: The "spacecraft cemetery" and the protection of the marine environment in areas beyond national jurisdiction" (2018) 49:2 *California Western International Law Journal* 345 at 367–69.

[31] Verspieren, op. cit.

it was well positioned to absorb the increased cost of safer missions. In the case of commercial missions, the costs associated with a move to controlled re-entries could affect the ability of a launch provider to compete. Yet this challenge, of increased costs arising when safety, environmental and other negative externalities are internalised, is one that has been faced by many industrial sectors in the past. This is where rules and regulations come in: when done well, they ensure a level playing field so that no single company, even a new entrant, loses out from improved practices.

### 4.3.3  Solving the Collective-Action Problem

National governments could raise the standards applicable to launches from their territory or by companies incorporated there. But individual governments might have competing incentives, such as reducing their own costs or growing a globally competitive domestic Space industry. Uncontrolled rocket body re-entries constitute a collective-action problem; solutions exist, but every launching state must adopt them.

There are numerous examples of national governments co-operating to ensure the adoption of technological 'fixes' to environmental problems. In the 1970s, scientists warned that chlorofluorocarbons (CFCs) used in refrigeration systems were converting and thus reducing ozone molecules in the atmosphere, which in turn allowed more cancer-causing ultraviolet radiation to reach the surface.[32] Fortunately, alternative technologies were available and, in 1985, the Vienna Convention for the Protection of the Ozone Layer was adopted.[33] This provided a framework for phasing out the use of CFCs, with the specific chemicals and timelines set out in the 1987 Montreal Protocol on Substances That Deplete the Ozone Layer.[34] These two treaties, which have been ratified by every single UN member state, have solved the collective-action problem. They have reduced the global use of CFCs by 98 per cent, prevented further

[32] US Environmental Protection Agency, 'Health and environmental effects of ozone layer depletion' (18 October 2021), online: www.epa.gov/ozone-layer-protection/health-and-environmental-effects-ozone-layer-depletion.

[33] Vienna Convention for the Protection of the Ozone Layer, 22 March 1985, 1513 UNTS 293 (entered into force 22 September 1988).

[34] Montreal Protocol on Substances That Deplete the Ozone Layer, 16 September 1987, 1522 UNTS 3 (entered into force 1 January 1989).

damage to the ozone layer, and thus prevented an estimated 2 million deaths from skin cancer every year.[35]

The 1970s also saw a growing risk to oceans and coastlines from oil spills, and, as a result, led to efforts, nationally and internationally, to adopt a requirement for double hulls on tankers. The shipping industry, however, concerned about increased costs, was able to stymie these efforts until 1989, when the *Exxon Valdez* spilled roughly 11 million gallons of oil into Alaska's Prince William Sound. Media coverage of the accident made the issue of oil spills a matter of public concern. The US National Transportation Safety Board concluded that a double hull would have significantly reduced, if not eliminated, the spill,[36] leading the US government to require all tankers calling at US ports to have double hulls.[37] This unilateral move then prompted the International Maritime Organization to amend the International Convention for the Prevention of Pollution from Ships (MARPOL Convention) in 1992 to require double hulls on new tankers and,[38] through further amendments in 2001 and 2003, to accelerate the retirement of single-hulled tankers.[39] The 1992 amendments to the MARPOL Convention have since been ratified by 150 states (including the United States, Liberia and Panama) which represent 98.33 per cent of the world's shipping tonnage.[40] This precedent, of oil spills and the double-hull requirement, is especially significant for uncontrolled rocket body re-entries because it concerns transport safety in an area beyond national jurisdiction. Oil spills pose risks for all coastal states in the same way that uncontrolled rocket body

---

[35] United Nations Environmental Programme (UNEP), 'Thirty years on, what is the Montreal Protocol doing to protect the ozone?' (15 November 2019), *UNEP*, online: www.unep.org/news-and-stories/story/thirty-years-what-montreal-protocol-doing-pro tect-ozone.

[36] US National Transportation Safety Board, 'Marine accident report: Grounding of the US tankship Exxon Valdez on Bligh Reef, Prince William Sound near Valdez, Alaska March 24, 1989' (31 July 1990) NTSB/MAR-90/04 at 163, online: www.ntsb.gov/investigations/ AccidentReports/Reports/MAR9004.pdf.

[37] Oil Pollution Act, 33 USC ch 40 (1990).

[38] International Convention for the Prevention of Pollution from Ships, 2 November 1973, 12 ILM 1319 as modified by the Protocol of 1978 Relating to the International Convention for the Prevention of Pollution from Ships, 1973, 17 February 1978, 1341 UNTS 3 (entered into force 2 October 1983) (MARPOL Convention).

[39] International Maritime Organization (IMO), 'Construction requirements for oil tankers – double hulls' (2019), *IMO*, online: www.imo.org/en/OurWork/Environment/Pages/ constructionrequirements.aspx.

[40] IMO, 'Status of Conventions' (2019), *IMO*, online: www.imo.org/en/About/Conventions/ Pages/StatusOfConventions.aspx.

re-entries do for the entire planet. It is our hope, however, that national governments will respond to the risks posed by uncontrolled rocket bodies now, rather than wait for the equivalent of an *Exxon Valdez* accident to occur.

Those national governments whose populations are being put at disproportionate risk from uncontrolled rocket bodies should demand that major spacefaring states mandate controlled rocket re-entries and create meaningful consequences for non-compliance, thus eliminating the risks for everyone. If necessary, they could initiate negotiations towards a non-binding resolution or even a treaty – because they have a majority at the United Nations General Assembly. Even if a multilateral treaty is not ratified by the major spacefaring states, it would still draw widespread attention to the issue and set new expectations for behaviour. This is what happened with the 1997 Anti-personnel Landmines Convention:[41] although not ratified by the United States, Russia or China, it led to a marked reduction in the global use of anti-personnel mines, with non-ratifiers also changing their behaviour.[42]

In any case, on the issue of uncontrolled rocket body re-entries, the states of the Global South hold the moral high ground: their citizens bear most of the risks, unnecessarily, since the technologies and mission designs needed to prevent casualties exist already.

---

[41] Convention on the Prohibition of the Use, Stockpiling, Production and Transfer of Anti-personnel Mines and on Their Destruction, 18 September 1997, 2056 UNTS 211 (entered into force 1 March 1999) (Anti-Personnel Landmines Convention).

[42] Adam Bower, *Norms without the Great Powers: International Law and Changing Social Standards in World Politics* (Oxford: Oxford University Press, 2017).

# Space Mining

## 5.1 Introduction

In the Netflix comedy series *Space Force*, China establishes a lunar base, starts mining Helium-3, and declares the Sea of Tranquility a 'territory of scientific research' off limits to other states. The United States ignores the Chinese declaration and establishes its own base nearby, and before the first season of *Space Force* ends, the astronauts from the two states proceed to destroy each other's bases. In reality, Space mining will be difficult and dangerous enough without any fighting. Yet concern over conflict is not limited to science fiction, and efforts to develop international rules for space mining are now under way.

At least 14 Space agencies have identified '*in situ* resource utilization' as a necessary capability for long-duration missions, including crewed missions to the Moon, Mars and deep Space.[1] Attention is currently focused on the potential production of rocket fuel from ice and water-bearing minerals. If rocket fuel can be sourced in Space, it will not need to be lifted, at great expense, from Earth's surface and transported throughout the solar system.

The Moon has long been the focus of Space mining studies.[2] Efforts are now under way to establish self-sustaining infrastructure and habitats in lunar orbit as well as on the surface, with eyes towards Mars. The NASA-led Artemis programme plans to use water sourced from the lunar south pole to provide fuel, radiation shielding and life support for surface and orbital operations.[3] In addition, 'regolith' – the loose layer

---

[1] International Space Exploration Coordination Group, 'ISECG Global Exploration Roadmap – 3rd ed' (20 January 2018), online: www.globalspaceexploration.org/wordpress/wp-content/isecg/GER_2018_small_mobile.pdf.

[2] John Billingham, William Gilbreath and Brian O'Leary, *Space Resources and Space Settlements* (Moffett Field, CA: NASA Ames Research Center, 1979).

[3] The Artemis Program incidentally aims 'to land the first woman and first person of color' on the Moon. See 'The Artemis Accords: Principles for a safe, peaceful, and prosperous

of rock on the surface of the Moon, or indeed of any moon, planet, or asteroid – can be mined for construction materials, and as a source of hydrogen and oxygen.[4]

China also has plans for lunar mining, and in 2020, as part of its Chang'e 5 mission, became the third state to bring samples from the Moon back to Earth.[5] The Soviet Union had done the same with its Luna programme between 1970 and 1976, preceded by the United States with Apollo between 1969 and 1972. In 2021, China and Russia signed a memorandum of understanding by which, according to a statement released by the China National Space Administration, they agreed to 'use their accumulated experience in space science research and development and use of space equipment and space technology to jointly formulate a route map for the construction of an international lunar scientific research station'.[6]

So far, all the lunar samples have been relatively small compared to the amounts envisaged with mining. But the distinction between scientific sampling and Space mining became less clear in 2020 when Jim Bridenstine, the NASA administrator during the Trump administration, announced that NASA was seeking to purchase small amounts of lunar regolith – after they had been extracted by private companies.[7] Those samples need not be returned to Earth. In the end, NASA signed contracts for future purchases with four companies.[8] As will be discussed later in this chapter, the stated purpose of these contracts was to create legally relevant 'subsequent practice' in support of an interpretation of

future' (March 2022), *NASA*, online: www.nasa.gov/specials/artemis-accords/index.html. Under the Trump administration, the goal was to land 'the first woman and the next man'.

[4] Michael B Duke, Lisa R Gaddis, G Jeffrey Taylor and Harrison H Schmitt, 'Development of the Moon' (2006) 60:1 *Reviews in Mineralogy & Geochemistry* 597.

[5] Jonathan Amos, 'China's Chang'e-5 mission returns Moon samples', *BBC News* (16 December 2020), online: www.bbc.com/news/science-environment-55323176.

[6] Steven Lee Myers, 'China and Russia agree to explore the Moon together', *New York Times* (10 March 2021), online: www.nytimes.com/2021/03/10/world/asia/china-russia-moon.html.

[7] Jeff Foust, 'NASA offers to buy lunar samples to set space resources precedent', *SpaceNews* (10 September 2020), online: spacenews.com/nasa-offers-to-buy-lunar-samples-to-set-space-resources-precedent.

[8] NASA, press release, 20-118, 'NASA selects companies to collect lunar resources for Artemis demonstrations' (3 December 2020), online: www.nasa.gov/press-release/nasa-selects-companies-to-collect-lunar-resources-for-artemis-demonstrations.

the 1967 Outer Space Treaty (OST) that would allow for property rights in extracted resources.[9]

In the case of water ice, we know that it exists within permanently shadowed regions of the Moon, such as the floors of craters located close to the poles.[10] Its existence in such regions is made possible because the Moon's rotational axis is nearly perpendicular to the Earth's orbital plane about the Sun (the ecliptic plane). To simulate this, you can shine a flashlight on a dimpled golf ball from a short distance and spin the ball so that its 'equator' is always directly illuminated. As you will see, the dimples near the 'poles' of the ball always have a shadow. On the Moon, these shadowed regions are always very cold and capable of supporting water ice, even in the absence of an atmosphere (see Figure 5.1). The Moon's southern pole seems to have the highest concentration of water ice because there are more permanently shadowed areas.[11]

Other regions of the Moon will be attractive for different reasons. For instance, the tops of some crater rims have nearly perpetual sunshine (i.e. solar energy).[12] Thus, while there might be many areas where it is possible to extract water, some of these areas will be more desirable than others, raising the prospect of competition for optimal mining locations among different states and different companies.

The Moon is hardly the only celestial body of interest. Many asteroids contain an abundance of water and minerals that could be used to support Space operations.[13] Robotic spacecraft have already rendez-voused with and examined several such bodies. Some have even brought samples back to Earth. The Japanese Space Agency's *Hayabusa-1* returned a small amount of regolith dust from the asteroid Itokawa in

---

[9] Treaty on Principles Governing the Activities of States in the Exploration and Use of Outer Space, Including the Moon and Other Celestial Bodies, 27 January 1967, 610 UNTS 205 (entered into force 10 October 1967) (Outer Space Treaty).

[10] Shuai Li, Paul G Lucey, Ralph E Milliken, Paul O Hayne, Elizabeth Fisher, Jean-Pierre Williams, Dana M Hurley and Richard C Elphic, 'Direct evidence of surface exposed water ice in the lunar polar regions' (2018) 115:36 *Proceedings of the National Academy of Sciences* 8907.

[11] Ibid.

[12] Brian Dunbar, 'Moon's south pole in NASA's landing sights' (15 April 2019), *NASA*, online: www.nasa.gov/feature/moon-s-south-pole-in-nasa-s-landing-sites.

[13] Eugene Jarosewich, 'Chemical analyses of meteorites: A compilation of stony and iron meteorite analyses' (1990) 25:4 *Meteoritics* 323; K Lodders, H Palme and HP Gail, 'Abundances of the elements in the solar system', in JE Trümper, ed, *Landolt-Börnstein: Group VI Astronomy and Astrophysics* (Berlin: Springer-Verlag, 2009) vol 4B, ch 4.4, 560.

**Figure 5.1** Map of the Moon's south (left) and north (right) poles, as taken by NASA's Moon Mineralogy Mapper instrument on India's *Chandrayaan-1* spacecraft. The grey colour shows temperature at the time of mapping, with cold regions shown in darker shades and hot regions in lighter ones. The cyan colour shows where water ice was detected. Credit: NASA.

2010, while *Hayabusa-2* returned a larger sample from the asteroid Ryugu in 2020. The latter sample included subsurface material that had not been degraded by eons of solar radiation. It was obtained by first firing a 'small carry-on impactor' into the asteroid to excavate a crater, and then touching down briefly to collect some of the pristine material that had been revealed. Then there is NASA's *OSIRIS-REx*, which rendezvoused with the asteroid Bennu in 2018 (see Figure 5.2). It spent 18 months flying alongside the asteroid (see Figure 5.3) before snatching a small amount of material from the surface. This sample should arrive on Earth in 2023.

In 2021, China and Russia announced a joint mission to Kamo'oalewa,[14] a 'quasi-satellite' of Earth. Kamo'oalewa is not a true moon but rather an asteroid with an eccentric orbit having a period of almost exactly one Earth year. As a result, it orbits the Sun in such a way that it never strays very far from Earth and, when viewed from here, has an apparent

---

[14] Andrew Jones, 'Russia joins China's mission to sample an asteroid and study a comet', *Space.com* (18 April 2021), online: www.space.com/russia-joins-china-asteroid-comet-mission.

**Figure 5.2**    This image of Bennu was taken by the *OSIRIS-REx* spacecraft from around 80 kilometres. Credits: NASA/Goddard/University of Arizona, www.nasa.gov/press-release/nasas-osiris-rex-spacecraft-arrives-at-asteroid-bennu

'orbit' (oscillation) about our planet.[15] The robotic spacecraft, due to launch in 2024, will also attempt to retrieve a sample and return it to Earth.

The scientific interest in asteroids is clear. For example, Ryugu and Bennu are composed of some of the oldest material in the Solar System,

[15] C de la Fuente Marcos and R de la Fuenta Marcos, 'Asteroid (469219) 2016 HO3, the smallest and closest Earth quasi-satellite' (2016) 462 *Monthly Notices of the Royal Astronomical Society* 3341.

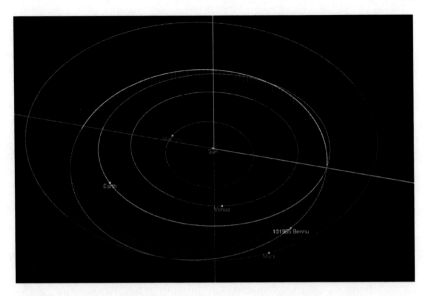

**Figure 5.3** Orbital diagram showing Mercury, Venus, Earth, Mars and Bennu on 3 December 2018 when *OSIRIS-REx* arrived within 20 kilometres of Bennu. In the diagram, brighter colouring signifies when an object is above Earth's orbital plane, while the fainter lines show when an object is below. Faint grey lines emphasise the distance between Bennu's orbit (white) and Earth's orbital plane. Because Bennu's orbit is inclined, the asteroid only approaches Earth during one part of its orbit. The yellow lines are references for describing orbital angles and positions. Credit: JPL. Orbital diagram accessed at ssd.jpl.nasa.gov/sbdb.cgi?sstr=bennu.

unaltered for over 4.5 billion years.[16] Meteorites, which are fragments of asteroids that have impacted Earth, reveal that such primitive asteroids contain organic molecules, including amino acids.[17] Whether they played a role in delivering precursors of life to Earth is still an open question. It is likely that asteroids similar to Ryugu and Bennu contributed to the formation of Earth's hydrosphere, as well as to the water on the Moon.

Asteroid science is also a matter of human survival. Close studies of asteroids provide knowledge about how radiation and other perturbative forces alter their trajectories, aiding close-approach predictions and Earth

[16]  Edward RD Scott, 'Chondrites and the protoplanetary disk' (2007) 35:1 *Annual Review of Earth and Planetary Sciences* 577.

[17]  John R Cronin and Sandra Pizzarello, 'Amino acids in meteorites' (1983) 3:9 *Advances in Space Research* 5.

impact warnings.[18] Bennu, for instance, is expected to pass by Earth at a distance closer than the Moon in 2135. The encounter with Earth's gravity will alter the trajectory of the 500 metre-wide asteroid as it orbits the Sun, perhaps leading to an impact risk in subsequent passes.[19] Don't panic! There are things that we can do to prevent this, with Chapter 6 of this book being devoted to the topic of 'planetary defence'.

Asteroid mining involves resource extraction beyond sampling, and while there is uncertainty as to when it might begin, there is clear momentum in that direction. NASA sees the *OSIRIS-REx* mission as a precursor to commercial operations, noting that 'asteroids like Bennu contain natural resources such as water, organics, and perhaps precious metals'.[20] Asteroids could potentially serve as deep Space fuelling stations and resource hubs. Under favourable conditions, it might also be possible to transport their resources elsewhere using low-cost, long-duration orbital manoeuvres such as solar sails and low-impulse thrusters. The potential for asteroid mining is central to plans for an off-Earth economy, with proponents of this vision including Jeff Bezos, one of the world's richest people.[21]

But while the mining of asteroids and other celestial bodies offers benefits, it will also create risks. For example, lunar mining conducted in a careful, scientifically informed manner could help us understand the Moon's history, including its record of bombardment by asteroids and comets, which in turn could help us understand Earth's history.[22] But mining that is motivated purely by resource extraction could overlook important scientific evidence or even destroy it.

A high level of care will also be required when mining asteroids, since any interference with near-Earth objects (NEOs) has the potential to create unique risks on and around Earth and the Moon. Asteroid mining

---

[18] NASA, news release, 'Planetary defense: The Bennu experiment' (6 December 2018), online: solarsystem.nasa.gov/news/782/planetary-defense-the-bennu-experiment.

[19] Steven R Chesley et al. 'Orbit and bulk density of the OSIRIS-REx target asteroid (101955) Bennu' (2014) 235 *Icarus* 5.

[20] Arizona Board of Regents, 'The mission' (2022), *OSIRIS-REx: Asteroid Sample Return Mission*, online: www.asteroidmission.org/objectives.

[21] Christian Davenport, 'Jeff Bezos pulls back the curtain on his plans for space', *Washington Post* (9 March 2016), online: www.washingtonpost.com/business/econ omy/jeff-bezos-pulls-back-the-curtain-on-his-plans-for-space/2016/03/09/a0716c7e-e5f4-11e5-a6f3-21ccdbc5f74e_story.html.

[22] William F Bottke and Marc D. Norman, 'The late heavy bombardment' (2017) 45 *Annual Review of Earth and Planetary Science* 619.

will almost inevitably create streams of debris, which under certain conditions could contribute to the meteoroid population in significant ways. Meteoroids already pose a hazard to satellites and other spacecraft, as well as to lunar operations, none of which benefit from the protection of Earth's atmosphere. Last, and perhaps most worryingly, most physical interactions with asteroids will alter their trajectories. Under certain circumstances, this could increase the uncertainty of the asteroid's orbit and even create a new, human-caused Earth impact risk.

As this discussion of risks makes clear, widely agreed rules on Space mining are needed – to protect other Space activities, the pursuit of scientific knowledge, and perhaps even humanity itself.

## 5.2 Space Mining and International Law

The 1967 Outer Space Treaty (OST) is at the centre of an ongoing debate about whether property rights may be acquired over extracted Space resources. Article II reads, in full, 'Outer space, including the moon and other celestial bodies, is not subject to national appropriation by claim of sovereignty, by means of use or occupation, or by any other means.'[23] The United States argues that the prohibition on national appropriation applies to natural resources only when they are 'in place' and that resources, once extracted, may be purchased and sold.[24]

Other states disagree. In 2020, Dmitry Rogozin, the director general of the Russian Space Agency (Roscosmos), said, 'We will not, in any case, accept any attempts to privatize the Moon. It is illegal, it runs counter to international law.'[25] In 2021, the Indonesian delegation to the United Nations Committee on the Peaceful Uses of Outer Space (COPUOS) stated,

> Since space resources are located beyond national jurisdiction, the existing international space law and principles shall apply in their

[23] Outer Space Treaty, Art. II.
[24] Brian J Egan, 'The next fifty years of the Outer Space Treaty' (address delivered at the Galloway Symposium on Critical Issues in Space Law, Washington, DC, 7 December 2016), US State Department, online: 2009–2017.state.gov/s/l/releases/remarks/264963 .htm.
[25] TASS Russian News Agency, 'Russia will not accept attempts to privatize the Moon, says Roscosmos CEO', TASS (25 May 2020), online: tass.com/science/1159969 (translated from Russian by the reporter).

exploration, exploitation, and utilization, including but not limited to:
non-appropriation, common heritage of [hu]mankind, exclusive use for
peaceful purposes, and for the benefits and interests of all countries.[26]

The Chinese delegation, for its part, joined the G77 group of developing
states in stressing the need for 'International cooperation in the development of space activities . . . for the benefit and in the interest of all States
taking in particular account the needs on [sic] developing countries'.[27]

In this section, we apply the rules of customary international law on
treaty interpretation, as codified in the 1969 Vienna Convention on the
Law of Treaties,[28] to the OST. We conclude that the US position is at
least tenable, insofar as the treaty does not specifically address Space
mining. We also explain how the United States is seeking to strengthen
its position by adopting national legislation allowing Space mining companies to obtain property rights, encouraging other states to do likewise,
negotiating bilateral statements (the 'Artemis Accords') in support of its
view, and contracting with private companies for the purchase of lunar
regolith with the explicit goal of creating legally relevant 'subsequent
practice'.

But while the OST does not specifically address Space mining, all Space
activities must still respect the various provisions of that treaty, including
the duties of consultation and 'due regard'. This means that Space mining
must be pursued in ways that guard against risks and consider the interests
of all states. The United States agrees with this. The problem is that the
applicable provisions of the OST are quite general, leaving room for
different states to interpret them differently, develop national rules that
differ from those of other states, or enforce those rules with differing
degrees of rigor and consistency. Leaving the regulation of Space mining

---

[26] Indonesia, 'Intervention made by the delegation of the Republic of Indonesia on the
Agenda Item 14: General exchange of views on potential legal models for activities in
exploration, exploitation and utilization of space resources at the 60th Session of Legal
Subcommittee of the United Nations Committee on the Peaceful Uses of Outer Space'
(1 June 2021), online: www.unoosa.org/documents/pdf/copuos/lsc/2021/statements/
item_14_Indonesia_ver.1_1_June_AM.pdf.

[27] G77 and China, 'G-77 and China statement during the Sixtieth Session of the Legal
Subcommittee of the United Nations Committee on the Peaceful Uses of Outer Space,
from 31 May–11 June 2021, delivered by HE Alejandro Solano Ortiz, ambassador,
permanent representative of Costa Rica' (31 May 2021), online: www.unoosa.org/docu
ments/pdf/copuos/lsc/2021/statements/item_3_5_6a_6b_8_10_11_13_14_G77_China_
ver.1_31_May_AM_LegalSC_280521.pdf.

[28] Vienna Convention on the Law of Treaties, 23 May 1969, 1155 UNTS 331 (entered into
force 27 January 1980) (Vienna Convention).

to national governments could result in a fragmentation of the governance regime, 'a race to the bottom' in terms of safety and environmental protections, or even the emergence of 'flag-of-convenience' states – with all these outcomes exacerbating the risks to Space exploration, science and the Earth itself noted above. Another possibility is that such a national approach could result in the development of rules of customary international law on Space mining that are based largely on the practice of one major spacefaring state, namely the United States, as well as the practice of companies incorporated there.

It is therefore desirable, even imperative, that states negotiate a multilateral treaty on Space mining. The good news is that a first possible step towards such negotiations has already been taken, with the creation of a Working Group on Space Resources within the Legal Subcommittee of COPUOS in 2021.

## 5.3   Interpreting the Outer Space Treaty

The international rules on treaty interpretation are found in the 1969 Vienna Convention on the Law of Treaties. Like most treaties, the Vienna Convention does not apply retrospectively; it therefore does not apply, as a treaty, to the 1967 OST. However, it is widely accepted as an accurate codification of the rules of customary international law on treaty interpretation,[29] which do apply to the OST. We therefore facilitate our analysis by referring to those customary rules as they appear in provisions of the Vienna Convention. This is standard practice among international lawyers. We will also, in our analysis, follow the steps of treaty interpretation in the order in which they are set out in the Vienna Convention.[30]

---

[29]   Anthony Aust, *Modern Treaty Law and Practice*, 2nd ed (Cambridge: Cambridge University Press, 2007) 12; Richard Gardiner, 'The Vienna Convention rules on treaty interpretation', in Duncan B Hollis, ed, *The Oxford Guide to Treaties*, 2nd ed (Oxford: Oxford University Press, 2020) 459 at 477; For US acceptance that the Vienna Convention reflects customary international law, see 'Letter of transmittal of Vienna Convention on the Law of Treaties to US Senate' (22 November 1971), Senate Executive L (92nd Cong, 1st Sess), available at (1972) 11:1 *International Law Materials* 234.

[30]   Steven Freeland and Ram Jakhu's interpretation of the OST begins with the negotiating history of the treaty, followed by the context, object and purpose, and meaning. Steven Freeland and Ram Jakhu, 'Article II' in Stephan Hobe, Bernhard Schmidt-Tedd and Kai-Uwe Schrog, eds., *Cologne Commentary on Space Law: Volume 1, Outer Space Treaty* (Cologne: Carl Heymanns Verlag, 2009) 44 at 59. However, Article 32 of the Vienna Convention stipulates that the negotiating history may only be used 'to confirm the

### 5.3.1   Ordinary Meaning

Article 31 of the Vienna Convention on the Law of Treaties reads, 'A treaty shall be interpreted in good faith in accordance with the ordinary meaning to be given to the terms of the treaty in their context and in the light of its object and purpose.' The first step in our interpretation therefore concerns the 'ordinary meaning' of the terms. We begin with Article I of the OST, which reads in full,

> The exploration and use of outer space, including the moon and other celestial bodies, shall be carried out for the benefit and in the interests of all countries, irrespective of their degree of economic or scientific development, and shall be the province of all [hu]mankind.
>
> Outer space, including the moon and other celestial bodies, shall be free for exploration and use by all States without discrimination of any kind, on a basis of equality and in accordance with international law, and there shall be free access to all areas of celestial bodies.
>
> There shall be freedom of scientific investigation in outer space, including the moon and other celestial bodies, and States shall facilitate and encourage international co-operation in such investigation.[31]

On its own, ordinary meaning provides little guidance for interpreting Article I. It does not tell us whether 'use' includes the extraction of Space resources, nor whether 'use' can be exclusive to a single actor – although there are words in Article I that at least suggest otherwise, i.e. 'shall be carried out for the benefit and in the interests of all countries, irrespective of their degree of economic or scientific development, and shall be the province of all [hu]mankind'. Nor does ordinary meaning tell us whether property rights can be acquired over extracted Space resources. Again, this last issue is the one under debate.

We turn now to Article II, where the term of greatest relevance is 'national appropriation': 'Outer space, including the moon and other celestial bodies, is not subject to national appropriation by claim of sovereignty, by means of use or occupation, or by any other means.'[32] There is no ordinary meaning for 'national appropriation', since the term is not used elsewhere in international law, or in day-to-day conversation.

---

meaning resulting from the application of article 31, or to determine the meaning when the interpretation according to article 31: (a) leaves the meaning ambiguous or obscure; or (b) leads to a result which is manifestly absurd or unreasonable.' Vienna Convention, Art. 32.

[31] Outer Space Treaty, Art. I.
[32] Outer Space Treaty, Art. II.

We do not know whether it means title to territory, or simply the use of an object or area by one state to the exclusion of others. As a result, this first stage of interpretation – 'ordinary meaning of the terms' – does not take us very far.

### 5.3.2   The Context of the Terms

We turn to the second stage of our interpretation, namely the 'context' of the terms being interpreted. According to the Vienna Convention, context includes the text of a treaty, its preamble and its annexes. With regard to the text of the OST, there are several provisions that might inform the interpretation of Articles I and II. The first of these is Article VI, the only provision of the OST to address the issue of non-state actors:

> States Parties to the Treaty shall bear international responsibility for national activities in outer space, including the moon and other celestial bodies, whether such activities are carried on by governmental agencies or by non-governmental entities, and for assuring that national activities are carried out in conformity with the provisions set forth in the present Treaty. The activities of non-governmental entities in outer space, including the moon and other celestial bodies, shall require authorization and continuing supervision by the appropriate State Party to the Treaty. When activities are carried on in outer space, including the moon and other celestial bodies, by an international organization, responsibility for compliance with this Treaty shall be borne both by the international organization and by the States Parties to the Treaty participating in such organization.[33]

'Non-governmental entities' will include international organisations, non-profit groups and private companies. But while mining is one possible profit-oriented activity that companies might pursue in Space, there are many others, including the use of satellites for communications – an activity that was already taking place at the time the OST was under negotiation and would therefore have been in the minds of the negotiators. The combination of Article VI with the possibility that Space mining could be conducted by non-governmental entities does not, on its own, make possible the acquisition of property rights. Indeed, there is nothing in Article VI that would either support or preclude this conclusion. Article VI simply makes states responsible for whichever Space activities their nationals, including private companies, undertake

---

[33] Outer Space Treaty, Art. IV.

(as well as any activities of non-nationals on their territory or in spacecraft registered by them).

Then there is Article IX of the OST, which reads in full,

> In the exploration and use of outer space, including the moon and other celestial bodies, States Parties to the Treaty shall be guided by the principle of co-operation and mutual assistance and shall conduct all their activities in outer space, including the moon and other celestial bodies, with due regard to the corresponding interests of all other States Parties to the Treaty. States Parties to the Treaty shall pursue studies of outer space, including the moon and other celestial bodies, and conduct exploration of them so as to avoid their harmful contamination and also adverse changes in the environment of the Earth resulting from the introduction of extraterrestrial matter and, where necessary, shall adopt appropriate measures for this purpose. If a State Party to the Treaty has reason to believe that an activity or experiment planned by it or its nationals in outer space, including the moon and other celestial bodies, would cause potentially harmful interference with activities of other States Parties in the peaceful exploration and use of outer space, including the moon and other celestial bodies, it shall undertake appropriate international consultations before proceeding with any such activity or experiment. A State Party to the Treaty which has reason to believe that an activity or experiment planned by another State Party in outer space, including the moon and other celestial bodies, would cause potentially harmful interference with activities in the peaceful exploration and use of outer space, including the moon and other celestial bodies, may request consultation concerning the activity or experiment.[34]

Article IX requires that states 'conduct all their activities in outer space, including the moon and other celestial bodies, with due regard to the corresponding interests of all other States Parties to the Treaty'.[35] However, there is no indication as to the level of care that 'due regard' requires. Is the obligation only to avoid reasonably foreseeable harm? Or is a higher standard of care required?

Article IX also foresees that some Space activities will have the potential to cause harmful contamination or interference, and it guards against these risks with a duty of consultation. However, there is no indication as to whether a state might be required to adjust its plans because of consultations. Nor does Article IX say anything, anywhere, about property rights.

---

[34] Outer Space Treaty, Art. IX.
[35] Ibid.

Article 31 of the Vienna Convention indicates that the preamble is also part of the context for the purposes of treaty interpretation. The preamble of the OST reads, in full,

> The States Parties to this Treaty,
>
> Inspired by the great prospects opening up before [hu]mankind as a result of man's entry into outer space,
>
> Recognizing the common interest of all [hu]mankind in the progress of the exploration and use of outer space for peaceful purposes,
>
> Believing that the exploration and use of outer space should be carried on for the benefit of all peoples irrespective of the degree of their economic or scientific development,
>
> Desiring to contribute to broad international co-operation in the scientific as well as the legal aspects of the exploration and use of outer space for peaceful purposes,
>
> Believing that such co-operation will contribute to the development of mutual understanding and to the strengthening of friendly relations between States and peoples,
>
> Recalling resolution 1962 (XVIII), entitled 'Declaration of Legal Principles Governing the Activities of States in the Exploration and Use of Outer Space', which was adopted unanimously by the United Nations General Assembly on 13 December 1963,
>
> Recalling resolution 1884 (XVIII), calling upon States to refrain from placing in orbit around the earth any objects carrying nuclear weapons or any other kinds of weapons of mass destruction or from installing such weapons on celestial bodies, which was adopted unanimously by the United Nations General Assembly on 17 October 1963,
>
> Taking account of United Nations General Assembly resolution 110 (II) of 3 November 1947, which condemned propaganda designed or likely to provoke or encourage any threat to the peace, breach of the peace or act of aggression, and considering that the aforementioned resolution is applicable to outer space,
>
> Convinced that a Treaty on Principles Governing the Activities of States in the Exploration and Use of Outer Space, including the Moon and Other Celestial Bodies, will further the Purposes and Principles of the Charter of the United Nations,
>
> Have agreed on the following . . .[36]

We see nothing in the preamble of the OST that supports or precludes the acquisition of property rights over extracted resources. The negotiators believed that the exploration and use of Space should benefit all peoples, but property rights are not necessarily incompatible with this belief.

---

[36] Outer Space Treaty, preamble.

### 5.3.3   Object and Purpose

The third step in a treaty interpretation is to examine whether the 'object and purpose' of the treaty cast any 'light' on the ordinary meaning of its terms. The most important evidence of a treaty's object and purpose is usually found in its preamble, which is reproduced directly above. It is clear from the preamble that the overall object and purpose of the OST is the promotion of peace and international co-operation in Space – something which property rights might, depending on the circumstances, either strengthen or weaken. In other words, the object and purpose provide no guidance to our interpretation.

### 5.3.4   Subsequent Agreement

We must now consider any 'subsequent agreement' or 'subsequent practice' establishing 'the agreement of the parties regarding' the interpretation of the OST, with Article 31(3)(a) and (b) of the Vienna Convention on the Law of Treaties reading,

> There shall be taken into account, together with the context:
>
> (a) any subsequent agreement between the parties regarding the interpretation of the treaty or the application of its provisions;
> (b) any subsequent practice in the application of the treaty which establishes the agreement of the parties regarding its interpretation ...[37]

One possible subsequent agreement of relevance is the 1979 Agreement Governing the Activities of States on the Moon and Other Celestial Bodies ('Moon Agreement'),[38] which Steven Freeland and Ram Jakhu argue provides some support for an interpretation of Article II OST in favour of the 'exploitation' of extracted resources not constituting 'national appropriation':

> the terms of the MOON [the 1979 Moon Agreement] suggest that the exploitation of the natural resources of the moon (and other celestial bodies within the solar system) does *not* constitute a means of appropriation. Article 11(2) of the MOON replicates the prohibitions contained in Article II of the Outer Space Treaty. Yet, one of the principal objects and

---

[37] Vienna Convention, Art. 31(3)(a)–(b).
[38] Agreement Governing the Activities of States on the Moon and Other Celestial Bodies, 5 December 1979, 1363 UNTS 13 (entered into force 11 July 1984) (Moon Agreement).

purposes of the MOON is to promote the "exploitation" of the natural resources of the moon, through the current provisions of the Agreement and eventual establishment of an international regime.

It is clear, therefore, that the prohibition of natural appropriation in Article 11(2) of the MOON does not in and of itself restrict the exploitation of natural resources, which will also involve removal of such resources from their "place" on the moon.[39]

However, the most relevant aspect of the Moon Agreement regarding the issue of resource exploitation would seem to be the deferral of negotiations on the issue until some later date. In our view, this deferral suggests not the existence of 'any agreement between the parties regarding the interpretation of the treaty or the application of its provisions', but rather an absence thereof. We therefore conclude that the Moon Agreement is of no assistance to our interpretation of the OST.

### 5.3.5  Subsequent Practice

We turn now to 'any subsequent practice in the application of the treaty which establishes the agreement of the parties regarding its interpretation'. Since Space mining as such has not yet taken place, there is very little to look at here – apart from the fate of a few lunar samples. In 1993, Sotheby's auctioned three moon rocks for $442,500.[40] The rocks had been collected by the Soviet Union's robotic Luna-16 mission in 1970 and given to the widow of Sergei Pavlovich Korolev, the former director of the Soviet Space programme, in his honour.[41] Two decades later, they somehow found their way to Sotheby's. The same rocks were auctioned again in 2018, this time for $855,000. However, there is no indication that the Soviet or Russian governments approved these sales, making them of little value as 'subsequent practice' establishing the 'agreement of the parties' regarding the interpretation of the OST.

In 2012, the US Congress granted former crew members of the Mercury, Gemini and Apollo programmes full ownership rights over equipment and spacecraft parts they had saved as souvenirs. However, the legislation specifically excluded 'lunar rocks and other lunar

---

[39] Freeland and Jakhu, op. cit. at 70, original emphasis.

[40] Douglas Martin, 'Space artifacts of Soviets soar at a $7 million auction', *New York Times* (12 December 1993), online: www.nytimes.com/1993/12/12/nyregion/space-artifacts-of-soviets-soar-at-a-7-million-auction.html.

[41] Agence France-Presse, 'Moon rocks sell for $855,000 in New York: Sotheby's', *Phys.org* (29 November 2018), online: phys.org/news/2018-11-moon-york-sotheby.html.

material'.[42] As an action taken by a national government, this exclusion would seem to be relevant as subsequent practice, but it is an isolated case. Five years later, in 2017, a bag containing a few particles of Moon dust was auctioned at Sotheby's for $1.8 million.[43] The bag, used by Neil Armstrong to collect lunar samples in 1969, was lent by NASA to a Space museum in Kansas. The bag then went missing and, years later, was misidentified and sold for just $995. When NASA found out what had happened, it challenged the purchaser's ownership, which led to litigation, a ruling against NASA, and ultimately the $1.8 million sale. It all makes for a great story, but there is no relevant subsequent practice here. NASA was not arguing that it did or did not have property rights over the lunar dust. It was simply arguing that the bag had been illegally acquired.

### 5.3.6   Negotiating Records

Our analysis above leads to the conclusion that the issue of property rights is not addressed in the OST. Having reached this stage, we can now review the negotiating record of the treaty to confirm our interpretation but not to overturn it, as Article 32 of the Vienna Convention explains:

> Recourse may be had to supplementary means of interpretation, including the preparatory work of the treaty and the circumstances of its conclusion, in order to confirm the meaning resulting from the application of article 31, or to determine the meaning when the interpretation according to article 31:
>
> (a) leaves the meaning ambiguous or obscure; or
> (b) leads to a result which is manifestly absurd or unreasonable.[44]

There was very little debate on Article II during the negotiation of the OST, probably because the provision was adopted almost verbatim from Article 3 of the 1963 United Nations General Assembly 'Declaration of Legal Principles Governing the Activities of States in the Exploration and Use of Outer Space', which reads, 'Outer space and celestial bodies are

---

[42] An Act to Confirm Full Ownership Rights for Certain United States Astronauts to Artifacts from the Astronauts' Space Missions, Public L No 112–185, 126 Stat 1425 (2012), online: www.congress.gov/112/plaws/publ185/PLAW-112publ185.pdf.

[43] Jacey Fortin, 'Bag with Moon dust in it fetches $1.8 million from a mystery buyer', *New York Times* (21 July 2017), online: www.nytimes.com/2017/07/21/us/moon-bag-auction-sothebys.html.

[44] Vienna Convention, Art. 32.

not subject to national appropriation by claim of sovereignty, by means of use or occupation, or by any other means.'[45]

The only change made to this text in the 1967 OST was the insertion of the words 'including the moon and other celestial bodies' after the term 'outer space', in recognition of the fact that all celestial bodies – including potentially mineral-rich asteroids – are part of Space and not distinct from it. The same change was made in Article I of the OST. As a result, the Moon, asteroids and other planets are all subject to the freedom of 'exploration and use' and other provisions of the treaty, in addition to the prohibition on national appropriation.

Despite the near absence of debate, an examination of the negotiating records (*travaux préparatoires*) reveals several interventions of relevance.[46] During a meeting of COPUOS on 13 July 1966, an Austrian delegate expressed the view that a proper differentiation was required between 'non-appropriation' and 'use'. He suggested that the text 'should go further and should regulate not only the exploration of the moon and other celestial bodies but also their use; that would obviate any contradiction between the terms "non-appropriation" and "use".'[47]

On 4 August 1966, a Belgian delegate said that he had 'taken note of the interpretation of the term "non-appropriation" advanced by several delegations – apparently without contradiction – as covering both the establishment of sovereignty and the creation of titles to property in private law.'[48]

---

[45] *Declaration of Legal Principles Governing the Activities of States in the Exploration and Use of Outer Space*, GA Res 1962 (XVIII), UNGAOR, 18th Sess, 1280th Plen Mtg, UN Doc A/RES/1962(XVIII) (1963). Resolution 1962 itself built on Resolution 1721 (XVI), adopted two years earlier, by providing examples of how the prohibited 'national appropriation' might occur, i.e. 'by claim of sovereignty, by means of use or occupation, or by any other means'. *International Cooperation in the Peaceful Uses of Outer Space*, GA Res 1721 (XVI), UNGAOR, 16th Sess, 1085th Plen Mtg, UN Doc A/RES/1721(XVI) (1961).

[46] The *travaux préparatoires* are at United Nations Office for Outer Space Affairs, 'Travaux Préparatoires – Treaty on Principles Governing the Activities of States in the Exploration and Use of Outer Space, Including the Moon and Other Celestial Bodies' (2022), online: www.unoosa.org/oosa/en/ourwork/spacelaw/treaties/travaux-preparatoires/outerspace treaty.html.

[47] Legal Subcommittee of the Committee on the Peaceful Uses of Outer Space, *Summary Record of the 58th Meeting*, UNGAOR, 5th Sess, 58th Mtg, UN Doc A/AC.105/C.2/SR.58 (13 July 1966) at 3.

[48] Legal Subcommittee of the Committee on the Peaceful Uses of Outer Space, *Summary Record of the 71st Meeting*, UNGAOR, 5th Sess, 71st Mtg, UN Doc A/AC.105/C.2/SR.71 (4 August 1966) at 10.

Ultimately, negotiations on the issue of 'extracting minerals' were deferred to some indefinite future date (i.e. after the conclusion of the OST), as the following exchange between French and Soviet delegates on 20 October 1966 made clear:

> Mr. Deleau (France) 'observed that it was most important to clarify the scope of the treaty. It was quite clear that the treaty was to apply both to the celestial bodies and to outer space, but what type of activity was it to regulate? The texts referred to exploration and "use". Did the latter term imply use for exploration purposes, such as the launching of satellites, or did it mean "use" in the sense of exploitation, which would involve far more complex issues? Space, of course, was already being used for meteorological research and telecommunications, but in the case of celestial bodies it was hard at present to conceive of utilizing the moon, say, for the extraction of minerals. It was important for all States, and not only those engaged in space exploration, to know exactly what was meant by the term "use". The word was, of course, to be found in the declaration of Principles, but the latter was by no means exhaustive and should not preclude further textual improvements'.[49]
>
> . . .
>
> In response to Mr. Deleau's comments on the Draft treaties submitted by the USSR and US, Mr. Morozov (USSR) had 'felt that the Soviet text covered the very interesting point raised by the representative of France. It was not possible to say everything in one article and he believed that adequate clarification was to be found in article II of the USSR draft, which specified that outer space and celestial bodies should not be subject to national appropriation by means of use or occupation, or by any other means. In other words, no human activity on the moon or any other celestial body could be taken as justification for national appropriation. Needless to say, a treaty could deal only with the problems arising at the current stage of human evolution, and future developments would give rise to new problems requiring subsequent solution. But it would be unwise to look too far ahead and to attempt to prescribe rules for situations on which it was impossible to form adequate judgement at the present stage . . .'[50]

As a conclusion to this section, we note that a full and systematic treaty interpretation, carried out in accordance with the customary international law codified in Articles 31 and 32 of the Vienna Convention on the Law of Treaties, supports the view that the OST does not address – and was not

---

[49] Legal Subcommittee of the Committee on the Peaceful Uses of Outer Space, *Summary Record of the 63rd Meeting*, UNGAOR, 5th Sess, 63rd Mtg, UN Doc A/AC.105/C.2/SR.63 (20 October 1966) at 8-9.

[50] Ibid. at 11.

intended to address – the issue of property rights over extracted Space resources. Rather, the issue was left until later, when Space mining had become a real prospect and the challenges involved were better understood.

A decade later, the initiation of negotiations leading to the 1979 Moon Agreement provided further confirmation that this was the intended approach. The preamble to the Moon Agreement acknowledges the 'benefits which may be derived from the exploitation of the natural resources of the moon and other celestial bodies' and the 'need to define and develop the provisions' of the four main Space treaties (the OST,[51] the Rescue Agreement,[52] the Liability Convention[53] and the Registration Convention[54]) 'having regard to further progress in the exploration and use of outer space'.

Indeed, the proposal that led to the negotiations, submitted to COPUOS by a representative from Argentina, Dr Aldo Armando Cocca, argued that the OST was deficient because it did not specifically regulate the use of the Moon's natural resources.[55]

The need for negotiations on Space mining was accepted by all the members of COPUOS, which operates on consensus, as well as all the members of the UN General Assembly, which adopted the Moon Agreement without a vote (i.e. by consensus) in 1979.[56] The fact that only 18 states subsequently ratified the Moon Agreement does not detract from this point, since decisions to refrain from ratifying usually concern the specific provisions of a treaty and not the general need for a treaty on the subject matter in question.

---

[51] Outer Space Treaty.

[52] Agreement on the Rescue of Astronauts, the Return of Astronauts and the Return of Objects Launched into Outer Space, 22 April 1968, 672 UNTS 119 (entered into force 3 December 1968) (Rescue Agreement).

[53] Convention on International Liability for Damage Caused by Space Objects, 29 March 1972, 961 UNTS 187 (entered into force 1 September 1972) (Liability Convention).

[54] Convention on Registration of Objects Launched into Outer Space, 12 November 1974, 1023 UNTS 15 (entered into force 15 September 1976) (Registration Convention).

[55] James R Wilson, 'Regulation of the outer space environment through international accord: The 1979 Moon Treaty' (1990) 2:2 Fordham Environmental Law Review 173 at 176.

[56] Agreement Governing the Activities of States on the Moon and Other Celestial Bodies, GA Res 34/68, UNGAOR, 34th Sess, 89th Plen Mtg, UN Doc A/RES/34/68 (5 December 1979), online: www.unoosa.org/oosa/oosadoc/data/resolutions/1979/general_assembly_34th_session/res_3468.html.

As mentioned above, the Moon Agreement itself does not provide a detailed set of rules for Space mining. Instead, it declares the Moon and other celestial bodies the 'common heritage of [hu]mankind' and provides a mechanism for initiating a multilateral negotiation on an 'international regime . . . to govern the exploitation of the natural resources of the moon as such exploitation is about to become feasible' (Article 11 (5)). According to Article 18, such a negotiating conference can be called 'at the request of one third of the States Parties to the Agreement and with the concurrence of the majority of the States Parties'.

Although the Moon Agreement was clearly intended to open the door to Space mining, the United States began opposing the new treaty shortly after its adoption,[57] as well as any other efforts to address the issue through multilateral negotiations. It adopted an alternative strategy of creating more 'subsequent practice' in favour of its position, which is that the OST does not preclude property rights over extracted resources, and that in the absence of international rules on the conduct of Space mining, these activities may be regulated solely through national laws. Again, the US position is not untenable, but this is hardly the end of the matter.

Our concerns are not with the US interpretation of the OST, but with the assumption that regulating Space mining solely through national laws is an appropriate approach, given the existence of serious risks, global interests and the possible emergence of flag-of-convenience states. We are also concerned that the United States and companies incorporated there could be uniquely positioned to shape the development of rules of customary international law on the conduct of Space mining, rules that could be heavily influenced by corporate interests and would be binding on most, if not all, states.

---

[57] The Moon Agreement is derided by the US mostly because it includes the term 'common heritage of [hu]mankind'. But the term is not unusual. It features centrally in the UN Convention on the Law of the Sea (UNCLOS), the so-called 'Constitution of the Oceans', which includes a detailed regime for deep seabed mining. United Nations Convention on the Law of the Sea, 10 December 1982, 1833 UNTS 3 Art. 136 (entered into force 16 November 1994) (UNCLOS). In 1987, the 'Brundtland report' of the World Commission on Environment and Development identified Space as 'a global commons and part of the common heritage of [hu]mankind'. Gro H Brundtland, 'Report of the World Commission on Environmental Development: Our Common Future' (1987), *United Nations*, online: sustainabledevelopment.un.org/content/documents/5987our-common-future.pdf.

## 5.4   Recent Efforts by the United States to Advance Its Position

Subsequent practice for the purposes of treaty interpretation includes not just physical acts, but also official statements, as well as the adoption of national law and regulations. The United States has long maintained that the OST 'does not preclude private ownership of resources extracted from a celestial body'.[58] In 1979, Secretary of State Cyrus Vance told the Senate Foreign Relations Committee that the 'non-appropriation' principle applies to the natural resources of celestial bodies only when such resources are 'in place' and does not limit 'ownership to be exercised by States or private entities over those natural resources which have been removed from their "place" on or below the surface of the moon or other celestial bodies.'[59] However, it still came as a surprise to many when, in 2015, the US government adopted national legislation in support of commercial Space mining despite the absence of widely agreed international rules.

### 5.4.1   Commercial Space Launch Competitiveness Act

Sponsored by Republican Senators Ted Cruz and Marco Rubio and signed by Democratic president Barack Obama, the 2015  Commercial Space Launch Competitiveness Act gives US citizens and companies the right to 'possess, own, transport, use, and sell [any] asteroid resource or space resource obtained in accordance with applicable law, including the international obligations of the United States'.[60] The legislation thus claims to be consistent with international law, though it does not necessarily take the interests of all countries into account.

The Commercial Space Launch Competitiveness Act was designed to bolster the United States' preferred interpretation of the OST and support US companies such as Planetary Resources, which, while now defunct, lobbied hard for this legislation.[61] As Brian Israel, one of the State Department lawyers involved in the legislation, later argued,

---

[58]  Egan, op. cit.

[59]  Quoted in ibid.

[60]  US Commercial Space Launch Competitiveness Act, Pub L No 114-90, 124 Stat 2806, 2820 (2015). See Mike Wall, 'New space mining legislation is "history in the making"', *Space.com* (20 November 2015), online: www.space.com/31177-space-mining-commercial-spaceflight-congress.html.

[61]  ProPublica, 'Lobbying by Planetary Resources, Inc – January 15, 2015 to March 31, 2017' (2017), *ProPublica*, online: projects.propublica.org/represent/lobbying/300931519.

'Absent international consensus on what the rule is, national legislatures are in the position of weighing in on one side or another of an unresolved interpretive debate'.[62]

Sometimes, national legislation can indeed help to clarify the interpretation of a treaty provision. Again, Article 31(3)(b) of the Vienna Convention on the Law of Treaties reads,

> There shall be taken into account, together with the context: . . .
>
> (b) any subsequent practice in the application of the treaty which establishes the agreement of the parties regarding its interpretation . . .[63]

However, no single state can develop international law on its own. For this reason, it helps the US interpretive effort that three countries have demonstrated support for its position by adopting similar domestic laws. In 2017, Luxembourg adopted legislation on commercial Space mining and offered subsidies to Space mining companies that incorporate there.[64] In 2019, the United Arab Emirates (UAE) adopted a law that foresees commercial Space mining, while postponing the creation of a licensing regime.[65] In 2021, Japan adopted a 'Law Concerning the Promotion of Business Activities Related to the Exploration and Development of Space Resources', under which Japanese companies may seek permission from the Japanese government to extract and use Space resources.[66]

One can understand why these states have become 'first movers' on this new economic frontier. The United States is the centre of 'NewSpace', with thousands of large and small companies focused on developing and generating profit from new technologies and applications. Luxembourg

---

[62]  Brian R Israel, 'Space resources in the evolutionary course of space lawmaking' (2019) 113 *AJIL Unbound* 114 at 116.

[63]  Vienna Convention, Art. 32(3)(b).

[64]  Luxembourg, Loi du 20 juillet 2017 sur l'exploration et l'utilisation des ressources de l'espace (20 July 2017), *Journal officiel du grand-duché de Luxembourg*, online: legilux .public.lu/eli/etat/leg/loi/2017/07/20/a674/jo/fr (with unofficial English translation). See Haroon Siddique, 'Luxembourg aims to be big player in possible asteroid mining', *The Guardian* (3 February 2016), online: www.theguardian.com/science/2016/feb/03/luxem bourg-aims-to-be-big-player-in-possible-asteroid-mining.

[65]  United Arab Emirates, Federal Law No. (12) of 2019 on the Regulation of the Space Sector (19 December 2019), *Ministry of Justice*, online: www.moj.gov.ae/assets/2020/ Federal%20Law%20No%2012%20of%202019%20on%20THE%20REGULATION%20OF %20THE%20SPACE%20SECTOR.pdf.aspx.

[66]  Jeff Foust, 'Japan passes space resources law', *SpaceNews* (17 June 2021), online: spacenews.com/japan-passes-space-resources-law.

has long provided a comfortable corporate home to the two largest operators of geosynchronous communications satellites, while the UAE is seeking to diversify its oil-based economy. It already operates three Earth observation satellites as well as a scientific probe named *Hope* that orbits Mars and collects data on that planet's atmosphere. The Japanese government, for its part, has long engaged in Space exploration, including on the International Space Station, and is now seeking to develop a globally competitive Space industry. One Japanese company, ispace, welcomed the new law with an ambitious statement of intent: 'This means that companies of Japanese nationality may operate continuously in a fixed location on the Moon for the purposes of mining or extraction, storage, processing, and other operations necessary for the development of space resources, as well as to freely use space resources.'[67] By adopting national legislation, all four states aim to provide companies and investors with some of the certainty they need to develop the expensive technologies and infrastructure required for Space mining.

However, Article 31(3)(b) of the Vienna Convention on the Law of Treaties includes the words 'which establishes the agreement of the parties'. Four states cannot, on their own, establish the agreement of the parties regarding the interpretation of a treaty, like the OST, that has been ratified by 110 states. Moreover, as with state practice in customary international law, 'subsequent practice' in treaty interpretation also includes the reactions of the other parties. How many states have expressed support for the US position? How many have expressed concerns, for instance, during meetings of COPUOS? How many have indicated a preference for a widely multilateral rather than unilateral or bilateral approach to the issue of Space mining? Although the United States, Luxembourg, the UAE and Japan have adopted legislation, what matters, more than these four instances of subsequent practice, is how the rest of the parties to the OST respond.

Again, it is important to recognise that the Commercial Space Launch Competitiveness Act is part of a deliberate effort to advance a particular interpretation of the OST. As Philip De Man cogently explains,

> Prominent spacefaring States are increasingly resorting to the adoption of domestic legislation that implements their international obligations according to an interpretation that best serves their own interests. This

---

[67] ispace, 'ispace applauds Japan's passage of space resources law' (15 June 2021), online: *ispace* ispace-inc.com/wp-content/uploads/2021/06/Release_SpaceMiningAct.pdf.

approach is obviously preferred over protracted multilateral negotiation processes that, apart from being cumbersome, risk upsetting the basic balance of the existing space law regime that favours spacefaring States in the first place.[68]

De Man also explains how a power imbalance between spacefaring states on the one hand, and non-spacefaring states on the other, raises a serious issue as to how we treat 'subsequent practice in the application of the treaty'. We can draw a parallel here with the role of power in the development and change of customary international law. Indeed, one of the authors of this book has argued that the actions and statements of less powerful states should be accorded disproportionate weight as state practice and evidence of *opinio juris* – the subjective element of customary international law – because taking positions in opposition to powerful states can entail 'costs' and doing so therefore indicates strong commitments to those positions.[69]

Further to this, De Man makes the important point that the OST is not a regular treaty. Instead, the OST and the other multilateral Space treaties contain 'fundamental principles' that 'concern all States, and indeed the whole of humanity'.[70] For this reason, De Man argues,

> the fundamental importance of the principles of the Outer Space Treaty as rules that guide the use and exploration of outer space by all States for the betterment of all [hu]mankind, warrants a particularly rigorous assessment of the conditions for subsequent practice to be taken into account for these principles. This consideration should hold in particular when the available practice is limited to conduct performed by a handful of States, whereas the treaty obligation at hand aims to safeguard the equality of all States in and through the performance of such practice.[71]

De Man finds support for his position in the first report of the United Nations International Law Commission's Working Group on Subsequent Agreements and Practice in Relation to the Interpretation of Treaties. According to the working group, 'the interpretation of treaties which establish rights for other States or actors is less susceptible to "authentic"

---

[68] Philip De Man, 'State practice, domestic legislation and the interpretation of fundamental principles of international space law' (2017) 42 *Space Policy* 92 at 93.
[69] Michael Byers, *Custom, Power and the Power of Rules* (Cambridge: Cambridge University Press, 1999) at 156–57.
[70] De Man, op. cit. at 98.
[71] Ibid. at 100.

interpretation by their parties'.[72] De Man goes so far as to argue that the second paragraph of Article I, and Article II, of the OST create obligations *erga omnes*, i.e. obligations owed 'towards the international community as a whole',[73] a category of rules that is well recognised in international law.[74]

To be clear, De Man is not arguing that the parties to the OST are unable to collectively modify its provisions, either formally through negotiations or informally through subsequent practice. His argument, instead, is that the subsequent practice of a small subset of the parties should not and cannot be treated as sufficient. The merit in this argument becomes apparent if we read the two provisions carefully again.

Article I, second paragraph:

> Outer space, including the moon and other celestial bodies, shall be free for exploration and use by all States without discrimination of any kind, on a basis of equality and in accordance with international law, and there shall be free access to all areas of celestial bodies.[75]

Article II:

> Outer space, including the moon and other celestial bodies, is not subject to national appropriation by claim of sovereignty, by means of use or occupation, or by any other means.[76]

The second paragraph of Article I recognises rights held by 'all States . . . on a basis of equality', while Article II maintains the internationalised character of Space against any effort to assert title, including by actions of

---

[72] International Law Commission, *First Report on Subsequent Agreements and Subsequent Practice in Relation to Treaty Interpretation*, UNGAOR, 65th Sess, UN Doc A/CN.4/660 (19 March 2013) at 14, fn 76.

[73] De Man, op. cit. at 101.

[74] *Barcelona Traction, Light and Power Company, Limited* (*Belgium v. Spain*), [1970] ICJ Rep 3 1970 at 32, para. 33; Michael Byers, 'Conceptualising the relationship between jus cogens and erga omnes rules' (1997) 66:2–3 *Nordic Journal of International Law* 211. The International Law Commission's 2001 'Draft Articles on Responsibility of States for Internationally Wrongful Acts, with Commentaries' make frequent reference to these 'obligations owed to the international community as a whole'. See International Law Commission, *Draft Articles on Responsibility of States for Internationally Wrongful Acts, with Commentaries*, UNGAOR, 56th Sess, Supp No 10, UN Doc A/56/10 (2001), online: legal.un.org/ilc/documentation/english/reports/a_56_10.pdf. These draft articles were commended to governments by the UN General Assembly in its resolution *Responsibility of States for Internationally Wrongful Acts*, GA Res 56/83, UNGAOR, 56th Sess, 85th Plen Mtg, UN Doc A/RES/56/83 (2001).

[75] Outer Space Treaty, Art. I, para. 2.

[76] Outer Space Treaty, Art. II.

a kind – 'use and occupation' – that could only be taken by powerful spacefaring states. All this leads De Man to conclude,

> The increasing importance of subsequent State practice as an interpretative tool to determine the current meaning of treaty provisions reflects a development in general international law with salient repercussions in international space law. The aim and content of the UN space treaties in combination with a marked shift in law-making dynamics from the multilateral to the domestic level renders a number of fundamental treaty principles particularly receptive to selective interpretation through subsequent practice by certain States.
>
> When national legislation is being pursued at the same time that proceedings at the intergovernmental level are losing their teeth, the danger for informal modification through State conduct becomes real. And when such practice can only be performed by a limited number of States, whereas the fundamental rules subject to interpretation stress the equal freedom of all States to carry out spacefaring activities in an inclusive environment, courts and States should be particularly wary of attaching authoritative importance to domestic space legislation as an interpretative tool.[77]

Although the United States' position on the OST and Space mining is not untenable, and while it is seeking to strengthen its position and develop new rules of customary international law through its own practice and those of a small group of like-minded states, it is important to remember that a much larger number of states disagree, including the G77, China and Russia. It is possible that two camps will emerge on the issue of Space mining and international law in the future: the United States and its allies on one side, and Russia, China and the Global South on the other. Such a divide would both weaken the OST and preclude the development of new customary international law. In the circumstances, the only globally responsible way forward is to negotiate a new multilateral treaty on Space mining. Brian Israel, indeed, anticipates such a negotiation – at some future point:

> It is foreseeable that space-resource utilization will again become the subject of major multilateral lawmaking, at such time as a critical mass of spacefaring states recognize a practical need and a practical basis for such lawmaking ... Such international lawmaking may also have the effect of straightening out the kinks in the regime as states revise their national laws for consistency with a new international agreement.[78]

[77] De Man, op. cit. at 101.
[78] Israel, op. cit. at 118.

The Commercial Space Launch Competitiveness Act has served an important, if unintended, purpose by drawing attention to these matters and mobilising voices in favor of a multilateral approach. Several expert groups and non-governmental organisations, representing a wide variety of stakeholders, have responded by proposing principles and frameworks for the multilateral governance of Space resources. For example, in November 2019, The Hague International Space Resources Governance Working Group adopted twenty 'Building Blocks for the Development of an International Framework on Space Resource Activities'.[79] This document advocates the establishment of an international framework which is consistent with international law, contributes to sustainable development, promotes and secures 'the orderly and safe utilization' of Space resources, and takes into 'particular account' the needs of developing states and science. In April 2020, the Outer Space Institute adopted the 'Vancouver Recommendations on Space Mining', which promote negotiations on a multilateral agreement that are open to all states.[80] It was in the context of these calls for multilateral negotiations that the United States decided to push harder, both for its preferred interpretation of the OST, and for new rules and practices developed among a small group of like-minded states.

### 5.4.2   Executive Order and Artemis Accords

In April 2020, President Donald Trump signed an 'Executive Order on Encouraging International Support for the Recovery and Use of Space Resources' (see Figure 5.4).[81] The executive order (EO) reiterated that it is 'the policy of the United States to encourage international support for the public and private recovery and use of resources in outer space, consistent with applicable law'. However, the EO went further than

[79] The Hague International Space Resources Governance Working Group, 'Building blocks for the development of an international framework on space resource activities' (12 November 2019), *Leiden University*, online: www.universiteitleiden.nl/binaries/con tent/assets/rechtsgeleerdheid/instituut-voor-publiekrecht/lucht–en-ruimterecht/space-resources/bb-thissrwg–cover.pdf.

[80] Outer Space Institute (OSI), 'Vancouver recommendations on space mining' (20 April 2020), *OSI*, online: www.outerspaceinstitute.ca/docs/Vancouver_Recommendations_on_ Space_Mining.pdf.

[81] Mike Wall, 'Trump signs executive order to support moon mining, tap asteroid resource', *Space.com* (6 April 2020), online: www.space.com/trump-moon-mining-space-resources-executive-order.html.

**Figure 5.4**    From left to right: NASA Administrator Jim Bridenstine, President Donald Trump, VP Mike Pence and Second Lady Karen Pence watch a SpaceX Falcon 9 rocket launch NASA astronauts Robert Behnken and Douglas Hurley on 30 May 2020. Credit: NASA (www.flickr.com/photos/nasahqphoto/49956153337/in/photostream).

the 2015 Commercial Space Launch Competitiveness Act by explicitly rejecting that Space is a 'global commons' and dismissing the 1979 Moon Agreement as irrelevant because it has not been ratified by major spacefaring states. The EO also instructed the US State Department to take 'all appropriate actions to encourage international support for the public and private recovery and use of resources in outer space'.[82]

---

[82] Ibid.

Just one month later, in May 2020, NASA announced the core principles of the 'Artemis Accords', which it said would 'establish a common
set of principles to govern the civil exploration and use of outer space'.[83]
Then, in October of 2020, the full text of the Artemis Accords was
released.[84]

The Trump administration clearly wanted the Artemis Accords to
provide strong support for the US position that the OST does not preclude
property rights over extracted resources, and that in the absence of
international rules on the conduct of Space mining, these activities may
be regulated solely through national laws. NASA negotiated bilaterally
with NASA partner states, with these being the states most likely to
support the US position. Yet the Artemis Accords as ultimately adopted
carry less weight, as subsequent practice, than NASA might have hoped.
Although Australia, Canada, Italy, Japan, Luxembourg, the UAE and the
UK all signed the document in an online ceremony at the International
Astronautical Congress in October 2020, the text explicitly states that the
Artemis Accords 'represent a political commitment'. In other words, they
do not constitute a multilateral treaty or even a series of bilateral treaties.
For this reason, the Artemis Accords are not that significant as 'subsequent
practice in the application of the treaty which establishes the agreement of
the parties regarding its interpretation', or as state practice and evidence of
*opinio juris* for the purposes of customary international law.

The text of the Artemis Accords also includes a sentence in Section 10
(2) that reads,

> The Signatories affirm that the extraction of space resources does not
> inherently constitute national appropriation under Article II of the Outer
> Space Treaty, and that contracts and other legal instruments relating to
> space resources should be consistent with that Treaty.[85]

The language used in this sentence differs from that used in the 'Artemis
Principles' as released by NASA in May 2020, before the negotiations
with NASA partner states began. There, NASA simply asserted, 'The

---

[83] Jeff Foust, 'NASA announces Artemis Accords for international cooperation in lunar
exploration', *SpaceNews* (15 May 2020), online: spacenews.com/nasa-announces-artemis-
accords-for-international-cooperation-in-lunar-exploration.

[84] The Artemis Accords: Principles for Cooperation in the Civil Exploration and Use of the
Moon, Mars, Comets, and Asteroids for Peaceful Purposes (13 October 2020), *NASA*,
online: www.nasa.gov/specials/artemis-accords/img/Artemis-Accords-signed-13Oct2020
.pdf.

[85] Artemis Accords, s 10(2).

Artemis Accords reinforce that space resource extraction and utilization can and will be conducted under the auspices of the Outer Space Treaty, with specific emphasis on Articles II, VI, and XI.' Although NASA was likely pushing for a similar statement that Space mining does not constitute 'national appropriation', the insertion of the word 'inherently' into Section 10(2) of the final text of the Artemis Accords introduces an element of ambiguity that the US negotiators would not have sought. Is Space mining sometimes 'national appropriation' and sometimes not? Was Space mining originally not 'national appropriation', but capable of becoming understood as 'national appropriation' as understandings and interests change? Can a term such as 'national appropriation', which has no 'ordinary meaning' because it is not used outside the Outer Space Treaty, 'inherently' mean anything? The appearance of this term in the final text of the Artemis Accords most likely represents a negotiated compromise, and specifically a 'constructive ambiguity' designed to accommodate different views by fudging the terminology.[86] The result, however, is to further reduce the weight of the Artemis Accords as subsequent practice, state practice and evidence of *opinio juris*.

Despite this ambiguity and their status as a 'political commitment', the Artemis Accords still had the effect of undermining the long and stable relationship of Space co-operation between Russia and the United States. The May 2020 announcement of the core principles of the Artemis Accords was quickly condemned by Dmitry Rogozin, the director general of Roscosmos, on Twitter: 'The principle of the invasion is the same, be it the moon or Iraq. Create a coalition of the willing and then, without the UN or even Nato, move forward to the goal. But this will only result in a new Afghanistan or Iraq.'[87] Two weeks later, in a radio interview, Rogozin spoke directly to the international law issue: 'We will not, in any case, accept any attempts to privatize the Moon. It is illegal, it runs counter to international law.'[88]

---

[86] The term 'constructive ambiguity' is generally attributed to Henry Kissinger. See GR Berridge and Lorna Lloyd, *Dictionary of Diplomacy*, 3rd ed (Basingstoke: Palgrave Macmillan, 2012) at 73. For more on this negotiating and drafting strategy, see Michael Byers, 'Still agreeing to disagree: International security and constructive ambiguity' (2020) 8:1 *Journal on the Use of Force and International Law* 91.

[87] Marc Bennetts, 'US plan for moon mining is like Iraq invasion, says Russia', *The Times* (10 May 2020), online: www.thetimes.co.uk/article/us-plan-for-moon-mining-is-like-iraq-invasion-says-russia-sqgvpvqvt (translated from Russian by the reporter).

[88] TASS Russian News Agency, op. cit.

China, for its part, did not offer an official response, although commentary in its state-run media described the Artemis Accords as a product of a Cold War mentality, focused on exerting dominance, and continuing the legacy of colonisation.[89] There is no indication or expectation that China might participate in the US-led effort to develop a governance regime for Space mining through practice and bilateral instruments.

As for the states of the Global South, most of them likely shared the view – expressed officially by Rogozin and unofficially by the Chinese state-run media – that the Artemis Accords were just another exercise of American hegemony, this time led by the proudly unilateralist and undiplomatic Donald Trump. As we will see below, many of these states later took part in a 'G77 and China' statement strongly supporting the creation of a Working Group on Space Resources at COPUOS, a possible first step towards multilateral negotiations.

The United States is, however, continuing its effort to advance its preferred interpretation of the OST, and to build on it by creating rules and practices for Space mining through agreements and other 'state practice' co-ordinated among a small group of like-minded states. Thirteen additional states – Brazil, New Zealand, South Korea, Ukraine, Poland, Israel, Mexico, Romania, Bahrain, Colombia, Singapore, France and Saudi Arabia – have signed the Artemis Accords since October 2020. However, the most significant further step in the US effort involves a call for proposals, issued to the Space industry, for the extraction and sale of lunar regolith to NASA.

### 5.4.3 NASA Contracting to Purchase Lunar Regolith

In September 2020, NASA announced that it was seeking proposals from private companies to extract small amounts of regolith from the surface of the Moon and sell them to NASA. Any selected company would be required to collect between 50 and 500 grams and provide imagery of the material and data concerning its location. NASA would then buy the material, through an 'in-place ownership transfer', without the company

---

[89] Elliot Ji, Michael B Cerny and Raphael J Piliero, 'What does China think about NASA's Artemis Accords?', *The Diplomat* (17 September 2020), online: thediplomat.com/2020/09/what-does-china-think-about-nasas-artemis-accords.

having to return the sample to Earth. NASA might then retrieve the material at some unspecified future time.[90] Or it might not.

None of this was about the regolith itself. NASA Administrator Jim Bridenstine admitted that the planned purchases were aimed at creating more subsequent practice in favour of the US interpretation of the OST: 'What we're trying to do is make sure that there is a norm of behavior that says that resources can be extracted and that we're doing it in a way that is in compliance with the Outer Space Treaty'.[91] The admission was remarkable for its candour: government officials are rarely transparent about efforts to change international law through actions rather than negotiations, perhaps because it draws attention to their efforts and can generate pushback from other state and non-state actors.

In December 2020, NASA signed contracts with four companies: Lunar Outpost and Masten Space Systems from the United States, and the Japanese company ispace and its Luxembourg-based subsidiary ispace Europe.[92] It aims to complete the purchases of regolith by 2024.

### 5.5   Risks of the US Approach

Former NASA Administrator Jim Bridenstine drew an analogy between Space mining and high-seas fishing, where a fish cannot be owned while in the ocean but can be owned as soon as it is caught.[93] The analogy is apt to the degree that it concerns the acquisition of ownership of something from an 'area beyond national jurisdiction'. Yet it does not lead to the conclusion that the exploitation of resources in such areas should be allowed and supported by national governments in the absence of a multilateral agreement providing specific rules for operators to follow.

Fishing without science-based regulation often leads to overexploitation and even destruction of stocks. For this reason, high-seas fisheries are now usually subject to international regulation, for instance under the 1995 United Nations Agreement on Straddling Fish Stocks and Highly

---

[90] NASA Shared Services Center, 'Request for quotation (RFQ) 80NSSC20737332Q, purchase of lunar regolith and/or rock materials from contractor' (10 September 2020), *System for Award Management*, online: sam.gov/opp/77726177617a45d0a196e23a587d7c14/view.

[91] Foust, 'NASA offers to buy lunar samples to set space resources precedent', op. cit.

[92] NASA, op. cit.

[93] Edward Helmore, 'NASA is looking for private companies to help mine the moon', *The Guardian* (11 September 2020), online: www.theguardian.com/science/2020/sep/11/nasa-moon-mining-private-companies.

Migratory Fish Stocks,[94] under regional treaties such as the 2018 International Agreement to Prevent Unregulated High Seas Fisheries in the Central Arctic Ocean,[95] and under numerous 'regional fisheries management organizations'.[96] These treaties often result in science-based quotas and sometimes moratoria. Other areas beyond national jurisdiction, such as the deep seabed and Antarctica, are also governed through specific multilateral agreements.[97] We are not arguing that these regimes are perfect; our point, simply, is that they exist – and that many states, including the United States and the Soviet Union, co-operated in their creation.

Space mining, if it occurs, will have to respect the interests of all states. Even the United States accepts this position, stressing the continued application of the duty to consult (Article IX OST) to any proposed Space mining activity. But while some shared interests are uncontroversial – for instance, avoiding the loss of science opportunities, the lofting of dust into lunar orbits, or the inadvertent redirecting of asteroids into Earth impact trajectories – the need for widely agreed safety and environmental standards for Space mining remains. Leaving the regulation of Space mining to individual states is unlikely to deliver the necessary protections. It also risks a regulatory race to the bottom and even the emergence of flag-of-convenience states, as governments compete to attract investments and technologies.[98]

---

[94] United Nations Agreement for the Implementation of the Provisions of the United Nations Convention on the Law of the Sea of 10 December 1982 relating to the Conservation and Management of Straddling Fish Stocks and Highly Migratory Fish Stocks, 4 August 1995, 2167 UNTS 3 (entered into force 11 December 2001).

[95] Agreement to Prevent Unregulated High Seas Fisheries in the Central Arctic Ocean, 3 October 2018, Can TS 2021 No (entered into force 25 June 2021). China, Russia and the United States are among the eight parties to the treaty.

[96] See e.g. 'Northwest Atlantic Fisheries Organization' (2022), online: www.nafo.int; 'Western & Central Pacific Fisheries Commission' (2022), online: www.wcpfc.int/home; 'Indian Ocean Tuna Commission' (2022), online: www.iotc.org.

[97] See UNCLOS, Part XI; also the 'International Seabed Authority' (2022), online: www.isa.org.jm/home; and the Antarctic Treaty, 1 December 1959, 402 UNTS 71 (entered into force 23 June 1961); also the Secretariat of the Antarctic Treaty, 'The Antarctic Treaty' (2022), online: www.ats.aq/e/antarctictreaty.html.

[98] So far, the world has been lucky on the latter front, with the availability of large government contracts incentivising Space companies to remain incorporated and active in the United States. But wealthy actors have options: Elon Musk recently moved his home and some of SpaceX and Tesla's operations from California to Texas, apparently because of its more favourable tax and regulatory regime. Bloomberg and Dana Hull, 'Why Elon Musk moved to Texas – and what he really thinks of California', *Fortune* (8 December 2020), online: fortune.com/2020/12/08/elon-musk-moving-to-texas-from-california.

### 5.5.1   Loss of Science Opportunities

Done well, Space mining could provide new science opportunities and unprecedented sampling of celestial bodies. For example, asteroids contain some of the oldest materials in the solar system, some of which have experienced little thermal processing since their incorporation into parent bodies. The Moon's ice deposits are a partial record of volatile delivery to Earth.

Done poorly, Space mining would hinder science. For example, water and oxygen could in the future be extracted from astromaterials by pyrolysis.[99] If systematic scientific sampling does not occur prior to their alteration or consumption, valuable information about the solar system could be lost, including information locked into cosmochemical or mineralogical signatures. A clear analogy exists on Earth where, in many jurisdictions, mining and construction companies are made to wait while archaeologists and biologists survey sites slated for development. A Space mining company's own analysis will be designed to maximise resource yields and not science opportunities. These risks would only be exacerbated by inconsistent practices of the kind likely to result from national regulations that are not co-ordinated under some kind of multilateral regime.

### 5.5.2   Planetary Protection

Some of the first efforts at private Space exploration have manifested an incautious approach to risk avoidance. In 2019, the Israeli non-profit SpaceIL crashed a robotic lander on the Moon. Unbeknown to SpaceIL, its partner – the Arch Mission Foundation – had placed thousands of tardigrades on board.[100] Tardigrades, commonly referred to as 'water bears' or 'moss piglets', are tiny (0.5 millimetre) eight-legged animals that are able to survive extreme temperatures, pressures and radiation, and even the vacuum of Space. In this instance, the act of putting life on the Moon is not the concern, thanks to the harsh environment on the lunar surface. Rather, the concern is that a non-governmental entity has

---

[99] Lukas Schlüter and Aidan Cowley, 'Review of techniques for in-situ oxygen extraction on the moon' (2020) 181 *Planetary and Space Science* 104753.

[100] Keren Shahar and Dov Greenbaum, 'Lessons in space regulations from the lunar tardigrades of the Beresheet hard landing' (2020) 4 *Nature Astronomy* 208.

already smuggled lifeforms onto a spacecraft destined for another celes
tial body.

In 2018, SpaceX launched a Tesla automobile on an orbit that extends
past Mars. Although no impact with Mars is expected,[101] there was an
initial lack of clarity on the mission profile and the potential for the
unsterilised payload to encounter the Red Planet.[102] Unlike the Moon,
the environment on Mars may allow certain forms of life to survive and
become established. Careful precautions are therefore needed and should
always involve full transparency and co-operation.

These examples of private risk-taking suggest that Space mining
companies might take shortcuts too if not carefully regulated according
to widely agreed rules. For example, they might choose not to fully
sterilise equipment sent to Mars or other celestial bodies having conditions potentially favorable to life, thus contravening the international
guidelines on planetary protection produced by the Committee on
Space Research (COSPAR) and studiously followed by national Space
agencies.[103] One could even imagine a company disregarding the guidelines in order to experiment by introducing lifeforms to an alien environment, as occurred with rabbits in Australia, starlings in the United
States and Canada Geese in the United Kingdom and New Zealand.
It is, in addition, very easy to imagine Space mining companies failing
to take the measures necessary to contain potentially dangerous dust
and debris.

### 5.5.3    Dust and Debris Streams

Lunar dust, which is very fine and highly abrasive, is a known challenge
to operations on the Moon. Any surface activity could exacerbate lunar
dust migration, including by lofting dust onto trajectories that cross lunar

---

[101] Hanno Rein, Daniel Tamayo and David Vokrouhlický, 'The random walk of cars and
their collision probabilities with planets' (2018) 5:2 *Aerospace* 57.

[102] Committee on the Review of Planetary Protection Policy Development Processes, *Review
and Assessment of Planetary Protection Policy Development Process* (Washington DC:
The National Academies Press, 2018).

[103] G Kminek, C Conley, V Hipkin and H Yano, 'COSPAR's Planetary Protection Policy'
(December 2017), *Committee on Space Research (COSPAR)*, online: cosparhq.cnes.fr/
assets/uploads/2019/12/PPPolicyDecember-2017.pdf. For more on COSPAR, which
operates at arm's length from many governments, see COSPAR, 'About' (20 May
2019), *COSPAR*, online: cosparhq.cnes.fr/about.

orbits, such as that of NASA's planned Lunar Gateway.[104] Moreover, without co-operation from all actors, the limited number of useful lunar orbits could quickly become filled with Space debris, interfering with humanity's access to the Moon.

On asteroids, limited gravity and low escape speeds will make it difficult to prevent the loss of surface material. Even if full enclosures are used, waste material might be purposefully jettisoned to reduce costs. Mining could also lead to uncontrolled outbursts of material due to volatile sublimation following the removal of surface layers or other processes.

Space mining will initially focus on the Moon and near-Earth asteroids, because of their accessibility. Asteroids on Earth-crossing orbits will be among the easiest to reach. Under certain conditions, the debris streams resulting from asteroid mining could contribute to the near-Earth meteoroid population and therefore threaten not only lunar operations but the thousands of satellites in Earth's orbit that support essential civilian and military activities, ranging from banking, agriculture and aviation to search and rescue and reconnaissance.[105] Even the dust from the Moon, if expelled at much higher than natural rates, could cause noticeable changes to the cis-lunar environment (which, as we explain in Chapter 7, is the region of Space between an altitude of 35,786 kilometres – where Earth's geosynchronous orbit is located – and the area around the Moon).

Space missions already provide some evidence of such risks, although so far these remain at negligible levels. As mentioned, a small impactor was used to make a crater on Ryugu in 2019, during Japan's *Hayabusa-2* mission.[106] Some of the anthropogenic meteoroids resulting from the impact could begin reaching Earth in 2033 during Ryugu's next close

---

[104] Philip T Metzger, 'Dust transport and its effects due to landing spacecraft' (paper delivered at the Impact of Lunar Dust on Human Exploration conference, Houston, 11–13 February 2020, Houston, LPI Contrib No 2141), online: www.hou.usra.edu/meetings/lunardust2020/pdf/5040.pdf.

[105] Logan Fladeland, Aaron C Boley and Michael Byers, 'Meteoroid stream formation due to the extraction of space resources from asteroids' (paper delivered at the First International Orbital Debris Conference, 9–12 December 2019, Sugar Land, TX), online: arxiv.org/pdf/1911.12840.pdf.

[106] Masahiko Arakawa et al., 'An artificial impact on the Asteroid (162173) Ryugu formed a crater in the gravity-dominated regime' (2020) 368:6486 *Science* 67.

approach to our planet.[107] In September 2022, NASA tested its ability to deflect an asteroid by striking (65803) Didymos B (Dimorphos) with the Double Asteroid Redirection Test (DART) spacecraft. This impact will also have produced anthropogenic meteoroids, with the possibility in this case of immediate delivery to Earth.[108] Again, while these risks are far less than those posed by existing meteoroids, they demonstrate that human actions can indeed change the near-Earth environment.

Nor are operational hazards the only consideration. For example, while dust launched into cis-lunar Space from the Moon might be too fine or too low in spatial density to pose a serious risk to spacecraft, at least compared to other hazards, it could, if launched in sufficient quantities, have implications for the brightness of Earth's sky and therefore for astronomy due to scattered light. Since we are just now beginning to understand how dust is naturally distributed in cis-lunar Space,[109] we are not yet at the point of considering its effects on sky brightness. But light pollution from satellites has emerged as a major concern, followed (most recently) by an awareness that light reflecting off orbital debris might also affect astronomy.[110]

### 5.5.4    Asteroid Trajectory Changes

Some of the risks associated with Space mining are small in terms of statistical risk but very high in consequence. As Chapter 6 explains, over the next decade we can expect about 50 asteroids with diameters greater than 100 metres to pass within ten lunar distances of Earth, a handful of which are in the 1,000-metre size range.[111] The positions and orbits of these asteroids are relatively well established and none of them poses any risk to us in this current century. However, these asteroids that approach

---

[107] M Kováčová, R Nagy, L Kornoš and J Tóth, '101955 Bennu and 162173 Ryugu: Dynamical modelling of ejected particles to the Earth' (2020) 185 *Planetary and Space Science* 104897.

[108] Paul Wiegert, 'On the delivery of DART-ejected material from Asteroid (65803) Didymos to Earth' (2019) 1:3 *Planetary Science Journal* 1.

[109] Charles Q Choi, 'Signs of Earth's weird, elusive "dust moons" finally spotted', *Space.com* (31 October 2018), online: www.space.com/42293-earth-orbiting-dust-clouds-confirmed .html.

[110] Miroslav Kocifaj, Frantisek Kundracik, John C Barentine and Salvador Bará, 'The proliferation of space objects is a rapidly increasing source of artificial night sky brightness' (2021) 504:1 *Monthly Notices of the Royal Astronomical Society: Letters* L40.

[111] Center for Near Earth Object Studies, 'NEO Earth close approaches' (May 2022), online: *NASA* cneos.jpl.nasa.gov/ca.

closest to Earth are also the ones most likely to be selected for Space mining. Since removing mass from an asteroid will almost inevitably change its trajectory, any mining operations that are not fully informed by science could potentially lead to an Earth impact emergency. Do we trust profit-oriented companies, which seek to reduce costs wherever possible, to conduct the careful scientific assessments and calculations needed to guard against this low-risk, very-high-consequence outcome? Do we trust national regulators from individual states to maintain up-to-date requirements based upon the best available science and the precautionary principle, and to monitor and enforce compliance? What about flag-of-convenience states that may see economic advantage in having more relaxed standards or less rigorous enforcement? Clearly, multilateral rules and oversight are required.

### 5.5.5   Space Companies as Actors in International Law-Making?

The accessibility of Space is increasing as a growing number of actors develop or purchase the technologies needed to launch and operate satellites and other spacecraft. Alongside the growth in spacefaring states is an even faster growth in the number of Space companies. The result, one might think, could be a certain democratisation of the Space environment.

However, most of the growth in Space companies is centred in one country.[112] This concentration of growth raises the possibility that the United States, as the launch and licensing state for most commercial Space activities, could be uniquely positioned to steer actual mining practice in support of its diplomatic efforts to secure broad acceptance among states that commercial Space mining is permissible under the OST. Such practice could further contribute to the development of customary international law standards for the conduct of mining operations.

This steering could happen in one of two ways, or even both. First, international Space law uniquely makes states responsible for the activities of companies incorporated within them. This feature might allow those activities to count both as 'subsequent practice' for the purposes of treaty interpretation, and as 'state practice', and even evidence of

---

[112] James Clay Moltz explains how the rapid growth in Space companies ('NewSpace'), and associated technological developments, are the principal factors keeping the United States ahead of China in the Space domain. James Clay Moltz, 'The changing dynamics of twenty-first-century space power' (2019) 12:1 *Journal of Strategic Security* 15.

*opinio juris*, for the purposes of customary international law. This is due to Article VI of the OST, which is reproduced in full above, and only partly here:

> States Parties to the Treaty shall bear international responsibility for national activities in outer space ... whether such activities are carried on by governmental agencies or by non-governmental entities, and for assuring that national activities are carried out in conformity with the provisions set forth in the present Treaty.[113]

The activities of most Space mining companies will comply from the outset with the laws, regulations and policy preferences of their state of incorporation, which again is likely to be the United States. In such a situation, one could – because of Article VI – understand the activities of the company as akin to those of an agent acting on behalf of the state. We note that a state can be legally accountable for the actions of actual agents, e.g. SpaceX when carrying NASA astronauts to the ISS under contract with that national Space agency, under the general rules of customary international law on state responsibility,[114] in parallel to (or even outside the scope of) Article VI.

In other situations, the laws, regulations and policy preferences of the state of incorporation might not yet be fully developed, in which case the activities of the company will either be met with acquiescence or prompt the state into adopting new rules or clarifying existing ones.[115] In the case of acquiescence, the activities of the company could be considered subsequent practice and state practice, since the state is thereby implicitly endorsing them. Activities that prompt the state to develop or reform its laws, in contrast, should not be so considered, because the state is responding in a manner that indicates a lack of endorsement. Instead, it is the adoption of new rules or the clarification of existing rules that is the relevant subsequent practice and state practice here. It may also

---

[113] Outer Space Treaty, Art. VI.

[114] International Law Commission, 'Draft Articles on the Responsibility of States for Internationally Wrongful Acts', op. cit., Art. 5.

[115] See Melissa J Durkee, 'Interstitial space law' (2019) 97:2 *Washington University Law Review* 423 at 428: 'Because private missions are defined by the Outer Space treaty as "national" missions, which are attributed to the home nation and for which home nations are responsible, these private acts can also be attributed to those nations for the purposes of customary law formation and treaty interpretation. This is because when a corporation whose activity is attributed to the state publicly asserts a legal rule and acts on it, and a nation does nothing, that nation implicitly accepts the corporate rule' (footnotes omitted).

provide evidence of *opinio juris* because it suggests a sense of obligation on the part of the state to bring its domestic law into compliance with developments in international law.

The second way that US steering could happen is that other states or foreign companies wishing to engage in Space mining might have little choice but to hire US companies, or to enter into joint ventures with them, in order to access technology or operational experience. As a result, their Space mining activities will then follow the laws and regulations of the United States.

There is a historical precedent for this. In the 1945 Truman Proclamation, the US government asserted that every coastal state has exclusive jurisdiction over the resources of the continental shelf off its coastline.[116] The claim, which was framed to be available to every coastal state, was soon repeated by many of them, leading to the rapid development of a new rule of customary international law and, just 13 years later, to its codification in the 1958 Convention on the Continental Shelf.[117] However, the reciprocally available character of the claim did more than attract the support of other states; it also worked to the advantage of US oil companies, which at the time were among the very few companies with offshore drilling technologies. As a result, most other coastal states could only exercise their newly recognised rights by partnering with a US oil company.[118] This situation also worked to the benefit of the US government, as overseas profits flowed home, and as US regulators found themselves regulating offshore drilling worldwide – via their regulatory powers over the US companies.

One can see a similar development currently in low Earth orbit (LEO), where SpaceX is occupying entire orbital shells under licences issued by

---

[116] 'Proclamation by the president with respect to the natural resources of the subsoil and sea bed of the continental shelf' (25 September 1945), reproduced in (1946) 40:S1 *American Journal of International Law* 45.

[117] Convention on the Continental Shelf, 29 April 1958, 499 UNTS 311 (entered into force 10 June 1964). On the Truman Proclamation's effects on customary international law, see Zdenek Slouka, *International Custom and the Continental Shelf* (The Hague: Martinus Nijhoff, 1968); James Crawford and Thomas Viles (1994) 'International law on a given day', in Konrad Ginther et al., eds., *Völkerrecht zwischen normativem Anspruch und politischer Realität: Festschrift für Karl Zemanek* (Berlin: Duncker and Humblot, 1994) 45.

[118] Even developed states had little choice but to co-operate with the US oil industry. As late as 1981, US companies were responsible for 50 per cent of production in the North Sea. See William H Millard, 'The legal environment of the British oil industry' (1982) 18:3 *Tulsa Law Review* 394.

the United States' Federal Communications Commission (FCC) as it builds a mega-constellation of up to 40,000 satellites. As a result, the FCC has become the most important regulator in LEO, notwithstanding the international character of that zone. The various challenges associated with mega-constellations are discussed in Chapters 2 and 3.

There are, however, two factors that could impede the influence of the United States and US companies on the development of new rules for Space mining. The first is the incredible mobility of high-tech companies, which can be attracted to states with generous subsidies, lower taxes or more relaxed regulatory regimes. The second factor is China, which has recently developed into a major spacefaring state.

### 5.5.6    Fragmentation of the Space Law Regime

As mentioned, the interpretation of the OST preferred by the United States risks a race to the bottom and even the emergence of flag-of-convenience states. Allowing Space mining to take place under national regulations – subject, at the international level, only to an undefined duty to consult – would enable states that wished to attract mining companies to do so by offering minimal regulation and lax enforcement.

There are examples here on Earth that support our concerns. For example, three-quarters of the world's terrestrial mining companies are incorporated in Canada, which exercises relatively little oversight of their operations in the Global South.[119] Inconsistencies among different national laws and regulations, along with weak enforcement, have led to human rights abuses, environmental damage and adverse health impacts. Meanwhile, in the maritime domain, flag-of-convenience states provide shipping companies with registrations for their vessels, as is required by international law, but do so with minimal regulation and lax enforcement. Not surprisingly, ships with flags of convenience  have poor safety records.[120] In Space, as we explain in Chapter 2, national regulation of corporate activities with little international involvement has already resulted in a debris crisis in LEO.

Established US companies such as  SpaceX are unlikely to change their place of incorporation anytime soon, because of the frequent and often

---

[119] See e.g. Todd Gordon and Jeffery R Webber, 'Imperialism and resistance: Canadian mining companies in Latin America' (2008) 29:1 *Third World Quarterly* 63.

[120] Alexandra Mandaraka-Sheppard, *Modern Maritime Law: Volume 2, Managing Risks and Liabilities*, 3rd ed (Abingdon: Informa Law from Routledge, 2013).

very large contracts they receive from NASA and the US Space Force. But the fact that Japan's ispace has established a subsidiary in Luxembourg suggests that other Space companies are willing to 'move' elsewhere in pursuit of subsidies, tax breaks or favourable regulations. It is also interesting that this Luxembourg subsidiary, ispace Europe, was one of the four recipients of a NASA contract for the extraction and sale of lunar regolith, since this suggests a certain lack of concern about 'regulatory flight' on the part of the US government. However, awarding this one contract to a foreign company might also have been a calculated move to involve another country in what, according to the then NASA administrator, was nothing more than an effort to create a legal precedent.[121]

Tax breaks and favourable regulation is one thing; little to no oversight is another. It is not difficult to imagine a national government seeking revenue through fees for incorporating Space companies or for registering spacecraft without making any serious effort to develop and enforce national laws and regulations. As we explain in Chapter 2, for example, Rwanda might be behaving as a flag-of-convenience state for the purposes of filings for radio spectrum at the International Telecommunication Union. We thus must ask whether a flag-of-convenience state would be acquiescing to all activities of one of its 'national' companies by failing to develop or enforce meaningful national laws for Space mining companies incorporated there. And would this then make the activities of that company subsequent practice for the purposes of treaty interpretation, and state practice and evidence of *opinio juris* for the purposes of customary international law? The answer, unfortunately, could well be 'yes'.

Then there is China, which has recently emerged as a major spacefaring state and is unlikely to support or accept new rules that have been crafted to suit US interests. China has ratified the Outer Space Treaty, is an active participant at COPUOS, and co-operates with the United States and other Western countries in Space-based search and rescue (COSPAS-SARSAT)[122] and disaster relief (the Disasters Charter).[123] But

---

[121] See discussion at *supra* note 91.

[122] See COSPAS-SARSAT, 'International Cospas-Sarsat Programme' (2014), online: www .cospas-sarsat.int/en/about-us/about-the-programme.

[123] See 'International charter space and major disasters' (2022), online: disasterscharter.org; For the text of this 'Charter on Cooperation to Achieve the Coordinated Use of Space Facilities in the Event of Natural or Technological Disasters', Rev 3 (25 April 2000), see *International Charter Space and Major Disasters*, online: disasterscharter.org/web/guest/ text-of-the-charter.

its considerable political and economic power, fast-growing Space cap
abilities and increasingly assertive approach to foreign relations all suggest that China will either go it alone on Space mining or – perhaps more
likely – seek to create its own group of like-minded states. The latter
approach would be consistent with China's creation of the Belt and Road
Initiative and the Asian Infrastructure Investment Bank, as well as its
open invitation to host foreign astronauts on its new Tiangong Space
station. A Chinese-led bloc of spacefaring states would likely develop its
own practices and procedures, different from the US-led approach under
the Artemis Accords, with even subtle differences – such as on safety
zones – being potentially important.

One thing is certain. In the absence of a multilateral process for
governing Space mining, the approach taken by the United States risks
the development of different, inconsistent and perhaps even conflicting
rules and practices. This could, in turn, destabilise the entire existing
Space governance regime, to the long-term detriment of international
peace and security. By marginalising input from developing and non-
spacefaring states, it could also replicate, perpetuate and even exaggerate
current economic and political inequities as humanity moves into Space.

### 5.5.7 Safety Zones and Long-Term Stewardship

'Safety zones' are used around oil platforms operating in exclusive economic zones (EEZs) to prevent accidents involving ships. Under Article
60 of the 1982 United Nations Convention on the Law of the Sea
(UNCLOS), a coastal state 'may, where necessary, establish reasonable
safety zones' around oil platforms and similar installations.[124] These
safety zones may not extend more than 500 metres from the structure,
and other states must be provided with 'due notice' of their extent. It
remains unsettled whether a coastal state may create a safety zone around
an oil platform on the extended continental shelf (i.e. beyond the 200-
nautical-mile EEZ) or around a ship in motion, such as a ship conducting
a seismic survey in support of oil and gas exploration.[125]

In the Artemis Accords, signatories express their intent to use 'safety
zones' around Space mining operations to provide notification of
their activities and to co-ordinate with other actors to avoid 'harmful

---

[124] UNCLOS, Art. 60.
[125] See Joanna Mossop, 'Protests against oil exploration at sea: Lessons from the Arctic
Sunrise arbitration' (2016) 31:1 International Journal of Marine and Coastal Law 60.

interference'.[126] Arguably, this notification is necessary to allow full implementation of the consultation, due regard, and notification obligations in Articles IX and XI of the OST.[127] The signatories say they will 'respect the principle of free access to all areas of celestial bodies and all other provisions of the Outer Space Treaty in their use of safety zones', which 'will ultimately be temporary, ending when the relevant operation ceases'.[128]

These assurances are appropriate, but they are expressed within a non-binding instrument that was negotiated among a small group of like-minded states. This leaves the door open to selective application, abuse or at least contestation regarding any safety zone that is established. There is also a question of how China and other non-Artemis Accord spacefaring states might regard the rights of others in any safety zones that they themselves might choose to establish – now that the United States has opened this door. On the oceans, the behaviour of coastal states concerning safety zones has given rise to several disputes, most notably between the Netherlands and Russia, when a Greenpeace ship and its crew were detained for months after protesting offshore oil drilling in the Russian EEZ.[129] Moreover, it is not clear that safety zones, as envisaged, are any better than the general duty to consult. Consultation could provide the desired notification of planned activities on the Moon and other celestial bodies without creating any boundaries, even if those boundaries are only non-binding and temporary.

The US effort to persuade other states to sign the Artemis Accords has undoubtedly been facilitated by the following provision: 'The Signatories intend to use their experience under the Accords to contribute to multilateral efforts to further develop international practices, criteria, and rules applicable to the definition and determination of safety zones and harmful interference.'[130] However, the United States might not be

---

[126] Artemis Accords, s 11. Safety zones were recommended in the final report of The Hague International Space Resources Governance Working Group, op. cit. See also Tanja Masson-Zwaan and Mark J Sundahl, 'The lunar legal landscape: Challenges and opportunities' (2021) 46 *Air and Space Law* 29.

[127] Lucas Mallowan, Lucien Rapp and Maria Topka, 'Reinventing treaty compliant "safety zones" in the context of space sustainability' (2021) 8:2 *Journal of Space Safety Engineering* 155.

[128] Artemis Accords, s 11(7)(b).

[129] *Arctic Sunrise Arbitration* (*The Netherlands* v. *Russia*) (Award on Merits), Permanent Court of Arbitration, Case No 2014-02 (14 August 2014), online www.pcacases.com/web/view/21.

[130] Artemis Accords, s 11(6).

disappointed if the envisaged multilateral law-making efforts are post poned, fail or never take place. As we explained above, the United States and US companies are uniquely positioned to influence the development of customary international law concerning the conduct of Space mining, including through actual mining and safety zones. It is also possible that this influence might be bolstered by the Artemis Accords' provisions on safety zones, not as treaty provisions, but as a weak form of state practice on the part of the signatories.

Of course, US-led efforts to 'develop international practices, criteria, and rules' for safety zones could also fail at the level of customary international law. Everything depends on the responses of other states, including non-spacefaring and developing states. Again, no single state or small group of states can make or change international law on its own, no matter how powerful and technologically capable they may be.

None of what is happening here is unusual in international law-making, including the fact that a powerful state is seeking to establish the framework within which state practice and any eventual multilateral negotiations will take place. Powerful states generally try to shape international law in their interests, rather than brazenly violating or simply ignoring the rules.[131] The postponement of negotiations until rules and practices can be shaped by a small group of like-minded states is one of the tried-and-tested strategies of hegemonic law-making. For this reason, less powerful states, including non-spacefaring and developing states, may wish to weigh in on this matter sooner rather than later.

There are long-term, global interests at stake. As prefigured in the Artemis Accords, safety zones could – depending on how they are applied in practice – provide a Space actor with some of the benefits of territory, while relieving it of long-term obligations of stewardship. It is easy to find analogies on Earth that support these concerns, including 'orphan' oil wells and abandoned mining tailings.[132] Moreover, since resource exploration and extraction could take considerable time in Space, a safety zone might remain in place for decades or even centuries, blurring any distinction between temporary use and de facto occupation.

---

[131] See generally Michael Byers and Georg Nolte, eds., *United States Hegemony and the Foundations of International Law* (Cambridge: Cambridge University Press, 2003).

[132] Robert Fife et al., 'Ottawa provides $2.4-billion to get oil and gas workers back on the job', *Globe and Mail* (17 April 2020), online: www.theglobeandmail.com/politics/article-ottawa-announces-17-billion-to-clean-up-orphan-oil-wells-in-western.

We agree that safety zones could reduce the risk of certain kinds of accident by ensuring that Space actors do not encroach on each other's operations. Geographic separation could be particularly important in low-gravity situations were dust and debris are easily dispersed. Our concern about the US-led push for an acceptance of safety zones does not deny their potential benefits, or that something like safety zones will be needed in some circumstances. Rather, our concern is that the development of safety zones, and standards for them, could be skewed in favour of powerful spacefaring states and companies from those states, enabling arbitrary boundaries, limits on access or other forms of unnecessary self-privileging. For this reason, safety zones, and Space mining operations in general, should be governed by rules informed by longer-term interests and diverse perspectives—including those of states in the Global South.

Current debates on international law and Space mining can benefit from the experience gained during the development of globally applicable rules on deep seabed mining. During the negotiation of UNCLOS, the United States demanded that private companies have access to deep seabed resources beyond the continental shelf. Most other states wished the deep seabed to be recognised as 'the common heritage of [hu]-mankind',[133] with mining subject to international regulation and oversight. The latter view prevailed, mostly due to co-ordinated negotiating by developing states.[134] This is not the place to defend how that exercise in multilateralism is playing out; we simply point to it as an opportunity for learning.[135] We also note that the United States' failure to ratify UNCLOS has not posed a barrier to the treaty's success: 168 other states have ratified the treaty and, since 1983, the United States has accepted that many of its provisions reflect customary international law.[136]

---

[133] UNCLOS, Art. 136.

[134] Gorana Draguljić, 'Power in numbers: The developing world and the construction of global commons institutions' (2020) 41:12 *Third World Quarterly* 1973; Surabhi Ranganathan, 'The common heritage of mankind: Annotations on a battle', in Jochen von Bernstorff and Philipp Dann, eds., *The Battle for International Law* (Oxford: Oxford University Press, 2019) 35.

[135] For an overview of the latest developments, see Pradeep A Singh, 'The two-year deadline to complete the International Seabed Authority's Mining Code: Key outstanding matters that still need to be resolved' (2021) 134 *Marine Policy* 104804.

[136] Ronald Reagan, 'Statement on United States Ocean Policy', 1 Pub Papers 378 (10 March 1983), online: www.reaganlibrary.gov/archives/speech/statement-united-states-oceans-policy: '[UNCLOS] contains provisions with respect to traditional uses of the oceans

## 5.6  The Working Group on Space Resources

In August 2020, more than 140 non-governmental experts, including three Nobel Laureates, signed an 'International Open Letter on Space Mining' addressed to the president of the United Nations General Assembly.[137] The concluding paragraph of the letter read,

> It is our opinion that the speed and scale of developments relating to the exploration, exploitation and utilization of space resources require more affirmative and urgent action. The undersigned therefore urge States to present for adoption at the United Nations General Assembly, a resolution which would request UNCOPUOS to negotiate, with all deliberate speed, a draft multilateral agreement on space resource exploration, exploitation and utilization for consideration by the General Assembly.[138]

In May 2021, a proposal to create a 'Working Group on Space Resources' was put before the Legal Subcommittee of COPUOS by eight states: Austria, Belgium, the Czech Republic, Finland, Germany, Greece, Slovakia and Spain.[139] The proposal was based on a recognition of 'the increased interest in activities on celestial bodies in general, and activities involving space resources in particular, and taking into account various initiatives to develop normative instruments applicable to space resources activities, as well as the desire for legal certainty and international cooperation in this regard'.[140] Its stated objective was to 'ensure that space resources activities are conducted in a safe, sustainable and peaceful manner, for the benefit and in the interests of all countries, irrespective of their degree of economic or scientific development, and in accordance with international law.'[141]

which generally confirm existing maritime law and practice and fairly balance the interests of all states'.

[137] Outer Space Institute (OSI), 'International open letter on space mining' (August 2020), *OSI*, online: www.outerspaceinstitute.ca/docs/InternationalOpenLetterOnSpaceMining .pdf. The authors of this book led the initiative and were the first two signatories.

[138] Ibid.

[139] United Nations Office for Outer Space Affairs (UNOOSA), 'Working paper on the establishment of a working group on space resources submitted by Austria, Belgium, Czech Republic, Finland, Germany, Greece, Slovakia and Spain' (27 May 2021), *UNOOSA*, online: www.unoosa.org/documents/pdf/copuos/lsc/space-resources/Non-paper-on-the-Establishment-of-a-Working-Group-on-Space_Resources-at-COPUOS_LSC-27-05-2021 .pdf.

[140] Ibid.

[141] Ibid.

The proposal was supported strongly by the G77 and China. The G77 presently includes 134 states, with the original name of the group being retained as a reminder of the considerable successes of collective bargaining by developing states since 1964. China has long been a de facto member of the G77, with the words 'G77 and China' being used to signal whenever the group and the newest superpower are speaking with one voice. Together, they represent 70 per cent of UN member states, 80 per cent of the world's population, and 25 per cent of global GDP.

In their joint statement, the G77 and China identified the need for a multilateral response to the national laws adopted by the United States, Luxembourg and the UAE, 'to avoid gaps or contradictions in the legal framework in this area and to provide a clear understanding of the legal obligations of the States in the space exploration.'[142] They also stressed the need for international co-operation in the development of Space activities 'for the benefit and in the interest of all States taking in particular account the needs on [sic] developing countries.'[143]

The statement was emphatic on the necessary role of developing states in any normative or legal developments:

> The Group is of the view that the discussions of this Subcommittee should not lead to any measures, including norms, guidelines and standards that would limit access to outer space by nations with emerging space capabilities, especially the developing countries. Accordingly, the Group believes that the international legal framework should be developed in a manner that addresses the concerns of all States. In this regard, the Group emphasizes the need for COPUOS to devote more efforts for legal capacity-building and make the required expertise available to developing countries, facilitated by UNOOSA.[144]

Indonesia, a member of the G77, made a second, parallel statement of its own that included the following two paragraphs:

> Since space resources are located beyond national jurisdiction, the existing international space law and principles shall apply in their exploration, exploitation, and utilization, including but not limited to: non-appropriation, common heritage of [hu]mankind, exclusive use for peaceful purposes, and for the benefits and interests of all countries.
>
> Indonesia encourages principles of equitable access and collaboration on the issue of space resources so that developing countries are not left

---

142 G77 and China, op. cit.
143 Ibid.
144 Ibid.

behind by spacefaring countries, also consider such arrangements must
include the regulation of potential conflicts between space actors.[145]

Russia also supported the creation of the working group. Just one week
after the end of the Legal Subcommittee meeting, Dmitry Rogozin, the
director general of Roscosmos, called for a 'system of regulations' to
address the issue of Space mining at an international level: 'Russia
believes that states mustn't adopt any laws and regulations on a unilateral
basis because space is our common heritage and belongs to everyone. We
consider the United Nations as a suitable [forum] to discuss these
issues.'[146]

With all this support, on 9 June 2021 the Legal Subcommittee of
COPUOS decided 'to establish, under a five-year workplan, a working
group under the agenda item on the general exchange of views on
potential legal models for activities in exploration, exploitation and
utilization of space resources'.[147] Since COPUOS operates based on
consensus, all 95 of its members consented to this decision. On 6 April
2022, the new working group adopted a 'five-year workplan and methods
of work of the working group'; again, this was done on the basis of
consensus, including the United States and Russia – six weeks after the
Russian invasion of Ukraine.[148]


## 5.7   Optimal Multilateral Outcomes

The Working Group on Space Resources and any subsequent multilateral
negotiations could lead to several possible outcomes. The ideal outcome
would be a binding treaty that is widely ratified, including by the major

---

[145] Indonesia, op. cit.
[146] Foust, 'Japan passes space resources law', op. cit.
[147] Legal Subcommittee of the Committee on the Peaceful Uses of Outer Space, *Draft Report – General Exchange of Views on Potential Legal Models for Activities in Exploration, Exploitation and Utilization of Space Resources*, UNGAOR, 60th Sess, UN Doc A/AC.105/C.2/L.314/Add.8 (10 June 2021), online: www.unoosa.org/res/oosadoc/data/documents/2021/aac_105c_2l/aac_105c_2l_314add_8_0_html/AC105_C2_L314Add08E.pdf.
[148] Legal Subcommittee of the Committee on the Peaceful Uses of Outer Space, *Draft Report Annex II: Report of the Chair and Vice-Chair of the Working Group Established under the Legal Subcommittee Agenda Item Entitled 'General Exchange of Views on Potential Legal Models for Activities in the Exploration, Exploitation and Utilization of Space Resources'*, UNGAOR, 61st Sess, UN Doc A/AC.105/C.2/2022/SRA/L.1 (5 April 2022), online: www.unoosa.org/res/oosadoc/data/documents/2022/aac_105c_2sra/aac_105c_22022sral_1_0_html/AC105_C2_2022_SRA_L01E.pdf.

spacefaring states. Such a treaty would build on the Outer Space
Treaty, as the Rescue Agreement, Registration Convention and Liability
Convention did within the issue areas they addressed. As mentioned
above, the 1979 Moon Agreement was a first attempt to create a treaty
providing greater specificity on Space mining; it failed to gain broad
support, due mostly to larger geopolitical issues – including the Soviet
invasion of Afghanistan the following year. However, the widespread
recognition that precipitated those negotiations in the late 1970s – that
a treaty on resource extraction is needed as humanity expands into
Space – is even more widespread and compelling today.

### 5.7.1   Clarifying Existing Obligations

The working group will want to take a broad approach to the issue of
Space mining, one that encompasses all extraction of Space resources,
whether conducted by governmental or non-governmental entities, and
whether for scientific, mission-critical or profit-oriented purposes.
Among the issues that it should address are necessary clarifications to
existing rights and obligations, including:

1 Freedoms in Space and the corresponding restrictions on them, as they
  pertain to resource extraction and use. These freedoms and restrictions
  are prefigured in Articles I and II of the Outer Space Treaty, but with
  Space mining now foreseeable, the time has come for the international
  community to elaborate on them.
2 Limits on the involvement of military personnel and equipment in
  Space resource extraction and use. Article IV of the Outer Space Treaty
  specifies that the Moon and other celestial bodies 'shall be used ...
  exclusively for peaceful purposes' and forbids 'the establishment of
  military bases, installations and fortifications, the testing of any type of
  weapons and the conduct of military manoeuvres on celestial
  bodies.'[149] However, Article IV does permit the use of military personnel 'for scientific research or for any other peaceful purposes', as
  well as the use of 'any equipment or facility necessary for peaceful
  exploration of the moon and other celestial bodies'.[150]
3 The obligation to ensure that 'national activities' carried out by 'non-
  governmental entities' are conducted in accordance with international

---

[149] Outer Space Treaty, Art. IV.
[150] Ibid.

law. Article VI of the Outer Space Treaty states, 'The activities of non-governmental entities in outer space, including the moon and other celestial bodies, shall require authorization and continuing supervision by the appropriate State Party to the Treaty.'[151] With Space mining now foreseeable, detailed requirements for the authorisation and supervision of companies and other non-state actors are needed to prevent or mitigate the many risks identified above.

4 The obligation of 'due regard'. Under Article IX of the Outer Space Treaty, states are required to 'conduct all their activities in outer space, including the moon and other celestial bodies, with due regard to the corresponding interests of all other States Parties to the Treaty'.[152] With Space mining now foreseeable, clarification is needed as to the level of care required. Is the obligation only to avoid reasonably foreseeable harm? Or does 'due regard' require the application of the 'precautionary principle'?

### 5.7.2   Applying the Precautionary Principle

The precautionary principle was set out in Principle 15 of the 1992 Rio Declaration:

> In order to protect the environment, the precautionary approach shall be widely applied by States according to their capabilities. Where there are threats of serious or irreversible damage, lack of full scientific certainty shall not be used as a reason for postponing cost-effective measures to prevent environmental degradation.[153]

Today, the precautionary principle is central to numerous treaties, including most recently the 2018 Central Arctic Ocean Fisheries Agreement to which the United States, Russia, China and the European Union are all parties.[154] This treaty prohibits all commercial fishing in the central Arctic Ocean until scientific research establishes that a sustainable fishery can take place.

---

[151] Outer Space Treaty, Art. VI.
[152] Outer Space Treaty, Art. IX.
[153] United Nations Conference on Environment and Development, *Rio Declaration on Environment and Development*, UNGAOR, UN Doc A/CONF.151/26 (Vol. I) (12 August 1992), Principle 15, online: www.un.org/en/development/desa/population/migration/gen eralassembly/docs/globalcompact/A_CONF.151_26_Vol.I_Declaration.pdf.
[154] Agreement to Prevent Unregulated High Seas Fisheries in the Central Arctic Ocean.

The precautionary principle has also become part of customary international law, even if the precise content of the principle remains a subject of debate. As Patricia Birnie and Alan Boyle explained two decades ago:

> Use by national and international courts, by international organizations, and in treaties, shows that the precautionary principle does have a legally important core on which there is international consensus – that in performing their obligations of environmental protection and sustainable use of natural resources states cannot rely on scientific uncertainty to justify inaction where there is enough evidence to establish the possibility of a risk of serious harm, even if there is as yet no proof of harm.[155]

Some of the main objections to the precautionary principle are that it is inherently unscientific because it requires action (for instance, regulatory action), or in some cases inaction (for instance, a moratorium on mining in a particular area), before certainty has been obtained, and thus it impedes progress. However, dealing with uncertainty is at the very heart of science, and making decisions based on identified and characterised uncertainty is not the same as making decisions based on conjecture. Nor does the principle require inaction except in grave circumstances; more often, it simply slows activities down so that uncertainties can be properly assessed.

Just as importantly, the precautionary principle (as set out in the Rio Declaration) calls for 'cost-effective' measures when science, with its uncertainty, identifies activities that are causing serious or irreversible damage. As humanity seeks to exploit other worlds for resources, let us be cognisant that we, as a species, might not know what we think we know, and acknowledge that there is far more about Space that we do not understand than that which we do. This is true even for the Moon.

Applying the precautionary principle to Space mining would make scientific assessments of risk necessary prior to any significant activity, including risks to materials of interest to science, risks associated with dust and debris, and risks to Earth and other celestial bodies. Sampling, for science or prospecting purposes, should be permitted, but always also used to inform risk assessment. The risks associated with dust and debris and asteroid trajectory alterations will require strict standards from the outset, at least until these risks become better understood and can be reassessed – not the other way around.

---

[155] Patricia Birnie and Alan Boyle, *International Law and the Environment*, 2nd ed (Oxford: Oxford University Press, 2002) 120.

Applying the precautionary principle would also require an acceptance that Space mining operations cannot be allowed to proceed in the face of an unfavourable risk assessment. That said, an operator should be allowed to rework a proposal and have it re-evaluated through a second risk assessment. The goal is not to prevent Space mining, but to make it safer and more sustainable – and therefore a success in the long term.

## 5.8   A New Multilateral Treaty

A new multilateral treaty could be based on a draft treaty text produced by the Working Group on Space Resources, which would be debated, amended and adopted by the Legal Subcommittee of COPUOS, and then forwarded to COPUOS as a whole and then to the First Committee of the United Nations General Assembly. Ultimately, the treaty would be adopted by a General Assembly resolution, at which point it would be open to states for signature and ratification. Now, it is possible that states might decide to adopt an instrument arising from this process as simply a non-binding General Assembly resolution and not proceed to then elevate its status to a binding multilateral treaty. Such an outcome would not constitute a failure. For the resolution could still influence state behaviour and contribute to customary international law, as Bin Cheng famously explained regarding the General Assembly resolutions on Space adopted in 1961 and 1963.[156] It could also smooth the path to an eventual treaty, perhaps not so very far in the future. Indeed, the adoption of those 1961 and 1963 resolutions provided a firm basis for the negotiation and adoption of the OST just a few short years later.

Alternatively, if it should prove impossible to achieve the consensus required within COPUOS, a treaty on Space mining could be advanced in the form of a protocol to the OST, with negotiations and voting taking place among the parties. Such a protocol would not automatically bind the parties; they would each have to ratify it, just as with a standalone treaty. For the same reason, such an approach would not require the support of each party, which could make it easier for progress to be achieved. A third way forward could involve ad hoc negotiations outside

---

[156] Bin Cheng, 'United Nations resolutions on outer space: "Instant" international customary law?' (1965) 5 *Indian Journal of International Law* 23. See both the 1961 International Cooperation in the Peaceful Uses of Outer Space and the 1963 Declaration of Legal Principles Governing the Activities of States in the Exploration and Use of Outer Space, op. cit.

any existing forum, as occurred for the Anti-personnel Landmines and Cluster Munitions conventions.[157]


## 5.9   Conclusion

Multilateral governance takes time and requires compromise, but it also helps to internalise externalities by solving 'collective-action' problems through scientifically grounded, widely agreed and implemented practices. Multilateral governance can also ensure a form of peer review with respect to the proposed actions of individual governments. To protect the Earth and its natural and cultural heritage, as well as Space, the Moon and other celestial bodies, we need rules that bind all space-faring states and companies. Such rules must take full account of astrophysical realities and their long timescales.

This latter point may be one of the most difficult hurdles on the way to sustainable and effective Space governance, as the effects of activities set in motion today could take a century or more to manifest. A particular danger concerns the demand for strictly data-driven approaches, rather than multifaceted approaches that are not driven solely by data but also seek input from models and analogues – such as terrestrial mining, deep seabed mining, high-seas fishing and the mix of national and international regulatory regimes that have been developed for them. A strictly data-driven approach and the resulting absence of strong changes or clear thresholds might prompt policy makers to continually defer regulatory action – until it is too late. It would be like climate change policy, but with even greater uncertainties and longer timescales.

The US-led effort to secure widespread acceptance that property rights may be acquired over extracted Space resources, and to develop rules and practices in support of commercial Space mining, is unlikely to succeed. As discussed above, the Artemis Accords have to date received support from only 21 of the 112 parties to the OST, with most of those states agreeing only to a 'political commitment', further qualified by the

---

[157] Timothea Turnbull, 'Prestige, power, principles and pay-off: Middle powers negotiating international conventional weapons treaties' (2022) 76:1 *Australian Journal of International Affairs* 98; Convention on the Prohibition of the Use, Stockpiling, Production and Transfer of Anti-personnel Mines and on Their Destruction, 18 September 1997, 2056 UNTS 211 (entered into force 1 March 1999); Convention on Cluster Munitions, 30 May 2008, 2688 UNTS 39 (entered into force 1 August 2010).

ambiguous statement 'the extraction of space resources does not inherently constitute national appropriation'.

None of this is sufficient for success because subsequent practice can only change the accepted interpretation of a treaty provision if it demonstrates the 'agreement of the parties'. Changes to customary international law likewise require widespread consent, which can be withheld through physical action as well as written or verbal statements. For these reasons, it is possible for other states to block changes to the accepted interpretation of a treaty provision or to the development or change of a rule of customary international law. Indeed, the redirection of the Space mining issue into a new Working Group on Space Resources is the immediate outcome of the Global South becoming involved in this matter, most notably through the statement issued by the G77 and China.

It is also significant that the United States, under the newly elected president Joe Biden, joined China and Russia in supporting the creation of this working group. It remains to be seen whether the result will be a draft treaty, a draft resolution or simply a final report. Regardless of the outcome, it matters that a multilateral discussion involving all the major spacefaring states is now under way.

# 6

## Planetary Defence

### 6.1 Introduction

This book was written in two locations in British Columbia, Canada. The first was on Salt Spring Island, against a background of birdsong from the neighbourhood robins, finches, warblers and the occasional pileated woodpecker. The second was on an oceanside bluff in Tsawwassen, south of Vancouver, where the chatter of bald eagles was constantly present. Both woodpeckers and eagles are formidable creatures, and for good reason. Modern birds are in fact dinosaurs, with the avian dinosaurs having survived a cataclysmic collision between the Earth and an asteroid with a diameter of about 10 kilometres some 66 million years ago. All other dinosaurs, the non-avian ones, either perished in the resulting firestorms or starved to death during the ensuing years of 'impact winter'.

Today, the field of 'planetary defence' involves the detection, characterisation, risk assessment and, if necessary, deflection or destruction of asteroids and comets that have the potential to strike Earth. Throughout its history, Earth has frequently been struck by such leftover 'planetesimals'. These remaining planetary building blocks formed from metals, rocks and ice that condensed and coalesced in the solar nebula – the disc of dust and gas that surrounded the nascent Sun. Impacts from asteroids and comets have served as an ongoing geological process, with almost 200 confirmed impact craters on Earth today (see Figure 6.1).

Fortunately, most Earth impactors are meteoroids and interplanetary dust. According to the International Astronomical Union definition, meteoroids range from 30 microns to one metre in diameter. These objects burn up harmlessly at high altitudes in Earth's atmosphere, producing a bright flash of light called a meteor. Interplanetary dust particles are also harmless because of their size – less than 30 microns. Curiously, this small size also enables them to survive atmospheric re-entry, because their large surface-area-to-mass ratio radiates away

**Figure 6.1** Lake Manicouagan was created by a five-kilometre-diameter asteroid approximately 214 million years ago. Located in Quebec, Canada, it is approximately 100 kilometres across, with the reservoir ring being approximately 70 kilometres across. This image was taken by the European Space Agency's Sentinel-2 satellite.

frictional heat. Interplanetary dust particles are found everywhere on Earth, including in our bodies and on the pages of this book. At the other end of the scale, objects larger than one metre in diameter are considered small asteroids, but this is a very imprecise definition. Sometimes, any natural body entering Earth's atmosphere is referred to as a meteoroid.

Each year, dozens of small asteroids with diameters greater than one metre strike Earth, exploding harmlessly in the upper atmosphere with energies of less than a few kilotons of TNT. Figure 6.2 depicts all such 'airbursts' detected by US government sensors over a 34-year period. Additional strikes would have escaped detection, especially if they occurred over the oceans. Only one of the airbursts depicted on the map caused injuries to people.

The larger the impactor, the longer the typical timescale between impact events. However, this is a 'stochastic process': statistically analysable but still random. Although the average time between strikes causing widespread damage is measured in tens of thousands of years, nothing precludes a major strike this century.

In 2013, a meteoroid about 19 metres in diameter exploded at an altitude of about 30 kilometres above the Russian city of Chelyabinsk, which is in the middle of the red dot in Figure 6.2. The resulting airburst

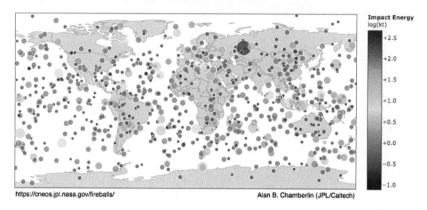

**Figure 6.2**　Alan B Chamberlin, 'Fireball and bolide data: Fireballs reported by US government sensors (1988-Apr-15 to 2022-Apr-21)', (April 2022), *Center for Near Earth Object Studies*, online: cneos.jpl.nasa.gov/fireballs. A fireball is a very bright meteor, reaching a brightness comparable to that of the planet Venus, while a bolide is a bright fireball that explodes.

had an energy equivalent to about 500 kilotons.[1] It blew out windows, caused minor structural damage to buildings, and sent over 1,000 people to hospital, most of them injured by shattered glass after they rushed to windows to observe the bright flash in the sky.[2] The airburst over Chelyabinsk was the first confirmed Earth impact in recorded history to cause a significant number of injuries. While objects of such size strike our planet on average once every handful of decades, they had – until 2013 – never done so over a populated city.[3] A slightly larger asteroid, just 30 metres or more, could cause serious damage to a large city.

---

[1] Peter G Brown, Jelle D Assink, Luciana Astiz, Rhiannon Blaauw, Mark B Boslough, Jiří Borovička, N Brachet, D Brown, M Campbell-Brown, L Ceranna and WD Cooke, 'A 500-kiloton airburst over Chelyabinsk and an enhanced hazard from small impactors' (2013) 503:7475 *Nature* 238.

[2] Ellen Barry and Andrew E Kramer, 'Shock wave of fireball meteor rattles Siberia, injuring 1,200', *New York Times* (15 February 2013), online: nytimes.com/2013/02/16/world/europe/meteorite-fragments-are-said-to-rain-down-on-siberia.html.

[3] The historical record is persuasive but inconclusive concerning the 'Ch'ing-yang event' of 1490, which occurred over the city of Qingyang in northwest China. According to some

In 1908, the so-called 'Tunguska event' levelled over 2,000 square kilometres of Siberian forest and probably involved an asteroid that was 50 to 70 metres in diameter.[4] More worrying, but less likely, would be an asteroid with a diameter above 140 metres that could devastate an entire region. Events like this can be expected about once every 30,000 years. Strikes from larger asteroids, with diameters above 1,000 metres, only occur about once every 500,000 years.

The perceived threat from asteroids and other 'near-Earth objects' (NEOs) like comets is often overblown. Journalists regularly report about upcoming 'near misses' that in fact pose no impact risk to Earth. They do so, in part, because the vast distances between Space objects can be confusing. In April 2020, the Internet was abuzz with reports of an upcoming near miss by an asteroid with a diameter of between two and four kilometres.[5] There was some excited newspaper reporting also, though most newspapers did at least mention that the asteroid would miss Earth – by 6.3 million kilometres,[6] which is about 16 times the distance between Earth and the Moon, or 1,000 times the distance between New York City and Berlin.

As international lawyer James Green explains, this 'asteroid paranoia' makes it 'easy to dismiss calamitous NEO impact as a concern that should be reserved for science fiction fans and conspiracy theorists'.[7] It probably does not help that astronomers categorise all objects that pass within 1.3 astronomical units of the Sun as NEOs. An 'astronomical unit'

---

reports, thousands of people were struck dead by a shower of small rocks that may have been fragments from an asteroid or comet.

[4] David Morrison, 'Tunguska workshop: Applying modern tools to understand the 1908 Tunguska impact' (December 2018) NASA Ames Research Center, NASA Technical Memorandum 220174, *NASA*, online: ntrs.nasa.gov/citations/20190002302.

[5] Surabhi Sabat, 'Fact check: Will an asteroid really hit Earth on April 29, 2020?', *Republic World* (31 March 2020), online: www.republicworld.com/fact-check/coronavirus/fact-check-will-asteroid-really-hit-earth-on-april-29.html.

[6] See e.g. Sebastian Kettely, 'Asteroid news: A 4km rock will zip past Earth this month – astronomers can already see it', *Daily Express* (10 April 2020), online: www.express.co.uk/news/science/1267536/Asteroid-news-4km-asteroid-Earth-close-approach-NASA-NEO; Jack Hobbs, 'Huge asteroid 52768 to fly by Earth the morning of April 29', *New York Post* (28 April 2020), online: nypost.com/2020/04/28/huge-asteroid-passing-earth-morning-of-april-29.

[7] James A Green, 'Planetary defense: Near-Earth objects, nuclear weapons, and international law' (2019) 42 *Hastings International and Comparative Law Review* 1 at 6; citing Evan R Seamone, 'When wishing on a star just won't do: The legal basis for international cooperation in the mitigation of asteroid impacts and similar transboundary disasters' (2002) 87 *Iowa Law Review* 1091 at 1108–11.

(au) is the semi-major axis (i.e. one-half of the longest axis) of Earth's elliptical orbit around the Sun.[8] This characteristic distance is 149.6 million kilometres, which is about 389 times the distance between Earth and the Moon (i.e. a 'lunar distance'), or 23,400 times the distance between New York City and Berlin.

But, as the dinosaurs discovered, large asteroids do strike the planet from time to time. With steady population growth and rapid urbanisation, which have resulted today in over 30 'mega-cities' with more than 10 million inhabitants, our vulnerability to large impactors continues to increase.[9] As with other low-probability, high-consequence events such as large earthquakes and global pandemics, preparing for NEO threats is good public policy. NEO threats are more like pandemics than they are like earthquakes, in that an Earth impact is potentially preventable – if the threat is detected early, a deflection capability has been prepared and action is taken quickly.

## 6.2    Detection

Good public policy begins with detection. Approximately 23,000 NEOs have been identified so far, with the detection of objects one kilometre in diameter or larger likely being nearly complete (i.e. well above 90 per cent) (see Figure 6.3). However, it is estimated that only about 30 per cent of NEOs with diameters between 140 metres and one kilometre have been identified. An even smaller fraction of NEOs of less than 140 metres will have been detected so far.

There are numerous efforts under way to detect and catalogue more NEOs, with the most significant ones being funded by the United States' National Aeronautics and Space Administration (NASA). The Pan-STARRS Project, located on a mountaintop in Hawaii, devotes 90 per cent of its time to NEO detection.[10] NASA also supports the Catalina Sky Survey, which operates from Arizona.[11] Then there is the Asteroid

---

[8]  Perhaps more simply, it is the average of the Earth's closest distance to the Sun (perihelion) and its farthest distance from the Sun (aphelion).

[9]  Joseph N Pelton, 'Global space governance and planetary defense mechanisms', in Nikola Schmidt, ed., *Planetary Defense: Global Space Collaboration for Saving Earth from Asteroids and Comets* (Cham: Springer, 2019) 339 at 348.

[10]  NASA Science Mission Directorate, 'Pan-STARRS across the sky' (5 April 2019), *NASA*, online: science.nasa.gov/pan-starrs-across-sky.

[11]  University of Arizona Lunar and Planetary Laboratory, 'Catalina sky survey' (2022), online: catalina.lpl.arizona.edu.

Terrestrial-Impact Last Alert System (ATLAS), a robotic early-warning system designed to detect smaller NEOs in the weeks or days before they impact Earth. Using two 0.5-metre telescopes located on Hawaiian mountaintops 160 kilometres apart, ATLAS provides repeat coverage of the observable sky on an almost nightly basis.[12]

Outside the United States, the Instituto de Astrofísica de Canarias hosts dozens of international telescopes on two mountaintops in the Canary Islands, several of which contribute to NEO detection as part of the International Asteroid Warning Network – as will be discussed below. Numerous other observatories also contribute globally, while additional capability will soon be provided by the Vera C. Rubin Observatory (previously known as the Large Synoptic Survey Telescope) under construction in Chile. It will be able to detect about 60 per cent of NEOs larger than 140 metres in diameter.[13] The Vera C. Rubin Observatory will also greatly help to address the shortage of NEO surveys providing coverage of the southern hemisphere sky. The same shortage explains why NASA is funding two additional telescopes for ATLAS, which will likewise be located in the southern hemisphere.[14]

Asteroids approaching Earth from the direction of the Sun can be difficult to spot, though this challenge can be addressed with Space-based sensors. In 2009, NASA's Wide-Field Infrared Survey Explorer (WISE) was launched to detect 'minor planets' – another term for asteroids and comets. But just two years later, the spacecraft was placed in hibernation after the frozen hydrogen used to cool the telescope was depleted. Then, in 2013, WISE was reactivated and renamed NEOWISE to reflect a new approach to its mission. Using its two shortest-wavelength detectors, it has since made more than 993,000 infrared measurements of 37,161 different Solar System objects, including 1,145 NEOs and 198 comets.[15] In July 2020, a long-period comet became visible to the naked eye from Earth, delighting sky watchers. The comet was named after NEOWISE,

[12] University of Hawaii Institute for Astronomy, 'Asteroid Terrestrial-Impact Last Alert System (ATLAS): How it works' (2020), *ATLAS*, online: atlas.fallingstar.com/how_atlas_works.php.

[13] NASA Planetary Defense Coordination Office, 'Planetary defense frequently asked questions' (22 April 2019), *NASA*, online: www.nasa.gov/planetarydefense/faq.

[14] Traci Watson, 'Project that spots city-killing asteroid expands to southern hemisphere', *Nature* (14 August 2018), online: www.nature.com/articles/d41586-018-05969-2.

[15] Infrared Processing and Analysis Center, 'The NEOWISE project: Finding, tracking and characterizing asteroids' (23 March 2022), *California Institute of Technology*, online: neowise.ipac.caltech.edu.

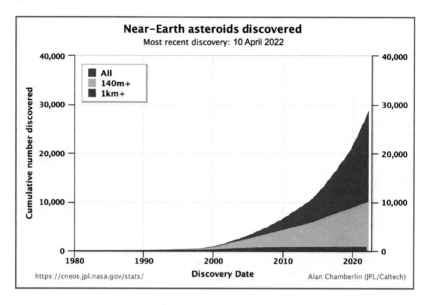

**Figure 6.3**  Near-Earth asteroid discovery plot, cumulative over time. The upward slope is due to the completeness of catalogued objects still being low for smaller bodies.

which had detected it just four months earlier. Around 2025, NEOWISE will be replaced with the Near-Earth Object Surveillance Mission (NEOSM), a 0.5-metre Space-based telescope that will operate in the infrared spectrum and be able to detect 'dark asteroids' – asteroids with low albedo (reflectivity) that are almost impossible to detect with optical telescopes but may be quite common.[16]

Another challenge concerns NEOs approaching from the opposite direction to the Sun, because they often do not show large sky motion relative to the stars. Such NEOs are often detected late, providing little time for a response. On 24 July 2019, the asteroid 2019 OK was detected when it was just 1.5 million kilometres away from Earth. One day later, it passed within 65,000 kilometres, which is just 0.17 of the distance between Earth and the Moon.[17] Travelling at around 24 kilometres per

---

[16] Paul Voosen, 'NASA to build telescope for detecting asteroids that threaten Earth', *Science* (23 September 2019), online: www.sciencemag.org/news/2019/09/nasa-build-tele scope-detecting-asteroids-threaten-earth.

[17] NASA Center for Near Earth Object Studies, 'Largest asteroid to pass this close to Earth in a century' (6 August 2019), *NASA*, online: cneos.jpl.nasa.gov/news/news203.html.

second, and with a diameter of between 57 and 130 metres, an asteroid this size could kill millions of people if it struck a large city.

Satellites also pose challenges to NEO detection, particularly mega-constellations such as Starlink – as discussed in Chapters 2 and 3. Sunlight reflecting off satellites creates light pollution for optical tele-scopes, while the heat signature of the satellites could create a similar problem for infrared telescopes. In both instances, the possible misiden-tification of satellites is not the primary concern. Rather, satellite streaks across images can render some of the data unusable, with multiple streaks having greater effects. Particularly bright satellites can cause 'artefacts' (disruptions of the astronomical data) across the entire detector. All these effects will frustrate NEO detection searches.

Refining the orbital uncertainties of known NEOs is also a primary concern, particularly if the object in question has a small 'minimum orbital intersection distance' (MOID) with Earth. To visualise a MOID, imagine two elliptical orbits as curves in Space, one representing Earth's orbit and the other an NEO's orbit. The smallest distance between the curves is the MOID (Figure 6.4). This does not represent, in general, the closest that Earth and the NEO will ever get, as their orbital phases matter (i.e. they will not necessarily arrive at the MOID at the same time). But it does highlight the potential for a close encounter. An NEO is classified as 'potentially hazardous' if it has a size larger than 140 metres and a MOID of less than 0.05 au (7.5 million kilometres, or about 20 times the distance between Earth and the Moon).[18] Many large asteroids pass harmlessly by Earth at distances much closer than this threshold. Such close encounters can, however, alter the MOID and thus the risk of a future impact.

Determining the MOID for Earth and a given NEO is one factor in calculating collision risks. But even if the MOID is essentially zero, i.e. the orbits do directly cross, this does not mean that there will be a collision in the foreseeable future. As noted above, a collision may only occur if Earth and the asteroid arrive at a sufficiently small MOID at the same time. Thus the detailed positions and movements of Earth and the asteroid are critical to evaluating the actual collision risk, which must be measured.

---

[18] NASA Center for Near Earth Object Studies, 'NEO basics' (2022), *NASA*, online: cneos.jpl.nasa.gov/about/neo_groups.html.

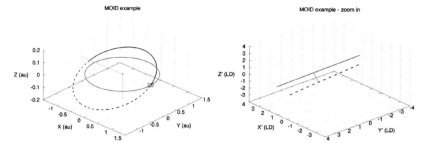

**Figure 6.4**    Visualisation of the minimum orbital intersection distance (MOID) between a Bennu-like asteroid orbit and Earth. The left panel shows the full view of the orbits, with Earth (blue curve) lying in the $X$–$Y$ plane and the Sun at the centre, indicated by the orange dot. The co-ordinates are in astronomical units (au). The asteroid is shown with the black curve. The solid portion depicts the orbit section that is above Earth's orbital plane, and the dashed section shows the section below. The projection alone gives the impression that the orbits intersect twice, even though they do not. The pink box highlights where the MOID occurs. The right panel shows a zoomed-in region of the MOID. The units are now in lunar distances (LD) and are arbitrarily centred. The primes are used to denote that the co-ordinate centre is different from the left panel. The short purple line segment is the MOID itself, i.e. the closest the two orbits ever come to each other. In this example, the MOID is about 0.003 au (just slightly larger than one LD). They appear closer at negative $Y'$ due to projection effects, with the black dashed curve crossing under the blue curve.

However, observations and measurements of an asteroid always come with uncertainties,[19] which means that there will always be uncertainty in our knowledge of the actual orbit of the asteroid. As a consequence, the impact risk is given as a probability, which might be low enough to suggest that an impact is essentially ruled out, or high enough to cause concern. An impact can only be predicted with certainty if the orbit of the potential impactor is very well known, which often is only the case just weeks or months before the actual impact. Dedicated observation campaigns could add years to this warning time. In addition, the evolution of orbits also needs to be considered. Although most asteroids identified as potential threats are eventually proven to be harmless once their trajectories have been precisely determined, constant vigilance is required. Gravitational effects from the planets can cause changes in

---

[19] Uncertainties in a measurement can result from a variety of factors, including physical constraints and limitations of the calibrations and detector performance.

asteroid trajectories over time, with Earth and Mars playing a major role for NEOs. Even the gravitational effects of some of the major asteroids could make the subtle difference between a collision and a close call.[20] Orbital changes can even be caused by micrometeoroid collisions,[21] asteroid surface activity, and the minute amounts of force transmitted by photons.[22] The last of these is possible because light carries momentum, with shorter wavelengths carrying more momentum than longer ones. For example, a rotating asteroid has a morning side that is cooler, and an afternoon side that is hotter due to the 'day'-long effects of solar heating. The hotter side will give off more short-wavelength radiation, and thus more momentum, than the cooler side. In this way, light behaves like a rocket impulse, and this so-called 'Yarkovsky effect' can move an asteroid away from or towards the Sun, i.e. grow or shrink the asteroid's orbital semi-major axis, depending on the direction of its rotation. Because of these perturbing forces, an accurate prediction of the impact risk of an object is usually only attempted for 100 years into the future.

For all these reasons, radar is used whenever asteroids pass close to Earth to provide more accurate assessments of their orbit, size and composition.[23] This information helps to determine whether subsequent flybys pose risks and, if so, what deflection method might work best. Information from radar proved to be critical in the determination that the 340-metre-diameter asteroid Apophis will not pose an impact risk for at least the next century.[24] In the future, potentially dangerous asteroids could be tagged with radio beacons, or have small spacecraft orbiting them or conducting frequent flybys. This would enable more precise studies of the asteroids' orbits and the various factors that influence them.

---

[20] Steven R Chesley, Davide Farnocchia, Michael C Nolan, David Vokrouhlický, Paul W Chodas, Andrea Milani, Federica Spoto, B Rozitis, LA Benner, WF Bottke and MW Busch, 'Orbit and bulk density of the OSIRIS-REx target Asteroid (101955) Bennu' (2014) 235 *Icarus* 5.

[21] Paul A Wiegert, 'Meteoroid impacts onto asteroids: A competitor for Yarkovsky and YORP' (2015) 252 *Icarus* 22.

[22] William F Bottke Jr, David Vokrouhlický, David P Rubincam and David Nesvorný, 'The Yarkovsky and YORP effects: Implications for asteroid dynamics' (2006) 34 *Annual Review of Earth and Planetary Sciences* 157.

[23] NASA Center for Near Earth Object Studies, 'NASA scientists use radar to detect asteroid force' (5 December 2003), *NASA*, online: cneos.jpl.nasa.gov/news/news141.html.

[24] NASA Center for Near Earth Object Studies, 'Earth is safe from asteroid Apophis for 100-plus years' (25 March 2021), *NASA*, online: www.jpl.nasa.gov/news/nasa-analysis-earth-is-safe-from-asteroid-apophis-for-100-plus-years.

In the next decade, we can expect over 50 asteroids with diameters greater than 100 metres to pass within ten lunar distances of Earth, a handful of which are in the 1,000-metre range.[25] Fortunately, the positions and orbits of these asteroids are fairly well established – and none of them poses any risk to us in this century. At some future time, however, we will likely discover a large asteroid on an Earth impact trajectory, at which point the mission will change from detection to deflection.

### 6.3   Deflection

If an impending Earth impact is discovered early enough, a deflection might be possible. Deflecting an asteroid involves slightly altering its orbit by perturbing its velocity, with astrodynamicists referring to a change in velocity as $\Delta v$, pronounced 'delta-v'. The most effective way to perturb an asteroid (or indeed any orbiting object) is to apply the $\Delta v$ along or against its orbital track, as opposed to perpendicular to it. For small perturbations, this can be thought of as a matter of timing, so that the asteroid's close approach is advanced or delayed, thus allowing Earth to be out of the way. To understand why this is the case, we need to briefly consider one of the fundamental concepts of planetary dynamics: Kepler's third law. By painstakingly going through Tycho Brahe's records of meticulous naked-eye planet observations, Johannes Kepler discovered that planets orbit in ellipses about the Sun and that the period, $P$, of the orbit is proportional to the semi-major axis, $a$, of the planet's orbital ellipse raised to the 3/2 power:

$$P \propto a^{\frac{3}{2}}.$$

Because the absolute distances between planets were not known at the time, Kepler scaled everything relative to Earth's orbit. An object that has a semi-major axis of four aus orbits the Sun in eight years, regardless of how eccentric the orbit might be. Kepler did not know why planets behaved in this way – it took Newton's law of gravitation and laws of physics to explain why – but his discoveries were a major feat of astronomy and data science.

[25] NASA Center for Near Earth Object Studies, 'NEO Earth close approaches' (2022), *NASA*, online: cneos.jpl.nasa.gov/ca.

It turns out that nudging an asteroid with a $\Delta v$ will also change the semi-major axis of that asteroid by a small amount. If the semi-major axis is increased, then the period is also increased. If it is decreased, the period is decreased. It is important to emphasise that the overall orbit remains essentially the same. For the purposes of planetary defence, the goal of deflection is to change the rate at which the asteroid goes around the Sun, so that after years, the small timing difference between the old and new periods amounts to spatial differences on a planetary scale, and a miss.

It is instructive to have a sense of the magnitude of $\Delta v$ needed for any given deflection. To do this, we need to introduce another concept called the B-plane, or body plane. Consider an asteroid's close approach as seen from Earth. If, for the moment, we ignore Earth's gravity, we can imagine that, during the flyby, the asteroid's trajectory is approximately a line passing by Earth. We can next imagine a plane that passes through the centre of the Earth and is oriented such that the line (asteroid trajectory) intersects the plane at 90° (in other words, the trajectory is normal to the plane).

The degree to which a potential impactor threatens Earth can be assessed by the object's passage through the B-plane, as well as whether the uncertainty of the orbit (down to some threshold) overlaps Earth. For example, the nominal (best-fit) orbit might clearly miss Earth, but for a very uncertain orbit there might be a 1 per cent chance that the asteroid hits Earth – based on the current knowledge of the dynamics. As we refine our knowledge of the orbit through additional observations, we hope to see the probability of an impact event drop to a level where it can be ruled out. However, it might also be the case that, as the orbit is refined, the possibility of an impact collapses to 100 per cent and motivates action.

If we want to move the location of the asteroid's closest approach on the B-plane by one Earth radius, the necessary $\Delta v$ perturbation along or against track can be estimated by considering the change in orbital rates due to the perturbation, yielding[26]

$$\Delta v = \frac{3.5 \ \frac{cm}{s}}{T_{yr}}$$

where $T_{yr}$ is the 'lead time' in years, i.e. the time between the closest approach and when the $\Delta v$ is applied. For comparison, the orbital speed for something going around the Sun at one au (again, an astronomical

[26] Steven R Chesley and Timothy B Spahr, 'Earth impactors: Orbital characteristics and warning time', in Michael JS Belton et al., eds., *Mitigation of Hazardous Comets and Asteroids* (Cambridge: Cambridge University Press, 2004) 22.

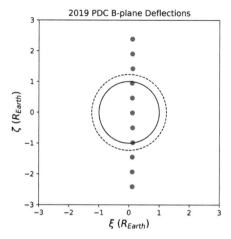

**Figure 6.5** B-plane showing simulation results of different deflection scenarios for the hypothetical impactor 2019 PDC. The B-plane co-ordinates are in units of Earth radii. The solid circle represents the cross section of Earth, and the dashed line is Earth's effective cross section when including gravitational focusing. Each point represents where the hypothetical 2019 PDC passed through the B-plane – if the point is within the dashed circle, then the impactor would have hit Earth. The central point represents no deflection attempt. Starting from the uppermost point moving downward, the deflections used are $\Delta v$ = –10, –8, –6, –4, –2, 0, 2, 4, 6, 8, 10 millimetres per second. Each $\Delta v$ was applied 7.7 years before the potential impact, with the results roughly consistent with the approximate relation in the text. Figure produced in collaboration with Edmond Ng.

unit is the semi-major axis of Earth's orbit) is about 30 kilometres per second. The longer the lead time, the greater the effect the small perturbation will have. And the shorter the lead time, the greater the perturbation needed to avoid an Earth impact.[27]

The Center for NEO Studies at NASA's Jet Propulsion Laboratory periodically releases impact scenarios for tabletop exercises.[28] The hypothetical impactor in the 2019 scenario discussed at the 2019 Planetary Defense Conference was called asteroid 2019 PDC. Figure 6.5 shows the results of

[27] The Center for NEO Studies has released a 'deflection app' to demonstrate some of these features. See Center for Near Earth Object Studies, 'NASA/JPL NEO deflection app' (2017), *NASA*, online: cneos.jpl.nasa.gov/nda.

[28] NASA Center for Near Earth Object Studies, 'Hypothetical impact scenarios' (2022), *NASA*, online: cneos.jpl.nasa.gov/pd/cs.

executing different $\Delta v$'s (each case only uses one $\Delta v$) along or against the orbital track 7.7 years before the hypothetical impact by 2019 PDC.

Presently, the two most feasible methods for perturbing an asteroid's velocity are kinetic impactors and nuclear explosive devices (NEDs). However, other methods exist and might be possible, such as ion beams, lasers, mass drivers (essentially, asteroid-mining machines) and 'gravity tractors'.[29]

### 6.3.1    Kinetic Impactors

A kinetic impactor works by transferring momentum from the spacecraft's motion to the target asteroid through a collision, which also causes secondary momentum 'kicks' through debris ejection during crater formation. Momentum is a conserved property in physics that depends on an object's mass and velocity. Like velocity, momentum is a vector quantity, meaning it has a magnitude ('how much') and a direction.[30] The overall effect of the kinetic impactor will depend on the total amount of momentum change imparted onto the asteroid and the direction in which the momentum change is applied relative to the asteroid's current motion.

To develop this idea further, first consider the effect of the spacecraft's collision alone. For simplicity, we only consider the case of a spacecraft hitting the asteroid directly along or against the asteroid's instantaneous direction of motion (i.e. its track).

Modelling the collision such that the spacecraft's momentum is perfectly absorbed by the asteroid, we can write the change in the asteroid's velocity immediately after the impact as

$$\Delta v = v_r \frac{m_{sc}}{m_{astr}}$$

---

[29] Edward T Lu and Stanley G Love, 'Gravitational tractor for towing asteroids' (2005) 438:7065 *Nature* 177.

[30] If you are not used to thinking about vectors, then consider velocity as a conceptual reference. Your velocity is your speed and direction of motion. Changing either your speed or your direction of motion requires an acceleration applied through a force. Note that you can move at a constant speed, but have your velocity continuously change, such as being in a turn. Extending this to momentum for most situations is straightforward. But because momentum is mass times velocity, a momentum change can be due to a change in mass or a change in velocity or both. Forces cause changes in momentum, and forces can be applied instantaneously, drawn out, or somewhere in between.

for asteroid mass $m_{astr}$, spacecraft mass $m_{sc}$, and spacecraft velocity relative to the asteroid $v_r$. The direction of the change is governed by the direction of $v_r$, with the against motion being represented by a negative value for the spacecraft's relative velocity.

The spacecraft's mass will be much smaller than the asteroid's mass, making very high-velocity impacts necessary for even modest deflections. Fortunately, as we saw above, even small changes can have a large effect when given enough time. Moreover, the momentum imparted onto the asteroid is larger than that given by the spacecraft alone. This is because the high speeds of the collision will result in a cratering event, causing the ejection of asteroid material during crater formation. The mass loss due to cratering provides a rocket-reaction-like 'kick' on the asteroid itself. Assuming the ejecta is released predominantly in the direction opposite to that taken by the incoming spacecraft, the crater ejecta enhances the overall $\Delta v$. However, it is also possible that waves will propagate through the asteroid and cause mass to be lost on the side opposite the impact, which would work against the desired momentum change and reduce the overall $\Delta v$.

Cratering effects in the kinetic impact method are taken into account using a parameterised approach, modifying the equation above by including an additional factor:

$$\Delta v = \beta v_r \frac{m_{sc}}{m_{astr}},$$

where $\beta$ (pronounced 'beta') is greater than unity if cratering enhances the kinetic impact method and less than unity if it works against it. Simulations show that $\beta > 1$ are very feasible,[31] but this depends on the type of asteroid and exactly how the shock waves propagate through the asteroid. To truly know, we need to perform tests.

NASA recently sent a spacecraft to an asteroid to do just that. The Double Asteroid Redirection Test (DART) mission targeted Didymos, a binary asteroid system consisting of a large asteroid accompanied by a 'moonlet': a smaller asteroid that orbits the larger one.[32] This moonlet,

---

[31] AM Stickle, ESG Rainey, M Bruck Syal, JM Owen, P Miller, OS Barnouin and CM Ernst, 'Modeling impact outcomes for the Double Asteroids Redirection Test (DART) mission' (2017) 204 *Procedia Engineering* 116.

[32] Andrew F Cheng, Andrew S Rivkin, Patrick Michel, Justin Atchison, Olivier Barnouin, Lance Benner, Nancy L Chabot, C Ernst, EG Fahnestock, M Kueppers and P Pravec, 'AIDA DART asteroid deflection test: Planetary defense and science objectives' (2018) 157 *Planetary and Space Science* 104.

now officially designated Dimorphos (but sometimes called 'Didymoon') is about 170 metres in diameter, a size scale that would pose a considerable threat if a comparable object were to hit Earth. (There is, it is important to note, no current threat to Earth from either Didymos or Dimorphos).

We can assume that Dimorphos has a mass of about 5 billion kilograms.[33] The DART spacecraft mass was 500 kilograms and was planned to collide with Dimorphos at about 6.6 kilometres per second. To get a feel for the numbers, if we assume that $\beta = 2$, then the expected $\Delta v$ would be approximately one millimetre per second. Why use a double asteroid for the test? Didymos has a very well-characterised light curve (variation of brightness over time) with easily discernible variation due to the passage of Dimorphos across and behind Didymos, as seen from Earth. A change in the period of Dimorphos due to DART was, indeed, quite noticeable using observations from the ground. In contrast, measuring the velocity change for a single asteroid orbiting the Sun would have been extremely difficult, at least without precise ranging equipment or years of meticulous observations.[34]

The kinetic impactor method for asteroid redirection has some clear advantages: the technology is relatively simple and the legal issues surrounding its implementation are (as we will see) largely uncontroversial. The downside is that the way the kinetic impactor strikes the asteroid matters significantly. As discussed in the previous section, the impact is most likely to be designed to be along or against the track of the asteroid. However, due to constraints set by the details of orbital dynamics, one of the directions will be much easier to accommodate than the other. This means that the kinetic impactor method has a preferred direction for deflection, a direction that might not be the same as what is needed on the B-plane. Consider Figure 6.5 again. Suppose we know that an asteroid will strike Earth at the first dot below the centre position. The best deflection strategy would accordingly be to perturb the asteroid such

---

[33] Andrew F Cheng, J Atchison, Brian Kantsiper, Andrew S Rivkin, A Stickle, Cheryl Reed Andres Galvez, Ian Carnelli, Patrick Michel, and S Ulamec, 'Asteroid Impact and Deflection Assessment mission: Kinetic impactor' (2016) 121 *Planetary and Space Science* 27.

[34] Andrew F Cheng et al., 'The Double Asteroid Redirection Test (DART): Planetary Defense Investigations and Requirements', (2021) 2 *Planetary Science Journal*, id. 173, online: https://ui.adsabs.harvard.edu/abs/2021PSJ.....2..173R/abstract. Confirmation of the success was announced during the proof stages of this book. NASA, 'NASA Confirms DART Mission Impact Changed Asteroid's Motion in Space', NASA, online: https://www.nasa.gov/press-release/nasa-confirms-dart-mission-impact-changed-asteroid-s-motion-in-space

that it moves downward on the B-plane, only needing to go a bit more than half of an Earth radius. But say such a deflection is not practical due to the details of the orbits, and instead the asteroid needs to be moved up on the diagram. This would mean that a larger perturbation is required (over 1.5 Earth radii), which in turn requires a more massive spacecraft, a higher impact speed, multiple impactors or a combination of two or more of these. In fact, multiple impactors might be the safest approach in this situation, since using a large $\Delta v$ all at once risks fragmenting the asteroid, which would in turn increase the collisional cross section of the material and could, potentially, cause multiple destructive airbursts when the fragments reach Earth.[35] Then there is uncertainty in the effective $\beta$, which can have a significant effect on the strength and number of impacts required. When looking at a larger motion on the B-plane, all these uncertainties could amount to an unsuccessful deflection. For these reasons – more flexibility and control over the perturbations – we should now consider the use of a nuclear explosive device.

### 6.3.2   Nuclear Explosive Devices

Nuclear explosive devices (NEDs) deflect an asteroid by vaporising a region of its 'regolith' – a layer of unconsolidated rock and dust found on the surface of most asteroids (as well as other celestial bodies such as the Moon). The newly formed vapour, bounded by the asteroid on one side and Space on the other, expands rapidly away from the asteroid's surface. The result is that the vapour acts just like the exhaust from a rocket, imparting a $\Delta v$ onto the asteroid, with the direction set by the location of the NED (and hence the location of regolith that becomes vaporised).

An NED spacecraft only needs to rendezvous with the asteroid, removing the directional bias inherent in the kinetic impactor method; the NED can be detonated along or against track. In addition, the spacecraft carrying the NED can first study the asteroid to best determine how far away the NED should be detonated, which will control the amount of regolith that is vaporised and thus the resulting $\Delta v$. In 2007, a NASA report prepared for the US Congress concluded, 'Nuclear

---

[35] Brent W Barbee, Megan Bruck Syal, David Dearborn, Galen Gisler, Kevin Greenaugh, Kirsten M Howley, Ron Leung, J Lyzhoft, PL Miller, JA Nuth and C Plesko, 'Options and uncertainties in planetary defense: Mission planning and vehicle design for flexible response' (2008) 143 *Acta Astronautica* 37 at 38.

standoff explosions are assessed to be 10–100 times more effective than the non-nuclear alternatives analyzed in this study.'[36]

Despite the clear advantages, NEDs have their own challenges. Just as in the kinetic impactor method, too large a single $\Delta v$ could fragment the asteroid; to reduce this risk, multiple, sequential NEDs may be necessary. Moreover, the perturbation will depend on the actual yield of regolith vaporisation, which may not behave as expected. A nuclear explosion close to Earth, such as an attempt to break up a small but still destructive asteroid, could also have unintended consequences, for instance delivering radioactive debris to Earth's atmosphere and possibly even to the surface.[37] Perhaps most pressing from an implementation standpoint, NEDs have legal and security implications, as will be discussed below.

Still, there are several reasons why NEDs are widely considered to be an attractive option for asteroid deflection: the necessary technology already exists in the form of nuclear warheads and large Space rockets, they can deliver far more energy than other conceivable methods, and they offer more flexibility in timing. The latter is significant, as perturbations have a maximum effectiveness if applied during certain parts of an asteroid's orbit; specifically, you get more orbital change for your $\Delta v$ if the 'kick' is applied at perihelion (the closest approach of the asteroid to the Sun), where the asteroid is moving the fastest in its orbit. This well-known 'Oberth effect' can thus cause larger changes to the asteroid location on the B-plane than an otherwise equivalent mission that perturbs the asteroid away from perihelion.

### 6.3.3  The Long Game: Mass Drivers and Gravity Tractors

The previous two sections explored 'impulsive' asteroid redirection methods, in which the desired $\Delta v$ is achieved more or less instantaneously. With enough lead time, however, a gentler approach could be taken, with a continuous application of small nudges accumulating over time into the desired movement of the asteroid on the B-plane. Although

[36] US National Aeronautics and Space Administration (NASA), 'Near-Earth object survey and deflection analysis of alternatives: Report to Congress' (Washington DC, NASA, March 2007) at 2, online: cneos.jpl.nasa.gov/doc/neo_report2007.html.

[37] Bohumil Doboš, Jakub Pražák and Marie Němečková, 'Atomic salvation: A case for nuclear planetary defense' (2020) 18:1 Astropolitics 73 at 84.

there are several such methods, we focus on two very different approaches to highlight the range of possibilities.

A mass driver is potentially the crudest approach. It involves landing one or more spacecraft on an asteroid and throwing mass in the opposite direction of the desired deflection.[38] With every throw, the 'recoil' due to Newton's third law (equivalent momentum conservation) imparts a small $\delta v$ ('little delta v') to the asteroid. This by itself is insufficient to redirect the asteroid, but after time all the little $\delta v$'s deliver a cumulative $\Delta v$ that is large enough to produce the desired effect.

The asteroid itself is the source of the mass. In the most basic form, you might imagine a mining-like apparatus that is continuously scooping up material and jettisoning it into Space. In a more sophisticated form, the material might be sorted, processed and used in a high-velocity ion engine.

Essentially, a mass driver turns the asteroid into a rocket. Under the assumption of rocket motion only, the change in speed of a rocket after throwing out some mass $\Delta M$ is

$$\Delta v = -v_e \, ln \left( \frac{M_0 - \Delta M}{M_0} \right),$$

where $M_0$ is the initial mass and $v_e$ is the exhaust speed of the propellant. And here we run into the harsh reality of rocketry: the velocity change is proportional to the logarithm of the mass change. This means we need to either throw out a lot of mass, or have high exhaust speeds, or both. Flipping the equation around, we see that

$$\Delta M = M_0 (1 - exp(-\Delta v / v_e)).$$

If we want to achieve a $\Delta v$ of approximately one millimetre per second (comparable to the kinetic impactor scenario discussed above), then for $v_e = 10$ metres per second, two kilometres per second, and 40 kilometres per second, we need to respectively use $\frac{\Delta M}{M_0} = 10^{-4}$, $5 \times 10^{-7}$, and $2.5 \times 10^{-8}$ of the asteroid's mass as fuel (note this is *useful* mass – the amount that

---

[38] George Friedman, John Lewis, Leslie Snively, Lee Valentine, Richard Gertsch and Dennis Wingo, 'Mass drivers for planetary defense' (paper delivered at the Planetary Defense Conference: Protecting Earth from Asteroids, Orange County, California, 23–26 February 2004); GK O'Neill and HH Kolm, 'High-acceleration mass drivers' (1980) 7 *Acta Astronautica* 1229.

needs to be processed may be much higher). The different speeds are
chosen to highlight those that (1) might be comparable to what will be used
to expel waste during mining, (2) reflect conventional rocketry nozzle
speeds and (3) are comparable to ion drive exhaust speeds. Although these
mass fractions are small, they might be challenging to mine. For an
asteroid such as Dimorphos, even the ion drive scenario requires consuming
125 kilograms of useful mass from the asteroid. The conventional rocket
scenario requires 2.5 tonnes (again this is useful mass), and the low-speed
mining ejection scenario requires 500 tonnes. The last approach literally
involves throwing rocks, so while large amounts are needed, no processing
is required.

The difficulty of the mass driver method rises quickly both with the
size of the asteroid and with the size of the desired $\Delta v$. It should also be
kept in mind that Dimorphos is fairly small. All other things being equal,
an asteroid twice as large would require eight times as much mass as fuel
to achieve comparable $\Delta v$'s. Achieving a higher $\Delta v$ would also require
considerably more mass: ten times more mass as fuel in the case of a
Dimorphos-like asteroid that we wanted to give a $\Delta v$ of about one
centimetre per second.

The benefit of a mass driver is that the spacecraft turns the asteroid
into a fuel source. Since each $\delta v$ is quite small, there is also no risk of
fragmenting the asteroid from the impulses themselves. Moreover,
should Space resource utilisation of asteroids become commonplace,
mining spacecraft could be repurposed for planetary defence, in a fortuit-
ous application of dual-use technology. There are, nonetheless, numerous
and potentially quite serious challenges. Physically touching the asteroid
is required, which could disturb the surface layers and potentially cause
instabilities, including an unwanted outburst of material. Moreover,
throwing any material off the asteroid will naturally cause a debris
stream, which in turn could have long-term unintended consequences –
as we explain in Chapter 5 on Space mining. The asteroid will also be
spinning and may need to be de-spun before mass drivers can be landed
or operated effectively.

Gravity tractors, by contrast, employ Newton's third law and momentum conservation in a manner that avoids having to physically touch the
asteroid. In this approach, gravity is a finicky tether that connects the
asteroid and a nearby spacecraft. Just as the mutual gravity between the
spacecraft and the asteroid accelerates the spacecraft towards the asteroid, it also accelerates the much more massive asteroid towards the
spacecraft. The gravity tractor's job is to fly in formation with the

asteroid, using thrusters to maintain a steady distance and direction. Gravity then provides a continuous supply of $\delta v$'s to the asteroid.

The benefits of a gravity tractor are clear. There is no need to physically touch the asteroid and therefore no risk of generating debris or inducing surface activity. Details such as the asteroid's spin rate or surface composition do not matter. But there are also at least two major challenges: a large spacecraft is needed, and it needs to carry enough fuel for a lengthy period of formation flying with the asteroid.

Since there is essentially no difference between the mass driver and the gravity tractor in terms of satisfying the rocketry equations, well over 100 kilograms of fuel would be needed for an effective $\Delta v$ of approximately one millimetre per second using an ion thruster (or something similar) on an asteroid like Dimorphos. Note that this is for the gravity 'tug' only. For further context, if there were a need to give a bigger asteroid like Apophis a larger $\Delta v$ of approximately one centimetre per second, then about ten or more tonnes of fuel would be required. In all likelihood, however, even more fuel would be needed – because the rockets cannot be fired in the optimal direction, since this would place the asteroid in the path of the exhaust. Moreover, we have again used the term 'effective' $\Delta v$ to signify that the impulse is not instantaneously applied, which can lead to some important differences in the detailed orbital evolution.

There is one further point to mention. With an impulsive technique such as a kinetic impactor or an NED, the full $\Delta v$ can be applied at an optimal orbital configuration, providing the maximal movement on the B-plane for the given momentum change. In contrast, low-impulse, long-duration techniques apply $\delta v$'s throughout the orbit. For this reason, the total $\Delta v$ for a mass driver or a gravity tractor could be larger than that needed for an impulsive technique, all other things being equal. Still, the low-impulse methods have many advantages – if there is sufficient lead time to implement them! A practical scientific demonstration of such a method, similar to the demonstration of a kinetic impactor being provided by DART, would be a major contribution to planetary defence.

## 6.4  Comets

Asteroids tend to be the focus of planetary defence discussions because of the high number that pass close to Earth. Yet comets also pose a risk, and should not be dismissed. Comets, which are composed of ice, rock and dust, are the leftover planetesimals that formed in the colder regions of the

solar nebula during planet building.[39] There are two primary comet reser-
voirs in the solar system. One is the Edgeworth–Kuiper Belt (often simply
referred to as the Kuiper Belt) that comprises icy bodies located just beyond
Neptune's orbit.[40] These comets orbit in roughly the same plane and
direction as the planets. The other reservoir, which is presumed to exist
based on an analysis of certain types of cometary orbits, as well as planet
formation calculations, is the Oort Cloud.[41] This can be thought of as a
spherical shell of cometary material that formed when bodies were almost
ejected from the solar system during planet building. They then had their
closest approach to the Sun (perihelion) increased through gravitational
perturbations by the Milky Way galaxy, decoupling the Oort Cloud from
the rest of the solar system's dynamics. The main Oort Cloud is thought to
have an inner edge around 20,000 au from the Sun, making it the most
distant material that is still part of the solar system. According to Kepler's
laws, an orbit about the Sun with a semi-major axis of 20,000 au will have a
period of about 3 million years. In other words, it will take that long, or
longer, for a comet in the Oort Cloud to make a single orbit around the Sun.

But just as the varying gravitational perturbations from stars and galactic
clouds of gas and dust helped to form the Oort Cloud, similar types of
perturbation can decrease the perihelia of Oort comet orbits, making them
very elliptical, and bringing these distant bodies well into the inner solar
system.[42] This is possible because the Sun's gravitational influence is weak at
such large distances, and small perturbations can have significant orbital
consequences. The result is 'long-period' comets, that is to say comets with
periods of more than (and in many cases much more than) 200 years. If
these bodies also have a strong interaction with a giant planet, such as
Jupiter, a Halley-type comet could be produced: one that, despite having a
highly inclined orbit, has a period of less than 200 years. In all these cases, the
orbits can have a wide range of orientations. They can even be 'retrograde',
meaning that the comet orbits in the opposite direction of the planets.

[39] Michael F A'Hearn, 'Comets as building blocks' (2011) 49 *Annual Review of Astronomy and Astrophysics* 281.

[40] Brett Gladman and Kathryn Volk, 'Transneptunian Space' (2021) 59 *Annual Review of Astronomy and Astrophysics* 203.

[41] Ibid.

[42] Luke Dones, Paul R Weissman, Harold F Levison and Martin J Duncan, 'Oort Cloud formation and dynamics', in Doug Johnstone, FC Adams, DNC Lin, DA Neufeeld and EC Ostriker, eds., *Star Formation in the Interstellar Medium: In Honor of David Hollenbach, Chris McKee and Frank Shu* (San Francisco: Astronomical Society of the Pacific, 2004) 371.

In contrast, many of the short-period comets (less than 200 years) are thought to originate from the Kuiper Belt. Over time, orbital evolutions of some of the icy bodies in the Kuiper Belt can lead to strong, multiple interactions with one or more of the giant planets. When this happens, an icy body can eventually be placed on an orbit that extends into the inner solar system. This mechanism is thought to produce comets with orbits that are roughly in the same orbital plane as the planets.

Regardless of their origin, when cometary bodies get close enough to the Sun, they 'turn on' due to the sublimation of frozen gas. The resulting 'outgassing',[43] which includes 'jetting' of material, releases gas and dust and produces a visible atmosphere ('coma') that surrounds the icy body (the core or 'nucleus'). It also produces a gas ion tail, which points away from the Sun along the solar wind, as well as a dust tail, which tends from the Sun but is curved due to orbital dynamics. While we think of comets as being bright objects, this is only true when they are active, and even then the cometary nucleus tends to be very dark and difficult to detect. This is especially true for comets that are making their first close approach to the Sun.

This discussion leads to a sobering point: we know little, if anything, about the existence and trajectories of most comets, even ones that will, one day, pass close to Earth.[44]

Efforts to detect and better understand comets are under way. In 2004, the European Space Agency (ESA) launched a robotic spacecraft (*Rosetta*) and a smaller lander (*Philae*) to study the comet 67P/Churyumov–Gerasimenko (see Figure 6.6), with *Philae* reaching the surface in November 2014. Importantly, *Rosetta* monitored the comet as it began outgassing and jetting as it approached the Sun.[45] In 2005, NASA sent the robotic spacecraft *Deep Impact* to the comet Tempel 1, where it deployed a small impactor to excavate material. The resulting crater revealed that the comet's interior was dustier and less icy than expected,[46] a fact which ultimately has planetary defence implications, at least for comets similar to Tempel 1.

---

[43] Jake Parks, 'Organic molecules make up half of Comet 67P', *Astronomy* (1 December 2017), online: astronomy.com/news/2017/12/comet-67p.

[44] NASA Science Mission Directorate, 'Comets' (19 December 2019), *NASA*, online: solarsystem.nasa.gov/asteroids-comets-and-meteors/comets/in-depth.

[45] Emily Baldwin, 'Comet jet in 3D' (9 October 2015), *ESA*, online: blogs.esa.int/rosetta/2015/10/09/comet-jet-in-3d.

[46] NASA Deep Impact Mission, 'Deep Impact Team reports first evidence of cometary ice' (3 February 2006), *NASA* , online: www.nasa.gov/mission_pages/deepimpact/media/dee pimpact_water_ice.html.

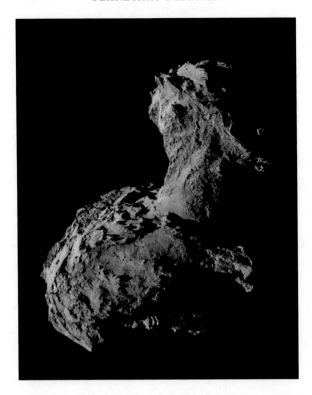

**Figure 6.6**    Comet 67P/Churyumov–Gerasimenko, in a mosaic of four photographs
from ESA's *Rosetta* spacecraft. The comet, which appears to be two icy bodies weakly
held together, is about 4.3 by 4.1 kilometres at its longest and widest dimensions. One
of *Rosetta*'s many discoveries was that the isotopic signature of the water on the comet
is quite different from that on Earth, which suggests that Earth's oceans did not come
from comets like 67P.[47]

Part of the interest in comets is driven by collisions that were observed
on the surface of Jupiter in 1994. The event derived from the short-
period comet Shoemaker–Levy 9, which was likely captured by Jupiter's
immense gravity around 1970 while passing close to the gas giant during
its aphelion (the point of the comet's orbit furthest from the Sun). There
it stayed in an evolving, highly elliptical Jovian-centric orbit. Then, in

[47] Ian Sample, 'Rosetta discovers water on Comet 67p like nothing on Earth', *The Guardian*
(11 December 2014), online: www.theguardian.com/science/2014/dec/10/water-comet-
67p-earth-rosetta.

1992, the planet's tidal forces overwhelmed the comet, breaking it into fragments, several of which were about two kilometres in diameter. Two years later, these fragments collided with Jupiter at 60 kilometres per second, leaving scars on its gaseous surface that remained visible for months.[48] The event is often cited as one of the main drivers for early planetary defence initiatives.[49]

An Earth impact scenario involving a comet was prepared by NASA scientists and shared with the attendees at the International Academy of Astronautics' (IAA) 2019 Planetary Defense Conference.[50] Although the scenario was not as developed as the exercise involving asteroid 2019 PDC, it illuminated the greater uncertainties and potentially greater risks of comets as compared to asteroids. Again, many comets have very long orbits, meaning that we have no prior knowledge of their existence, trajectories or composition. Comets also tend to be larger than asteroids, travel much faster, and be composed of a combination of solid and gaseous materials that lends itself to fragmentation events.[51] All of these factors make it difficult to predict whether a comet passing close to Earth will fly by harmlessly or collide destructively, and equally difficult to predict where on Earth any such impact would occur.

For all these reasons, a comet would be much more difficult to deflect or destroy than an asteroid. The only good news is that comets pass by Earth much less frequently than asteroids. Still, it is good public policy to develop mechanisms for the early detection of comets, for determining their orbits with as much precision as possible, and for deflecting or destroying them should such a need ever arise.

[48] NASA Science Mission Directorate, 'P/Shoemaker-Levy 9' (19 December 2019), NASA, online: solarsystem.nasa.gov/asteroids-comets-and-meteors/comets/p-shoemaker-levy-9/in-depth.

[49] Lindley N Johnson, 'Preparing for planetary defense: Detection and interception of asteroids on collision course with Earth' (paper delivered at the 32nd Space Congress, Cocoa Beach, Florida, 25 April 1995), online: commons.erau.edu/space-congress-proceedings/proceedings-1995-32nd/april-25-1995/18.

[50] NASA Center for Near Earth Object Studies, 'Hypothetical comet impact scenario – PDC 2019' (2019), NASA, online: cneos.jpl.nasa.gov/pd/cs/pdc19c.

[51] Claire Andreoli, Ray Villard, David Jewitt and Quanzhi Ye, 'Hubble watches comet ATLAS disintegrate into more than two dozen pieces' (28 April 2020), NASA, online: www.nasa.gov/feature/goddard/2020/hubble-watches-comet-atlas-disintegrate-into-more-than-two-dozen-pieces.

## 6.5 International Co-operation

The challenges of detecting and characterising dangerous asteroids and comets, assessing risks and, if necessary, deflecting or destroying them are likely to exceed the capabilities of any single state and therefore call for international co-operation. Should mitigation turn to disaster management, even a city-wide or regional impact from a near-Earth object (NEO) could have worldwide economic and social effects.[52] Yet there has been a lack of high-level diplomacy on this issue, with the low-probability character of Earth impact making planetary defence a low priority for political leaders whose timelines seldom extend beyond the next four to five years. Such international co-operation on planetary defence as is currently taking place is occurring among national Space agencies, observatories and even amateur astronomers rather than among foreign ministries.

In 1999, the Third UN Conference on the Exploration and Peaceful Uses of Outer Space recommended improvements to international co-ordination on planetary defence.[53] As a response, 'Action Team 14' – a co-ordinated effort by 19 countries to study potentially hazardous NEOs – was formed by the UN Committee on the Peaceful Uses of Outer Space (COPUOS) in 2001.[54] After the airburst over Chelyabinsk, Russia, in February 2013, which injured more than 1,000 people, the work done by Action Team 14 enabled a prompt response from higher levels of the United Nations. In December 2013, the UN General Assembly adopted Resolution 68/75 in which it welcomed recommendations from COPUOS to establish the International Asteroid Warning Network (IAWN) and the Space Mission Planning Advisory Group (SMPAG).[55]

---

[52] R Albrecht and MHJ Dore, 'Toward plans for mitigating possible socio-economic effects due to a physical impact of an asteroid on Earth' (paper delivered at the 7th IAA Planetary Defense Conference, virtual, 26–30 April 2021), online: ui.adsabs.harvard .edu/abs/2021plde.confE..74A/abstract.

[53] United Nations Office for Outer Space Affairs, *Report of the Third United Nations Conference on the Exploration and Peaceful Uses of Outer Space (Vienna, 19–30 July 1999)*, UN Doc A/CONF.184/6 (18 October 1999) at res 1(I) para. 1(c)(i)–(iii), online: digitallibrary.un.org/record/287788.

[54] *Report of the Committee on the Peaceful Uses of Outer Space*, UN GAOR, 56th sess, Supp No 20, UN Doc A/56/20 (2001) at paras. 44–61, online: www.unoosa.org/pdf/gadocs/A_ 56_20E.pdf; Pelton, op. cit. at 348.

[55] *International Cooperation in the Peaceful Uses of Outer Space*, GA Res 68/75, 68th sess, UN Doc A/RES/68/75 (16 December 2013) at para. 8, online: www.unoosa.org/oosa/ oosadoc/data/resolutions/2013/general_assembly_68th_session/ares6875.html.

### 6.5.1   International Asteroid Warning Network

The International Asteroid Warning Network (IAWN) connects astronomers, observatories and other institutions that were already engaged in identifying and studying potentially hazardous NEOs. By pooling existing capabilities, IAWN aims to 'discover, monitor, and physically characterize' the entire population of potentially hazardous NEOs using 'optical and radar facilities and other assets based in both the northern and southern hemispheres and in space'.[56] It also serves as an international clearing house for NEO observations,[57] co-ordinates campaigns for the observation of NEOs of particular concern, and recommends criteria and thresholds for when emerging impact threats should be communicated to national governments and general publics. Finally, IAWN aims to develop a database of potential 'impact consequences', to assess 'hazard analysis results', to communicate them to governments and to assist in the planning of 'mitigation responses'.[58] These latter activities, it should be noted, are directed at dealing with the effects of an impact after it occurs.

Participation in IAWN is open to all governmental and nongovernmental entities with relevant capabilities, including survey telescopes, follow-up observations, orbit computations, hazard analysis, data distribution, processing and archiving. However, participants must accept a policy of free and open communication. If someone identifies an NEO threat, they must tell everyone else about it! The network's 'Statement of Intent' currently has more than 40 signatories, ranging from highly skilled 'amateur' astronomers to NASA, ESA, the China National Space Administration and the Special Astrophysical Observatory of the Russian Academy of Sciences.[59] In terms of participation in IAWN, a shared interest in knowing about cataclysmic threats has superseded national rivalries.

---

[56] Elizabeth Warner, 'History' (31 March 2022), *IAWN*, online: iawn.net/about.shtml.

[57] IAWN works closely with the International Astronomical Union's Minor Planet Center, which is hosted by the Harvard and Smithsonian Center for Astrophysics, located at the Smithsonian Astrophysical Observatory and funded primarily by NASA. See 'International Astronomical Union Minor Planet Center' (18 April 2022), *Center for Astrophysics*, online: minorplanetcenter.net.

[58] Warner, 'History', op. cit.

[59] Elizabeth Warner, 'Membership' (31 March 2022), *IAWN*, online: iawn.net/about/members.shtml.

### 6.5.2 Space Mission Planning Advisory Group

The Space Mission Planning Advisory Group (SMPAG, generally pronounced 'same page') was created to 'prepare for an international response to an NEO impact threat through the exchange of information, development of options for collaborative research and mission opportunities, and NEO threat mitigation planning activities'.[60] Currently composed of representatives from 18 Space agencies, including NASA, ESA, Roscosmos and the China National Space Administration, SMPAG addresses issues such as the feasibility of and options for mitigating an impact threat through a Space mission, and the length of time that it would take to build and launch a spacecraft to deflect an NEO. SMPAG is grounded on a shared conviction that the 'threat of an asteroid or comet impact is a real and global issue demanding an international response'. Recognising that states 'already share a number of common interests in NEO threat identification and mitigation', SMPAG aims 'to develop cooperative activities among its members and to build consensus on recommendations for planetary defense measures'.[61] In other words, unlike IAWN, which focuses on international co-operation in the detection of potentially hazardous NEOs, SMPAG focuses on co-ordinating the capabilities that might be needed to deflect or destroy them.

That said, SMPAG is not working to marshal a fleet of asteroid deflection spacecraft and rockets in preparation for a planetary emergency. Nor would it fulfil any decision-making role should such an emergency arise. Rather, SMPAG would respond to a credible impact threat by proposing 'mitigation options and implementation plans for consideration by the international community'.[62] This means that the decision makers would be national governments, whether acting unilaterally, in some ad hoc coalition, or through an existing international mechanism such as the United Nations Security Council. No predeterminations have been made as to who would contribute, and what they would contribute, in the event of an Earth impact emergency. These issues, of who decides and who acts, will be discussed below. First, however, we should consider the kinds of decisions that would have to be taken.

---

[60] Space Mission Planning Advisory Group (SMPAG), 'Terms of reference for the Near-Earth Object Threat Mitigation Space Mission Planning Advisory Group – Version 2.0' (13 September 2019), *ESA*, online: www.cosmos.esa.int/web/smpag/terms_of_reference_v2.

[61] Ibid.

[62] Ibid.

## 6.6   Tabletop Exercises

The fictional asteroid 2021 PDC was developed for the 2021 Planetary Defense Conference,[63] in a scenario that quite deliberately provided a very short timeline for reacting to an impact emergency, in order to highlight several new issues of concern. The exercise played out as follows.

- IAWN announced the discovery of 2021 PDC, which posed an impact risk to Earth within approximately six months. At the time, the estimated impact risk was 5 per cent and the size of the asteroid was very uncertain – somewhere between 35 and 700 metres, which corresponds to very localised to widespread (a few kilometres to hundreds of kilometres) severe damage potential.
- One week later, ground-based follow-up observations confirmed that an impact would take place. However, the impact corridor remained uncertain and stretched from Scandinavia to North Africa. Nor was there any more information on the size of the asteroid. SMPAG began to explore Space mission options.
- Four months before the impact, Space-based observations by NEOWISE narrowed the impact corridor to a swath across Central Europe. They also constrained the size of the asteroid to between 35 and 500 metres, with a likely size of 160 metres in diameter. At the same time, SMPAG determined that 'no space mission can be launched in time to deflect or disrupt the asteroid'. Nor could any reconnaissance mission be launched.
- With the lack of deflection options, mitigation became disaster management, with a focus on refining the impact location and size of the asteroid, as well as implementing civil responses. The estimated size of the asteroid meant that a '[l]arge airburst or impact is likely to cause extensive blast damage over areas extending from tens to hundreds of kilometers in radius', affecting 'hundreds of thousands of people, potentially up to several million in rare worst-cases'.[64]

---

[63] NASA Center for Near Earth Object Studies, 'Planetary Defense Conference Exercise – 2021' (2021), *NASA*, online: cneos.jpl.nasa.gov/pd/cs/pdc21.

[64] Lorien Wheeler, Jessie Dotson, Michael Aftosmis, Eric Stern, Donovan Mathias and Paul Chodas, '2021 PDC Hypothetical Impact Exercise: probabilistic asteroid impact risk, scenario day 3' (paper delivered at the 7th IAA Planetary Defense Conference, virtual, 26–30 April 2021), *NASA*, online: cneos.jpl.nasa.gov/pd/cs/pdc21/pdc21_day3_briefing2 .pdf.

. The Goldstone Solar System Radar in California was able to observe the asteroid for the last six days before the impact and narrow the impact location to the tri-border region of Germany, Austria and the Czech Republic. Fortunately, the asteroid was smaller than previously thought, though still sizeable at 100 metres in diameter. Within the remaining uncertainty, the object could cause serious damage to a region 300 kilometres across for the highest plausible impact energies and 150 kilometres across for the average estimated impact energy. Serious damage refers to window breakage, some structural damage and possible second-degree burns. The 'unsurvivable' region, closest to the impact centroid, would be about 10 per cent of the serious-damage extent.

Several important things were learned as a result of this exercise. First, reliable and ready-to-launch spacecraft for planetary defence reconnaissance are needed and currently lacking. Second, had sensitive all-sky surveys been operational a decade before the hypothetical discovery, the asteroid could have been discovered with sufficient lead time to launch one or more deflection missions. Third, access to reliable archival data is fundamental to planetary defence, allowing for the possibility of 'pre-recoveries', i.e. finding the asteroid in older data, in the form of observational information about a previous pass by Earth. But a pre-recovery of archival data could be precluded for many reasons, and might only become possible when new real-time information about the asteroid's location comes in.

Although the 2021 PDC exercise was important for exploring disaster response, it was not designed to raise or address issues of mitigation. For this, we need to turn to the fictional asteroid 2019 PDC,[65] as developed for the 2019 Planetary Defense Conference.[66] That tabletop exercise, which provided an optimistic eight-year timeline between detection and impact, identified a series of questions that would have to be addressed in any such situation:

. What type of space missions should be used to rapidly improve our understanding of the asteroid's orbit, to determine whether and where it will impact Earth?

---

[65] Note that this is the same hypothetical asteroid used in Figure 6.5 for introducing the B-plane.
[66] NASA Center for Near Earth Object Studies, 'Planetary Defense Conference Exercise – 2019' (2019), NASA, online: cneos.jpl.nasa.gov/pd/cs/pdc19.

- Are flyby missions sufficient or do we need a rendezvous with the asteroid?
- Who will build the spacecraft? Who will launch?
- Should a nuclear explosive device be part of the reconnaissance spacecraft, to provide an immediate deflection option, or should the deflection options be restricted to non-nuclear methods?
- Who decides whether a deflection is needed?
- Who decides what method will be used?
- What if there is substantial disagreement on the need for a deflection or the method used?
- Who will be responsible for any negative consequences of a failed or only partial deflection?
- If the asteroid is on course to impact a non-spacefaring state, do spacefaring states have an obligation to mount a deflection mission?

To this list we might add: what is the most reliable way to characterise the asteroid, in terms of its composition and therefore the suitability and safety of different deflection methods?

In the 2019 exercise, flyby and rendezvous reconnaissance spacecraft were considered, as well as immediate-deflection scenarios. The immediate-deflection options involved significant uncertainties due to incomplete knowledge about the asteroid. Indeed, at the time SMPAG began looking at mission possibilities, the impact probability was still only 10 per cent. Yet the optimal orbital characteristics for the use of kinetic impactors were only present for an early launch. During the exercise, it was also noted that an NED-capable rendezvous spacecraft would have the greatest flexibility – combining asteroid characterisation with the option of deflection – but that it would also introduce a number of legal and policy issues, as discussed below. Regardless of the method chosen, the scenario anticipated that more than a year would be required to build the necessary spacecraft. Ultimately, the shortest-timeline reconnaissance mission was performed, which was a flyby. This still left uncertainty about the asteroid's mass but removed any doubt that an impact would occur: a 140- to 220-metre asteroid striking the Greater Denver, Colorado area.

Although an NED could have been launched, a sub-optimal but still-feasible kinetic impactor mission was chosen instead. Between them, NASA, ESA, Roscosmos and the Chinese and Japanese Space agencies built and launched six spacecraft – a number designed to provide redundancy and prevent the need for a single, large $\Delta v$. Three of the six

## Day 5 Ground Zero; Central Park NYC, NY*

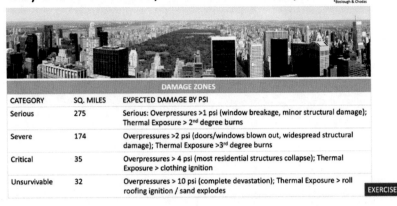

*Boslough & Chodas

| DAMAGE ZONES | | |
| --- | --- | --- |
| CATEGORY | SQ. MILES | EXPECTED DAMAGE BY PSI |
| Serious | 275 | Serious: Overpressures >1 psi (window breakage, minor structural damage); Thermal Exposure > 2nd degree burns |
| Severe | 174 | Overpressures >2 psi (doors/windows blown out, widespread structural damage); Thermal Exposure >3rd degree burns |
| Critical | 35 | Overpressures > 4 psi (most residential structures collapse); Thermal Exposure > clothing ignition |
| Unsurvivable | 32 | Overpressures > 10 psi (complete devastation); Thermal Exposure > roll roofing ignition / sand explodes |

**Figure 6.7** The area of expected damage due to an airburst from a 60-metre asteroid, arranged by increasing severity. The region of 'severe' damage is enclosed by the region of 'serious' damage, and so forth. Regions need not be circular, and they depend on several factors. The term 'overpressure' refers to the pressure, in pounds per square inch (psi), in excess of the ambient pressure prior to the arrival of the blast wave. From Barbara Jennings, 'Day 5 at Risk Critical Infrastructure Effects' (paper delivered at the 6th Planetary Defense Conference, College Park, Maryland, 29 April–3 May 2019), *NASA*, online: cneos.jpl.nasa.gov/pd/cs/pdc19/pdc19_briefing5c.pdf.

spacecraft reached the asteroid, but despite using multiple impactors, one of the collisions caused the asteroid to fragment. And so, while the deflection effort prevented the entire asteroid from striking Boulder, a 60-metre fragment remained on course to strike Earth and, more precisely, New York City. With the decision makers having failed to agree on sending an NED, even as a back-up option ('due to widespread controversy that was not resolved in time'[67]), they were unable to save New York City and the surrounding area. Figure 6.7, prepared for the exercise, gives a sense of the destruction that could be caused by a 60-metre asteroid.

---

[67] Brent Barbee, Paul Chodas, Joshua Lyzhoft, Anastassios E. Petropoulos, Javier Roa and Bruno Sarli, '2019 PDC mitigation mission options' (paper delivered at the 6th IAA Planetary Defense Conference, College Park, Maryland, 29 April–3 May 2019), *NASA*, online cneos.jpl.nasa.gov/pd/cs/pdc19/pdc19_briefing4c.pdf.

Quite a few tabletop exercises similar to this have taken place,[68] as well as one *ex post facto* legal analysis conducted by an Ad-Hoc Working Group on Legal Issues established by SMPAG. In its 2020 'Legal Overview and Assessment', the Ad-Hoc Working Group took a tabletop exercise from the 2017 Planetary Defense Conference, where the legal issues were not addressed, and conducted its own analysis of the legal issues that would have arisen – had the scenario played out in real life.[69] Some of this analysis will be discussed below.

### 6.7   Legal Issues

Some difficult legal issues can be expected to arise in the context of planetary defence. Most of these are discussed in an excellent 2020 report from the Ad-Hoc Working Group on Legal Issues established by SMPAG.[70] This section follows the structure of that report and reproduces some of its content, while adding commentary and raising a few additional issues.

### 6.7.1   *Information sharing*

If an NEO with a potentially dangerous orbit is discovered, it is almost inconceivable that the astronomers involved would not promptly inform the global astronomical community of their find. There are strong ethical obligations to share information that could potentially save millions of lives. Moreover, science relies on the international circulation of discoveries and data, and careers are made through peer-reviewed publications leading to global reputations. The astronomers who discovered a significant NEO threat would thus have powerful incentives to share that information; indeed, if the NEO were a comet, it would be named after them. But even in the absence of strong ethical and professional motivations, keeping secret the existence of a possible Earth-impacting asteroid or comet is not a real possibility. After observations of an NEO

---

[68] NASA Center for Near Earth Object Studies, 'Hypothetical comet impact scenario – PDC 2019' (29 April 2019), *NASA*, online: cneos.jpl.nasa.gov/pd/cs/pdc19c.

[69] Space Mission Planning Advisory Group (SMPAG), 'Planetary defence legal overview and assessment: Report by the Ad-Hoc Working Group on Legal Issues to the Space Mission Planning Advisory Group' (8 April 2020), *ESA*, online: www.cosmos.esa.int/documents/336356/336472/SMPAG-RP-004_1_0_SMPAG_legal_report_2020-04-08.pdf.

[70] Ibid.

are taken, the data are almost universally submitted to the International Astronomical Union's Minor Planet Center and made publicly available, and for good reason. Initial observations are typically unable to yield reliable orbit solutions. Publicly accessible announcements of new objects are circulated so that astronomers worldwide, including highly skilled 'amateurs', can acquire more observations of the object. Several independent groups also focus on computing orbital solutions with known data. Even independently of formal collaborations, the detection and characterisation of NEOs is a team effort and thus involves many people with open information.

National governments are unlikely to interfere because they, too, would have powerful incentives to share the information. Even if the data are sufficient to determine whether an impact will happen, the resulting orbit solutions are unlikely, at first, to be accurate enough to determine an impact location with actionable certainty. With everyone (or at least many) at equal risk, all states would have an equal interest in seeing the full deployment of the international astronomical community's capabilities to determine whether an impact were forthcoming, and where exactly it would take place.

International law augments these reasons for information sharing with a binding legal obligation that can be inferred from two articles of the 1967 Outer Space Treaty. Article IX reads,

> In the exploration and use of outer space, including the Moon and other celestial bodies, States Parties to the Treaty shall be guided by the principle of cooperation and mutual assistance and shall conduct all their activities in outer space, including the Moon and other celestial bodies, with due regard to the corresponding interests of all other States Parties to the Treaty.[71]

As we explained in Chapter 3, observatories are engaged in the 'exploration' of Space. It is also clearly in the interests of all parties to the treaty to be promptly informed of any new NEO threat.

Further to this, Article XI sets out a general obligation to share information:

> In order to promote international cooperation in the peaceful exploration and use of outer space, States Parties to the Treaty conducting activities in

---

[71] *Treaty on Principles Governing the Activities of States in the Exploration and Use of Outer Space, Including the Moon and Other Celestial Bodies*, 27 January 1967, 610 UNTS 205 (entered into force 10 October 1967) (Outer Space Treaty).

outer space, including the Moon and other celestial bodies, agree to inform the Secretary-General of the United Nations as well as the public and the international scientific community, to the greatest extent feasible and practicable, of the nature, conduct, locations and results of such activities. On receiving the said information, the Secretary-General of the United Nations should be prepared to disseminate it immediately and effectively.[72]

This treaty obligation is uncontroversial and may well have contributed to the development of a parallel rule of customary international law that binds all states and not just the parties to the Outer Space Treaty. This process, of treaties contributing to parallel customary obligations, is well established in the international legal system – and will be discussed at greater length below.

Treaties and customary international law are the first two 'sources of international law', as identified by the Statute of the International Court of Justice. The third source of international law – 'the general principles of law recognized by civilized nations' – is also relevant here.[73] This is because the International Court of Justice (ICJ) has held that the obligation to share information in life-and-death situations is supported by 'elementary considerations of humanity' that constitute 'general and well-recognized principles' of law. As the Ad-Hoc Working Group on Legal Issues explains, in the 1949 *Corfu Channel Case*,

> The ICJ found that Albania was under the obligation to inform foreign vessels about the existence of a minefield in its territorial waters. This obligation was, according to the Court, based on *'general and well-recognized principles, namely: elementary considerations of humanity'.*[74] In this case, the failure to notify foreign ships led to the death or injury of over 80 persons. Since *'nothing was attempted by the Albanian authorities to prevent the disaster'*[75], the Court found that Albania was responsible

---

[72] Ibid. Art. IX.

[73] Art. 38(1) of the Statute of the International Court of Justice identified three primary sources of international law, with the third being 'the general principles of law recognized by civilized nations'. See Statue of the International Court of Justice, 26 June 1945, Can TS 1945 No 7 Art. 38(1) (entered into force 24 October 1945); The phrase 'civilized nations' is, of course, colonial terminology. In 2019, the United Nations International Law Commission noted that the term is generally agreed to be inappropriate and outdated, and suggested it should be read as 'community of nations'. See *Report of the International Law Commission: Seventy-First Session 29 April–7 June and 8 July–9 August 2019*, UNGAOR, 74th Sess, Supp No 10, UN Doc A/74/10 (2019) at 336, para. 243, online: digitallibrary.un.org/record/3827355?ln=en.

[74] *Corfu Channel Case* (*UK* v. *Albania*), [1949] ICJ Reports 4 at 22, SMPAG's emphasis.

[75] Ibid. at 23, SMPAG's emphasis.

under international law for the damage and loss of human life which resulted from the explosion of the minefield and that there was a duty upon Albania to pay compensation.[76]

This led the Ad-Hoc Working Group to conclude, 'While the case does not address the specific situation of an NEO impact threat, it can nevertheless support the argument that elementary considerations of humanity can form the basis of a duty to share information in order to avoid the loss of human lives.'[77]

The obligation to share information promptly and publicly about NEO threats is thus strongly supported on ethical, professional, practical and legal grounds.

### 6.7.2   Assisting Other States

If an asteroid on an Earth impact trajectory is identified, and if the asteroid is small enough that the damage will be limited to one state or a small number of states, those states clearly have the right to attempt a deflection mission. They might then be responsible for any damage caused to third states, for instance if the mission altered the trajectory of the asteroid only slightly, causing it to strike a state or states which had not initially been threatened. This issue of 'state responsibility' will be addressed below, along with the question whether this damage could be excused by either a United Nations Security Council resolution or 'circumstances precluding wrongfulness'.

The Ad-Hoc Working Group raises another issue, namely whether states having the capability to mount a deflection mission are legally obligated to come to the assistance of states that lack this capability but discover that they will be the location of an NEO impact. We will turn to this issue of a possible legal obligation in a moment, but first there are compelling reasons to believe that the issue is unlikely ever to arise. Indeed, there are at least three reasons to believe that spacefaring states would always seek to prevent an NEO impact even if their own territories and populations were not directly threatened. First, an asteroid large enough to cause significant damage in one state will have indirect effects in other states. These effects could include alterations to the climate, if large amounts of material are lofted into the atmosphere, leading to a

---

[76] SMPAG, 'Planetary defence', op. cit. at 20.
[77] Ibid.

consequential diminishment of global food supplies. They could impact the broader economy, if international trade, investment and travel are disrupted. They could also lead to migration, if an asteroid strike in one country forced large numbers of people to flee to other countries, either before or after the impact. Such sudden and dramatic changes could, in turn, affect the political stability or national security of multiple states. Second, the random nature of NEO threats means that an impeding strike on a non-spacefaring state or states would provide an excellent opportunity for spacefaring states to test their deflection capabilities, knowing that another NEO will, sooner or later, eventually threaten them. Third, governments everywhere are responsive to public opinion. It is difficult to imagine that the public in the United States, Europe, Russia or China, would – if accurately informed about the situation – abide their leaders abandoning millions of fellow human beings to a preventable NEO threat.

Now we turn to the Ad-Hoc Working Group's analysis of the issue, which concluded that, 'in the absence of specific and clear obligations under international law, States are free to decide whether they provide assistance to other States that are threatened by a possible NEO impact'.[78] Unfortunately, by limiting its analysis to the search for 'specific and clear obligations under international law',[79] the Ad-Hoc Working Group did not consider the third source of international law, i.e. 'the general principles of law recognized by civilized nations'.[80] Interestingly, this is the same Ad-Hoc Working Group that, on the issue of information sharing, referred approvingly to the International Court of Justice's finding in the *Corfu Channel Case* that 'elementary considerations of humanity' constitute 'general and well-recognized principles' of law.[81] Had the Ad-Hoc Working Group conducted a similar and necessary analysis with regard to a duty to rescue human beings in distress, they might have reached a very different conclusion, which we will expand on now.

The duty to rescue exists in many national legal systems. For example, section 323c(1) of the German Civil Code states,

> Whoever does not render assistance in the case of an accident or a common danger or emergency although it is necessary and can

---

[78] Ibid. at 24.
[79] Ibid.
[80] Statute of the International Court of Justice, op. cit., Art. 38(1).
[81] *Corfu Channel Case*, op. cit. at 23.

reasonably be expected under the circumstances, in particular if it is
possible without substantial danger to that person and without breaching
other important duties, incurs a penalty of imprisonment for a term not
exceeding one year or a fine.[82]

Similarly, in the Canadian province of Quebec, its provincial Charter of
Human Rights and Freedoms states,

> Every human being whose life is in peril has a right to assistance. Every
> person must come to the aid of anyone whose life is in peril, either
> personally or calling for aid, by giving him the necessary and immediate
> physical assistance, unless it involves danger to himself or a third person,
> or he has another valid reason.[83]

Many other Civil Law systems, from France to Argentina to Egypt,
contain the same duty to rescue.

Common Law systems do not have a general duty to rescue, although
such a duty has been found in the context of pre-existing relationships,
for instance teachers vis-à-vis their students, or parents vis-à-vis their
children.[84] In the United States, numerous states have 'Good Samaritan'
statutes, and some of these contain a duty to rescue.[85] In Vermont, for
instance,

> A person who knows that another is exposed to grave physical harm shall,
> to the extent that the same can be rendered without danger or peril to
> himself or without interference with important duties owed to others, give
> reasonable assistance to the exposed person unless that assistance or care
> is being provided by others.[86]

Other US states, however, only go so far as to provide immunity from
civil liability to a person who acts to rescue another and, in doing so,
inadvertently causes harm.

Internationally, the duty to rescue is included in numerous treaties.
The International Convention for the Safety of Life at Sea (SOLAS
Convention) was adopted in 1914, with the negotiations having been
prompted by the sinking of the *Titanic* two years earlier. Although it has

---

[82] German Criminal Code, 13 November 1998 (Federal Law Gazette I, p 3322), s 323c(1).
[83] Charter of Human Rights and Freedoms, CQLR c C-12, s 2.
[84] Martin Vraken, 'Duty to rescue in civil law and common law: Les extrêmes se touchent'
(1998) 47:4 *International & Comparative Law Quarterly* 934.
[85] Patricia Grande Montana, 'Watch or report? Livestream or help? Good Samaritan laws
revisited: The need to create a duty to report' (2017) 66:3 *Cleveland State Law Review* 533.
[86] *Vermont Statues Annotated*, Title 12 § 519(a) (2017).

been updated many times since then, the SOLAS Convention has always required each party 'to ensure that any necessary arrangements are made for coast watching and for the rescue of persons in distress at sea round its coasts'.[87] The 1944 Convention on International Civil Aviation (Chicago Convention) has an entire annex devoted to search and rescue. Parties to the Chicago Convention are required to assist survivors of accidents regardless of nationality.[88] The 1979 International Convention on Maritime Search and Rescue (SAR Convention) requires states parties, individually or co-operatively, to 'participate in the development of search and rescue services to ensure that assistance is rendered to any person in distress at sea'.[89]

The 1982 United Nations Convention on the Law of the Sea reinforces these earlier treaties, with Article 98(1) reading,

> Every State shall require the master of a ship flying its flag, in so far as he can do so without serious danger to the ship, the crew or the passengers:
>
> (a) to render assistance to any person found at sea in danger of being lost;
> (b) to proceed with all possible speed to the rescue of persons in distress, if informed of their need of assistance, in so far as such action may reasonably be expected of him;
> (c) after a collision, to render assistance to the other ship, its crew and its passengers and, where possible, to inform the other ship of the name of his own ship, its port of registry and the nearest port at which it will call.[90]

The duty to rescue is also found in numerous regional and bilateral treaties, and not just between allies. For instance, in 1988 the United States and the Soviet Union concluded a bilateral treaty on maritime

---

[87] International Convention for the Safety of Life at Sea, 1 November 1974, 1184 UNTS 278 (entered into force 25 May 1980) (SOLAS Convention) ch V, reg 15. For a brief history of the SOLAS Convention and its many updates, see 'SOLAS' (2019), *International Maritime Organization*, online: www.imo.org/en/KnowledgeCentre/ConferencesMeetings/Pages/SOLAS.aspx.

[88] Convention on International Civil Aviation, 7 December 1944, 15 UNTS 295 Annex 12 (7th ed., 2001), Art. 2.1.2 (entered into force 4 April 1947) (Chicago Convention), Annex 12 (7th ed., 2001).

[89] International Convention on Maritime Search and Rescue, 27 April 1979, 1405 UNTS 119 Annex, ch 2, Art. 2.1.1 (entered into force 22 June 1985, including amendments adopted in 1998 and 2004).

[90] United Nations Convention on the Law of the Sea, 10 December 1982, 1833 UNTS 397, Art. 98 (1) (entered into force 16 November 1994).

search and rescue.[91] Then, after the loss of the Russian nuclear attack submarine *Kursk* in the year 2000, Russia and NATO signed an agreement on submarine rescues in 2003.[92] Two years later, a British submersible was used to free seven Russian sailors whose mini submarine had become tangled in a fishing net 190 metres below the surface of the Pacific Ocean off the Kamchatka peninsula.[93] There is also the 2011 Agreement on Cooperation on Aeronautical and Maritime Search and Rescue in the Arctic, which reiterates the obligations of the Chicago Convention and the SAR Convention in a regional context among the eight Arctic states, and includes five NATO states as well as Russia.[94]

The duty to rescue is found in the 1967 Outer Space Treaty, with the first sentence of Article V reading, 'States Parties to the Treaty shall regard astronauts as envoys of mankind in outer space and shall render to them all possible assistance in the event of accident, distress, or emergency landing on the territory of another State Party or on the high seas'.[95] Indeed, the duty to rescue was considered so fundamental that, the very next year, the same states concluded the 1968 Agreement on the Rescue of Astronauts, the Return of Astronauts and the Return of Objects Launched into Outer Space (Rescue Agreement).[96] The Rescue Agreement elaborates on Article V of the Outer Space Treaty. It explains that, in any given situation, the duty to rescue requires that 'those Contracting Parties which are in a position to do so shall, if necessary, extend assistance in search and rescue operations for such personnel to assure their speedy rescue'.[97] As we explain in Chapter 1, this duty applies everywhere: within the jurisdiction of each respective state party as well as in areas beyond national jurisdiction, such as the high seas and Space.

---

[91] Agreement between the Government of the United States of America and the Government of the Union of Soviet Socialist Republics on Maritime Search and Rescue, 12 December 1986, 2191 UNTS 115 (entered into force 1 January 1989).

[92] NATO Update, 'NATO and Russia sign submarine rescue agreement' (8 February 2003), *North Atlantic Treaty Organization*, online: www.nato.int/docu/update/2003/02-febru ary/e0208a.htm.

[93] 'Russians saved in deep-sea rescue', *BBC News* (7 August 2005), online: news.bbc.co.uk/1/ hi/world/europe/4128614.stm.

[94] Agreement on Cooperation on Aeronautical and Maritime Search and Rescue in the Arctic, 12 May 2011, 50 ILM 1119 (entered into force 19 January 2013).

[95] Outer Space Treaty, op. cit., Art. V.

[96] Agreement on the Rescue of Astronauts, the Return of Astronauts and the Return of Objects Launched into Outer Space, 22 April 1968, 672 UNTS 119 (entered into force 3 December 1968) (Rescue Agreement).

[97] Ibid. Art. 3.

For all these reasons, the Ad-Hoc Working Group was wrong to conclude that 'States are free to decide whether they provide assistance to other States that are threatened by a possible NEO impact'.[98] States have a general duty to rescue people in distress that would most certainly be engaged by an impending asteroid or comet strike. Of course, the duty is not absolute: no state would be required to develop a deflection capability in order to come to the assistance of another state. However, what if a state already had a deflection capability, including both spacecraft and rockets, on standby? Balancing the duty to rescue against any risks and expenses associated with acting is a fact-specific determination, one that does not detract from the existence of this duty as a general principle of law among the community of nations.

### 6.7.3   Nuclear Explosive Devices

The potential use of NEDs for deflecting or destroying asteroids is debated among international lawyers, with this debate connecting to a larger one about the legality of using or even possessing nuclear weapons.[99] In this section, we will demonstrate that most of the legal discussion about using NEDs for planetary defence is of limited relevance. This is because a nuclear explosion in Space would constitute a clear violation of the 1963 Limited Test Ban Treaty,[100] which binds the two states most likely to attempt such an action, namely the United States and Russia. It is also possible that the prohibition on nuclear explosions in Space has become a rule of customary international law, in which case it would bind non-parties to the Limited Test Ban Treaty, most notably China – which tested its first atomic bomb in 1964 but has never conducted a nuclear test in Space.[101] China has signed but not ratified the 1996 Comprehensive Test Ban Treaty, which, if it ever comes into force, will ban all nuclear tests including in Space.[102]

---

[98] SMPAG, 'Planetary defence', op. cit. at 24.

[99] See Bryce G Poole, 'Against the nuclear option: Planetary defence under international Space law' (2020) 45:1 *Air and Space Law* 55.

[100] Treaty Banning Nuclear Weapon Tests in the Atmosphere, in Outer Space and under Water, 5 August 1963, 480 UNTS 43 (entered into force 10 October 1963) (Limited Test Ban Treaty).

[101] James Martin Center for Nonproliferation Studies, 'China nuclear overview fact sheet' (29 April 2015), *Nuclear Threat Initiative*, online: www.nti.org/analysis/articles/china-nuclear.

[102] Comprehensive Test Ban Treaty, 24 September 1996, 35 ILM 1439 (not yet entered into force).

This is not the end of the discussion, however, since the United Nations Security Council could still authorise the use of an NED, with resolutions adopted under Chapter VII of the UN Charter prevailing over conflicting rules of international law. Moreover, if the Security Council failed to adopt a resolution – for instance because of a veto cast by one of its five permanent members – a state could still use an NED and claim 'necessity'.[103] Necessity, as we will explain below, is a 'circumstance precluding wrongfulness' within the international law of state responsibility. The relevant questions, at that point, would concern whether the criteria for necessity had been fulfilled.

### 6.7.4   Nuclear Explosive Devices and the Outer Space Treaty

Most legal discussions concerning the use of NEDs in planetary defence start with the first paragraph of Article IV of the Outer Space Treaty, which reads,

> States Parties to the Treaty undertake not to place in orbit around the earth any objects carrying nuclear weapons or any other kinds of weapons of mass destruction, install such weapons on celestial bodies, or station such weapons in outer space in any other manner.[104]

It is important to note that this paragraph does not prohibit the launch of nuclear weapons into Space if they do not make an orbit around the Earth. Nor does it say anything about whether NEDs used for planetary defence should be distinguished from nuclear weapons. However, the absence of any such provisions has not stopped international lawyers from debating whether an NED should be considered a weapon. The Ad-Hoc Working Group looks to dictionaries, writing, 'Generally, the term "weapon" can be defined as *"any object used in fighting or war, such as a gun, bomb, knife"* (Cambridge English Dictionary) or as *"an instrument*

---

[103] It is also conceivable that, in the event of a veto being cast in the Security Council, the UN General Assembly could adopt a resolution supporting the use of a NED. There are precedents here, most notably Resolution 377A(V), the so-called 'Uniting for Peace' resolution, which was adopted in 1950 in support of 'collective measures ... to maintain or restore international peace and security' on the Korean peninsula. See *Uniting for Peace*, GA Res 377(V), UNGAOR, 5th Sess, 302nd Plen Mtg, UN Doc A/RES/377 (3 November 1950) Art. 1.

[104] Outer Space Treaty, op. cit., Art. IV.

*of any kind used in warfare or in combat to attack and overcome an enemy"* (Oxford English Dictionary)'.[105]

Both these definitions require that the object be used to fight or wage war, which an NED would not. The Ad-Hoc Working Group concedes this point,[106] but then moves past the dictionary definitions to come to the opposite conclusion:

> However, not only the purpose for which something is used determines its qualification as a weapon. Any possible dual-use applications would not change the inherent nature of 'weapons', 'nuclear weapons' or 'weapons of mass destruction', which result from their initial designation. A 'weapon' remains a 'weapon' irrespective of whether it may be used for non-destructive civilian purposes. The problem arising in this context is that it is difficult to construct a device that could be used only against a NEO and not have some applicability against other targets. A planetary defence device could also be used as a weapon.[107]

This then leads the Ad-Hoc Working Group to conclude, 'Since, following the analysis above, NEDs can be qualified as "nuclear weapons", their use in the context of planetary defence missions falls under the scope of this provision' (i.e. Article IV, first paragraph).[108]

Again, this conclusion is contestable. As terrorists have demonstrated, cars and passenger planes can be used as weapons, even though they are not designed or considered as such. More to the point, a kitchen knife is not considered a weapon, unless wielded with hostile intent. Even firearms used for hunting – especially subsistence hunting (i.e. for food) – are not generally considered weapons.

Other international lawyers have taken a more nuanced approach. James Green engages in a lengthy exercise in treaty interpretation, including a foray into the negotiating records (*travaux préparatoires*) of the Outer Space Treaty, before concluding that an NED launched directly from Earth towards an asteroid would be permissible, but an NED stationed in Space in anticipation of an Earth impact emergency would not.[109] He bases

---

[105] SMPAG, 'Planetary defence', op. cit. at 29, SMPAG's emphasis.

[106] 'Generally, planetary defence devices are not developed for use in warfare to attack or overcome an enemy. They are also not intended to cause widespread devastation and loss of life. On the contrary, planetary defence methods are intended to be specifically targeted at a potentially hazardous asteroid or comet in order to save lives and prevent widespread devastation on Earth.' Ibid.

[107] Ibid.

[108] Ibid.

[109] Green, 'Planetary defense', op. cit.

the former conclusion on the text of Article IV's first paragraph , as well as the fact that it was negotiated at the height of the Cold War when both the United States and the Soviet Union would have wished 'to retain the possibility of undertaking nuclear strikes against each other via intercontinental ballistic missiles launched out of the atmosphere on a trajectory that then returned them to their terrestrial target'.[110] ICBMs existed before the Outer Space Treaty was negotiated. However, permanently stationing nuclear weapons in Space would have escalated the Cold War, and this, Green explains, was something that both superpowers were cognisant to avoid.

One could quibble with some of Green's analysis. Like the Ad-Hoc Working Group, he argues that an NED cannot be distinguished from a nuclear weapon for the purposes of the Outer Space Treaty, since the components would be identical. But again, these arguments may not actually matter, since another treaty is much clearer on the key point in question.

### 6.7.5   The Limited Test Ban Treaty

Although the Outer Space Treaty may not necessarily pose an obstacle to the use of an NED against an NEO, Article I(1)(a) of the 1963 Limited Test Ban Treaty is unequivocal:

1. Each of the Parties to this Treaty undertakes to prohibit, to prevent, and not to carry out any nuclear weapon test explosion, or any other nuclear explosion, at any place under its jurisdiction or control:
   (a) in the atmosphere; beyond its limits, including outer space; or under water, including territorial waters or high seas ...[111]

Note that the prohibition is not limited to nuclear weapon tests but encompasses 'any other nuclear explosion', including in Space. This conclusion is supported by the Preamble, which states that 'the principal aim' of the Limited Test Ban Treaty is 'the speediest possible achievement of an agreement on general and complete disarmament', and that a further aim is 'to put an end to the contamination of man's environment by radioactive substances.' Moreover, the *travaux préparatoires* reveal that the words 'or any other nuclear explosion' were inserted into Article

---

[110] Ibid. at 32.
[111] Limited Test Ban Treaty, op. cit.

I(1)(a) to prevent the prohibition being circumvented through an assertion of 'peaceful use'.[112]

Russia, the United States, the United Kingdom and India are all parties
to the Limited Test Ban Treaty; China, France and North Korea are not.
The Limited Test Ban Treaty thus poses a legal obstacle to four of the
states currently able to attempt an NEO deflection with an NED. But
China also has nuclear warheads and large Space rockets, while France
has warheads and potential access to rockets via ArianeSpace – the
European launch provider.

### 6.7.6   Nuclear Explosive Devices and Customary International Law

It is well established that treaty provisions can contribute to parallel rules
of customary international law. In the *North Sea Continental Shelf Cases*,
the International Court of Justice considered whether a provision in the
1958 Geneva Convention on the Continental Shelf could have given rise
to a parallel rule of customary international law.[113] It wrote,

> Although the passage of only a short period of time is not necessarily, or
> of itself, a bar to the formation of a new rule of customary international
> law on the basis of what was originally a purely conventional rule, an
> indispensable requirement would be that within the period in question,
> short though it might be, State practice, including that of States whose
> interests are specially affected, should have been both extensive and
> virtually uniform in the sense of the provision invoked; and should
> moreover have occurred in such a way as to show a general recognition
> that a rule of law or legal obligation is involved.[114]

It is significant that, while several states tested nuclear weapons in Space
before the Limited Test Ban Treaty was adopted in 1963, none has done
so since. Moreover, those states that acquired the capability to test
nuclear weapons in Space after 1963 have refrained from doing so.
Most significantly, two of these states – China and France – have
refrained from nuclear weapon testing in Space despite never having
acceded to the Limited Test Ban Treaty. However, it is uncertain whether

---

[112] Green, 'Planetary defense', op. cit. at 41, citing Arthur H Dean, *Test Ban and
Disarmament: The Path of Negotiation*, 1st ed. (New York: Published for the Council
on Foreign Relations by Harper & Row, 1966) at 100–10.

[113] Convention on the Continental Shelf, 29 April 1958, 499 UNTS 311 (entered into force
10 June 1964).

[114] *North Sea Continental Shelf Cases* (*Germany* v. *Denmark*; *Germany* v. *Netherlands*)
[1969] ICJ Reports 3 at 44, para. 74.

this avoidance of nuclear weapon testing in Space has been driven by 'a general recognition that a rule of law or legal obligation is involved' (in the words of the ICJ),[115] or whether states simply became aware that such tests have dangerous consequences.

The Soviet Union conducted five nuclear weapon tests in Space in 1961 and 1962. The latter of these, which occurred at an altitude of 230 kilometres, generated such a strong electromagnetic pulse that it caused a fire in a power plant on the ground and disabled hundreds of kilometres of telephone lines. That same year – 1962 – the United States detonated a 1.44 megaton thermonuclear weapon at an altitude of 400 kilometres over the Pacific Ocean.[116] The test, dubbed Starfish Prime, was one of five tests in Operation Fishbowl, which sought to determine whether an artificial intensification of the Van Allen radiation belts could disable intercontinental ballistic missiles.[117] It provided a surprising result: the electromagnetic pulse from the explosion shut down power grids in Hawaii and disabled Telstar 1, which had just begun broadcasting live television between the United States and Europe, as well as five other satellites from the US, the United Kingdom and the Soviet Union.[118]

However, even were the subsequent avoidance of nuclear explosions in Space the result of an awareness of risk rather than a specific legal obligation, this avoidance is occurring in a legal context that includes not only the Limited Test Ban Treaty, but also a general obligation in customary international law to not cause damage to the property of another state. The existence of this obligation is recognised in Article VII of the Outer Space Treaty, which provides that launch states are 'internationally liable for damage to another State Party to the Treaty or to its natural or juridical persons by such [Space] object or its component parts on the Earth, in air space or in outer space, including the moon and other celestial bodies'. The 1972 Convention on the International Liability for Damage Caused by Space Objects (Liability Convention) elaborates on this provision by providing for absolute liability for damage

---

[115] Ibid.

[116] David Portree, 'Starfish and Apollo (1962)', *Wired* (21 March 2012), online: www.wired.com/2012/03/starfishandapollo-1962.

[117] Daniel G Dupont, 'Nuclear explosions in orbit', *Scientific American* 290:6 (2004) 100; Phil Plait, 'The Fiftieth anniversary of Starfish Prime: The nuke that shook the world', *Discover Magazine* (9 July 2012), online: www.discovermagazine.com/the-sciences/the-50th-anniversary-of-starfish-prime-the-nuke-that-shook-the-world.

[118] Portree, op. cit.

on Earth, and fault-based liability for damage in Space.[119] It is easy to imagine a nuclear explosion that is caused by one state damaging or disabling satellites owned by others – as, indeed, occurred with Starfish Prime. States that can conduct nuclear weapon tests in Space and choose not to do so based on a recognition of the risks to others are, therefore, engaged in state practice and demonstrating *opinio juris* in support of a rule of customary international law prohibiting such explosions.

Further support for the existence of a rule of customary international law prohibiting nuclear explosions in Space can be found in the 1996 Comprehensive Test Ban Treaty, Article I(1) which reads, 'Each State Party undertakes not to carry out any nuclear weapon test explosion or any other nuclear explosion, and to prohibit and prevent any such nuclear explosion at any place under its jurisdiction or control'.[120] The inclusion of Space within this prohibition is confirmed by the Preamble, where the states parties are: '*Noting* the aspirations expressed by the Parties to the 1963 Treaty Banning Nuclear Weapon Tests in the Atmosphere, in Outer Space and Under Water to seek to achieve the discontinuance of all test explosions of nuclear weapons for all time'.

According to Article XIV, the Comprehensive Test Ban Treaty will not come into force until it is ratified by 44 specific states. These 'Annex 2 states' are those that participated in the negotiation of the treaty in 1994–1996 and possessed nuclear reactors at that time. Of these 44 states, eight have not yet ratified the treaty, although five of them – the United States, China, Egypt, Iran and Israel – have signed it. They are therefore obligated to 'refrain from acts which would defeat the object and purpose' of the treaty, with this general obligation in customary international law (binding on the signatories of any treaty) being recognised in Article 18 of the Vienna Convention on the Law of Treaties.[121]

The three remaining Annex 2 states – India, North Korea and Pakistan – have neither signed nor ratified the Comprehensive Test Ban Treaty and seem unlikely to do so. But what is more relevant for the purposes of customary international law is that 168 states have

---

[119] Convention on International Liability for Damage Caused by Space Objects, 29 March 1972, 961 UNTS 187 Arts. II–III (entered into force 1 September 1972) (Liability Convention).

[120] Comprehensive Test Ban Treaty, op. cit., Art. I(1).

[121] Vienna Convention on the Law of Treaties, 23 May 1969, 1155 UNTS 331 Art. 18 (entered into force 27 January 1980).

ratified the Comprehensive Test Ban Treaty, while another 16 have signed but not yet ratified. This means that 95 per cent of countries – 184 of 193 member states of the United Nations – have thereby indicated their support for a prohibition on nuclear weapon tests that extends to Space. Considering all this, we conclude that a rule of customary international law prohibiting nuclear explosions in Space exists, with North Korea (but not India or Pakistan, because they have ratified the Limited Test Ban Treaty) perhaps remaining outside its scope as a so-called 'persistent objector'.[122]

## 6.8   Who Decides?

Within this legal context, a number of key questions arise. Who should be responsible for vetting the science, assessing the risks and making decisions if Earth were faced with an actual NEO threat? How can we maximise international co-operation to ensure a positive outcome? Who should be responsible for mounting a deflection mission, and how can we guard against things going wrong?

Depending on the amount of time between detection and potential impact, a deflection mission might need to be launched before the orbit of the NEO has been determined with precision and before any impending impact can be confirmed. Since any deflection mission will be expensive, decision makers may have to spend large amounts of money based on risk rather than on certainty. These challenges of time, uncertainty and expense could be mitigated by forward-deploying spacecraft in cis-lunar orbit, in advance of the detection of any specific threat. The spacecraft could be designed with both scientific and deflection capabilities, enabling operators to determine whether an Earth impact is actually impending, and, if it is not, to collect other kinds of valuable information – including about the risk of an Earth impact on subsequent passes of an NEO.

Improved detection and orbit determination capabilities will also assist decision makers in determining when deflections are unnecessary for other reasons, for instance if the impact will take place in a sparsely populated region. Even then, any potential climate-altering effects, such as through lofting of material into the atmosphere, will have to be assessed. Similarly, impacts at sea could lead to dangerous and damaging

---

[122] James A Green, 'India and a customary comprehensive nuclear test-ban: Persistent objection, peremptory norms and the 123 agreement' (2011) 51:3 *Indian Journal of International Law* 3 at 9–18.

tsunamis. All of this would need to be further weighed against the risks of a failed or only partially successful deflection.

### 6.8.1 Space Agencies Acting Collectively

The ideal response to an NEO threat would be for Space agencies to collectively determine the feasibility and risks of different mitigation options, decide on the best approach and implement it. As discussed above, Space agencies are already working together on these issues through an International Asteroid Warning Network that reports to the Space Mission Planning Advisory Group, currently made up of representatives from 18 Space agencies. Both bodies were created in 2013 at the recommendation of the UN Committee on the Peaceful Uses of Outer Space.[123] The IAWN connects Space agencies, observatories and other groups engaged in discovering, monitoring and characterising potentially hazardous NEOs; it also serves as a 'clearing house' for NEO observations and recommends criteria and thresholds for notification of emerging threats.[124] The SMPAG prepares for an international response to an NEO threat by exchanging information, developing options for collaborative research and mission opportunities, and conducting threat mitigation planning activities. Yet it is unclear whether Space agencies would be allowed to lead on these issues in the event of an actual NEO threat, given that militaries are also active in Space and often have much greater political influence. However, as we will explain, militaries are poorly suited for planetary defence. For this reason, states should commit in advance to keeping Space agencies in charge during such eventualities, with this commitment expressed in a multilateral declaration or, better yet, treaty. This commitment could then be implemented in national legal systems, to bind militaries directly.

### 6.8.2 A Decision-Making Matrix

The Ad-Hoc Working Group recognised that responses to NEO threats will be complicated because of the absence of international legal instruments explicitly addressing this issue and because of the short time that might be available to make decisions and to act at the international level. For these reasons, it suggested the drafting of a template for decision

---

[123] SMPAG, 'Terms of reference', op. cit.
[124] Warner, 'History', op. cit.

making that could quickly be adapted and adopted by the international community in the face of a specific threat. This template could include 'modalities for the organization of cooperation among States and inter-governmental organizations', as well as for the dissemination of information regarding NEO threats.[125] As the Ad-Hoc Working Group explained, any such decision-making matrix would have to balance between the need for transparency and inclusion and 'the importance of avoiding a lengthy process that inhibits an effective response and of providing the flexibility and the resilience that is required'.[126]

The Ad-Hoc Working Group issued its report before the COVID-19 pandemic exposed the weakness of multilateral co-operation in the field of global health. Given the rapid sidelining of the World Health Organization, how confident can we be that SMPAG – another voluntary mechanism designed to co-ordinate state responses – will operate effectively during an equally significant global crisis? Will national political struggles or leadership failings impair collective decision making? Will powerful states turn away from international co-operation as they prioritise national preservation? These last questions become even more relevant with regard to the most powerful international body, the United Nations Security Council, where the five permanent members each hold a veto over decision making.

### 6.8.3   The UN Security Council

One hundred and ninety-three states have ratified the 1945 United Nations Charter and are consequently bound to accept Security Council decisions made under Chapter VII of that treaty. Chapter VII gives the Security Council the power to 'determine the existence of any threat to the peace, breach of the peace, or act of aggression' and to 'decide what measures shall be taken ... to maintain or restore international peace and security'. Such measures can include 'action by air, sea, or land forces', including within the territory of non-consenting states.[127]

---

[125]  SMPAG, 'Planetary defence', op. cit. at 26.
[126]  Ibid. at 59.
[127]  Charter of the United Nations, 26 June 1945, Can TS 1945 No 7 (entered into force 24 October 1945).

For decades, the Security Council has taken a broad view of international security. It has invoked Chapter VII to impose an embargo on the racist government of Southern Rhodesia in 1968,[128] to deliver humanitarian aid in Somalia in 1992,[129] and to require measures against terrorist financing in all national legal systems in 2001.[130] In 2010, the Security Council invoked Chapter VII in response to an earthquake in Haiti, authorising the deployment of 680 police to augment the existing UN peacekeeping and humanitarian mission in that country.[131] There is no question that the Security Council could decide that an NEO was a threat to international peace and security and make decisions – such as authorising the use of an NED – that would otherwise violate international law. The Security Council could even provide the acting states with a waiver of liability for any resulting damage, liability that might otherwise flow from the 1967 Outer Space Treaty, the 1972 Liability Convention or customary international law.

The peremptory effect of Chapter VII resolutions comes from Article 103 of the UN Charter, which reads, 'In the event of a conflict between the obligations of the Members of the United Nations under the present Charter and their obligations under any other international agreement, their obligations under the present Charter shall prevail.' The only limiting factor here is that Security Council resolutions require the support of at least nine of its 15 members, including the concurring votes (or abstentions) of all five permanent members. In other words, China, France, Russia, the United Kingdom and the United States all hold vetoes over Security Council resolutions. In the literature on planetary defence, the veto is generally regarded as a bad thing, since it could prevent the Security Council from authorising necessary action. However, the veto can also serve as a check on precipitous or incautious action, such as a deflection mission that is not supported by a careful scientific assessment of the risks involved.

In any event, if Security Council decision making is blocked because of a veto, it is conceivable that one or more states might proceed with an unauthorised deflection mission.

---

[128] *Question Concerning the Situation in Southern Rhodesia*, SC Res 253, UNSCOR, 1428th mtg, UN Doc S/RES/253 (29 May 1968).
[129] SC Res 794, UNSCOR, 3145th mtg, UN Doc S/RES/794 (3 December 1992).
[130] SC Res 1373, UNSCOR, 4385th mtg, UN Doc S/RES/1373 (28 September 2001).
[131] SC Res 1927, UNSCOR, 6330th mtg, UN Doc S/RES/1927 (4 June 2010).

### 6.8.4 Individual States

The DART mission (discussed above) was led by NASA, with some participation from the European Space Agency and the Italian Space Agency.[132] Although there was no risk that the targeted moonlet would inadvertently be directed onto an Earth impact trajectory, it is noteworthy that the United States did not seek the consent of other states during the mission-planning process. It did consult with them, however, including by informing the SMPAG.

If an NEO is discovered on an actual Earth impact trajectory, one or more states might take it upon themselves to mount a deflection mission. Some experts have pointed to the right of self-defence, a rule of customary international law that is codified in Article 51 of the UN Charter, as providing a legal avenue for unilateral action. However, as Green correctly explains,

> Self-defense, conceptually, is focused on a defensive response to human-authored attacks or threats of attack, and exists as an exception to the *ad bellum* prohibition on the use of force. That prohibition is set out in Article 2(4) of the UN Charter, which outlaws 'the threat or use of force against the territorial integrity or political independence of any state . . . .' Forcible action against an asteroid or comet would not be directed 'against . . . any state,' but, instead, against a large space rock. This means that the prohibition of the use of force would not be breached by a planetary defense action. Resorting to self-defense therefore would amount to an attempt to employ an exception to a rule that would not be violated by the action undertaken.[133]

No rule of international law directly prohibits a unilateral deflection mission directed against an asteroid or comet. Rather, the legal issues concern the rights of other states to be consulted, not to be exposed to increased risk, and to obtain compensation in the event of an accident. There are other legal issues concerning the use of NEDs, concerning the role of the UN Security Council in this regard (and in relation to possible waivers of liability), and concerning the possibility that 'circumstances precluding wrongfulness' might excuse a breach of international law. We will delve deeper into some of these issues below.

The possibility of a unilateral deflection mission is real, given the panic and selfishness that can arise in crisis situations. Adding to the risk,

---

[132] Andrew F Cheng et al., 'AIDA DART asteroid deflection test: Planetary defense and science objectives' (2018) 157 *Planetary and Space Science* 104.

[133] Green, 'Planetary defense', op. cit. at 52–53.

militaries could insist on being involved in national decision making concerning an NEO threat, because of the scale of the threat, the kind of equipment that could be used – especially NEDs – and the fact that the political influence of militaries always exceeds that of Space agencies.

Militaries, however, are poorly suited for planetary defence. They tend to favour forceful actions over more subtle interventions such as diplomacy. In the context of planetary defence, they might favour kinetic impactors or NEDs over slow-moving mass drivers or gravity tractors. Militaries are not involved in current NEO detection and mission-planning exercises at the international level, notably IAWN and SMPAG, and therefore might not be fully informed on these matters – and more likely to make mistakes. Finally, militaries tend to co-operate with smaller circles of states than Space agencies, making them poorly suited for multilateral initiatives that include non-allies. There is a reason why the International Space Station, where Americans and Russians work side by side, is operated by civilian Space agencies rather than militaries.

Fortunately, even a unilateral military-led response to an NEO threat would be constrained by international law. First, any state planning a unilateral deflection mission would have to consult with other states. Article IX of the Outer Space Treaty reads, in part,

> States Parties to the Treaty shall be guided by the principle of co-operation and mutual assistance and shall conduct all their activities in outer space, including the moon and other celestial bodies, with due regard to the corresponding interests of all other States Parties to the Treaty ... If a State Party to the Treaty has reason to believe that an activity or experiment planned by it or its nationals in outer space, including the moon and other celestial bodies, would cause potentially harmful interference with activities of other States Parties in the peaceful exploration and use of outer space, including the moon and other celestial bodies, it shall undertake appropriate international consultations before proceeding with any such activity or experiment.[134]

Consultation offers many benefits, one of which is an increased likelihood that careful scientific analyses of the risks of any proposed action will take place. Militaries acting unilaterally have done incautious things in the past in Space. For example, between 1961 and 1963, the US military launched 480 million copper needles into orbit, in an attempt

---

[134] Outer Space Treaty, op. cit., Art. IX.

to create an artificial ring around Earth for relaying radio signals.[135] Most of these needles have long since re-entered the atmosphere, driven by the effects of solar radiation, but clumps of them remain in orbit today – contributing to the serious and growing problem of Space debris. Consultation is critical in the context of an NEO threat since it might well lead to an initial rendezvous mission to determine the asteroid's precise orbit, shape and composition, and thus serve as the basis for a considered response.

In lieu of consulting other states and taking their interests into account, what would happen if a military decided to act unilaterally? What if the NED were launched without pooling scientific knowledge and mission capabilities with other states, and before carefully consider-ing other methods? Does international law empower other states to prevent a powerful state from acting in this way? One possible step would be economic countermeasures, up to and including sanctions, especially if the acting state was a party to the 1963 Limited Test Ban Treaty (which, again, clearly prohibits the use of an NED).[136] However, economic countermeasures are unlikely to have any immediate effect on a powerful state that sees itself responding to a serious threat. A more interesting question concerns pre-emptive self-defence. If other states had scientific evidence that the unilateral deflection mission would increase the risk to their territory and populations, for instance by changing the impact location, could they take pre-emptive military action to prevent the launch?

This scenario, it should be noted, is fundamentally different from discussions of self-defence as a justification for deflection missions, as dismissed by Green at the beginning of this section. Here, the threat comes from another state interfering with the asteroid.

The existence and extent of a right of pre-emptive self-defence is hotly contested in international law, with the United States leading the push for a more expansive approach, and many smaller, less powerful states

---

[135] NASA Orbital Debris Program Office, 'West Ford needles: Where are they now?' (2013) 17:4 *Orbital Debris Quarterly* 3, online: orbitaldebris.jsc.nasa.gov/quarterly-news/pdfs/odqnv17i4.pdf.

[136] On countermeasures, see 'Draft Articles on the Responsibility of States for Internationally Wrongful Acts' in *Yearbook of the International Law Commission 2001*, vol. II, part 2 (New York: UN, 2007), Arts. 22, 49–54 (UN Doc A/CN.4/SER.A/2001/Add.1 (Part 2)), online: legal.un.org/ilc/publications/yearbooks/english/ilc_2001_v2_p2.pdf.

resisting its efforts.[137] We will not repeat that debate here. It is, however, readily conceivable that a state might claim pre-emptive self-defence in circumstances where it feels threatened by another state interfering with a natural force. Imagine if a state had reason to believe that another state was preparing to attack a hydroelectric dam upstream from a population centre. However, if a right of pre-emptive self-defence exists, and if it were invoked to justify military action to prevent the launch of an asteroid deflection mission by another state, that action would still be subject to the usual constraints imposed on self-defence under customary international law, namely that the response must be both 'necessary' and 'proportionate'.[138]

Although the issue of pre-emptive self-defence is interesting in this context, it is unlikely ever to arise. Militaries cannot simply launch their existing nuclear missiles against incoming NEOs, since ballistic missiles cannot achieve escape velocity. There will always be time to consult with other states, receive additional scientific input and engage in sober second thought. As this happens, international law will move to the forefront of the deliberation process, not least because of rules on state responsibility and liability, rules that would apply to any damage caused on Earth by a failed deflection mission.

## 6.9    State Responsibility

As the Ad-Hoc Working Group on Legal Issues explained, 'Any violation of an international obligation in the course of a planetary defence mission, such as the use of NEDs, entails the international responsibility of the States involved and may provide the basis for claims for compensation'.[139] 'State responsibility' is governed by rules of customary international law that were codified by the International Law Commission in its 2001 Draft Articles on State Responsibility, as commended to governments by the UN General Assembly later that

---

[137] For an overview of the pre-emptive self-defence debate, see Christine Gray, *International Law and the Use of Force*, 4th ed. (Oxford: Oxford University Press, 2018) at 248–253.

[138] The right of self-defence, including the criteria of necessity and proportionality, are discussed at length in Chapter 8 in the context of anti-satellite weapons.

[139] SMPAG, 'Planetary defence', op. cit. at 3.

same year.[140] The rules on 'circumstances precluding wrongfulness' are of primary interest in the context of planetary defence.

### 6.9.1   Circumstances Precluding Wrongfulness

Sometimes in the international realm, just as in the domestic, lawbreakers are excused for their actions because of the unusual circumstances they found themselves in. If a state chose to violate international law while engaging in planetary defence, for example by using an NED, it is possible that the violation would be excused because it took place under 'circumstances precluding wrongfulness'. The different circumstances that can preclude wrongfulness are identified in the International Law Commission's Draft Articles on State Responsibility, with 'consent' and 'necessity' being of greatest potential relevance here.[141] It is also important to note that, according to Article 27 of the Draft Articles, the invocation of a circumstance precluding wrongfulness does not relieve the acting state of any obligation to provide compensation for any material loss caused by the otherwise illegal act in question. In other words, being excused for the wrong does not relieve the state of any obligation to pay compensation.

#### 6.9.1.1   Consent

Article 20 of the International Law Commission's Draft Articles on State Responsibility reads, 'Valid consent by a State to the commission of a given act by another State precludes the wrongfulness of that act in relation to the former State to the extent that the act remains within the limits of that consent.'[142] This means that, if a state facing an NEO threat consents to another state using a planetary defence method that violates international law, that act will no longer be wrongful as between those two states. As the Ad-Hoc Working Group explains, consent can either be expressed or implied, for example through the provision of support for the mission.

---

[140] 'Draft Articles on the Responsibility of States for Internationally Wrongful Acts', in *Responsibility of States for Internationally Wrongful Acts*, GA Res 56/83, UNGAOR, 56th Sess, 85th Plen Mtg, UN Doc A/RES/56/83 Annex (28 January 2002), online: undocs .org/en/A/RES/56/83.

[141] Ibid., Arts. 20, 25.

[142] Ibid., Art. 20.

This is not the end of the issue, however, since the international rule being violated will still apply between the acting state and third states, unless each of them has also consented. For this reason, the Ad-Hoc Working Group suggests that a UN General Assembly resolution could be used to express 'broad consent to a particular planetary defence mission'.[143]

### 6.9.1.2   Distress

The Ad-Hoc Working Group also identifies 'distress' as a condition precluding wrongfulness that might be relevant to planetary defence. Article 24 of the International Law Commission's Draft Articles on State Responsibility reads,

1. The wrongfulness of an act of a State not in conformity with an international obligation of that State is precluded if the author of the act in question has no other reasonable way, in a situation of distress, of saving the author's life or the lives of other persons entrusted to the author's care.
2. Paragraph 1 does not apply if: (a) the situation of distress is due, either alone or in combination with other factors, to the conduct of the State invoking it; or (b) the act in question is likely to create a comparable or greater peril.[144]

As the Ad-Hoc Working Group explains, 'Thus, in situations where the lives of persons are threatened by the possible impact of an NEO, the use of a planetary defence method in violation of international law could be justified if there is "*no other reasonable way*" of saving the lives'.[145]

It is questionable, however, whether distress would ever be a relevant circumstance precluding wrongfulness in the context of planetary defence. Distress is most often invoked when ships or aircraft are suddenly forced to enter another state's airspace or internal waters because of a storm or accident.[146] The discovery of an NEO threat is unlikely to require similarly sudden action, since spacecraft will have to be built and launched. For this reason, the opportunity to seek consent will almost

---

[143] SMPAG, 'Planetary defence', op. cit. at 38.

[144] 'Draft Articles on the Responsibility of States', op. cit., Art. 24.

[145] SMPAG, 'Planetary Defence', op. cit. at 38, SMPAG's emphasis.

[146] International Law Commission, 'Draft Articles on Responsibility of States for Internationally Wrongful Acts, with Commentaries 2001' (2008) at 78–80, *United Nations*, online: legal.un .org/ilc/texts/instruments/english/commentaries/9_6_2001.pdf.

always be available. The more appropriate circumstance precluding wrongfulness for situations where the issue is not the time available to secure consent but rather the use of an illegal method, such as an NED, would seem to be necessity.

### 6.9.1.3   Necessity

Article 25(1) of the International Law Commission's Draft Articles on State Responsibility reads,

> Necessity may not be invoked by a State as a ground for precluding the wrongfulness of an act not in conformity with an international obligation of that State unless the act:
>
> a. Is the only way for the State to safeguard an essential interest against a grave and imminent peril; and
> b. Does not seriously impair an essential interest of the State or States towards which the obligation exists, or of the international community as a whole.[147]

As the Ad-Hoc Working Group notes, necessity as a ground for precluding wrongfulness was recognised by the International Court of Justice in the 1997 *Case Concerning the Gabčíkovo-Nagymaros Project*.[148] The dispute concerned Hungary's abandonment of a joint project to construct a dam and a series of locks on the river Danube, and the Slovak Republic's decision to proceed with its part of the project – the dam, located on its territory – regardless. Hungary argued that its decision to abandon the project was justified under the criteria for necessity, and particularly the existence of an 'imminent peril'. The ICJ disagreed, and Hungary was therefore not excused for violating the treaty that served as the legal basis for the joint project. The absence of an imminent peril provided Hungary with time to find another, legal way in which to safeguard its 'essential interest'.

Whether all the criteria have been met in the case of any NEO threat, including the existence of a grave and imminent peril and an essential interest, will depend on the specifics of the threat. Moreover, as the Ad-Hoc Working Group explains, the fulfilment of these criteria must be 'objectively established and not merely apprehended as possible'.[149]

---

[147] 'Draft Articles on the Responsibility of States', op. cit., Art. 25(1).
[148] *Gabčíkovo-Nagymaros Project* (*Hungary* v. *Slovakia*) [1997] ICJ Reports 7 at 37, para. 51.
[149] SMPAG, 'Planetary defence', op. cit. at 39.

In other words, it is not sufficient for the acting state simply to believe that the criteria for necessity have been fulfilled. We should also note that circumstances precluding wrongfulness are generally considered after the fact, when there will be ample time to determine whether the criteria were actually met.

The Ad-Hoc Working Group identifies an example, again from the ICJ, of how the very survival of a state could constitute a situation of necessity. Asked by the UN General Assembly to provide an advisory opinion on the *Legality of the Threat or Use of Nuclear Weapons*, a split decision – ultimately determined by the casting vote of the court's president – saw the ICJ advise that it 'cannot conclude definitively whether the threat or use of nuclear weapons would be lawful or unlawful in an extreme circumstance of self-defence, in which the very survival of a State would be at stake'.[150] While recognising the very different context of this advisory opinion, the Ad-Hoc Working Group claims that the ICJ's failure to come to a clear conclusion 'can nevertheless support the argument that a use of planetary defence methods which is not in conformity with international obligations could be justified if it is, in extreme situations, the only way to safeguard the survival of a State or the entire planet'.[151] We disagree, because a judicial *lacuna* (failure to decide) does not provide support for anything. Each potential circumstance precluding wrongfulness must be assessed on its own facts, not on the basis of any precedent or, in the case of this advisory opinion of the ICJ, an absence thereof.

One might also ask whether necessity could justify the use of an NED as a first choice of deflection method rather than as a last resort, for example after kinetic impactors had failed to alter the asteroid's orbit sufficiently to prevent an Earth impact. What if an NED was the most likely method to give a successful outcome? Again, Draft Article 25(1)(a) specifies that the act must be '*the only way* for the State to safeguard an essential interest against a grave and imminent peril'.[152] In the 2017 table-top exercise undertaken at that year's Planetary Defense Conference on which the Ad-Hoc Working Group based their later legal analysis, several states (fictionally) decided to use an NED without UN Security Council authorisation and without having first attempted a kinetic deflection.

---

[150] *Legality of the Threat or Use of Nuclear Weapons*, Advisory Opinion, [1996] ICJ Rep 226 at 44.

[151] SMPAG, 'Planetary defence', op. cit. at 40.

[152] 'Draft Articles on the Responsibility of States', op. cit., Art. 25(1)(a), added emphasis.

Although the use of the NED proved successful in this hypothetical scenario, it was, in the circumstances, almost certainly illegal.

More realistically, an NEO threat might be identified too late for any deflection method other than an NED. Kinetic impactors will take time to build, and multiple impactors might be needed. Low-impulse methods would take even longer, unless (in the case of mass drivers) they are already deployed for Space mining purposes on asteroids that are dynamically accessible (i.e. from which a small $\Delta v$ would be sufficient to redirect the spacecraft onto a rendezvous orbit), with a means – and sufficient fuel – for transporting them to the threatening asteroid. A gravity tractor might take even longer again, both to build and launch and to have the necessary, slowly accumulating effect on the asteroid's orbit. In the absence of any viable alternative, the use of an NED could, perhaps, meet the criteria of necessity.

Then there is Article 25(1)(b) of the International Law Commission's Draft Articles on State Responsibility, which specifies that necessity may only be invoked as a circumstance precluding wrongfulness if it does not 'seriously impair an essential interest of the State or States towards which the obligation exists, or of the international community as a whole'.[153] In other words, necessity cannot excuse an action, by one state, that causes serious harm to other states. On this, the Ad-Hoc Working Group wrote,

> it must be ensured that the deflection of the asteroid does not lead to an impact on other States and that no other serious dangers are caused to the international community as a whole, such as harm to the Earth or to the Earth and outer space environment through radioactive contamination or space debris.[154]

Given the uncertainties associated with asteroid deflection, we have to question the Ad-Hoc Working Group's addition of the words 'must be ensured' to this criterion. Clearly, the acting state must do *everything practicable* to ensure that the deflection mission does not 'seriously impair an essential interest', including by characterising the asteroid and precisely determining its orbit in advance of the deflection attempt. 'Everything practicable' will also include conducting the deflection in the least risky way by, for instance, using a gravity tractor if sufficient time is available and, if it is not, a kinetic impactor rather than an NED. But to read a higher standard of care into Article 25(1)(b) seems like a mistake.

---

[153] Ibid. Art. 25(1)(b).
[154] SMPAG, 'Planetary defence', op. cit. at 91.

It may also be unnecessary, since the consequences on Earth of a Space-based action are subject to absolute liability under the Liability Convention. Absolute liability could be a powerful incentive for cautious, science-based action, as will be discussed below.

### 6.9.2   States Are Responsible for Non-State Actors

There is one important difference in the international law of state responsibility as it applies in Space as compared to elsewhere, and this concerns non-state actors. Generally speaking, the conduct of private actors is not attributable to a state under international law. But according to Article VI of the Outer Space Treaty,

> States Parties to the Treaty shall bear international responsibility for national activities in outer space, including the moon and other celestial bodies, whether such activities are carried on by governmental agencies or by non-governmental entities, and for assuring that national activities are carried out in conformity with the provisions set forth in the present Treaty. The activities of non-governmental entities in outer space, including the moon and other celestial bodies, shall require authorization and continuing supervision by the appropriate State Party to the Treaty. When activities are carried on in outer space, including the moon and other celestial bodies, by an international organization, responsibility for compliance with this Treaty shall be borne both by the international organization and by the States Parties to the Treaty participating in such organization.[155]

It is easy to imagine SpaceX mounting an asteroid-deflection mission if Elon Musk felt that national governments were moving too slowly or taking the wrong approach. But if SpaceX undertook such a mission, responsibility for complying with international law and providing compensation for any damage would rest with the US government, since SpaceX is incorporated in the United States. The same rule would apply, self-evidently, to the conduct of any private contractor taking part in a state-led mission. The point, however, is to ensure that national governments have a strong incentive to regulate private companies, and exercise strong oversight, because it is the governments that will carry the legal and financial burdens internationally if something goes wrong.

---

[155] Outer Space Treaty, op. cit., Art. VI.

## 6.10    Liability

A state is liable for damage caused by any Space object for which it is a 'launching state', with this term being defined in Article I(c) of the 1972 Convention on the International Liability for Damage Caused by Space Objects (Liability Convention) as meaning:

 (i)  A State which launches or procures the launching of a space object;
 (ii)  A State from whose territory or facility a space object is launched.[156]

It will be clear from this that an individual Space object can have several launching states.

Any deflection attempt against an asteroid or comet would take place beyond Earth orbit and necessarily entail the use of 'space objects', which the Outer Space Treaty makes clear is any object launched into Space.[157] As mentioned above, an ICBM would not suffice because such missiles do not achieve escape velocity.

As also mentioned, liability is based on 'fault' when the damage is inflicted on other Space objects. However, when the damage is inflicted on Earth, the liability is 'absolute', in that it exists even without wrongdoing. For this reason, a deflection mission that goes wrong – causing the asteroid to strike a different location, or perhaps fragmenting it and creating multiple large airbursts with a wider scope of destruction (in terms of the number of people killed or the amount of damage to infrastructure) – would entail liability for damage even if the damage was unforeseen or the result of an accident.

At the same time, the extent of liability takes on a potentially surreal dimension in the context of failed or only partially successful asteroid deflections. It is possible to imagine a state paying for damage on the scale of the Chelyabinsk airburst or even the Tunguska event. States have paid very large reparations in the past, for instance after losing a war in which they were the aggressor. But an asteroid large enough to justify a deflection attempt could cause damage on a scale that is beyond the financial ability of any state to compensate.

### 6.10.1    Liability for False Alarms?

Another liability issue identified by the Ad-Hoc Working Group concerns false alarms. A warning about an NEO threat could cause a government to

---

[156] Liability Convention, op. cit., Art. 1(c).
[157] Outer Space Treaty, op. cit., Arts. VII–VIII, X.

launch a deflection mission or evacuate a city or region. Is anyone legally responsible for the associated expenses and disruptions if the warning proves to be a false alarm? But while this question is interesting, it is only of limited relevance, since the astronomical community quickly verifies or disproves any newly identified NEO threat, thus reducing the time during which an alarm which turns out to be false is perceived to be real enough to entail unnecessary expenses or disruptions.

For more than three decades, Brian Marsden directed the Central Bureau for Astronomical Telegrams, the body created by the International Astronomical Union to serve as an international clearing house for information on transient astronomical events. In 1992, Marsden warned of a possible Earth impact from Comet Swift Tuttle in 2126.[158] This would have been an extinction-level event, because Swift Tuttle has a nucleus with a diameter of about 26 kilometres, making it the largest object in the Solar System that repeatedly passes close to Earth, doing so with a relative velocity of about 60 kilometres per second. Fortunately, information obtained from historical Chinese reports in 69 BCE and 188 CE, combined with further observations, enabled the astronomical community to rapidly determine that there is, in fact, no impact risk from Comet Swift Tuttle for the next two millennia.[159]

In 1998, Marsden issued another warning that also turned out to be a false alarm, this time concerning a possible impact with the asteroid 1997 $XF_{11}$ in 2028. The warning caused a media frenzy, partly because it was issued by press release rather than circulated within the astronomical community, and partly because 1997 $XF_{11}$ has a diameter of approximately one kilometre. Fortunately, it took less than a day for other astronomers to resolve the asteroid's orbit with greater precision, after one of them found an eight-year-old image of the same asteroid. It will indeed pass by Earth in 2028, but at about 2.4 lunar distances (930,000 kilometres) from us.[160]

These false alarms demonstrated how quickly the astronomical community reacts to possible Earth impacts, by providing new data and analysis and almost immediately verifying or disproving the existence of a threat. The cost of a false alarm is therefore quite limited, while the

---

[158] Brian G Marsden, 'International Astronomical Union Circular, 5536: 1992t' (15 October 1992), *Central Bureau for Astronomical Telegrams*, online: www.cbat.eps.harvard.edu/ iauc/05600/05636.html.

[159] John Maddox, 'Comfort for next century but one' (1994) 367:6465 *Nature* 681.

[160] Tony Reichhardt, 'Asteroid watchers debate false alarm' (1998) 392:6673 *Nature* 215.

benefit of an early warning of an actual strike – i.e. more time in which to act – would be preserved.

In any case, as the Ad-Hoc Working Group points out, the issue of liability for false alarms does not fall within the scope of the Outer Space Treaty or the Liability Convention, since there is no 'space object' – in the legal sense of a human-made spacecraft or parts thereof – involved here. Rather, the issue is governed by the general rules of international law on state responsibility and liability, at least in cases where the warning has been issued by a state, including a national Space agency, or experts acting on behalf of a group of states or Space agencies, as with IAWN. These rules involve fault-based rather than strict liability, leading the Ad-Hoc Working Group to conclude,

> NEO threat warnings may be treated similar to warnings regarding the likelihood of (other) natural disasters, tsunami warnings serving as a potential analogy. As long as States do not willingly or in a grossly negligent manner provide false data, it will be difficult to hold them internationally responsible or liable, it being understood however that any concrete legal appraisal depends on the context and circumstances and no general rule or conclusion can therefore be established.[161]

But if states and Space agencies are protected, what about false alarms issued by non-governmental organisations? Brian Marsden, for example, worked for a non-governmental organisation, namely the International Astronomical Union. Many other astronomers work for universities, some of them private. What about amateur astronomers, hundreds of whom are actively and very ably involved in NEO detection?

International law principally applies among nation states. As a result, the question of liability for false alarms issued by non-state groups and individuals is one of national law, which varies from state to state. The good news is that liability in most national legal systems is fault-based, and as a result a warning issued in good faith will not generate liability. Just as importantly, a warning issued by a reputable non-governmental organisation or amateur astronomer will attract the attention of the astronomical community almost as fast as a warning issued by a state, meaning that new data and analysis will be brought to bear quickly – before a false alarm can result in unnecessary expenses or disruptions. For all these reasons, liability for false alarms is not much of an issue. Astronomers, it turns out, have each other's backs.

---

[161] SMPAG, 'Planetary defence', op. cit. at 54.

## 6.11   Developing Capabilities for Planetary Defence

Effective planetary defence demands a wide range of capabilities, from improved NEO detection, characterisation and orbit resolution to the development of safe and effective technologies for use in deflections. All these things require international co-operation, with telescopes located around the planet, as well as redundant detection and deflection capabilities in the event that equipment fails – or that the commitment or decision-making capability of a leading state falters. The ways in which different states can contribute to planetary defence will vary greatly, but clearly it is necessary to have an internationally organised, well-tested, widely accepted system for NEO detection and threat response.

More Space-based NEO detection telescopes are needed, including from countries other than the United States. In 2013, Canada launched the Near Earth Object Surveillance Satellite (NEOSSat), equipped with a 15-centimetre telescope especially designed to detect NEOs approaching from the direction of the Sun. Unfortunately, NEOSSat was launched prematurely, without the 'fine-pointing' software module required to fulfil its primary mission, and while subsequent efforts to upload software fixes reduced the problem, they did not fully solve it.[162] Canada has not replaced NEOSSat, even though it cost only CA$25 million to build and launch.

Developing mission-ready planetary defence assets should also be a priority. It would be relatively easy for a consortium of states, companies, universities or private foundations to provide a set of low-cost but still reliable flyby spacecraft with interchangeable instrumentation and rapid launch capabilities, and to test them by conducting flybys of non-hazardous NEOs. Particularly dangerous asteroids could be tagged in some way, or have small spacecraft stationed around them, to enable long-term monitoring of their orbital evolutions. Information gained in this way would also contribute greatly to scientific knowledge of asteroid behaviour and therefore planetary defence in general. Finally, a widely accepted decision-making protocol on NEO threats is needed, in the form of either a soft law declaration, a binding treaty or a UN Security Council resolution. Such a protocol might require that any deflection effort (1) be based on science and respect the precautionary principle, (2)

---

[162] Canadian Space Agency, 'Evaluation of the Near Earth Object Surveillance Satellite (NEOSSat) project' (February 2014), *Government of Canada*, online: https://open.canada.ca/data/en/dataset/dd76f7c5-42e7-4b8e-846b-0a227150ad7b.

employ the safest technology possible in the time frame available, (3) be led by national Space agencies rather than militaries and (4) be multilaterally rather than unilaterally organised and implemented.

## 6.12    Precautionary Planetary Defence

So far, we have been discussing different interventions that could be attempted if an asteroid were about to strike Earth. In this section, we discuss interventions with asteroids that are not on immediately dangerous trajectories. In particular, we consider two possibilities: (1) limiting missions to an asteroid due to the risk of creating a human-caused Earth impact, and (2) actively managing asteroids to place them in 'safe harbours', even when impact risks are otherwise below 'decision-to-act' thresholds. We use Apophis as a case study for illustrative purposes and address the two possibilities in turn.

Apophis will pass within approximately 38,010 kilometres of Earth's centre (the 'geocentre') in 2029,[163] bringing it momentarily about as close as communications and Earth observation satellites in geosynchronous orbit. The 'near miss' will present rare science opportunities for studying how very close encounters can both alter the way in which asteroids spin and lead to changes in their surfaces. It may even create opportunities for probing the asteroid's interior structure.

But the rarity, at least as measured in human lifetimes, does not lie in Apophis's close approach alone. Close approaches have been observed before, including the even closer flyby of the 30-metre asteroid 367943 Duende (2012 DA14) in 2013.[164] Rather, it is the size of Apophis (about 340 metres in diameter) that makes this particular approach so interesting. Indeed, portions of the world's population will be able to see Apophis with the unaided eye, appearing like a bright satellite moving across the sky. We can therefore expect that governments and scientists will engage in considerable outreach before the event, both as an educational opportunity and as a pre-emptive move against inaccurate reporting and public anxiety.

---

[163] See Apophis close approach tables: Jet Propulsion Laboratory, 'Small-body database lookup – 99942 Apophis (2004 MN4)' (29 June 2021), *NASA*, online: ssd.jpl.nasa.gov/tools/sbdb_lookup.html#/?sstr=Apophis.

[164] Tony Greicius, 'Asteroid 2012 DA14 – Earth flyby reality check' (15 February 2013), *NASA*, online: www.nasa.gov/topics/solarsystem/features/asteroidflyby.html.

The science potential associated with Apophis's close approach is currently motivating many different teams to propose a variety of missions,[165] including rendezvous and flybys, with some proposed missions being primarily technology demonstrations rather than research efforts. All are potentially problematic because Apophis's B-plane for the 2029 encounter (recall the discussion above) has multiple 'keyholes'[166] – as shown in Figure 6.8.

The curve in Figure 6.8 is generated by taking Apophis's nominal (best-fit) orbit and perturbing (nudging) it along and against its orbit using systematically increasing $\Delta v$'s.[167] This is done to explore the parameter space of the encounter. The reported minimum distance in the figure ($y$ axis), given in Earth radii, is the closest approach distance that Apophis would have with Earth in the next 100 years following the 2029 flyby if it were to go through the given B-plane location. The minimum distances are shown with respect to the $\zeta$ co-ordinate of the B-plane (Figure 6.5 above), with $\Delta\zeta$ representing the deviation relative to the nominal orbit.

The keyholes are those areas on a B-plane where, were an asteroid to pass through one during a given flyby, its orbit would evolve in such a manner that it would hit Earth on a subsequent encounter. Different keyholes are associated with different impact dates, and while the specific locations of keyholes are intricately connected to the dynamics of the asteroid, the existence of keyholes is a general property of any close encounter.

For impact hazard assessment, the immediate priority is to rule out an impact during the encounter in question. Once it is determined that the asteroid will pass safely by Earth, attention can turn to the much more

---

[165] For example, see the T-9 Apophis workshop program conference abstracts at Lunar and Planetary Institute, 'Apophis T-9 Years: Knowledge opportunities for the science of planetary defense' (virtual, November 2020), *Universities Space Research Association (USRA)*, online: www.hou.usra.edu/meetings/apophis2020.

[166] Davide Farnocchia, Steven R Chesley, Paul W Chodas, M Micheli, DJ Tholen, A Milani, GT Elliott and F Bernardi, 'Yarkovsky-driven impact risk analysis for asteroid (99942) Apophis' (2013) 224:1 *Icarus* 192.

[167] Simulations were run using a modified version of Rebound/X. See Hanno Rein and David S Spiegel, 'IAS15: A fast, adaptive, high-order integrator for gravitational dynamics, accurate to machine precision over a billion orbits' (2015) 446:2 *Monthly Notices of the Royal Astronomical Society* 1424; This included GR, Earth's J2 and J4 components, and perturbations from the list of asteroids given in Farnocchia et al., op. cit. The initial conditions for Apophis are the Horizons orbit solution ref. JPL211, epoch 2021-April-7.0.

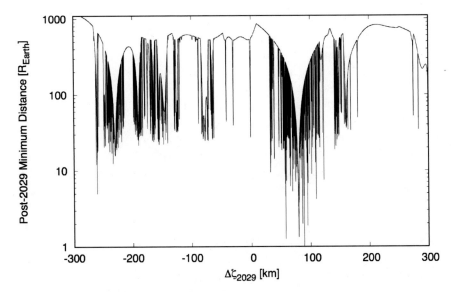

**Figure 6.8** Keyhole map for the 2029 flyby of Apophis. The *x* axis shows the change in the $\zeta$ co-ordinate on the B-plane, relative to the location of the nominal orbit. The *y* axis shows the closest to Earth that Apophis would come after the 2029 encounter for the next 100 years upon passing through the noted location on the B-plane. The downward spikes represent the orbital structure. Spikes that get within about 10 per cent of Earth's radius will collide with Earth in that 100-year timeframe, depending on the amount of gravitational focusing (which draws the asteroid even closer to the planet). The broad downward dip with multiple spikes is an example of a 'keyhole complex', where there is the potential for multiple keyholes to reside. To a very high degree of certainty, the orbit of Apophis will not pass through a keyhole in 2029.

difficult task of ruling out keyhole passages. Indeed, it was not until 2021 that a keyhole passage by Apophis in 2029 was ruled out, using ground-based radar measurements.[168]

But even with such a reassurance, we still need to ask: to what degree are missions to the asteroid wise, if even a small perturbation could knock the asteroid into a keyhole? For if a mission to an asteroid like Apophis, with a rich set of keyholes, goes awry and the spacecraft unintentionally collides with the asteroid, there is a risk (albeit a low-probability one) that

---

[168] Ian J O'Neill and Joshua Handel, 'NASA analysis: Earth is safe from asteroid Apophis for 100-plus years' (26 March 2021), *NASA*, online: www.nasa.gov/feature/jpl/nasa-analysis-earth-is-safe-from-asteroid-apophis-for-100-plus-years.

this will create a future impact emergency.[169] Of course, one could just as easily knock the asteroid away from a keyhole. The point, however, is that the result is uncertain. For this reason, if we know the asteroid is on a safe orbit, any uncontrolled alteration – and any possibility of an uncontrolled alteration – involves an unnecessary gamble.

The perturbation required to knock an asteroid into a keyhole will depend on multiple factors, including the distance between the actual B-plane intersection and the location of the keyhole on that plane. As discussed above, the lead time of the perturbation and the strength of the $\Delta v$ are all critical details. Some asteroids are safer to 'play' with than others. Fortunately for us, Apophis, as best as we can tell, is a relatively safe one.

Other asteroids will not be so safe. Although well-co-ordinated missions to riskier asteroids could be conducted safely and, from a planetary defence point of view might in fact *need* to be conducted, the prospects of competition between actors could result in a relaxation of the necessary stringent caution. Moreover, the publicity associated with very close approaches, like that already starting for Apophis, could prompt non-state actors to launch their own missions – as technology demonstrations or profile-raising exercises, much like the infamous launch of a Tesla car by SpaceX in 2018.

Applying the precautionary principle and exercising restraint might be the best policy in these cases. This would by no means preclude missions to asteroids such as Apophis,[170] but it would demand a high level of co-ordination among all Space actors, including governments, industry and other non-governmental entities. It would also require that some missions be modified and, in extreme cases, severely limited – notwithstanding the scientific or technology demonstration benefits that might otherwise be obtained. This leads us to ask, who should make such decisions?

As discussed above, SMPAG does not have decision-making authority. Not even SMPAG members themselves require permission from the group to carry out a mission. Rather, national governments make the

---

[169] S Chesley and D Farnocchia, 'Apophis impact hazard assessment and sensitivity to spacecraft contact' (paper delivered at the Apophis T-9 Years workshop, virtual, November 2020), Lunar and Planetary Institute Contrib No 2242, *USRA*, online: www.hou.usra.edu/meetings/apophis2020/pdf/2049.pdf.

[170] Again, Apophis itself appears to be in a reasonably safe-for-Earth position on the B-plane.

decision whether to proceed with a mission, either on their own or in co-operation with others. But while SMPAG lacks decision-making author-ity, it serves – much like the International Space Station – as a focus for co-operation among spacefaring states. It is therefore an appropriate venue for sharing information about planned missions to asteroids and having those plans and the associated scientific assessments vetted by experts from other states. If that process reveals the need for limitations on a particular mission, and the launch state is reluctant to change its plans, the usual range of diplomatic pressures and incentives could be deployed (as they are daily among states on thousands of other issues).

A completely new dimension to decision making comes with NewSpace, an era defined by the growing reach and influence of Space companies, with some private actors expected to possess advanced exploration capabilities well before 2029. In 2019, SpaceIL became the first non-state entity to place a spacecraft on the Moon, albeit via a hard landing. SpaceX is already flight-testing Starship, a reusable spacecraft for Earth orbit, the Moon and Mars. Multiple tourism ventures are under way, with trips to the ISS occurring already and trips around the Moon likely to occur soon. One or more of these increasingly capable private Space actors may wish to use Apophis or other asteroids for their own purposes. The prospect of eventual asteroid mining adds yet another dimension, as this could be a benefit or a risk to planetary defence, depending on the degree to which companies share information (some of which they may consider proprietary) and guard against the risk of knocking an asteroid into an Earth impact orbit.

Although the Outer Space Treaty makes the 'launching state' respon-sible for the actions of non-state actors, such actors might have different approaches to scientific uncertainty and risk. They might not engage, or be required to engage, in the same level of co-ordination as national Space agencies do through SMPAG. Nor are all national regulatory frameworks necessarily prepared for a much higher level of commercial Space activity. For these reasons, national regulators should be strongly encouraged to take planetary defence considerations into account when issuing launch licences to non-state actors, including adopting practices that require both the non-state actor and the regulator to consult with IAWN and SMPAG. This approach could be encouraged and bolstered by a United Nations General Assembly resolution on planetary defence, which could, among other things, recommend that any state planning or licensing an asteroid mission consult with SMPAG and satisfy any concerns they might have.

Having made the case for restraint, we can also ask whether the purposeful redirection of asteroid orbits might sometimes be warranted even when the asteroid does not pose a clear impact risk. Such active management or 'shepherding' would ideally be conducted with a gravity tractor to ensure minimal interference with the asteroid. This possibility was explored in the context of Apophis when there was still some worry that it might pass through a 2029 keyhole.[171] One of the ideas addressed in that research was the so-called 'safe harbour' for an asteroid, i.e. placing it on an orbit that precludes it entering a keyhole. Building on this idea, we might ask whether there is an accessible orbit that not only misses keyholes but also minimises the long-term risk posed by a given asteroid. Put differently, any harbour will do in a storm, but if we have fair weather, what harbour should we pick?

Again, Figure 6.8 illustrates some of the dynamical complexities involved in understanding the long-term risk posed by an asteroid. From this keyhole map we can see that Apophis is close to a downward spike in the minimum-distance profile (corresponding to the year 2116 encounter), potentially dropping below a 30 Earth radii minimum distance. Importantly, it is not an impact keyhole, so the location is safe despite the potential for a future close encounter. At slightly higher $\zeta$, Apophis can be kept farther from Earth over the next 100 years than at its current nominal location. However, such a change would place the asteroid closer to a keyhole complex. At lower $\zeta$, a small 'hill' exists that is free from close encounters and known keyholes.

If you could choose, where would you want Apophis to pass on the B-plane? Which is the safest harbour?

One could argue against moving Apophis to higher $\zeta$ on the ground that this is closer to a keyhole. A response to this concern might be that a rendezvous with a gravity tractor should enable a precise orbit to be determined, in which case the shepherding could always be reassessed. This might include aborting the mission if the orbital uncertainty remains too high. Moving to lower $\zeta$ does not raise the same concern, though it also does not lead to a much better situation than the current orbit. Perhaps more interesting, one might question whether some of the downward spikes (not keyholes) could be used to help keep track of the

---

[171] D Yeomans, S Bhaskaran, SB Broschart, SR Chesley, PW Chodas, TH Sweetser and R Schweickart, 'Deflecting a hazardous near-Earth object' (paper delivered at the 1st IAA Planetary Defense Conference, Granada, Spain, 27–30 April 2009), *NASA*, online: cneos .jpl.nasa.gov/doc/PDC_proceedings_062009.pdf.

asteroid, ensuring that it has a regular close but safe approach to Earth. Finally, we might further re-pose the question by imagining what our reaction would be if Apophis were in a narrow, safe region within the keyhole complex at, for example, $\Delta\zeta_{2029} = 75$ km. Would this motivate deflection to lower $\zeta$ to find a safer harbour?

Two things are clear. If we have the means to safely decrease the long-term risk of an asteroid strike, then we should at least consider doing so. And if we do not have the means to safely decrease the long-term risk, the asteroid should be left alone.

Despite raising these intentionally provocative questions, we acknowledge that the precautionary principle could support an argument against any active management because such an approach might create new risks. For example, if a failure happened while using a gravity tractor, a given asteroid could be dropped into a keyhole.[172] It is also possible that there are as yet unknown risks that we do not therefore understand. For these reasons, any decision to actively manage an asteroid into a safe harbour should only be taken after peer-reviewed scientific assessment, full international collaboration and broad agreement.

A detailed model for a gravity tractor has been developed by others, with Apophis deflection scenarios shown to be feasible with a 1,000-kilogram spacecraft.[173] We note that SpaceX's Starship is about 100 tonnes empty, and that it is fully automated and reusable. Designed to transport and land cargo and people on the Moon and Mars, a version of Starship could be reconfigured as a highly effective and reusable gravity tractor. The Starship HLS, the version designed for lunar landings with high-thrust oxygen- and methane-fuelled thrusters located mid-body, might be a good place to start.

'The dinosaurs did not have a Space program' is an oft-used phrase in planetary defence. Woodpeckers, eagles and other birds are proof that a few species of dinosaurs survived. And yet the direction of life on Earth was radically changed when, without astronomy, rockets and worldwide co-ordination, their ancestors were unable to ward off the tremendous energy locked into asteroids.

[172]  Ibid.
[173]  Ibid.

# Space Security

## 7.1 Introduction

The entire world sat up and took notice when, in 2018, President Donald Trump directed the creation of the United States Space Force.[1] The move was subject to widespread ridicule, including through a Netflix comedy series starring Steve Carell and John Malkovich. In reality, this new sixth branch of the US armed forces was little more than a renamed US Air Force Space Command (a conclusion supported, among other things, by the fact that the 'chief of space operations' reports to the Secretary of the Air Force). While there is no denying that the US military is a significant Space actor – it has about 200 operational spacecraft[2] and an annual Space-related budget of approximately US$20 billion[3] – this is not new, since militaries have always accounted for a large portion of human Space activity.

Humanity's ascent into Space began in 1929 when the German Army tested its first rocket, the A-1.[4] The size and reliability of the German rockets were gradually increased until, in 1942, the first test launches of the A-4 took place.[5] Two years later, the A-4 was renamed the V-2 and deployed against Paris, London and Antwerp. Although the V-2 was

---

[1] Katie Rogers, 'Trump orders establishment of Space Force as sixth military branch', *New York Times* (18 June 2018), online: www.nytimes.com/2018/06/18/us/politics/trump-space-force-sixth-military-branch.html.

[2] According to the Union of Concerned Scientists' Satellite Database, there are 157 operational US military satellites. The US military also operates an additional 40 satellites jointly with civil, commercial and governmental entities. See Union of Concerned Scientists (UCS), 'UCS Satellite Database' (1 January 2022), online: www.ucsusa.org/resources/satellite-database.

[3] European Space Policy Institute (ESPI), *EPSI Yearbook 2020: Space Policies, Issues and Trends* (Vienna: ESPI, 2020), online: espi.or.at/publications/espi-yearbook.

[4] Michael J Neufeld, *The Rocket and the Reich: Peenemünde and the Coming of the Ballistic Missile Era* (New York: Simon and Schuster, 1995).

[5] Ibid.

inaccurate and therefore not militarily decisive, it was still a major technological achievement. Capable of carrying a one-tonne payload 320 kilometres, it travelled on a ballistic trajectory that took it far beyond the reach of anti-aircraft guns.[6] In 1944, a V-2 reached an apogee of about 180 kilometres, making it the first human-made object to reach Space (using the most widely accepted definition of 100 kilometres, often called the Kármán line). More than 3,000 V-2s were launched during the last year of the Second World War.[7]

As the war drew to a close, both the United States and the Soviet Union raced to capture German rocket engineers. The lead engineer, Wernher von Braun, made sure that he fell into American hands. The United States also captured enough parts to build around 80 rockets. In 1949 a modified V-2 launched by the US Army became the first US-launched object to reach Space.[8] Further modifications led to the Redstone rocket, which carried the first American satellite into orbit in 1958. That same year, the Redstone was deployed in West Germany as a tactical missile armed with a nuclear warhead.[9] The Soviet Union, meanwhile, had also captured German rocket engineers. In 1957 it launched Sputnik, the world's first artificial satellite, on an R-7 rocket that was based on the V-2 design. Two years later, the R-7 went into operation as the Soviet Union's first intercontinental ballistic missile (ICBM).

While militaries have always accounted for a large portion of human Space activity, their use of the Space environment has been constrained by a mutual self-interest in preserving access to it for a broad range of purposes. As James Clay Moltz explains, the United States and the Soviet Union 'gradually accepted mutual constraints on deployable weapons in return for safe access to the space environment for military reconnaissance, weather forecasting, tracking, early warning, and a range of civilian uses'.[10] This chapter traces the development of these constraints while also considering several new issues, including the growing need for a new treaty to ban kinetic anti-satellite (ASAT) weapon tests, and the potentially destabilising effects of an imminent extension of military

---

[6] John W Bullard, *History of the Redstone Missile System* (Huntsville: Army Missile Command, 1965).

[7] Norman Longmate, *Hitler's Rockets: The Story of the V-2s* (London: Hutchinson, 1985).

[8] Dieter K Huzel and Wernher von Braun, *Peenemünde to Canaveral* (Englewood Cliffs, NJ: Prentice-Hall, 1962).

[9] Bullard, op. cit.

[10] James Clay Moltz, *The Politics of Space Security*, 3rd ed. (Stanford: Stanford University Press, 2019) at 4.

activities to cis-lunar Space. The following chapter will evaluate existing international law, including international humanitarian law, as it concerns the testing and use of ASAT weapons.

## 7.2    Preserving Safe Access to Space: The 1963 Limited Test Ban Treaty

The sky above the Pacific Ocean turned red for an hour on 9 July 1962, after the United States detonated a 1.4-megaton hydrogen bomb at an altitude of 400 kilometres to test, in part, whether an artificial intensification of the Van Allen radiation belts – where highly charged particles from the solar wind are captured by Earth's magnetic field – could disable intercontinental ballistic missiles.[11] The Starfish Prime nuclear test worked much better than expected, generating a powerful electromagnetic pulse that disabled six satellites – one Soviet, one British, and four American. All three countries drew the same lesson from the test: nuclear explosions in Space posed a major and indiscriminate threat to new Space-based technologies.

Some of the technologies had commercial applications. One of the disabled satellites was Telstar 1, which had just begun transmitting the first live television broadcasts between North America and Europe. Other technologies were of fast-growing military importance, including reconnaissance satellites able to track the activities of adversaries from beyond the reach of fighter–interceptor jets and anti-aircraft guns. These reconnaissance satellites enabled the United States and the Soviet Union to avoid a classic 'security dilemma' in which a state is compelled to make a choice between building up its military, or not, in response to another state's suspected but uncertain build-up.[12] Radiation from the Starfish Prime nuclear test, moreover, not only dispersed along the Van Allen Belts, but persisted there. The presence and persistence of this additional radiation posed a potential threat to human spaceflight at a time when

---

[11] Gilbert King, 'Going nuclear over the Pacific', *Smithsonian Magazine* (15 August 2012), online: www.smithsonianmag.com/history/going-nuclear-over-the-pacific-24428997; Phil Plait, 'The Fiftieth anniversary of Starfish Prime: The nuke that shook the world', *Discover Magazine*, 9 July 2012, online: www.discovermagazine.com/the-sciences/the-50th-anniversary-of-starfish-prime-the-nuke-that-shook-the-world.

[12] John H Herz, 'Idealist internationalism and the security dilemma' (1950) 2:2 *World Politics* 157; Robert Jervis, 'Cooperation under the security dilemma' (1978) 30:2 *World Politics* 167; Ken Booth and Nicholas J Wheeler, *The Security Dilemma: Fear, Cooperation, and Trust in World Politics* (Basingstoke: Palgrave Macmillan, 2007).

the United States and the Soviet Union were competing to put the first humans on the Moon.

The lessons of Starfish Prime were taken up almost immediately in the 1963 Treaty Banning Nuclear Weapon Tests in the Atmosphere, in Outer Space and under Water.[13] This Limited Test Ban Treaty (also known as the Partial Test Ban Treaty) was negotiated by the United States, the Soviet Union, and the United Kingdom – the same three countries that had lost satellites as a result of the nuclear test.[14] For almost six decades now, the treaty's provisions have been fully complied with, because they serve the interests of every modern military and national Space agency.

The Limited Test Ban Treaty was the first of a series of arms control treaties based on a recognition that keeping weapons out of Space is a prerequisite for avoiding nuclear conflict on Earth. In 1967, the Outer Space Treaty prohibited the deployment in Space of 'any objects carrying nuclear weapons or any other kinds of weapons of mass destruction'.[15] In the 1972 Strategic Arms Limitation Talks Agreement (SALT I),[16] the United States and the Soviet Union limited the number of silos and launch tubes available for ground- and sea-based ICBMs, i.e. missiles that transit Space en route to their targets.

The same talks led to the 1972 Anti-Ballistic Missile Treaty,[17] in which the United States and the Soviet Union limited missile defence systems to 200 interceptors each, protecting a maximum of two locations.[18] This

---

[13] Treaty Banning Nuclear Weapon Tests in the Atmosphere, in Outer Space and under Water, 5 August 1963, 480 UNTS 43 (entered into force 10 October 1963) (Limited Test Ban Treaty).

[14] The Cuban missile crisis, which occurred in October 1962 and brought the US and the USSR to the brink of nuclear war, was another factor leading to the negotiations. King, op. cit.

[15] Treaty on Principles Governing the Activities of States in the Exploration and Use of Outer Space, Including the Moon and Other Celestial Bodies, 27 January 1967, 610 UNTS 205 (entered into force 10 October 1967) (Outer Space Treaty).

[16] Interim Agreement on Certain Measures with Respect to the Limitation of Strategic Offensive Arms, United States and USSR, 26 May 1971, 944 UNTS 3 (entered into force 3 October 1972) (Strategic Arms Limitation Talks Agreement (SALT I)).

[17] Treaty on the Limitation of Anti-Ballistic Missile Systems, United States and USSR, 26 May 1971, 944 UNTS 13 (entered into force 3 October 1972) (Anti-Ballistic Missile Treaty (ABM Treaty)).

[18] In 1974, the US and USSR negotiated a protocol to the ABM Treaty that limited each of them to just one location and no more than 100 interceptors. The US system, located in North Dakota, was shut down after one year. The Soviet system, located around Moscow, remained in place for decades. Protocol to the Treaty between the United States of America and the Union of Soviet Socialist Republics on the Limitation of Anti-Ballistic Missile Systems, 3 July 1974, 1042 UNTS 424 (entered into force 24 May 1976).

ABM Treaty, which also specifically prohibited Space-based anti-ballistic missile systems, was designed to preserve 'mutually assured destruction' by ensuring that most ICBMs would reach their targets regardless of whether they were launched as part of a first or a second strike. It also had the consequence of preserving Space as a region through which weapons would travel, rather than one in which armed conflict would take place. SALT I and the ABM Treaty further prohibited interference with 'national technical means of verification'.[19] In other words, states party to the treaty could not interfere with any reconnaissance satellites used to verify treaty compliance. This amounted to a ban on the use of weapons of any type against an entire category of satellites.

### 7.3   ASAT Weapons and Space Debris

Satellites are indispensable tools for providing global security, but travelling as they do on predictable paths, they are also vulnerable. Their use in surveillance, reconnaissance, communications and high-precision targeting, and in the operation of armed drones and 'fifth-generation' fighter jets such as the F-35, all make them attractive military targets. Indeed, destroying just a few such satellites should be relatively easy, and could render an enemy's armed forces both deaf and blind, particularly if a state's dependence on satellites is asymmetrical to that of its adversaries.

Several types of ASAT weapons were developed during the early years of the Cold War. The first American test took place in 1959 as part of Bold Orion, a program involving air-launched ballistic missiles.[20] The Soviet Union for its part conducted 20 Space-based ASAT weapon tests between 1968 and 1982.[21] Practically speaking, any ground-, sea- or air-based missile can be used to destroy a satellite, if it has sufficient range and an accurate enough guidance system. At the same time, any satellite can, at least in principle, also be used as an ASAT weapon – if it has sufficient propulsion, control and targeting to manoeuvre itself onto a collision course with another object. In this chapter, we focus on these

---

[19]   SALT I, op. cit., Art. V(2); ABM Treaty, op. cit., Art. XII(2).

[20]   Andreas Parsch, 'WS-199' (1 November 2005 2010), *Directory of US Military Rockets and Missiles – Appendix 4: Undesignated Vehicles*, online: www.designation-systems.net/dusrm/app4/ws-199.html.

[21]   Nicholas L Johnson and David M Rodvold, *Europe and Asia in Space 1993–1994*, 2nd ed. (Colorado Springs: Kaman Sciences Corp, 1993).

kinds of 'kinetic' ASAT weapons that employ violent impacts and therefore create Space debris; in the next chapter, we also discuss 'non-kinetic'
methods of disabling satellites or interrupting their communications,
such as cyber actions and jamming.

As the United States and the Soviet Union continued to develop and
test both 'direct-ascent' and Space-based ASAT weapons, a major problem emerged: any single 'kinetic' impact can create tens of thousands to
hundreds of thousands of individual pieces of dangerous Space debris.
Only the largest of these, corresponding to hundreds to thousands of
pieces for a single impact event, are trackable. Most of the debris is too
small for Earth- or Space-based sensors to detect, but these small pieces
can still be lethal.

Debris and satellites orbit the Earth at speeds of up to approximately
28,000 kilometres per hour (about 7.8 kilometres per second), with
relative speeds of up to twice that. For this reason, even pieces of debris as
small as three to five millimetres in diameter can disable operational
satellites, including ones belonging to the same country that has tested or
used a kinetic ASAT weapon, thus putting its own Space assets at risk.

An even greater problem was recognised in 1978, when Donald
Kessler and Burton Cour-Palais, building on ideas from solar system
dynamics, identified that every collision, explosion or other debris-
generating event in orbit increases the cross-sectional area of the material
involved and therefore the risk of further collisions, further fragmentations and so on.[22] Known today as the 'Kessler syndrome', or, more
accurately, the 'Kessler–Cour-Palais syndrome',[23] this phenomenon of
the runaway proliferation of Space debris has the potential to render
entire orbits unsafe for centuries.[24] The Kessler–Cour-Palais syndrome
thus threatens all military and civilian satellites, including those used
for weather forecasting, navigation, aircraft and ship communications,

---

[22] Donald J Kessler and Burton G Cour-Palais, 'Collision frequency of artificial satellites:
The creation of a debris belt' (1978) 83:A6 *Journal of Geophysical Research* 2637.

[23] Burton Cour-Palais, a NASA scientist who specialised in high-velocity impacts, was put
in charge of meteoroid protection during the Apollo programme. He was a full co-author
of the seminal 1978 paper.

[24] A collisional runaway was dramatized in the movie *Gravity*, although it did so by
drastically speeding up the timescale of the cascade and taking many other liberties with
physics and the overall context of Earth orbit. See Caitlin Dewey, 'Here's what 'Gravity'
gets right and wrong about space', *Washington Post* (21 October 2013), online: www.
washingtonpost.com/news/wonk/wp/2013/10/21/heres-what-gravity-gets-right-and-
wrong-about-space; Cameron Byers, '"Gravity": It's not rocket science!', *The Tyee* (2
March 2014), online: https://thetyee.ca/ArtsAndCulture/2014/03/02/Gravity-Check.

financial services, agriculture, forestry, fisheries, environmental science, search and rescue, and disaster relief. Even a limited conflict in Space could be devastating to the global economy, food supply and human security.

Increased debris also poses a risk to human spaceflight. Already, the International Space Station has been boosted out of the way of Space debris on some 30 occasions.[25] These manoeuvres were in response to larger pieces of debris, since only pieces about ten centimetres in diameter or more can be identified and tracked. Millions of smaller pieces of debris also pose a significant threat, for something as small as a paint fleck or metal chip can penetrate an astronaut's spacesuit at orbital speeds.

Kessler and Cour-Palais's article had an almost immediate effect on international co-operation. Just one year after it was published, negotiators from the United States and the Soviet Union came to a preliminary agreement on banning the testing and use of ASAT weapons.[26] The agreement, however, was never finalised due to the Soviet invasion of Afghanistan in December 1979,[27] and the subsequent election of Ronald Reagan as US president in November 1980.

## 7.4   From Reagan to Clinton

The 1980 election of Ronald Reagan was a major setback for international Space co-operation. The new administration was populated with 'hawks' who had little respect for multilateralism and international law. In 1983, Reagan announced the Strategic Defense Initiative (SDI). Widely referred to as 'Star Wars', this massively expensive programme sought to render ICBMs obsolete through the development of ground-, sea-, air- and Space-based missile defence systems.

Experts on Space security in the United States have long been divided into two camps. The first advocates for the United States to seek to

---

[25] See Mark Garcia, 'Space debris and human spacecraft' (26 May 2021), *National Aeronautics and Space Administration (NASA)*, online: www.nasa.gov/mission_pages/ station/news/orbital_debris.html; Mark Garcia, 'Station separates from debris after orbital maneuver' (3 December 2021), *NASA*, online (blog): blogs.nasa.gov/spacesta tion/2021/12/03/station-separates-from-debris-after-orbital-maneuver.

[26] Moltz, op. cit. at 186, citing Paul Stares, *The Militarization of Space: U.S. Policy 1945– 1984* (Ithaca, NY: Cornell University Press, 1985) at 198–99.

[27] Ibid. at 187.

dominate Space, including by displaying an ability to destroy an adversary's Space assets in response to any aggression. The second camp understands that any armed conflict in Space could render key parts of that region unusable for everyone and recognises that spacefaring states have long been co-operating to prevent this from happening. The first camp benefits from the popular image of Space as an inherently violent region, while the second finds support in the fact that Space remains peaceful after more than six decades of human activity. Indeed, no country has ever deliberately struck another country's spacecraft.

Although the risk of the Kessler–Cour-Palais syndrome had already been publicly identified, both the Reagan administration and US military leaders were in wilful denial of the Space debris problem. When the US Air Force decided to test an air-launched missile against a satellite in 1985, it did so over the strong objections of NASA scientists. The scientists' concerns were validated when the test created 285 pieces of trackable debris and many thousands of smaller pieces.[28] This brief period of wilful denial ended abruptly: further tests were cancelled, and within a year the US Department of Defense was adopting its first debris mitigation guidelines. By 1989, the George H. W. Bush administration was promoting Space debris mitigation with other spacefaring states and international organisations. This included the creation of a new US–Soviet Orbital Debris Working Group.

During the 1991 Gulf War, satellites proved to be of considerable military utility. Earth-imaging satellites enabled US forces to track Iraqi units from Space, while an early global positioning system (GPS) enhanced situational awareness and assisted with precision targeting. These US successes contributed to a global awareness of the value of Space-based assets, and with it of the critical importance of safe access to Earth orbit. In 1993, the Bill Clinton administration led the creation of the Inter-Agency Space Debris Coordination Committee (IADC).[29] The Russian Space agency (known today as Roscosmos) was a member from the start, and the China National Space Administration (CNSA) joined two years later.

---

[28] Ibid. at 202.
[29] Ibid. at 237. The IADC remains active today with its 13 member Space agencies. See Hae-Dong Kim, 'Inter-Agency Space Debris Coordination Committee' (2019), *IADC*, online: www.iadc-home.org.

## 7.5   China's 2007 ASAT Weapon Test

In 2001, the Reagan-era hawks returned to Washington as part of the George W. Bush administration. They promptly initiated a programme of US Missile Defense: a scaled-back version of SDI focused on ground- and sea-based interceptors. They also withdrew the United States from the ABM Treaty, recognising that their new program would have violated it. These moves created strategic uncertainties for other countries, uncertainties that may have contributed to China's decision to test a ground-based missile against a defunct satellite in 2007.[30]

Just as the United States' 1985 test was conducted by its Air Force over the objections of NASA scientists, China's 2007 test may have been conducted by the Peoples' Liberation Army without the fully informed support of the Chinese Ministry of Foreign Affairs and other civilian government departments.[31] The test involved a ground-based missile and a defunct Chinese satellite. It resulted in 3,527 pieces of debris large enough to be logged in the US military's satellite catalogue and about 150,000 inferred pieces greater than one centimetre. Making things worse, the strike took place at an altitude around 850 kilometres, which meant that some of the debris will remain in orbit for centuries. At the time, the US Air Force Space Command estimated that over 700 satellites, including the International Space Station (ISS), were at risk of being struck by debris from the Chinese test.[32] Sure enough, in 2013, one of the pieces collided with and disabled a Russian satellite.[33]

[30] Marc Kaufman and Dafna Linzer, 'China criticized for anti-satellite missile test', *Washington Post* (19 January 2007), online: www.washingtonpost.com/wp-dyn/content/article/2007/01/18/AR2007011801029.html.

[31] Bates Gill and Martin Kleiber, 'China's space odyssey: What the antisatellite test reveals about decision-making in Beijing' (2007) 86:3 *Foreign Affairs* 2, online: www.foreignaffairs.com/articles/china/2007-05-01/chinas-space-odyssey-what-antisatellite-test-reveals-about-decision; Philippe C Saunders and Charles D Lutes, 'China's ASAT test: Motivations and implications' (2007) 46:3 *Joint Force Quarterly* 39 at 40, online: apps.dtic.mil/sti/pdfs/ADA517485.pdf ('The uncoordinated Chinese response suggests that the Ministry of Foreign Affairs (MFA) was not aware of the January ASAT test in advance.')

[32] Christopher Stone, 'Chinese intentions and American preparedness', *Space Review* (13 August 2007), online: www.thespacereview.com/article/930/1.

[33] Melissa Gray, 'Chinese space debris hits Russian satellite, scientists say', *CNN* (9 March 2013), online: www.cnn.com/2013/03/09/tech/satellite-hit.

### 7.6   The United States' 2008 Satellite Intercept

Just one year after China's ASAT weapon test, the US Navy used a sea-based SM-3 missile defence interceptor to destroy a malfunctioning reconnaissance satellite, USA 193.[34] The interceptor struck the satellite at an altitude of about 240 kilometres, with the aim of producing no long-lasting debris. That aim, however, was not achieved, with 174 pieces of trackable debris subsequently listed in the US military's satellite catalogue. While about 90 per cent of that debris de-orbited within two months, it took 20 months before the last pieces did so.

The United States claimed that the intercept had been necessary for public safety reasons, since the satellite was about to re-enter Earth's atmosphere loaded with highly toxic hydrazine thruster fuel, some of which might have reached the surface. It is possible that China's ASAT weapon test of the previous year was a factor in the United States' decision, even though this has been strongly denied.[35] What is certain, however, is that, since 1985, the US military has been consistent on the issue of Space debris. As General John E. Hyten, the commander of the Air Force Space Command, said in 2015, 'Kinetic [anti-satellite weaponry] is horrible for the world ... the one limiting factor is no debris. Whatever you do, don't create debris.'[36]

### 7.7   India's 2019 ASAT Weapon Test

In 2019, India tested a ground-based missile defence interceptor against a satellite (Microsat-R) that it had launched for that purpose.[37] It designed the impact to occur about 283 kilometres above the Earth and assured

---

[34] 'US missile hits spy satellite', *New Scientist* (21 February 2008), online: www.newscientist .com/article/dn13359-us-missile-hits-spy-satellite.

[35] Nicholas Johnson, 'Operation Burnt Frost: A view from inside' (May 2021) 56 *Space Policy* 101411. In what might well have been another coincidence, the US action came just one week before China and Russia introduced a draft Treaty on the Prevention of the Placement of Weapons in Outer Space and of the Threat or Use of Force against Outer Space Objects in the Conference on Disarmament. See discussion, section 7.9 below.

[36] General Hyten went on to serve as vice chair of the Joint Chiefs of Staff from 2019 to 2021.

[37] Jeffery Gettleman and Hari Kumar, 'India shot down a satellite, Modi says, shifting balance of power in Asia', *New York Times* (27 March 2019), online: www.nytimes .com/2019/03/27/world/asia/india-weather-satellite-missle.html.

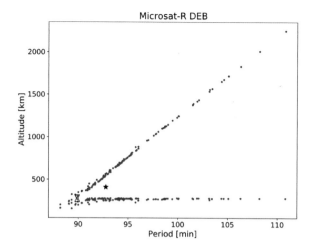

**Figure 7.1**    Gabbard plot showing the apogee–perigee distribution of tracked fragments resulting from India's ASAT weapon test (destruction of Microsat-R). The approximate altitude of the ISS is shown with a star. The apogee and perigee of Microsat-R just prior to the impact are shown by the downward and upward triangle. Despite the impact occurring at about 280 kilometres, tracked debris extended above LEO (i.e. above 2,000 kilometres in altitude). Note that if an object (such as an operational satellite) is between the red and blue points on this plot, then the debris crosses that object's orbital altitude.

other countries that no long-lasting debris would result.[38] The actual outcome was quite different.

Figure 7.1 shows the result of the impact, with debris extending above low Earth orbit (LEO) at apogee. It should be stressed that this is just the debris that can be tracked. There are roughly 130 such pieces in the US military's satellite catalogue, meaning that they were in orbit long enough to be tracked and assigned an identifier. It is reasonable to assume that there was at least one order of magnitude more pieces between one and ten centimetres in size, all of them still potentially lethal to satellites, Space stations and astronauts.

Figure 7.2 demonstrates that much of the debris from India's ASAT weapon test remained in orbit for months, taking over a year for 90 per

[38]  Sanjeev Miglani, 'India says space debris from anti-satellite test to "vanish" in 45 days', *Reuters* (28 March 2019), online: https://www.reuters.com/article/us-india-satellite-idUSKCN1R91DM.

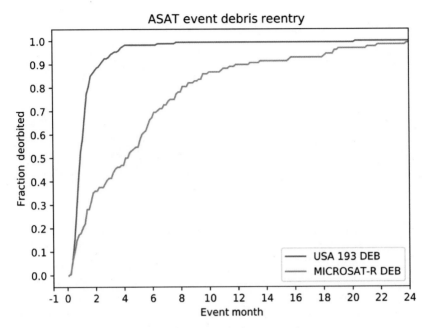

**Figure 7.2** Fraction of USA 193 and Microsat-R debris de-orbited by the number of months after the events. The USA 193 strike took place at an altitude of about 240 kilometres, leading to a relatively rapid loss of the debris, with about 90 per cent of the trackable debris pieces having de-orbited after about two months. In contrast, the Microsat-R strike occurred at about 280 kilometres, leading to much longer-lived debris, with 90 per cent of the debris de-orbiting only after 13 months. Data: USSPACECOM.

cent of the tracked debris to de-orbit. This can be compared with the USA 193 event in 2008, which took place at a lower altitude, and saw 90 per cent of the material de-orbiting in about two months. Neither situation was ideal, and both led to debris that went to high apogees. Regardless, the USA 193 event should have been a clear indication that some long-lived debris would be produced by a weapon test at the altitude of Microsat-R.

Initially, the international response to India's ASAT weapon test was muted, presumably because of the assurances that no long-lasting debris would result. This changed when it became apparent that considerable debris had remained in orbit. Then NASA Administrator Jim Bridenstine was especially critical because (as Figure 7.1 shows) many of the pieces crossed the International Space Station's altitude. Describing this as 'a terrible, terrible thing,' Bridenstine said, 'it is not acceptable for us to allow people to create orbital debris fields that put at risk our people'.[39]

India's ASAT weapon test was likely intended to demonstrate to China, its larger and more powerful regional rival, that any attacks on Indian satellites could be responded to in kind.[40] Regardless of India's motives, its actions also had the result of heightening international concerns about kinetic ASAT weapon tests, concerns that are only destined to grow as LEO becomes busier.

### 7.8  Russia's 2021 ASAT Weapon Test

On 15 November 2021, Russia's military used a ground-based missile to strike Kosmos 1408, a defunct Soviet-era satellite with a mass of about 1,750 kilograms orbiting at an altitude of about 480 kilometres. Again, due to the high impact energies involved, debris from a kinetic ASAT weapon test such as this inevitably ends up on highly eccentric orbits that cross the orbital altitudes of thousands of other satellites twice per revolution. Over time, as the debris from the test de-orbits, it will all pass through the altitudes of the International Space Station and China's new Tiangong Space station, placing astronauts, cosmonauts and taikonauts at deadly risk.

Figure 7.3 highlights how debris from this test crosses the orbits of the two Space stations, satellite mega-constellations currently being deployed, and many operational Russian satellites. This last point is especially important: the action was contrary to Russia's own investments and interests in Space.

The figure has been produced using Kosmos 1408 debris from two-line elements (TLEs) available through the United States Space Command (USSPACECOM) as of 7 December 2021. The grey curves show the path of each debris piece based on its first available TLE. Only about 340 of the estimated 1,500 tracked debris pieces are included in the figure, for clarity (and were the only ones available as of 7 December 2021).

---

[39] Sarah Lewin, 'India's anti-satellite test created dangerous debris, NASA chief says', *Space. com* (1 April 2019), online: www.space.com/nasa-chief-condemns-india-anti-satellite-test .html.

[40] Rajeswari Pillai Rajagopalan, 'Changing space security dynamics and governance debates', in Melissa De Zwart and Stacey Henderson, eds., *Commercial and Military Uses of Outer Space* (Singapore: Springer, 2021) 153 at 161.

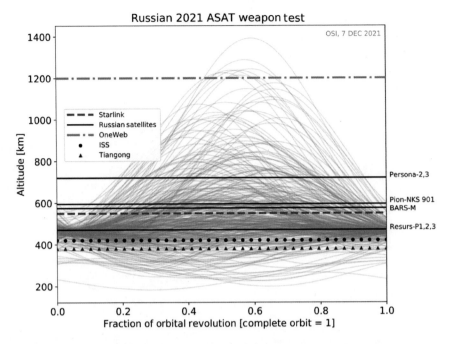

**Figure 7.3** Orbital trajectories for 340 pieces of debris from the Russian ASAT weapon test. The debris fragments cover a large range of low Earth orbits, crossing critical infrastructure, including the ISS, the Tiangong Space station and Russian satellites. Moreover, due to the high altitude of the test, all of the debris fragments will pass through the orbital space of the ISS and the Tiangong Space station as they decay.

We estimate that at least 50 operational Russian satellites are at altitudes traversed by the debris from the November 2021 test. Twenty-five of these are operated by the Russian Ministry of Defence, five by Roscosmos and five by Lomonosov Moscow State University. These are not small satellites: 21 of them have masses greater than a tonne. Moreover, at least 30 of these satellites are at altitudes that experienced a significant increase in the debris field due to the test. For reference, we have included the approximate orbital altitudes of select satellites and satellite constellations on the above plot, as well as the two Space stations.

Not included on the plot is the lethal, non-trackable debris, which is of particular concern because it will be more abundant than the trackable debris by at least an order of magnitude. Since small debris cannot be detected, collision avoidance manoeuvers cannot be used to protect against them. And again, at typical relative speeds of about 10 kilometres

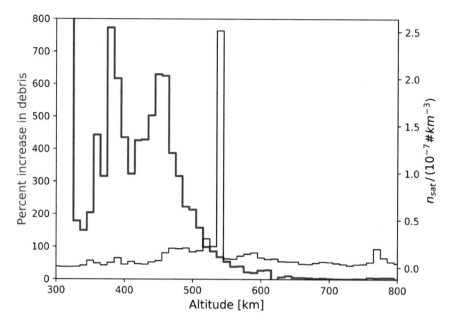

**Figure 7.4** The blue, thick line shows the increase in tracked debris across different altitudes due to the Russian ASAT weapon test. The increase is determined by comparing the USSPACECOM satellite catalogues as of 17 November 2021 (just after the event but before event debris was catalogued) and as of 27 January 2022. The grey, thin line shows the satellite number density as a function of altitude, with Starlink clearly visible. Ten-kilometre bins are used for determining the debris and satellite densities, weighted by the time the object spends within a given altitude bin. (This figure was made in collaboration with Outer Space Institute junior fellow Sarah Thiele).

per second (36,000 kilometres per hour), even a tiny piece can disable a satellite or kill an astronaut, cosmonaut or taikonaut.

To demonstrate the degree to which the 15 November 2021 test endangered Russian and all other orbital assets, we compared the debris field before the test with the debris field shortly after. In Figure 7.4, the blue line shows the percentage increase in the debris density across all altitudes, taken at face value using the catalogued debris as of 27 January 2022. The background grey line shows the satellite density distribution as of 17 November 2021, with Starlink clearly visible.

It bears repeating that every collision increases the cross-sectional area of the material involved and therefore the risk of further collisions. The most extreme outcome is, again, the Kessler–Cour-Palais syndrome.

But there are other serious, less dramatic concerns. For example, even at low-altitude orbits, sudden injections of material will proliferate small debris through knock-on collisions that could significantly interfere with satellite operations and human spaceflight.

Some of the debris from the November 2021 test will de-orbit quickly. Indeed, debris curves in the first plot that appear to be 'detached' from their birth altitude have already experienced substantial orbital evolution due to atmospheric drag. However, a significant fraction will remain in orbit for years or even decades, with the precise 'clearing time' dependent on the characteristics of the fragments and the behaviour of the atmosphere.

Such debris does not produce a consistent level of threat either. Earth is not a perfect sphere, which results in the orientation of orbits evolving with time, while keeping the same overall inclination. Astrophysicists would say that the orbit 'precesses'. To visualise this, imagine the edge of a coin as representing an orbit, and a spinning and wobbling coin representing the orbit's precession. Now, when the orientation of the debris orbit becomes nearly anti-aligned with another satellite's orbit (i.e. the debris and the satellite are moving towards each other), there can be episodic periods of very high 'conjunction' activity (close approaches between objects) involving clusters of debris.

Several such 'conjunction squalls' arising from the Russian ASAT weapon test have been predicted by COMSPOC,[41] one of several new companies offering 'Space situational awareness' (SSA) – essentially, knowledge about the Space environment and human activities in Space. Even if these squalls only create a modest increase in the collision risk, the sheer number of conjunctions could overload SSA efforts or trigger excessive collision avoidance manoeuvres by other actors. This strains Space safety and could lead to secondary failures or accidents.

As we have explained above, the Russian military is not the only military to have tested a kinetic ASAT weapon in a manner that was certain to create long-lasting debris. But the action was more imprudent in 2021 than it was in 1985, 2007 or even 2019. This is because the fast-changing orbital environment has made such activities significantly more dangerous than before. There are currently over 7,000 satellites (active and defunct) in LEO, as compared to just over 3,000 three years ago. And

---

[41] Jeff Foust, 'Russian ASAT debris creating "squalls" of close approaches with satellites', *SpaceNews* (18 February 2022), online: spacenews.com/russian-asat-debris-creating-squalls-of-close-approaches-with-satellites.

this number is projected to grow quickly – to over 100,000 satellites by 2030 – largely because of the construction and completion of numerous satellite mega-constellations. It is thus clear that any additional kinetic ASAT weapon tests, by anyone, will threaten the interests of all space-faring states – including Russia, India and China. It is therefore imperative that the international community move forward on this issue, with all deliberate speed.

### 7.9   Diplomatic Initiatives

In 1979, the United States and the Soviet Union negotiated the preliminary text of a treaty that would have banned the testing and use of ASAT weapons (as we noted above).[42] More recently, in 2008 and again in 2014, China and Russia jointly introduced a draft Treaty on the Prevention of the Placement of Weapons in Outer Space, the Threat or Use of Force against Outer Space Objects (PPWT) at the Conference on Disarmament.[43] The draft treaty is quite simple, centring on a commitment to not 'place any weapons in outer space', with a 'weapon in outer space' being defined in the 2014 draft document as

> any outer space object or its component produced or converted to eliminate, damage or disrupt normal functioning of objects in outer space, on the Earth's surface or in the air, as well as to eliminate population, components of biosphere important to human existence, or to inflict damage to them by using any principles of physics.[44]

The China–Russia draft treaty also reaffirms within the Space context the UN Charter's Article 2(4) prohibition on the threat or use of force, with a prohibition on 'the threat or use of force against outer space objects of States Parties'.[45] As with the UN Charter, the draft treaty

---

[42] Moltz, op. cit. at 186, citing Stares, op. cit. at 198–99.

[43] Draft Treaty on the Prevention of the Placement of Weapons in Outer Space, the Threat or Use of Force against Outer Space Objects (submitted by China and Russia to the Conference on Disarmament) UN Doc CD/1985 (12 June 2014) (2014 PPWT), online: documents-dds-ny.un.org/doc/UNDOC/GEN/G14/050/66/PDF/G1405066.pdf; Treaty on the Prevention of the Placement of Weapons in Outer Space and of the Threat or Use of Force against Outer Space Objects (submitted by China and Russia to the Conference on Disarmament) UN Doc CD/1839 (29 February 2008) (2008 PPWT), online: documents-dds-ny.un.org/doc/UNDOC/GEN/G08/604/02/PDF/G0860402.pdf.

[44] 2014 PPWT, Art. I(b).

[45] Charter of the United Nations, 26 June 1945, Can TS 1945 No 7 Art. 2(4) (entered into force 24 October 1945).

makes clear that this prohibition 'shall by no means affect the States Parties' inherent right to individual or collective self-defence, as recognized by Article 51 of the UN Charter'.[46] The right of self-defence is part of customary international law, and its implications for ASAT weapons are explored in the next chapter.

The United States, along with some non-governmental experts, criticised the China–Russia draft treaty for failing to provide verification measures and for not addressing direct-ascent ASAT weapons.[47] Such criticisms were relied on by the United States to justify blocking negotiations on the draft treaty in the Conference on Disarmament, which operates on a consensus basis.

In our assessment, the criticisms of the China–Russia draft treaty were misplaced, for two reasons. First, the ability to detect the use and even the deployment of kinetic ASAT weapons is constantly improving because of technological improvements in Space situational awareness. These improvements are being driven, in part, by the fast-growing need to identify and track satellites and Space debris to prevent accidental collisions. Numerous ground-based sensors and some Space-based sensors are now dedicated to this purpose.[48] There is no need for a treaty provision requiring countries to acquire verification tools that they already possess and are quickly improving.

Second, direct-ascent ASAT weapons are in fact dealt with in the China–Russia draft treaty through the prohibition on the 'threat or use of force against outer space objects of States Parties'. Although this is a prohibition of the use of such weapons rather than of their deployment, the prohibition needs to be focused in this way because missile defence interceptors can be used as ASAT weapons, as China, India and Russia have already demonstrated through tests and, in the case of the United States, through the destruction of a defunct re-entering satellite loaded

---

[46] Ibid. Art. 51.

[47] Jinyuan Su, 'The legal challenge of arms control in space', in Cassandra Steer and Matthew Hersch, eds., *War and Peace in Outer Space: Law, Policy, and Ethics* (Oxford: Oxford University Press, 2020) 181 at 186; Michael Listner and Rajeswari Pillai Rajagopalan, 'The 2014 PPWT: A new draft but with the same and different problems', *Space Review* (11 August 2014), online: www.thespacereview.com/article/2575/1.

[48] Most of these assets are military, such as Canada's *Sapphire* satellite, which is dedicated entirely to SSA. But there are also new commercial providers such as LeoLabs, COMSPOC and Privateer. The use of commercial assets for arms control verification is already well established with Earth-imaging satellites, with militaries being some of the largest customers for such services.

with toxic thruster fuel. In other words, one could not prohibit the existence of direct-ascent ASAT weapons without also banning surface-based missile defence systems such as the SM-3 missiles on US Aegis class naval vessels, which is something the United States would never accept.

For these reasons, it seems likely that US opposition to the China–Russia draft treaty was politically motivated, and not by concerns about the scope and likely effectiveness of the instrument. Of course, there would have been political reasons behind China and Russia proposing the treaty in the first place, including concerns about the United States possibly developing a Space-based missile defence system after its denunciation of the 1972 Anti-Ballistic Missile Treaty in 2002. Political reasons may also explain why China and Russia have not taken their draft treaty to another forum, one where decisions are not based on consensus and the United States is unable to block negotiations. That said, it is possible that China and Russia regard the United States as a necessary partner in any treaty on Space weapons, in which case moving to another forum would offer them no advantage.

The China–Russia draft treaty is consistent with a resolution that has been adopted, annually and with near unanimity, by the United Nations General Assembly on the Prevention of an Arms Race in Outer Space (PAROS).[49] It is also consistent with a resolution on No First Placement of Weapons in Outer Space, which the General Assembly has adopted on five occasions since 2015.[50]

Several individual countries have also made specific proposals that align with the China–Russia draft treaty. After India's 2019 ASAT weapon test, the German delegation to the Legal Subcommittee of the UN Committee on the Peaceful Uses of Outer Space (COPUOS) called for a 'legally binding prohibition of the intentional destruction of space objects resulting in the generation of long-lasting debris, including in situations of armed conflict'.[51]

---

[49] For the most recent iteration, see *Prevention of an Arms Race in Outer Space*, GA Res 76/22, UNGAOR, 76th Sess, 45th Plen Mtg, UN Doc A/RES/76/22 (8 December 2021), online: documents-dds-ny.un.org/doc/UNDOC/GEN/N21/377/75/PDF/N2137775.pdf.

[50] For the most recent iteration, see *No First Placement of Weapons in Outer Space*, GA Res 76/23, UNGAOR, 76th Sess, 45th Plen Mtg, UN Doc A/RES/76/23 (8 December 2021), online: documents-dds-ny.un.org/doc/UNDOC/GEN/N21/377/82/PDF/N2137782.pdf.

[51] Stefan Talmon, 'Germany criticizes India over anti-satellite missile test', *German Practice in International Law* (20 May 2019), online: gpil.jura.uni-bonn.de/2019/05/germany-criticizes-india-over-anti-satellite-missile-test/. The German position is also expressed,

Other proposals have focused on banning the *testing* of kinetic ASAT weapons rather than their deployment or use. In January 2020, Canada's representative at the Conference on Disarmament spoke about the desirability of negotiations on specific arms control issues in Space, 'such as negotiating a potential end to ASAT testing causing space debris'.[52]

The Russian diplomat Alexey Arbatov has proposed that Russia and the United States take the first step with a bilateral agreement against the 'testing of anti-satellite systems involving the actual destruction of target satellites (space objects)'.[53] Such a treaty is possible, Arbatov says, because the two countries have a shared interest in limiting the development of weapons that threaten satellites designed to provide early warning of nuclear strikes.[54] He calls for the inclusion of clear transparency and co-operation requirements and argues that verification could be provided by existing missile detection systems, modified, if necessary, so that they can also monitor for kinetic ASAT weapon tests.[55]

Ross Liemer and Christopher Chyba have proposed that kinetic ASAT weapon tests be prohibited above a set altitude, to prevent the creation of Space debris without banning testing completely.[56] They suggested that the altitude cap could be set by the Inter-Agency Space Debris Coordination Committee (IADC), and that Space powers could negotiate this partial test ban in a venue such as the Conference on Disarmament. They argued that an altitude cap, rather than an outright ban on testing, is more likely to garner broad international support because it would not discriminate against those countries that currently lack kinetic ASAT weapons, since they could develop and test their new systems below the set altitude. Liemer and Chyba also argued that an altitude cap would

without attribution, in Committee on the Peaceful Uses of Outer Space, *Report of the Legal Subcommittee on Its Fifty-Eighth Session, Held in Vienna from 1 to 12 April 2019*, UNGAOR, 62nd Sess, UN Doc A/AC.105/1203 (18 April 2019) at para. 184, online: www .unoosa.org/oosa/oosadoc/data/documents/2019/aac.105/aac.1051203_0.html.

[52] Reported in Paul Meyer, 'Arms control in outer space: Mission impossible or unrealized potential?' (20 October 2020), Canadian Global Affairs Institute Policy Perspective, online: www.cgai.ca/arms_control_in_outer_space_mission_impossible_or_unrealized_ potential.

[53] Alexey Arbatov, 'Arms control in outer space: The Russian angle, and a possible way forward' (2019) 75:4 *Bulletin of the Atomic Scientists* 151.

[54] Ibid. at 158.

[55] Ibid. at 158.

[56] Ross Liemer and Christopher F Chyba, 'A verifiable limited test ban for anti-satellite weapons' (2010) 33:3 *Washington Quarterly* 149. See also Jesse Oppenheim, 'Danger at 700,000 feet: Why the United States needs to develop a kinetic anti-satellite missile technology test-ban treaty' (2013) 38:2 *Brooklyn Journal of International Law* 761.

enable countries to maintain existing ASAT weapon and missile defence capabilities, and to destroy their own satellites in the event of a hazardous uncontrolled re-entry by doing so at a low altitude where Space debris would not be created. Finally, they asserted that a widely supported total test ban (i.e. one that covered all altitudes) would be difficult to achieve if it forbade 'debris-producing ASAT tests [by all countries] but permitted midcourse-interception ballistic missile defence tests, which China and the USA may view as essential to their national security'.[57]

However, even low-altitude tests will result in Space debris, because the large amount of energy imparted in the impacts can kick small pieces of debris into highly elliptical orbits, as the Indian ASAT weapon test and even the USA 193 event demonstrated. Most of this debris might not stay in Space very long, because of the effects of gas drag at perigee,[58] but the debris could stay on mega-constellation- and Space station-crossing orbits for weeks to months. Going to lower and lower orbits will reduce the de-orbit timescale, but it does not eliminate initial high-altitude debris. And while debris with a high area-to-mass ratio might de-orbit in days or weeks, pieces with a lower area-to-mass ratio will remain in Space for longer. This sort of variation is to be expected, since the debris resulting from any single ASAT weapon test will have a wide range of characteristics.

The idea of an altitude cap for ASAT weapon tests thus depends on states finding common ground on an acceptable risk threshold. Explosions at an altitude of, for example, 150 kilometres will ensure very rapid de-orbits, but not without any risk due to the lofting into orbit of uncontrolled material, however temporary. For all these reasons, anything less than an absolute ban on kinetic ASAT weapon testing will leave some risk, including for astronauts, cosmonauts and taikonauts.

---

[57] Liemer and Chyba, op. cit. at 157.

[58] Earth's upper atmosphere extends into LEO, albeit with very low gas densities. An object moving through gas feels a resistance against its motion, called 'gas drag'. The strength of the drag depends on a number of details about the interaction, but the drag is stronger for higher gas densities and for faster motion through the gas. While gas drag operates at all altitudes where gas is present, objects at lower altitudes experience stronger gas drag due to the increasing density of gas with decreasing altitude. An object's orbital motion is also faster for lower altitudes. Objects on elliptical orbits thus experience the strongest gas drag effects at perigee (closest approach to Earth), causing the apogee (farthest part of the orbit from Earth) to lower over time until the orbit is approximately circular. The orbit continues to decay from that point but remains roughly circular.

Geoffrey Forden has suggested several ways in which a ban on kinetic ASAT weapon tests could be achieved.[59] One way would be for states to 'pledge to avoid creating persistent space debris by following the guidelines of the Inter-Agency Space Debris Coordination Committee'. This approach has the attraction of not requiring a renegotiation of the required behaviour. There are two ways in which similar pledges have created legal obligations in the past. First, 'unilateral declarations' can be binding on countries, as the International Court of Justice explained in the *Nuclear Test Cases*: 'When it is the intention of the State making the declaration that it should become bound according to its terms, that intention confers on the declaration the character of a legal undertaking, the State being thenceforth legally required to follow a course of conduct consistent with the declaration.'[60] The threat of Space debris is so very great that one could imagine a spacefaring state unilaterally declaring its intention to treat the IADC guidelines as legally binding.[61] And while these kinds of declarations are unusual, Forden has to be credited with foresight and perhaps even influence because, in April 2022, the United States announced that it would unilaterally impose an ASAT weapon test ban on itself.[62] We will discuss this development in the next chapter.

A more usual law-making path would involve a number of spacefaring states agreeing to make the IADC guidelines legally binding, among themselves, through a new treaty. Guidelines and other forms of 'soft law' are often transformed into hard law through the treaty-making process, with the subsequent adoption of all the provisions of the UN General Assembly's Declaration of Legal Principles Governing the

---

[59] Geoffrey Forden, 'After China's test: Time for a limited ban on anti-satellite weapons' (April 2007) 37 *Arms Control Today*, online: www.armscontrol.org/act/2007-04/features/after-chinas-test-time-limited-ban-anti-satellite-weapons.

[60] *Nuclear Tests* (*Australia v. France*), [1974] ICJ Rep 253 at 19, para. 43; *Nuclear Tests* (*New Zealand v. France*), [1974] ICJ Rep 457 at 19, para. 46.

[61] The day after the Russian ASAT test, the Secure World Foundation (SWF) issued a statement in which it called upon the United States, Russia, China and India 'to declare unilateral moratoriums on further testing of their antisatellite weapons that could create additional orbital debris and to work with other countries towards solidifying an international ban on destructive ASAT testing'. Secure World Foundation, 'SWF statement on Russian ASAT test' (16 November 2021), *SWF*, online: swfound.org/news/all-news/2021/11/swf-statement-on-russian-asat-test.

[62] The White House, fact sheet, 'Vice President Harris advances national security norms in space – New US commitment on destructive direct-ascent anti-satellite missile testing' (18 April 2022), online: www.whitehouse.gov/briefing-room/statements-releases/2022/04/18/fact-sheet-vice-president-harris-advances-national-security-norms-in-space/.

Activities of States in the Exploration and Use of Outer Space into articles of the Outer Space Treaty being a case in point.

Forden's second suggestion was 'to ban one spacecraft from approaching another orbiting spacecraft at excessive speeds'.[63] He suggested a threshold of 100 metres per second for spacecraft located within 100 kilometres of each other. As Forden explained,

> These speeds and distances are great enough not to interfere with much of the normal operating procedures in space and yet would still obstruct the development of the tracking, guidance, and control of any ASAT weapon. At the same time, they do not prevent the testing and deployment of ground-based missile defenses because the target is not in orbit.

It is important to recognise that Forden made this suggestion in 2007, when LEO was not as crowded as it is today. 'Conjunctions' – when two satellites come within a few kilometres of each other at high relative speeds – now occur every few minutes,[64] a situation that will only be exacerbated by mega-constellations.

Proposals also exist for a prohibition on all ASAT weapon testing, including the testing of non-kinetic ASAT weapons, to prevent a broader arms race in Space.[65] Unfortunately, such proposals immediately encounter problems with respect to verification, namely the detection of cyber and other non-kinetic tests, as well as the potential dual-use character of some Space systems, such as those proposed for the active removal of Space debris. That said, there are many multilateral treaties that have been adopted despite verification problems, with the Convention against Torture being a case in point.[66] We know that the existence of such a treaty can shape state practice, both by 'marshalling shame' and by forcing violators to conceal and deny their actions.[67]

In any event, these proposals for a prohibition on all ASAT weapon testing provide additional evidence of growing concerns about ASAT

---

[63] Forden, op. cit.

[64] See Advanced Sciences and Technology Research in Astronautics, 'Conjunction streaming service demo' (2022), *University of Texas at Austin*, online: astriacss.tacc.utexas.edu/ui/min .html.

[65] Peter van Ness, 'The time has come for a treaty to ban weapons in space' (2010) 34:3 *Asian Perspective* 215 at 224.

[66] Convention against Torture and Other Cruel, Inhuman or Degrading Treatment or Punishment, 10 December 1984, 1465 UNTS 85 (entered into force 26 June 1987).

[67] John Humphrey, *Human Rights and the United Nations: A Great Adventure* (Epping: Bowker, 1984); Louis Henkin, *The Age of Rights* (New York: Columbia University Press, 1990) at 29.

weapons and their negative consequences, especially Space debris and the Kessler–Cour-Palais syndrome. Together with all the other evidence considered above, they suggest that an intermediate step – a treaty banning kinetic ASAT weapon tests – could receive widespread support.

Now it would be easy to assume that the November 2021 Russian ASAT weapon test will set back efforts to negotiate a ban on kinetic testing. But there are several reasons to hope that this will not be the case. First, it is possible that Russia wished to test (and, perhaps more importantly, demonstrate) the effectiveness of its new PL-19 Nudol missile system as an ASAT weapon before negotiating a test ban with other spacefaring states.[68]

Second, it is possible, perhaps even likely, that the Russian military conducted the test without the support or even the knowledge of the Russian Space agency (Roscosmos) and the Russian Foreign Ministry.[69] If so, the influence of the latter two branches of the Russian government may have been strengthened by the fact that the test created over a thousand pieces of trackable and many thousands of pieces of untrackable debris in orbits that create non-trivial risks for valuable Russian satellites and cosmonauts on the International Space Station. Although it is difficult to assess the internal politics of the Vladimir Putin regime, we know that Roscosmos is concerned about Space debris and that the Russian Foreign Ministry has participated constructively in COPUOS and UN General Assembly negotiations on this issue.[70]

---

[68] It has likewise been suggested that one of the motives for India's 2019 test may have been 'to convey credible proof of Indian capabilities before any international efforts to ban kinetic, debris-producing ASAT tests were consummated'. Ashely J Tellis, 'India's ASAT test: An incomplete success' (15 April 2019), *Carnegie Endowment for International Peace*, online: carnegieendowment.org/2019/04/15/india-s-asat-test-incomplete-success-pub-78884.

[69] According to the *Washington Post*, NASA Administrator Bill Nelson 'said he would not be surprised if his counterpart at the Russian space agency, Dmitry Rogozin, didn't "know a thing about this, and it's the Russian military doing their thing".' Paul Soone, Missy Ryan and Christian Davenport, 'In first, Russian test strikes satellite using Earth-based missile', *Washington Post* (16 November 2021), online: www.washingtonpost.com/national-security/russia-satellie-weapon/2021/11/15/0695621c-4648-11ec-973c-be864f938c72_story.html.

[70] In November 2021, a compromise was reportedly brokered between the United States, China and Russia in the lead-up to the First Committee of the UN General Assembly voting to create an Open Ended Working Group (OEWG) on Reducing Space Threats Through Norms, Rules and Principles of Responsible Behaviours. According to Breaking Defense, 'Washington now has accepted the possibility the OEWG might recommend legally codified norms of behavior. In exchange, while Beijing and Moscow voted "No" on the OEWG's formation, they at the same time refrained from pushing a competing UN

Third, Russia has strenuously denied that their November 2021 test created risks for operational satellites or the Space stations. Such a position is not supported by the measured distribution of Kosmos 1408 debris, as we discussed above. Yet the denial itself constitutes an acknowledgement, by the Russian government, that the deliberate creation of dangerous debris is unacceptable today. For international lawyers, such denials are significant as evidence of *opinio juris*, the subjective element of customary international law. They can also count as 'state practice' that, in terms of its law-creating effect, is just as significant as the action being denied.

Again, the prohibition on torture, which is widely accepted as having achieved the heightened, peremptory status of a *jus cogens* rule of customary international law, provides a powerful example of how such rules can develop. As Anthony D'Amato wrote,

> It seems . . . important to ask whether the states that engage in torture are (a) disclosing that they are torturing people, (b) proclaiming that what they are doing is legally justified, and (c) implicitly inviting other states to do likewise on the ground that, if torture is legally permissible for them, it is legally permissible for all states.[71]

D'Amato went on to explain that 'hiding, cover-up, minimization, and non-justification . . . betoken a violation of law' and therefore constitute legally relevant state practice *in support of* a rule prohibiting the actions in question.[72] Denials are, in short, the tribute that vice pays to virtue – and they can have law-creating effects.

Russia, by denying that it created dangerous debris in November 2021, was strengthening, not weakening, a possible new customary rule against testing ASAT weapons in ways that create long-lasting debris. In the next chapter of this book, we will consider the rest of the state practice and

---

venue for discussions based on their long-proposed treaty barring the placement of weapons in space, known as the PPWT.' Theresa Hitchens, 'UN committee votes "yes" on UK–US-backed space rules group', *Breaking Defense* (1 November 2021), online: breakingdefense.com/2021/11/un-committee-votes-yes-on-uk-us-backed-space-rules-group.

[71] Anthony D'Amato, 'Custom and treaty: A response to Professor Weisburd' (1988) 21:3 *Vanderbilt Journal of Transnational Law* 459 at 466.

[72] Ibid. at 469. D'Amato's analysis was validated a decade later when the George W. Bush administration argued – implausibly – that it was not committing torture because techniques such as waterboarding did not fit the legal definition of the term. See Jose E Alvarez, 'Torturing the law' (2006) 37:2 *Case Western Reserve Journal of International Law* 175.

evidence of *opinio juris* that could be contributing to such a new rule today, including the United States' announcement, in April 2022, that it would unilaterally impose an ASAT weapon test ban on itself.[73]

Before doing so, however, we turn to a related and often overlooked issue, namely the possibility that missile defence tests may also be contributing to the crisis of Space debris.

## 7.10   Missile Defence and Space Debris

Increasingly, the same type of ground-based missiles that can be used as ASAT weapons are being developed, tested, and deployed for ballistic missile defence. The SC-19 missile used by China to strike a satellite in 2007 was designed primarily for missile defence, as was the SM-3 missile used by the United States in 2008, the PDV Mk-II missile used by India in 2019, and the PL-19 Nudol missile used by Russia in 2021.

Of all these ballistic missile defence programmes, that of the United States is the most advanced of any country. The US Air Force currently has 44 Ground-Based Midcourse Defense interceptors in Alaska and California that are designed to impact incoming ICBMs as they transit LEO. The US Navy has a much larger number of SM-3 missiles deployed on 41 Aegis class cruisers and destroyers. SM-3 missiles are also deployed at two 'Aegis Ashore' sites in Romania and Poland. While SM-3s are designed for intercepting intermediate-range ballistic missiles, they have been successfully tested for use against ICBMs.

We have already discussed the Space debris hazard posed by ground-based missiles when tested or used as ASAT weapons. However, the testing or use of the same type of missiles against incoming ballistic missiles can also create Space debris, at least under certain conditions, if the strike occurs above the atmosphere during the mid-course phase of a ballistic missile's flight. This issue of ballistic missile defence and Space debris has not previously been publicly addressed, though it may well have been analysed and discussed within government circles.

It would be easy to make two assumptions about ballistic missile defence and Space debris:

(1) The trajectories of ballistic missiles are notably different from low Earth orbits (Figures 7.5 and 7.6), and it would thus seem reasonable,

---

[73] The White House, op. cit.

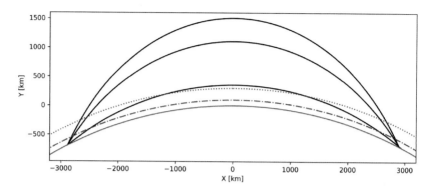

**Figure 7.5**  Ballistic trajectories for three different profiles, showing a depressed, an efficient and a high-altitude trajectory. The blue curve represents the surface of the Earth, while the dot-dashed curve is at an altitude of 100 kilometres and the dotted line is at 300 kilometres.

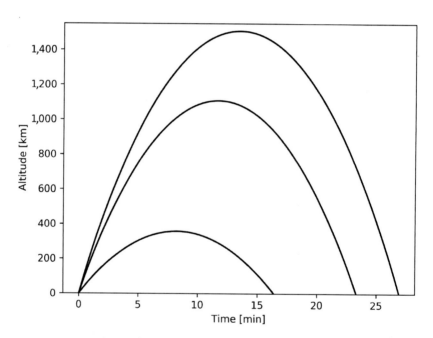

**Figure 7.6**  Simplified example of the flight times corresponding to the depressed, efficient and high-altitude trajectories in Figure 7.5. The times are based on Keplerian arcs, so they do not account for the time needed to accelerate the ICBMs to burnout (at around 100 kilometres). Nonetheless, this introduces a timing difference of only one to a few minutes, so the overall scale of the flight times is preserved.

at first glance, to assume that any fragmentation of the missile will only result in pieces that will enter the atmosphere essentially on the same trajectory as before the fragmentation.

(2) A ballistic missile defence interception can take place at relatively low altitudes (e.g. 225 kilometres), where fragments will be subject to strong gas drag forces. It thus seems reasonable, at first glance, to assume that no long-lived Space debris generation will occur.

Both these assumptions require scrutiny.

Multiple factors will affect whether ballistic missile defence tests produce orbital debris and the degree of danger such debris will cause: the shape of the ballistic missile trajectory, the point of impact between interceptor and ballistic missile, and their relative velocities, which will then affect the nature and number of fragments produced, as well as the change in velocity ($\Delta v$) of each fragment, which in turn will affect trajectories for debris that achieve orbital velocities. The analysis of these factors and the danger they pose to the Space environment is complex but telling.

The mid-course phase of an ICBM's flight begins when it is no longer under power and is following a ballistic trajectory. This can begin at a range of altitudes, depending on the flight profile. However, the maximum altitude reached along its arc is typically between 300 and 1,300 kilometres. Recall that the International Space Station orbits at an altitude of around 400 kilometres, while the majority of commercial and military satellites orbit at altitudes between 300 and 800 kilometres. Even a 'depressed' trajectory, which requires more energy but might reduce the exposure to missile defence interceptors, will see the missile spend most of its flight above 200 kilometres, where – as we have seen above and will revisit below – an impact can still create Space debris that imperils satellites higher up.

US ballistic missile defence tests have been conducted at several different altitudes and speeds. Variation in test conditions is important to ensure effectiveness across a range of scenarios, such as the time of day, altitude and closing speeds (the relative speed of the two objects as they approach each other). Quite a few tests have taken place at an altitude of 225 kilometres, although the highest and fastest test interception to date has been FTG-15, which took place in 2017 at an altitude of 740 kilometres (after the target missile had begun its descent from a peak altitude of 1,250 kilometres). A schematic of the FTG-15 interception is shown in Figure 7.7.

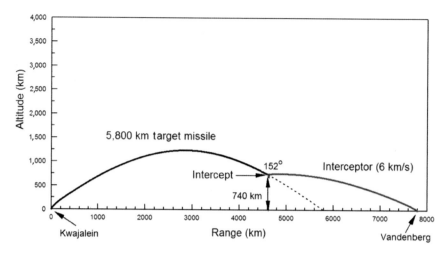

**Figure 7.7** Depiction of the FTG-15 interception test. Credit: Laura Grego and David Wright, 'Incremental Progress but No Realistic Capability: Analysis of the Ground-Based Midcourse Missile Defense Test FTG-15' (2018) *Union of Concerned Scientists Report*, online: www.ucsusa.org/resources/analysis-gmd-missile-defense-test-ftg-15. Reproduced with permission.

In the case of FTG-15, the closing speed of the target missile and the interceptor was approximately 10.2 kilometres per second.[74]

Despite the missiles being suborbital, we know from the discussion above concerning ASAT weapon tests that debris can be given very high-velocity 'kicks' during the explosion that results from the collision. Should these kicks be in the 'right' direction, orbital speeds can in principle be achieved. To explore the conditions in which debris might be placed into orbit, we make the following 'toy model' – a term used in physics for a deliberately simplistic model with many details removed, to enable a concise explanation.

We assume an FTG-15-like high-altitude trajectory with an apogee of 1,250 kilometres and a collision with the kill vehicle at 740 kilometres. The trajectory follows a Keplerian orbital arc for simplicity, and is given a speed of approximately 5.2 kilometres per second. The total break-up mass is assumed to be one tonne, and we further assume that the collision is sufficiently energetic to be catastrophic, i.e. the target and

---

[74] Closing speeds in general will vary based on the details of the interception.

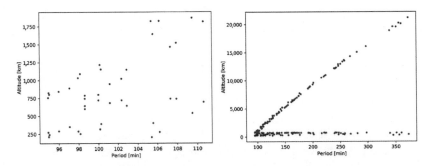

**Figure 7.8** Surviving debris resulting from the catastrophic break-up of a missile during an FTG-15-like ICBM interception test. Fragments are determined according to the NASA standard break-up model. The model only considers fragments between the sizes of one centimetre and one metre. Almost 47,000 debris pieces are produced in the model, 19 of which survive in LEO and about 100 on altitudes below 22,000 kilometres (GPS orbits at approximately 20,000 kilometres). The vast majority of the fragments re-enter the atmosphere, but, clearly, long-lived Space debris is produced by such tests (taken to be fragments with perigees higher than 250 kilometres)

the 'kill vehicle' are both completely destroyed. We use the NASA 'standard break-up model' for collisional catastrophic fragmentation to determine the number of fragments, the distribution of area-to-mass ratios, and the change in velocity ($\Delta v$) for each simulated debris particle (which depends on the area-to-mass ratios in the break-up model).[75] The $\Delta v$ is applied to the velocity of the debris at the moment of the collision (the 'instantaneous velocity vector'), with each debris piece being given a random direction (assuming 'isotropy' – i.e. no variation based on direction). The new total velocities can then be used to determine new 'instantaneous orbits', i.e. the orbits resulting immediately after the explosion. If the perigees of the fragments – the lowest part of their orbits – are at a high enough altitude, they are potentially long-lived debris.

Figure 7.8 demonstrates that the FTG-15 interception in 2017 likely produced long-lived debris. Most of the material does re-enter the atmosphere, as would typically be expected, including the trackable debris. However – and this is the critical point – some centimetre-size debris is given sufficient $\Delta v$ to place these small objects into orbit. And while the long-lived debris may only be a small fraction of the total

---

[75] Heiner Klinkrad, *Space Debris: Models and Risk Analysis* (Berlin: Springer, 2006).

fragmentation debris from the impact event, which consists of tens of thousands of pieces, the debris is still potentially lethal to satellites, Space stations and astronauts.

Now let us consider a different profile altogether, namely a depressed trajectory. This toy model has an apogee altitude of 350 kilometres and an interception altitude of 225 kilometres (similar range). If we likewise assume a one-tonne target and a catastrophic collision, long-lived debris is again generated among the centimetre-size population. We have not reproduced plots for this second toy model here, because they look similar to those in Figure 7.8.

It thus seems plausible that ballistic missile defence tests will result in long-lived debris, despite the missiles themselves being suborbital. The fraction of surviving material is much less than that seen in ASAT weapon tests, due to the underlying dynamics. The debris is also limited to smaller pieces, although these are still potentially lethal. The duration that this Space debris will survive in orbit depends on the resulting area-to-mass ratios. However, since the surviving debris has very high apogee, it could spend considerable time in orbit.

So why has Space debris not previously been discussed in the context of ballistic missile defence testing? It may be that the absence of any long-lived trackable debris leads to the impression that such tests will never create any long-lived debris. However, if the NASA standard break-up model applies, our analysis shows that pieces of smaller, untrackable debris can indeed survive – and therefore pose a lethal risk. Admittedly, the severity of this risk is reduced as a result of the long-lived debris being relegated to the so-called 'tails' of the distributions, making these events relatively minor contributors to Space debris. But they are *purposeful* additions of Space debris, and they exacerbate an already dangerous situation in orbit.

Ultimately, the detailed trajectories of the missile and the interceptor, and the specifics of the break-up, will control the amount of material that enters orbit. There is no single threshold for this. But one thing is clear: If we wish to avoid the creation of long-lived Space debris, we need to conduct ballistic missile defence tests at low altitudes only *and* manage the energy of the impacts.

## 7.11   Are Debris Concerns Outweighed by the Purpose of Missile Defence Systems?

A second reason why Space debris is rarely discussed in the context of ballistic missile defence may concern the purpose of these systems, which is to prevent nuclear warheads from reaching the Earth's surface and causing mass destruction there. In other words, it may be assumed that any concerns about Space debris are outweighed by the number of lives that would be lost if an incoming missile were not intercepted.

This assumption can be questioned from the outset with a historical fact. The only US ballistic missile defence system built during the Cold War protected ICBM silos in North Dakota. Its purpose was not directly to save lives, but to ensure that the United States maintained a 'second strike' capability in the event of a Soviet first strike. Today, US ballistic missile defence interceptors in Alaska, California and Eastern Europe, and on naval vessels, are considered by many to be a destabilising factor. This is because they might cause potential adversaries to develop new technologies, such as hypersonic cruise missiles that can evade attempted interceptions, or to deploy more missiles to ensure that any missile defence system would be overwhelmed by the sheer number of incoming targets.

Still, one can envisage scenarios where intercepting an incoming ballistic missile would save many lives, for instance if North Korea launched a missile towards a city in the United States. It may be instructive to consider whether the purpose of the interception would feed into a legal analysis. Consider the right of self-defence: an incoming nuclear warhead would meet the threshold of an 'armed attack', and the scale of destruction prevented by a defensive interception would very likely fulfil the criteria of necessity and proportionality – even if some long-lasting Space debris were likely to result. For as the analysis above shows, a ballistic missile interception will produce significantly less Space debris than a strike against a satellite. The same conclusion would result from an analysis of the *jus in bello*, which is also known as either the 'law of armed conflict' or 'international humanitarian law' and concerns the conduct of armed conflicts that are already under way. A *jus in bello* analysis involves the principles of military necessity, distinction and proportionality. We will come back to the right of self-defence and the *jus in bello* in much greater depth in the next chapter, within the context of ASAT weapons.

But use is one thing, and *testing* is another. The two toy models above suggest that kinetic mid-course missile defence tests will create a small amount of untrackable long-lasting Space debris and therefore increase the risks to satellites, Space stations and astronauts. Such tests should therefore be avoided. Indeed, there is a strong argument for including the topic of ballistic missile defence testing in any negotiations on a treaty banning kinetic ASAT weapon testing. That ban should probably include mid-course missile defence tests above certain relative-speed and combined-mass thresholds, all with the goal of preventing long-lasting Space debris.

## 7.12   Militarisation of Cis-lunar Space

Cis-lunar Space is about to be developed due to an emerging Space race between China and the United States. Although the race is currently between civilian Space agencies, all the conditions exist for yet another security dilemma.[76]

Cis-lunar (Latin for 'this side of the moon') Space is the volume that extends from Earth's geosynchronous orbits and encompasses the Moon, the Moon's orbits, the Earth–Moon Lagrange points, and certain types of transfer orbits.[77] The Lagrange points, or 'L points', are defined as locations where the combined gravitational acceleration due to the Earth and the Moon allows a small object, such as a spacecraft, to orbit the Earth at the same rate as the Moon. Due to these unique features, L points will be important for future lunar activities as locations where communications and monitoring equipment, refuelling depots and even Space stations can be maintained at relatively low energy output. Even though cis-lunar Space is very large, extending more than ten times further than geosynchronous orbit, the optimal regions near the five Lagrange points are limited in size. Consequently, they are highly desirable and potentially contested locations (see Figure 7.9).

Due to the distances involved, Earth-based telescopes and radar are not adequate for monitoring spacecraft in cis-lunar Space. Nor can they monitor the far side of the Moon. Sensors to provide Space situational awareness will be required in cis-lunar Space itself.

The Lagrange point known as L2 offers an ideal location to place a spacecraft for surveillance or as a communications relay. Satellites are not placed directly at L2 because it is an unstable equilibrium point, like a pencil placed on its tip. But they can maintain a 'halo' orbit around L2

---

[76] See discussion, supra note 12.

[77] Cis-lunar Space can also be defined as including all Earth orbits, with the term 'xGEO' being used specifically to denote the Space beyond GEO. In much of our discussion, we are focused on the region beyond GEO.

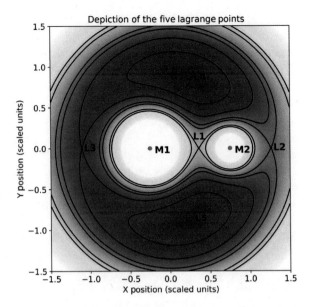

**Figure 7.9** A depiction of the Lagrange points for a simple dynamical model involving two massive bodies (M1 > M2), such as the Earth and the Moon. The curves and colours represent constraints on the motion of a third essentially (i.e. by comparison) 'massless' body, such as a spacecraft. The image itself is in the 'rotating frame'; that is, M1 and M2 appear to be stationary even though they are orbiting each other about their centre of mass. X marks the spot for the L1, L2 and L3 Lagrange points. L4 and L5 are shown as the darker 'islands' on the plot. An object at exactly those points will appear to be stationary in this rotating frame. In practice, the objects are placed on orbits that oscillate about the L points. This example sets M2 to be one-third the mass of M1 to accentuate the structure (the actual Moon-to-Earth mass ratio is about one to 81).

without expending much fuel. Since these orbits are physically large, satellites in L2 halo orbits are able to communicate with Earth at the same time as they observe operations on the far side of the Moon. In 2019, China became the first nation to use L2 in support of a lunar lander, called the *Chang'e 4*.

So far, only civilian science spacecraft have ventured into cis-lunar Space. However, the United States' Air Force Research Laboratory recently announced plans to build two spacecraft to do just that. The first, known as the Cislunar Highway Patrol Satellite (CHPS), will be placed at one of the L points. From there, it will track other spacecraft in cis-lunar Space and lunar orbits.[78] The second, known as the Defense Deep Space Sentinel (D2S2), is described as a highly manoeuverable spacecraft able to conduct 'rendezvous/proximity operations' as well as 'space object removal and recovery, and other applications in defensive space operations'.[79]

Arguably, any improved Space situational awareness in cis-lunar Space would be a good thing, providing more information as to what other Space actors are doing – and what they are not. Yet such a role could just as easily be fulfilled by civilian spacecraft that could also engage in scientific studies, including detecting and tracking asteroids and comets for the purposes of planetary defence.

As for D2S2, there is nothing inherently wrong with Space debris removal and recovery technology. But such technology is inherently 'dual-use' and could be employed to interfere with other spacecraft. For this reason, the necessary and daunting task of cleaning up Space debris should be led by national Space agencies. D2S2 is also suspect because there is no current need for debris removal in cis-lunar Space, and there is unlikely to be any such need for decades to come. The situation in LEO is, of course, quite different, as we explained above.

Perhaps just as important are two closely related questions: (1) where, exactly, would the debris be moved to? And (2) should any individual state be allowed to make these decisions on its own? Answers to these questions will be required at some point, since the two other most feasible options – leaving derelict spacecraft to drift uncontrolled in cis-lunar Space or redirecting them so that they crash into the lunar surface – are unsustainable practices. A further option, sending debris into a heliocentric (i.e. Sun-centred) orbit, might seem like a better idea but would present its own challenges, including that the debris might come back to the Earth–Moon system.[80]

Meanwhile, the Defense Advanced Research Projects Agency (DARPA), within the United States Department of Defense, has announced that it is

---

[78] Theresa Hitchens, 'AFRL satellite to track up to the Moon; Space Force–NASA tout cooperation', *Breaking Defense* (21 September 2020), online: breakingdefense.com/2020/09/afrl-satellite-to-track-up-to-the-moon-space-force-nasa-tout-cooperation.

[79] Theresa Hitchens, 'Space Force, AFRL to demo mobile lunar spy sat', *Breaking Defense* (30 November 2020), online: breakingdefense.com/2020/11/space-force-afrl-to-demo-mobile-lunar-spy-sat.

[80] Mary Beth Griggs, 'Earth's next mini-moon might be space junk from the 1960s' *The Verge* (12 October 2020), online: www.theverge.com/2020/10/12/21512725/mini-moon-space-junk-nasa.

**Figure 7.10**   Artist's illustration of plans for a new DARPA program to develop designs and materials for building large structures in orbit and on the moon. Image courtesy of Darpa.mil according to the DARPA User Agreement (www.darpa.mil/policy/usage-policy).

starting up a Novel Orbital and Moon Manufacturing, Materials and Mass-Efficient Design (NOM4D) program, which 'seeks to pioneer technologies for adaptive, off-earth manufacturing to produce large space and lunar structures'.[81] According to DARPA, 'The NOM4D program will pioneer new materials and manufacturing technologies for construction on orbit and on the lunar surface'. Although the program does not presently include an actual military base, the announcement on DARPA's website was originally accompanied by an artist's depiction that included a sizeable building, a landing pad and at least six vehicles – with the building and one of the vehicles sporting the letters DARPA on their sides (see Figure 7.10).[82]

[81]   DARPA Public Affairs, 'Orbital construction: DARPA pursues plan for robust manufacturing in space' (5 February 2021), *Defense Advanced Research Projects Agency*, online: www.darpa.mil/news-events/2021-02-05.

[82]   This image was later cropped to exclude the equipment and infrastructure on the surface. It is reasonable to infer that the change is due in part to domestic and international pressure, including work by the authors on which this section of the book is based. Importantly, cropping the figure is an implicit acknowledgment of the concerns discussed in this section. See Michael Byers and Aaron Boley, 'Cis-lunar space and the security dilemma' (2022) 78:1 *Bulletin of the Atomic Scientists* 17–21.

Even if DARPA is not planning to actually engage in surface operations, it is easy to imagine other countries reading the announcement as
a statement of intent to militarise the Moon. The NOM4D program will
consequently create uncertainty with regard to US plans and therefore,
quite possibly, create security dilemmas for both China and Russia. As
Jessica West commented, 'Blurring of civil, military, and commercial
capabilities and intentions in space is exactly what the U.S. accuses other
countries such as China of doing. It doesn't build trust, and it doesn't
build confidence. And these two qualities are already in short supply.
I don't see how this ends well.'[83]

Then, in April 2021, DARPA awarded three contracts aimed at the
development of a nuclear thermal propulsion (NTP) system for fast, highly
manoeuverable, long-duration spacecraft that would be deployed in cis-
lunar Space. The contracts, awarded to General Atomics, Blue Origin and
Lockheed Martin, are part of the Demonstration Rocket for Agile Cislunar
Operations (DRACO) programme. According to programme manager
Major Nathan Greiner, it aims to 'provide agile, responsive maneuverability (potentially across vast distances) within the cislunar domain for a
variety of missions' and 'conduct space domain awareness within the
cislunar domain in a timely fashion'.[84] As the DARPA website explains,

> Rapid maneuver is a core tenet of modern Department of Defense (DoD)
> operations on land, at sea, and in the air ... [The] NTP system has the
> potential to achieve high thrust-to-weight ratios similar to in-space chem-
> ical propulsion and approach the high propellent efficiency of electric
> systems. This combination would give a DRACO spacecraft greater agility
> to implement DoD's core tenet of rapid maneuver in cislunar space.

In other words, it is hoped that nuclear thermal propulsion will provide
both high power and high efficiency, and thus manoeuverability and
longevity. The plan is to launch the DRACO spacecraft in 2025.

The US military's plans for cis-lunar Space are being justified as
protection for NASA's Artemis Program,[85] which will include a Space

[83] Theresa Hitchens, 'DARPA space manufacturing project sparks controversy', *Breaking Defense* (12 February 2021), online: breakingdefense.com/2021/02/darpa-space-manufac turing-project-sparks-controversy.

[84] Theresa Hitchens, 'DARPA nuke set to target cislunar monitoring mission', *Breaking Defense* (19 April 2021), online: breakingdefense.com/2021/04/darpa-nuke-sat-to-target-cislunar-monitoring-mission.

[85] Theresa Hitchens, 'Space Force–NASA accord highlights cooperation beyond Earth orbit', *Breaking Defense* (22 September 2020), online: breakingdefense.com/2020/09/space-force-nasa-accord-highlights-cooperation-beyond-earth-orbit.

station in a special type of halo orbit around the Moon as well as permanent human presence on the surface. China is seen as the principal threat to the programme,[86] even though it is unclear what would motivate that country to interfere with NASA's activities.

Extracting resources from the Moon, other than rock for construction and water for survival and fuel, is unlikely to be economically viable for quite some time. The remote location and extreme environment combine to make any activities extremely expensive. And while helium-3 and precious minerals do exist on the Moon, their concentrations are so low that large-scale mining and processing would be required. All this suggests that China's lunar programme is focused on pursuing scientific knowledge and stoking national pride – just as the United States' Apollo programme did in the 1960s.

US military leaders are also using the perceived threat from China as an argument for developing new rules of lunar access and behaviour from a position of strength. In August 2020, Steven Butow, who leads the Space Portfolio within the Defense Innovation Unit,[87] said, 'Much of our law that we follow today is established on precedents. And one of the things we don't want to do, is we don't want to let our peer competitors and adversaries go out and establish the precedent of how things are gonna [sic] be done in the solar system, beginning with the Moon.'[88]

However, there is already an extensive body of international law that applies in cis-lunar Space and on the Moon, including the UN Charter and the   Outer Space Treaty. Article IV of the latter categorically prohibits all military activities on the Moon and other celestial bodies, with its second paragraph reading,

[86] Liane Zivitski, 'China wants to dominate space, and the US must take countermeasures', *Defense News* (23 June 2020), online: www.defensenews.com/opinion/commentary/2020/06/23/china-wants-to-dominate-space-and-the-us-must-take-countermeasures.

[87] The Defense Innovation Unit of the US Department of Defense was established in 2015 in Silicon Valley with the mission of accelerating the adoption of emerging commercial technology throughout the US military, and has been described as '[t]he Pentagon's Innovation Experiment'. See Fred Kaplan, 'The Pentagon's Innovation Experiment', *MIT Technology Review* (19 December 2016), online: www.technologyreview.com/2016/12/19/155246/the-pentagons-innovation-experiment.

[88] Theresa Hitchens, 'Industry says "meh" to DoD cislunar space push', *Breaking Defence* (28 August 2020), online: breakingdefense.com/2020/08/industry-says-meh-to-dod-cislunar-space-push.

> The moon and other celestial bodies shall be used by all States Parties to the Treaty exclusively for peaceful purposes. The establishment of military bases, installations and fortifications, the testing of any type of weapons and the conduct of military manoeuvres on celestial bodies shall be forbidden. The use of military personnel for scientific research or for any other peaceful purposes shall not be prohibited. The use of any equipment or facility necessary for peaceful exploration of the moon and other celestial bodies shall also not be prohibited.

It should be noted that the second paragraph of Article IV is both detailed and categorical, with military installations, the testing of any type of weapon and military manoeuvres all specifically 'forbidden'. Article IV's second paragraph is thus quite different from the references in Articles IX and XI to the 'peaceful exploration and use of outer space'.

The last two sentences of the second paragraph of Article IV do allow for some military involvement in lunar activities, provided it is limited to the use of personnel, such as US military personnel serving as NASA astronauts. Moreover, facilities and equipment can be established and used on the Moon, provided they are for peaceful purposes only and are not part of a military base, installation or fortification. Thus collaboration between a military and a civilian Space agency does not necessarily contravene Article IV's second paragraph, while a military carrying out an independent programme on the Moon likely does. As Christopher Johnson explained in the context of the NOM4D programme,

> If DARPA (or its contractors) are conducting activities on the Moon which are temporarily peaceful in nature (like refining in situ resources into fuel or other useful material), this is still a MILITARY activity, and therefore pretty clearly prohibited. It's not done under the banner of NASA, or part of an Artemis program with international partners, or any principally civil activity – it's just the US military conducting activities, with military aims and objectives in mind. On the surface of the Moon, this is strictly proscribed and prohibited.[89]

We can only conclude that the NOM4D programme is inconsistent with the United States' legal commitments. In addition to taking steps that risk creating security dilemmas for China and Russia, US military leaders are challenging foundational treaties designed to promote peace and security in international affairs.

---

[89] Hitchens, 'DARPA space manufacturing project sparks controversy', op. cit.

### 7.12.1   Other Risks

The US military's plans for cis-lunar Space will also create serious risks outside the security domain, including for the future of radio astronomy. Terrestrial[90] and satellite-borne[91] signal contamination of radio observations already limits the radio astronomy that can be done from Earth. Interference from Earth orbit is growing, due to the construction of mega-constellations of communications satellites – as discussed in Chapters 2 and 3. Not surprisingly, the idea of placing radio observatories on the far side of the Moon has been around for quite some time and is now seeing concepts in development.[92] The Breakthrough Listen project is particularly interested in using the Moon as a unique and unspoiled opportunity for conducting search for extraterrestrial intelligence (SETI) science.[93]

However, spacecraft in lunar orbits, orbiting about L points or stationed elsewhere in cis-lunar Space could cause radio interference for these Moon-based observatories in bands that have already been lost to Earth-based facilities. Even a lunar surface-based communication network could cause substantial interference unless designed with the protection of radio astronomy in mind.[94]

Radio interference is a foreseeable issue that could be adequately mitigated, but to succeed in this, all lunar actors will have to respect radio quiet zones. They will also have to limit the number of satellites as well as the portions of the spectrum and the directions of the beams they use. Having militaries racing to position their own spacecraft in cis-lunar Space could complicate this necessarily co-operative exercise.

There are also potential risks involving congestion and debris. Although cis-lunar Space is very large, the locations of greatest utility are restricted

---

[90] National Radio Astronomy Observatory (NRAO), 'Radio frequency interference' (2022), *NRAO*, online: public.nrao.edu/telescopes/radio-frequency-interference.

[91] Toni Feder, 'Iridium satellite system poses threat to radio astronomy' (1996) 49:11 *Physics Today* 71.

[92] Saptarshi Bandyopadhyay, 'Lunar crater radio telescope (LCRT) on the far-side of the Moon' (7 April 2020), *NASA*, online: www.nasa.gov/directorates/spacetech/niac/2020_Phase_I_Phase_II/lunar_crater_radio_telescope.

[93] Eric Michaud, 'Breakthough listen: Lunar opportunities for SETI' (2020), *University of California Berkeley*, online: seti.berkeley.edu/lunarseti.

[94] Emma Alexander, 'A 4G network on the Moon is bad news for radio astronomy', *The Conversation* (23 October 2020), online: theconversation.com/a-4g-network-on-the-moon-is-bad-news-for-radio-astronomy-148652.

in size and therefore have physical carrying limits, even if we do not yet know what they are.

Many of the orbits are unstable and therefore subject to uncontrolled self-cleaning, including halo orbits about L points as well as many lunar orbits. By self-cleaning, we mean that the objects cannot remain at their location without active management and will eventually enter a new orbital trajectory, which could include one that crashes into the Moon or meanders in cis-lunar Space. For this reason, the few lunar orbits that are stable will attract human activity, which could lead to congestion, collisions and debris – creating operational hazards both in those orbits and on the lunar surface. Collisions or fragmentation events will create even more debris, just as they do in Earth orbit. Debris streams could even develop between lunar and Earth orbits. Challenges such as spacecraft disposal in the cis-lunar environment therefore need to be addressed in advance, with safe procedures being followed by all spacefaring states. This situation calls for restraint and close international co-ordination, which competing militaries are rarely able to provide.

### 7.12.2  *Possible Solutions*

Space situational awareness in cis-lunar Space should be shared freely, as a public good that will help to prevent accidents. Eventually, some kind of mechanism will be needed to monitor the use of L points and lunar orbits and possibly to assign 'slots' to prevent congestion, as occurs in geosynchronous orbit today. International planning for this kind of co-ordination should begin now. At the same time, the US government should terminate the CHPS, D2S2 and NOM4D programmes, or reassign them to NASA to avoid the potentially destabilising militarisation of cis-lunar Space.

The United States should also support the negotiation of a treaty prohibiting weapons in cis-lunar Space, including dual-use technologies operated by militaries. Space has long been a focus for arms control, beginning with the 1963 Limited Test Ban Treaty that prohibited nuclear explosions in Space.[95] In 1967, the Outer Space Treaty banned all weapons of mass destruction from being stationed in Space and designated the Moon 'exclusively for peaceful purposes'.[96] Today, there is a similar opportunity to keep weapons out of cis-lunar Space. The demarcation of Earth

---

[95] Limited Test Ban Treaty, op. cit.
[96] Outer Space Treaty, op. cit., Art. IV.

orbit and cis-lunar Space provides a clear line upon which such a commitment could be based.

We can still develop the Moon and its associated orbits. But as we have learned from decades of human activity in Earth orbit, developing Space in a sustainable way requires foresight, planning and co-operation. Space must be recognised as an environment that is worth preserving, and as one in which fast-paced alterations can have a myriad of unintended consequences. From avoiding security dilemmas, to maintaining radio quiet zones, to co-ordinating the use of orbital slots, in cis-lunar Space, we still have the chance to get things right.

# 8

# Anti-satellite Weapons and International Law

Prohibitions on specific types of weapons can sometimes arise very quickly in international law, and with universal effect. On 22 April 1915, the German Army released 168 tonnes of chlorine gas near the Belgian city of Ypres.[1] Five thousand soldiers died in the Allied trenches that day while another 10,000 were grievously injured. Three months later, the British Army launched its own first chlorine gas attack. By the end of the First World War, chemical weapons had killed nearly 100,000 people and wounded an estimated one million.[2] After the war, these horrors prompted the negotiation of the 1925 Protocol for the Prohibition of the Use in War of Asphyxiating, Poisonous or Other Gases, and of Bacteriological Methods of Warfare.[3] Today, the prohibition on the use of chemical weapons is regarded as a *jus cogens* rule – a customary international law 'taboo' that tolerates no exceptions, not even exceptions created by way of treaty.[4]

Compliance with the rule has not been perfect: Saddam Hussein used mustard gas against Iranian forces in the 1980s and then against Kurdish civilians in northern Iraq.[5] The international community responded with the 1992 Convention on the Development, Production, Stockpiling and

---

[1] David Hughes, 'Chemical weapons: The day the first poison gas attack changed the face of warfare forever', *The Independent* (28 April 2016), online: www.independent.co.uk/news/ world/politics/chemical-weapons-warfare-remembrance-day-poison-mustard-gas-first-world-war-ypres-isis-a7005416.html.

[2] Ibid.

[3] Protocol for the Prohibition of the Use in War of Asphyxiating, Poisonous or Other Gases, and of Bacteriological Methods of Warfare, 17 June 1925, 94 LNTS 65 (entered into force 9 May 1926).

[4] Richard M Price, *The Chemical Weapons Taboo* (Ithaca, NY: Cornell University Press, 2007).

[5] Ibid.

Use of Chemical Weapons and on Their Destruction.[6] Eleven years later, Saddam was removed from power by a US-led coalition that justified its actions based on allegations (which proved to be false) that Iraq was stockpiling 'weapons of mass destruction'. In the Syrian Civil War, Bashar al-Assad has used sarin gas while remaining in power, thanks to Russian support. But the general picture is clear: there is opprobrium attached to the use of chemical weapons today,[7] and to biological and nuclear weapons also. The best evidence for this is that, although the United States, Russia and China long had stockpiles of chemical weapons, they were hardly ever used, with the employment of Agent Orange in the Vietnam War and an unknown chemical in the 2002 Moscow Theatre hostage crisis being two borderline exceptions. Russia and China have both reported the destruction of their stockpiles in fulfilment of their commitments under the 1992 Chemical Weapons Convention, although the publicly voiced concerns of US officials about the possible use of chemical weapons in Ukraine suggest that some secret Russian stocks may have been retained.[8] Meanwhile, the few remaining US chemical weapons are due for elimination by September 2023.[9]

Anti-personnel landmines are another category of weapons against which a general prohibition has emerged. During the twentieth century, countless innocent civilians were killed, sometimes long after the conflicts in which they were deployed had come to an end.[10] In 1997, the Canadian government took the issue of anti-personnel landmines out of the Conference on Disarmament, where it had languished due to the consensus decision making used there. An ad hoc negotiating conference held in Ottawa produced the 1997 Convention on the Prohibition of the

---

[6] Convention on the Development, Production, Stockpiling and Use of Chemical Weapons and on Their Destruction, 3 September 1992, 1975 UNTS 45 (entered into force 29 April 1997) (Chemical Weapons Convention).

[7] The 1992 Chemical Weapons Convention has been ratified by 193 states, including China, Russia and the United States. See Organisation for the Prohibition of Chemical Weapons (OPCW), 'Member States' (2022), *OPCS*, online: www.opcw.org/about-us/member-states.

[8] Sam Fossum and Betsy Klein, 'Biden warns Russia will pay a "severe price" if it uses chemical weapons in Ukraine', *CNN* (11 March 2022), online: www.cnn.com/2022/03/11/politics/joe-biden-warning-chemical-weapons/index.html.

[9] Arms Control Association (ACA), 'Chemical and biological weapons status at a glance' (March 2022), *ACA*, online: www.armscontrol.org/factsheets/cbwprolif.

[10] Maxwell A Cameron, Robert J Lawson and Brian W Tomlin, eds., *To Walk without Fear: The Global Movement to Ban Landmines* (Toronto: Oxford University Press, 1998).

Use, Stockpiling, Production and Transfer of Anti-personnel Mines and on Their Destruction.[11] The 'Ottawa Convention' currently has 164 parties, although the United States, Russia and China are not among them.[12] The lack of ratifications or accessions by these militarily powerful states was readily foreseeable at the time of the negotiations; what was perhaps not as foreseeable was that the use of anti-personnel landmines has declined markedly in the past two decades, including among non-parties to the Ottawa Convention (although not, it would seem, Russia in Ukraine).[13] For international lawyers, this development is not a huge surprise, since the conclusion of multilateral treaties often leads to state practice, evidence of *opinio juris* (i.e. sense of legal obligation), and the consequent development of parallel rules of customary international law.[14] Even in the absence of a binding new rule, a change in a community's view of the ethical acceptability of an action can have powerful behavioural consequences.

Weapons that cause indiscriminate and long-lasting harm have also been tested in Space, including – as discussed in the previous chapter – nuclear devices as anti-ballistic-missile weapons. These weapons have, in turn, prompted efforts to prohibit or limit their testing and use. The 1962 discovery that nuclear explosions in Space threaten all satellites created momentum for the negotiation of the Limited Test Ban Treaty the very next year.[15]

A second indiscriminate threat to satellites was identified in the 1970s in the form of orbital debris, including the Kessler–Cour-Palais syndrome of knock-on collisions discussed in the previous chapter. As we also saw in that chapter, kinetic ASAT weapon tests – i.e. tests of anti-satellite weapons that rely on violent impacts – have contributed to the

---

[11] Convention on the Prohibition of the Use, Stockpiling, Production and Transfer of Anti-personnel Mines and on Their Destruction, 18 September 1997, 2056 UNTS 211 (entered into force 1 March 1999) (Ottawa Convention).

[12] Anti-personnel Mine Ban Convention, 'Convention on the Prohibition of the Use, Stockpiling, Production and Transfer of Anti-personnel Mines and on Their Destruction – Membership' (2018), online: new.apminebanconvention.org/en/membership.

[13] Adam Bower, *Norms without the Great Powers: International Law and Changing Social Expectations in World Politics* (Oxford: Oxford University Press, 2017).

[14] Bing Bing Jia, 'The relations between treaties and custom' (2010) 9:1 *Chinese Journal of International Law* 81.

[15] Treaty Banning Nuclear Weapon Tests in the Atmosphere, in Outer Space and under Water, 5 August 1963, 480 UNTS 43 (entered into force 10 October 1963) (Limited Test Ban Treaty).

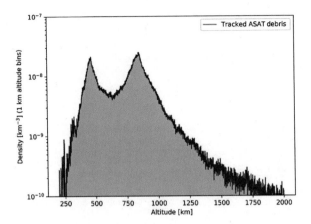

**Figure 8.1**    Density of debris in orbit as of 27 January 2022 due to ASAT weapon tests. While a number of tests contribute to the structure, the shape is dominated by two distinct events: the Russian 2021 and the Chinese 2007 weapon tests at about 480 kilometres and 850 kilometres respectively. The densities are determined using methods similar to those used for Figures 2.2 and 2.3 in Chapter 2. ASAT weapon test debris contributes a large fraction of the total on-orbit debris.

debris crisis in low Earth orbit (LEO). Indeed, as of February 2022, approximately 2,850 trackable pieces remain in orbit from the most significant of these events, a Chinese test in 2007. Another major injection of debris occurred after the November 2021 Russia test (See Figure 8.1).

ASAT weapons are now regarded as a major threat to the exploration and use of Space, including the communications and Earth-imaging provided by military satellites. As a result, international momentum towards negotiations on a kinetic ASAT weapon test ban treaty has been growing. However, that is not the only way in which a ban could come into being. Two distinct but related strands of legal development will be examined in this chapter.

The first considers whether a test ban already exists, or might soon develop, as the result of a reinterpretation of the Outer Space Treaty. The accepted interpretation of Article I, second paragraph, of the Outer Space Treaty may be evolving as a result of the changing practice of the parties to that treaty. In short, many states are behaving as if ASAT weapon tests that create long-lasting debris are contrary to the 'freedom of exploration and use of space'. For this reason, we will end up concluding that the accepted interpretation of this second paragraph of Article I is indeed changing.

**Figure 8.2** Defence Research and Development Organisation ballistic missile defence interceptor being launched for ASAT weapon test in March 2019. Photograph credit: Government of India.

The second strand, emerging from the same practice and an accompanying *opinio juris* may be the development of a parallel rule of customary international law. Ultimately, our analysis leads us to the conclusion that this change, too, is now under way.

Before we embark on this analysis, it is important to note that the *use* of ASAT weapons, as opposed to their *testing*, is governed by two further, separate bodies of international law. These are the *jus ad bellum* governing the recourse to armed force, which includes self-defence, and the *jus in bello* governing the conduct of armed conflict itself. The *jus ad bellum* and the *jus in bello* will be discussed towards the end of this chapter, where we conclude that any use of a kinetic ASAT weapon in armed conflict would be illegal today because of the growing crisis of Space debris. This chapter does not consider the legality of *possessing* ASAT weapons, because many potential ASAT weapons are dual-use. Indeed, a spacecraft designed to retrieve defunct satellites and other Space debris could also be used to destroy or disable another active satellite.

## 8.1    Kinetic ASAT Weapon Tests and the Outer Space Treaty

The freedom of exploration and use of Space began as a rule of customary international law, developing shortly after the 1957 launch of Sputnik when other states acquiesced to having their territory overflown by the Soviet satellite.[16] The launch the following year of the first American satellite was met with a similarly passive and therefore permissive response. The freedom of exploration and use of Space was then made central to two landmark United Nations General Assembly resolutions adopted in 1961 and 1963. Resolution 1721 (XVI) stated, 'Outer space and celestial bodies are free for exploration and use by all States in conformity with international law ...'.[17] The subsequent Resolution 1962 (XVIII) similarly stated, 'Outer space and celestial bodies are free for exploration and use by all States on a basis of equality and in accordance with international law.'[18] States were so quick to accept these two resolutions as reflective of customary international law that Bin Cheng coined the term 'instant customary international law'.[19]

When the Outer Space Treaty was adopted in 1967, it included as the second paragraph of Article I,

> Outer space, including the Moon and other celestial bodies, shall be free for exploration and use by all States without discrimination of any kind,

---

[16]  Eugène Pépin, 'Legal problems created by the Sputnik' (1957) 4 *McGill Law Journal* 66 at 67; Anthony D'Amato, *The Concept of Custom in International Law* (Ithaca, NY: Cornell University Press, 1971) at 89; Stuart Banner, *Who Owns the Sky? The Struggle to Control Airspace from the Wright Brothers On* (Cambridge, MA: Harvard University Press, 2008) at 278–79.

[17]  *International Co-operation in the Peaceful Uses of Outer Space*, GA Res 1721 (XVI), UNGAOR, 16th Sess, 1085th Plen Mtg, UN Doc A/RES/1721(XVI) (1961) at para. 1(b).

[18]  *Declaration of Legal Principles Governing the Activities of States in the Exploration and Use of Outer Space*, GA Res 1962 (XVIII), UNGAOR, 18th Sess, 1280th Plen Mtg, UN Doc A/RES/1962(XVIII) (1963) at para. 2.

[19]  Bin Cheng, 'United Nations resolutions on outer space: "Instant" international customary law?' (1965) 5 *Indian Journal of International Law* 23.

on a basis of equality and in accordance with international law, and there shall be free access to all areas of celestial bodies.[20]

Most rights or freedoms exist together with obligations. In this case, the obligation is to not interfere with other states' exploration and use of Space. This obligation of non-interference is recognised and supported by Article IX of the Outer Space Treaty, the first sentence of which reads,

> In the exploration and use of outer space, including the moon and other celestial bodies, States Parties to the Treaty shall be guided by the principle of co-operation and mutual assistance and shall conduct all their activities in outer space, including the moon and other celestial bodies, with due regard to the corresponding interests of all other States Parties to the Treaty.

The rest of Article IX sets out a duty to consult, which helps to protect the freedom of exploration and use by ensuring that states do not carry out insufficiently informed actions that might interfere with this shared freedom. Responses to possible violations of Article I, second paragraph, sometimes focus on a failure to consult in advance of the problematic behaviour,[21] perhaps because it is easier to establish an absence of consultation than it is to establish a violation of the obligation of non-interference. In any event, it is important to treat the duty to consult as separate from the freedom of exploration and use (and the related obligation of non-interference), with the latter constituting the primary obligation of the two.

The Outer Space Treaty was negotiated and adopted before the risk of Space debris was understood, and before Donald Kessler and Burton Cour-Palais clearly described the risk of knock-on collisions in 1978.[22] Yet treaty obligations designed for general application can and often do apply to specific issues that emerge at later times. For example, there is no question that the provisions of the 1945 United Nations Charter that

---

[20] Treaty on Principles Governing the Activities of States in the Exploration and Use of Outer Space, Including the Moon and Other Celestial Bodies, 27 January 1967, 610 UNTS 205 Art. I (entered into force 10 October 1967) (Outer Space Treaty).

[21] In an article written just after the 2007 Chinese ASAT test, Michael Mineiro focused on the duty to consult and US, Russian and Chinese failures in that regard, concluding that Article IX was weakened but still operative. Michael C Mineiro, 'FY-1C and USA-193 ASAT intercepts: An assessment of legal obligations under Article IX of the Outer Space Treaty' (2008) 34:2 *Journal of Space Law* 321.

[22] Donald J Kessler and Burton G Cour-Palais, 'Collision frequency of artificial satellites: The creation of a debris belt' (1978) 83:A6 *Journal of Geophysical Research: Space Physics* 2637.

prohibit the use of force (Article 2(4)) while allowing for a right of self-defence (Article 51) apply to modern cyber attacks.[23]

We therefore need to consider how the freedom of exploration and use of Space as set out in the second paragraph of Article I of the Outer Space Treaty is being interpreted and applied to kinetic ASAT weapon testing. Doing so requires not only a careful assessment of the 'subsequent practice' of the parties in conducting ASAT weapon tests – the Chinese in 2007, the Indians in 2019 and the Russians in 2021 – but also what those states said, the international responses to them, and the avoidance of actual strikes during other, similar tests.[24]

This subsequent practice is relevant because of Article 31 of the 1969 Vienna Convention on the Law of Treaties,[25] which reads,

1. A treaty shall be interpreted in good faith in accordance with the ordinary meaning to be given to the terms of the treaty in their context and in the light of its object and purpose.
2. The context for the purpose of the interpretation of a treaty shall comprise, in addition to the text, including its preamble and annexes:
   (a) any agreement relating to the treaty which was made between all the parties in connexion with the conclusion of the treaty;
   (b) any instrument which was made by one or more parties in connexion with the conclusion of the treaty and accepted by the other parties as an instrument related to the treaty.
3. There shall be taken into account, together with the context:
   (a) any subsequent agreement between the parties regarding the interpretation of the treaty or the application of its provisions;
   (b) *any subsequent practice in the application of the treaty which establishes the agreement of the parties regarding its interpretation*;
   (c) any relevant rules of international law applicable in the relations between the parties.

---

[23] Khatuna Burkadze, 'A shift in the historical understanding of armed attack and its applicability to cyberspace' (2020) 44:1 *Fletcher Forum of World Affairs* 33.

[24] The US Navy's use of a ship-based missile to destroy a re-entering satellite in 2008 is also discussed below, though it remains uncertain whether that strike was a test or, as the United States claimed, motivated by safety and environmental concerns.

[25] Although the 1969 Vienna Convention on the Law of Treaties does not apply retrospectively to the 1967 Outer Space Treaty, its provisions are generally treated as codifying pre-existing customary international law regarding treaty interpretation. See Richard K Gardiner, *Treaty Interpretation*, 2nd ed. (Oxford: Oxford University Press, 2015) 477.

4. A special meaning shall be given to a term if it is established that the parties so intended.[26]

For present purposes, the relevant provision is Article 31(3)(b) (which we have italicised) since there are no agreements (2(a)) or instruments (2 (b)) or subsequent agreements (3(a)) of relevance here.

It should be noted that all of this 'subsequent practice' will also constitute 'state practice' as well as potential evidence of *'opinio juris'* – the objective and subjective elements of customary international law. As a result, the review of practice in which we are about to engage – regarding the interpretation of the second paragraph of Article I of the Outer Space Treaty – will also enable us to consider, in the second part of this chapter, whether a prohibition on kinetic ASAT weapon testing is also developing as a rule of customary international law.

To save readers a great deal of repetition, we do *not* conduct two separate reviews of practice. Instead, in this first part we review the 'subsequent practice' for the purposes of treaty interpretation. We then refer to this review in the next part, which addresses the 'state practice' and *opinio juris* elements of customary international law. We can take this approach because almost all the spacefaring states, and all the major spacefaring states, are parties to the Outer Space Treaty. Nearly all the relevant practice is therefore both subsequent practice and state practice.

### 8.1.1   Kinetic ASAT Weapon Tests This Century

As soon as the first satellites were placed into orbit, states began exploring how to destroy them, with the first kinetic ASAT weapon test taking place as early as 1959. These efforts were led by the United States and the Soviet Union, with China and India following in the 2000s. A comprehensive list of ASAT weapon tests, made available by the Secure World Foundation, is worth taking time to review online.[27]

Several things can be learned from the Secure World Foundation list. First, most ASAT weapon tests have generated no Space debris, mainly because they were conducted without a physical target. Second, those that have involved strikes on physical targets have generated debris, and in

---

[26] Vienna Convention on the Law of Treaties, 23 May 1969, 1155 UNTS 331 Art. 31 (entry into force 27 January 1980).

[27] Secure World Foundation, 'History of ASAT Tests in Space' (2022), *Google Docs*, online: docs.google.com/spreadsheets/d/1e5GtZEzdo6xk41i2_ei3c8jRZDjvP4Xwz3BVsUHwi48/edit#gid=0.

doing so have had a lasting impact on the orbital environment. Third, single events, such as the 2007 Chinese ASAT weapon test, can create substantial changes to the debris population. Fourth, the cumulative effects of multiple events can also be serious and long-lasting. Indeed, there are about as many fragments from Soviet-era ASAT weapon tests still in orbit today as there are fragments added by the November 2021 Russian ASAT test. And when those two debris populations are added together, they are comparable in number to that produced by the 2007 Chinese test, the single worst debris-generating event of all time.

As states have become aware of the long-term Space debris created by ASAT weapon tests, and the associated hazards, opposition to those tests that involve physical strikes has also begun to grow.

### 8.1.2   Responses to the 2007 Chinese ASAT Weapon Test

The 2007 Chinese test was the first strike by a kinetic ASAT weapon in more than two decades.

It could be argued that the debris-creating test, as a prominent instance of 'subsequent practice', confirmed and thus bolstered an interpretation of the Article I, second paragraph, freedom of exploration and use that allows for such testing. But an examination of the international response to the test leads to a different conclusion.

Any assessment of subsequent practice associated with an ASAT weapon test must also include the responses from other treaty parties because, in accordance with Article 31(3)(b) of the Vienna Convention on the Law of Treaties, we are looking for 'any subsequent practice in the application of the treaty *which establishes the agreement of the parties regarding its interpretation*' (emphasis added). No single act, such as a missile strike, can establish an agreement of the parties. Taken collectively, the responses to the Chinese test reveal that (1) states are concerned about the creation of long-lasting Space debris; (2) some states consider the deliberate creation of long-lasting debris to be illegal; (3) no state, not even China, is willing to assert that the deliberate creation of long-lasting debris is legal.

The response of the United States unfolded over several stages, first in public and then behind closed doors. Immediately after the Chinese test, US National Security Council spokesperson Gordon Johndroe stated, 'The United States believes China's development and testing of such weapons is inconsistent with the spirit of cooperation that both countries aspire to in the civil space area. We and other countries have expressed our concern to the Chinese.'[28]

Later, once it became clear just how much debris had been created, the US embassy in Beijing was instructed to make a *démarche* to the Chinese government based on a set of 'talking points' to be left with the Chinese as a 'non-paper'. For the purposes of this chapter, the relevant talking points listed in this deliberately unofficial document were:

- Debris from China's ASAT test has increased hazards to other peaceful uses of space in low earth orbit by the United States and other space-faring nations.
- This is a very serious matter for the entire international community.
- Unfettered access to space and the capabilities provided by satellites in orbit are vital to United States national and economic security.
- The United States considers space systems to have the rights of unhindered passage through, and operations in, space without interference.[29]

The last of these talking points shows the United States expressing the view that kinetic ASAT weapon tests impede the freedom of exploration and use of Space when they create long-lasting debris.

Japan came to the same conclusion, with Prime Minister Shinzo Abe stating that the Chinese test violated the Outer Space Treaty, though he did not indicate which specific article had been contravened.[30] Foreign Minister Taro Aso warned of the danger from debris, saying, 'I doubt if we could call this a peaceful use.'[31] The European Union also cited the Outer Space Treaty when urging the Chinese to 'abide by their commitment to exercise their Space activities in accordance with international law'.[32] Madhavan Nair, the chair of the Indian Space Research Organisation,

---

[28] William J Broad, David E Sanger and Joseph Kahn, 'Missile test puts China on path to militarizing space', *New York Times* (19 January 2007), online: www.nytimes.com/2007/01/19/world/asia/19iht-china.4269526.html.

[29] United States Secretary of State, diplomatic cable, 'Second demarche for China regarding China's January 2007 anti-satellite test' (6 January 2007), *WikiLeaks*, online: wikileaks.org/plusd/cables/08STATE1264_a.html.

[30] Carin Zissis, 'China's anti-satellite test' (22 February 2007), *Council on Foreign Relations*, online: www.cfr.org/backgrounder/chinas-anti-satellite-test.

[31] Broad, Sanger and Kahn, op. cit. (citing the Japanese newspaper *Asahi Shimbun*).

[32] Council of the European Union, press release, 5602/1/07 REV1 (Presse 10), 'Declaration by the presidency on behalf of the European Union on a Chinese test of an anti-satellite weapon' (24 January 2007), online: www.consilium.europa.eu/ueDocs/cms_Data/docs/pressData/en/cfsp/92512.pdf.

similarly stated that China 'should not have done this as it goes against international convention'.[33]

Other states expressed alarm at the Chinese ASAT weapon test without expressing any specific legal concerns, and these statements, while still relevant, therefore count for less in our legal analysis than the ones above. Australian foreign minister Alexander Downer said his country was 'concerned about the militarisation of outer space on the one hand and secondly concerned about the impact that debris from destroyed satellites could have on other satellites, which are very expensive pieces of equipment'.[34] Canada 'expressed its strong concerns to the Chinese authorities over the reported anti-satellite test and the possible negative effects'.[35] A spokesperson for the United Kingdom said, 'We are concerned about the impact of debris in space and we expressed that concern.'[36]

For the purposes of a complete analysis, it should be noted that several states responded to the Chinese ASAT weapon test without addressing the legal or Space debris issues. Russian deputy prime minister Sergei Ivanov stated, 'The use of outer space for security and defense purposes is one thing, and the placement of weapons there is quite another. The latter is absolutely unacceptable in our view, as it makes the global security situation unpredictable.'[37] Since the Chinese test was conducted with a ground-based missile, Ivanov's comment was somewhat off-point. It was, however, soon supplemented by a public acknowledgement of the risks posed by Space debris and knock-on collisions by scientists from the

---

[33] Joseph E Lin, 'Regional reactions to ASAT missile test & China's renewed activities in the East China Sea' (17 October 2007), *Jamestown Foundation*, online: jamestown.org/pro gram/regional-reactions-to-asat-missile-test-chinas-renewed-activities-in-the-east-china-sea.

[34] Agence France-Presse, 'Australia summons China envoy over satellite', *Space Daily* (19 January 2007), online: www.spacedaily.com/reports/Australia_Summons_China_Envoy_ Over_Satellite_999.html.

[35] Geoffrey York, 'China's anti-satellite weapon fuels anxiety', *Globe and Mail* (22 January 2007), online: www.theglobeandmail.com/news/world/chinas-anti-satellite-weapon-fuels-anxiety/article677375.

[36] Richard Spencer, 'Chinese missile destroys satellite in space', *The Telegraph* (19 January 2007), online: www.telegraph.co.uk/news/worldnews/1539948/Chinese-missile-destroys-satellite-in-space.html.

[37] 'Russia opposes militarizing space', *United Press International* (6 February 2007), online: www.upi.com/Defense-News/2007/02/06/Russia-opposes-militarizing-space/ 77401170778644.

Russian Space Agency, who, in 2009, made a presentation which included the following verbatim text:

Man-made orbital debris poses an increasing risk to space vehicles

- The time have come when space debris poses the real risk for long term sustainable space activity, also for people safety and property on the Earth surface.
- Each following launch of a space vehicle at long last leads to creation of new space debris. Moreover, studies indicate that beyond the middle of current century the self-collision fragments will outnumber decaying debris, and force the total debris population to increase.
- Taking into account that space have got more deeply in all fields of activity of states and individuals, any limitation of space activity can lead to negative influence on economy of states and international relations up to development of potential conflicts.
- So, space debris problem that have to be decided, concerns not only aspects of space engineering and space technologies, but also affects the social and economic development of states and their national security.[38]

China eventually responded to the concerns expressed by other states and did so in a conciliatory manner. Foreign Ministry spokesperson Liu Jianchao said, 'China consistently advocates peaceful utilization of the outer space, and opposes to weaponization of arms race in the outer space. Neither has China has participated, nor will it participate in arms race of the outer space in any form.'[39] Some observers believe that the Chinese government had underestimated the negative responses the ASAT weapon test would generate, because of the lack of protests after previous debris-creating tests conducted by the United States and Soviet Union during the 1970s and 1980s.[40] Others believe that the People's Liberation Army conducted the test without first securing the agreement of the Chinese Foreign Ministry or fully informing the

---

[38] Yuriy Makarov, Dmitriy Gorobets and Michael Yakovlev, 'Space debris and challenges to safety of space activity' (presentation delivered at the International Interdisciplinary Congress on Space Debris, Montreal, 7–9 May 2009), online: www.mcgill.ca/iasl/files/iasl/Session_3_Michael_Yakovlev.pdf.

[39] Liu Jianchao, 'Foreign Ministry spokesperson Liu Jianchao's regular press conference on 23 January 2007' (24 January 2007), *Embassy of The People's Republic of China in the United States of America*, online: http://toronto.china-consulate.gov.cn/eng/fyrthhz/lxjzzdh/200701/t20070124_7253368.htm.

[40] Phillip C Saunders and Charles D Lutes, 'China's ASAT test: Motivations and implications' (2007) 46 *Joint Force Quarterly* 39.

Chinese leadership about the likely creation of large amounts of Space debris.[41] Significantly, China did not respond to the concerns of other states by asserting that it had a legal right to test ASAT weapons in an unrestricted manner.

### 8.1.3  Changes in Practice after the 2007 Chinese ASAT Weapon Test

After the 2007 Chinese ASAT weapon test, which revealed that even a single kinetic weapon can create tens of thousands of pieces of Space debris, subsequent tests were conducted in ways that sought to avoid creating long-lasting debris. In 2008, when the United States employed a missile defence interceptor to destroy a malfunctioning satellite,[42] it did so at a very low altitude.[43] It also justified its action on the basis that the satellite was about to re-enter the atmosphere with a large amount of highly toxic hydrazine thruster fuel on board.[44] For these reasons, and despite some observers speculating that the US action was a response to the 2007 Chinese test,[45] it did not attract protests from other states.

In 2013, China tested a missile by directing it to 'nearly geosynchronous orbit'.[46] However, no attempt was made to strike a satellite, in an apparently deliberate effort to avoid creating Space debris. Then, in 2014, China conducted a missile defence test that would have contributed to its ASAT capabilities.[47] However, the missile-to-missile impact took place at a very low altitude.

Since 2007, in China and elsewhere, most ASAT development efforts have focused on highly manoeuvrable spacecraft designed to nudge or pull satellites off course, as well as non-kinetic technologies such as lasers,

---

[41] Bates Gill and Martin Kleiber, 'China's space odyssey: What the antisatellite test reveals about decision-making in Beijing' (May/June 2007) 86:3 *Foreign Affairs* 2; Saunders and Lutes, op. cit. at 40 ('The unco-ordinated Chinese response suggests that the Ministry of Foreign Affairs (MFA) was not aware of the January ASAT test in advance').

[42] 'US missile hits spy satellite', *New Scientist* (21 February 2008), online: www.newscientist .com/article/dn13359-us-missile-hits-spy-satellite.

[43] Lee Billings, 'War in space may be closer than ever', *Scientific American* (10 August 2015), online: www.scientificamerican.com/article/war-in-space-may-be-closer-than-ever.

[44] Thom Shanker, 'Pentagon is confident missile hit satellite tank', *New York Times* (21 February 2008), online: www.nytimes.com/2008/02/21/us/21cnd-satellite.html.

[45] Karanpreet Kaur, 'China's anti-satellite warfare programme: Implications and lessons' (Spring 2014) *Scholar Warrior* 112.

[46] Harsh Vasani, 'How China is weaponizing outer Space', *The Diplomat* (1 January 2017), online: thediplomat.com/2017/01/how-china-is-weaponizing-outer-space.

[47] Ibid.

jammers and cyber actions.[48] None of these methods or technologies contributes directly to the creation of Space debris. However, it is possible that a redirected satellite could incidentally collide with another satellite or with debris, while a satellite subject to a cyber action might be permanently disabled and thus transformed into a substantial piece of long-lived Space debris.

The Space debris crisis is motivating some spacefaring states and companies to include technologies in satellites that allow them to be de-orbited at the end of their operational lives or boosted to sparingly used 'graveyard' orbits. 'Active debris removal' is also the subject of considerable research. In October 2021, China launched the *Shijian-21* spacecraft, which two months later docked with the defunct Beidou-2 G2 navigation satellite in geosynchronous Earth orbit (GEO), about 36,000 kilometres above the equator. In January 2022, *Shijian-21* performed an engine burn which raised its altitude – and that of the defunct satellite – by about 3,000 kilometres.[49] *Shijian-21* then undocked and returned to GEO, leaving Beidou-2 G2 behind in a very high graveyard orbit. Although the Chinese spacecraft is clearly 'dual-use' technology, its employment to remove a defunct satellite from a crowed orbit demonstrates China's concern about Space debris.[50]

The European Space Agency is also testing methods to de-orbit derelict satellites and other Space debris. In 2025, it will launch a spacecraft named *ClearSpace-1* equipped with four robotic arms to experimentally capture a piece of debris—a 100-kilogram payload adapter left in an 800 × 660-kilometre orbit following the launch of an ESA remote-sensing satellite

---

[48] See Billings, op. cit; David A Koplow, *Death by Moderation: The U.S. Military's Quest for Useable Weapons* (Cambridge: Cambridge University Press, 2009) at 168–72; Madeleine Moon, 'The space domain and allied defence' (8 October 2017), NATO Parliamentary Assembly Defence and Security Committee, Report 162 DSCFC 17 E rev.1 fin at 6-8, online: www.nato-pa.int/document/2017-space-domain-and-allied-defence-moon-report-162-dscfc-17-e-rev1-fin.

[49] Andrew Jones, 'China's Shijian-21 towed dead satellite to a high graveyard orbit', *SpaceNews* (27 January 2022), online: spacenews.com/chinas-shijian-21-spacecraft-docked-with-and-towed-a-dead-satellite/.

[50] A related technological effort involves 'on-orbit servicing'. US-based Northrop Grumman has twice conducted test dockings of its 'Mission Extension Vehicle' with satellites operated by Intelsat. Once fully operational, the technology will be used to refuel satellites in geosynchronous orbit, thus extending their operational lives. Northrop Grumman, 'SpaceLogistics: Our life extension services' (2022), online: www.northropgrumman.com/space/space-logistics-services.

in 2013.[51] NASA too has similar research projects under way.[52] All of these measures indicate a fast-growing concern about collisions that lead to Space debris, and thus contribute to developing a prohibition on ASAT weapon testing that creates long-lasting debris, as a matter both of treaty reinterpretation and, as we will see later, of customary international law.

### 8.1.4   Debates and Decisions within Intergovernmental Organisations

Recent debates within intergovernmental organisations demonstrate widespread concern about kinetic ASAT weapon tests that create long-lasting debris as well as growing support for a ban. Some of these statements constitute subsequent practice in support of a reinterpretation of the second paragraph of Article I of the Outer Space Treaty, as well as state practice and evidence of *opinio juris* for the purposes of customary international law, as discussed below. Decisions taken by intergovernmental organisations can also constitute subsequent practice, as well as state practice and evidence of *opinio juris*, on the part of their member states, even if the decisions are not themselves legally binding – as with United Nations General Assembly resolutions.[53] This is particularly the case in the Space context, where all spacefaring states are members of both the General Assembly and the United Nations Committee on the Peaceful Uses of Outer Space (COPUOS). Nearly all of them are also parties to the Outer Space Treaty, which explicitly refers to its parties undertaking Space activities within the framework of international organisations.[54] Finally, decisions taken by international organisations can prompt states to engage in legally relevant subsequent practice beyond the framework of those organisations, with this practice also

---

[51] ClearSpace Today, 'Shaping sustainability beyond Earth' (2022), online: clearspace.today; Samantha Matthewson, 'ESA partners with startup to launch first debris removal mission in 2025', *Space.com* (16 May 2021), online: www.space.com/esa-startup-clearspace-debris-removal-2025.

[52] NASA Astromaterials Research & Exploration Science, 'Orbital Debris Program Office' (2022), *NASA*, online: orbitaldebris.jsc.nasa.gov.

[53] Following the report of a working group of the International Law Commission into the 'Identification of customary international law', the UN General Assembly in 2018 adopted Resolution 73/203 which found, 'In certain cases, the practice of international organizations also contributes to the formation, or expression, of rules of customary international law'. *Identification of Customary International Law*, GA Res 73/203, UNGAOR, 73rd Sess, 62nd Plen Mtg, UN Doc A/RES/73/203 (2018).

[54] Outer Space Treaty, op. cit., Arts. VI, XIII.

constituting state practice as well as, perhaps, evidence of *opinio juris*. An example is a state taking the guidelines adopted by an intergovernmental organisation and making them part of its domestic law.

This is exactly what occurred after COPUOS adopted seven Space Debris Mitigation Guidelines in 2007, including this guideline (their fourth):

> Recognizing that an increased risk of collision could pose a threat to space operations, the intentional destruction of any on-orbit spacecraft and launch vehicle orbital stages or other harmful activities that generate long-lived debris should be avoided. When intentional break-ups are necessary, they should be conducted at sufficiently low altitudes to limit the orbital lifetime of resulting fragments.[55]

Since COPUOS operates on a consensus basis, the guidelines were supported by all of its then 67 member states, which included almost all the spacefaring states (except for Israel, which joined COPUOS in 2015).[56] This support is subsequent practice for the purposes of treaty interpretation (and state practice for the purposes of customary international law). Then, when the UN General Assembly endorsed the Space Debris Mitigation Guidelines later in 2007, it stated that the guidelines themselves 'reflect the existing practices as developed by a number of national and international organizations'.[57]

Now this is where things get interesting: China responded to the Space Debris Mitigation Guidelines by immediately adopting Space debris mitigation requirements for all Chinese entities engaged in Space activities.[58] Then, in 2009, it released domestically binding Interim Measures on Space Debris Mitigation and Protective Management with the aim, according to Yun Zhao, 'of guaranteeing the normal operation of spacecraft and protection of the Space environment'.[59]

---

[55] United Nations Office for Outer Space Affairs (UNOOSA), *Space Debris Mitigations Guidelines of the Committee on the Peaceful Uses of Outer Space* (Vienna: United Nations, 2010), guideline 4, online: www.unoosa.org/oosa/oosadoc/data/documents/2010/stspace/stspace49_0.html.

[56] If one considers spacefaring states as those which have launched orbital spacecraft, currently North Korea (which achieved orbital launch capability in 2012) is the only spacefaring state that is not also one of the now 102 members of COPUOS.

[57] *International Co-operation in the Peaceful Uses of Outer Space*, GA Res 62/217, UNGAOR, 62nd Sess, 79th Plen Mtg, UN Doc A/RES/62/217 (2007) at para. 27.

[58] Yun Zhao, *National Space Law in China* (Leiden: Brill Nijhoff, 2015) at 218.

[59] Ibid. at 220.

Russia introduced its own General Requirements on Space Systems for the Mitigation of Human-Produced Near-Earth Space Pollution in 2008. These requirements, which are binding in Russian domestic law, are explicitly based on the UN Space Debris Mitigation Guidelines.[60]

Prior to this, in 1995, NASA was the first Space agency to issue a set of orbital debris mitigation guidelines. Then, in 2001, the binding Orbital Debris Mitigation Standard Practices (ODMSP) became the principal debris-related requirements applicable to all Space activities under the supervision and control of the US government.[61] The ODMSP influenced both the subsequent Space debris mitigation guidelines of COPUOS in 2007 and the Inter-Agency Space Debris Coordination Committee (IADC) in 2002.[62] They were updated by the US government in November 2019,[63] a development that could potentially spur updates to these multilateral guidelines in the years ahead.

Australia's 2018 Space (Launches and Returns) Act includes as a launch requirement a Space debris mitigation strategy, which must be based on internationally recognised standards or guidelines, such as those of COPUOS and the IADC.[64] Similarly, the Space debris mitigation requirements of Canada's 2007 Remote Sensing Space Systems Regulations are consistent with both the COPUOS and IADC Space debris mitigation guidelines, with the Canadian Space Agency adopting the latter in 2012 as directly applicable to all its operations.[65]

The IADC, noted above, was created even earlier, in 1993, to co-ordinate efforts to deal with orbital debris. It is currently made up of

---

[60] Russian Federation, 'National standard of the Russian Federation GOSTR52925–2008', cited in Y Makarov, G Raykunov, S Kolchin, S Loginov, M Mikhailov and M Yakovlev, 'Russian Federation activity on space debris mitigation', Federal Space Agency of Russia (2010), online: www.tsi.lv/sites/default/files/editor/science/Conferences/SPACE/makarov.pdf.

[61] NASA Orbital Debris Program Office, 'Debris mitigation' (2022), *NASA*, online: orbitaldebris.jsc.nasa.gov/mitigation.

[62] Michael P Gleason, 'A short guide for understanding and assessing US space sustainability initiatives' (April 2021), *Center for Space Policy and Strategy*, online: aerospace.org/sites/default/files/2021-04/Gleason_SpaceSustainability_20210407.pdf.

[63] NASA, 'US government orbital debris mitigation standard practices, November 2019 update' (2019), *NASA*, online: orbitaldebris.jsc.nasa.gov/library/usg_orbital_debris_mitigation_standard_practices_november_2019.pdf.

[64] UNOOSA, 'Compendium: Space debris mitigation standards adopted by states and international organizations' (17 June 2021), *UNOOSA*, online: www.unoosa.org/documents/pdf/spacelaw/sd/Space_Debris_Compendium_COPUOS_17_june_2021.pdf     at 8–9.

[65] Ibid. at 16–19.

representatives from the European Space Agency and 12 national Space agencies, including those of the United States, Russia, China and India. In 2002, and again (with small revisions) in 2007, 2020 and 2021, the IADC adopted a set of its own Space Debris Mitigation Guidelines.[66] Guideline 5.2.3 on the 'Avoidance of intentional destruction and other harmful activities' reads,

> Intentional destruction of a spacecraft or orbital stage, (self-destruction, intentional collision, etc.), and other harmful activities that may significantly increase collision risks to other spacecraft and orbital stages should be avoided. For instance, intentional break-ups should be conducted at sufficiently low altitudes so that orbital fragments are short lived.

The International Organization for Standardization (known as the ISO) is an international non-governmental organisation with 165 members – all of them national standards bodies, some of which are closely connected to governments, others of which are not.[67] In 2010 the ISO adopted a stringent set of Space Debris Mitigation Requirements which apply to all unmanned satellites and spacecraft 'launched into, or passing through, near-Earth space'.[68] These requirements were updated by the ISO the following year and are 'intended to reduce the growth of space debris by ensuring that spacecraft and launch vehicle orbital stages are designed, operated and disposed of in a manner that prevents them from generating debris throughout their orbital lifetime'.[69] Among other things, all new satellites must be able to de-orbit to Earth, or boost themselves into graveyard orbits at the end of their lifespan.

The ISO Space Debris Mitigation Requirements are not legally binding. However, in 2015 they were adopted by the European Cooperation for Space Standardization, an initiative, led by the 22 member-state European Space Agency (ESA), that seeks to develop a coherent, single set of user-friendly standards for use in all European

---

[66] Inter-Agency Space Debris Coordination Committee (IADC), 'Space Debris Mitigation Guidelines – third revision' (2021), *IADC*, online: https://www.iadc-home.org/documents_public/file_down/id/5249.

[67] International Organization for Standardization (ISO), 'About us' (2022), *ISO*, online: www.iso.org/about-us.html.

[68] ISO, 'ISO 24113:2010, Space systems – Space debris mitigation requirements' (July 2010), *ISO*, online: www.iso.org/standard/42034.html.

[69] ISO, 'ISO 24113:2011, Space systems – Space debris mitigation requirements' (May 2011), *ISO*, online: www.iso.org/standard/57239.html.

Space activities.[70] The standards adopted by the European Cooperation for Space Standardization are applied to all ESA projects,[71] a step which constitutes both state practice and perhaps also evidence of *opinio juris* – not on the banning of kinetic ASAT weapon tests specifically, but rather on the avoidance of debris-creating Space activities in general as legally appropriate behaviour at the global level. In 2019, the ISO released a third edition of its Space Debris Mitigation Requirements,[72] with a fourth edition currently in development.[73]

Making a set of international guidelines binding in domestic law, or within the 22 member-state ESA, is subsequent practice. It is also state practice and, most importantly, evidence of *opinio juris*, since it suggests that national governments feel an obligation to ensure that the guidelines are followed.

Other debates and decisions within international organisations provide less direct but still significant evidence of a shift in international opinion (although probably not evidence of *opinio juris*) concerning Space debris and kinetic ASAT weapon testing. For example, in 2012 the UN secretary general established a Group of Governmental Experts on Transparency and Confidence-Building Measures in Outer Space Activities. The group's consensus report, released the following year, observed that 'in the context of international peace and security, there is growing concern that threats to vital space capabilities may increase during the next decade as a result of both natural and man-made hazards and the possible development of disruptive and destructive counter-space capabilities'.[74] It then stated, 'Intentional destruction of any on-orbit spacecraft and launch vehicle orbital stages or other harmful activities that generate long-lived debris should be avoided.'[75]

---

[70] European Space Agency (ESA), 'European Cooperation for Space Standardization (ECSS)' (2022), *ECSS*, online: ecss.nl.

[71] ESA, 'Mitigating space debris generation' (2022), *ESA*, online: www.esa.int/Safety_Security/Space_Debris/Mitigating_space_debris_generation.

[72] ISO, 'ISO 24113:2019, Space systems – Space debris mitigation requirements' (July 2019), *ISO*, online: www.iso.org/standard/72383.html.

[73] ISO, 'ISO/DIS 24113 Space systems – Space debris mitigation requirements' (2022), *ISO*, online: www.iso.org/standard/83494.html.

[74] *Report of the Group of Governmental Experts on Transparency and Confidence-Building Measures in Outer Space Activities*, UNGAOR, 68th Sess, UN Doc A/68/189 (2013) at para. 6.

[75] Ibid. at para. 45.

In 2014, the European Union released a draft International Code of Conduct for Outer Space Activities.[76] At its core, the draft code included a set of principles, including 'the responsibility of states to refrain from the threat or use of force against the territorial integrity or political independence of any state' and the 'inherent right of states to individual or collective self-defence'.[77] In this context, the draft code identified that states are required 'to take all appropriate measures and cooperate in good faith to avoid harmful interference with outer space activities' and 'to take all appropriate measures to prevent outer space from becoming an arena of conflict'.[78]

In 2019, COPUOS adopted 21 guidelines for the long-term sustainability (LTS) of Space activities.[79] Although the guidelines do not refer specifically to kinetic ASAT weapon testing, they express considerable concern about Space debris, the operational stability of the environment, and the need to ensure that defence and security measures are 'compatible with preserving outer space for peaceful exploration and use'. They also refer to the 2013 report of the Group of Governmental Experts on Transparency and Confidence-Building Measures in Outer Space Activities, discussed above. For the purposes of our analysis, the LTS guidelines provide yet further evidence that states are changing their practice and views on this issue, thus contributing to the development of a ban on ASAT weapon testing that creates long-lasting debris. We will return to COPUOS shortly when we review the responses of state delegations to another significant 2019 development: the Indian ASAT weapon test.

---

[76] European External Action Service, 'EU proposal for an international space code of conduct, draft' (31 March 2014), *European Union*, online: www.eeas.europa.eu/node/14715_en.

[77] Ibid. at para. 26.

[78] Ibid. at paras. 27–28. The EU's draft code, it must be said, has not received widespread support, in part because states outside the EU, especially developing states, were not involved in the negotiations. See Rajeswari Pillai Rajagopalan, 'International Code of Conduct for Outer Space Activities: Major Asian perspectives', *Asia Dialogue* (27 October 2014), online: theasiadialogue.com/2014/10/27/international-code-of-conduct-for-outer-space-activities-major-asian-perspectives.

[79] Committee on the Peaceful Uses of Outer Space, 'Guidelines for the Long-term Sustainability of Outer Space Activities', Annex II in *Report of the Committee on the Peaceful Uses of Outer Space, Sixty-Second Session (12–21 June 2019)*, UNGAOR, 74th Sess, Supp No 20, UN Doc A/74/20, online: www.unoosa.org/res/oosadoc/data/documents/2019/a/a7420_0_html/V1906077.pdf.

### 8.1.5   The Indian ASAT Weapon Test: Conduct and Responses

As mentioned, in 2007 the chair of the Indian Space Research Organisation said that China should not have tested a kinetic ASAT weapon in a manner that created long-lasting debris 'as it goes against international convention'.[80] Then, in 2012, Vijay Kumar Saraswat, the scientific adviser to the Indian defence minister, told *India Today* that the country possessed ASAT technology but '[w]e will not do a physical test (actual destruction of a satellite) because of the risk of space debris affecting other satellites.'[81] Yet seven years later, on 27 March 2019, India conducted exactly such a kinetic ASAT weapon test against one of its own satellites.[82] The test is relevant to our legal analysis in several respects, beginning with the way it was conducted.

The satellite was struck at an altitude of about 283 kilometres, which according to Indian officials was low enough that the resulting debris would quickly decay and fall back to Earth. In an interview with Reuters, the chair of India's Defence Research and Development Organisation, G. Satheesh Reddy, asserted that the debris will 'vanish in no time' and 'should be dying down within 45 days'.[83] He repeated that assurance at a press conference on 6 April 2019, stating that the debris 'will decay in [a] few weeks' and 'won't cause problem to any existing space assets'.[84] At that same press conference, Reddy explained that the interception was 'specially designed' to strike the satellite at an angle so as to ensure 'minimal debris'.[85] It is possible that these assertions were based, in part, on the perceived results of the 2008 US satellite strike – as discussed above.

---

[80] Lin, op. cit.

[81] Sandeep Unnithan, 'India has all the building blocks for an anti-satellite capability', *India Today* (27 April 2012), online: www.indiatoday.in/india/story/agni-v-drdo-chief-dr-vijay-kumar-saraswat-interview-100405-2012-04-27 (quoting Vijay Kumar Saraswat).

[82] Jeffery Gettleman and Hari Kumar, 'India shot down a satellite, Modi says, shifting balance of power in Asia', *New York Times* (27 March 2019), online: www.nytimes.com/2019/03/27/world/asia/india-weather-satellite-missle.html.

[83] Sanjeev Miglani, 'India says space debris from anti-satellite test to "vanish" in 45 days', *Reuters* (28 March 2019), online: https://www.reuters.com/article/us-india-satellite-idUSKCN1R91DM.

[84] India Today Web Desk, 'Mission Shakti: ASAT test debris will decay within 45 days, says DRDO chief Satheesh Reddy', *India Today* (6 April 2019), online: www.indiatoday.in/science/story/mission-shakti-asat-satellite-debris-decay-45-days-drdo-gs-reddy-1495670-2019-04-06.

[85] Rahul Bedi, 'India's DRDO reveals additional details of recent ASAT missile test', *Jane's 360* (8 April 2019), online: https://www.janes.com/defence-news/news-detail/indias-drdo-reveals-additional-details-of-recent-asat-missile-test.

As we explained in the previous chapter, the Indian military's effort to minimise debris did not fully succeed. There are roughly 130 pieces of debris from the test in the USSPACECOM catalogue, meaning that they were in orbit long enough to be tracked and assigned an identifier. It is reasonable to assume that there was at least one order of magnitude more (i.e. 1,300) pieces between one and ten centimetres in size, a size range too small to track but still potentially lethal to satellites, Space stations and astronauts. Some of this long-lived debris, placed on highly eccentric orbits with apogees greater than 1,000 kilometres, remained in Space for over a year (see Figure 7.2 in Chapter 7) – crossing multiple orbital shells twice per orbit.

As with the 2007 Chinese ASAT weapon test, it could be argued that the 2019 Indian ASAT weapon test, as a prominent instance of subsequent practice, confirmed and thus bolstered an interpretation of the Article I, second paragraph, freedom of exploration and use that would allow such testing. But two factors lead to a different conclusion. First, India sought to *avoid* creating long-lasting debris. As a result, its conduct supports an interpretation of the second paragraph of Article I that prohibits tests that do this. The same conduct concurrently contributes to the development of a parallel rule of customary international law. Second, an examination of the responses to the Indian test confirms that the positions of states on this matter are changing.

### 8.1.6   Responses to the 2019 Indian ASAT Weapon Test

The Indian ASAT weapon test initially escaped criticism, presumably because of the assurances that no long-lasting debris would result. The United States' response began with a State Department spokesperson affirming that 'the issue of space debris is an important concern for the U.S. government. We took note of Indian government statements that the test was designed to address the debris issues'.[86] Then, NASA Administrator James Bridenstine weighed in. He explained that there were 400 identified pieces of trackable debris and 24 of them were in elliptical orbits that extended above the International Space Station,[87] increasing

---

[86] Frank A Rose, 'India's anti-satellite test presents a window of opportunity for the Trump administration: Will it take advantage?' (10 May 2019), *The Brookings Institution*, online (blog): www.brookings.edu/blog/order-from-chaos/2019/05/10/indias-anti-satellite-test-presents-a-window-of-opportunity-for-the-trump-administration.

[87] Of the 400 noted debris pieces, only 130 were eventually included in the public catalogue.

the risk of collisions with the ISS by an estimated 44 per cent.[88] Bridenstine called this 'a terrible, terrible thing',[89] and stated that this 'kind of activity is not compatible with the future of human spaceflight that we need to see happen ... It is not acceptable for us to allow people to create debris fields that put at risk our people'.[90] US Defense Secretary Patrick Shanahan was also critical of India's test: 'we all live in space, let's not make it a mess. Space should be a place where we can conduct business. Space is a place where people should have the freedom to operate'.[91]

The Russian Foreign Ministry issued a press release the day after the test in which it acknowledged India's peaceful intent but noted that the test was nonetheless the result of a larger deterioration in arms control.[92] It urged India to support the Chinese–Russian draft treaty on Space weapons.[93] Pakistan, India's regional rival, expressed 'grave concern' about the test and the threat posed by the resulting Space debris to orbital installations such as the ISS.[94]

As the Indian ASAT weapon test took place just before the annual session of the Legal Subcommittee of COPUOS in early April 2019, several states expressed concerns during the session about debris-generating ASAT weapon testing. Germany stated,

> it is appropriate to recall that any intentional destruction of an on-orbit space craft generating additional space debris poses a major safety threat to space activities conducted for the benefit and in the interest of all humankind. It must therefore be avoided. Due to the energy converted during the impact of anti-satellite weapons, even in low earth orbit, any

[88] Kai Schultz, 'NASA says debris from India's antisatellite test puts space station at risk', *New York Times* (2 April 2019), online: www.nytimes.com/2019/04/02/world/asia/nasa-india-space-debris.html.

[89] Ibid.

[90] Rose, op. cit.

[91] 'Mission Shakti: Space debris warning after India destroys satellite', *BBC News* (28 March 2019), online: www.bbc.com/news/world-asia-india-47729568.

[92] Andrew Korybko, 'Russia's response to India's ASAT missile test wasn't what New Delhi expected', *Global Research* (1 April 2019), online: www.globalresearch.ca/russias-response-to-indias-asat-missile-test-wasnt-what-new-delhi-expected/5673254.

[93] Ibid.

[94] Government of Pakistan, media briefing, 'Record of press briefing by spokesperson on Friday, 05 April 2019' (2019), *Ministry of Foreign Affairs*, online: mofa.gov.pk/record-of-press-briefing-by-spokesperson-on-friday-05-april-2019. See also Asad Hashim, 'Pakistan expresses "grave concern" over Indian space weapons test', *Al Jazeera* (3 April 2019), online: www.aljazeera.com/news/2019/4/3/pakistan-expresses-grave-concern-over-indian-space-weapons-test.

resulting space debris is uncontrollable and increases collision risk, including in higher orbits. Therefore, generally accepted international standards such as the Space Debris Mitigation Guidelines of COPUOS and the ESA as well as the recommendations of the group of governmental experts on transparency and confidence building measures in outer space activities urge responsible space actors to refrain from intentional destruction of space objects. Like already done in other forums, Germany calls for a legally binding prohibition of the intentional destruction of space objects resulting in the generation of long-lasting debris, including in situation[s] of armed conflict.[95]

France said that it is 'the obligation of states to abstain ... [from] the intentional destruction of space objects'.[96] Finland observed, 'Any unnecessary or voluntary creation or increase of in-orbit space debris population can be viewed ... to run counter to the norms and principles of responsible behaviour in outer space.'[97] A delegate from the Netherlands stated,

> My government is concerned with the deliberate and unnecessary creation of space debris through the destruction of space objects. In our view, this would constitute a threat to the safety and sustainable use of outer space, and would not be in line with guideline 4 of the Space Debris Mitigation Guidelines.[98]

Canada said, 'Impacts and collisions involving space debris present a serious challenge to our continued exploration and use of outer space.'[99] Austria commented, 'The intentional destruction of spacecraft, in contradiction to the abovementioned Space Debris Mitigation Guidelines, may therefore be an indicator of fault when it comes to determining the liability of the launching state for damage caused by space debris created

---

[95] Legal Subcommittee of the Committee on the Peaceful Uses of Outer Space (COPUOS), *Digital Recording of 9 April 2019 from 10:00 to 13:00*, 58th Sess (statement of German delegate at 0:49:21 to 0:51:01), *United Nations*, online: https://www.unoosa.org/oosa/en/ourwork/copuos/lsc/2019/index.html. The German position is also expressed, without attribution, by the Legal Subcommittee of COPUOS in its 2019 report of its annual session. Committee on the Peaceful Uses of Outer Space, *Report of the Legal Subcommittee on Its Fifty-Eighth Session, Held in Vienna from 1 to 12 April 2019*, UNGAOR, 62nd Sess, UN Doc A/AC.105/1203 (2019) at 26, para. 184.

[96] Legal Subcommittee of the COPUOS, *Digital Recording of 9 April 2019 from 10:00 to 13:00*, 58th Sess (statement of French delegate at 0:56:45 to 0:56:55), *United Nations*, online: https://www.unoosa.org/oosa/en/ourwork/copuos/lsc/2019/index.html (translation by the authors).

[97] Ibid. (statement of Finish delegate at 0:58:00 to 0:58:16).

[98] Ibid. (statement of the Netherlands delegate at 0:63:17 to 0:63:38).

[99] Ibid. (statement of the Canadian delegate at 0:73:13 to 0:73:21).

by the intentional destruction.'[100] Last but not least, the European Space Agency, which holds observer status within COPUOS, stated, 'Intentional destructions, which will generate long-lived debris, should not be planned or conducted.'[101]

Collectively, these responses to India's test constitute subsequent practice for the purposes of a reinterpretation of the second paragraph of Article I of the Outer Space Treaty against ASAT weapon testing that creates long-lasting debris. They also constitute state practice and evidence of *opinio juris* in support of a developing rule of customary international law, as will be discussed below.

### 8.1.7    The 2021 Russian ASAT Weapon Test

As we explained in the previous chapter, the Russian military used a ground-based missile to strike Kosmos 1408 on 15 November 2021. It had previously tested the PL-19 Nudol missile's capabilities as an ASAT weapon through 'flybys', i.e. without attempting to strike an actual satellite, thereby demonstrating at least some concern about the creation of long-lasting Space debris.[102] No such concern was manifest this time.

The defunct Soviet-era satellite had a mass of about 1,750 kilograms and was orbiting at an altitude of about 480 kilometres. Due to the  high impact energies involved in such a strike, debris ended up on highly eccentric orbits that cross the orbital altitudes of thousands of other satellites twice per revolution. Moreover, as the debris de-orbits with time, it will all pass through the altitudes of the International Space Station and China's new Tiangong Space station. Indeed, shortly after test, the crew members of the ISS – four Americans, one German and two Russians – were woken up by their respective mission controls, told that there had been a 'satellite break-up', and asked to close the hatches to the

---

[100] Legal Subcommittee of the COPUOS, *Digital Recording of 9 April 2019 from 15:00 to 17:36*, 58th Sess (statement of the Austrian delegate at 0:77:37 to 0:77:58), *United Nations*, online: https://www.unoosa.org/oosa/en/ourwork/copuos/lsc/2019/index.html.

[101] Legal Subcommittee of the COPUOS, *Digital Recording of 9 April 2019 from 10:00 to 13:00*, 58th Sess (statement of the European Space Agency delegate at 0:71:37 to 0:71:45), *United Nations*, online: https://www.unoosa.org/oosa/en/ourwork/copuos/lsc/2019/index.html.

[102] See Secure World Foundation, op. cit.

radial modules on the station.[103] The crew members were then directed into their hardened Crew Dragon and Soyuz capsules for two hours as the ISS passed through the debris cloud.

Remarkably, the Russian Defence Ministry denied that debris from the test threatened other satellites. '[E]merging fragments at the time of the test and in terms of the orbit's parameters did not and will not pose any threat to orbital stations, satellites and space activity', it said.[104] It also noted, 'Earlier, such tests in outer space were already conducted by the United States, China, and India.'

In response, US Secretary of State Anthony Blinken issued a statement that read, in part,[105]

> The long-lived debris created by this dangerous and irresponsible test will now threaten satellites and other space objects that are vital to all nations' security, economic, and scientific interests for decades to come. In addition, it will significantly increase the risk to astronauts and cosmonauts on the International Space Station and other human spaceflight activities . . .
>
> We call upon all responsible spacefaring nations to join us in efforts to develop norms of responsible behavior and to refrain from conducting dangerous and irresponsible destructive tests like those carried out by Russia.

NASA Administrator Bill Nelson said,

> I'm outraged by this irresponsible and destabilizing action. With its long and storied history in human spaceflight, it is unthinkable that Russia would endanger not only the American and international partner astronauts on the ISS, but also their own cosmonauts. Their actions are reckless and dangerous, threatening as well the Chinese space station and the taikonauts on board. All nations have a responsibility to prevent the purposeful creation of space debris from ASATs and to foster a safe, sustainable space environment.[106]

---

[103] Elizabeth Howell, 'Hear how NASA alerted astronauts to incoming space debris after Russian anti-satellite test', *Space.com* (17 November 2021), online: www.space.com/space-station-crew-russian-space-debris-audio.

[104] 'Russia's top brass reports on successfully striking defunct satellite in tests', TASS Russian News Agency (16 November 2021), online: tass.com/science/1362125.

[105] Anthony J Blinken, press statement, 'Russia conducts destructive anti-satellite missile test' (15 November 2021), *US Department of State*, online: www.state.gov/russia-conducts-destructive-anti-satellite-missile-test.

[106] NASA, press release, 21-156, 'NASA administrator statement on Russian ASAT test' (15 November 2021), *NASA*, online: www.nasa.gov/press-release/nasa-administrator-statement-on-russian-asat-test.

NATO secretary general Jens Stoltenberg said the test was reckless, posed a threat to the ISS and the Chinese Space station, and showed that Russia was developing new weapons systems.[107] The North Atlantic Council, made up of representatives from all 30 NATO states, then released the following statement:[108]

1. The North Atlantic Council strongly condemns the Russian Federation's reckless and irresponsible anti-satellite missile test on 15 November 2021. This test caused an orbital debris field that significantly increases risk to human life and to the space-based assets of numerous nations and entities.
2. Russia's actions demonstrate a pattern of irresponsible behaviour and endanger the security, economic, scientific, and commercial interests of all nations and actors seeking to explore and use outer space for peaceful purposes.
3. This dangerous behaviour directly contradicts Russia's claims to oppose the "weaponisation" of space, and undermines the rules-based international order.
4. NATO Allies remain committed to protecting and preserving the peaceful access to and exploration of space for all humanity. We call upon all nations, including Russia, to join the international efforts to develop norms, rules and principles of responsible behaviour in order to reduce space threats, and to refrain from conducting dangerous and irresponsible destructive tests like those carried out by the Russian Federation.

Separate from this, France's Defence and Foreign Ministries issued a joint statement in which they said the test was 'destabilising, irresponsible and likely to have consequences for a very long time in the space environment and for all actors in space'.[109] In an earlier tweet, French defence minister Florence Parly went so far as to call the Russian military 'space vandals' who 'generate debris that pollutes and puts our astronauts and satellites in danger'.[110]

---

[107] North Atlantic Treaty Organization (NATO), press statement, 'Doorstep statement by NATO secretary general Jens Stoltenberg at the Council of the EU' (16 November 2021), *NATO*, online: www.nato.int/cps/fr/natohq/opinions_188605.htm.

[108] NATO, press release, (2021) 170, 'Statement by the North Atlantic Council on the recent anti-satellite missile test conducted by the Russian Federation' (19 November 2021), *NATO*, online: www.nato.int/cps/en/natohq/news_188780.htm.

[109] 'Germany and France slam Russia for satellite strike', *Straits Times* (17 November 2021), online: www.straitstimes.com/world/europe/germany-and-france-slam-russia-for-satellite-strike.

[110] Florence Parly, 'L'Espace est un bien commun, celui des 7,7 milliards d'habitants de notre planète: Les saccageurs de l'Espace ont une responsabilité accablante en générant

Josep Borrell, the high representative of the European Union for Foreign Affairs and Security Policy, issued a statement on behalf of all 27 EU Member States that read, in part,[111]

> The European Union strongly condemns the Russian Federation's conduct of a kinetic direct-ascent anti-satellite (ASAT) weapon test against its own satellite, COSMOS 1408, resulting in its destruction by a missile, as a clear act of irresponsible behaviour in outer space. It generated a large amount of space debris that constitute a long-lasting risk for crewed and un-crewed space activities, including for the safety of astronauts and cosmonauts at the International Space Station. This action goes also against the principles reflected in the UN Space Debris Mitigation Guidelines and will jeopardize the free access to and use of space for all States for many years. It also contradicts the position expressed by the Russian Federation in multilateral fora, including in its contribution to the report of the UN Secretary General on responsible behaviour in outer space. This puts the credibility of its stance into question.
>
> The conduct of such tests are dangerous and highly destabilising, as potentially leading to deteriorating the confidence between space actors, increasing the perception of threats. This could lead to potential catastrophic consequences. The European Union continues to urge all States to refrain from the irresponsible behaviour of destructing space objects that generate space debris in order to preserve the safe, secure and sustainable use of outer space for present and future generations.

Nine non-EU states – North Macedonia, Montenegro, Albania, Iceland, Liechtenstein, Norway, Ukraine, Moldova and Georgia – aligned themselves with this declaration.[112]

The British defence minister also weighed in, saying that the test 'shows a complete disregard for the security, safety and sustainability of space. The debris resulting from this test will remain in orbit putting satellites and human spaceflight at risk for years to come'.[113] A joint

---

des débris qui polluent et mettent nos astronautes et satellites en danger' (16 November 2021 at 07:30), *Twitter*, online: twitter.com/florence_parly/status/1460586002230263822 (authors' translation).

[111] Council of the European Union, press release, 'Statement by the high representative of the Union for foreign affairs and security policy on behalf of the EU on the Russian anti-satellite test on 15 November 2021' (19 November 2021), *European Union*, online: www.consilium.europa.eu/en/press/press-releases/2021/11/19/statement-by-the-high-representative-of-the-union-for-foreign-affairs-and-security-policy-on-behalf-of-the-eu-on-the-russian-anti-satellite-test-on-15-november-2021.

[112] Ibid.

[113] 'Russian anti-satellite missile test draws condemnation', *BBC News* (16 November 2021), online: www.bbc.com/news/science-environment-59299101.

media release from the Australian defence and foreign ministers described the Russian test as 'a provocative and dangerous act that demonstrated the threats to space systems are real, serious and growing'.[114] The German foreign minister was equally critical:

> This irresponsible behaviour carries a risk of error of judgement and escalation. The test underlines the risks and growing threats for security and stability in space and the urgent need for the international community to agree on rules for the peaceful and lasting use of space and on measures aimed at reinforcing safety and confidence.[115]

In Japan, the Ministry of Foreign Affairs issued a statement that read, in part,[116]

> The destruction of a satellite that generates a large amount of space debris indiscriminately increases the risk of collisions of on-orbit space objects and is an irresponsible behavior that undermines sustainable and stable use of outer space. As the importance of outer space is increasing, the Government of Japan is concerned about the destruction also from the perspective of peaceful use of outer space and security. In addition, Space Debris Mitigation Guidelines adopted unanimously by the member states of the United Nations Committee on the Peaceful Uses of Outer Space (COPUOS), including Russia, in 2007 require that the intentional destruction of any on-orbit space objects that generates long-lived space debris should be avoided. In this respect, the test runs counter to the guidelines.
>
> The Government of Japan expresses concerns towards the test and calls upon the Government of Russia not to conduct this kind of test in the future.
>
> As it is important to ensure the peaceful use of outer space, the international rule-making is necessary for sustainable and stable use of outer space. The Government of Japan will continue to call upon relevant countries for their responsible behavior in preventing the generation and diffusion of long-lived space debris and to engage actively in the discussions in the international arena on responsible behavior in outer space.

---

[114] Australian minister for defence and minister for foreign affairs, joint media release, 'Russian anti-satellite weapons testing' (17 November 2021), *Australian Department of Defence*, online: www.minister.defence.gov.au/minister/peter-dutton/media-releases/russian-anti-satellite-weapons-testing.

[115] 'Germany and France slam Russia for satellite strike', op. cit.

[116] Yoshida Tomoyuki, press release, 'An anti-satellite test conducted by the government of Russia' (18 November 2021), *Ministry of Foreign Affairs of Japan*, online: www.mofa.go.jp/press/release/press3e_000270.html.

In South Korea, the Foreign Ministry sent a text message to reporters that read, 'We are concerned about the anti-satellite weapon test that took place Nov. 15 and in particular numerous pieces of debris created in space as a result of the test.'[117] In the same message, it urged 'all nations to act responsibly in space to ensure peaceful and sustainable use of space, and work together to advance related international rules'.

Then, there was China. When asked about the Russian test during a press conference the following day, Foreign Ministry spokesperson Zhao Lijian said, 'We noted relevant reports and that Russia has yet to respond. I think it is too early to make any comment.'[118] Two months later, a report from the Chinese state-controlled *Global Times* – widely regarded as a mouthpiece for the government – signalled that China was very concerned about Russia's action, not least after a close conjunction between one of its scientific satellites and a piece of debris from the test. A long excerpt from that report is reproduced here, because of its considerable importance:[119]

> The Space Debris Monitoring and Application Center of the China National Space Administration sent out a warning on an extremely dangerous rendezvous on Tuesday between the Tsinghua Science satellite and Russia's Kosmos 1408 debris. An expert on space debris told the Global Times on Wednesday that the data released showed that there was a high chance of collision between the debris and the satellite on Tuesday.
>
> 'Currently, they keep a safe distance but the chance for these two getting close in the future cannot be excluded,' Liu Jing, a space debris expert said.
>
> The closest distance between Tsinghua's satellite and the Russian debris was 14.5 meters, with a relative speed of 5.27 kilometers per second. Liu told the Global Times that it is very rare to see the distance between space debris and spacecrafts within just a dozen of meters, as normally during the debris–spacecraft rendezvous, the two keep a distance of several tens of kilometers . . .

---

[117] Park Si-soo, 'China silent, South Korea "concerned" over debris created by Russia's anti-satellite missile test', *SpaceNews* (17 November 2021), online: spacenews.com/china-silent-south-korea-concerned-over-debris-created-by-russias-anti-satellite-missile-test/.

[118] Ibid.

[119] Fan Wei, 'Following "extremely dangerous rendezvous" between Russian space debris and Chinese satellite, Chinese expert says it's possible the two get closer again', *Global Times* (20 January 2022), online: www.globaltimes.cn/page/202201/1246440.shtml.

The debris came from a Russian anti-satellite test on November 15, 2021. Russia's anti-satellite test produced an estimated 1,600 pieces of debris larger than 10 centimeters, most of which were distributed in an orbital altitude range of 400 to 1,100 kilometers, according to media reports.

Experts said that China has launched hundreds of satellites within this orbital altitude. In theory, these space debris may pose a threat to China's spacecraft. Since Russia's anti-satellite tests last November, China has been closely monitoring the space debris created and calculated their locations daily based on the latest data to predict if there is a risk of collision between these debris and Chinese satellites, Liu said. He also highlighted that 'if there is [a possibility of collision] we need to quickly notify our satellites and make some evasive maneuvers in advance to avoid these debris. This is the most feasible method at present.'

Huang Zhicheng, an aerospace expert, said that as space debris has an increasingly frequent impact on human spaceflights, the tasks of reducing and removing space debris should be put on the corresponding agenda.

'It is not only necessary to conduct research on experimental devices or spacecraft to remove space debris, but also to formulate corresponding international laws and regulations on the generation of space debris under the framework of the UN,' Huang said.

This report from *Global Times* and the responses summarised above demonstrate that Russia's 2021 ASAT weapon test generated considerable concern among other states, including all the other major spacefaring states. Indeed, as Nivedita Raju observed, 'India's destructive ASAT test in March 2019 generated fewer and much softer responses than Russia's.'[120] Many of the responses to the Russian test will constitute subsequent practice for the purposes of interpreting the second paragraph of Article I of the Outer Space Treaty, as well as state practice and evidence of *opinio juris* for the purposes of customary international law. Just as importantly, not a single state responded to the Russian ASAT weapon test by saying that it was an appropriate or internationally legal action.

In terms of international law-making, it is especially significant that Russia denied that the ASAT weapon test created risks for operational satellites or Space stations. As we demonstrated in the previous chapter, the denial was scientifically implausible. Yet it also constitutes a clear, if implicit, acknowledgement, by the Russia government, that the deliberate

---

[120] Nivedita Raju, 'Russia's anti-satellite test should lead to a multilateral ban' (7 December 2021), *Stockholm International Peace Research Institute*, online: www.sipri.org/commentary/essay/2021/russias-anti-satellite-test-should-lead-multilateral-ban.

creation of dangerous debris is unacceptable today. The denial was, in short, more legally relevant than the test itself as subsequent practice for the purpose of interpreting the second paragraph of Article I, and as state practice and evidence of *opinio juris* for customary international law.

As we explained in the previous chapter, the prohibition on torture (a rule found in numerous treaties as well as customary international law) provides a powerful example of how denials of actions can contribute to those actions being, or becoming, illegal. To quote Anthony D'Amato again:

> It seems . . . important to ask whether the states that engage in torture are (a) disclosing that they are torturing people, (b) proclaiming that what they are doing is legally justified, and (c) implicitly inviting other states to do likewise on the ground that, if torture is legally permissible for them, it is legally permissible for all states.[121]

D'Amato went on to explain that 'hiding, cover-up, minimization, and non-justification . . . betoken a violation of law' and therefore constitute legally relevant state practice *in support of* a rule prohibiting the actions in question.[122] Russia, by denying that it created dangerous debris in November 2021, was strengthening, not weakening, a possible new rule against testing ASAT weapons in ways that create long-lasting debris.

### 8.1.8   United Nations General Assembly Resolutions 75/36 and 76/231

In December 2020, the United Nations General Assembly adopted Resolution 75/36 on Reducing Space Threats through Norms, Rules and Principles of Responsible Behaviours.[123] The resolution:

> Encourages Member States to study existing and potential threats and security risks to space systems, including those arising from actions, activities or systems in outer space or on Earth, characterize actions and activities that could be considered responsible, irresponsible or threatening and their potential impact on international security, and share their ideas on the further development and implementation of norms, rules and principles of responsible behaviours . . .

---

[121] Anthony D'Amato, 'Custom and treaty: A response to Professor Weisburd' (1988) 21:3 *Vanderbilt Journal of Transnational Law* 459 at 466.

[122] Ibid. at 469.

[123] *Reducing Space Threats through Norms, Rules and Principles of Responsible Behaviours*, GA Res 75/36, UNGAOR, 75th Sess, 37th Plen Mtg, UN Doc A/RES/75/36 (2020).

The resolution further requested that the UN secretary general 'seek the views of Member States'. Those views, compiled in a report to the General Assembly at its 76th session in September 2021, show strong support for restrictions on kinetic ASAT weapon testing.[124]

Russia called for 'a complete and comprehensive ban on space-based strike weapons as well as on any land-, air-, or sea-based systems designed to destroy objects in outer space'. China expressed a similar view. Australia, Canada, France, Germany, Italy, Japan, Luxembourg, the Netherlands, Norway, Slovenia, the United Kingdom and the European Union all expressed the view that kinetic ASAT weapon tests should be avoided. Ireland, New Zealand and the United States identified kinetic ASAT weapon tests as a category of behaviour 'that could be considered during further development and implementation of norms, rules, and principles of responsible behaviours'. Brazil, Mexico, Sweden and Switzerland expressed support for multilateral negotiations leading to legally binding constraints on kinetic ASAT weapon testing.[125] Most importantly, not a single state in its response submitted for this United Nations report considered the testing of kinetic ASAT weapons to be an appropriate or internationally legal action.

Then, in December 2021, the United Nations General Assembly adopted Resolution 76/231,[126] which created an open-ended working group:

> (a) To take stock of the existing international legal and other normative frameworks concerning threats arising from State behaviours with respect to outer space;

---

[124] *Report of the Secretary-General: Reducing Space Threats through Norms, Rules and Principles of Responsible Behaviours*, UNGAOR, 76th Sess, UN Doc A/76/77 (2021).

[125] It should be noted that expressing support for treaty negotiations does not indicate a lack of belief in the existence of customary international law on the same point. A treaty can provide clarity and therefore certainty that customary international law cannot provide. It can also serve to 'crystallise' customary international law, turning a newly emerged rule into a concrete standard, or contribute to the 'progressive development' of a new rule.

[126] *Reducing Space Threats through Norms, Rules and Principles of Responsible Behaviours*, GA Res 76/231, UNGAOR, 76th Sess, 54th Plen Mtg, UN Doc A/RES/76/231 (2021). There were 150 votes in favour, eight against (China, Cuba, the Democratic People's Republic of Korea, Iran, Nicaragua, the Russian Federation, Syria and Venezuela), and seven abstentions (Armenia, Belarus, Central African Republic, India, Israel, Pakistan and Tajikistan). See United Nations (UN), Meetings Coverage, GA/12398, 'Approving $3.12 billion programme budget, General Assembly adopts 26 resolutions, 2 decisions, as main part of seventy-sixth session concludes' (24 December 2021), *UN*, online: www.un .org/press/en/2021/ga12398.doc.htm.

(b) To consider current and future threats by States to space systems, and actions, activities and omissions that could be considered irresponsible;

(c) To make recommendations on possible norms, rules and principles of responsible behaviours relating to threats by States to space systems, including, as appropriate, how they would contribute to the negotiation of legally binding instruments, including on the prevention of an arms race in outer space;

(d) To submit a report to the General Assembly at its 78th session.

It is possible that the open-ended working group will negotiate a draft treaty banning kinetic ASAT weapon testing, as recommended in an international open letter co-ordinated by the Outer Space Institute in September of that year.[127] That letter, signed by former prime ministers, Nobel laureates, retired astronauts and hundreds of other experts, was addressed to the president of the General Assembly.

The open-ended working group did not, however, experience a smooth launch. At their first organisational meeting, in early February 2022, the members of the group decided to postpone the first substantive session from mid-February to May. According to a report from Breaking Defense, 'Russia raised a litany of procedural complaints', arguing that national delegations needed more time to prepare and seeking 'new limitations preventing representatives of non-governmental organizations (NGOs) from speaking or providing direct input'. The author of the report, the well-informed Theresa Hitchens, added some extra colour when she explained that the latter issue 'was left unresolved when the formal meeting adjourned to a private venue, after the clock ran out on interpretation services at the Palais de[s] Nations and building management threatened to kill the lights on the diplomatic squabbling'.[128]

It is important to note that early February 2022 was a time of newly heightened tension between Russia and Western states, with missiles, tanks and nearly 200,000 Russian troops massed on Ukraine's borders. Aidan Liddle, the British ambassador to the Conference on Disarmament in Geneva, took to Twitter to express a more optimistic view of the squabbling within the working group. '[T]hat's the nature of multilateral

---

[127] 'International open letter on kinetic anti-satellite (ASAT) testing' (2 September 2021), *Outer Space Institute*, online: outerspaceinstitute.ca/docs/OSI_International_Open_Letter_ASATs_PUBLIC.pdf.

[128] Theresa Hitchens, 'No love from Russia for UN military space norms meeting', *Breaking Defense* (9 February 2022), online: breakingdefense.com/2022/02/no-love-from-russia-for-un-military-space-norms-meeting.

diplomacy', he wrote. '[A]nd when it works, it's worth the wait'.[129] Russia's subsequent invasion of Ukraine on February 24 and the corresponding near breakdown in relations with Western states simultaneously make the new working group even more relevant, while creating major uncertainty for its future.[130]

### 8.1.9   The 2022 United States 'Unilateral Declaration'

Something quite unusual happened on 18 April 2022 when, during a speech at Vandenberg Space Force Base in California, US Vice President Kamala Harris solemnly declared that 'as of today, the United States commits not to conduct destructive direct ascent anti-satellite missile testing'.[131] In international law, statements such as these are called 'unilateral declarations' and are legally binding.

In the 1974 *Nuclear Tests Cases*, the International Court of Justice wrote,

> One of the basic principles governing the creation and performance of legal obligations, whatever their source, is the principle of good faith. Trust and confidence are inherent in international co-operation, in particular in an age when this co-operation in many fields is becoming increasingly essential. Just as the very rule of *pacta sunt servanda* in the law of treaties is based on good faith, so also is the binding character of an international obligation assumed by unilateral declaration. Thus interested States may take cognizance of unilateral declarations and place confidence in them, and are entitled to require that the obligation thus created be respected.[132]

---

[129] Aidan Liddle, 'No, but that's the nature of multilateral diplomacy – and when it works, it's worth the wait' (10 February 2022 at 17:12), *Twitter*, online: twitter.com/AidanLiddle/status/1491897924564967430.

[130] We address the implications of Russia's attack on Ukraine further in the Conclusion to this book.

[131] The White House, speeches and remarks, 'Remarks by Vice President Harris on the ongoing work to establish norms in space' (18 April 2022), *The White House*, online: www.whitehouse.gov/briefing-room/speeches-remarks/2022/04/18/remarks-by-vice-president-harris-on-the-ongoing-work-to-establish-norms-in-space. See also the White House, 'Vice President Harris delivers remarks about our ongoing work to establish norms for space' (18 April 2022), *YouTube*, online: https://www.youtube.com/watch?v=oATgItF2CFQ. For the associated 'fact sheet', see the White House, statements and releases, 'Fact sheet: Vice President Harris advances national security norms in space' (18 April 2022), *The White House*, online: www.whitehouse.gov/briefing-room/statements-releases/2022/04/18/fact-sheet-vice-president-harris-advances-national-security-norms-in-space.

[132] *Nuclear Tests Case (Australia v. France)*, [1974] ICJ Rep 253 at 268, para. 46; *Nuclear Tests Case (New Zealand v. France)*, [1974] ICJ Rep 457 at 473, para. 49.

The unilateral declaration at issue in the *Nuclear Tests Cases* was a commitment not to test nuclear weapons in the atmosphere, made publicly by both the French president and the French foreign minister. The parallel with Vice President Harris's declaration, which also involves weapons testing in an 'area beyond national jurisdiction', is striking.

In 2006, the United Nations International Law Commission (ILC) completed a decade-long study on unilateral declarations and issued a set of ten Guiding Principles. These principles confirmed that a unilateral declaration, if made publicly, in clear and specific terms, and by an authority vested with the power to do so, constitutes a binding commitment vis-à-vis all other states.[133] Those states 'may then take them into consideration and rely on them; such States are entitled to require that such obligations be respected'.[134] The ILC also confirmed that a unilateral declaration 'cannot be revoked arbitrarily', with arbitrariness being determined, in part, by 'the extent to which those to whom the obligations are owed have relied on such obligations'.[135]

It is therefore clear that the United States is now bound, under international law, not to engage in direct-ascent ASAT missile tests. Importantly, other states may now rely on the US commitment, for instance, while deciding not to develop or test ground-based kinetic ASAT weapons themselves.

At the same time, it is important to note that the US unilateral declaration does not extend to, and therefore does not commit the United States to avoid, the testing of Space-based kinetic ASAT weapons or the testing of non-kinetic technologies such as lasers, jammers or cyber attacks, whether destructive or not. We also note that the United States already possesses the capability that it has committed not to test, as demonstrated by the use of a ship-based missile in 2008 to destroy a malfunctioning satellite. Nor does the unilateral declaration extend to the testing of missile defence interceptors, which are effectively dual-use ASAT weapons and, as demonstrated in the previous chapter, capable of generating long-lasting Space debris. But while the US unilateral declaration is tightly focused, this is not necessarily a bad thing, since it should make it easier for other states to follow suit, either by making

---

[133] International Law Commission, *Report of the Working Group on Unilateral Acts of States: Guiding Principles Applicable to Unilateral Declarations of States Capable of Creating Legal Obligations*, UNGAOR, 58th Sess, UN Doc A/CN.4/L.703 (2006).

[134] Ibid., principle 1.

[135] Ibid., principle 2.

their own declarations, or by refraining from testing such weapons themselves, or both.

The intent of the US government to create momentum and persuade others to make similar unilateral declarations is clear. As Vice President Harris said in the same speech,

> We are the first nation to make such a commitment. And today, on behalf of the United States of America, I call on all nations to join us.
>
> Whether a nation is spacefaring or not, we believe this will benefit everyone, just as space benefits everyone.
>
> In the days and months ahead, we will work with other nations to establish this as a new international norm for responsible behaviour in space ...[136]

Canada, New Zealand, Japan, Germany, South Korea, the UK, and Australia soon made similar declarations. Now, a series of unilateral declarations cannot in themselves make a 'new international norm' that binds all states, but they can contribute to generally applicable rules in two ways. First, they count as 'subsequent practice' for the purposes of interpretating the second paragraph of Article I of the Outer Space Treaty, and specifically the 'freedom of exploration and use of space', in a manner that precludes kinetic ASAT weapon tests that create long-lasting debris. Second, they can contribute to the development of customary international law as both state practice and expressions of *opinio juris*.

## 8.2   Kinetic ASAT Weapon Tests and Customary International Law

In the first part of this chapter, we considered whether a ban on kinetic ASAT weapon tests that create long-lasting debris already exists, or might soon develop, as the result of a reinterpretation of the second paragraph of Article I of the Outer Space Treaty. We examined a range of 'subsequent practice' of the parties to that treaty and found that many of them are behaving as if ASAT weapon tests that create long-lasting debris are contrary to the 'freedom of exploration and use of space'. In this second part of the chapter, we consider whether 'state practice' and an accompanying *opinio juris* are contributing to the development of a parallel rule of customary international law.

---

[136] The White House, 'Remarks by Vice President Harris on the ongoing work to establish norms in space', op. cit. As this book was in press the UN General Assembly, on 7 Dec 2022, adopted Res 77/41 by a vote of 155 to 9. It: 'Calls upon all States to commit not to conduct destructive direct-ascent anti-satellite missile tests'.

The main difference between subsequent practice and state practice concerns the range of practice that must be examined. With treaty interpretation, it is the practice of the parties to the treaty that matters, whereas, in the case of customary international law, it is the practice of all states. Again, since nearly all spacefaring states are parties to the Outer Space Treaty,[137] we are saving readers a great deal of repetition by combining the analysis of subsequent practice for the purposes of treaty interpretation with the analysis of state practice for the purposes of customary international law.

Moreover, a treaty reinterpretation and the development of a rule of customary international law can occur in parallel to, and reinforce, each other. It is well established that a rule of customary international law can exist alongside a treaty provision to the same effect. As the International Court of Justice recognised in the *Nicaragua Case*: 'customary international law continues to exist and to apply, separately from international treaty law, even where the two categories of law have an identical content'.[138] Customary international law can even be generated by treaty provisions acting as state practice, as recognised by the same court in the *North Sea Continental Shelf Cases*.[139]

State practice can include both actions and inactions – for example, states saying or doing nothing in response to an action by another state.[140] But state practice cannot create a rule of customary international law on its own. One must also find evidence of *opinio juris*, a belief that the practice in question is legally required, or at least legally relevant.[141]

---

[137] A notable exception is Iran, which has signed but not ratified the treaty.

[138] *Military and Paramilitary Activities in and against Nicaragua (Nicaragua v. United States)*, [1986] ICJ Rep 14 at 96, para. 179.

[139] *North Sea Continental Shelf Cases (Germany v. Denmark; Germany v. Netherlands)*, [1969] ICJ Rep 3 at 41, para. 71.

[140] Iain MacGibbon, 'The scope of acquiescence in international law' (1954) 31 *British Yearbook of International Law* 143; Ian MacGibbon, 'Customary international law and acquiescence' (1957) 33 *British Yearbook of International Law* 115. The consent provided by acquiescence is inferred rather than implied, with many writers arguing that states – as full participants in the international legal system – have consented to 'secondary' procedural rules including the process by which customary international law is made and changed. See, e.g., D'Amato, *The Concept of Custom in International Law*, op. cit. at 41–44; Vaughan Lowe, 'Do general rules of international law exist?' (1983) 9:3 *Review of International Studies* 207; Serge Sur, *La coutume internationale, 2e cahier* (Paris: Librairies techniques, 1990) at 5, 10.

[141] Art. 38(1)(b) of the Statute of the International Court of Justice says the Court shall apply 'international custom, as evidence of a general practice accepted as law'. Statute of the International Court of Justice, 26 June 1945, Can TS 1945 No 7 Art. 38(1)(b)

Often, the same behaviour will constitute both state practice and evidence of *opinio juris*. This will often be the case with statements of national governments. It will also often be the case with positions articulated in the debates, decisions, declarations and statements of the member states of international organisations, whether made individually or collectively.[142] Even domestic laws, and the decisions of national courts, can sometimes constitute state practice and provide evidence of *opinio juris*.[143]

However, not all states are able to contribute equally to the making or changing of a rule of customary international law.[144] Any analysis must consider the vast differences between the technologies and activities of the major spacefaring states, as compared to those of a much larger number of other states. The United States, Russia, China, India, Japan and the 22 member states of the European Space Agency (collectively) have large Space programmes, conduct multiple launches each year, operate large numbers of satellites and conduct deep Space missions. Quite a few other states operate satellites that have been launched on their behalf, while nearly all states benefit from Space-based services

---

(entered into force 24 October 1945); *North Sea Continental Shelf Cases* (*Germany v. Denmark*; *Germany v. Netherlands*), [1969] ICJ Rep 3 at 44, para. 77. The challenge of identifying *opinio juris* when states acquiesce is addressed again (see previous footnote) by the argument that states consent to the process of customary international law, which includes shared understandings – often based on context – as to which behaviour is legally relevant, and which is not. See discussion and sources in Michael Byers, *Custom, Power and the Power of Rules* (Cambridge: Cambridge University Press, 1999) at 147–51.

[142] As Michael Akehurst explained, state practice 'covers any act or statement by a State from which views can be inferred about international law'. Michael Akehurst, 'Custom as a source of international law' (1975) 47:1 *British Yearbook of International Law* 1 at 10.

[143] In 1950, the United Nations International Law Commission included treaties, the decisions of international and domestic courts, national legislation, diplomatic correspondence and the opinions of foreign ministry legal advisers as examples of the various possible forms of state practice. 'Ways and means for making the evidence of customary international law more readily available', in *Yearbook of the International Law Commission 1950*, vol. 2 (New York: UN, 1957) at 368–72.

[144] See generally Byers, op. cit. See also the recent work of the International Law Commission on this topic, which led to General Assembly Resolution 73/203 and the statement, 'The requirement of a general practice, as a constituent element of customary international law, refers primarily to the practice of States that contributes to the formation, or expression, of rules of customary international law'. *Identification of Customary International Law*, GA Res 73/203, UNGAOR, 73rd Sess, UN Doc A/RES/73/203 (2018) at conclusion 4(1).

provided by other states or private companies. Roughly half of all states, most of them in the Global South, have no national Space programmes as such.

Clearly, the actions of the major spacefaring states will feature heavily in any analysis of customary international law within the Space context. So, too, will their considerable engagement in other forms of state practice, including their involvement in treaty making, 'soft law' instruments such as IADC and COPUOS guidelines, diplomatic protests and other public statements. But other, less powerful, spacefaring states also matter, as indeed do non-spacefaring states. - especially when they speak in unison. Like other forms of international law, customary international law is grounded in the consent of states. If non-spacefaring states are opposed to a potential new or changed rule of customary international law, their views - expressed through public statements of various kinds - count as both state practice and evidence of *opinio juris*.

Two qualifying observations must be made here. First, no single state can prevent the development of a new or changed rule of customary international law. Instead, single or very small numbers of opposing states can become 'persistent objectors' to a new or changed rule, in which case they remain bound by the pre-existing rule of customary international law in their relations with other states.[145] Second, non-spacefaring states should pay close attention to developments in international law concerning Space - because silence is often treated as acquiescence during the making and changing of customary international law.[146] For this reason, it is concerning that to date only 102 states have chosen to become members of COPUOS. Although that number has steadily grown, just slightly more than half of the member states of the United Nations are as yet fully engaged in diplomacy and international law-making concerning Space. In some cases, this lack of full engagement reflects the fact that less wealthy states tend to have smaller and less resourced foreign ministries. Civil society can help in this regard: numerous non-governmental organisations have observer status at COPUOS and can monitor developments and alert the broader international community when attempts at legal change are under way.

---

[145] James A Green, *The Persistent Objector Rule in International Law* (Oxford: Oxford University Press, 2016).

[146] DW Greig, 'Reflections on the role of consent' (1989) 12 *Australian Yearbook of International Law* 125 at 137; Robert Kolb, 'Selected problems in the theory of customary international law' (2003) 50:2 *Netherlands International Law Review* 119 at 141.

Another aspect of customary international law is also relevant here: state practice cannot, in the absence of *opinio juris*, either contribute to or impede the development or change of a customary rule. For example, the 2007 Chinese ASAT weapon test might, as state practice, have little impact on customary international law if, as mentioned, the People's Liberation Army did indeed fail to secure the agreement of the Chinese Foreign Ministry in advance of the test or fully inform the Chinese leadership about the likely creation of large amounts of Space debris.[147] Just as significantly, China's response to the concerns expressed by other states did not include an assertion that the test was carried out in a legal way. The fact that subsequent Chinese ASAT weapon tests have avoided striking satellites confirms that the 2007 test lacked the requisite *opinio juris* to impede the development of a new rule of customary international law prohibiting such behaviour.

A similar point can be made about the United States' use of a ship-based missile against a satellite in 2008. Although the United States might or might not have been responding to the Chinese test the previous year, the strike was designed to occur at a very low altitude to prevent or at least reduce the creation of long-lasting Space debris.[148] Moreover, the United States justified its actions on the basis that the satellite was fully loaded with highly toxic thruster fuel and needed to be destroyed for health and environmental protection reasons. These aspects of the US strike thus provide evidence of *opinio juris* in favour of a developing rule not for, but against, ASAT weapon tests that create long-lasting debris.

Then there is the 2019 Indian ASAT weapon test, the most legally relevant aspects of which were the effort to avoid creating Space debris and the assurances to this effect provided to other states in advance. Again, this behaviour constitutes both state practice and evidence of *opinio juris* in favour of a developing rule of customary international law against ASAT weapon tests that create long-lasting debris. Further state practice and evidence of *opinio juris* came from the responses of other states, once it became clear that long-lasting debris had in fact been created.

Finally, there is the 2021 Russian ASAT weapon test, as discussed in the previous chapter and above. The test generated negative responses from many states, including all the major spacefaring states. These responses constitute state practice for the purposes of customary

---

[147] Gill and Kleiber, op. cit.
[148] See discussion, Chapter 7, section 7.6.

international law, while those that address the legality of the test or at
least refer to the legal context will also constitute evidence of *opinio juris*.
Just as importantly, not a single state responded to the Russian ASAT
weapon test by saying that it was an appropriate or internationally
legal action.

Perhaps most importantly, Russia strenuously denied that the test
created dangerous Space debris, with its defence ministry stating,
'emerging fragments at the time of the test and in terms of the orbit's
parameters did not and will not pose any threat to orbital stations,
satellites and space activity'.[149] This constitutes an acknowledgement
that the deliberate creation of long-lasting debris is unacceptable today,
with the denial constituting both state practice and evidence of *opinio
juris* in support of a developing rule of customary international law to
this effect.

### 8.3   Non-kinetic Technologies

Developing rules on kinetic ASAT weapon testing is made easier by the
existence of non-kinetic technologies that can disable satellites or interrupt
their communications without creating Space debris. These can involve
using a laser to 'dazzle' (temporarily interfere with) or 'blind' (permanently damage) the satellite's sensors, sending competing signals to 'spoof'
(misdirect) or 'jam' (interrupt) the satellite's communications, or engaging
in cyber actions such as 'hacking' (gaining access to the computing systems
of the satellite or one of its ground stations).[150] They can also involve
physical interference that does not involve violent impacts. All these
technologies are broadly referred to as counterspace capabilities.

In 1997, the US Navy's Mid-Infrared Advanced Chemical Laser was
tested against a US Air Force satellite.[151] Although it failed in its mission,
a second, lower-power chemical laser was able to temporarily blind the
satellite's sensors.[152] In 2006, China directed a laser at a US satellite,

---

[149] 'Russia's top brass reports on successfully striking defunct satellite in tests', op. cit.

[150] Todd Harrison, Kaitlyn Johnson, Zack Cooper and Thomas G Roberts, 'Escalation
and deterrence in the second space age' (October 2017) Center for Strategic and
International Studies (CSIS) Project Report, *CSIS*, online: www.csis.org/analysis/escal
ation-and-deterrence-second-space-age at 17.

[151] Matthew Mowthorpe, *The Militarization and Weaponization of Space* (Lanham, MD:
Lexington Books, 2004) at 152.

[152] Ibid.

blinding the satellite for a few minutes.[153] Electronic interference has already occurred on occasion in geostationary orbit, when one satellite begins broadcasting on the same frequency as a nearby satellite, but it is not known whether this interference was intended.[154] Jamming is also used by multiple governments to prevent their citizens from accessing uncensored satellite television and Internet,[155] while in 2018 Russia jammed GPS signals to interfere with a NATO naval exercise in the Norwegian Sea.[156] More recently, in February 2022, Russian forces began jamming GPS signals in Ukraine.[157] Commenting on the situation, State Department official Eric Desautels said that 'the United States has our own communications jammer known as the CCS [Counter Communications System] … We think that jamming is probably a normal part of conflict'.[158]

In recent years, Russia, the United States, China and the European Space Agency have all engaged in 'proximity missions' where they manoeuvre one spacecraft close to another spacecraft. Such exercises are often benign, indeed necessary, such as the docking of supply and crew change spacecraft with the International Space Station. Others can

---

[153] Michael P Pillsbury, 'An assessment of China's anti-satellite and space warfare programs, policies and doctrines' (19 January 2007) US–China Economic and Security Review Commission (USCC) Report, *USCC*, online: https://www.uscc.gov/research/assessment-chinas-anti-satellite-and-space-warfare-programs-policies-and-doctrines.

[154] Conference on Disarmament, *Report of the Conference on 'Building the Architecture for Sustainable Space Security' Held on 30–31 March 2006 in Geneva*, UN Doc CD/1786 (22 June 2006); Deborah Housen-Couriel, 'Disruption of satellite transmissions *ad bellum* and *in bello*: Launching a new paradigm of convergence' (2012) 45:3 *Israel Law Review* 431.

[155] See Pavel Velkovsky, Janani Mohan and Maxwell Simon, 'Satellite jamming: A technology primer' (3 April 2019), *CSIS*, online: res.cloudinary.com/csisideaslab/image/upload/v1565982911/on-the-radar/Satellite_Jamming_Primer_FINAL_pdf_bdzxwn.pdf; Peter B de Selding, 'Eutelsat blames Ethiopia as jamming incidents triple', *SpaceNews* (6 June 2014), online: spacenews.com/40818eutelsat-blames-ethiopia-as-jamming-incidents-triple/; Paul Sonne and Farnaz Fassihi, 'In skies over Iran, a battle for control of satellite TV', *Wall Street Journal* (27 December 2011), online: www.wsj.com/articles/SB10001424052970203501304577088380199787036.

[156] Ryan Browne, 'Russia jammed GPS during major NATO military exercise with US troops', *CNN* (14 November 2018), online: www.cnn.com/2018/11/14/politics/russia-nato-jamming/index.html.

[157] Theresa Hitchens, 'Satellite jamming "normal" by militaries during conflict, not peacetime: State Dept. official', *Breaking Defense* (21 March 2022), online: breakingdefense.com/2022/03/satellite-jamming-normal-by-militaries-during-conflict-not-peacetime-state-dept-official.

[158] Ibid.

be explained as involving research into 'on-orbit servicing' or 'active debris removal', with the latter including methods for capturing derelict satellites and other Space debris and sending them into re-entry or graveyard orbits – as discussed above. Of course, the same technology could be used for military purposes, to capture satellites or simply nudge them off course. But while such actions involve physical contact, in the absence of a violent impact they generally do not create Space debris, and for this reason are – for all practical and legal purposes – properly categorised as involving non-kinetic technologies rather than kinetic ASAT weapons.

There is no move to prohibit states from testing non-kinetic technologies against their own satellites, presumably because such tests pose no threat to other Space objects (provided control of the Space object is maintained). As for the deployment of non-kinetic technologies against satellites from other states, such actions are governed by the standard rules of international law on the use of force and on interference falling short of armed force. We will discuss these rules in the section on self-defence below.

As mentioned, cyber actions are another form of non-kinetic technology. Such actions might involve disrupting transmissions, corrupting data or even taking over a satellite's control systems to repurpose, shut down or direct it into a disadvantageous orbit.[159] Some states undoubtedly possess such capabilities already. China is suspected of having engaged in cyber actions against several US satellites, though the US government has never publicly attributed responsibility.[160] In February 2022, Russia was suspected of being behind a cyber action against the satellite company Viasat, which provides Internet connectivity in Ukraine.[161] Cyber actions against Space systems could be a serious problem, but the practical and legal constraints that apply to them are no different to those which apply to cyber actions directed at critical infrastructure on the Earth's surface, such as hospitals or electrical grids.

---

[159] David Livingstone and Patricia Lewis, 'Space, the final frontier for cybersecurity?' (22 September 2016) Chatham House research paper, online: www.chathamhouse.org/2016/09/space-final-frontier-cybersecurity.

[160] Anthony H Cordesman and Joseph Kendall, 'Chinese space strategy and developments' (18 August 2016) CSIS Report, *CSIS*, online: www.csis.org/analysis/china-space-strategy-and-developments at 28.

[161] Hitchens, 'Satellite jamming "normal" by militaries during conflict, not peacetime', op. cit.

For the most part, such actions are governed by the general rules on the use of force, including the right of self-defence.

## 8.4    ASAT Weapons and the Right of Self-Defence

A rule against ASAT weapon testing that creates long-lasting debris would not prohibit all uses of such weapons. Although an unprovoked strike against a foreign-owned or -registered satellite would always be illegal, a state could, conceivably, use an ASAT weapon in self-defence – in response to an armed attack either in Space or, perhaps more likely, on the surface of the Earth itself. The right of self-defence is a rule of customary international law affirmed in Article 51 of the UN Charter, which also applies in Space.[162] However, the right of self-defence includes the criteria of necessity and proportionality, and heightened awareness and concern about Space debris will change how these criteria are applied in the context of ASAT weapons.

Any use of an ASAT weapon against a foreign-owned or -registered satellite will violate the prohibition on the threat or use of force set out in Article 2(4) of the UN Charter, or alternatively, at a lower threshold, violate the general prohibition on interference with property under the

---

[162] Art. III of the Outer Space Treaty reads, 'States Parties to the Treaty shall carry on activities in the exploration and use of outer space, including the moon and other celestial bodies, in accordance with international law, including the Charter of the United Nations'. For recognition that the right of self-defence, specifically, extends to Space, see European External Action Service, 'EU proposal for an international space code of conduct, draft', op. cit., para. 26; Conference on Disarmament, *Letter dated 12 February 2008 from the Permanent Representative of the Russian Federation and the Permanent Representative of China to the Conference on Disarmament addressed to the Secretary-General of the Conference transmitting the Russian and Chinese texts of the draft 'Treaty on Prevention of the Placement of Weapons in Outer Space and the Threat or Use of Force against Outer Space Objects (PPWT)' introduced by the Russian Federation and China*, UN Doc CD/1839 (29 February 2008); Conference on Disarmament, *Letter Dated 10 June 2014 from the Permanent Representative of the Russian Federation and the Permanent Representative of China to the Conference on Disarmament addressed to the Acting Secretary-General of the Conference transmitting the Updated Russian and Chinese texts of the draft Treaty on Prevention of the Placement of Weapons in Outer Space and of the Threat or Use of Force against Outer Space Objects (PPWT) Introduced by the Russian Federation and China*, UN Doc CD/1985 (12 June 2014); United States Department of Defense, 'Directive 3100.10 – space policy' (9 July 1999) at para. 4.2.1.

jurisdiction of a foreign state within customary international law.[163] But this is not the end of the matter, because Article 51 declares,

> Nothing in the present Charter shall impair the inherent right of individual or collective self-defence if an armed attack occurs against a Member of the United Nations, until the Security Council has taken measures necessary to maintain international peace and security.[164]

What constitutes an 'armed attack' with respect to satellites? Under what circumstances would targeting a satellite in response to an armed attack elsewhere, such as on the Earth's surface, fulfil the necessity and proportionality criteria within the right of self-defence? To answer these questions, we must turn again to customary international law – as the word 'inherent' in Article 51 instructs us to do – and, with that, the criteria of necessity and proportionality. How are these criteria applied to ASAT weapons? Is their application changing due to heightened awareness and concern about Space debris?

### 8.4.1   Armed Attack

A military vessel is treated as an extension of a state's territory; as a result, the use of force against such a vessel generally constitutes an 'armed attack' giving rise to a right of self-defence.[165] The use of force against a military satellite, therefore, should have the same consequence, subject to several contextual factors.[166] Whether any particular use of force constitutes an armed attack will, for example, depend upon its gravity. As the

---

[163]   One could, of course, imagine scenarios where the foreign state explicitly consents to the use of an ASAT weapon against its satellite, with the United States' shooting down of its own malfunctioning hydrazine-laden satellite in 2008 providing an example of how such a situation could arise. In such a case, no violation of international law would occur.

[164]   Charter of the United Nations, 26 June 1945, Can TS 1945 No 7 Art. 51 (entered into force 24 October 1945).

[165]   Article 3(d) of the UN General Assembly Resolution on the Definition of Aggression includes 'An attack by the armed forces of a State on the land, sea or air forces . . . of another State.' Definition of Aggression, GA Res 3314(XXIX), UNGAOR, 29th Sess, 2319th Plen Mtg, UN Doc A/RES/29/3314(XXIX) (1974), Art. 3(d); Art. 6 of the North Atlantic Treaty provides for collective self-defence against 'an armed attack on the territory . . . or on the forces . . . of any of the parties.' North Atlantic Treaty, 4 April 1949, 34 UNTS 213 Art. 6 (entered into force 24 August 1949).

[166]   Christopher M Petras, 'The use of force in response to cyber-attack on commercial space systems: Reexamining "self-defense" in outer space in light of the convergence of U.S. military and commercial space activities' (2002) 67:4 Journal of Air Law and Commerce 1213 at 1254–55.

International Court of Justice held in the *Nicaragua Case*, 'It is necessary to distinguish the most grave forms of the use of force (those constituting an armed attack) from other less grave forms.'[167]

This threshold for an armed attack is needed to help prevent small incidents from escalating into large conflicts, since the state being attacked may (if it respects the criteria of necessity and proportionality, as discussed below) respond to an armed attack by using force against elements of the attacking state's military that were not used in the initial attack. To illustrate the point, consider what happens when a missile system on a military vessel from one state 'locks on' to a military aircraft from another state. Although the act of locking on is considered to demonstrate hostile intent and could well constitute a violation of Article 2(4) as a threat to use force, it would not normally constitute an armed attack because the gravity threshold will not have been reached. As a result, the state subject to the locking on will not be entitled to use force in response, either against the military vessel or against additional elements of the other state's armed forces. It may, however, be entitled to engage in non-forceful 'countermeasures' (i.e. measures that would otherwise be contrary to international law, but which are permitted if taken in response to an internationally wrongful act in order 'to procure cessation and reparation').[168]

Border incursions, where a small number of troops briefly cross into the territory of another state, are treated in a similar manner. In the *Nicaragua Case*, the Court explained that 'scale and effects' are what distinguish an armed attack from a 'mere frontier incident'.[169] The gravity requirement was reaffirmed in the subsequent *Oil Platforms Case*, where the Court held that Iran's deployment of a mine without the specific intent to damage a US military vessel was insufficiently grave to constitute an armed attack.[170]

---

[167] *Military and Paramilitary Activities in and against Nicaragua* (*Nicaragua v. United States*), [1986] ICJ Rep 14 at 101, para. 191.

[168] 'Draft Articles on the Responsibility of States for Internationally Wrongful Acts', in *Responsibility of States for Internationally Wrongful Acts*, GA Res 56/83, UNGAOR, 56th Sess, 85th Plen Mtg, UN Doc A/RES/56/83 Annex (28 January 2002) at Part Three, ch. II (Countermeasures), online: undocs.org/en/A/RES/56/83.

[169] *Military and Paramilitary Activities in and against Nicaragua* (*Nicaragua v. United States*), [1986] ICJ Rep 14 at 103, para. 195.

[170] *Oil Platforms* (*Iran v. United States*), [2003] ICJ Rep 161 at 195, para. 72. However, in the same paragraph, the Court expressly did 'not exclude the possibility' that the planting of a mine, which subsequently struck a single military vessel, 'might be sufficient to bring into play "the inherent right of self-defense".'

Now consider how the gravity requirement might apply to actions taken against a foreign military satellite in peacetime. What if the satellite were only temporarily disabled by dazzling or jamming? Or what if the satellite were destroyed by a missile but there was no direct loss of life or significant damage to assets or people on the ground? At first glance, neither situation would reach the gravity threshold for an 'armed attack' and thus trigger the right of self-defence. However, it is unlikely that any use of a kinetic ASAT weapon against a military satellite would be directed solely at the machinery of the satellite. It would, most likely, also be directed at degrading the situational awareness, communications and control of armed forces on the ground – in other words, core military capabilities made possible by the satellite. Since the use of kinetic ASAT weapons against military satellites would almost always be directed at these core capabilities, the scale and effects of their use would almost always reach the gravity threshold and constitute an armed attack.

The same logic – focusing on the scale and effects of the strike on military capabilities, rather than on the satellite itself – could lead to the conclusion that strikes against dual-use satellites might also constitute armed attacks, even if the satellites are owned by private companies. That said, some dual-use satellites might only provide occasional service to military customers. The fact that a satellite is dual-use will not determine whether a strike against it constitutes an armed attack. What matters is the scale and effects of the use of force in terms of its impact on the targeted satellite's contributions to a state's military activities.

The analysis becomes even more difficult with purely civilian satellites that form no part of a state's military apparatus, but in many cases constitute key economic infrastructure or serve as tools for search and rescue and disaster relief. International law has addressed this issue in the past, albeit in the context of oceans rather than Space: a military action against a single civilian vessel will not usually constitute an armed attack, but a military action against an entire merchant fleet could.[171] Similarly, cyber actions against civilian computers can constitute an armed attack, but only if they cause significant economic damage or imperil essential

---

[171] Art. 3(d) of the UN General Assembly Resolution on the Definition of Aggression refers to an attack on the 'marine and air fleets of another State'. For a comprehensive discussion, see Tom Ruys, *Armed Attack and Article 51 of the UN Charter: Evolutions in Customary Law and Practice* (Cambridge: Cambridge University Press, 2010) at 204–11.

state functions such as power grids, hospitals or air traffic control.[172] Applying the same logic to civilian satellites, an action that causes economic damage or imperils essential functions could be considered an armed attack, provided the scale and effects are serious enough.[173]

This conclusion raises further, highly context-dependent issues of redundancy and resilience, since some states are better able than others to withstand the loss of one satellite or a small number of them. Does a state with many civilian satellites have a higher threshold for suffering an armed attack, given that any satellites that are not targeted could continue providing economic and essential services? The answer would seem to be yes, though it is impossible to identify the exact number or percentage of satellites that would need to be lost before a right of self-defence would arise. Each situation will have to be assessed on its own terms, and again, a consideration of scale and effects will be determinative. It is clear, however, that militaries developing satellite constellations to provide redundancy for security purposes are *reducing* the chances of the threshold of 'armed attack' being achieved. Satellite constellations might thus help to prevent escalations for any single attack. Attacks designed to disable entire constellations, though, will need to be considered differently.

Even if a particular use of an ASAT weapon against a satellite constitutes an 'armed attack' and thus triggers a right of self-defence, this does not give the attacked state *carte blanche* in its response. The right of self-defence includes the criteria of necessity and proportionality, which limit the type and scale of any permissible reaction.

### 8.4.2    Necessity and Proportionality

As the International Court of Justice held in the *Nicaragua Case*, 'whether the response to the [armed] attack is lawful depends on

---

[172] James P Farwell and Rafal Rohozinski, 'Stuxnet and the future of cyber war' (2011) 30:1 *Survival* 23 at 30; Burkadze, op. cit.

[173] Christopher M Petras argues that *any* attack on a commercial satellite gives rise to a right of self-defence. Focusing on the fact that the Outer Space Treaty requires each state to maintain a national registry of satellites and retain jurisdiction over them, he writes, 'just as the right of the State to forcefully defend vessels attacked on the high seas extends to all vessels registered in the State (i.e., without regard to whether the vessel that is the target of the attack is a State or private instrumentality), so too must the State's right to defend satellites in space apply equally to all satellites carried on its national registry, including commercial satellites.' Petras, op. cit. at 1256.

observance of the criteria of the necessity and the proportionality of the measures taken in self-defence'.[174] Applying these criteria – essentially balancing the reasons for taking military action against its negative impacts on other states as well as civilians – is always a fact-specific exercise. For this reason, as Christine Gray explains, 'There was until recently relatively little general academic discussion of these essential characteristics of self-defence, as opposed to discussion in application to particular incidents.'[175] It is possible, however, to make two general observations about the application of necessity and proportionality to ASAT weapons that lead to specific conclusions.

First, when it comes to necessity and proportionality applied to ASAT weapons, the armed attack and the response might well occur in different domains. It is possible that both the armed attack and the response will occur in Space. For instance, a satellite operated by one state might be used to attack a satellite operated by another state, and in response the state that has been attacked destroys either the attacking satellite (if it was not initially destroyed) or another satellite operated by the aggressor state. Alternatively, it is also possible that the state that has been attacked in Space will engage in a 'cross-domain' response directed at targets on Earth, such as a satellite ground station belonging to the aggressor state. However, the most likely scenario is that the armed attack will occur on Earth and the responding state will engage in a cross-domain response in Space, targeting one or more satellites to interrupt the aggressor state's situational awareness, communications and control. As we will see below, factors specific to one domain, such as Space debris, can influence the application of the criteria of necessity and proportionality in ways that do not occur in another domain.

---

[174] *Military and Paramilitary Activities in and against Nicaragua (Nicaragua* v. *United States)*, [1986] ICJ Rep 14 at 103, para. 194. See also *Legality of the Threat or Use of Nuclear Weapons*, Advisory Opinion, [1996] ICJ Rep 226 at 245, para. 41; *Oil Platforms (Iran* v. *United States)*, [2003] ICJ Rep 161 at 198, para. 76; *Armed Activities on the Territory of the Congo (Democratic Republic of the Congo* v. *Uganda)*, [2005] ICJ Rep 168 at 223, para. 147.

[175] Christine Gray, *International Law and the Use of Force*, 4th ed. (Oxford: Oxford University Press, 2018) at 159. The recent discussions concern terrorism and other use-of-force situations on the Earth's surface. They include David Kretzmer, 'The inherent right to self-defence and proportionality in jus ad bellum' (2013) 24:1 *European Journal of International Law* 235; Dapo Akande and Thomas Lieflander, 'Clarifying necessity, imminence, and proportionality in the law of self-defense' (2013) 107:3 *American Journal of International Law* 563.

Second, it is not easy to apply the criteria of necessity and proportionality in the context of ASAT weapons. One might, for example, see an analogy between military and dual-use satellites, on the one hand, and remotely-controlled communications towers and radar facilities, on the other, in that taking military action against a satellite could not only disable a potential adversary's situational awareness, communications and control, but also do so without causing direct casualties. However, the analogy does not hold, because military and dual-use satellites have distinctive attributes.

### 8.4.2.1 Military Satellites

The importance of satellites for modern militaries would be difficult to exaggerate. They contribute to core military capabilities such as surveillance, situational awareness, communications and control and targeting. Thus, when engaging in an armed response against Space-based assets, the criteria of necessity and proportionality must be applied to balance the central importance of military and dual-use satellites against the damage caused by an armed attack. Just like destroying the main military headquarters of a state would be a disproportionate response to most armed attacks, destroying military satellites that support surveillance, situational awareness, communications and control and targeting capabilities would also be disproportionate – in most cases. Like the need to consider the scale and effect of the initial military action when determining whether it amounts to an armed attack, one needs to consider whether a responsive disablement or destruction of a satellite or satellites has disproportionate consequences.

Disproportionate consequences might include more than consequences for military capabilities. States direct very large amounts of money and effort to the development, launch, maintenance and protection of their military satellites, money that might otherwise have been spent on more traditional military equipment and personnel.[176] Some US military satellites are as large as a school bus and cost more than US$1

---

[176] For example, the global positioning system cost US$10 billion–12 billion to establish. Rick W Sturdevant, 'NAVSTAR, the global positioning system: A sampling of its military, civil, and commercial impact', in Steven J Dick and Roger D Launius, eds., *Societal Impact of Spaceflight* (NASA: Washington, DC, 2007) 331 at 332, online: history .nasa.gov/sp4801-part2.pdf. Satellites are still added to the system periodically, increasing the overall cost.

billion to construct and launch.[177] Arguably, both the importance of military satellites and their considerable expense must be taken into account with regard to the criteria of necessity and proportionality, so as to avoid introducing an excessively punitive element into any self-defence action involving ASAT weapons.

### 8.4.2.2   Dual-Use Satellites

Many satellites are dual-use in that they serve civilian as well as military functions. For instance, the global positioning system (GPS) was developed for military purposes and is provided by US military satellites. However, it has become an essential service for commercial aviation and shipping, financial services and the personal travel of billions of people, who are connected to the service via their mobile phones and automobiles.[178]

At the same time, militaries constitute some of the largest customers of commercial satellite services.[179] More than 80 per cent of the communications resources currently used by the US military in overseas operations are supplied by commercial satellites. Even some of the bandwidth used for the operation of US armed drones comes from commercial providers.[180] The US military also purchases large amounts of Earth-imaging data collected by commercial satellites, often from other countries. To provide just one example, RadarSat-2, a synthetic aperture radar satellite built and launched by a Canadian private company with financial support from the Canadian government, has been heavily used by the US military – to the point where a bilateral treaty was deemed necessary.[181]

---

[177] According to a 2015 report, Lockheed Martin was seeking to reduce the cost of military satellites to US$1.1 billion each. Andrea Shalal, 'Lockheed seeks to cut costs of U.S. military satellites', *Reuters* (16 March 2015), online: www.reuters.com/article/us-lock heed-satellites-idUSKBN0MC20W20150316.

[178] Sturdevant, op. cit. at 332.

[179] Greg Berlocher, 'Military continues to influence commercial operators', *Satellite Today* (1 September 2008), online: www.satellitetoday.com/publications/via-satellite-magazine/ supplement/2008/09/01/military-continues-to-influence-commercial-operators.

[180] Andrew A Adams and Rachel J McCrindle, *Pandora's Box: Social and Professional Issues of the Information Age* (Chichester: John Wiley & Sons, 2008) at 253.

[181] Agreement between the Government of Canada and the Government of the United States of America Concerning the Operation of Commercial Remote Sensing Satellite Systems, 16 June 2000, Can TS 2000 No 14 (entered into force 16 June 2000), online: www.treaty-accord.gc.ca/text-texte.aspx?id=103522. An unpublished annex to the treaty is rumoured to provide the US with 'priority access' as well as 'shutter control', i.e. the ability to deny access to others.

The US and other militaries also use commercial facilities for downloading data from satellites. The largest such facility, located at 78 degrees north on the Svalbard archipelago, is owned and operated by Kongsberg Satellite Services (KSAT) and connected to the Norwegian mainland by two fibre optic cables that were paid for mostly by the US government.[182] As a whole, the US government is the world's single largest consumer of commercial satellite services, spending US$1.34 billion in 2015.[183] The militaries of other countries are also increasingly dependent on civilian satellites. As David Koplow explains, 'The clear trend around the world is for ever-increasing integration of military and civilian space programs and assets.'[184]

Applying the criteria of necessity and proportionality to dual-use satellites will always be difficult. Will the necessity requirement be fulfilled if a state responds to an armed attack by targeting military communications satellites, while knowing that its opponent can quickly obtain the same services from commercial satellites? Could the proportionality requirement be fulfilled if the commercial satellites are then targeted, given the negative economic and other impacts on civilians that are likely to result? Even attacks on military satellites could have civilian impacts exceeding the limits of proportionality; consider for example the consequences that would result from targeting GPS satellites.

Then there is the issue of satellites used for national technical means (NTMs) of verification under arms control treaties.[185] Although these satellites fulfil other functions, including providing Earth imaging to military forces, targeting one or more of them could be a matter of real

---

[182] Steven M Buchanan, Jayson W Cabell and Daniel C McCrary, *Acquiring Combat Capability through Innovative Uses of Public Private Partnerships* (MBA professional report, Naval Postgraduate School, 2006) at 11–12, online: calhoun.nps.edu/handle/10945/384.

[183] 'US government and military satellite market 2017, forecast to 2022: The US government accounted for $1.34 billion in purchases of commercial satellite services – research and markets', *PRNewswire* (20 January 2017), online: www.prnewswire.com/news-releases/us-government-and-military-satellite-market-2017-forecast-to-2022-the-us-government-accounted-for-134-billion-in-purchases-of-commercial-satellite-services—research-and-markets-300394107.html.

[184] David A Koplow, 'ASAT-isfaction: Customary international law and the regulation of anti-satellite weapons' (2009) 30 *Michigan Journal of International Law* 1187 at 1194.

[185] David A Koplow, 'An inference about interference: A surprising application of existing international law to inhibit anti-satellite weapons' (2014) 35:3 *University of Pennsylvania Journal of International Law* 737 at 768–81.

consequence for international peace and security. Applying the criteria of necessity and proportionality in these circumstances would be challenging indeed.

Once the full range of military and civilian impacts are included in an assessment of ASAT weapons and the right of self-defence, it becomes clear that most satellites are not the necessary, proportionate, low-collateral-effects targets they might seem at first glance. Some satellites are low-impact and therefore unnecessary targets because of the redundancy and resiliency provided by other satellites, including commercial ones. Other satellites are high-collateral-effects targets because of their importance to search and rescue, disaster relief, shipping, aviation, agriculture, fisheries and other core economic activities. Much will depend on what a particular satellite is used for, and in almost all circumstances the criteria of necessity and proportionality will be difficult to fulfil.

### 8.4.2.3   Self-Defence and Space Debris

The military and civilian effects of an ASAT weapon could be greatly magnified if it creates long-lasting Space debris, thus imperilling other satellites and contributing to the risk of knock-on collisions (i.e. the Kessler–Cour-Palais syndrome). In a worst-case scenario, the use of ASAT weapons could result in the loss of access to portions of low Earth orbit, including for Earth-imaging satellites essential for global food security and disaster relief. These and other impacts might well preclude future Space applications that have yet to be discovered and developed, at least for some time. Perhaps most importantly, many of these negative consequences would affect third states – that is, states not involved in the circumstances giving rise to the decision to use an ASAT weapon.

The international responses to the 2007 Chinese, 2019 Indian and 2021 Russian ASAT weapon tests and surrounding changes in the practice of states demonstrate heightened awareness and concern about Space debris, to the point where it becomes difficult to imagine any use of an ASAT weapon in a manner that created long-lasting debris being considered necessary and proportionate. This development, it should be noted, is not driven by any change in the law of self-defence, but rather a change in knowledge that affects its application. In other words, states now know that a single fragmentation event can create tens of thousands of pieces of Space debris that will imperil other satellites, including civilian satellites, dual-use satellites, NTM satellites and satellites belonging to other states, with potentially serious consequences for otherwise uninvolved states, companies and ordinary people. Even India, which sought to test a ground-based missile as an ASAT weapon without creating long-lasting Space debris, failed in that effort and created debris. In the context of necessity and proportionality, this developing knowledge is decisive. Accordingly, most uses of ASAT weapons that involve kinetic impacts are today unlikely to meet the criteria for self-defence under international law.

## 8.5 ASAT Weapons and International Humanitarian Law

The use of kinetic ASAT weapons could also violate the *jus in bello*, which is the body of law that applies to all sides once an armed conflict has begun. Also known as the 'law of armed conflict' or 'international humanitarian law', it seeks to limit the human suffering that is the inevitable consequence of war. The rules of the *jus in bello* are codified within a series of multilateral treaties, primarily The Hague Conventions of 1907, the Geneva Conventions of 1949 and the Additional Protocols of 1977,[186] which are complemented by a parallel body of customary international law.[187]

In this section, we consider how the core *jus in bello* principles of military necessity, distinction and proportionality apply in an increasingly busy orbital environment that includes satellite mega-constellations, Space debris and a growing risk of knock-on collisions. More specifically, we ask whether the heightened risks posed to civilians – through the potential loss of satellites supporting food production, disaster relief and other essential services – lead to the conclusion that the *jus in bello* precludes the extension of ground-based conflicts to Space via kinetic ASAT weapons today.

### 8.5.1 *Military Necessity*

The principle of military necessity is central to the *jus in bello*. In the words of Article 52(2) of Additional Protocol I to the Geneva Conventions, belligerents may lawfully target 'those objects which by their nature,

---

[186] See International Committee of the Red Cross (ICRC), 'Treaties, state parties and commentaries' (2022), *ICRC IHL Databases*, online: ihl-databases.icrc.org/applic/ihl/ihl.nsf.

[187] See ICRC, 'Customary IHL Database' (2005), *ICRC IHL Databases*, online: ihl-databases.icrc.org/customary-ihl/eng/docs/home.

location, purpose or use make an effective contribution to military action and whose total or partial destruction, capture or neutralization, in the circumstances ruling at the time, offers a definite military advantage'.[188] Military satellites could well qualify as such objects under this legal definition. So too might some dual-use satellites, if they are being employed by an adversary for military purposes including communications, situational awareness or targeting.

### 8.5.2  Distinction

The principle of distinction is also central to the *jus in bello*, with Additional Protocol I prohibiting indiscriminate attacks, including those that 'employ a method or means of combat which cannot be directed at a specific military objective'[189] or 'may be expected to cause incidental loss of civilian life, injury to civilians, damage to civilian objects, or a combination thereof, which would be excessive in relation to the concrete and direct military advantage anticipated'.[190]

As Bill Boothby explains,

> a space weapon is unlawful if, when used in its normal or designed circumstances, it cannot be directed at a specific military objective or if its effects cannot be reasonably restricted to the target, and, if as a result, its nature is to strike lawful targets, such as military objectives, and protected persons and objects without distinction.[191]

Boothby concludes that ASAT weapons 'that are likely to cause debris clouds in areas of outer space that civilian satellites may be expected to use are likely to be regarded as breaching the indiscriminate attacks rule'.[192] We further note, as discussed in the previous chapter, that a fragmentation event at one orbital altitude will affect a broad range of altitudes, such that it is infeasible to distinguish military orbital Space from civilian orbital Space. Indeed, such a distinction does not exist.

---

[188] Protocol Additional to the Geneva Conventions of 12 August 1949, and Relating to the Protection of Victims of International Armed Conflicts, 8 June 1977, 1125 UNTS 3 (7 December 1978) (Additional Protocol I).

[189] Ibid., Art. 51(4)(b).

[190] Ibid., Art. 51(5)(b).

[191] Bill Boothby, 'Space weapons and the law' (2017) 93 *International Law Studies* 179 at 187–88.

[192] Ibid. at 208.

### 8.5.3   Proportionality

A third core principle of the *jus in bello* is proportionality – between military advantage on the one hand and the protection of civilians and civilian objects on the other. This long-standing rule of customary international law also finds expression in Additional Protocol I, with Article 57 (2)(a) stipulating that 'those who plan or decide upon an attack shall':

(ii)   take all feasible precautions in the choice of means and methods of attack with a view to avoiding, and in any event to minimizing, incidental loss of civilian life, injury to civilians and damage to civilian objects;

(iii)   refrain from deciding to launch any attack which may be expected to cause incidental loss of civilian life, injury to civilians, damage to civilian objects, or a combination thereof, which would be excessive in relation to the concrete and direct military advantage anticipated.

Today, the principle of proportionality must be applied to ASAT weapons within the context of an increasingly busy orbital environment, Space debris and the risk of knock-on collisions, as well as the severe consequences for civilians that would result from the loss of essential satellite services. We can only conclude that the use of an ASAT weapon in a manner that creates long-lasting Space debris would be disproportionate and therefore illegal under the *jus in bello*.

Sometimes, the principle of proportionality can require states to choose different kinds of weapons, or different targets. APV Rogers provides an example of proportionality at work in the planning of a US airstrike on a hydroelectric dam during the Vietnam War:

> [The dam] was estimated to supply up to 75 per cent of Hanoi's industrial and defense needs. On the other hand, it was thought that if the dam at the site were breached, as many as 23,000 civilians could die, presumably in the resultant floods. President Nixon's military advisers said that if laser-guided bombs were used there was a 90 per cent chance of the mission's being accomplished without breaching the dam. On that basis, the President authorized the attack, which successfully destroyed the electricity generating plant without breaching the dam.[193]

In other words, the principle of proportionality required the United States to choose a different kind of weapon to reduce the risk of civilian

---

[193]   APV Rogers, *Law on the Battlefield*, 3rd ed. (Manchester: Manchester University Press, 2012) at 22, citing W Hays Parks, 'Air war and the law of war' (1990) 32 *Air Force Law Review* 1 at 168–69.

harm. Michael Schmitt has explained how the same rebalancing might operate in the context of ASATs:

> In strikes against space-based assets, the primary concern in this regard is ... creation of space debris. As a result, an attacker might be required to employ a soft kill technique, such as computer network attack, in lieu of kinetic means if the former would result in less collateral damage while yielding a similar military advantage.[194]

As for the choice of targets, the awkwardly worded Article 57(3) of Additional Protocol I states, 'When a choice is possible between several military objectives for obtaining a similar military advantage, the object-ive to be selected shall be that the attack on which may be expected to cause the least danger to civilian lives and to civilian objects.' On this, Schmitt writes,

> As an example, if a satellite can be reliably neutralized through a strike on a ground-based control node in a remote area, it would not be permissible to attack the satellite kinetically and thereby create dangerous space debris. Much like attacks against terrestrial targets, space warfare necessi-tates deconstructing space systems to make such determinations.[195]

Again, the principle of proportionality could rule out the use of ASAT weapons involving violent impacts, and push states towards other types of weapons and other types of targets.

For all these reasons, we agree with the International Committee of the Red Cross. In 2021, the ICRC submitted a position paper to the secretary general of the United Nations in which it wrote, 'When assessing the lawfulness of such [ASAT weapon] attacks, all foreseeable direct and indirect incidental harm or damage to civilian objects must be considered, including when targeting a dual-use space object. The risk of creating debris and its indirect effects ... should also be considered when applying these rules.'[196]

It is difficult to imagine circumstances where a kinetic ASAT weapon could be used without violating the *jus in bello*, which, again, is often referred to as international humanitarian law.

---

[194] Michael N Schmitt, 'International law and military operations in space' (2006) 10 *Max Planck Yearbook of United Nations Law* 89 at 120–21.

[195] Ibid. at 121.

[196] ICRC, 'The potential human cost of the use of weapons in outer space and the protection afforded by international humanitarian law' (2021), position paper submitted by the ICRC to the secretary general of the United Nations on the issues outlined in General Assembly Resolution 75/36, *ICRC*, online: www.icrc.org/en/document/potential-human-cost-outer-space-weaponization-ihl-protection.

# 9

## Conclusion

### Where To from Here?

As is evident throughout this book, the global governance regime for Space is grounded in six decades of co-operation between the Soviet Union and then Russia on the one hand, and the United States and its allies on the other. The Apollo–Soyuz 'handshake in Space',[1] planned during the Vietnam War and carried out shortly after the fall of Saigon, reminds us of the depths of this co-operation. China and India's rapid rise as spacefaring states has occurred within this governance regime.

But continued co-operation is not guaranteed. Significant divisions exist, such as those between the Artemis Program and the Russia–China International Lunar Research Station.[2] The US Congress's ban on direct co-operation between NASA and the China National Space Administration (CNSA), which is known as the 'Wolf Amendment' and dates to 2011, may be helping this division to grow.[3] Moreover, as China, India and Russia form stronger ties in Space, it is reasonable to question whether the long-stable Space governance regime will fracture into two parallel systems, one led by the United States and the other by Russia and China.

The Ukraine War has the potential to be the bifurcation point.

Russia launched a full-scale invasion of Ukraine on 24 February 2022, sending tanks, artillery and some 200,000 soldiers into the country. As Ukrainians fought back, the United States and its allies adopted deep-reaching sanctions. Co-operation between Russia and Western states stopped abruptly, including in the United Nations Security Council where

---

[1] Anatoly Antonov, 'With the Apollo–Soyuz handshake in space, the Cold War thawed a little', *Smithsonian Magazine* (15 July 2020), online: www.smithsonianmag.com/air-space-magazine/apollo-soyuz-cold-war-thawed-little-180975321.

[2] Jeff Foust, 'Russia continues discussions with China on lunar exploration cooperation', *SpaceNews* (4 April 2022), online: spacenews.com/russia-continues-discussions-with-china-on-lunar-exploration-cooperation.

[3] Jeff Foust, 'Defanging the Wolf Amendment', *Space Review* (3 June 2019), online: www.thespacereview.com/article/3725/1.

Russia holds a veto. Vladimir Putin went so far as to threaten the use of nuclear weapons if third states interfered in his 'special military operation'.[4]

As a result of these actions, some elements of international Space co-operation broke down immediately. Russia refused to launch a Soyuz rocket that was already on the pad in Kazakhstan with a payload of satellites owned by the British–Indian company OneWeb.[5] It also cancelled all Soyuz launches from French Guiana, which had for years been conducted in partnership with the French company Arianespace.[6] Then, the European Space Agency (ESA) suspended plans to launch the ExoMars lander on a Russian rocket in September 2022[7] and stopped collaborating with Russia on the Lunar 25, 26 and 27 landers.[8] At the United Nations, Russian diplomats postponed the first substantive session of a new Open Ended Working Group on Reducing Space Threats through Norms, Rules and Principles of Responsible Behaviours by raising a 'litany of procedural complaints'.[9]

Nevertheless, despite these developments, other more established forms of Space co-operation continued, including on the International Space Station (ISS) and with Cospas-Sarsat.

[4] According to a translation of Putin's speech on 24 February 2022, published by the *New York Times*, the Russian president said, 'I would now like to say something very important for those who may be tempted to interfere in these developments from the outside. No matter who tries to stand in our way or all the more so create threats for our country and our people, they must know that Russia will respond immediately, and the consequences will be such as you have never seen in your entire history.' Max Fisher, 'Putin's case for war, annotated', *New York Times* (24 February 2022), online: www.nytimes.com/2022/02/24/world/europe/putin-ukraine-speech.html.

[5] Joey Roulette, 'Russia's isolation on Earth moves up into space' *New York Times* (3 March 2022), online: www.nytimes.com/2022/03/03/science/russia-oneweb-launch.html.

[6] Jeff Foust, 'Russia halts Soyuz launches from French Guiana', *SpaceNews* (26 February 2022), online: spacenews.com/russia-halts-soyuz-launches-from-french-guiana.

[7] Tereza Pultarova, 'European Space Agency suspends Mars rover launch on Russian rocket', *Space.com* (17 March 2022), online: www.space.com/europe-suspends-exomars-mars-rover-launch-russia.

[8] Tereza Pultarova, 'Europe halts moon exploration partnership with Russia, looks to replace Ukraine-built rocket engines', *Space.com* (13 April 2022), online: www.space.com/europe-moon-partnership-russia-ukraine-rocket-engines.

[9] Theresa Hitchens, 'No love from Russia for UN military space norms meeting', *Breaking Defense* (9 February 2022), online: breakingdefense.com/2022/02/no-love-from-russia-for-un-military-space-norms-meeting.

## 9.1 The International Space Station

On 18 March 2022, three Russian cosmonauts arrived on the ISS wearing bright yellow flight suits with blue trim,[10] causing widespread speculation on social media that they were protesting the invasion of Ukraine. Both the Russian space agency (Roscosmos) and the cosmonauts themselves denied the colours were chosen for this reason, and a US astronaut, Mark Vande Hei , also on board, later confirmed their account.[11] But the idea that the suits were a protest still appeals to many, as the ISS is a powerful symbol of peace.

The most expensive structure ever built by humanity, the ISS has been continuously inhabited for more than two decades by Russian cosmonauts and Western astronauts. If you know where and when to look,[12] you can see the ISS sail across the sky, even in light-polluted cities. This beacon of light is a reminder of what humanity can do when it chooses peace and co-operation over conflict and division. Indeed, the ISS was conceived largely as a peace mission.

Russia's involvement in the ISS helped to prevent the proliferation of expertise and technology to terrorists and rogue states following the dissolution of the Soviet Union, while giving Western states access to Russian expertise in long-duration spaceflight as well as reliable Soyuz rockets for resupply and crew rotations. Indeed, for nine years after the Space Shuttle program was shut down in 2011, Soyuz was the only way to access the ISS, including for American astronauts. Even during the Crimean crisis in 2014, the West and Russia co-operated on the ISS.

But the 2022 Ukraine War appears to be different, and it is not immediately clear whether Russian–Western relations in Space will remain as resilient as before.

When US president Joe Biden announced the first round of new sanctions against Russia on 24 February 2022, he emphasised that a ban

---

[10] Kenneth Chang, 'Russia's astronauts enter the space station in yellow and blue flight suits', *New York Times* (18 March 2022), online: www.nytimes.com/2022/03/18/science/russian-astronauts-yellow-blue-flight-suits-ukraine.html.

[11] Christian Davenport, 'NASA astronaut: Russians were "blindsided" by reaction to yellow suits', *Washington Post* (5 April 2022), online: www.washingtonpost.com/technology/2022/04/05/mark-vande-hei-russia-ukraine-yellow-suits.

[12] We recommend NASA's 'Spot the Station' webpage where you can enter your location to see upcoming viewing opportunities: spotthestation.nasa.gov/home.cfm.

on high-tech exports would 'degrade their aerospace industry, including their space program'.[13] Dmitry Rogozin, the director general of Roscosmos, responded by pointing out that the ISS is dependent on propulsion from Russian spacecraft, with regular boosts countering the effect of gas drag and preventing an atmospheric re-entry. 'If you block cooperation with us, who will save the ISS from an uncontrolled de-orbit and fall into the United States or Europe?' Rogozin wrote on Twitter.[14]

While this tweet was written in Rogozin's typical bombastic style, it was not without substance. Should Russia (wilfully or otherwise) stop providing regular boosts, the other ISS partner states would have difficulty keeping the station in orbit. At a minimum, new equipment and procedures would need to be developed at breakneck speeds to prevent an uncontrolled re-entry.

All the ISS partner states, especially Russia, have invested too much money, effort and national prestige into the project to allow it to fail. Russian propaganda has suggested that the Russian modules might be detached, presumably forming their own Space station,[15] but Roscosmos would then have to replace electrical power currently provided by the rest of the ISS. This would probably require a new module – one that would take years to build and launch. Joining the Russian modules to China's new Tiangong Space station is not an option, either, because of a ten-degree difference in the inclination of the orbits.

With these realities in mind, on 25 February 2022 – just one day after Rogozin's threatening tweet – Russia quietly conducted a pre-scheduled boost: to raise the orbit of the ISS, not crash it into the ocean.[16] The following week, Vande Hei made a pre-scheduled return to Earth in a

---

[13] White House, 'Remarks by President Biden on Russia's unprovoked and unjustified attack on Ukraine' (24 February 2022), online: www.whitehouse.gov/briefing-room/speeches-remarks/2022/02/24/remarks-by-president-biden-on-russias-unprovoked-and-unjustified-attack-on-ukraine.

[14] Steve Gorman, 'NASA shrugs off Roscosmos leader's rant over U.S. sanctions and space station', *Reuters* (25 February 2022), online: www.reuters.com/world/europe/nasa-shrugs-off-roscosmos-leaders-rant-over-us-sanctions-space-station-2022-02-26.

[15] India Today Web Desk, 'Russia detaches from International Space Station in propaganda video', *India Today* (6 March 2022), online: www.indiatoday.in/world/russia-ukraine-war/story/russia-detaches-international-space-station-propaganda-video-watch-1921266-2022-03-06.

[16] Mark Garcia, 'Crew works robotics, spacesuits as station orbits higher for crew swap' (28 February 2022), *NASA Space Station*, online (blog): blogs.nasa.gov/spacestation/2022/02.

Soyuz capsule, landing in Kazakhstan, before being whisked off in a NASA aircraft back to the United States.[17]

Shortly after Vande Hei's return, Rogozin took to Twitter again, threatening to suspend ISS co-operation if Western sanctions are not lifted and stating that Roscosmos would decide on a date to end Russia's involvement.[18] While tweets from the director general of Roscosmos cannot be ignored, it should be recognised that, just before Vande Hei and two Russian cosmonauts returned to Earth, three additional cosmonauts – the ones with the yellow flight suits – joined the ISS crew.

It is difficult to overstate the depth of the rift caused by the Ukraine War, or the dangers associated with it. The ISS will eventually be decommissioned and safely de-orbited. Russia might try to make that day come sooner than the United States would like, but it does not yet have another clear and achievable plan for maintaining a Russian presence in Space. Eventually Russia and China might forge their own path forward in low Earth orbit (LEO), and perhaps on the Moon, but for now some co-operation between Russia and Western states continues in Space, and not just on the ISS.

## 9.2   Cospas-Sarsat

Around the globe, individuals venturing into the wilderness for work or recreation are encouraged to carry satellite search-and-rescue beacons, while most ships and airplanes are required to be equipped with such beacons by law. The beacons save literally thousands of lives each year by taking the 'search' out of search and rescue. But they are only able to do so because of a unique international organisation that was created during the Cold War.

The International Cospas-Sarsat Programme co-ordinates the detection and location of activated beacons and ensures that this information is promptly sent to the relevant authority responsible for search and rescue in the territory or maritime zone from which the distress signal is

---

[17] Chelsea Gohd, 'NASA astronaut Mark Vande Hei back on Earth after record-breaking mission', *Space.com* (31 March 2022), online: www.space.com/nasa-astronaut-mark-vande-hei-lands-earth-misses-wife.

[18] Emma Roth, 'Russia says it will suspend ISS cooperation unless sanctions are lifted', *The Verge* (4 April 2022), online: www.theverge.com/2022/4/2/23007575/russia-suspend-iss-cooperation-sanctions-lifted-ukraine-space-nasa.

received.[19] It uses a network of satellites that provide coverage of the entire planet, including five satellites in LEO polar orbits, 17 in geosynchronous orbit, and more than 50 in medium Earth orbit.[20] The instruments providing this service travel as secondary payloads on the satellites, which have other missions such as collecting meteorological data or providing global positioning signals. The satellites in the network are owned and operated by the United States, Russia, France, Canada, India, the European Union and EUMETSAT, the European Organisation for the Exploitation of Meteorological Satellites. Dozens of ground stations track the satellites and receive signals relayed by them, including at least one in China.[21] Information about distress signals and their locations is distributed to search-and-rescue centres in over 200 countries and territories – at no cost to the owners of the beacons or to the governments that conduct the rescues.

The International Cospas-Sarsat Programme was created by Canada, France, the United States and the Soviet Union in 1979.[22] The first rescue took place in 1982, just weeks after the first satellite in the system, COSPAS-1, was launched by the Soviet Union. In 1988, the four states decided to ground the system in a treaty: the International Cospas-Sarsat Programme Agreement.[23] Cospas-Sarsat is now a small but important international organisation with a permanent secretariat located in Montreal.[24] Since 1982, it has helped rescue at least 45,000 people by guiding more than 13,000 search-and-rescue missions worldwide.[25]

---

[19] See Daniel Levesque, ed., *The History and Experience of the International Cospas-Sarsat Programme for Search and Rescue* (Paris: International Astronautical Federation, 2016), online: https://cospas-sarsat.int/images/content/articles/Cospas-Sarsat-Report_ReducedSize_Jan-2019 .pdf.

[20] 'Current space segment status and SAR payloads', *International Cospas-Sarsat Programme*, online: www.cospas-sarsat.int/en/current-space-segment-status-and-sar-payloads.

[21] Levesque, op. cit., Annex 3: 'States and organisations associated with or contributing to the Cospas-Sarsat programme'.

[22] Richard JH Barnes and Jennifer Clapp, 'Cospas-Sarsat: A quiet success story' (1995) 11:4 *Space Policy* 261 at 262–63; Levesque, op. cit.

[23] The International Cospas-Sarsat Programme Agreement, 1 July 1988, 1518 UNTS 209 (entered into force 30 August 1988).

[24] In 2005, Canada concluded a headquarters agreement for the organisation. See 'Arrangement between Canada, the Republic of France, the Russian Federation and the United States of America Regarding the Headquarters of the International Cospas-Sarsat Programme' (2005), *Government of Canada*, online: laws-lois.justice.gc.ca/eng/regula tions/SOR-2005-112/page-2.html.

[25] See the website of the International Cospas-Sarsat Programme: www.cospas-sarsat.int/en.

The most interesting part of the Cospas-Sarsat story is that such a body was established during the Cold War – and that it survived through the extreme tensions of the early 1980s, which included the Soviet invasion of Afghanistan and US President Ronald Reagan's Strategic Defense Initiative ('Star Wars').[26] There are several possible explanations, the most obvious of which is that all of the partner states benefited from the programme, since combining all of their satellites and ground stations provided greater coverage and therefore faster notification of distress signals than would otherwise have been the case. These benefits were significant, since the four founding states have immense maritime zones, including around Canada and Russia's Arctic islands and France and the United States' overseas possessions, as well as global shipping interests. However, this explanation is not sufficient, as Richard Barnes and Jennifer Clapp have explained: 'Search and rescue satellite-aided tracking ... was attractive to the Soviets because of their world-wide fishing fleet *and* because it provided them with an opportunity to demonstrate their space capability in a humanitarian application.'[27]

In other words, Cospas-Sarsat has succeeded because it implements the 'Good Samaritan' principle of assisting strangers in distress. As we explained in Chapter 6, this principle had already been set out in several major treaties, beginning with the International Convention for the Safety of Life at Sea,[28] which was prompted by the sinking of the *Titanic* in 1912 and adopted in 1914. As we write this several months into the Ukraine War, it seems that the humanitarian principle is just as powerful as it was before. Russia remains an active partner in Cospas-Sarsat, with four of its satellites listed as having fully operational search-and-rescue payloads on the programme's website in April 2022.[29] And yet, despite this co-operation, in Cospas-Sarsat and on the ISS, Space is also part of the Ukraine War.

---

[26] Barnes and Clapp, op. cit. at 266.

[27] Ibid. at 263 (emphasis added).

[28] International Convention for the Safety of Life at Sea, 1 November 1974, 1184 UNTS 278 (entered into force 25 May 1980).

[29] The four satellites are *Cospas-14*, *Electro-L No. 2*, *Electro-L No. 3*, and *Louch-5A*. One other Russian satellite is identified as 'available for ground segment testing' while three more are identified as 'under test'. See 'Current space segment status and SAR payloads', op. cit.

### 9.3    Space and the Ukraine War

Russia's anti-satellite (ASAT) weapon test of 15 November 2021 featured prominently in Chapters 7 and 8 of this book. Seen from a post-invasion perspective, the test was clearly meant as a warning to NATO states that Russia was willing to incur the increased risks from Space debris that would result from any use of kinetic ASAT weapons, including risks to its own cosmonauts in orbit. General David Thompson, the vice chief of Space operations for the US Space Force, admitted in April 2022 that this is also how the United States interprets the Russian test today: 'They [the Russians] were also making a very clear statement to us about their intention to threaten our capabilities.'[30] But the ASAT weapon test might not have been Russia's only threat against Space assets.

On 7 January 2022, one of the two subsea cables that connect the satellite ground station on the Svalbard archipelago to the Norwegian mainland suffered a disruption – at a location where the ocean depths drop sharply to about 2,700 metres.[31] After an investigation, the Norwegian police concluded that the disruption was no accident, stating, 'Preliminary investigations strengthen our hypothesis about human impact leading to the loss of communication in one of the cables', they said.

The satellite ground station on Svalbard is the largest such commercial facility in the world, with more than 100 receiving dishes. Located at 78 degrees north, it is perfectly located to download the vast amount of data produced by Earth-imaging satellites in polar orbit, with much of that imagery being used by NATO militaries. Since the second cable was not disrupted, the only loss was one of redundancy, which KSAT, the company that operates the station, was able to restore 11 days later. But there is little doubt that whoever used a submarine to interfere with the cable could have caused a complete disruption, had they wished to do so. It is reasonable to infer that the action was a warning, to Norway as well as other NATO states, that Russia could cut the ground station off at will. Given that this incident occurred just six weeks before the invasion of Ukraine, it should probably be considered as part of the Russian build-up to that action.

---

[30] Tom Costello, 'Russia is jamming U.S.-provided GPS signals in Ukraine, U.S. general says', *NBC News* (11 April 2022), online: www.nbc.com/nbc-nightly-news/video/russia-is-jamming-us-provided-gps-signals-in-ukraine-us-general-says/519685976.

[31] Atle Staalesen, '"Human activity" behind Svalbard cable disruption', *Barents Observer* (11 February 2022), online: thebarentsobserver.com/en/security/2022/02/unknown-human-activity-behind-svalbard-cable-disruption.

At the exact same time as Russia invaded Ukraine, early in the morning of 24 February 2022, a cyber attack was launched against the communications services provided to Ukraine by the US satellite company Viasat.[32] The attack, which exploited a misconfiguration in a VPN (virtual private network) appliance to obtain network access, targeted ground-based modems only. Ultimately, tens of thousands of them were forced off the network. Most of these modems were in Ukraine, but a 'substantial number' were in other parts of Europe.

A few days later, SpaceX sent hundreds of Starlink ground terminals to the Ukrainian government, in an apparent response to the cyber attack on Viasat, as well as to concerns about the vulnerability of ground-based cables. According to Elon Musk, as later corroborated by the director of electronic warfare for the Office of the US Secretary of Defense,[33] Russia proceeded to jam the terminals for hours at a time, until SpaceX responded with a software update that restored normal operability.[34] On 25 March 2022, Musk tweeted, 'Starlink, at least so far, has resisted all hacking & jamming attempts.'[35]

Russia, however, has been able to jam transmissions from the US military's global positioning system (GPS) satellites. In the interview he gave on 11 April 2022, General David Thompson said, 'Ukrainians may not be able to use GPS because there are jammers around that prevent them from receiving and using the signal effectively.'[36]

At the same time, Russia will, of course, be using its own satellites for global positioning, communications, situational awareness and signals intelligence in and around Ukraine. This is not entirely a bad thing, since having reliable information about what NATO forces are doing outside Ukraine could help to prevent the conflict from spreading. Satellites have long played a role in helping to prevent security dilemmas, which is why

---

[32] Viasat Corporate, 'KA-SAT network cyber attack overview' (30 March 2022), *Viasat Inc*, online (blog): www.viasat.com/about/newsroom/blog/ka-sat-network-cyber-attack-overview.

[33] Kate Duffy, 'A top Pentagon official said SpaceX Starlink rapidly fought off a Russian jamming attack in Ukraine', *Business Insider* (22 April 2022), online: www.businessinsider .com/spacex-starlink-pentagon-russian-jamming-attack-elon-musk-dave-tremper-2022-4.

[34] See Elon Musk, 'SpaceX reprioritized to cyber defense & overcoming signal jamming. Will cause slight delays to Starship & Starlink V2' (4 May 2022 at 23:59), *Twitter*, online: twitter.com/elonmusk/status/1499972826828259328.

[35] See Elon Musk, 'Starlink, at least so far, has resisted all hacking & jamming attempts' (25 March 2022 at 19:25), *Twitter*, online: twitter.com/elonmusk/status/1507505633259630599.

[36] Costello, op. cit.

some satellites are protected as 'national means of verification' in certain arms control treaties, as discussed in Chapter 7.

But there is a major difference between satellites used by Russia and those relied upon by Ukraine, in that many of the latter are commercially owned and operated. Viasat, SpaceX and literally dozens of other Western satellite companies are playing significant roles in the Ukraine War. In addition to aiding the Ukrainian military with communications and situational awareness, these companies are lifting the 'fog of war' by making high-resolution images accessible to everyone, and thus exposing indiscriminate attacks, atrocities against civilians, mass graves and Russian denials. More prominently than ever before, this development raises the question, discussed in Chapter 8, of the role of dual-use satellites in armed conflict. Are these commercial satellites now legitimate targets under international humanitarian law (*jus in bello*), which applies notwithstanding Russia's clear violation of the law governing the recourse to force (*jus ad bellum*)? And if commercial Space assets are targeted at any point – perhaps a Russian missile attack on a Western satellite, or the severing of both subsea cables to Svalbard – could this then trigger the right of self-defence?

## 9.4   War in Space Has No Good Outcomes

Given the rapidly growing number of satellites, one might be tempted to think that soon there will be too many satellites for any single military to be able to target all of them, and that this might then have a stabilising effect on global security. And to some extent, it might. For why would a state attack another state's satellites if it could not achieve its military aims and would only open itself up to retaliation? Nor could the deliberate creation of Space debris be seen as a quick path to victory (notwithstanding the self-harm it would cause), since the destruction of one or even dozens of satellites would not immediately initiate a collisional cascade.

However, distribution of Space capabilities across thousands of satellites still does not provide perfect security, since all of LEO remains susceptible to a primitive, but catastrophically effective, ASAT weapon. Indeed, should a state determine that its adversaries would be more disadvantaged by the loss of Space-based assets than it would be, it might decide to deny the use of large swathes of LEO to everyone. This could be quickly achieved using a 'pellet ring' – a potential weapon that was identified during the Cold War and that might have seen further development if the US Strategic Defense Initiative ('Star Wars') had been realised.[37]

A pellet ring involves dispersing a very large number of particles – such as three-millimetre steel balls – into an orbit that ensures many crossings of satellites in a constellation chosen for targeting. A nearly polar orbit dispersal would work well in attacking constellations with low to moderate inclinations, while a low-inclination orbit dispersal would work well against a constellation with polar orbits.

For illustration purposes, let us assume that a pellet weapon disperses 100 million particles with a low change in velocity ($\Delta v$). An approximate timescale for disabling a constellation is found by $T \approx \frac{P}{(2N\sigma)}$, where $N$ is the 'column density' of particles released in the attack (i.e. the number of particles per area);[38] $\sigma$ is the typical satellite cross section, including solar panels; and $P$ is the orbital period at the altitude of the attack. The factor of two arises because each satellite will pass through the ring's column density twice per orbit. To provide some definitive numbers, consider an attack at an altitude of 550 kilometres. Further assume that $\sigma$ is ten square metres and the dispersal of particles is confined to an altitude range of about ten kilometres. In this case, $N$ is approximately 230 per

---

[37] The idea of using pellet swarms, Space mines and Space shrapnel as counterspace measures is well known, with pellets and shrapnel being part of Soviet ASAT weapons, although these were not designed to be pellet ring weapons. See Kurt Gottfried and Richard N Lebow, 'Anti-satellite weapons: Weighing the risks', in Franklin A Long, Donald Hafner and Jeffrey Boutwell, eds., *Weapons in Space*, 1st ed. (New York: WW Norton & Company, 1986) 147. A broad overview of ASAT weapons and ballistic missile defence can be found in the following publication of the Soviet Scientists' Committee for the Defense of Peace against the Nuclear Threat: Yevgeni Velikhov, Roald Sagdeev and Andrei Kokoshin, eds., *Weaponry in Space: The Dilemma of Security*, translated by Alexander Repyev (Moscow: Mir Publishers, 1986). Brief but specific references to pellet rings are found in Tom Wilson, 'Threats to United States space capabilities' (2001), Commission to Assess United States National Security Space Management and Organization, online: spp.fas.org/eprint/article05.html; David Evans, '"Star Wars" Will It Work?' *Chicago Tribune* (23 May 1987) online: https://www.chicagotribune .com/news/ct-xpm-1987-05-24-8702080800-story.html.

[38] If 'column density' is an unfamiliar term, think of the following: Suppose you enter a dusty room, with small dust particles uniformly suspended in air throughout the room. The volume density of the dust in this case is just the number of dust particles in the room divided by the room's volume. Now instead, imagine looking at a wall directly across the room and imagine a column extending from the wall to you. All the particles in the column can be counted to give a number of particles per column area (with the area being the base of the column). If you were to walk across the room to the wall, the total number of dust particles you would go through can be estimated by taking the cross section of your body (your area) times the column density. A satellite going through a pellet ring is similar.

square kilometre. The orbital period is about 96 minutes, so the typical time for a collision with any given satellite is about 15 days. This leads to a reasonable expectation that the entire constellation will be effectively destroyed in about one month, while suffering losses of individual satellites almost immediately.

Of course, the ring of particles takes a bit of time to form. A ring ten kilometres wide would require about a month to fully form through 'orbital shear', which occurs because different altitudes orbit at different rates, thus spreading an initial clump of material into a ring. But because this timescale is similar to the timescale for destroying the constellation, and because impacts will begin as soon as some shearing occurs, the time involved in ring formation is not a major limiting factor.

Finally, we should assess whether 100 million is a plausible number of particles. Assuming randomly packed spheres of about three millimetres in diameter, we would need just over two cubic metres of volume. If they are steel balls, then the mass would be around 11 tonnes – about half the payload capacity (to LEO) of a Proton-M rocket. Even then, coarse sand might be easier, weigh a bit less, and work just as well. At any of these particle sizes, collision avoidance manoeuvres are not practical, since the particles are too small to be tracked. The constellation operator might try to change the altitudes of some or all the satellites to avoid the pellet ring, but doing so would be highly disruptive, likely cause accidents, and thus make the attack at least partially successful.

As the target constellation became disabled, dead satellites would undergo collisions with the existing debris field and add to the effectiveness of the attack. Should the attack be at a sufficiently low altitude, such as 550 kilometres, gas drag would then cause the debris to decay, destroying all satellites below that altitude over time. Moreover, nothing prevents multiple pellet rings from being launched at once, to target different altitudes simultaneously.

If dispersing 100 million steel pellets seems like an unfeasible act, it is not. As we explained in Chapter 6, the United States did something similar in Project West Ford, dispersing nearly 500 million copper dipoles in Earth orbit in 1963, intended for enabling long-range communications.

A pellet ring was deemed impractical during the Cold War because mega-constellations did not exist and a constellation of 'battle stations' for Space-based missile defence initiatives was never realised. But recent changes in Earth's orbital environment and in the use of Space assets could make actions that were impractical in the past more than conceivable today, including not only this but other types of counterspace activities.

We began this book with the observation that long-term solutions to grand challenges in Space require approaches that integrate multiple disciplines. We end with a discussion of the pellet ring, not to be disheartening, but to emphasise the essential nature of transdisciplinary, policy-oriented research. Instead of focusing their efforts on international arms control, policy makers have, until very recently, seized upon satellite constellations as providing protection against ASAT weapons – while overlooking their vulnerability to something as simple as dumping a playground's worth of sand into orbit.

# BIBLIOGRAPHY

Abraham, Kenneth S, 'Environmental liability and the limits of insurance' (1988) 88:5 *Columbia Law Review* 942.

Adams, Andrew A & Rachel J McCrindle, *Pandora's Box: Social and Professional Issues of the Information Age* (Chichester: John Wiley & Sons, 2008).

A'Hearn, Michael F, 'Comets as building blocks' (2011) 49 *Annual Review of Astronomy and Astrophysics* 281.

Ailor, William H, 'Large constellation disposal hazards' (20 January 2020), Center for Space Policy and Strategy, *The Aerospace Corporation*, online: aerospace .org/sites/default/files/2020-01/Ailor_LgConstDisposal_20200113.pdf.

Akande, Dapo & Thomas Lieflander, 'Clarifying necessity, imminence, and proportionality in the law of self-defense' (2013) 107:3 *American Journal of International Law* 563.

Akehurst, Michael, 'Custom as a source of international law' (1975) 47:1 *British Yearbook of International Law* 1.

Albrecht, R & MHJ Dore, 'Toward plans for mitigating possible socio-economic effects due to a physical impact of an asteroid on Earth' (paper delivered at the 7th IAA Planetary Defense Conference, virtual, 26–30 April 2021), online: ui.adsabs.harvard.edu/abs/2021plde.confE..74A/abstract.

Alexander, Emma, 'A 4G network on the Moon is bad news for radio astronomy', *The Conversation* (23 October 2020), online: theconversation.com/a-4g-net work-on-the-moon-is-bad-news-for-radio-astronomy-148652.

Alvarez, Jose E, 'Torturing the law', (2006) 37:2 *Case Western Reserve Journal of International Law* 175.

American Astronomical Society, 'Impact of satellite constellations on optical astronomy and recommendations towards mitigations' (2020), ed. Constance Walker & Jeffrey Hall ['SATCON1 Report'], online: aas.org/sites/default/files/2020-08/ SATCON1-Report.pdf.

American Astronomical Society, 'Report of the SATCON2 Workshop' (2021), ed. Constance Walker & Jeffrey Hall ['SATCON2 Report'], online: baas.aas.org/ pub/2021i0205/release/1.

Anz-Meador, Phillip D, John N Opiela, Debra Shoots & J-C Liou, *History of On-Orbit Satellite Fragmentations*, 15th ed. (Houston: NASA, 2018).

Aoki, Setsuko, 'Satellite ownership transfers and the liability of the launching states' (presentation delivered at the IISL/ECSL Symposium at the 51st Session of the Legal Subcommittee of the Committee on the Peaceful Uses of Outer Space, Vienna, 19 March 2012), online: www.unoosa.org/pdf/pres/lsc2012/symp-03E.pdf.

Arakawa, M, T Saiki, K Wada, K Ogawa, T Kadono, K Shirai et al., 'An artificial impact on the asteroid (162173) Ryugu formed a crater in the gravity-dominated regime' (2020) 368:6486 *Science* 67.

Arbatov, Alexey, 'Arms control in outer space: The Russian angle, and a possible way forward' (2019) 75:4 *Bulletin of the Atomic Scientists* 151.

Aust, Anthony, *Modern Treaty Law and Practice*, 2nd ed. (Cambridge: Cambridge University Press, 2007).

Azzarelli, Tony, 'Obtaining landing licenses and permission to operate LEO constellations on a global basis', in Joseph N Pelton & Scott Madry, eds., *Handbook of Small Satellites* (Cham: Springer, 2020) 1287.

Banner, Stuart, *Who Owns the Sky? The Struggle to Control Airspace from the Wright Brothers On* (Cambridge, MA: Harvard University Press, 2008).

Barbee, Brent W, Megan Bruck Syal, David Dearborn, Galen Gisler, Kevin Greenaugh, Kirsten M Howley et al., 'Options and uncertainties in planetary defense: Mission planning and vehicle design for flexible response' (2008) 143 *Acta Astronautica* 37.

Barbee, Brent, Paul Chodas, Joshua Lyzhoft, Anastassios E Petropoulos, Javier Roa & Bruno Sarli, '2019 PDC mitigation mission options' (paper delivered at the 6th IAA Planetary Defense Conference, College Park, Maryland, 29 April–3 May 2019), *NASA*, online: cneos.jpl.nasa.gov/pd/cs/pdc19/pdc19_briefing4c.pdf.

Barnes, Richard JH & Jennifer Clapp, 'Cospas-Sarsat: A quiet success story' (1995) 11:4 *Space Policy* 261.

Beyerlin, Ulrich & Thilo Marauhn, *International Environmental Law* (Oxford: Hart, 2011).

Billingham, John, William Gilbreath & Brian O'Leary, eds., *Space Resources and Space Settlements* (Moffett Field, CA: NASA Ames Research Center, 1979).

Birnie, Patricia & Alan Boyle, *International Law and the Environment*, 2nd ed. (Oxford: Oxford University Press, 2002).

Boley, Aaron & Michael Byers, 'Satellite mega-constellations create risks in low Earth orbit, the atmosphere and on Earth' (2021) 11 *Scientific Reports* 10642.

Boley, Aaron C, Ewan Wright, Samantha Lawler, Paul Hickson & Dave Balam, 'Plaskett 1.8 metre observations of Starlink satellites' (2022) 163:5 *Astronomical Journal* 199.

Booth, Ken & Nicholas J Wheeler, *The Security Dilemma: Fear, Cooperation, and Trust in World Politics* (Basingstoke: Palgrave Macmillan, 2007).

Boothby, Bill, 'Space weapons and the law' (2017) 93 *International Law Studies* 179.

Bottke, William F & Marc D Norman, 'The late heavy bombardment' (2017) 45 *Annual Review of Earth and Planetary Science* 619.

Bottke, William F, Jr, David Vokrouhlický, David P Rubincam & David Nesvorný, 'The Yarkovsky and YORP effects: Implications for asteroid dynamics' (2006) 34 *Annual Review of Earth and Planetary Sciences* 157.

Bower, Adam, *Norms without the Great Powers: International Law and Changing Social Standards in World Politics* (Oxford: Oxford University Press, 2017).

Brown, PG, JD Assink, L Astiz, R Blaauw, MB Boslough, J Borovička et al., 'A 500-kiloton airburst over Chelyabinsk and an enhanced hazard from small impactors' (2013) 503:7475 *Nature* 238.

Brundtland, Gro H, 'Report of the World Commission on Environmental Development: Our Common Future' (1987), *United Nations*, online: sustainabledevelopment.un.org/content/documents/5987our-common-future.pdf.

Buchanan, Steven M, Jayson W Cabell & Daniel C McCrary, *Acquiring Combat Capability through Innovative Uses of Public Private Partnerships* (MBA professional report, Naval Postgraduate School, 2006), online: calhoun.nps .edu/handle/10945/384.

Bullard, John W, *History of the Redstone Missile System* (Huntsville: Army Missile Command, 1965).

Burkadze, Khatuna, 'A shift in the historical understanding of armed attack and its applicability to cyberspace' (2020) 44:1 *Fletcher Forum of World Affairs* 33.

Burton, Michael G, 'Astronomy in Antarctica' (2010) 18:4 *Astronomy and Astrophysics Review* 417.

Byers, Michael, 'Conceptualising the relationship between jus cogens and erga omnes rules' (1997) 66:2–3 *Nordic Journal of International Law* 211.

   *Custom, Power and the Power of Rules* (Cambridge: Cambridge University Press, 1999).

   'Still agreeing to disagree: International security and constructive ambiguity' (2020) 8:1 *Journal on the Use of Force and International Law* 91.

Byers, Michael & Aaron Boley, 'Cis-lunar space and the security dilemma' (2022) 78:1 *Bulletin of the Atomic Scientists* 17.

Byers, Michael & Cameron Byers, 'Toxic splash: Russian rocket stages dropped in Arctic waters raise health, environmental and legal concerns' (2017) 53:6 *Polar Record* 580.

Byers, Michael, Kelsey Franks & Andrew Gage, 'The internationalization of climate damages litigation' (2017) 7:2 *Washington Journal of Environmental Law and Policy* 264.

Byers, Michael & Georg Nolte, eds., *United States Hegemony and the Foundations of International Law* (Cambridge: Cambridge University Press, 2003).

Byers, Michael & Andrew Simon-Butler, 'Outer space', in Anne Peters, ed., *Max Planck Encyclopedia of Public International Law* (Oxford: Oxford University Press, article last modified October 2020), online: opil.ouplaw.com/view/10.1093/law:epil/9780199231690/law-9780199231690-e1202.

Byers, Michael, Ewan Wright, Aaron Boley & Cameron Byers, 'Unnecessary risks created by uncontrolled rocket reentries' (2022) 6 *Nature Astronomy* 1–5, online: https://www.nature.com/articles/s41550-022-01718-8.

Cameron, Maxwell A, Robert J Lawson & Brian W Tomlin, eds., *To Walk without Fear: The Global Movement to Ban Landmines* (Toronto: Oxford University Press, 1998).

Capone, Francesca, 'Remedies', in Anne Peters, ed., *Max Planck Encyclopedia of Public International Law* (Oxford: Oxford University Press, article last modified October 2020), online: opil.ouplaw.com/view/10.1093/law:epil/9780199231690/law-9780199231690-e1089.

Cheng, Andrew F, P Michel, M Jutzi, AS Rivkin, A Stickle, O Barnouin et al., 'Asteroid impact & deflection assessment mission: Kinetic impactor' (2016) 121 *Planetary and Space Science* 27.

Cheng, Andrew F, P Michel, C Reed, A Galvez & I Carnelli, 'DART: Double Asteroid Redirection Test' (paper delivered at the European Planetary Science Congress, Madrid, September 2012), online: meetingorganizer.copernicus.org/EPSC2012/EPSC2012-935-1.pdf.

Cheng, Andrew F, Andrew S Rivkin, Patrick Michel, Justin Atchison, Olivier Barnouin, Lance Benner et al., 'AIDA DART asteroid deflection test: Planetary defense and science objectives' (2018) 157 *Planetary and Space Science* 104.

Cheng, Bin, 'The legal regime of airspace and outer space: The boundary problem. Functionalism versus spatialism: The major premises' (1980) 5 *Annals of Air & Space Law* 323.

'The 1968 astronauts agreement or how not to make a treaty' (1969) 23 *Year Book of World Affairs* 185.

*Studies in International Space Law* (Oxford: Oxford University Press, 1999).

'United Nations resolutions on outer space: "Instant" international customary law?' (1965) 5 *Indian Journal of International Law* 23.

Chesley, SR & D Farnocchia, 'Apophis impact hazard assessment and sensitivity to spacecraft contact' (paper delivered at the Apophis T-9 Years workshop, virtual, November 2020), Lunar and Planetary Institute Contrib No 2242, *Universities Space Research Association*, online: www.hou.usra.edu/meetings/apophis2020/pdf/2049.pdf.

Chesley, Steven R, Davide Farnocchia, Michael C Nolan, David Vokrouhlický, Paul W Chodas, Andrea Milani et al., 'Orbit and bulk density of the OSIRIS-REx target asteroid (101955) Bennu' (2014) 235 *Icarus* 5.

Chesley, Steven R & Timothy B Spahr, 'Earth impactors: orbital characteristics and warning time', in Michael JS Belton, Thomas H Morgan, Nalin H

Samarasinha & Donald K Yeomans, eds., *Mitigation of Hazardous Comets and Asteroids* (Cambridge: Cambridge University Press, 2004) 22.

Christol, CQ, *The Modern International Law of Outer Space* (New York: Pergamon Press, 1982).

Committee on the Review of Planetary Protection Policy Development Processes, *Review and Assessment of Planetary Protection Policy Development Process* (Washington, DC: The National Academies Press, 2018).

Cordesman, Anthony H & Joseph Kendall, 'Chinese space strategy and developments' (18 August 2016) CSIS report, *Center for Strategic & International Studies* (*CSIS*), online: www.csis.org/analysis/china-space-strategy-and-developments.

Craven, Matthew, *The Decolonization of International Law: State Succession and the Law of Treaties* (Oxford: Oxford University Press, 2009).

Crawford, James & Thomas Viles (1994) 'International law on a given day', in Konrad Ginther, Gerhard Hafner, Winfried Lang, Hanspeter Neuhold & Lilly Sucharipa-Behrmann, eds., *Völkerrecht zwischen normativem Anspruch und politischer Realität: Festschrift für Karl Zemanek* (Berlin: Duncker and Humblot, 1994) 45.

Cronin, John R & Sandra Pizzarello, 'Amino acids in meteorites' (1983) 3:9 *Advances in Space Research* 5.

Dallas, JA, S Raval, JP Alvarez Gaitan, S Saydam & AG Dempster, 'The environmental impact of emissions from space launches: A comprehensive review' (2020) 255 *Journal of Cleaner Production* 120209.

D'Amato, Anthony, *The Concept of Custom in International Law* (Ithaca, NY: Cornell University Press, 1971).

'Custom and treaty: A response to Professor Weisburd' (1988) 21:3 *Vanderbilt Journal of Transnational Law* 459.

'International law, intertemporal problems', in R Bernhardt, ed., *Encyclopedia of Public International Law* (Oxford: Oxford University Press, 1992) 1234.

Dean, Arthur H, *Test Ban and Disarmament: The Path of Negotiation*, 1st ed. (New York: Published for the Council on Foreign Relations by Harper & Row, 1966).

De la Fuente Marcos, C, & R de la Fuenta Marcos, 'Asteroid (469219) 2016 HO3, the smallest and closest Earth quasi-satellite' (2016) 462 *Monthly Notices of the Royal Astronomical Society* 3341.

De Lucia, Vito & Viviana Iavicoli, 'From outer space to ocean depths: The "spacecraft cemetery" and the protection of the marine environment in areas beyond national jurisdiction' (2019) 49:2 *California Western International Law Journal* 345.

De Man, Philip, 'State practice, domestic legislation and the interpretation of fundamental principles of international space law' (2017) 42 *Space Policy* 92.

Dembling, Paul G & Daniel M Arons, 'The Treaty on Rescue and Return of Astronauts and Space Objects' (1968) 9:3 *William and Mary Law Review* 649.

Doboš, Bohumil, Jakub Pražák & Marie Němečková, 'Atomic salvation: A case for nuclear planetary defense' (2020) 18:1 *Astropolitics* 73.

Dones, L, PR Weissman, HF Levison & MJ Duncan, 'Oort Cloud formation and dynamics', in D Johnstone, Fred C Adams, Doug NC Lin, David A Neufeld & Eve C Ostriker, eds., *Star Formation in the Interstellar Medium: In Honor of David Hollenbach, Chris McKee and Frank Shu* (San Francisco: Astronomical Society of the Pacific, 2004) 371.

Draguljić, Gorana, 'Power in numbers: The developing world and the construction of global commons institutions' (2020) 41:12 *Third World Quarterly* 1973.

Drolshagen, Gerhard, Detlef Koschny, Sandra Drolshagen, Jana Kretschmer & Björn Poppe, 'Mass accumulation of Earth from interplanetary dust, meteoroids, asteroids, and comets' (2017) 143 *Planetary and Space Science* 21.

Duke, Michael B, Lisa R Gaddis, Jeffrey Taylor & Harrison H Schmitt, 'Development of the Moon' (2006) 60:1 *Reviews in Mineralogy & Geochemistry* 597.

Dupont, Daniel G, 'Nuclear explosions in orbit' (2004) 290:6 *Scientific American* 100.

Durkee, Melissa J, 'Interstitial space law' (2019) 97:2 *Washington University Law Review* 423.

Egan, Brian J, 'The next fifty years of the Outer Space Treaty' (address delivered at the Galloway Symposium on Critical Issues in Space Law, Washington, DC, 7 December 2016), *US State Department*, online: 2009-2017.state.gov/s/l/releases/remarks/264963.htm.

ESA Space Debris Office, 'ESA's Annual Space Environment Report' (2022) European Space Agency (ESA) Ref No GEN-DB-LOG-00288-OPS-SD, online: www.sdo.esoc.esa.int/environment_report/Space_Environment_Report_latest.pdf.

European Space Policy Institute (ESPI), *EPSI Yearbook 2020: Space Policies, Issues and Trends* (Vienna: ESPI, 2020), online: espi.or.at/publications/espi-yearbook.

Evans, David, '"Star Wars" Will It Work?' Chicago Tribune (23 May 1987) online: https://www.chicagotribune.com/news/ct-xpm-1987-05-24-8702080800-story.html.

Faber, Daniel, *Capitalizing on Environmental Injustice: The Polluter–Industrial Complex in the Age of Globalization* (Lanham, MD: Rowman & Littlefield, 2008).

Farnocchia, D, SR Chesley, PW Chodas, M Micheli, DJ Tholen, A Milani et al., 'Yarkovsky-driven impact risk analysis for asteroid (99942) Apophis' (2013) 224:1 *Icarus* 192.

Farwell, James P & Rafal Rohozinski, 'Stuxnet and the future of cyber war' (2011) 30:1 *Survival* 23.

Feder, Toni, 'Iridium satellite system poses threat to radio astronomy' (1996) 49:11 *Physics Today* 71.

Feynman, RP, 'Volume 2: Appendix F – Personal observations on reliability of shuttle', *Report of the Presidential Commission on the Space Shuttle Challenger Accident* (1986), online: history.nasa.gov/rogersrep/v2appf.htm.

Fladeland, Logan, Aaron C Boley & Michael Byers, 'Meteoroid stream formation due to the extraction of space resources from asteroids' (paper delivered at the First International Orbital Debris Conference, Sugar Land, TX, 9–12 December 2019), online: arxiv.org/pdf/1911.12840.pdf.

Forden, Geoffrey, 'After China's test: Time for a limited ban on anti-satellite weapons' (2007) 37:April *Arms Control Today*, online: www.armscontrol.org/act/2007-04/features/after-chinas-test-time-limited-ban-anti-satellite-weapons.

Freeland, Steven, 'Up, up and . . . back: The emergence of space tourism and its impact on the international law of outer space' (2005) 6:1 *Chicago Journal of International Law* 10.

Freeland, Steven & Ram Jakhu, 'Article II', in Stephan Hobe, Bernhard Schmidt-Tedd, Kai-Uwe Schrogl & Gérardine Meishan Goh, eds., *Cologne Commentary on Space Law: Volume 1, Outer Space Treaty* (Cologne: Carl Heymanns Verlag, 2009) 44.

Friedman, George, John Lewis, Leslie Snively, Lee Valentine, Richard Gertsch & Dennis Wingo, 'Mass drivers for planetary defense' (paper delivered at the Planetary Defense Conference: Protecting Earth from Asteroids, Orange County, California, 23–26 February 2004).

Gardiner, Richard, 'The Vienna Convention rules on treaty interpretation', in Duncan B Hollis, ed., *The Oxford Guide to Treaties*, 2nd ed. (Oxford: Oxford University Press, 2020) 459.

Gardiner, Richard K, *Treaty Interpretation*, 2nd ed. (Oxford: Oxford University Press, 2015).

Gill, Bates & Martin Kleiber, 'China's space odyssey: What the antisatellite test reveals about decision-making in Beijing' (2007) 86:3 *Foreign Affairs* 2, online: www.foreignaffairs.com/articles/china/2007-05-01/chinas-space-odyssey-what-antisatellite-test-reveals-about-decision.

Givel, Michael & Stanton A Glantz, 'The "global settlement" with the tobacco industry: Six years later' (2004) 94:2 *American Journal of Public Health* 218.

Gladman, Brett & Kathryn Volk, 'Transneptunian space' (2021) 59 *Annual Review of Astronomy and Astrophysics* 203.

Gleason, Michael P, 'A short guide for understanding and assessing US space sustainability initiatives' (April 2021), *Center for Space Policy and Strategy*, online: aerospace.org/sites/default/files/2021-04/Gleason_SpaceSustainability_20210407.pdf.

Gordon, Todd & Jeffery R Webber, 'Imperialism and resistance: Canadian mining companies in Latin America' (2008) 29:1 *Third World Quarterly* 63.

Gottfried, Kurt & Richard N Lebow, 'Anti-satellite weapons: Weighing the risks', in Franklin A Long, Donald Hafner & Jeffrey Boutwell, eds., *Weapons in Space*, 1st ed. (New York: W. W. Norton & Company, 1986) 147.

Gray, Christine, *International Law and the Use of Force*, 4th ed. (Oxford: Oxford University Press, 2018).

Green, James A, 'India and a customary comprehensive nuclear test-ban: Persistent objection, peremptory norms and the 123 Agreement' (2011) 51:3 *Indian Journal of International Law* 3.

The Persistent Objector Rule in International Law (Oxford: Oxford University Press, 2016).

'Planetary defense: Near-Earth objects, nuclear weapons, and international law' (2019) 42 *Hastings International and Comparative Law Review* 1.

Grego, Laura & David Wright, 'Incremental progress but no realistic capability: Analysis of the ground-based midcourse missile defense test FTG-15' (2018) Union of Concerned Scientists report, online: www.ucsusa.org/resources/analysis-gmd-missile-defense-test-ftg-15.

Greig, DW, 'Reflections on the role of consent' (1989) 12 *Australian Yearbook of International Law* 125.

Grün, E, HA Zook, H Fechtig & RH Giese, 'Collisional balance of the meteoritic complex' (1985) 62:2 *Icarus* 244

Hall, R Cargill 'Rescue and return of astronauts on Earth and in outer space' (1962) 63:2 *American Journal of International Law* 197.

The Hague International Space Resources Governance Working Group, 'Building blocks for the development of an international framework on space resource activities' (12 November 2019), *Leiden University*, online: www.universiteitleiden.nl/binaries/content/assets/rechtsgeleerdheid/instituut-voor-publiekrecht/lucht-en-ruimterecht/space-resources/bb-thissrwg–cover.pdf.

Hardin, Garrett, 'The tragedy of the commons' (1968) 162:3859 *Science* 1243.

Harrison, Todd, Zack Cooper, Kaitlyn Johnson & Thomas G Robert, 'Escalation and deterrence in the second space age' (October 2017) CSIS Project report, *Center for Strategic & International Studies (CSIS)*, online: www.csis.org/analysis/escalation-and-deterrence-second-space-age.

Henkin, Louis, *The Age of Rights* (New York: Columbia University Press, 1990).

Herz, John H, 'Idealist internationalism and the security dilemma' (1950) 2:2 *World Politics* 157.

Hobe, Stephan, 'Legal aspects of space tourism' (2007) 86:2 *Nebraska Law Review* 442.

Housen-Couriel, Deborah, 'Disruption of satellite transmissions ad bellum and in bello: Launching a new paradigm of convergence' (2012) 45:3 *Israel Law Review* 431.

Humphrey, John, *Human Rights and the United Nations: A Great Adventure* (Epping: Bowker, 1984).

Huzel, Dieter K & Wernher Von Braun, *Peenemünde to Canaveral* (Englewood Cliffs, NJ: Prentice-Hall, 1962).

International Astronomical Union & United Nations Office for Outer Space Affairs, 'Dark and quiet skies for science and society – Report and recommendations' (2021), ed. Constance Walker & Simonetta Di Pippo ['Dark and Quiet Skies I Report'], online: www.iau.org/static/publications/dqskies-book-29-12-20.pdf.

'Dark and quiet skies II for science and society – Working group reports' (2022), ed. Constance Walker & Piero Benvenuti ['Dark and Quiet Skies II Report'], online: doi.org/10.5281/zenodo.5874725.

International Committee of the Red Cross (ICRC), 'The potential human cost of the use of weapons in outer space and the protection afforded by international humanitarian law' (2021), position paper submitted by the ICRC to the secretary general of the United Nations on the issues outlined in General Assembly Resolution 75/36, *ICRC*, online: www.icrc.org/en/document/poten tial-human-cost-outer-space-weaponization-ihl-protection.

International Law Commission, 'Ways and means for making the evidence of customary international law more readily available', in *Yearbook of the International Law Commission 1950, Volume 2* (New York: UN, 1957).

Israel, Brian R, 'Space Resources in the Evolutionary Course of Space Lawmaking' (2019) 113 *AJIL Unbound* 114.

Jarosewich, Eugene, 'Chemical analyses of meteorites: A compilation of stony and iron meteorite analyses' (1990) 25:4 *Meteoritics* 323.

Jennings, Barbara, 'Day 5 at risk critical infrastructure effects' (paper delivered at the 6th Planetary Defense Conference, College Park, Maryland, 29 April–3 May 2019), *NASA*, online: cneos.jpl.nasa.gov/pd/cs/pdc19/pdc19_briefing5c .pdf.

Jervis, Robert, 'Cooperation under the security dilemma' (1978) 30:2 *World Politics* 167.

Jia, Bing Bing 'The relations between treaties and custom' (2010) 9:1 *Chinese Journal of International Law* 81.

Johnson, Christopher D, 'The legal status of megaLEO constellations and concerns about appropriation of large swaths of earth orbit', in Joseph N Pelton & Scott Madry, eds., *Handbook of Small Satellites* (Cham: Springer, 2020) 1337.

Johnson, Lindley N, 'Preparing for planetary defense: Detection and interception of asteroids on collision course with Earth' (paper delivered at the 32nd Space Congress, Cocoa Beach, Florida, 25 April 1995), online: commons.erau.edu/space-congress-proceedings/proceedings-1995-32nd/ april-25-1995/18/.

Johnson, Nicholas L, 'Operation Burnt Frost: A view from inside' (2021) 56 *Space Policy* 101411.

Johnson, Nicholas L & David M Rodvold, *Europe and Asia in Space 1993–1994*, 2nd ed. (Colorado Springs: Kaman Sciences Corp, 1993).

Kaplan, Fred, 'The Pentagon's innovation experiment' *MIT Technology Review* (19 December 2016), online: www.technologyreview.com/2016/12/19/155246/ the-pentagons-innovation-experiment.

Kaur, Karanpreet, 'China's anti-satellite warfare programme: Implications and lessons' (Spring 2014) *Scholar Warrior* 112.

Keith, David W, 'Geoengineering the climate: History and prospect' (2000) 25 *Annual Review of Energy and the Environment* 245.

Kessler, Donald J & Burton G Cour-Palais, 'Collision frequency of artificial satellites: The creation of a debris belt' (1978) 83:A6 *Journal of Geophysical Research* 2637.

Klinkrad, Heiner, *Space Debris: Models and Risk Analysis* (Berlin: Springer, 2006).

Kocifaj, Miroslav, Frantisek Kundracik, John C Barentine & Salvador Bará, 'The proliferation of space objects is a rapidly increasing source of artificial night sky brightness' (2021) 504:1 *Monthly Notices of the Royal Astronomical Society: Letters* L40.

Kolb, Robert, 'Selected problems in the theory of customary international law' (2003) 50:2 *Netherlands International Law Review* 119.

Koplow, David A, 'ASAT-isfaction: Customary international law and the regulation of anti-satellite weapons' (2009) 30 *Michigan Journal of International Law* 1187.

*Death by Moderation: The U.S. Military's Quest for Useable Weapons* (Cambridge: Cambridge University Press, 2009).

'An inference about interference: A surprising application of existing international law to inhibit anti-satellite weapons' (2014) 35:3 *University of Pennsylvania Journal of International Law* 737.

Kováčová, M, R Nagy, L Kornoš & J Tóth, '101955 Bennu and 162173 Ryugu: Dynamical modelling of ejected particles to the Earth' (2020) 185 *Planetary and Space Science* 104897.

Kretzmer, David, 'The inherent right to self-defence and proportionality in jus ad bellum' (2013) 24:1 *European Journal of International Law* 235.

Larson, Erik JL, Robert W Portmann, Karen H Rosenlof, David W Fahey, John S Daniel & Martin N Ross, 'Global atmospheric response to emissions from a proposed reusable space launch system' (2017) 5:1 *Earth's Future* 37.

Lawler, Samantha M, Aaron C Boley & Hanno Rein, 'Visibility predictions for near-future satellite megaconstellations: Latitudes near 50° will experience the worst light pollution' (2022) 163:1 *Astronomical Journal* 21.

Le May, S, S Gehly, BA Carter & S Flegel, 'Space debris collision probability analysis for proposed global broadband constellations' (2018) 151 *Acta Astronautica* 445.

Levesque, Daniel, ed., *The History and Experience of the International Cospas-Sarsat Programme for Search and Rescue* (Paris: International Astronautical Federation, 2016), online: https://cospas-sarsat.int/images/content/articles/Cospas-Sarsat-Report_ReducedSize_Jan-2019.pdf.

Lewis, Hugh G, 'Understanding long-term orbital debris population dynamics' (2020) 7:3 *Journal of Space Safety Engineering* 164.

Li, Shuai, Paul G Lucey, Ralph E Milliken, Paul O Hayne, Elizabeth Fisher, Jean-Pierre Williams et al., 'Direct evidence of surface exposed water ice in the lunar polar regions' (2018) 115:36 *Proceedings of the National Academy of Sciences* 8907.

Liemer, Ross & Christopher F Chyba, 'A verifiable limited test ban for anti-satellite weapons' (2010) 33:3 *Washington Quarterly* 149.

Liou, J-C & NL Johnson, 'Risks in space from orbiting debris' (2006) 311 *Science* 340.

Liou, J-C, M Matney, A Vavrin, A Manis & D Gates, 'NASA ODPO's large constellation study' (2018) 22:3 *Orbital Debris Quarterly News* 4.

Livingstone, David & Patricia Lewis, 'Space, the final frontier for cybersecurity?' (22 September 2016) Chatham House research paper, online: www .chathamhouse.org/2016/09/space-final-frontier-cybersecurity.

Lodders, K, H Palme & HP Gail, 'Abundances of the elements in the solar system', in JE Trümper, ed., *Landolt-Börnstein: Group VI Astronomy and Astrophysics* (Berlin: Springer-Verlag, 2009), Volume 4B, ch. 4.4, 560.

Lodders, Katharina, 'Solar system abundances of the elements', in Aruna Goswami & B Eswar Reddy, eds., *Principles and Perspectives in Cosmochemistry* (Berlin: Springer, 2010) 379.

Longmate, Norman, *Hitler's Rockets: The Story of the V-2s* (London: Hutchinson, 1985).

Lowe, Vaughan, 'Do general rules of international law exist?' (1983) 9:3 *Review of International Studies* 207.

Lu, Edward T & Stanley G Love, 'Gravitational tractor for towing asteroids' (2005) 438:7065 *Nature* 177.

Lyall, Francis & Paul B Larsen, *Space Law: A Treatise* (Farnham: Ashgate Publishing, 2009).

McDowell, Jonathan C, 'The edge of space: Revisiting the Karman Line' (2018) 151 *Acta Astronautica* 668.

MacGibbon, Iain C, 'Customary international law and acquiescence' (1957) 33 *British Yearbook of International Law* 115.

'The scope of acquiescence in international law' (1954) 31 *British Yearbook of International Law* 143.

McNair, Lord, *The Law of Treaties* (Oxford: Oxford University Press, 1961) (republished 1986).

Maddox, John, 'Comfort for next century but one' (1994) 367:6465 *Nature* 681.

Mallowan, Lucas, Lucien Rapp & Maria Topka, 'Reinventing treaty compliant "safety zones" in the context of space sustainability' (2021) 8:2 *Journal of Space Safety Engineering* 155.

Mandaraka-Sheppard, Alexandra, *Modern Maritime Law: Volume 2, Managing Risks and Liabilities*, 3rd ed. (Abingdon: Informa Law from Routledge, 2013).

Marboe, Irmgard, ed., *Soft Law in Outer Space: The Function of Non-binding Norms in International Space Law* (Vienna: Böhlau Verlag, 2012).

Marchisio, Sergio, 'Article IX', in Stephan Hobe et al., eds., *Cologne Commentary on Space Law: Volume 1* (Cologne: Carl Heymanns Verlag, 2009) 169.

Massey, Robert, Sara Lucatello & Piero Benvenuti, 'The challenge of satellite megaconstellations' (2020) 4 *Nature Astronomy* 1022.

Masson-Zwaan, Tanja & Mark J Sundahl, 'The lunar legal landscape: Challenges and opportunities' (2021) 46 *Air and Space Law* 29.

Metzger, Philip T, 'Dust transport and its effects due to landing spacecraft' (paper delivered at the Impact of Lunar Dust on Human Exploration conference, Houston, 11–13 February 2020, LPI Contrib No. 2141), online: www.hou .usra.edu/meetings/lunardust2020/pdf/5040.pdf.

Meyer, Paul, 'Arms control in outer space: Mission impossible or unrealized potential?' (20 October 2020), Canadian Global Affairs Institute Policy Perspective, online: www.cgai.ca/arms_control_in_outer_space_mission_ impossible_or_unrealized_potential.

Millard, William H, 'The legal environment of the British oil industry' (1982) 18:3 *Tulsa Law Review* 394.

Mineiro, Michael C, 'FY-1C and USA-193 ASAT intercepts: An assessment of legal obligations under Article IX of the Outer Space Treaty' (2008) 34:2 *Journal of Space Law* 321.

Moltz, James Clay, 'The changing dynamics of twenty-first-century space power' (2019) 12:1 *Journal of Strategic Security* 15.

The Politics of Space Security, 3rd ed. (Stanford: Stanford University Press, 2019).

Montana, Patricia Grande, 'Watch or report? Livestream or help? Good Samaritan laws revisited: The need to create a duty to report' (2017) 66:3 *Cleveland State Law Review* 533.

Moorhead, Althea V, Aaron Kingery & Steven Ehlert, 'NASA's meteoroid engineering Model 3 and its ability to replicate spacecraft impact rates' (2020) 57:1 *Journal of Spacecraft and Rockets* 160.

Morrison, David, 'Tunguska Workshop: Applying modern tools to understand the 1908 Tunguska impact' (December 2018), NASA Ames Research Center, NASA Technical Memorandum 220174, *NASA*, online: ntrs.nasa.gov/cit ations/20190002302.

Mossop, Joanna, 'Protests against oil exploration at sea: Lessons from the Arctic Sunrise arbitration' (2016) 31:1 *International Journal of Marine and Coastal Law* 60.

Mowthorpe, Matthew, *The Militarization and Weaponization of Space* (Lanham, MD: Lexington Books, 2004).

Nadarajah, Hema, '*Soft law and international relations: The Arctic, outer space, and climate change*' (PhD thesis, University of British Columbia, 2020), online: dx.doi.org/10.14288/1.0394919.

NASA Orbital Debris Program Office, 'West Ford needles: Where are they now?' (2013) 17:4 *Orbital Debris Quarterly* 3, online: orbitaldebris.jsc.nasa.gov/quarterly-news/pdfs/odqnv17i4.pdf.

National Aeronautics and Space Administration (NASA), *'Near-Earth object survey and deflection analysis of alternatives – Report to Congress'* (Washington, DC, NASA, March 2007), online: cneos.jpl.nasa.gov/doc/neo_report2007.html.

National Aeronautics and Space Administration (NASA), 'NASA Confirms DART Mission Impact Changed Asteroid's Motion in Space', NASA (11 Oct 2022), online: https://www.nasa.gov/press-release/nasa-confirms-dart-mission-impact-changed-asteroid-s-motion-in-space.

Neufeld, Michael J, *The Rocket and the Reich: Peenemünde and the Coming of the Ballistic Missile Era* (New York: Simon and Schuster, 1995).

Newman, Christopher, Ralph Dinsley & William Ralston, 'Introducing the law games: Predicting legal liability and fault in satellite operations' (2021) 67:11 *Advances in Space Research* 3785

Nicolls, Michael J & Darren McKnight, 'Collision risk assessment for derelict objects in low-Earth orbit' (paper delivered at the First International Orbital Debris Conference, Sugar Land, TX, 9–12 December 2019), online: www.hou.usra.edu/meetings/orbitaldebris2019/orbital2019paper/pdf/6096.pdf.

O'Neill, GK & HH Kolm, 'High-acceleration mass drivers' (1980) 7 *Acta Astronautica* 1229.

Oppenheim, Jesse, 'Danger at 700,000 feet: Why the United States needs to develop a kinetic anti-satellite missile technology test-ban treaty' (2013) 38:2 *Brooklyn Journal of International Law* 761.

Pardini, Carmen & Luciano Anselmo, 'Uncontrolled re-entries of spacecraft and rocket bodies: A statistical overview over the last decade' (2019) 6 *Journal of Space Engineering Safety* 30.

Park, Seong-Hyeon, Javier Navarro Laboulais, Pénélope Leyland, Stefano Mischler, 'Re-entry survival analysis and ground risk assessment of space debris considering by-products generation' (2021) 179 *Acta Astronautica* 604.

Parks, W Hays, 'Air war and the law of war' (1990) 32 *Air Force Law Review* 1.

Parson, Edward A & David W Keith, 'End the deadlock on governance of geoengineering research' (2013) 339 *Science* 1278.

Patera, Russell P, 'Hazard analysis for uncontrolled space vehicle reentry' (2008) 45:5 *Journal of Spacecraft and Rockets* 1031.

Pelton, Joseph N, 'Global space governance and planetary defense mechanisms', in Nikola Schmidt, ed., *Planetary Defense: Global Space Collaboration for Saving Earth from Asteroids and Comets* (Cham: Springer, 2019) 339.

Pépin, Eugène, 'Legal problems created by the Sputnik' (1957) 4 *McGill Law Journal* 66.

Petras, Christopher M, 'The use of force in response to cyber-attack on commercial space systems: Reexamining "self-defense" in outer space in light of the convergence of U.S. military and commercial space activities' (2002) 67:4 *Journal of Air Law and Commerce* 1213.

Phillips, Catherine & Jaideep Sirkar, 'The International Conference on Safety of Life at Sea, 1914' (Summer 2012) 69:2 *Coast Guard Proceedings: Journal of Safety & Security at Sea* 27, online: www.dco.uscg.mil/Portals/9/DCO%20Documents/ Proceedings%20Magazine/Archive/2012/Vol69_No2_Sum2012.pdf.

Pillsbury, Michael P, 'An assessment of China's anti-satellite and space warfare programs, policies and doctrines' (19 January 2007), US–China Economic and Security Review Commission (USCC) Report, *USCC*, online: www.uscc .gov/research/assessment-chinas-anti-satellite-and-space-warfare-pro grams-policies-and-doctrines.

Pisani, Donald J, "'I am resolved not to interfere, but permit all to work freely": The Gold Rush and American resource law' (Winter 1998–1999) 77:4 *California History* 123.

Poole, Bryce G, 'Against the nuclear option: Planetary defence under international space law' (2020) 45:1 *Air and Space Law* 55.

Price, Richard M, *The Chemical Weapons Taboo* (Ithaca, NY: Cornell University Press, 2007).

Rajagopalan, Rajeswari Pillai, 'Changing space security dynamics and governance debates', in Melissa De Zwart & Stacey Henderson, eds., *Commercial and Military Uses of Outer Space* (Singapore: Springer, 2021) 153.

Raju, Nivedita, 'Russia's anti-satellite test should lead to a multilateral ban' (7 December 2021), *Stockholm International Peace Research Institute*, online: www.sipri.org/commentary/essay/2021/russias-anti-satellite-test-should-lead-multilateral-ban.

Ranganathan, Surabhi, 'The common heritage of mankind: Annotations on a battle', in Jochen von Bernstorff & Philipp Dann, eds., *The Battle for International Law* (Oxford: Oxford University Press, 2019) 35.

Rapp, Lucien & Maria Topka, 'Small satellite constellations, infrastructure shift and space market regulation', in Annette Froehlich, ed., *Legal Aspects around Satellite Constellations, Volume 2* (Cham: Springer, 2021) 1.

Rawls, Meredith L, Heidi B Thiemann, Victor Chemin, Lucianne Walkowicz, Mike W Peel & Yan G Grange, 'Satellite constellation internet affordability and need' (2020) 4:10 *Research Notes of the AAS* 189.

Reichhardt, Tony, 'Asteroid watchers debate false alarm' (1998) 392:6673 *Nature* 215.

Reiland, Nathan, Aaron J Rosengren, Renu Malhotra & Claudio Bombardelli, 'Assessing and minimizing collisions in satellite mega-constellations' (2021) 67:11 *Advances in Space Research* 3755.

Rein, Hanno & David S Spiegel, 'IAS15: A fast, adaptive, high-order integrator for gravitational dynamics, accurate to machine precision over a billion orbits' (2015) 446:2 *Monthly Notices of the Royal Astronomical Society* 1424.

Rein, Hanno, Daniel Tamayo & David Vokrouhlický, 'The random walk of cars and their collision probabilities with Planets' (2018) 5:2 *Aerospace* 57.

Rogers, APV, *Law on the Battlefield*, 3rd ed. (Manchester: Manchester University Press, 2012).

Ross, Martin, Michael Mills & Darin Toohey, 'Potential climate impact of black carbon emitted by rockets' (2010) 37:24 *Geophysical Research Letters* L24810.

Ross, Martin & Patti Sheaffer, 'Radiative forcing caused by rocket engine emissions' (2014) 2:4 *Earth's Future* 117.

Ross, Martin & James Vedda, 'The policy and science of rocket emissions', Center for Space Policy and Strategy, the Aerospace Corporation (2018), online: aerospace.org/sites/default/files/2018-05/RocketEmissions_0.pdf.

Rossi, A, A Petit & D McKnight, 'Short-term space safety analysis of LEO constellations and clusters' (2020) 175 *Acta Astronautica* 476.

Rotola, Giuliana & Andrew Williams, 'Regulatory Context of Conflicting Uses of Outer Space: Astronomy and Satellite Constellations' (2021) 46:4/5 *Air and Space Law* 545.

Ruys, Tom, *Armed Attack and Article 51 of the UN Charter: Evolutions in Customary Law and Practice* (Cambridge: Cambridge University Press, 2010).

Saunders, Philippe C & Charles D Lutes, 'China's ASAT test: Motivations and implications' (2007) 46:3 *Joint Force Quarterly* 39, online: apps.dtic.mil/sti/pdfs/ADA517485.pdf.

Schlüter, Lukas & Aidan Cowley, 'Review of techniques for in-situ oxygen extraction on the Moon' (2020) 181 *Planetary and Space Science* 104753.

Schmidle, Nicholas, *Virgin Galactic and the Making of a Modern Astronaut* (New York: Henry Holt & Co, 2021).

Schmitt, Michael N, 'International law and military operations in space' (2006) 10 *Max Planck Yearbook of United Nations Law* 89.

Schulz, Leonard & Karl-Heinz Glassmeier, 'On the anthropogenic and natural injection of matter into Earth's atmosphere' (2021) 67:3 *Advances in Space Research* 1002.

Scott, Edward RD, 'Chondrites and the Protoplanetary Disk' (2007) 35:1 *Annual Review of Earth and Planetary Sciences* 577.

Seamone, Evan R, 'When wishing on a star just won't do: The legal basis for international cooperation in the mitigation of asteroid impacts and similar transboundary disasters' (2002) 87 *Iowa Law Review* 1091.

Shahar, Keren & Dov Greenbaum, 'Lessons in space regulations from the lunar tardigrades of the Beresheet hard landing' (2020) 4 *Nature Astronomy* 208.

Singh, Pradeep A, 'The two-year deadline to complete the International Seabed Authority's Mining Code: Key outstanding matters that still need to be resolved' (2021) 134 *Marine Policy* 104804.

Slouka, Zdenek, *International Custom and the Continental Shelf* (The Hague: Martinus Nijhoff, 1968).

Sokol, Joshua, 'The fault in our stars: Satellite swarms are threatening the night sky. Is low-Earth orbit the next great crucible of environmental conflict?', *Science* (7 October 2021), online: www.science.org/content/article/satellite-swarms-are-threatening-night-sky-creating-new-zone-environmental-conflict.

Space Mission Planning Advisory Group (SMPAG), 'Planetary defence legal overview and assessment: Report by the Ad-Hoc Working Group on Legal Issues to the Space Mission Planning Advisory Group' (8 April 2020), *ESA*, online: www.cosmos.esa.int/documents/336356/336472/SMPAG-RP-004_1_0_SMPAG_legal_report_2020-04-08.pdf.

Stares, Paul, *The Militarization of Space: U.S. Policy 1945–1984* (Ithaca, NY: Cornell University Press, 1985).

Stickle, AM, ESG Rainey, M Bruck Syal, JM Owen, P Miller, OS Barnouin et al., 'Modeling impact outcomes for the Double Asteroids Redirection Test (DART) mission' (2017) 204 *Procedia Engineering* 116.

Stucke, Maurice & Allen Grunes, *Big Data and Competition Policy* (Oxford: Oxford University Press, 2016).

Sturdevant, Rick W, 'NAVSTAR, the global positioning system: A sampling of its military, civil, and commercial impact', in Steven J Dick & Roger D Launius, eds., *Societal Impact of Spaceflight* (NASA: Washington DC, 2007) 331, online: history.nasa.gov/sp4801-part2.pdf.

Su, Jinyuan, 'The legal challenge of arms control in space', in Cassandra Steer & Matthew Hersch, eds., *War and Peace in Outer Space: Law, Policy, and Ethics* (Oxford: Oxford University Press, 2020) 181.

Sundahl, Mark J, 'The duty to rescue space tourists and return private spacecraft' (2009) 35:1 *Journal of Space Law* 169.

Sur, Serge, *La coutume internationale, 2e cahier* (Paris: Librairies techniques, 1990).

Tellis, Ashley J, 'India's ASAT test: An incomplete success' (15 April 2019), *Carnegie Endowment for International Peace*, online: carnegieendowment.org/2019/04/15/india-s-asat-test-incomplete-success-pub-78884.

Thirlway, Hugh, *Sources of International Law*, 2nd ed. (Oxford: Oxford University Press, 2019).

Turnbull, Timothea, 'Prestige, power, principles and pay-off: Middle powers negotiating international conventional weapons treaties' (2022) 76:1 *Australian Journal of International Affairs* 98.

United Nations Office for Outer Space Affairs (UNOOSA), 'Compendium – Space debris mitigation standards adopted by states and international organizations' (17 June 2021), *UNOOSA*, online: www.unoosa.org/documents/pdf/spacelaw/sd/Space_Debris_Compendium_COPUOS_17_june_2021.pdf.

United Nations Office for Outer Space Affairs (UNOOSA), 'Working paper on the establishment of a working group on space resources submitted by Austria, Belgium, Czech Republic, Finland, Germany, Greece, Slovakia and Spain' (27 May 2021), *UNOOSA*, online: www.unoosa.org/documents/pdf/copuos/lsc/space-resources/Non-paper-on-the-Establishment-of-a-Working-Group-on-Space_Resources-at-COPUOS_LSC-27-05-2021.pdf.

Van Ness, Peter, 'The time has come for a treaty to ban weapons in space' (2010) 34:3 *Asian Perspective* 215.

Vasani, Harsh, 'How China is weaponizing outer space', *The Diplomat* (1 January 2017), online: thediplomat.com/2017/01/how-china-is-weaponizing-outer-space.

Vavrin, D & A Manis, 'CubeSat study project review' (2018) 22: 1 *Orbital Debris Quarterly News* 6.

Velikhov, Yevgeni, Roald Sagdeev & Andrei Kokoshin, eds., *Weaponry in Space: The Dilemma of Security*, translated by Alexander Repyev (Moscow: Mir Publishers, 1986).

Velkovsky, Pavel, Janani Mohan & Maxwell Simon, 'Satellite jamming: A technology primer' (3 April 2019), *Center for Strategic & International Studies (CSIS)*, online: res.cloudinary.com/csisideaslab/image/upload/v1565982911/on-the-radar/Satellite_Jamming_Primer_FINAL_pdf_bdzxwn.pdf.

Venkatesan, Aparna, James Lowenthal, Parvathy Prem & Monica Vidaurri, 'The impact of satellite constellations on space as an ancestral global commons' (2020) 4 *Nature Astronomy* 1043.

Vereschetin, Vladlen S, 'Astronauts', in Anne Peters, ed., *Max Planck Encyclopedia of Public International Law* (Oxford: Oxford University Press, article last modified January 2006), online: opil.ouplaw.com/view/10.1093/law:epil/9780199231690/law-9780199231690-e1141.

Verspieren, Quentin, 'The US Air Force compliance with the Orbital Debris Mitigation Standard Practices' (paper delivered at the Advanced Maui Optical and Space Surveillance Technologies Conference, virtual, 16–18 September 2020), online: amostech.com/TechnicalPapers/2020/Orbital-Debris/Verspieren.pdf.

Volynskaya, Olga A, 'Landmark space-related accidents and the progress of space law' (2013) 62 *Zeitschrift für Luft- und Weltraumrecht* (German Journal of Air and Space Law) 220.

Vraken, Martin, 'Duty to rescue in civil law and common law: Les extrêmes se touchent' (1998) 47:4 *International & Comparative Law Quarterly* 934.

Wheeler, Lorien, Jessie Dotson, Michael Aftosmis, Eric Stern, Donovan Mathias & Paul Chodas, '2021 PDC hypothetical impact exercise: Probabilistic asteroid impact risk, scenario day 3' (paper delivered at the 7th IAA Planetary Defense Conference, virtual, 26–30 April 2021), *NASA*, online: cneos.jpl.nasa.gov/pd/cs/pdc21/pdc21_day3_briefing2.pdf.

Wiegert, Paul, 'On the delivery of DART-ejected material from asteroid (65803) Didymos to Earth' (2019) 1:3 *Planetary Science Journal* 1.

Wiegert, Paul A, 'Meteoroid impacts onto asteroids: A competitor for Yarkovsky and YORP' (2015) 252 *Icarus* 22.

Wilson, James R, 'Regulation of the outer space environment through international accord: The 1979 Moon Treaty' (1990) 2:2 *Fordham Environmental Law Review* 173.

Wilson, Tom, 'Threats to United States space capabilities' (2001), Commission to Assess United States National Security Space Management and Organization, online: spp.fas.org/eprint/article05.html.

Wood, Steven, 'The scope of international obligations to extend rescue assistance to "astronauts" and "personnel" under the Outer Space Treaty and the Return and Rescue Agreement', in Jan Wouters, Philip De Man & Rik Hansen, eds., *Commercial Uses of Space and Space Tourism: Legal and Policy Aspects* (Cheltenham: Edward Elgar, 2017) 44.

Yeomans, DK, S Bhaskaran, SB Broschart, SR Chesley, PW Chodas, TH Sweetser et al., 'Deflecting a hazardous near-Earth object' (paper delivered at the 1st IAA Planetary Defense Conference, Granada, Spain, 27–30 April 2009), *NASA*, online: cneos.jpl.nasa.gov/doc/PDC_proceedings_062009.pdf.

Zedalis, Rex J & Catherine L Wade, 'Anti-satellite weapons and the Outer Space Treaty of 1967' (1978) 8:3 *California Western International Law Journal* 454.

Zhao, Yun, *National Space Law in China* (Leiden: Brill Nijhoff, 2015).

Zissis, Carin, 'China's anti-satellite test' (22 February 2007), *Council on Foreign Relations*, online: www.cfr.org/backgrounder/chinas-anti-satellite-test.

# INDEX

Note: page references in **bold** denote figures and photographs.

Note: dates glossed for the United Nations Space treaties (Liability Convention, Moon Agreement, Outer Space Treaty, Registration Convention, and Rescue Agreement) are the dates the treaties were opened for signatures.

101955 Bennu (asteroid), 1, 133–34, **135**
1997 XF11 (asteroid), 248
2019 OK (asteroid), 192–93
367943 Duende (2012 DA14, asteroid), 251
67P/Churyumov–Gerasimenko (comet), 208, **209**

A-1 (Germany), 258
A-4 (Germany), 258
Abe, Shinzo (prime minister, Japan), 310
ABM Treaty (1972), 261–62, 266, 276
Additional Protocols to the Geneva Conventions (1977), 355–56
Advisory Opinion on the Legality of the Threat or Use of Nuclear Weapons, 244
Agreement Governing the Activities of States on the Moon and Other Celestial Bodies (1979); *see* Moon Agreement (1979)
Agreement on Cooperation on Aeronautical and Maritime Search and Rescue in the Arctic (2011), 225
Agreement on Straddling Fish Stocks and Highly Migratory Fish Stocks (UN, 1995), 163
Amazon/Kuiper, 49, 59, 63, 68

Anderson, Eric (CEO, Space Adventures), 20
Ansari X-Prize, 12
Antarctic Treaty (1959), 103
Anti-Ballistic Missile Treaty (ABM Treaty, 1972), 261–62, 266, 276
anti-satellite weapons; *see also* international humanitarian law (*jus in bello*); *see also* right of self-defence
ASAT ban, 276–81, 320, 333
ASAT development, post-2007, 313
China test (2007), 53, 266, 303, 312–13
China test (2007), responses, 308–9
China test (2013), 313
China test (2014), 313
counterspace capabilities, 335–43
cumulative effects of testing, 308–9
cyber intrusions, 344
deployment and use verification, 275
direct-ascent weapons, 267, 275, 283, 324–25, 335
electronic countermeasures, 335–43
IADC guidelines, 317–18
India test (2019), 61, 267–70, **304–22**
India test (2019), responses, 322
intergovernmental organizations, decisions, 315–16, 319
international law, 303, 322, 324–25, 335–37

Kessler–Cour-Palais syndrome, 263–64
kinetic weapons, 262–63
laser tests, 335–43
Outer Space Treaty (1967), 307
pellet ring, 368–70
proximity missions, 343–44
Russia test (2021), 2–3, 53, 280–81, 303, 324–25
Russia test (2021), responses, 326–31
space debris and kinetic weapons, 262–63, 278, 281–82, 310–13, 315
subsequent practice, 307–9, 313, 315–16, 319, 322, 324–25, 331–32, 337
UN Charter and self-defense, 345–46
unilateral declaration, United States, 335
US test (1985), 265
US test (2008), 267, 313
Apophis (asteroid), 195, 251–57
Arbatov, Alexey, 277
Arch Mission Foundation (USA), 164–65
ArianeSpace, 230, 360
Artemis Accords: China reaction to, 160
duty to consult, 174
Global South reaction to, 161
lunar mining, 130–31
multilateral law-making, 174
national appropriation, 159
political accord, 159
rationale, 159
safety zones, 3, 173–76
safety zones and non-signatory countries, 174
US military, cis-lunar Space, 294–95
US–Russia relationship undermined, 160
Asian Infrastructure Investment Bank, 173
Aso, Taro (foreign minister, Japan), 310
Asteroid Terrestrial-Impact Last Alert System (ATLAS), 190–91
Astra Space, 49

astronomy; *see also* international law, astronomy
anthropogenic occultations, 93
Dark and Quiet Skies, 92
data loss, 92
definition of, 101
ghost streaks, 92
industry guidelines, informal, 93
light pollution, 46–47, **47**, 117–18, **117–18**, 167
mega-constellation visibility, 94–96
mega-constellations, altitude limit concerns, 96
mega-constellations, threats of, 91–92
natural heritage, 97
radio astronomy, 92
satellite brightness, 94–97
transient interference, 92–93
Atlas V (USA), 121
Australia, 159, 311, 328–29
Space (Launches and Returns) Act (2018), 81, 317
Austria, 324–25
Axiom, 17, 45

Barnes, Richard, 365
Behnken, Robert (astronaut, NASA), **158**
Beidou-2 G2 (navigation satellite, China), 314
Belgium, 147
Belt and Road Initiative, 173
Bennu (101955 Bennu, asteroid), 1, 133–34, **135**
*Beresheet* (Israel), 4–5, 164–65
Bezos, Jeff, 1, 14–16, 38, 136
Biden, Joe (president, USA), 185, 361
Bin Cheng, 305
Birnie, Patricia, 182
Blinken, Anthony (Secretary of State, USA), 326
Blue Origin: DRACO program, 34
FAA registration, 36–37
lunar lander contract, 16
New Shepard, 13–14, 16, 33–34, 36–37
Space tourism, 11, 13–14

Boothby, Bill, 356
Borrell, Josep (high representative of
    the European Union for foreign
    affairs and security policy), 327–28
Boyle, Alan, 182
Brahe, Tycho, 91, 196
Branson, Sir Richard, 12–13, 15, 38, 44
Braun, Wernher von, 259
Breakthrough Listen (SETI project),
    297
Bridenstine, Jim (NASA
    Administrator), 20, 131, **158**, 162,
    172, 269–70, 322–23
Butow, Steven, 295

Canada: Artemis Accords signatory,
    159
ASAT test ban proposal,
    276–77
Canadian Space Agency, 317
Kosmos 954 impact, 63–64, 88
Near Earth Object Surveillance
    Satellite (NEOSSat), 250
Pikialasorsuaq (North Water
    Polynya), 64
RadarSat-2, 352
Remote Sensing Space Systems
    Regulations (2007), 317
response to 2007 China ASAT test,
    311
response to 2019 India ASAT test,
    324
terrestrial mining companies, 171
Canadian Space Agency, 317
Canary Islands, 191
Capone, Francesca, 108
Case Concerning the Gabčíkovo-
    Nagymaros Project (1997),
    243
Catalina Sky Survey, 190
Center for NEO Studies (Jet Propulsion
    Laboratory, NASA), 198
Central Bureau for Astronomical
    Telegrams, 248
Chang Zheng 3B (China), 119
Chang'e 4 (lunar lander, China), 291
Chang'e 5 (lunar lander, China), 131
Chelyabinsk event, 187–88, 211

Chicago Convention (1944): aircraft,
    definition, 35
duty to rescue, 28, 31, 33–34, 37, 225
international law, 50
SpaceShipTwo, 37
Chile, 91–92, 191
China: anti-satellite weapon test (2007),
    53, 77, 303
Asian Infrastructure Investment
    Bank, 172–73
Belt and Road Initiative, 172–73
Chang'e 4 (lunar lander), 291
Chang'e 5 (lunar lander), 131
China National Space
    Administration (CNSA), 56–57,
    79, 265, 330–31, 359
collision avoidance maneuver, 56–57
Global Times, 330–31
Interim Measures on Space Debris
    Mitigation and Protective
    Management (2009), 316
lunar mining, 131, 295
PPWT (2014), 274–75
response to 2021 Russia ASAT test,
    330–31
Space-faring state, emergence as,
    172–73
Tiangong Space station, 3, 41, 56–57,
    74–75, 172–73, 270, 325
Working Group on Space Resources,
    177–78
China National Space Administration
    (CNSA), 57, 79, 265, 330, 359
CHPS (USA), 291–92, 298
Chyba, Christopher, 277–78
Cislunar Highway Patrol Satellite
    (CHPS, USA), 291–92, 298
cis-lunar Space: arms control, 298
blurring of intentions, 294
Chang'e 4 (lunar lander, China), 291
Cislunar Highway Patrol Satellite
    (CHPS, USA), 291, 331–32
congestion and debris, 297–98
DARPA, 292, 296, 298
debris removal, 291–92
Defense Deep Space Sentinel (D2S2,
    USA), 291, 298
definition, 290

international law, 295–96
Lagrange points, 290, 297
radio astronomy, 296
Space situational awareness, 290–91, 298
Space-based monitoring, 290
Clapp, Jennifer, 365
*ClearSpace-1* (European Space Agency), 314
CNSA, 57, 79, 265, 330, 359
Commercial Space Launch Competitiveness Act (USA, 2015), 151–54, 157–58
Committee on Space Research (COSPAR), 165
Committee on the Peaceful Uses of Outer Space (COPUOS): Action Team 14 (hazardous NEO investigation), 211
creation of, 6
Declaration of Legal Principles, 78–104
Guidelines for the Long-Term Sustainability of Outer Space Activities (2018, 2019), 83, 121
IAWN and SMPAG recommendations, 211–34
legal subcommittee, 32–33, 177, 179, 276, 323–24
long-term sustainability of Space activities (LST, 2019), 320
membership, 78–81, 315, 340
property rights, 137–38
ROSCOSMOS, 281
soft law, 78–79
Space Debris Mitigation Guidelines (2007, 2010), 78–81, 121, 315, 317, 329
Space mining, 138–39, 147–49
Comprehensive Test Ban Treaty (1996), 226, 232–33
Conference on Disarmament, 274–75, 277, 301, 334
Connor, Larry, 17
Convention against Torture (1984), 79, 282, 332
Convention on Cluster Munitions (2008), 184

Convention on International Civil Aviation (1944); *see* Chicago Convention (1944)
Convention on Registration of Objects Launched into Outer Space (1974), 37
Convention on the Continental Shelf (1958), 170, 230
Convention on the Development, Production, Stockpiling and Use of Chemical Weapons and on Their Destruction (1992), 301
Convention on the International Liability for Damage Caused by Space Objects (1972); *see* Liability Convention (1972)
Convention on the International Regulations for Preventing Collisions at Sea (1972), 70–71
Convention on the Law of the Sea (1982); *see* UNCLOS (1982)
Convention on the Prohibition of the Use, Stockpiling, Production and Transfer of Anti-personnel Mines and on Their Destruction (1997), 129, 184, 301–2
COPUOS; *see* Committee on the Peaceful Uses of Outer Space (COPUOS)
*Corfu Channel Case*, 220–21
COSPAS-1 (satellite), 364
Cour-Palais, Burton, 263, 306
Crew Dragon (SpaceX): astronaut transport to ISS, 16
duty to rescue, 28
environmental impacts, 39–40
passenger/crew distinction, 17–18
rescue capability, 38–39
Space debris, 39–40
Space tourism, 19–20
spacesuits, 15
Cruise, Tom, 20
Cruz, Ted (senator, USA), 151
customary international law: chemical weapons, 300–1
deep seabed mining, 176
duty to rescue, 43
environmental protection, 106–8

customary international law: chemical
weapons (cont.)
    hard law, 78
    international law, source of, 220
    *jus cogens* rules, 282
    kinetic ASAT weapons testing, 282
    multilateral negotiations, 183
    persistent objectors, 340
    precautionary principle, 181–82
    proportionality, 357
    right of self-defence, 237, 240,
        345–46
    silence as acquiescence, 340
    soft law, relationship to, 78–79
    Space mining, 138, 148–49
    state practice, 112, 150, 170, 172, 302,
        316, 322, 325, 338–39, 341–42
    state responsibility, 99, 240–41
    subsequent practice, 153–54, 156,
        159, 168–69, 175, 185, 331–32
    treaty interpretation, 28, 30, 138–39
    Vienna Convention (1969), 24

D2S2 (USA), 292, 298
D'Amato, Anthony, 282, 332
DARPA (USA), 292–94, 296, 298
DART (NASA), 167, 200–1
Deep Impact (comet probe, NASA),
    208
Defence Research and Development
    Organisation (India), 321
Defense Advanced Research Projects
    Agency (DARPA, USA), 292–94,
    296, 298
Defense Deep Space Sentinel (D2S2,
    USA), 292, 298
Delta IV (USA), 126
De Man, Philip, 153–54
Demonstration Rocket for Agile
    Cislunar Operations (DRACO,
    DARPA), 294
Desautels, Eric, 343
Dimorphos (asteroid), 167, 200–1
Disasters Charter, 172
Double Asteroid Redirection Test
    (DART, NASA), 167, 200–1
Downer, Alexander (Foreign Minister,
    Australia), 311

Draft Articles on State Responsibility
    (2001), 240–46
duty to rescue; *see also* under Rescue
    Agreement (1968); *see also* under
    Liability Convention (1972); *see
    also* under Outer Space Treaty
    (1967)
    Agreement on Cooperation on
        Aeronautical and Maritime Search
        and Rescue in the Arctic (2011),
        225
    Chicago Convention (1944), 28, 31,
        33–34, 37, 223–24
    commercial spacecraft, 28
    Cospas-Sarsat, 365
    non-governmental passengers,
        31
    planetary defence, 222–23
    regional and bilateral treaties,
        224
    SAR Convention (1979), 28, 34, 37,
        223–25
    SOLAS Convention (1914), 28, 31,
        33–34, 37, 223–24
    UN Charter, 43
    UNCLOS (1982), 28, 34, 37
    universal applicability, 37

Edgeworth–Kuiper Belt (Kuiper Belt),
    207–8
environmental impacts: aluminium
    from satellite demise, 64
    aluminium from solid fuel rockets,
        67
    anthropogenic atmospheric injection
        modeling, 66–67
    black carbon, 38, 41, 67
    commercial travel, volume, 38
    deorbiting space objects, 63–64
    mesospheric cloud formation, 33–41,
        66–67
    ozone layer depletion, 67
    satellite demise, 64
    Space debris, 41
ESA; *see* European Space Agency (ESA)
European Organisation for the
    Exploitation of Meteorological
    Satellites (EUMETSAT), 364

European Space Agency (ESA):
  collision avoidance maneuver, 57
  COPUOS observer status, 325
  DART test, 237
  debris clearance, 314–15
  European Cooperation for Space
    Standardization, 82, 318–19
  IADC member, 79
  ISO, 82, 318
  response to 2019 India ASAT test,
    324
  *Rosetta/Philae (probe/lander)*, 208,
    **209**
  termination of co-operation with
    Russia, 360
European Union, 310, 320, 327–28; *see
  also* European Space Agency (ESA)
Exxon Valdez, 83, 128

FAA, 14, 36–37
Falcon 9 (SpaceX), 20, 38, 41, 67, 114
FCC: categorical exclusion, claim of,
    110
  collision risk underestimation, 61
  de facto regulator of LEO, 170–71
  orbital shell assignment, 69
  SpaceX, 60
  Starlink, 48–49, 63, 108, 110
  *Viasat, Inc. v. Federal
    Communications Commission*,
    111–12
Federal Aviation Administration
    (FAA), 14, 36–37
Federal Communications Commission
    (FCC); *see* FCC
Fédération Aéronautique
    Internationale, 13
Finland, 324
flag-of-convenience states:
  Luxembourg, 4
  maritime law, 171
  Rwanda, 172
  Space mining, 138–39, 168,
    171–72
  suppression of, 98
Forden, Geoffrey, 278–80
France, 148, 324, 327
Funk, Wally, 16, 32

G77 states, 138
Galileo (EU GPS system), 74
General Atomics, 294
Geneva Conventions (1949), 355
GEO (geosynchronous orbit), 52, 58,
    70, 111–12
Geosynchronous Satellite Launch
    Vehicle, 62–63
Germany, 258–59, 276, 323–24, 329
Glassmeier, Karl-Heinz, 66–67
global positioning system (GPS); *see*
  GPS
Global South, **124**, 125–26, 129, 161,
    171, 176
*Global Times*, 330–31
GPS, 48, 265, 352, 367
Gray, Christine, 350
Green, James, 189, 228–29, 237
Guidelines for the Long-term
    Sustainability of Outer Space
    Activities (COPUOS, 2018, 2019),
    83, 121
Guiding Principles Applicable to
    Unilateral Declarations (UN,
    International Law Commission,
    2006), 336
Guo Wang/StarNet, 49, 59, 185

Hagle, Sharon and Mark, 2
Hague Conventions, The (1907), 355
Hague International Space Resources
    Governance Working Group, The,
    157
Harris, Kamala (vice president, USA),
    335, 337
*Hayabusa-1* probe (Japan), 132
*Hayabusa-2* probe (Japan), 133, 166
Hirano, Yozo (filmmaker), 20
Hitchens, Theresa, 334
Hobe, Stephan, 35
Huang Zhicheng, 331
Hurley, Douglas (astronaut, NASA),
    **158**
Hyten, General John E., 267

IADC: ASAT tests, 277, 307–18
  creation of, 265
  deorbiting guidelines, 74, 84–85

IADC: ASAT tests (cont.)
  kinetic ASAT ban, 279
  law-making, 279
  mega-constellations, 50
  ODMSP influence, 317
  Space debris mitigation guidelines,
    307–18
India, 61–63, 118–19, 304–22, **304–22**
Indonesia, 119–20, 137–38, 178–79
Instituto de Astrofísica de Canarias
    (Canary Islands), 191
Inter-Agency Space Debris
    Coordination Committee (IADC);
    see IADC
International Agreement to Prevent
    Unregulated High Seas Fisheries
    in the Central Arctic Ocean
    (2018), 163, 181
International Asteroid Warning
    Network (IAWN), 211–34
International Astronautical Congress, 159
International Astronomical Union, 93,
    103–4, 186, 219, 248
International Civil Aviation
    Organization (ICAO), 70
International Code of Conduct for
    Outer Space Activities (EU), 320
International Committee of the Red
    Cross, 358
International Convention for the
    Prevention of Pollution from
    Ships (MARPOL Convention,
    1992, 2001, 2003), 128
International Convention for the Safety
    of Life at Sea (1914); see SOLAS
    Convention (1914)
International Convention on Maritime
    Search and Rescue (1979); see SAR
    Convention (1979)
International Cospas-Sarsat
    Programme, 172, 363–65
International Court of Justice: *Advisory
    Opinion on the Legality of the
    Threat or Use of Nuclear Weapons*
    (1996), 244
  *Case Concerning the Gabčíkovo-
    Nagymaros Project* (1997), 243
  *Corfu Channel Case* (1949), 220–21

environmental protection, 107
information sharing, 220–21
judicial decisions, 112
*Nicaragua Case* (1986), 338, 346–47,
    349–50
*North Sea Continental Shelf Cases*
    (1969), 230, 338
*Nuclear Test Cases* (1974), 279,
    335–36
*Oil Platforms Case*, 347
International Covenant on Civil and
    Political Rights (1976), 79
international humanitarian law (*jus in
    bello*): Additional Protocols to the
    Geneva Conventions (1977),
    355–57
  ASAT weapons, 355, 358
  distinction, 355–56
  Geneva Conventions (1949), 355
  military necessity, 355–56
  proportionality, 357
  proportionality and ASAT use,
    357–58
  proportionality, example of,
    357–58
international law, astronomy: Antarctic
    Treaty (1959), 103
  compliance, 112–13
  customary international law, 106
  Declaration of Legal Principles
    (COPOUS), 78–104
  due regard, context, 104–5
  due regard, duty of, 98, 104–6,
    108–9
  due regard, ordinary meaning, 104–5
  environmental impact assessments,
    98, 107–9
  exploration and use, 98–100, 102
  exploration and use, context, 101–2
  exploration and use, ordinary
    meaning, 99–100
International Court of Justice, 106–7
  mega-constellations, 77–78
  negotiation required, 108–9
  precautionary principle (Rio
    Declaration (1992)), 98
  Rio Declaration (1992), 106–7
  Stockholm Declaration (1972), 106

UN Framework Convention on
Climate Change (1992), 106–7
West Ford Experiment (1961-63),
78–104, 238–39
international law, satellite collisions:
causation, 77, 89–90
disaster response, 83, 90–91
enforcement, 87–88
fault, determination of, 84
hard law, 78–79
IADC guidelines, 74, 79
indirect damage (knock-on
collisions), 85–87
ISO standard, 81
liability, 87
liability and national courts, 89
national implementation of
COPUOS guidelines, 81
negligence, determination of, 77
soft law, 78
Space Debris Mitigation Guidelines
(COPUOS, 2007), 78–82
state recovery of compensation,
87–88
sustainability guidelines, 83
tort law, 89
International Law Commission (ILC,
United Nations), 154–55, 240–43,
245, 336
International Maritime Organization,
83, 128
International Organization for
Standardization (ISO), 82, 318
International Space Station (ISS); see
ISS
International Telecommunication
Union (ITU); see ITU
Iridium, 8, 48, 51, 53, 92
Iridium 33 (satellite), 8
Isaacman, Jared, 19–20
ISO, 82, 318
ispace (Japan), 153, 162, 172
Israel, 4–5, 164–65, 255
Israel, Brian, 151–52, 156
ISS: civilian control, 238
collision risks, 74–75, 264, 266,
269–70, 281, 322–23, 325–26, 328
feature film production, 2, 20

Space debris, 3, 41
Space tourism, 2, 11
Italian Space Agency, 237
Italy, 159, 237
Itokawa (asteroid), 132
ITU: communication satellites, orbital
assignments, 70
Constitution and Convention, 71
LEO regulatory role, 70
mega-constellations, 49
mega-constellations, milestone-
based regulatory approach, 71–72
milestone-based regulatory
approach, problems, 72–73, 75–76
Radio Regulations, 71–72
radio spectrum allocation, 71, 172
Radiocommunication Bureau, 71–72
Rules of Procedure, 71–72
Ivanov, Sergei (deputy prime minister,
Russia), 311
Ivory Coast, 118

Jakhu, Ram, 144–45
Japan: Artemis Accords signatory, 159
Hayabusa-1 probe, 132–33
Hayabusa-2 probe, 132–33, 166
ispace, 153, 162, 172
Japanese Space Agency, 132–33
response to 2007 China ASAT test,
310
response to 2021 Russia ASAT test,
329
Space mining, 152
Japanese Space Agency, 132–33
Jet Propulsion Laboratory (NASA), 198
Johndroe, Gordon (NSC
spokesperson), 309–10
Johnson, Christopher, 296

Kamo'oalewa (asteroid), 133–34
Kármán Line, 13, **153**, 259
Kepler Communications, 49, 62, 75
Kepler, Johannes, 91, 196, 207
Kessler, Donald, 263, 306
Kessler–Cour-Palais Syndrome, 54,
263–65, 272, 281, 302, 306
Kongsberg Satellite Services (KSAT,
Norway), 352–53, 366

Koplow, David, 353
Korolev, Sergei Pavlovich, 145
Kosmos 1408 (Russia), 2, 270, 282, 325,
    328, 330
Kosmos 2251 (Russia), 8, 54
Kosmos 954 (Russia), 63–64, 88
K–T extinction event, 186, 257

Lagrange points, 64, **290**, 297
Laliberté, Guy, 44
Law of Treaties, The (McNair, 1986),
    106
LEO; see also mega-constellations
    automated collision avoidance, 8
    debris-generating events, 8
    GEO transfer orbits, 41, 58, 111–12
    inter-operator communications, 55,
        57–58
    Kessler–Cour-Palais Syndrome,
        54–55
    orbital congestion, 7–8, 54–55, **55**,
        58, 75
    satellites prior to 2019, 48
    satellite–satellite collision, 8, 53
    situational awareness, 55, 90
LeoLabs, 90
Liability Convention (1972): absolute
    liability, 34–35
    damage on return, 36
    enforcement, 88–89
    fault, 84
    indirect damage (knock-on
        collisions), 86–87
    planetary defence, 247
    rocket bodies, 121
    space object, 36
    state liability, 87
    suborbital flights, 36–37
Liemer, Ross, 277–78
Liman, Doug, 20
Limited Test Ban Treaty (1963), 226,
    229–30, 239, 261, 298, 302
Liu Jianchao (Foreign Ministry, China),
    312
Liu Jing, 330
Lockheed Martin, 294
Long March (China), 63, 118
low Earth orbit (LEO); see LEO

Lunar Gateway (NASA), 166
Lunar Outpost, 162
Luxembourg: Artemis Accords
    signatory, 159
    flag-of-convenience state, 4
    GEO communication companies,
        152
    ispace Europe, 162
    Space mining, 152, 162, 172

McDowell, Jonathan, 13, 119
McNair, Lord, 106
    The Law of Treaties (1986), 106
Maezawa, Yusaku, 20–21
Marsden, Brian, 248–49
Marvel Space Communications, 49,
    73–74
Masten Space Systems, 162
mega-constellations; see also
    international law, satellite
    collisions; see also ITU; see also
    international law, astronomy; see
    also OneWeb, see also Starlink
    Amazon/Kuiper, 49, 59–60
    Astra Space, 49
    automated collision avoidance,
        59–60
    collision risks, 58–60, 74–75
    congestion/collision mitigation, 62
    consumer electronic product model,
        49, 58
    deorbiting satellites, 58–60
    deorbiting satellites, safety, 63
    differential access, 51
    environmental effects of rocket
        launches, 68–69
    environmental effects of satellite
        demise, 64
    fragmentation events, 60–61
    governance, 49, 70
    Guo Wang/StarNet, 49, 59–60
    ITU regulatory approach, 72
    Kepler Communications, 49
    market change, 51
    Marvel Space Communications, 49,
        73–74
    meteoroid collisions, 60–61
    military use, 50–51

new services, 51
NewSpace, **53**, 54
OneWeb, 49, 59–60
orbital shell assignment, 70
radio astronomy, interference with,
    91–93
satellites, brightness mitigation, 47,
    91–92
satellites, light pollution, 46–47, **47**
Space debris, 51
SpaceX, collision assessments, 60
user base, 50
*Viasat, Inc. v. Federal Communications
    Commission*, 111–12
mesopause, 12
mesosphere, 12, 66
Microsat-R (ASAT target, India), 267,
    **268**
Minor Planet Center (International
    Astronomical Union), 219
Montreal Protocol on Substances that
    Deplete the Ozone Layer (1987),
    127
Moon Agreement (1979), 144–45,
    149–50, 158, 180
Musk, Elon, 16, 41, 52, 66, 246, 367

Nair, Madhavan (Indian Space
    Research Organization), 310–11
NASA; *see also* Artemis Accords
    Catalina Sky Survey, 190
    cometary impact scenario, 210
    Commercial Crew Program, 20
    Deep Impact, 208
    Double Asteroid Redirection Test
        (DART), 167, 200–1, 211–37
    IADC membership, 79
    Jet Propulsion Laboratory, 198
    Lunar Gateway, 166
    lunar lander contract, 16
    lunar regolith purchase, 131–32,
        161–62, 172
    Near-Earth Object Surveillance
        Mission (NEOSM), 192
    NEOWISE, 191–92
    Orbital Debris Mitigation Standard
        Practices (ODMSP, 2001), 81,
        120–21, 317

*OSIRIS-REx* probe, 133, 136
Pan-STARRS Project, 190
SpaceX, collision avoidance co-
    ordination, 57–58
US ASAT test (1985), objections to,
    265
Wolf Amendment (2011), 359
National Aeronautics and Space
    Administration (NASA); *see*
    NASA
National Environmental Policy Act
    (USA), 110–11
National Transportation Safety Board
    (USA), 128
NATO, 326–27, 343, 366
Near Earth Object Surveillance Satellite
    (NEOSSat, Canada), 250
Near-Earth Object Surveillance Mission
    (NEOSM, NASA), 192
NED: advantages of use, 203
    challenges to use, 203
    claim of necessity, 226
    Comprehensive Test Ban Treaty
        (1996), 226, 232–33
    deflection method, 202
    Limited Test Ban Treaty (1963), 226,
        229–30, 239
    NEO rendezvous, 202
    *North Sea Continental Shelf Cases*,
        230
    Oberth effect, 203
    Outer Space Treaty (1967), 226
    Space-based nuclear weapons tests,
        230
    Space-based testing moratorium,
        231–32
    UN Security Council authorisation,
        226
Nelson, Bill (NASA Administrator),
    326
NEOWISE (comet), 191–92
NEOWISE (NASA satellite), 191–92
Netherlands, 324
New Shepard (Blue Origin), 14, 16, 33,
    37
NewSpace, **53**, 54, 152, 255
*Nicaragua Case*, 338, 346–47, 349–50
NOM4D, **293**, 293–94, 296, 298

North Atlantic Council (NATO), 327
North Sea Continental Shelf Cases, 230, 338
Norway, 9, 352–53, 366
Novel Orbital and Moon Manufacturing, Materials and Mass-Efficient Design (NOM4D, DARPA), 293–94, **293**, 296, 298
nuclear explosive device (NED); see NED
*Nuclear Test Cases*, 279, 335–36

Obama, Barack (president, USA), 151
Oberth effect, 203
Office for Outer Space Affairs, 93
*Oil Platforms Case*, 347
OneWeb: collision avoidance, 60
  collision risks, 75
  environmental impact statements, 99
  Geosynchronous Satellite Launch Vehicle, use of, 62–63
  Greg Wyler (CEO), 74–75
  mega-constellation, 49, 59
  Soyuz rocket, use of, 62–63
  Ukrainian war, 360
Oort Cloud, 207
Operation Burnt Frost, 64
Orbital Debris Mitigation Standard Practices (ODMSP, USA, 2001), 81, 120–21, 317
*OSIRIS-REx* probe (NASA), 1, 133, **135**
OST; see Outer Space Treaty (1967)
Outer Space Institute, 157
Outer Space Treaty (1967): collision avoidance, 56–57
  duty of due regard, 105, 141–42
  duty to consult, 142, 163, 306
  duty to rescue, 21
  duty to rescue, celestial bodies, 42
  duty to rescue, commercial spacecraft, 28
  duty to rescue, non-governmental passengers, 33
  exploration and use, 101–2, 146, 305–6
  geographic scope of rescue, 23
  information sharing, 219–20
  liability, Space tourism, 34
  mega-constellations, 50
  NEDs, 227–29
  non-state actors, 246
  object and purpose, 102, 106, 143
  orbital shells, *de facto* use, 69–70
  origins, 279–80
  principles, 154–56
  property rights, 137, 141–43, 146, 148–49
  Space mining, 1, 138–41
  Space security, 261, 279–98
  subsequent practice, 153
  unilateral action against NEO, 238

Pan-STARRS Project, 190
Parly, Florence (defence minister, France), 327
PDV Mk-II (India), 283
pellet ring, 368–70
Pence, Karen, **158**
Pence, Mike (vice president, USA), **158**
Peresild, Yulia, 20
PL-19 Nudol (Russia), 281, 283, 325
Planet Labs, 48
planetary defence; see also NED; see also Space Mission Planning Advisory Group (SMPAG)
  airbursts, 187
  anthropogenic environmental degradation, 192
  asteroid deflection, 196
  Asteroid Terrestrial-Impact Last Alert System (ATLAS), 190–91
  B-plane, 196, **198**, 201–2
  Catalina Sky Survey, 190
  Chelyabinsk event, 187, 211
  circumstances precluding wrongfulness, 241
  circumstances precluding wrongfulness, consent, 241–42
  circumstances precluding wrongfulness, distress, 242–43
  circumstances precluding wrongfulness, necessity, 243–46
  collective Space agency action, 234
  cometary impact scenario, NASA, 209–10
  comets, 206–7

dark asteroids, 192
decision-making matrix, 234
Deep Impact (NASA), 208
defence capability, development of, 250
direction of approach, 191–92
Double Asteroid Redirection Test (DART, NASA), 200–1, 211
duty to rescue, international law, 223–26
Earth impactors, **186**, 186
Edgeworth–Kuiper Belt (Kuiper Belt), 206–8
fault-based liability, 249
gravity tractors, 205–6
impact timescales, 187–88
information sharing, 211
information sharing, international law, 219–20
Instituto de Astrofísica de Canarias (Canary Islands), 191
International Asteroid Warning Network (IAWN), 211–12
international cooperation, 211
keyholes, 251–53, **253**, 256
kinetic impactors, 199–202
K–T extinction event, 186, 257
liability, 247
liability and false alarms, 247–49
mass drivers, 204–5
minimum orbital intersection distance (MOID), 192, **194–96**
mission-ready assets, 250–51
multilateral assistance, 221–22
Near-Earth Object Surveillance Mission (NEOSM, NASA), 192
NEO identification, 190
NEOWISE (NASA), 191
NGO liability, 249
non-state actors and state responsibility, 246, 255
Oort Cloud, 206–7
Pan-STARRS Project, 190
precautionary defence, mission restriction, 251–53
precautionary defence, NEO deflection, 255
precautionary principle, 254, 257

pre-emptive self-defence, 239–40
risk assessment, 188, 194–96, 233–34
Rosetta/Philae (probe/lander), 208, **209–10**
safe harbours, 256
Shoemaker–Levy 9 (comet), 209–10
Space Mission Planning Advisory Group (SMPAG), 211, 213
Space-based sensors, 191, 250
state responsibility, 221
tabletop exercise (2017), NED use, 217, 244–45
tabletop exercise (2019), deflection mission, 215–17, **217**
tabletop exercise (2021), impact emergency, 214–15
Tunguska event, 188
UN Security Council, 235–36
unilateral action, 211
unilateral action and military involvement, 237–38
unilateral action, international law, 237–38
Vera C. Rubin Observatory (Large Synoptic Survey Telescope, Chile), 191
waiver of liability (UN Security Council), 236
Yarkovsky effect, 195
PPWT (2014), 274–75
precautionary principle (Rio Declaration [1992]):
environmental degradation, 107
environmental impact assessments, 98–99, 107–8
planetary defence, 250–51, 254, 257
Space mining, 168, 181–83
Privateer, 90
Protocol for the Prohibition of the Use in War of Asphyxiating, Poisonous or Other Gases, and of Bacteriological Methods of Warfare (1925), 300
Putin, Vladimir (president, Russia), 281, 360

R-7 (Russia), 259
RadarSat-2 (Canada), 352

radio astronomy, 92–93, 297
Raju, Nivedita, 331
Reagan, Ronald (president, USA), 264,
    365
Reddy, G. Satheesh, 321
Redstone (USA), 259
Registration Convention (1974), 37
Remote Sensing Space Systems
    Regulations (Canada, 2007), 317
Rescue Agreement (1968): alighted,
    interpretation of, 22
  cost reimbursement, 37
  duty to rescue, 21–22, 31, 34, 37
  duty to rescue, celestial bodies, 42
  duty to rescue, commercial
    spacecraft, 30–31
  duty to rescue, non-governmental
    passengers, 32–33
  duty to rescue, *travaux préparatoires*,
    32–33
  geographic scope of rescue, 22
  *travaux préparatoires*, 28
right of self-defence: ASAT use on
    civilian satellite, 348
  ASAT use on dual-use satellite, 348
  ASAT use on military satellite,
    347–48
  gravity threshold, 346–47, 349, 354
  necessity and proportionality,
    350–51
  necessity and proportionality, debris
    creation, 354–55
  necessity and proportionality, dual-
    use satellites, 352–54, 368
  necessity and proportionality,
    military satellites, 351–52
  Space debris, 354
  UN Charter and ASAT weapons,
    345–46
Rio Declaration (1992), 106–7, 181
rocket bodies: casualty risk assessment,
    120, **122–23**
  casualty risk assessment, future risk,
    122–23, **124**
  controlled re-entry, 114
  controlled re-entry, switch to, 124
  environmental risks, 62, 68–69
  generic term, 114

Global South, 121, **124**, 124
Guidelines for the Long-Term
    Sustainability of Outer Space
    Activities (2018), 120–21
Liability Convention (1972), 121
liability risk, 121
light pollution, 117–18, **117–18**
low-risk, high-consequence events,
    120–21
negotiation before disaster, 128–29
on-orbit abandonment, 114, 120
Orbital Debris Mitigation Standard
    Practices (ODMSP, USA), 120–21
re-entry safety risks, 62
Space debris, 53–54, 114, **116**
Space Debris Mitigation Guidelines
    (2010), 120–21
SpaceX, best practices, 62
tragedy of the commons, prevention
    of, 127–29
uncontrolled re-entry,
    62, 114, 120
uncontrolled re-entry, casualty
    expectations, 122–23
uncontrolled re-entry, surface
    impacts, 118–20, **119**
Rogers, A.P.V., 357–58
Rogozin, Dmitry (ROSCOSMOS
    director general), 20, 137, 160,
    179, 362–63
ROSCOSMOS: IADC membership, 79,
    265
  property rights, 137–38, 160
  Russia (2021) ASAT test, 281
  Space debris, 281, 311–12
  Space tourism, 17, 20–21
  Ukrainian war, 362–63
*Rosetta/Philae* (probe/lander, ESA),
    208, **209**
Rubio, Marco (senator, USA), 151
Russia; *see also* ISS; *see also* Soyuz
    (Russia); *see also* ROSCOSMOS
  anti-satellite weapon test (2021), 2–3,
    53, 270–71, 281–82, 303
  ASAT tests (1968-1982), 262
  bilateral Russia/US ASAT test ban
    proposal, 277
  Chelyabinsk event, 187–88, 211

Cospas–Sarsat rescue programme, 364

General Requirements on Space Systems for the Mitigation of Human-Produced Near-Earth Space Pollution (2008), 317

knock-on collision, 77

Kosmos 954 impact, 63–64, 88

Luna-16 probe, 145

NED testing, 231

Outer Space Treaty, *travaux préparatoires*, 148

Pikialasorsuaq (North Water Polynya), 64

PPWT (2014), 274–75

response to 2007 China ASAT test, 311

response to 2019 India ASAT test, 323

Salyut-7 Space station, 118

satellite–debris collision, 266

satellite–satellite collision, 8, 53

Space mining, 131, 145

Tunguska event, 188–89

Ukrainian war, 6, 334, 343–44, 359–60

West Ford Experiment, reaction to, 103

Working Group on Space Resources, 179

Russia–China International Lunar Research Station, 359

Russian Space Agency (ROSCOSMOS); *see* ROSCOSMOS

Rwanda, 49, 73–74, 172

Ryugu (asteroid), 133–34, 166

Salyut-7 Space station, 118

SAR Convention (1979), 29, 34, 37, 224–25

Saraswat, Vijay Kumar, 321

SC-19 (China), 283

Scaled Composites, 12

Schmitt, Michael, 358

Schulz, Leonard, 66–67

Sea Launch project, 64

Shanahan, Patrick (Defense Secretary, USA), 323

*Shijian-21* (spacecraft, China), 314

Shipenko, Klim, 20

Shoemaker–Levy 9 (comet), 209–10

SiriusXM, 48

SM-3 missile (US), 267, 276, 283

SOLAS Convention (1914): duty to rescue, 28, 31, 33–34, 37, 223–24, 365

international law, 50

South Korea, 330

Soviet Union; *see* Russia

Soyuz (Russia): ISS resupply and crew rotation, 361

Space tourism, 11, 17, 20–21, 44

Ukrainian war, 360, 362–63

uncontrolled re-entry, 62–63

Space; *see also* Space tourism; *see also* environmental impacts; *see also* LEO; *see also* GEO (Geosynchronous Orbit); *see also* rocket bodies; *see also* astronomy; *see also* Space mining; *see also* planetary defence; *see also* Space security; *see also* IADC; *see also* ISS; *see also* Committee on the Peaceful Uses of Outer Space (COPUOS); *see also* Space debris; *see also* anti-satellite weapons

definition of boundary, 12–13

determining astronaut title, 13–14

freedom of exploration and use, 305

governance, 6, 9, 49–50, 70–71, 184, 359

governance breakdown, 359

grand challenges, 7

LEO denial of safe access, 368–70

ownership, 5–6

rules of the road, 70–71

satellite companies, national registration, 71

satellite–satellite collision, 8, 53–54

spacefaring states, 339–40

sustainable development, 9

traffic management, 58

Ukrainian war, 366–68

Space (Launches and Returns) Act (Australia, 2018), 81, 317

Space Adventures, 11, 17, 20

Space debris; *see also* Kessler–Cour-
  Palais Syndrome
 active debris removal, 54, 344
 anti-satellite weapons tests, 3, 53,
   60–61, 265–69, **268**, 271–73, 278,
   281–82, 322
 cis-lunar Space, 297–98
 debris-generating events, 8, 60–61
 gas drag clearance, 53
 graveyard orbits, 314, 318
 mega-constellations, 52
 meteoroid collisions, 60–61
 missile defence systems and debris
   generation, **273**, 283–85, 287–90
 national implementation of UN
   guidelines, 316–17
 on-orbit infrastructure, 52, **53**, 75–76
 rocket bodies, 53
 tracked debris, 52
 tragedy of the commons, 7
 untrackable debris, 8, 60
Space Debris Mitigation Guidelines
  (COPUOS, 2007, 2010), 78–82,
  121
Space Force (USA), 4, 171–72, 366–67
Space mining; *see also* Space mining,
  US approach
 accidents, 1
 asteroid mining, 133–36
 asteroid trajectory change, 167
 asteroids, scientific interest, 134–35
 China–Russia joint mission
   (Kamo'oalewa asteroid), 134–35
 debris streams, 165–66
 deep seabed mining as example, 176
 duty to consult, 142
 exploration and use, 146
 flag-of-convenience states, 172
 freedoms and restrictions, 180
 invasive-species protection, 164–65
 light pollution, 167
 low-risk, high-consequence events,
   167
 lunar mining, 130–36
 lunar orbits, 165–66
 lunar regolith purchase, NASA, 131,
   161–62, 172
 military resource use, 180

 mining, duty of due regard, 141–42,
   181
 mining, duty to consult, 162–63
 mining, non-state actors, 141
 mining, ordinary meaning, 140–41
 Moon Agreement (1979), 144–45,
   148–49
 multilateral agreement required,
   162–63, 173, 179–80, 183
 national policy, 152–53, 156
 opposition, 1, 156
 planetary defence, 205
 precautionary principle, 181
 property rights, 137, 141–43, 146,
   148–49, 184–85
 risks, 136
 scientific knowledge, potential loss, 164
 Space-based fuel production, 130,
   136
 subsequent agreement, 144–45
 subsequent practice, 131–32, 138,
   145–46, 150–51, 153–54, 156, 162,
   168–69, 172, 184–85
 *travaux préparatoires*, 147
 treaty negotiations, 156–57
 Working Group on Space Resources,
   177–79, 183
Space mining, US approach: China as
  counter-balance, 172
 Commercial Space Launch
   Competitiveness Act (2015),
   151–54, 156–57
 de facto regulatory regime, 170–71
 global commons, rejection of, 157–58
 NewSpace, 152
 obligations *erga omnes*, 154–56
 power imbalance, 153–54
 property rights, 151
 regulatory flight, 171–72
 Space companies as non-state actors,
   168, 180
 Space companies, US concentration,
   168
Space Mission Planning Advisory Group
  (SMPAG): Ad-Hoc Working
  Group on Legal Issues, 211
 creation of, 211
 DART mission, 211

non-state actors, 255
planetary defence, 213, 234
potential sidelining in emergency, 235
Space agency cooperation, 211, 254
Space security; *see also* cis-lunar Space
ABM Treaty (1972), 261, 265, 276
ASAT ban, 277–81
ASAT limitation proposals, 276
ASAT weapons, kinetic, 262–63, 267, 270, 273–74
bilateral Russia–US ASAT test ban proposal, 277
China ASAT test (2007), 265
FTG-15 (US interception test), 273, **273, 287**
IADC, 265
increased collision risk, **270, 271–72,** 272–73
India ASAT test (2019), 267
Kessler–Cour-Palais Syndrome, 263–64
Limited Test Ban Treaty (1963), 261
military Space activity, historical, 258–59
missile defence systems, 283
missile defence systems and debris generation, **273,** 283–85, 287–90
missile defence systems, permitted use, 288–89
Outer Space Treaty (1967), 261
PPWT (2014), 273–74
Russia ASAT test (2021), 270, 280–81
space debris and kinetic weapons, 262–63, 265, 267, **268,** 271–73, 278, 281–82
spacecraft approach speeds, 279
Starfish Prime, 260–61
Strategic Arms Limitation Talks Agreement (SALT 1, 1972), 261
Strategic Defense Initiative (SDI), 264
UN General Assembly resolutions, 276
US ASAT test (1985), 265
US ASAT test (2008), 267
US unilateral ASAT test ban, 279, 283
US-Soviet Orbital Debris Working Group, 265

Space Systems - Space Debris Mitigation Requirements (ISO, 2010), 82, 318
Space tourism; *see also* duty to rescue
environmental impacts, 2, 11, 38–39
extinction tourism, 44–45
international law, 11
liability, 34–38
liability regime, determination of, 34–36
orbital tourism, **16–21**
safety, 14–15
Space debris, 11
suborbital tourism, 12–16, **16–21**
types, 2, 11
SpaceIL (Israel), 164–65, 255
*SpaceShipOne* (Virgin Galactic), 12
*SpaceShipTwo* (Virgin Galactic):
altitude limit, 12, 14
carrying capacity, 12
Chicago Convention, 36–37
environmental impacts, 38–39, 67
FAA registration, 36–37
launch, 12
liability regimes, 35
SpaceX; *see also* Starlink; *see also* Crew Dragon (SpaceX); *see also* Falcon 9 (SpaceX)
astronaut transport to ISS, 16, 29
collision assessments, 60
control of orbits, 4
Falcon 9, 20, 38, 41, 114
lunar lander contract, 16
movement of operations, 4
NASA contracts, 4, 171–72
NASA, collision avoidance coordination, 57–58
orbital tourism, 16–17, 19–20
rocket body best practices, 62
Space Force contracts, 4, 171–72
Space tourism, 11
Starship, 20–21, 41, 67–68, 255, 257
Tesla automobile launch, 165
*SS Titanic*, 33, 223, 365
Starfish Prime (US NED test), 232

Starlink: aluminium from satellite
        demise, 64
    automated collision avoidance,
        59–60
    brightness mitigation, 91–92
    Chinese collision avoidance
        maneuver, 56–57
    collision risks, 74–75
    deorbiting satellites, 58
    deployment, 48–49
    environmental impact assessments,
        98–99, 107–8
    ESA collision avoidance maneuver,
        55–57
    FCC licence, 110
    orbital congestion, 59–60
    Ukrainian war, 367
Starship, 20–21, 41, 67–68, 255, 257
Statute of the International Court of
        Justice, 112
Stockholm Declaration (1972), 107
Stoltenberg, Jens (NATO Secretary-
        General), 326–27
Strategic Arms Limitation Talks
        Agreement (SALT 1, 1972), 261
Strategic Defense Initiative (SDI), 264,
        365
stratosphere, 66, 68
Suffredini, Michael, 17
Sundahl, Mark, 30–31
Swift Tutle (comet), 248

tardigrades (water bears), 4–5, 164–65
Telstar 1 (communications satellite),
        231, 260
thermosphere, 12
Thompson, General David (Vice-Chief
        of Space Operations, US Space
        Force), 366–67
Tiangong Space station, 3, 41, 56–57,
        74–75, 173, 270, 325
Titanic, 33, 223, 365
Tito, Dennis, 11, 17
tragedy of the commons, 7, 50, 70, 78,
        90–91, 127–29, 184
Transparency and Confidence-Building
        Measures in Outer Space Activities
        (UN, 2012), 319–20

Treaty on the Prevention of the
        Placement of Weapons in Outer
        Space, the Threat or Use of Force
        Against Outer Space Objects
        (PPWT [2014]), 274–75
Truman Proclamation (1945), 170
Trump, Donald (President, USA),
        157–58, **158**, 161, 258
Tunguska event, 188–89

Ukrainian war, 6, 334, 343–44, 359–60
UN Charter, 227, 236–37, 274–75, 295,
        345–46
UN Framework Convention on
        Climate Change (1992), 107–8
UN General Assembly resolutions:
        Declaration of Legal Principles
        Governing the Activities of States
        in the Exploration and Use of
        Outer Space (1962 [XVIII]),
        78–104, 143, 280
    No First Placement of Weapons in
        Outer Space, 276
    Prevention of an Arms Race in Outer
        Space (PAROS), 276
    resolution 110 (II), 143
    resolution 1721 (XVI), 303–5
    resolution 1884 (XVIII), 143
    resolution 1962 (XVIII), 303–5
    resolution 68/75, 211
    resolution 76/231, 333–34
UN Space treaties; see Outer Space
        Treaty (1967); see Liability
        Convention (1972); see Moon
        Agreement (1979); see Rescue
        Agreement (1968); see
        Registration Convention (1974)
UNCLOS (1982), 29, 34, 37, 173, 176,
        224
United Arab Emirates (UAE), 159
United Kingdom, 74, 99, 108, 159, 311,
        328–29
United States; see also NASA; see also
        ISS; see also Blue Origin; see also
        SpaceX; see also FCC; see also
        Virgin Galactic
    Cislunar Highway Patrol Satellite
        (CHPS, USA), 291–92, 298

Counter Communications System (CCS), 343
DARPA, 292–94, 296, 298
Defense Deep Space Sentinel (D2S2, USA), 291–92, 298
Demonstration Rocket for Agile Cislunar Operations' (DRACO, DARPA), 294
FAA, 14, 36–37
military Space activity, 258
NewSpace, 152, 255
response to 2007 China ASAT test, 309–10
response to 2019 India ASAT test, 322
response to 2021 Russia ASAT test, 326
Space Force, 4, 171–72, 366–67
Space security advocacy, 264–65
unilateral declaration on ASAT tests, 279, 283, 335–37
United States Air Force Research Laboratory, 291–92
United States Space Command (USSPACECOM), 60, 90, 258, 270, 322
Wolf Amendment (2011), 359
United States Air Force Research Laboratory, 291–92
United States Space Command (USSPACECOM), 60, 90, 258, 270, 322
Universal Declaration of Human Rights (1948), 79
USA 193 (US reconnaissance satellite), 267, 269

V-2 (Germany), 258–59
V-2 (US), 259
Van Allen radiation belts, 231, 260–61
Vance, Cyrus (Secretary of State, USA), 151
Vande Hei, Mark (astronaut), 361, 363
Vera C. Rubin Observatory (Large Synoptic Survey Telescope, Chile), 191

Viasat, 110–11, 344, 366–67
*Viasat, Inc. v. Federal Communications Commission*, 110–11
Vienna Convention (1969): astronomy, 98, 100–2
Outer Space Treaty (1967), 142–43
Rescue Agreement (1968), 24–25, 31–32
Space mining, 138–39, 141, 146, 152
subsequent agreement/practice, 144
subsequent practice, 153, 307–8
*travaux préparatoires*, 25
Vienna Convention for the Protection of the Ozone Layer (1985), 127
Vienna Convention on the Law of Treaties (1969); *see* Vienna Convention (1969)
Virgin Galactic: altitude flight limits, 34
environmental impacts, 40
landing site, 34
safety, 15
Space tourism, 11
*SpaceShipTwo*, 12–14, 35, 37–40, 67
Vulcan Centaur (USA), 63, 68

West Ford Experiment (USA, 1961-63), 103–4, 238–39, 370
West, Jessica, 294
*WhiteKnightTwo* (Virgin Galactic), 39–40
Wood, Steven, 25, 27–28, 33
Working Group on Space Resources, 139, 177–79, 183
Wyler, Greg, 74

Yarkovsky Effect, 195
Yun Zhao, 316

Zhao Lijian, 330

CAMBRIDGE STUDIES IN INTERNATIONAL
AND COMPARATIVE LAW

*Books in the Series*

176 *Who Owns Outer Space? International Law, Astrophysics and the Sustainable Development of Space* Michael Byers and Aaron Boley

175 *Intervening in International Justice: Third States before Courts and Tribunals* Brian McGarry

174 *Reciprocity in Public International Law* Arianna Whelan

173 *When Environmental Protection and Human Rights Collide* Marie-Catherine Petersmann

172 *The International Law of Sovereign Debt Dispute Settlement* Kei Nakajima

171 *The Everyday Makers of International Law: From Great Halls to Back Rooms* Tommaso Soave

170 *Virtue in Global Governance: Judgment and Discretion* Jan Klabbers

169 *The Effects of Armed Conflict on Investment Treaties* Tobias Ackermann

168 *Investment Law's Alibis: Colonialism, Imperialism, Debt and Development* David Schneiderman

167 *Negative Comparative Law: A Strong Programme for Weak Thought* Pierre Legrand

166 *Detention by Non-state Armed Groups under International Law* Ezequiel Heffes

165 *Rebellions and Civil Wars: State Responsibility for the Conduct of Insurgents* Patrick Dumberry

164 *The International Law of Energy* Jorge Viñuales

163 *The Three Ages of International Commercial Arbitration* Mikaël Schinazi

162 *Repetition and International Law* Wouter Werner

161 *State Responsibility and Rebels: The History and Legacy of Protecting Investment against Revolution* Kathryn Greenman

160 *Rewriting Histories of the Use of Force: The Narrative of 'Indifference'* Agatha Verdebout

159 *The League of Nations and the Protection of the Environment* Omer Aloni

158 *International Investment Law and Legal Theory: Expropriation and the Fragmentation of Sources* Jörg Kammerhofer

157 *Legal Barbarians: Identity, Modern Comparative Law and the Global South* Daniel Bonilla Maldonado

156 *International Human Rights Law beyond State Territorial Control* Antal Berkes

155 *The Crime of Aggression under the Rome Statute of the International Criminal Court* Carrie McDougall

154 *Minorities and the Making of Postcolonial States in International Law* Mohammad Shahabuddin

153 *Preclassical Conflict of Laws* Nikitas E. Hatzimihail

152 *International Law and History: Modern Interfaces* Ignacio de la Rasilla

151 *Marketing Global Justice: The Political Economy of International Criminal Law* Christine Schwöbel-Patel

150 *International Status in the Shadow of Empire* Cait Storr

149 *Treaties in Motion: The Evolution of Treaties from Formation to Termination* Edited by Malgosia Fitzmaurice and Panos Merkouris

148 *Humanitarian Disarmament: An Historical Enquiry* Treasa Dunworth

147 *Complementarity, Catalysts, Compliance: The International Criminal Court in Uganda, Kenya, and the Democratic Republic of Congo* Christian M. De Vos

146 *Cyber Operations and International Law* François Delerue

145 *Comparative Reasoning in International Courts and Tribunals* Daniel Peat

144 *Maritime Delimitation as a Judicial Process* Massimo Lando

143 *Prosecuting Sexual and Gender-Based Crimes at the International Criminal Court: Practice, Progress and Potential* Rosemary Grey

142 *Capitalism as Civilisation: A History of International Law* Ntina Tzouvala

141 *Sovereignty in China: A Genealogy of a Concept since 1840* Adele Carrai

140 *Narratives of Hunger in International Law: Feeding the World in Times of Climate Change* Anne Saab

139 *Victim Reparation under the Ius Post Bellum: An Historical and Normative Perspective* Shavana Musa

138 *The Analogy between States and International Organizations* Fernando Lusa Bordin

137 *The Process of International Legal Reproduction: Inequality, Historiography, Resistance* Rose Parfitt

136 *State Responsibility for Breaches of Investment Contracts* Jean Ho

135 *Coalitions of the Willing and International Law: The Interplay between Formality and Informality* Alejandro Rodiles

134 *Self-Determination in Disputed Colonial Territories* Jamie Trinidad

133 *International Law as a Belief System* Jean d'Aspremont

132 *Legal Consequences of Peremptory Norms in International Law* Daniel Costelloe

131 *Third-Party Countermeasures in International Law* Martin Dawidowicz

130 *Justification and Excuse in International Law: Concept and Theory of General Defences* Federica Paddeu

129 *Exclusion from Public Space: A Comparative Constitutional Analysis* Daniel Moeckli

128 *Provisional Measures before International Courts and Tribunals* Cameron A. Miles

127 *Humanity at Sea: Maritime Migration and the Foundations of International Law* Itamar Mann

126 *Beyond Human Rights: The Legal Status of the Individual in International Law* Anne Peters

125 *The Doctrine of Odious Debt in International Law: A Restatement* Jeff King

124 *Static and Evolutive Treaty Interpretation: A Functional Reconstruction* Christian Djeffal

123 *Civil Liability in Europe for Terrorism-Related Risk* Lucas Bergkamp, Michael Faure, Monika Hinteregger and Niels Philipsen

122 *Proportionality and Deference in Investor–State Arbitration: Balancing Investment Protection and Regulatory Autonomy* Caroline Henckels

121 *International Law and Governance of Natural Resources in Conflict and Post-conflict Situations* Daniëlla Dam-de Jong

120 *Proof of Causation in Tort Law* Sandy Steel

119 *The Formation and Identification of Rules of Customary International Law in International Investment Law* Patrick Dumberry

118 *Religious Hatred and International Law: The Prohibition of Incitement to Violence or Discrimination* Jeroen Temperman

117 *Taking Economic, Social and Cultural Rights Seriously in International Criminal Law* Evelyne Schmid

116 *Climate Change Litigation: Regulatory Pathways to Cleaner Energy* Jacqueline Peel and Hari M. Osofsky

115 *Mestizo International Law: A Global Intellectual History 1842–1933* Arnulf Becker Lorca

114 *Sugar and the Making of International Trade Law* Michael Fakhri

113 *Strategically Created Treaty Conflicts and the Politics of International Law* Surabhi Ranganathan

112 *Investment Treaty Arbitration as Public International Law: Procedural Aspects and Implications* Eric De Brabandere

111 *The New Entrants Problem in International Fisheries Law* Andrew Serdy

110 *Substantive Protection under Investment Treaties: A Legal and Economic Analysis* Jonathan Bonnitcha

109 *Popular Governance of Post-conflict Reconstruction: The Role of International Law* Matthew Saul

108 *Evolution of International Environmental Regimes: The Case of Climate Change* Simone Schiele

107 *Judges, Law and War: The Judicial Development of International Humanitarian Law* Shane Darcy

106 *Religious Offence and Human Rights: The Implications of Defamation of Religions* Lorenz Langer

105 *Forum Shopping in International Adjudication: The Role of Preliminary Objections* Luiz Eduardo Salles

104 *Domestic Politics and International Human Rights Tribunals: The Problem of Compliance* Courtney Hillebrecht

103 *International Law and the Arctic* Michael Byers

102 *Cooperation in the Law of Transboundary Water Resources* Christina Leb

101 *Underwater Cultural Heritage and International Law* Sarah Dromgoole

100 *State Responsibility: The General Part* James Crawford

99 *The Origins of International Investment Law: Empire, Environment and the Safeguarding of Capital* Kate Miles

98 *The Crime of Aggression under the Rome Statute of the International Criminal Court* Carrie McDougall

97 *'Crimes against Peace' and International Law* Kirsten Sellars

96 *Non-legality in International Law: Unruly Law* Fleur Johns

95 *Armed Conflict and Displacement: The Protection of Refugees and Displaced Persons under International Humanitarian Law* Mélanie Jacques

94 *Foreign Investment and the Environment in International Law* Jorge E. Viñuales

93 *The Human Rights Treaty Obligations of Peacekeepers* Kjetil Mujezinović Larsen

92 *Cyber Warfare and the Laws of War* Heather Harrison Dinniss

91 *The Right to Reparation in International Law for Victims of Armed Conflict* Christine Evans

90 *Global Public Interest in International Investment Law* Andreas Kulick

89 *State Immunity in International Law* Xiaodong Yang

88 *Reparations and Victim Support in the International Criminal Court* Conor McCarthy

87 *Reducing Genocide to Law: Definition, Meaning, and the Ultimate Crime* Payam Akhavan

86 *Decolonising International Law: Development, Economic Growth and the Politics of Universality* Sundhya Pahuja

85 *Complicity and the Law of State Responsibility* Helmut Philipp Aust

84 *State Control over Private Military and Security Companies in Armed Conflict* Hannah Tonkin

83 *'Fair and Equitable Treatment' in International Investment Law* Roland Kläger

82 *The UN and Human Rights: Who Guards the Guardians?* Guglielmo Verdirame

81 *Sovereign Defaults before International Courts and Tribunals* Michael Waibel

80 *Making the Law of the Sea: A Study in the Development of International Law* James Harrison

79 *Science and the Precautionary Principle in International Courts and Tribunals: Expert Evidence, Burden of Proof and Finality* Caroline E. Foster

78 *Transition from Illegal Regimes under International Law* Yaël Ronen

77 *Access to Asylum: International Refugee Law and the Globalisation of Migration Control* Thomas Gammeltoft-Hansen

76 *Trading Fish, Saving Fish: The Interaction between Regimes in International Law* Margaret A. Young

75 *The Individual in the International Legal System: Continuity and Change in International Law* Kate Parlett

74 *'Armed Attack' and Article 51 of the UN Charter: Evolutions in Customary Law and Practice* Tom Ruys

73 *Theatre of the Rule of Law: Transnational Legal Intervention in Theory and Practice* Stephen Humphreys

72 *Science and Risk Regulation in International Law* Jacqueline Peel

71 *The Participation of States in International Organisations: The Role of Human Rights and Democracy* Alison Duxbury

70 *Legal Personality in International Law* Roland Portmann

69 *Vicarious Liability in Tort: A Comparative Perspective* Paula Giliker

68 *The Public International Law Theory of Hans Kelsen: Believing in Universal Law* Jochen von Bernstorff

67 *Legitimacy and Legality in International Law: An Interactional Account* Jutta Brunnée and Stephen J. Toope

66 *The Concept of Non-international Armed Conflict in International Humanitarian Law* Anthony Cullen

65 *The Principle of Legality in International and Comparative Criminal Law* Kenneth S. Gallant

64 *The Challenge of Child Labour in International Law* Franziska Humbert

63 *Shipping Interdiction and the Law of the Sea* Douglas Guilfoyle

62 *International Courts and Environmental Protection* Tim Stephens

61 *Legal Principles in WTO Disputes* Andrew D. Mitchell

60 *War Crimes in Internal Armed Conflicts* Eve La Haye

59 *Humanitarian Occupation* Gregory H. Fox

58 *The International Law of Environmental Impact Assessment: Process, Substance and Integration* Neil Craik

57 *The Law and Practice of International Territorial Administration: Versailles to Iraq and Beyond* Carsten Stahn

56 *United Nations Sanctions and the Rule of Law* Jeremy Matam Farrall

55 *National Law in WTO Law: Effectiveness and Good Governance in the World Trading System* Sharif Bhuiyan

54 *Cultural Products and the World Trade Organization* Tania Voon

53 *The Threat of Force in International Law* Nikolas Stürchler

52 *Indigenous Rights and United Nations Standards: Self-Determination, Culture and Land* Alexandra Xanthaki

51 *International Refugee Law and Socio-economic Rights: Refuge from Deprivation* Michelle Foster

50 *The Protection of Cultural Property in Armed Conflict* Roger O'Keefe

49 *Interpretation and Revision of International Boundary Decisions* Kaiyan Homi Kaikobad

48 *Multinationals and Corporate Social Responsibility: Limitations and Opportunities in International Law* Jennifer A. Zerk

47 *Judiciaries within Europe: A Comparative Review* John Bell

46 *Law in Times of Crisis: Emergency Powers in Theory and Practice* Oren Gross and Fionnuala Ní Aoláin

45 *Vessel-Source Marine Pollution: The Law and Politics of International Regulation* Alan Khee-Jin Tan

44 *Enforcing Obligations Erga Omnes in International Law* Christian J. Tams

43 *Non-governmental Organisations in International Law* Anna-Karin Lindblom

42 *Democracy, Minorities and International Law* Steven Wheatley

41 *Prosecuting International Crimes: Selectivity and the International Criminal Law Regime* Robert Cryer

40 *Compensation for Personal Injury in English, German and Italian Law: A Comparative Outline* Basil Markesinis, Michael Coester, Guido Alpa and Augustus Ullstein

39 *Dispute Settlement in the UN Convention on the Law of the Sea* Natalie Klein

38 *The International Protection of Internally Displaced Persons* Catherine Phuong

37 *Imperialism, Sovereignty and the Making of International Law* Antony Anghie

36 *Principles of the Institutional Law of International Organizations* C. F. Amerasinghe

35 *Necessity, Proportionality and the Use of Force by States* Judith Gardam

34 *International Legal Argument in the Permanent Court of International Justice: The Rise of the International Judiciary* Ole Spiermann

33 –

32 *Great Powers and Outlaw States: Unequal Sovereigns in the International Legal Order* Gerry Simpson

31 *Local Remedies in International Law (second edition)* Chittharanjan Felix Amerasinghe

30 *Reading Humanitarian Intervention: Human Rights and the Use of Force in International Law* Anne Orford

29 *Conflict of Norms in Public International Law: How WTO Law Relates to Other Rules of International Law* Joost Pauwelyn

28 –

27 *Transboundary Damage in International Law* Hanqin Xue

26 –

25 *European Criminal Procedures* Edited by Mireille Delmas-Marty and J. R. Spencer

24 *Accountability of Armed Opposition Groups in International Law* Liesbeth Zegveld

23 *Sharing Transboundary Resources: International Law and Optimal Resource Use* Eyal Benvenisti

22 *International Human Rights and Humanitarian Law* René Provost

21 *Remedies against International Organisations* Karel Wellens

20 *Diversity and Self-Determination in International Law* Karen Knop

19 *The Law of Internal Armed Conflict* Lindsay Moir

18 *International Commercial Arbitration and African States: Practice, Participation and Institutional Development* Amazu A. Asouzu

17 *The Enforceability of Promises in European Contract Law* James Gordley

16 *International Law in Antiquity* David J. Bederman

15 *Money Laundering: A New International Law Enforcement Model* Guy Stessens

14 *Good Faith in European Contract Law* Reinhard Zimmermann and Simon Whittaker

13 *On Civil Procedure* J. A. Jolowicz

12 *Trusts: A Comparative Study* Maurizio Lupoi and Simon Dix

11 *The Right to Property in Commonwealth Constitutions* Tom Allen

10 *International Organizations before National Courts* August Reinisch

9 *The Changing International Law of High Seas Fisheries* Francisco Orrego Vicuña

8 *Trade and the Environment: A Comparative Study of EC and US Law* Damien Geradin

7 *Unjust Enrichment: A Study of Private Law and Public Values* Hanoch Dagan

6 *Religious Liberty and International Law in Europe* Malcolm D. Evans

5 *Ethics and Authority in International Law* Alfred P. Rubin

4 *Sovereignty over Natural Resources: Balancing Rights and Duties* Nico Schrijver

3 *The Polar Regions and the Development of International Law* Donald R. Rothwell

2 *Fragmentation and the International Relations of Micro-states: Self-Determination and Statehood* Jorri C. Duursma

1 *Principles of the Institutional Law of International Organizations* C. F. Amerasinghe

Made in the USA
Middletown, DE
23 August 2023

37195254R00239